The Essays of

MONTAIGNE

in three volumes

·

VOLUME ONE

containing Book One

and

the first half of Book Two

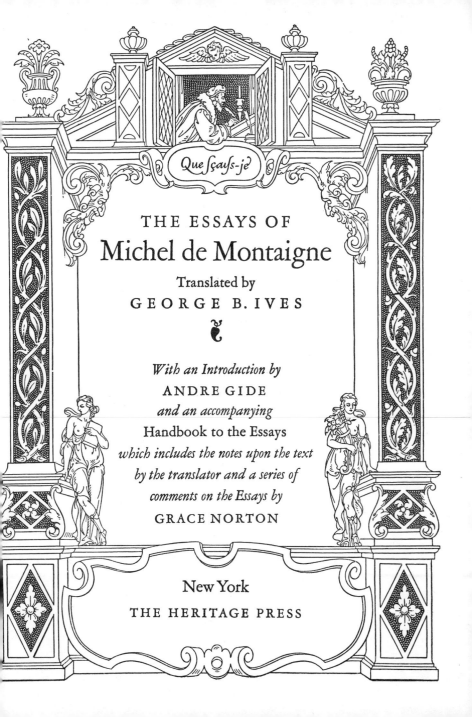

Que sçaufs-je

THE ESSAYS OF
Michel de Montaigne
Translated by
GEORGE B. IVES

With an Introduction by
ANDRE GIDE
and an accompanying
Handbook to the Essays
which includes the notes upon the text
by the translator and a series of
comments on the Essays by
GRACE NORTON

New York
THE HERITAGE PRESS

Contents

OF BOOK ONE

··

Contents

Contents

Contents

Contents

OF BOOK TWO

. .

BOOK TWO IS CONTINUED IN VOLUME TWO

THE TRANSLATOR'S

Preface

THERE have been two translations of Montaigne's Essays: that of John Florio, first published in 1603, and that of Charles Cotton, about 1670. The Florio translation was reissued in 1613 and 1632, but no other edition of it appeared until late in the nineteenth century. Within the past forty or fifty years it has been reprinted a number of times, but always without modification of the language.

The Cotton translation, on the other hand, has been "edited" by various hands, notably by William Hazlitt and O. W. Wight, and more recently by William Carew Hazlitt, by all of whom it has been considerably changed to suit their conceptions of Montaigne's meaning.

It was while assisting in the production of the Riverside Press limited edition, in folio, of the Florio translation, some twenty-odd years ago, that the present translator became convinced of its entire inadequacy, in many places, as a faithful interpretation of Montaigne's thought, and of its failure to reproduce what may, for lack of a better word, be called the essayist's style.

"Florio, the first English translator and the one of late most frequently reprinted, has a freedom and fluency that is often called 'Elizabethan'; but it is a fatal freedom and fluency for a translator; and it has little of Elizabethan weight and fullness of meaning; his abundance is constantly redundance; he has a tiresome use of clumsy compounds and is fond of useless synonyms, while with Montaigne one

IX

Preface

word is seldom the 'synonym' of another; each added word is an added thought. To illustrate this fully would take too much space, but a fair example may be found toward the close of the third chapter of the first Book, where in one sentence, that about Diomedon, Florio inserts the words 'ruthless,' 'exemplar,' 'cruelly,' 'bloody,' 'I say,' 'earnestly,' 'revenge'; translates *faict* by 'success' instead of 'action,' making the sense unintelligible; translates *paisable* by 'plausible' (probably a misprint, but one that Mr. Henry Morley, as editor, accepts); and translates *descouvrir* (here meaning 'to lay bare') by 'exasperate,' again obscuring the meaning. The character—the quality—of the writing is thus changed throughout. . . . The passage, a part of which was just quoted above in the original, Florio translates as follows: 'All this galiemafry which I huddle up here is but a register of my live-essayes, which in regard of the internal health are sufficiently exemplary to take the instruction against the hair.' It could hardly be guessed that Montaigne's meaning, paraphrased, is that the reader may profit by the author's example if he reverse it."*

The Cotton translation, while in some respects much more faithful to the original, is marred by not infrequent, unexplained omissions, generally of obscure or puzzling passages.

For ten years following the publication of the Riverside Florio, the need, or desirability, of a new translation was always present at the back of the present writer's mind, coupled with what seemed a hopeless ambition to undertake it. But finally, some twelve years ago, at the suggestion of Miss Grace Norton of Cambridge, who has been well

*Grace Norton, *Studies in Montaigne* (1904), p. 256, note.

Preface

known for many years, in France no less favorably than at home, as a devoted student of Montaigne, he set out upon the enterprise which is at last approaching completion.

It must be said that the work was done throughout with the continued unfailing encouragement and assistance of Miss Norton, without which it could hardly have been carried to an end. Every page of the first draft of the manuscript was read by her, and the rendering of many passages is due to mutual discussion. While it is in no sense such a translation as she herself would have made had conditions permitted, whatever merit it may possess is due chiefly to her advice. Moreover, the value of her learned and suggestive introductions to the several Essays can hardly be exaggerated.

II

The first edition of the Essays was published in 1580 and included only the first two books. The second, in 1582, contained some few slight, though not unimportant, additions; the third edition (1587) was practically a reprint of the second. The third book first appeared in 1588, in an edition called on the title-page the fifth, although no fourth has ever been discovered. In addition to the third book, this edition contained very considerable and important additions to, and changes in, the first two. This was the last edition published in Montaigne's lifetime. He died in 1592.

In 1595 appeared the first posthumous edition, which contained additions even more numerous and significant, to the third book as well as to the others. This edition was the one used by both Florio and Cotton as the basis of their translations, and it has been reprinted, in French, innumerable

Preface

times. The question of the authorship of, or responsibility
for, the changes embodied therein aroused no special interest
until the discovery, late in the eighteenth century, in a con-
vent near Bordeaux, of a copy of the edition of 1588, which
Montaigne had evidently used in preparing for a new edition. The title-page has been changed by substituting
"sixth edition" for "fifth edition," and adding the motto,
"Vires atque eundo"; on the back of the title-page is a list
of directions to the printer, and on every page of the volume
are interlineations and marginal additions, erasures, substitutions, and re-writings, which, in many cases, leave almost
no white paper visible. The volume is not in the original
binding, and there are places where a careless binder's knife
has trimmed the page so closely as to cut off some of the
written words, thus leaving something to conjecture.

The stupendous task of transcribing these manuscript additions was duly accomplished, with the result that a very
large majority of them are found to be included in the posthumous edition of 1595. But that edition contains an appre-
ciable number of other additions, together with some modifications of the manuscript emendations on the Bordeaux
copy. It has been conjectured that these may have been written on loose or detached sheets, which became separated
from the volume, or that they were made upon still another
copy of the 1588 edition, which has never been found. But
some doubt has been aroused by evidence that Montaigne's
fille d'alliance, Mademoiselle de Jars de Gournay,* had a

*In 1635, she published an edition of the Essays, with a very long intro-
duction signed by herself. She is referred to by Montaigne in affectionate
and eulogistic terms near the end of chapter 17 of Book II. The term *fille
d'alliance* did not, in this case, indicate any kinship, or even an adoption,
properly speaking. Her introduction to her edition of 1635 is dithyrambic
in praise of the Essays.

XII

Preface

hand in some of them; so that it is the general consensus of opinion at this day that the Bordeaux copy represents the most authentic version available of Montaigne's proposed revision; and the Bordeaux municipality has adopted it as the basis of its recently published sumptuous edition of the Essays, known as the "Edition Municipale." This text, therefore, has been used in the present translation; but any variations from the edition of 1595, other than mere verbal ones, are given in the notes, where the term "Edition Municipale" is used, for brevity's sake, instead of "Bordeaux copy of 1588," except where the use of the latter phrase is made necessary for the sake of clearness. The problem of paragraphing has been one of considerable difficulty, for in none of the early editions of the Essays was there any division into paragraphs at all. In attempting to solve the problem, the constant aim has been to assist the reader.

The foot-notes are of four classes [in the current edition, these are printed in Volume III which is called "A Handbook to the Essays]. (1) The passages quoted by Montaigne, chiefly from the Latin, of which translations have been placed in the text. The attempt has been made to fit them into the context, in accordance with Montaigne's manifest purpose. "It is worth while," says Miss Norton, "to give this hint to the reader with regard to Montaigne's quotations from the ancient poets. They are always as accurate as is needful, but not infrequently the essayist makes such use of them as disguises or even alters their original significance. He expresses by the words of another his own different thought. Those who trace these quotations to their source find an unlooked-for pleasure in discovering the skill with which Montaigne adorned his pages with them, in accord-

Preface

ance with the fashion of the time. He repeatedly takes notice himself of the multitude of his quotations, sometimes with open satisfaction in their noble birth and in their interpretive nature, sometimes with amused recognition of their easy multiplication."

(2) Citations of the authorities from whom Montaigne derived the facts and anecdotes and theories set forth in the text; and of the passages, chiefly from classical authors, which seem to have influenced his ideas and opinions in one way or another. Annotation of the Essays in this sense was first undertaken by Peter Coste, who was responsible for five editions in French in the first half of the eighteenth century. His work was very far from complete and his citations left much to be desired in the way of accuracy, but they have been generally accepted by editors of Cotton's translation—one must believe, without a serious attempt to verify them. Later French editors have revised and amplified Coste's work to some extent, but it remained for M. Pierre Villey, in his Notes to the Edition Municipale, to carry the work of annotation to a point that can hardly be surpassed. M. Villey had already published, under the most severe handicap imaginable,—that of total blindness,—two works of vast labor and erudition: *Les Sources et l'Evolution des Essais,* in two volumes, and *Livres de l'Histoire Moderne utilisés par Montaigne.* It is in the Notes based upon the second of these works, that he has carried the annotation of the Essays into a new field. The present translator has drawn rather freely upon these references to Montaigne's *modern* sources; and in this respect the work differs from all previous editions of the Essays in English.

(3) The original text of obscure or doubtful words or sen-

Preface

tences, and of passages with which some liberty has been taken in the way of paraphrase or a free rendering, so that the reader may, if he choose, translate for himself.

(4) Cross-references to other passages in the Essays with which comparison may, for one reason or another, be worth while. The examples given in the notes are merely illustrative; it would have been possible to add largely to their number.

An occasional reference to the variant readings of the Bordeaux copy will give some idea of Montaigne's method of revision, and of the phases through which his thought was wont to pass. It would be quite impossible within reasonable limits to offer anything more than a very few suggestive examples.

The writer is deeply indebted to Mrs. Elizabeth Gilpatrick Stewart and Miss Charlotte Heath of the Harvard University Press for their faithful and most helpful work on the proofs, and to his friend and former associate, Lanius D. Evans of the Riverside Press, for reading the proofs in page form, correcting many errors, and making many suggestions of great importance. As the work of translating and preparing for the press has lasted so many years, it has been almost impossible to preserve entire consistency in such matters as the method of citing authorities and of printing quoted passages. Such inconsistencies as may be found are not of a sort likely to mislead, or even, perhaps, to attract the attention of anybody but a printer.

GEORGE B. IVES

XV

An Addendum

FROM THE PUBLISHER

AS Mr. Ives sets forth, the two well-known translations of Montaigne's Essays were, before his appeared, that of John Florio in 1603, and that of Charles Cotton in 1670. The Cotton translation was later edited, by William Hazlitt, by O. W. Wight, by W. C. Hazlitt.

In most modern reprints (the World's Classics edition and the Everyman's Library edition notably) the Florio translation is reprinted. It is likely that the reason is the same as that given by J. I. M. Stewart when he edited the Florio version for the superlatively handsome Nonesuch Press edition: "The object is less that of bringing the reader nearer to Montaigne than of displaying the method and merit of Florio as a translator."

In the preparation of the edition which you now hold in your hands the object *is* to bring the reader nearer to Montaigne. It was felt that this object would best be served by the printing of the translation into modern English made by George B. Ives at Harvard in 1925—despite the fact that two other modern translations followed that of Mr. Ives: one, by E. J. Trechmann in London in 1927, the other by Jacob Zeitlin in New York in 1934; and despite the additional melancholy fact that Mr. Ives had earned for his translation the sobriquet "the figleaf edition".

It is a melancholy fact that Mr. Ives left many passages in the original French, the passages treating of matters of sex. His later rivals did not miss the opportunity to refer lugubriously to his incomprehensible action. But the pres-

XVI

Publisher's Addendum

ent publisher feels that, because Mr. Ives suffered from an excess of timidity, people may have failed to observe, and pay admiring respect to, the happiness of his English.

One quotation is here noted, therefore, out of dozens which are at hand. The sentence is in the opening paragraph of Chapter II in Book I, "Of Sadness". Montaigne tells us it is absurd to admire the emotion; he tells us the Italians did not admire it; then he makes reference to the Stoics; and this reference has been translated thus:

by Florio in 1603: "the Stoics inhibit their Elders and Sages to be therewith tainted"

by Cotton-Hazlitt in 1670-1892: "it is by the Stoics expressly and particularly forbidden to their sages"

by Trechmann in 1927: "the Stoics will not allow their sage to entertain this feeling"

by Zeitlin in 1934: "the Stoics forbid the feeling to their wise man"

AND *by Ives in 1925:* "the Stoics forbid the feeling to their ideal wise man"

It seems interesting that Mr. Zeitlin's rendering follows that of Mr. Ives exactly except for the word "ideal"; yet it is the reference to "the ideal wise man" which illuminates the thought; it is "the ideal" and not the Elder or the Sage, who must not be sad among the Stoics.

No translation can be perfect; but that of Mr. Ives seems to me the happiest of all. So I have selected it to be printed here; but I have appropriated from Mr. Trechmann's version the English of the sections Mr. Ives failed to translate, and incorporated it into the Ives translation so that this may no longer be considered fig-leaved.   GEORGE MACY

A Chronological Table

AS COMPOSED BY J. I. M. STEWART FOR THE
NONESUCH EDITION OF THE FLORIO MONTAIGNE

1477 *Ramon Eyquem, merchant of Bordeaux and great-grandfather of Montaigne, bought the property of Montaigne in Perigord.*

1495 *Pierre Eyquem, Montaigne's father, born. He followed François I in the Marignano campaign of 1515: on his journey back to France he met and married Antoinette de Louppe, a girl of Jewish family and a convert to Protestantism.*

1525 *Martin Luther encouraged the merciless suppression of the Peasant Revolt in Germany.*

1533 *Michel de Montaigne, third son of Pierre, born at Montaigne on the 28th of February.*

1536 *The Inca Atahualpa murdered by Pizarro. Erasmus died. Calvin at Geneva.*

1539 *Montaigne, hitherto reared and educated according to the system devised by his father, was sent to the College de Guienne at Bordeaux. Among his teachers were George Buchanan and Mark Antoine Muret.*

1546 *Luther died. Etienne Dolet was burnt at Paris.*

1548 *Montaigne began to study law. The insurrection against the gabelle in Bordeaux was suppressed by extensive civil execution.*

XVIII

A Chronological Table

1553 *Michel Servet was burnt at Geneva. Rabelais died. Mary succeeded to the throne of England.*

1556 *Cranmer burnt. Abdication of Charles V. Ignatius of Loyola died.*

1557 *Montaigne became a Councillor of the Parlement of Bordeaux.*

1557-8 *Montaigne met Etienne de La Boëtie. Elizabeth came to the throne of England.*

1559 *Amyot's French translation of Plutarch's* Lives *published. Peace of Le Cateau. Accession of François II. Montaigne visited Paris and accompanied the king to Bar-le-Duc.*

1560 *Accession of Charles IX.*

1561-2 *Montaigne again visited Paris and followed the Court to Rouen, meeting the savages on whose information he was to base on his essay on Cannibals.*

1561-92 *The struggle for religious unity in France became the pretext for thirty years almost unintermitted civil warfare.*

1563 *Etienne de La Boëtie died.*

1564 *Shakespeare and Galileo born.*

1565 *Montaigne married Françoise de la Chassaigne, an accomplished housekeeper and of some fortune. Of five daughters, only one, Léonore, survived.*

A Chronological Table

1568   *Pierre Eyquem died. Michel, the eldest surviving son, succeeded to the estates.*

1568-73   *Alva and the Council of Blood in the Netherlands. Alva boasted the execution of 18,000 heretics and rebels: 60,000 emigrated to England.*

1569   *Montaigne published the translation, made by him at his father's request, of the* Theologia Moralis *of Raimond Sebond.*

1570   *Signature of the peace of Saint-Germain. The prospect of a liberal settlement drew Montaigne to Paris, probably in the hope of an active political career.*

1571   *Montaigne returned to a retired life at home and began the composition of the* Essais.

1572   *The Massacre of Saint Bartholomew. The capture of Brill by the Sea Beggars assured the revolt of the Netherlands.*

1574   *Accession of Henri III.*

1576   *Formation of the Catholic League. The Spanish Fury in Antwerp.*

1577   *Montaigne, already a Gentleman of the Chamber of Henri III, received a like title at the Court of Henri of Navarre.*

1580   *Publication of the first two Books of the* Essais.

1580-81   *Montaigne travelled in Switzerland, Germany and Italy. At Rome he was requested by the Sacred College to remove certain passages from the* Essais: *these appeared in the later editions somewhat augmented.*

A Chronological Table

*On hearing of his election as Mayor of Bordeaux Montaigne
returned to France and held the office, exceptionally, for two
successive terms.*

1584 *Henri of Navarre, now heir to the French crown,
visited Montaigne at his chateau.*

      Assassination of William the Silent.

1585 *Ronsard died.*

1587 *Execution of Mary Stuart.*

1588 *Montaigne went to Paris and published the fourth
known edition of the Essais, containing for the first
time the third Book. He met Mlle. de Gournay, whom he
came to name his adopted daughter.*

      The Spanish Armada.

1589 *Henry III. assassinated. Henri of Navarre became
king of France.*

1592 *Michel de Montaigne died at the Chateau de Montaigne on the 13th of September at the age of fifty-
nine.*

1595 *Mlle. de Gournay and Pierre de Brach published the
authorised posthumous edition of the Essais.*

1597 *Bacon's Essayes.*

1605 *Sir Thomas Browne born.*

1611 *Authorised Version of the English Bible.*

1616 *Shakespeare died.*

Introduction

By ANDRE GIDE

MONTAIGNE is the author of a single book—the *Essays*. But in this one book, written without preconceived plan, without method, as events or his reading chanced to suggest, he claims to give us his whole self. He published four successive editions of it—the first in 1580, when he was forty-seven years old. This text he revised, he corrected, he perfected and, at his death in 1592, left yet another copy of his work loaded with emendations and addenda which were incorporated in later editions. Meanwhile Montaigne travelled through South Germany and Italy (1580-1581) and then filled the important post of Mayor of Bordeaux; he gives his readers the benefit of the observations he gathered in foreign lands and of the experiences of his public life at a period when the wars of religion were profoundly troubling his country.

From this time onwards, leaving public affairs in order to occupy himself only with his own thoughts, he shut himself up in his library and for the rest of his life never left the little château in Périgord where he was born. Here he wrote the additional chapters that constitute the third book of the *Essays;* he revised the old ones, corrected, improved them and introduced six hundred additions. He occasionally encumbered his first text too with a load of quotations gathered in the course of his continual reading; for Montaigne was persuaded that everything had already been thought and

Introduction

said, and was anxious to show that man is always and everywhere one and the same. The abundance of these quotations which turn some of his chapters into a compact pudding of Greek and Latin authors might cast a doubt on Montaigne's originality. It must indeed have been exceptionally great to triumph over such a jumble of antiquities.

This show of erudition was not peculiar to Montaigne, for it was a time when men's heads had been turned by Greek and Latin culture. Gibbon has very justly remarked that the study of the classics, which dates from much further back than the beginning of the Renaissance, retarded rather than hastened the intellectual development of the peoples of the West. The reason for this is that writers were then hunting for models rather than for inspiration and stimulus. Learning in the days of Boccaccio and Rabelais weighed heavily on men's minds and far from helping to liberate, stifled them. The authority of the ancients, and of Aristotle in particular, drove culture into a rut and during the sixteenth century the University of Paris turned out almost nothing but bookworms and pedants.

Montaigne does not go so far as to rebel against this bookish culture, but he succeeded so well in assimilating and making it his own that it was never a hindrance to his mind, and in this he differs from all other writers of his time. At most, he follows the fashion by interlarding his works with quotations. But, "What does it avail us" he asks, "to have a stomach full of food if it does not digest, if it does not become transformed within us, if it does not increase our size and strength?" (Book I, Chapter 25.)

The success of the *Essays* would be inexplicable but for the author's extraordinary personality. What did he bring

Introduction

the world then that was so new? Self-knowledge—and all other knowledge seemed to him uncertain; but the human being he discovers—and uncovers—is so genuine, so true, that in him every reader of the *Essays* recognizes himself.

In every historical period an attempt is made to cover over this real self with a conventional figure of humanity. Montaigne pushes aside this mask in order to get at what is essential; if he succeeds it is thanks to assiduous effort and singular perspicacity; it is by opposing convention, established beliefs, conformism, with a spirit of criticism that is constantly on the alert, easy and at the same time tense, playful, amused at everything, smiling, indulgent yet uncompromising, for its object is to know and not to moralize.

"Montaigne is the frankest and honestest of all writers," says Emerson, who places him among his constellation of six *Representative Men* with Plato, Swedenborg, Shakespeare, Goethe, and Napoleon. In his study on *Montaigne: or, the Skeptic,* he tells us that the *Essays* "is the only book which we certainly know to have been in the poet's library" (the poet here being Shakespeare). "Leigh Hunt," he adds, relates of Lord Byron, that Montaigne was the only great writer of past times whom he read with avowed satisfaction"; and further on, "Gibbon reckons, in these bigoted times" (the sixteenth century) "but two men of liberality in France: Henry IV and Montaigne."

For Montaigne, the body is as important as the mind; he does not separate the one from the other and is constantly careful never to give us his thoughts in the abstract. It is particularly incumbent on us therefore to see him before we listen to him. It is he himself who furnishes us with all the elements of a full-length portrait. Let us look at it.

Introduction

He is rather short; his face is full without being fat; he wears a short beard according to the fashion of the period. All his senses are "sound, almost to perfection." Although he has used his robust health licentiously, it is still very hearty and only slightly affected by gravel at the age of forty-seven. His gait is assured, his gestures brusque, his voice loud and sonorous. He is fond of talking and always talks vehemently and excitedly. He eats of everything and anything so gluttonously that he sometimes bites his own fingers, for in those days forks were not in use. He rides a great deal and even in his old age he is not fatigued by long hours in the saddle. Sleep, he tells us, takes up a great portion of his life. And I would on no account omit a little detail which may make American readers smile: when he sits down, he likes to have his "legs as high as my seat, or higher." (Book III, Chapter 13.)

The importance of an author lies not only in his personal value but also and greatly in the opportuneness of his message. There are some whose message is only of historical importance and finds no echo among us today. In past times, it may have stirred men's conscience, fed their enthusiasms, aroused revolutions; we have no ears for it now. Great authors are not only those whose work answers to the needs of one country and one period, but those who provide us with a food which is able to satisfy the different hungers of various nationalities and successive generations. "A competent reader," says Montaigne, "often discovers in another's writings other perfections than those which the author has consciously imparted to them, and lends to them a richer meaning and aspect." (Book I, Chapter 24.) Is he himself such an author and will he be able to answer such new questions

Introduction

as the competent reader may wish to put to him? I take leave to hope so.

In our time and in all countries whatsoever, constructive minds are in particular request; the authors who are most admired are those who offer us a carefully composed system, a method for solving the agonizing political, social, and moral problems which are tormenting almost all peoples and every one of us individually. Montaigne, it is true, brings us no method (how could a method that might have been valid at his time be practicable in ours?), no philosophical or social system. No mind could be less ordered than his. He lets it free to play and run wild as it pleases. And even his perpetual doubt which made Emerson consider him as the most perfect representative of skepticism (that is to say of antidogmatism, of the spirit of enquiry and investigation) may be compared, it has been said, to those purgative medicines which the patient ejects together with the stuff of which they rid him. So that some people have seen in his *"Que sçais-je?"* at once the highest mark of his wisdom and of his teaching. Not that it satisfies me. It is not their skepticism that pleases me in the *Essays,* nor is that the lesson I draw from them. A "competent reader" will find in Montaigne more and better than doubts and questions.

To Pilate's cruel question which re-echoes down the ages, Montaigne seems to have assumed, though in a quite human and profane manner, and in a very different sense, Christ's divine answer: *"I* am the truth." That is to say he thinks he can know nothing *truly* but himself. This is what makes him talk so much about himself; for the knowledge of self seems to him indeed as important as any other. "We must remove the mask," he says, "from things as from

Introduction

persons." (Book I, Chapter 21.) He paints himself in order to unmask himself. And as the mask belongs much more to the country and the period than to the man himself, it is above all by the mask that people differ, so that in the being that is really unmasked, it is easy to recognize our own likeness.

He even comes to think that the portrait he paints of himself may be more generally interesting in proportion as it is more peculiar to himself; and it is by reason of this profound truth that we do in effect take so great an interest in his portrait; for "every man has in himself the whole form of human nature." (Book III, Chapter 2.) And more than this: Montaigne is convinced that, "as Pindar said, being truthful is the beginning of great virtue." (Book II, Chapter 18.) These admirable words which Montaigne borrowed from Plutarch, who himself took them from Pindar, I adopt as my own; I should like to inscribe them in the forefront of the *Essays*, for there above all lies the important lesson I draw from them.

And yet Montaigne does not seem to have himself at first grasped the boldness and reach of this resolve of his to admit only the truth about himself and to paint himself as nature made him. This accounts for a certain early hesitation in his drawing, for his attempt to find shelter in the thick undergrowths of history, for his piling up of quotations and examples—authorizations, I was tempted to say—for his endless gropings. His interest in himself is at first vague and confused, with no very clear idea as to what is important, and with a suspicion that perhaps the things that are most negligible in appearance and the most commonly disdained may in reality be just those that are most worthy of attention. Everything in himself is an object of curiosity, amusement, and astonishment: "I have seen no monster or miracle on earth more evident than myself; we become wonted to all strangeness by habit and time; but the more familiar I am with myself and the better I know myself, the more my misshapenness astonishes me, and the less do I comprehend myself." (Book III, Chapter 11.) And how delightful it is to hear him talking like this of his "deformity," when what we like about him is precisely what enables us to recognize him as one of ourselves—just an ordinary man.

It is only when he gets to the third and last book of the *Essays* (which does not figure in the first edition) that Montaigne, in full possession, not of himself (he will never be that—no one can be) but of his subject, ceases to grope his way; he knows what he wants to say, what he must say, and he says it admirably, with a grace, a playfulness, a felicity and ingenuity of expression that are incomparable. "Others," he says, "shape the man; I narrate him." (Book III, Chapter 2.) And a few lines further on and more subtly, "I do not paint his being; I paint his passing." (Book III, Chapter 2.) (The Germans would say the "*werden.*") For Montaigne is constantly preoccupied by the perpetual flux of all things, and in these words he points to the non-stability of human personality which never *is,* but only conscious of itself in the evanescent moment of *becoming.* And as all other certainties break down around him, this one at least grows greater and stronger, that on this subject, at any rate —the subject of himself—he is "the most learned man alive" and that "no one ever went deeper into his subject" nor "arrived more exactly and more completely at the end which he had proposed to himself of his work" for which he has

Introduction

"need to bring to it only fidelity"; and he immediately adds "the most sincere and purest that can be found." (Book III, Chapter 2.)

I think the great pleasure we take in Montaigne's *Essays* comes from the great pleasure he took in writing them, a pleasure we feel, so to speak, in every sentence. Of all the chapters that compose the three books of the *Essays*, one alone is distinctly tedious; it is by far the longest and the only one he wrote with application, care, and a concern for composition. This is the *Apology for Raimond Sebond*, a Spanish philosopher who lived in the fifteenth century and professed medicine in France at the University of Toulouse, and whose *Theologia Naturalis* Montaigne had laboriously translated at his father's request. "It was a very strange and novel occupation for me; but being, by chance, at leisure at the time, and being unable to refuse any thing to the bidding of the best father that ever was, I accomplished it as I could." (Book II, Chapter 12.) This chapter is the first that Montaigne wrote. It is one of the most celebrated and oftenest quoted, for Montaigne's mind, by nature so rambling and unorderly, here strives to develop a sort of doctrine and give apparent consistency to his inconsistent skepticism. But just because he is keeping his mind on the lead, it loses almost all its grace, the exquisite charm of its indolent progress; he is directing it, we feel, towards an object, and we are never enchanted as we are later on when he allows it to venture tentatively down untraced paths and gather all the casually encountered flowers that grow by the wayside. No works, I should like here to remark, are more naturally perfect and beautiful than those which the author has most delighted in writing, those in which difficulty and effort are

Introduction

least apparent. In art, *seriousness* is of no avail; the surest of guides is enjoyment. In all, or almost all, the other writings which go to make up the different chapters of the *Essays,* Montaigne's thought remains as it were in the fluid state, so uncertain, so changing, and even contradictory, that the most diverse interpretations of it were subsequently given. Some writers as, for instance, Pascal and Kant, attempt to see in him a Christian; others, like Emerson, an exemplar of skepticism; others a precursor of Voltaire. Sainte-Beuve went so far as to look upon the *Essays* as a sort of preparation, an ante-chamber to Spinoza's *Ethics.* But Sainte-Beuve seems to me nearest the truth when he says: "With an appearance of making himself out peculiar, of reducing himself to a bundle of odd manias, he has touched each one of us in his most secret part, and while portraying himself with careless, patient and incessantly repeated strokes, he has cunningly painted the majority of mankind, and all the more successfully as he has the more minutely dissected his single self—'wavering and diverse' as he says. Each one of us finds a morsel of his own property in Montaigne." (*Port-Royal,* Book III, Chapter 2.)

I consider it a mark of great strength in Montaigne that he succeeded in accepting his own inconsistencies and contradictions. At the beginning of the second book of the *Essays* the following sentence strikes the alarm: "Those who employ themselves in observing the actions of men find themselves nowhere so embarrassed as in piecing them together and placing them in the same light; for they are wont to contradict one another in such strange fashion that it seems impossible that they should come from the same person." (Book II, Chapter 1.) Not one of the great special-

Introduction

ists of the human heart, be his name Shakespeare, Cervantes, or Racine, has failed to have at any rate fleeting glimpses of the inconsequence of human beings. But no doubt, it was necessary to establish for the time being a somewhat rudimentary psychology, on general and sharply defined lines, as a preliminary to the construction of a classical art. Lovers had to be nothing but lovers, misers wholly misers, and jealous men a hundred per cent jealous, while good care had to be taken that no one should have a share of all these qualities at once. Montaigne speaks of those "good authors" (and what he says is even truer of those who followed him than of those he was acquainted with) "who select a prevailing characteristic of a man, and adapt and interpret all his actions in accordance with that image; and if they can not sufficiently bend them, they attribute them to dissimulation." (Book II, Chapter 1.) And he adds, "Augustus hath escaped their hands" much in the same tone as Saint-Evremond who, nearly a century later, says, "There are corners and twists in our soul which have escaped him [Plutarch]. . . He judged men too much in the rough and did not believe them to be so different from themselves as they are. . . What he thinks contradictory he attributes to external causes . . . which Montaigne understood far better." It seems to me that Montaigne, unlike Saint-Evremond, saw more than mere 'inconstancy'; I think that it is precisely under cover of this word that the real question lies hidden, and that it was not until much later that Dostoievsky, and then Proust, attacked it, so that some people say, "What is at issue here is the very conception of man on which we are now living," a conception which Freud and some others are now in process of breaking down. Perhaps the most surprising thing

Introduction

about Montaigne, the thing that touches us most directly, is those few, sudden lights he casts unexpectedly, and as it were involuntarily, upon the uncertain frontiers of human personality and upon the instability of the ego.

Montaigne's contemporaries no doubt skated over the few passages which shake us most today without having eyes to see them, or at any rate to judge of their importance. And no doubt Montaigne himself partly shared their indifference, just as he shared their curiosity for things which no longer interest us, and if he were to come back to earth today, he might very well say, "If I had known that that was what you would care about, there is a great deal more I might have told you!" Why in the world didn't you then? It was not your contemporaries it was important to please, but *us*. The points which were criticized or overlooked by his own epoch are often the very points by which a writer succeeds in reaching and communicating with us across the ages. To foresee in the midst of the day's preoccupations what will still deserve the interest of coming generations demands indeed peculiar penetration.

Love does not seem to have played much part in Montaigne's life; sensuality a greater one. He seems to have married without much enthusiasm. And if, in spite of this, he was a good husband, he nevertheless wrote towards the end of his life, "It is, perchance, easier to do without the sex altogether than to comport oneself properly in all points in companionship with one's wife," (Book II, Chapter 33), which does not point exactly to his having done so. He had the lowest opinion of women, and beyond the pleasure he takes with them, confines them to the cares of the household.

Introduction

I have noted all the passages in the *Essays* in which he speaks of them; there is not one that is not insulting. And yet towards the end of his life he made an exception to this severity in favor of Mlle Marie de Gournay, his "daughter in alliance, and truly of me beloved with more than a fatherly love, and as one of the best parts of my being enfeofed in my home and solitariness." And he even adds, "There is nothing in the world I esteeme more than her." She was only twenty and Montaigne fifty-four when she was taken with an affection "more than superabounding" for the author of the *Essays*. It would be ungrateful not to mention this mutual attachment which was entirely spiritual in its nature, for it is to Mlle de Gournay's care and devotion that we owe the third and extremely important edition of the *Essays* (1595) which appeared three years after Montaigne's death, as well as the preservation of the manuscripts which served later for the establishment of the most authoritative text.

As to his own children, "they have all died at nurse," he tells us perfunctorily. (Book II, Chapter 8.) An only daughter "escaped that misfortune," and these successive bereavements do not seem to have greatly affected him.

Montaigne, however, was by no means incapable of sympathy, and particularly towards small and humble folk: "I readily associate with men of humble condition . . . from innate compassion, which in me is infinitely powerful." (Book III, Chapter 13.)

But, for equilibrium's sake, his reason immediately demands a correction. "I very tenderly compassionate the afflictions of another and could easily weep for company if, for any cause whatever, I were able to weep." (Book II, Chap-

Introduction

ter 11.) La Rochefoucauld says at a later date, forestalling Nietzsche's famous "Let us be hard": "I am little susceptible to pity and wish I were not so at all." But such declarations as these touch me particularly when they come from those who, like Montaigne and Nietzsche, are naturally tender-hearted.

Of Montaigne's sentimental life, friendship alone has left any trace in his work. Etienne de la Boëtie, his elder by three years, and author of a single short work entitled *On Voluntary Servitude,* inspired him with a feeling which seems to have occupied an important place in his heart and mind. This little book is not enough to make us consider La Boëtie "the greatest man of the age," as Montaigne did, but no doubt it helps us to understand the nature of the attachment which the future author of the *Essays* felt for a singularly generous and noble character.

Notwithstanding the beauty of this friendship, we may wonder whether it did not put some constraint upon Montaigne, and ask ourselves what the voluptuous author of the *Essays* would have been like if he had not met La Boëtie, and above all what the *Essays* would have been like if La Boëtie had not died so young (at the age of thirty-three) and if he had continued to exercise his influence over his friend. Sainte-Beuve, our great critic, quotes a very fine saying of the younger Pliny's: "I have lost the witness of my life. I fear I may henceforth live more carelessly." But this 'carelessly' is just what we like so much about Montaigne. Under La Boëtie's eyes, he draped himself a little in the antique fashion. In this, too, he was as sincere as ever, for he was greatly enamored of heroism; but he did not like a man to be artificial, and liked it less and less; more and more he

Introduction

came to fear that to grow in height must mean to increase in narrowness.

La Boëtie, in a piece of Latin verse addressed to Montaigne, says: "For you, there is more to combat, for you, our friend, whom we know to be equally inclined both to outstanding vices and virtues." Montaigne, when once La Boëtie had disappeared, withdrew more and more from the combat, as much from natural inclination as from philosophy. There is nothing Montaigne dislikes more than a personality—or rather an impersonality—obtained artificially, laboriously, contentiously, in accordance with morals, propriety, custom, and what he likens to prejudices. It is as though the true self which all this hampers, hides, or distorts, keeps in his eyes a sort of mystic value, and as if he were expecting from it some surprising kind of revelation. I understand, of course, how easy it is here to play upon words and to see in Montaigne's teaching nothing but a counsel to abandon oneself to nature, to follow one's instincts blindly, and even to grant precedence to the vilest, which always seem the sincerest, that is, the most natural, those which by their very density and thickness are invariably to be found at the bottom of the recipient, even when the noblest passions have shaken it. But I believe this would be a very wrong interpretation of Montaigne who, though he concedes a large allowance, too large perhaps, to the instincts we have in common with animals, knows how to take from them in order to rise, and never allows himself to be their slave or their victim.

It is natural that with such ideas, Montaigne should feel very little inclined to repentance and contrition. "I have grown older by a number of years since my first publication,

Introduction

which was in the year one thousand five hundred and
eighty; but I doubt whether I am one whit wiser." (Book
III, Chapter 9.) And again: "The excesses in which I have
found myself engaged are not, thank God, of the worst sort.
I have condemned them in myself, according as they deserve it." (Book II, Chapter 11.) Such declarations abound
in the last part of the *Essays,* and later on he adds again, to
some people's great indignation: "Had I to live again, I
should live as I have lived; I neither lament the past, nor fear
the future." (Book III, Chapter 2.) These declarations are
certainly as little Christian as possible. Every time Montaigne speaks of Christianity it is with the strangest (sometimes one might almost say with the most malicious) im-
pertinence. He often treats of religion, never of Christ. Not
once did he refer to His words; one might almost doubt
whether he had ever read the Gospels—or rather, one cannot
doubt that he never read them seriously. As for the respect
he shows Catholicism, there undoubtedly enters into it a
large amount of prudence. (We must remember that the
great massacre of Protestants throughout the whole kingdom of France on the eve of St. Bartholomew took place in
1572.) The example of Erasmus (d. 1536) was a warning to
him, and it is easy to understand that he was far from anxious to be obliged to write his *Retractions.* I know that as a
matter of fact Erasmus never did write his, but he had to
promise the Church that he would. And even a promise of
this kind is a nuisance. Far better to be wily.

In the editions of 1582 and 1595 a multitude of concilia-
tory additions have been introduced into the chapter entitled *Of Prayers and Orisons.* During his travels in Italy
in 1581, he had presented his book to Pope Gregory XIII,

Introduction

who was the founder of the Gregorian Calendar now in use. The Pope complimented him but made a few reservations of which Montaigne took account in the passages he afterwards introduced into the *Essays*. In these, and in others as well, Montaigne insists to excess and with much repetition on his perfect orthodoxy and submission to the Church. The Church indeed showed herself at that time extremely accommodating; she had come to terms with the cultural development of the Renaissance; Erasmus, in spite of the accusation of atheism which caused his books to be condemned in Paris, was put up as a candidate for the Cardinalate; the works of Macchiavelli, notwithstanding their profoundly irreligious character, had been printed in Rome by virtue of a 'brief' of Clement VII. This tolerance and relaxation on the part of the Church incited the great leaders of the Reformation to a corresponding increase of intransigence. Montaigne could come to an understanding with Catholicism but not with Protestantism. He accepted religion provided it was satisfied with a semblance. What he wrote about princes applied in his mind to ecclesiastical authorities as well: "All deference to them and bowing before them is their due, except with the understanding; my reason is not framed to bend and stoop—that is for my knees." (Book III, Chapter 8.)

In order still further to protect his book, he felt impelled to insert further passages of a very reassuring nature, in which he is hardly recognizable, into those very parts of the *Essays* which are most likely to arouse alarm in the hearts of sincere Christians: "This sole aim of another, happily immortal, life justly deserves that we should give up the satisfaction and charms of this life of ours." (Book I, Chapter 39.)

Introduction

This passage (which for that matter was left in manuscript and only published after his death) and other similar ones seem to have been stuck into his book like so many lightning-conductors, or better still, like labels of lemonade or ginger-ale fixed upon bottles of whiskey when a régime has gone dry. And in fact a few lines after the lightning-conductor come the words: "We must hold on with all our strength to the enjoyment of the pleasures of life, which our years tear from our grasp one after another." (Book I, Chapter 39.)

This passage of the first edition, which the added lines attempt in vain to disguise, shows the true Montaigne, that "sworn foe of every sort of falsification." (Book I, Chapter 40); and I should be indignant at this cautious recantation, if I did not think that it had perhaps been necessary in order to get his wares safely through to us. Sainte-Beuve says of him very justly: "He may have appeared a very good Catholic except for not having been a Christian." So that one might say of Montaigne what he himself said of the Emperor Julian: "In the matter of religion he was in error throughout; he had been surnamed the Apostate, because he abandoned our form; yet the opinion seems to me more probable that he had never believed it in his heart, but had pretended to do so, in obedience to the laws." (Book II, Chapter 19.) And later, quoting Marcellinus, again about Julian: "He cherished . . . paganism in his heart; but, all his army being Christians, he dared not let it be known." (Book II, Chapter 19.) What he likes about Catholicism, what he admires and praises, is its order and ancientness. "In this dissension which now agitates France with civil war, the best and sanest party is, doubtless, that which upholds the old time religion and government of the country." (Book

Introduction

II, Chapter 19.) For "all great mutations share a state and disorder it." (Book III, Chapter 9.) And "the oldest and best known evil is always more endurable than one new and untried." (Book III, Chapter 9.) There is no need to look for any other explanation of his ignorance of the Gospels and his hatred of Protestant reformers. He wishes to keep the Church's religion—France's religion—as it is, not because he thinks it the only good one but because he thinks it would be bad to change it.

In the same way we feel throughout Montaigne's life and writings a constant love of order and moderation, care for the public good, a refusal to let his own personal interest prevail over the interest of all. But he believes that the honesty of his own judgment and the preservation of that honesty are more valuable than any other considerations and should be set above them. "I would rather let things go to destruction than pervert my faithfulness in their service." (Book II, Chapter 17.) And I prefer to believe in the sincerity of this statement rather than ask myself whether he is not bragging a little; for it is as important nowadays that such words should be listened to as it was important in Montaigne's troubled times that there should be men to keep the integrity of their conscience and maintain their independence and autonomy above the herd instincts of submission and cowardly acceptance. "All general judgments are weak and imperfect." (Book III, Chapter 8); or again: "There is no course of life so foolish and feeble as that which is guided by rules and discipline." (Book III, Chapter 13.) Passages of this kind abound in the *Essays,* and as they seem to me of the highest importance, particularly nowadays, I will quote one more: "The public good demands

Introduction

that some men betray and lie and kill; let us resign this commission to the more obedient and compliant." (Book III, Chapter 1.)

When he resigned his post of magistrate and later on, too, when he left the mayoralty of Bordeaux to occupy himself henceforth exclusively with himself, he judged very rightly that the elaboration of his *Essays* would be the greatest service he could render to the State, and—let me add—to all mankind. For it must be observed that the idea of mankind for Montaigne predominates greatly over that of country. After a wonderful panegyric of France, or at any rate of Paris, "the glory of France and one of the noblest ornaments of the world" which "I love . . . tenderly, even to her warts and blemishes," (Book III, Chapter 9), he takes care to say that his love of the human race is greater still. . . "I regard all men as my compatriots and embrace a Pole as a Frenchman making less account of the national, than of the universal and common, bond." (Book III, Chapter 9.) "Pure friendships acquired by us usually surpass those in which the being of the same region or of the same blood joins us. Nature has put us into the world free and unfettered; we imprison ourselves within certain narrow limits, as did the kings of Persia, who bound themselves to drink no other water than that of the river Choaspes, foolishly renouncing their right of usage over all other streams, and dried up all the rest of the world so far as they were concerned." (Book III, Chapter 9.)

"Each of us inevitable;
 Each of us limitless; each of us with his or her right upon
 the earth,"

XL

Introduction

says Walt Whitman. (Ah! how Montaigne would have delighted—Montaigne who was so unblushing on the subject of his person, so anxious not to oppose the soul to the flesh and to proclaim the latter's legitimate and healthy pleasures—how he would have delighted to hear Whitman sing, indecently and gloriously, the beauties and robust joys of his body!)

One never comes to an end with Montaigne. As he speaks of everything without order or method, any man can glean what he likes from the *Essays,* which will often be what some other would leave aside. There is no author it is easier to give a twist to without incurring the blame of betraying him, for he himself sets the example and constantly contradicts and betrays himself. "In truth, and I am not afraid to confess it, I would readily, at need, offer a candle to St. Michael and another to his dragon." (Book III Chapter 1.) This, it must be admitted, is more likely to please the Dragon than Saint Michael. Montaigne, indeed, is not beloved by partisans, whom he certainly did not love, which explains why he was not held in much favor after his death, in France, at any rate, which was torn in two by the bitterest factions. Between 1595 (he died in 1592) and 1635, there were only three or four re-editions of the *Essays.* It was abroad, in Italy, in Spain, and particularly in England, that Montaigne soon became popular during this period of French disfavor or semi-favor. In Bacon's *Essays* and Shakespeare's plays there are unmistakable traces of Montaigne's influence.

It is well known that there exists in the British Museum a copy of Florio's translation of Montaigne which bears one of the rare signatures of the author of *Hamlet.* It is in this

Introduction

play in particular that English critics have found traces of Montaigne's philosophy. And in *The Tempest* he makes Gonzalo say:

> "Had I plantation of this isle . . .
> And were the king on't, what would I do? . . .
> I' the common wealth I would by contraries
> Execute all things; for no kind of traffic
> Would I admit; no name of magistrate;
> Letters should not be known; riches, poverty,
> And use of service, none; contract, succession,
> Bourn, bound of land, tilth, vineyard, none;
>
> No occupation; all men idle, all;
> And women too, but innocent and pure;
> No sovereignty. . .
> All things in common nature should produce
> Without sweat or endeavour; treason, felony,
> Sword, pike, knife, gun, or need of any engine,
> Would I not have; but nature should bring forth,
> Of its own kind, all foison, all abundance,
> To feed my innocent people."
>
> Act II, Sc. I.

This passage is practically translated, or at any rate greatly inspired by a chapter of the *Essays* of which an extract will be found in the following pages. Everything that Montaigne says here on *Cannibals*—the title of this chapter—will no doubt particularly interest Americans, for his subject is the New World which had been recently discovered, and towards which Europe was turning ecstatic

Introduction

glances. It hardly matters that countless illusions went to make up the prestige of these distant lands. Montaigne delights in describing their inhabitants and the purity of their manners and customs, just as Diderot, two centuries later, painted the manners of the Tahitians in order to shame those of the Old World. Both the one and the other understand what instruction and guidance the whole of humanity might gather from the sole example of a happy man.

In his drift away from Christianity, it is to Goethe that Montaigne draws near by anticipation. "For my own part, then, I love life and cultivate it, as it has pleased God to bestow it upon us. . . Nature is a gentle guide, but not more gentle than prudent and just." (Book III, Chapter 13.) Goethe would no doubt gladly have endorsed these sentences which are almost the last of the *Essays*. This is the final flowering of Montaigne's wisdom. Not a word of it is useless. How very careful he is to add the idea of prudence, justice, and culture to his declaration of the love of life!

What Montaigne teaches us especially is what was called at a much later date, *liberalism,* and I think that it is the wisest lesson that can be drawn from him at the present time when political or religious convictions are so miserably dividing all men and opposing them to each other. "In the present confusion of this state my personal concern has not made me ignore either the praiseworthy qualities in my adversaries or those that are reprehensible in the leaders whom I have followed." (Book III, Chapter 10.) He adds a little later: "If they have come to hate an orator, the next day he becomes to them not eloquent." (Book III, Chapter 10.) And further on these admirable lines: "They desire . . . our

Introduction

conviction and our judgment to subserve not truth, but an idea proceeding from our desires. I should err rather toward the other extreme, so greatly do I fear that my desire may mislead me." (Book III, Chapter 10.) These qualities of mind and soul are never more wanted and would never be of greater service than at the times when they are most generally disregarded.

This rare and extraordinary propensity, of which he often speaks, towards listening to, and even espousing, other people's opinions, to the point of letting them prevail over his own, prevented him from venturing very far along the road that was afterwards to be Nietzsche's. He is held back by a natural prudence from which, as from a safeguard, he is very loth to depart. He shrinks from desert places and regions where the air is too rarefied. But a restless curiosity spurs him on, and in the realm of ideas he habitually behaves as he did when travelling. The secretary who accompanied him on his tour kept a journal. "I never saw him less tired," he writes, "nor heard him complain less of his pain," (he suffered at that time from gravel, which did not prevent him from remaining for hours in the saddle) "with a mind, both on the road and in our halting places, so eager for any encounters, so on the lookout for opportunities to speak to strangers, that I think it distracted him from his ills." He declared he had "no project but to perambulate through unknown places," and further, "He took such great pleasure in travelling that he hated the neighbourhood of the place where he was obliged to rest." Moreover, he "was accustomed to say that after having passed a restless night, when in the morning it came to his mind he had a town or new country to visit, he would rise with eagerness and alacrity."

Introduction

Montaigne was very nearly fifty years old when he undertook the first and only long journey of his life through South Germany and Italy. This journey lasted seventeen months and in all probability would have lasted still longer, considering the extreme pleasure he took in it, if his unexpected election to the mayoralty of Bordeaux had not suddenly recalled him to France. From that moment he directed towards ideas the high-spirited curiosity that had sent him hurrying along the roads.

It is very instructive to follow through the successive editions of the *Essays* the modifications of his attitude towards death. He entitles one of the first chapters of his book, "That to Think As a Philosopher is to Learn to Die." (Book I, Chapter 20), in which we read: "There is nothing with which I have always been more occupied than with thoughts of death; yes, even in the most wanton season of my days." (Book I, Chapter 20.) His idea was that, by familiarizing himself with these imaginations, he would diminish their horror. But in the last edition of his *Essays* he reached the point of saying: "I am at this hour in such a state, God be praised, that I can dislodge whenever it may please him, without regret for anything whatsoever. I am untying myself from all things; my farewells are now said to everyone save myself. Never did man prepare to leave this world more wholly and entirely, or to detach himself from it more completely, than I endeavour to do." (Book I, Chapter 20.) He almost gets to love this death as he loves all that is natural.

We are told that Montaigne made a very Christian end. All we can say that he was by no means on the road to it. It is true that his wife and daughter were present at his last moments and no doubt they induced him, out of sympathy,

Introduction

as often happens, to die, not that "death withdrawn into itself, peaceful and solitary, belonging to me alone, suited to
my retired and secluded life," (Book III, Chapter 9), with
which he would have been more satisfied, but more devoutly
than he would have done of himself. Is it a presentiment of
this that made him write, "If, however, I had to choose, my
choice would be, I think, that it should be on horseback
rather than in bed, away from my house and far from my
family and friends." (Book III, Chapter 9.)

If I am accused of having sharpened Montaigne's ideas to
excess, my answer is that numbers of his commentators have
busied themselves with blunting them. I have merely removed their wrappings and disengaged them from the wad-
ding that sometimes chokes the *Essays* and prevents their
shafts from reaching us. The great preoccupation of pedagogues, when they are faced with authors of some boldness
who yet are classics, is to render them inoffensive; and I
often wonder that the work of years should so naturally
contribute to this. After a little it seems as though the edge
of new thoughts gets worn away, and on the other hand,
from growing in some sort accustomed to them, we are able
to handle them without fear of injury.

Montaigne, during his travels in Italy, is often surprised
to see the loftiest monuments of ancient Rome half buried
in a mass of fallen litter. Their summits have been the first
to crumble and it is their own fragments that strew the earth
around them and gradually raise its level. If, in our day,
they do not seem to tower so high above us, it is also because
we do not stand so far below them.

"To the Reader"

HIS is an honest book, reader. It gives you to know, at the outset, that I have proposed to myself only an intimate and private end; I have not considered what would be serviceable for you or for my renown; my powers are not equal to such a design. I have devoted these pages to the particular pleasure of my kinsmen and friends; to the end that, when they have lost me (which they must do ere long), they may find herein some touches of my qualities and moods, and that, by this means, they may cherish more completely and more vividly the knowledge they have had of me. Had I purposed to seek public favour, I should have better adorned myself, and presented myself in a studied attitude. I desire to be seen in my simple, natural, everyday guise, without effort and artifice; for it is my own self that I portray. My imperfections will be seen herein to the life, and my personal nature,* so far as respect for the

*Ma forme naïve.

public has permitted this. I assure you that, had I been living among those nations which are said still to dwell under the benign license of the primal laws of nature, I should very readily have painted myself quite completely, and quite naked. Since, reader, I am thus, myself, the subject of my book, it is not reasonable that you should employ your leisure on so trivial and empty a matter.

So, farewell. From Montaigne, this first March, 1580.*

*Other dates are affixed to different editions.

THE PUBLISHER OF THIS EDITION TO THE READER: The superior numbers which you will encounter in the text are references to the Notes by Mr. Ives; and you will find these Notes printed in the separate volume which is called A Handbook to the Essays—and which you can keep open before you for ready reference as you read the text.

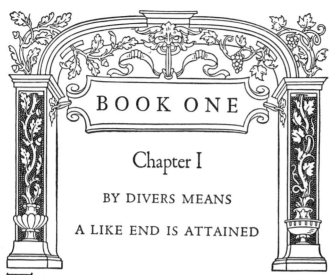

BOOK ONE

Chapter I

BY DIVERS MEANS
A LIKE END IS ATTAINED

THE most usual way to soften the hearts of those we have offended, when, having vengeance in their hand, they hold us at their mercy, is to move them by submission to commiseration and pity; defiance, courage, and resolution —means altogether different—have sometimes served the same purpose. Edward, Prince of Wales,[1] who so long governed our Guienne, a personage whose qualities and whose fortune show many notable characteristics of greatness, having been much harmed by the Limousins and having taken their city by force, could not be stayed by the outcries of the people and of the women and children given over to slaughter, crying for mercy and throwing themselves at his feet; until, as he went on through the city, he became aware of three French gentlemen who, with incredible valour, withstood alone the power of his victorious army. The sight of such notable courage and the respect that it aroused primarily

3

blunted the edge of his wrath, and beginning with those three, he shewed mercy to all the other inhabitants of the city.[2] Scanderbeg, Prince of Epirus,[3] pursuing one of his own soldiers, to put him to death, this soldier, having tried by every sort of humble expression and supplication to soften him, determined, in the last extremity, to await him, sword in hand. This action of his cut short his master's rage, who, seeing him play so honourable a part, received him into favour. The incident may suffer another interpretation by those who have not heard of this prince's prodigious strength and bravery. The Emperor Conrad the Third, having besieged Guelph, Duke of Bavaria, would vouchsafe no milder conditions—whatever base and dastardly terms of satisfaction were offered him—than to permit the gentlewomen who were besieged with the duke to go forth on foot, their honour secure, with whatever they could carry on their persons. And they, in greatness of heart, bethought them to take upon their backs their husbands and children and the duke himself. The emperor received such keen delight from witnessing the adroitness[4] of their courage, that he wept for joy, and quenched the bitterness of the mortal and capital hatred he had cherished against the duke, and thenceforth treated him and his courteously.[5]

Either of these methods would readily prevail with me, for I have a wonderful propensity toward mercy and mildness; so much so that I believe I should more instinctively yield to compassion than to admiration. Yet pity is a vicious sentiment, according to the Stoics:[6] they would have us succour the afflicted, but not be bowed down in sympathy with them.[7] Now these examples seem to me the more apt, inasmuch as we see in them these souls, when assailed and

A Like End is Attained

tested in these two ways, encounter the one without being shaken, and bend under the other. It may be said that to give way to commiseration and pity is the sign of an easy-going, kindly, and weak disposition; whence it happens that the feebler natures, as those of women and children and the common people, are most subject to this; but that, holding tears and prayers in contempt, to yield only to veneration for the sacred impersonation of courage is the sign of a strong and inflexible soul, which holds in admiration and honour virile and unyielding vigour. However, in less generous souls, astonishment and admiration may give birth to a like effect; witness the Thebans, who, having brought a capital charge against their captains for continuing to hold office beyond the time prescribed and preordained, absolved, not without much ado, Pelopidas, who bowed his head beneath the weight of such charges, and employed only entreaties and supplications to save himself. Whereas, on the contrary, in regard to Epaminondas, who eloquently recounted his achievements and taunted the people with them in a haughty and arrogant fashion, they had not the courage even to take the ballots in their hands, and the meeting broke up, greatly praising the high-heartedness of this personage.[8] Dionysius the elder, having taken the city of Reggio after extreme delays and difficulties, and therein the commander, Phyton, a man of great worth, who had very obstinately defended the city, determined to make use of the occasion for an example of terrible vengeance. First, he told him that, on the day before, he had caused his son and all his kindred to be drowned. To which Phyton replied only that they were more fortunate than himself by one day. Then he caused him to be stripped and seized by the executioners and dragged through

5

the city, scourging him most ignominiously and cruelly all the while, and in addition heaping violent and contumelious words upon him. But his courage never failed, or his self-possession; but, on the contrary, with steadfast mien, he continually declared in a loud voice the honourable and glorious cause of his death—that he would not surrender his country into the hands of a tyrant, whom he threatened with speedy punishment by the gods. Dionysius, reading in the eyes of his soldiers that, instead of being roused by the defiant words of this conquered foe in scorn of their leader and his triumph, they were becoming softened by their amazement at such rare courage, and were on the point of mutiny and even of snatching Phyton from the hands of the officials, consequently caused his martyrdom to come to an end, and sent him away secretly to be drowned in the sea.[9]

Truly man is a marvellously volatile, various, and wavering creature; it is difficult to base a stable and uniform judgement upon him. Look at Pompey, who pardoned the whole city of Mamertines, against which he was greatly roused, in view of the courage and magnanimity of the citizen Zeno, who took upon himself alone the public misdeed, and sought no other favour than to bear alone the penalty of it.[10] And Sylla's host, having displayed the like courage in the city of Perugia, gained nothing thereby, either for himself, or for others.[11] And, directly contrary to my first examples, the bravest of men, and the most merciful to the vanquished, Alexander, having forced the city of Gaza after many great difficulties, found there Betis, who was in command, of whose valour he had seen marvellous proofs during the siege, all covered with blood and wounds, still fighting in the midst of a number of Macedonians, who attacked him pell-mell.[12]

6

A Like End is Attained

Alexander, irritated by so costly a victory (for among other mischances he had received two fresh wounds on his body), cried out to him: "You shall not die as you have desired, Betis; be assured that you must suffer every kind of torture that can be invented for a prisoner." The other, with a countenance not only undismayed, but arrogant and haughty, said no word in reply to these threats. Whereupon Alexander, seeing his proud and persistent silence, cried: "Bends he not the knee? Has no sound of entreaty escaped him? Truly I will conquer this silence, and if I cannot extort a word from him, at least I will extort groans." And, his wrath becoming frenzy, he ordered that his heels should be pierced, and a cord passed through them, and had him dragged thus, alive, torn, and dismembered, at the tail of a cart.[13] May it be that courage was so natural and common a thing to him [Alexander] that, because he did not wonder at it, he thought less highly of it? or that he considered it to belong so peculiarly to himself, that he could not endure seeing it at this height in another without the irritation of an emotion of envy? or that the natural impetuosity of his wrath could not brook opposition? In truth, if it could have been checked, we must believe that it would have been so in the capture and desolation of the city of Thebes, upon seeing so many valiant men destroyed, and having no longer any means of defence, cruelly put to the sword. Nor was one seen who did not strive on to his last breath to avenge himself, and with the weapons of despair to console his own death with the death of some enemy. The carnage lasted till the last drop of blood was shed, and stopped only at those who were unarmed,—old men, women, and children,—to make of them thirty thousand slaves.[14]

Chapter II

OF

SADNESS

I AM one of those least subject to this emotion,[1] and I neither like nor respect it, although the world has undertaken, as if by agreement, to favour it with special honour. They clothe with it wisdom and virtue and knowledge: an absurd and deforming garment. The Italians have more aptly baptised malignity with its name;[2] for it is a quality always harmful, always foolish; and as being always cowardly and vile, the Stoics forbid the feeling to their ideal wise man.[3] But the story says that Psammenitus, King of Egypt, having been defeated and captured by Cambyses, King of Persia, seeing his daughter pass by, a prisoner, dressed as a servant sent to draw water, all his friends around him weeping and lamenting, stood motionless and silent, his eyes fixed on the ground; and soon after, seeing his son led to death, he maintained the same demeanour. But, having perceived one of his household among the captives, he beat his head and gave way to extreme lamentation.[4] This might be coupled with what we recently saw to be the case with one of our princes,[5] who, having heard at Trent, where he was, of the death of his eldest brother,—a brother upon whom, indeed, rested the support and honour of his family,

8

Of Sadness

—and very soon afterward of the death of a younger brother, its next hope; and having sustained these two assaults with exemplary firmness, when, some days later, one of his servants died, he allowed himself to be overcome by this last event, and, losing all his self-control, abandoned himself to mourning and regret, in such a way that it was argued by some that he had been touched to the quick only by the last blow; but the truth was that, being already full and over-full of sorrow, the slightest addition broke down the barriers of his endurance. The like might be thought, let me say, of our other tale, were it not that it adds that, when Cambyses asked Psammenitus why it was that, not being moved by the unhappy fate of his son and his daughter, he bore with so little patience that of his friend, "Because," he replied, "only that last grief could be shewn by tears; the first two far surpassed all means of expression." Perhaps, in this connection, we might recall the conceit of that ancient painter,[6] who, having to represent the mourning of those present at the sacrifice of Iphigenia according to the degree of each person's interest in the death of that innocent fair maid, having exhausted the last resources of his art, when it came to the maiden's father, he painted him with his face covered, as if no visage could evince that degree of grief. This is why poets described that wretched mother Niobe, when she had lost, first, seven sons, and straightway as many daughters, over-burdened with her losses, as having at last been transformed to stone,—

As having been petrified by calamity,[7]

to express that sombre, dumb, and deaf torpor that paralyses us when events surpassing our capability overwhelm us. In truth, the effect of an affliction, if it be extreme,

9

must wholly stun the mind and deprive it of freedom of action; as, on the startling alarm of some very ill news, it happens to us to feel dazed and deadened, and, as it were, completely paralysed, in such wise that the mind, upon giving way later to tears and lamentations, seems to relax and disperse itself, and take a wider sweep, more at its ease.

And at last, with difficulty, a passage for words is opened by grief.[8]

In the war that King Ferdinand waged against the widow of King John of Hungary, near Buda, Raïsciac, a trooper whom every one had noticed as having borne himself with exceeding gallantry, joined in the universal commiseration; but, sharing the general interest in seeing who he might be, after his armour was removed, he found that he was his own son. Amid the universal lamentation, he alone stood erect, without uttering a word or shedding a tear, his eyes fixed, gazing steadfastly upon him, until the violence of his grief congealed his vital powers, and felled him, stone dead, to the ground.[9]

He who can say how he burns is in no hot fire,[10]

say the lovers who would describe an unendurable passion.

Wretched man that I am, this [delight] deprives me of all my senses; as soon as I look upon thee, Lesbia, I can, in my delirium, utter nothing; my tongue is benumbed; a subtle flame spreads through my veins, my ears ring, darkness covers my eyes.[11]

It is not in the most poignant and penetrating heat of

Of Sadness

the attack that we are in a fitting state to set forth our lamentations and our persuasions: the mind is then overloaded by intense thought and the body prostrated and languishing with love. Hence there comes sometimes that sudden faintness which so unseasonably surprises the lover, and that chill which seizes him, by force of extreme ardour, even in the very lap of enjoyment. All passions which suffer themselves to be understood and marshalled in order[12] are but lukewarm.

Light griefs can speak; great ones are dumb.[13]

The surprise of an unhoped-for joy stuns us equally.

When she beheld me approaching, and saw me surrounded by Trojan arms, she was terror-struck; aghast at the wonder, she fainted at the sight; warmth abandoned her limbs, and she fell; then, after a long time, she spoke with difficulty.[14]

Besides the Roman woman who died of glad surprise on seeing her son return from the rout of Cannæ, and Talva, who died in Corsica on reading the news of the honours which the Roman Senate had bestowed upon him,[15] we learn in our own day that Pope Leo X, having been informed of the taking of Milan, which he had most ardently desired, felt such transports of joy that he was attacked by a fever and died of it.[16] Diodorus the Dialectician died suddenly, seized by an overwhelming sense of shame, when he could not explain a proposition put before him.

I am little subject to such violent emotions. My sensitiveness[17] is naturally not keen, and I harden and deaden it every day intentionally.[18]

Chapter III

OUR FEELINGS
EXTEND THEMSELVES
BEYOND OUR PERCEPTIONS[1]

THOSE[2] who accuse men of ever looking eagerly toward future things, and instruct us to lay hold of present possessions and to establish ourselves in them, as having no grip upon what is to come, much less, indeed, than upon what is past, put their finger on the most common of human errors—if we dare give the name of error to what Nature herself impels us to, in the interest of the continuation of her work, impressing upon us this false attitude of mind as well as many others; being more jealous of our doings than of our wisdom. We are never in our true abiding-place, we are always somewhere else. Fear, desire, hope drive us toward the future and deprive us of the perception and consideration of what is; and we waste our time thinking of what will be, when in truth we ourselves shall be no more. *Unfortunate is the mind that is troubled about the future.*[3]

This great principle is often cited by Plato: "Do what thou hast to do, and know thyself."[4] Each of these phrases includes, in general terms, our whole duty; and, likewise, each includes its companion. He who would do what it is his duty to do would see that his first lesson is to find out what he is and what is proper to him; and he who knows

12

himself does not see an action as belonging to him which is foreign to him, and he loves and cultivates himself before all else, declining superfluous occupations and futile ideas and suggestions. *Whilst folly, although she has acquired what she desired, none the less never thinks that she has obtained enough, wisdom, on the contrary, is always content with whatever happens, and is never displeased by anything.*[5] Epicurus exempts the wise man from forethought and care for the future.[6] Among the laws concerning the dead, that one seems to me very well founded which requires that the acts of princes be closely scrutinised after their death:[7] they are peers but not masters of the laws; since justice has little power over their lives, it is reasonable that it should have control over their reputations and over what belongs to their successors—matters which we often value more than life itself. It is a custom which affords peculiar advantages to those nations by which it is observed, and is desirable in the eyes of all good princes who have cause to complain that the memory of bad princes is treated like their own. We owe submission and obedience equally to all kings, for those are due to the kingly office; but esteem, like affection, we owe to their virtue alone. Let us yield to political necessity so far as to endure them patiently when unworthy, to conceal their vices, to assist with our commendation their unimportant acts so long as their authority needs our support; but when this intercourse is at an end, it is not reasonable to deny to justice and our liberty the expression of our real sentiments, and particularly to refuse to good subjects the glory of having reverently and loyally served a master whose imperfections were so well known to them; for then would posterity be cheated of a useful example. And those

13

who, through respect for some private indebtedness, basely espouse the memory of an unpraiseworthy prince, do private justice at the expense of public justice. Livy says truly,[8] that the speech of men brought up under a monarchy is always full of foolish boasting and worthless witness, each one equally exalting his king to the utmost degree of supreme worth and greatness. One may blame the great courage of those two soldiers who answered Nero to his face; the one, being asked why he wished him ill: "I loved you when you deserved it; but since you have become a parricide, an incendiary, a mountebank, and a coachman, I hate you as you deserve"; the other, being asked why he wished to kill him: "Because I see no other remedy for your constant evil deeds."[9] But what sound understanding can blame the public and universal testimonies to his tyrannical and degrading conduct, which were borne after his death, and will be for all time, against him and all evil-doers like him?[10]

I can but regret that in so immaculate a polity as the Lacedæmonian there should have been introduced such an insincere ceremony at the death of their kings. All the federated states and their neighbours, and all the Helots, men and women pell-mell, slashed their foreheads as evidence of their grief, and declared amid their cries and lamentations that this king, whatever he had been, was the best of all their kings, ascribing to rank the praise which belonged to merit, and that which belongs to the highest merit, to the lowest degree.[11] Aristotle, who touches on all subjects, questions about the saying of Solon, that "no one before he is dead can be said to be happy," whether even the man who has lived and died as he could wish can be called happy if his renown grow less, if his posterity be wretched. While we are alive, we are by anticipation wherever we choose; but having ceased to be, we have no communication with what is; and therefore Solon had better have said that man is never happy, since he is so only after he has ceased to exist.[12]

The man who imperfectly uproots himself from life and casts himself out of it, but who unconsciously conceives something of himself to survive, does not sufficiently remove himself from the body that is thrown out, and lays claim to it.[13]

Bertrand du Guesclin died at the siege of the castle of Rancon, near Le Puy in Auvergne.[14] The besieged, having surrendered later, were compelled to carry the keys of the citadel on the dead man's body. Barthelemys d'Alviano, commanding the army of the Venetians, having met death during their wars in La Bresse, and his body having to be taken back to Venice through Verona, a hostile territory, most of the army were of opinion that they should ask the Veronese for a safe-conduct for their march; but Theodore Trivulzio demurred, and chose rather to pass through by force, at the risk of a fight, "as it was not fitting," he said, "that he who had never in his life dreaded his enemies, being dead, should show fear of them."[15]

In a similar matter, in fact, the Greek law provided that he who asked the enemy for a dead body, in order to bury it, by so doing renounced the victory, and therefore it was not permissible for him to erect a trophy: to him of whom the request was made, it was a proof of success. Thus Nicias lost the advantage he had clearly won over the Corinthians;[16] and, on the other hand, Agesilaus confirmed his very questionable victory over the Bœotians.[17]

15

Our Feelings Extend Themselves

These acts might appear strange, had it not been the accepted practice in all ages, not only that we extend our care for ourselves beyond this life, but also to believe that very often the favours of Heaven accompany us to our grave and continue to our bones; of which there are so many ancient examples, to say nothing of our own time, that there is no need for me to enlarge upon the subject. Edward I, King of England, having experienced in the long wars between himself and Robert, King of Scotland, how great an advantage his presence gave to his affairs, having always been victorious in whatever he undertook in person, when he was dying, compelled his son to swear solemnly that, when dead, his body should be boiled,—in order to separate the flesh from the bones,—and the flesh buried; and as for the bones, that they should be preserved, to be carried with him [the king] and the army whenever it should happen that there was war with the Scotch; as if destiny had linked victory inevitably to his bones. Jean Vischa,[18] who embroiled Bohemia in defence of the heresies of Wyclif, ordered that his body should be flayed after death, and a drum be made of his skin, to be borne in war with his enemies, believing that it would help to continue the successes he had won in the wars waged by him against them. Certain Indian peoples in like manner carried into battle against the Spaniards the bones of one of their leaders, from consideration of the good fortune he had had in his lifetime.[19] And other nations in that same part of the world bear with them in war the bodies of the brave men who have fallen in their battles, to give them good luck and encourage them. The first of these instances would seem to indicate a retention in the tomb only of the reputation acquired by past deeds; but the last would

16

seem to conjoin therewith the power of continued action.

The act of Captain Bayard is of a finer description, who, feeling himself to be mortally wounded by a shot from an arquebus, and being urged to withdraw from the battle, replied that he would not begin at the end of his life to turn his back to the enemy; and having fought as long as his strength lasted, feeling that he was fainting and about to fall from his horse, he bade his servant lay him at the foot of a tree, but in such wise that he would die facing the enemy, as he did.[20] I must add this other example, which is as remarkable for the sort of thing under consideration as any of the preceding. The Emperor Maximilian, great-grandfather of the present King Philip,[21] was a prince endowed to the full with noble qualities, among others with singular physical beauty. But among his humours was this one,— quite the opposite of that of most princes, who, for the transaction of the most important affairs, make a throne of their close-stool,—that he never had a servant so familiar that he would allow him to see him in his closet: he would go apart to make water, being as modest as a maid in not exhibiting, to a physician or anybody else, the parts which we are wont to keep hidden. I myself, who am so brazen of speech, am none the less naturally inclined to this same modesty: except under great pressure of necessity or of passion, I rarely put before another's eyes the organs and the acts which our manners ordain shall be kept out of sight; I constrain myself more about this than I think very fitting for a man, and especially for a man of the opinions I profess. But he[22] reached such a pitch of superstition that he expressly ordered in his testament that they should put drawers on him when he was dead. He should have added a codicil to the effect that he who should put them on should be blind-folded.[23]

Cyrus's behest to his children, that neither they nor any other person should see or touch his body after his soul had departed,[24] I attribute to some religious emotion of his; for both his biographer and himself, among their great qualities, gave indications throughout the whole course of their lives of a peculiar regard and veneration for religion. I was not pleased with the tale told me by a great prince, of a kinsman of mine, a man well known both in peace and in war: it was to the effect that, when dying, very old, at court, and suffer-ing extreme pain from stone, he employed all his last hours in arranging, with eager care, the honours and the ceremony of his burial, and urged all the nobles who visited him to promise to be present at his funeral. He made an urgent entreaty to this same prince, my informant, who saw him during these last hours, that he would order his household to attend, alleging many precedents and arguments to prove that it was a thing due to such a man as he was; and he seemed to die content, having extorted that promise and having provided according to his desire for the arrangement and order of his parade. I have rarely known such persistent inanity. The other opposite crotchet (of which I am not lacking in examples near home) seems to me akin to this—namely, the taking great pains and being excited about this last matter to be arranged,—one's funeral train,—and re-ducing it to some peculiar and unaccustomed degree of parsimony, to one servant and a lantern. I hear people praise this whim, and the injunction of Marcus Æmilius Lepi-dus,[25] who forbade his heirs to go through the ceremonial which was customary on such occasions. Is it, indeed, moderation and frugality to avoid expense and luxury, the use and knowledge of which are beyond our ken? An easy reform that, and not costly. If there were need to make rules about this matter, I should be of opinion that in this, as in all the acts of our lives, each man should make the rule correspond to the amount of his fortune. The philosopher Lycon wisely instructed his friends to put his body where they should think best, and, as to his obsequies, to let them be neither superfluous nor mean.[26] I would leave it simply to custom to regulate this ceremonial,[27] and I shall trust myself to the discretion of any one into whose hands I shall fall in charge. *All this matter is to be entirely disregarded for ourselves, but not to be neglected for those dear to us.*[28] And, as was said like a saint by a saint: *The ordering of a funeral, the nature of the burial-place, and the procession are more for the solace of the living than for the succour of the dead.*[29] Thus, when Crito asked Socrates, in his last hour, how he wished to be buried, Socrates answered: "As you please."[30] If I had to occupy myself more about this, it would seem to me more spirited[31] to imitate those persons who, while living and breathing, entertain themselves about the order and honourableness of their burial, and who take pleasure in seeing in marble their dead features. Happy they who can rejoice and gratify their minds by insensibility, and live in their death!

I am almost moved to irreconcilable hatred against every sort of popular domination, although it seems the most natural and equitable, when I remember the inhuman injustice of the Athenian people in putting to death without mercy, and refusing even to hear in their own defence, the gallant officers who had just beaten the Lacedæmonians in

the naval battle near the Arginusæ Islands,—the most hotly
contested and the hardest battle that the Greeks ever fought
on the sea,—because they [the officers] had followed up
such opportunities as the laws of war offered them rather
than stay to collect and bury their dead. And the behaviour
of Diomedon makes this punishment the more odious: he
was one of the condemned—a man of noteworthy excellence
both military and political; he, coming forward to speak
after having heard the decree of condemnation, and finding
only then an opportunity to be heard without interruption,
instead of taking advantage of it to the profit of his own
cause and to lay bare the patent iniquity of so barbarous a
judgement, expressed only solicitude for the salvation of
his judges, beseeching the gods to turn that judgement to
their advantage; and lest, by the non-performance of the
vows that he and his companions had made in gratitude
for their eminent good-fortune, they[32] might draw down
upon themselves the wrath of the gods, he told them what
those vows were; and without other words, and without
discussion, he went boldly to his doom.[33] Some years later
fortune punished them with a taste of the same sauce;[34]
for Chabrias, the captain-general of their naval force, having had the upper hand in the battle against Pollis, the
Spartan admiral, off the island of Naxos, lost the whole
fruit, absolutely and completely,[35] of his victory (which
was of great importance to their affairs), in order not to
incur the ill-fortune of the foregoing instance; and, in order
not to lose a few dead bodies of his friends which were
floating on the sea, he allowed a multitude of living enemies to sail away unharmed, who afterward made them pay
dear for that ill-timed superstition.

Our Feelings Extend Themselves

You ask where you will be after death? Where the unborn are.[36]

These other verses restore the sense of repose to a body without a soul:—

He has no tomb to receive him, no refuge for his body, where, released from human life, it may repose from ills;[37]

just as nature shows us that many dead things have still occult relations with life. Wine becomes different in the cellar, in accordance with some variations of the seasons of the wine; and the flesh of the deer changes its condition and taste in the salting-house, according to the laws that govern living flesh, so it is said.

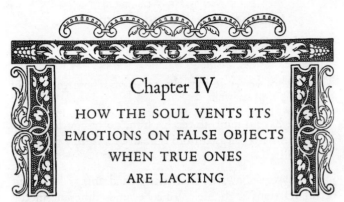

Chapter IV

HOW THE SOUL VENTS ITS
EMOTIONS ON FALSE OBJECTS
WHEN TRUE ONES
ARE LACKING

A GENTLEMAN of our day, who was terribly subject to gout, being urged by his physicians to abstain
altogether from salt meats, was wont to reply jocosely that
in the paroxysms and torture of the disease, he wanted to
have something to lay the blame on; and that, storming
and cursing at one time about sausage, at another about
tongue, and again about ham, he felt greatly relieved. But
in all seriousness, as, when the arm is raised to strike, it
annoys us if the blow meets no object but is wasted on the
air; and as, to make a view pleasant to the eye, it must not
be lost and spread out to the dim horizon, but should have
rising ground to limit it within a reasonable distance,—

As a wind loses its strength, meeting with no opposition from a dense forest, and is dissipated in the
void,[1]—

so it would seem that the mind, when disturbed and excited, goes astray of itself, if we do not give it something to
lay hold of; and it must always be supplied with some object to seize and work upon. Plutarch says,[2] speaking of
those who become attached to monkeys and little dogs,

22

How the Soul Vents its Emotions

that the affectionate part of us, in this way, for lack of a legitimate object, fashions a false and frivolous one rather than remain useless. And we see that the mind, when most excited, deceives itself, setting up a false and fanciful object, even contrary to its own belief, rather than not act against something. So the anger of wild animals drives them to attack the stone or the spear which has wounded them, and to take vengeance on themselves with their own teeth for the pain they suffer.

> So the Pannonian bear, the fiercer after being wounded by the Libyan lance hurled at her by its slender thong, turns upon the wound and furiously assaults the shaft lodged in her, and circles about the dart that flees with her.[3]

What causes do we not invent for the misfortunes that befall us! What do we not take offence at, rightly or wrongly, in order to have something to spar with! It was not those fair locks that you are tearing, or the whiteness of that breast which in anger you beat so cruelly, that killed your beloved brother with a miserable bit of lead; turn your wrath elsewhere.

Livy, speaking of the Roman army in Spain after the loss of the two brothers, its great captains, says: *All burst into tears and beat their heads.*[4] That is a common custom. And the philosopher Bion—did he not remark facetiously of that king who in his grief tore out his hair, "Does he think that baldness is a cure for grief?"[5] Who has not seen men chew and swallow cards and gulp down dice, by way of revenge for the loss of their money? Xerxes whipped the Hellespont, and branded it, and caused numberless insults to be heaped upon it, and sent a challenge to Mount Athos;[6] and Cyrus delayed a whole army for several days, that he might avenge himself on the river Gyndus for the alarm he had had in crossing it;[7] and Caligula destroyed a very beautiful house because of the suffering[8] his mother had endured in it. In my youth it was said by the common people that one of our neighbouring kings, having received a scourging at God's hands, swore to be revenged upon him, and decreed that for ten years no one should pray to or speak of him, and that, so long as he himself had authority, no one should believe in him; the intention of which tale was not so much to depict the folly as the vain-glory natural to the nation of which it was told. These vices are always found together, but such actions are due, in truth, rather more to presumption than to stupidity. Augustus Cæsar, having been beaten about by a storm at sea, undertook to brave the god Neptune, and, in the celebration of the games in the Circus, had his statue removed from its place among the other gods, as his revenge upon him.[9] In which he was even less excusable than those already spoken of, and less than he himself was later, when, Quintilius Varus having lost a battle in Germany, he went about in rage and despair, beating his head against the wall and shouting, "Varus, give me back my soldiers![10] For they go beyond all degrees of folly—since impiety is added to it—who attack God himself.[11] Now, as that poet of old says, quoted by Plutarch,

> Tis vain to be angered with things,
> They care not a rap for our wrath.

But we shall never say enough in derision of the disorderliness of our mind.

24

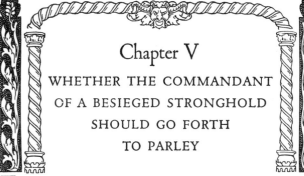

Chapter V

WHETHER THE COMMANDANT
OF A BESIEGED STRONGHOLD
SHOULD GO FORTH
TO PARLEY

LUCIUS MARCIUS, the Roman legate during the war against Perseus, King of Macedon, wishing to gain the time required to put the Roman army in condition, scattered suggestions of future agreement,[1] whereby the king was thrown off his guard and agreed to a truce for several days, thus affording his enemy an opportunity and leisure to prepare himself; as a result the king was utterly overthrown.[2] But the elders of the Senate, mindful of the customs of their fathers, denounced this device as contrary to their former practice, which was, they said, to fight with valour, not with cunning, nor by surprises and night attacks; nor by counterfeited retreats and unexpected returns; never entering into a war until they had proclaimed it, and often not until they had appointed the time and place of the battle. On this principal they sent back to Pyrrhus his treacherous physician,[3] and to the Faliscans their disloyal schoolmaster.[4] Such were the characteristically Roman methods, not those of Greek subtlety and Punic craft, which hold it to be less glorious to conquer by force than by fraud. To deceive may serve for the moment; but he alone considers himself vanquished who knows that he has been so, neither by stratagem nor by chance, but by valour, array against array, in a loyal and just war.[5] It is plain enough, from this language on the part of those good people, that they had not as yet accepted this fine saying,—

> What matters it whether cunning or courage be used against an enemy?[6]

The Achaians, says Polybius,[7] detested all manner of deceit in their wars, deeming that no victory when the courage of the enemy was not cast down. *A conscientious and wise man must know the only true victory to be that which is won without the violation of good faith and honour,*[8] says another.

> Let us test by valour whether all-powerful Fortune wills that you or that I shall reign, or what she brings us.[9]

In the kingdom of Ternates, among those nations whom we so unhesitatingly[10] call Barbarians, it is the custom not to enter into war without having first proclaimed it, adding a full declaration of the means, of all kinds, that they have at their command—how many men, what supplies, what weapons, offensive and defensive. But also, that being done, if their enemies do not yield and come to an agreement, they feel at liberty to do their worst, and do not think that they can be reproached with treason or cunning, whatever means they make use of to conquer.[11] The ancient Florentines were so far from desiring to obtain advantage over their enemies by surprise, that they gave them warning a month before putting their army in the field, by the constant ringing of the bell they called "Martinella."[12]

26

Should the Commandant go Forth to Parley

As for our less superstitious selves, who hold the honour of war to be his who has the benefit of it, and who, following Lysander, say that, where the lion's skin does not suffice, we must add to it a piece of the fox's,[13] the most common occasions of surprise are derived from such doing, and there is no time, we say, when a commander should have a more watchful eye than that of parleys and treaties of peace; and for that reason, it is a rule echoed by all the military men of our day, that the commandant of a besieged stronghold must never himself go outside the gates to parley. In the time of our fathers, the lords of Montmord and of Assigni, who were defending Mousson against the Count of Nassau, were blamed for so doing.[14] But yet, in this matter, he would be excusable who should manage his going out in such a way that safety and advantage would remain with him, as Count Guy de Rangon did in the city of Reggio (if we are to believe du Bellay about it, for Guicciardini says[15] that it was he himself), when the Lord of l'Escut approached the walls to parley; for he was so far from abandoning his safe ground that, a disturbance having arisen during the negotiation, not only did Monsieur de l'Escut and his soldiers, who had come out with him, find themselves the weaker party, so that Alessandro Trivulzio was killed, but he himself was forced, as the safest course, to follow the count, and, upon faith in his word, to seek shelter in the town.

Eumenes, in the city of Nora, being urged by Antigonus, who was besieging him, to come forth to treat with him, Antigonus alleging, after many other pretences, that it was right that he should come to him since he [Antigonus] was the greater and stronger,—having made this noble re-

Should the Commandant go Forth to Parley

sponse: "I shall never deem any man greater than myself so long as my sword is mine,"—did not consent to come out until Antigonus had given him, at his demand, his own nephew, Ptolomæus, as a hostage.[16] It is indeed true that there have been others who have found it very advisable to go out on the word of the assailant: witness Henry de Vaux, a knight of Champagne, who being beseiged in the Castle of Commercy, and Barthelemy de Bonnes, who commanded the besiegers, having from outside caused the greater part of the castle to be mined, so that nothing was needed, to bury the besieged under the ruins, but to fire the train—he summoned the said Henry to come out to parley with him for his own advantage, which he did, with three others; and his certain destruction being made plain to his own eyes, he perceived himself to be deeply indebted to his enemy, by whose direction, after he and his troop had surrendered, the mine being fired, and the wooden props giving way, the castle was destroyed from roof to cellar.[17]

I readily trust to the word of another, but I should be slow to do so when it could be thought that I had done it more from despair and lack of courage, than in freedom of spirit and from confidence in his loyalty.

Chapter VI

THE HOUR OF PARLEY

IS A DANGEROUS TIME

TO continue, I saw lately in my neighbourhood, at Mussidan, that those whom our army expelled thence by force, and also others of their party, cried out on treachery because, during the negotiations and while the parleying was still going on, they had been surprised and cut to pieces[1]—a point of view which might perchance have been reasonable in another age. But, as I just said, our ways are entirely unlike former rules of conduct, and we should not expect to place confidence in one another until the last pledge of engagement has been given; even then there is enough to look after.

It has always been a dangerous decision to entrust to the unbridled liberty of a victorious army the observance of the faith pledged to a city which has surrendered on mild and favourable terms, and to allow the troops free entry in hot blood. Lucius Æmilius Regillus, the Roman prætor, having wasted much time trying to take the city of Phocæa by force, because of the extraordinary prowess of the people in defending themselves, made an agreement with them to receive them as friends of the Roman people, and to make his entry as into an allied city, relieving them from all fear of hostile action. But having taken his army into the city, in order to present himself with greater pomp, it was not in his power, whatever effort he might make, to bridle his soldiers; and he saw a large part of the city sacked before his eyes, the claims of avarice and vengeance overriding those of his authority and of military discipline.[2]

Cleomenes said that, whatever injury one can inflict on the enemy in war is above the realm of justice and not subject to it, whether before gods or men; and having made a truce with the Argives for seven days, the third night after, he fell upon them when they were all asleep, and killed them declaring that in the truce no mention was made of nights;[3] but the gods avenged this treacherous sophistry.

During the parley, and while they were deliberating upon their guaranties, they of Casilinum were taken by surprise;[4] and that nevertheless in the age of the most honourable captains and of the most perfect military discipline among the Romans; for there is no rule that according to time and place we may not take advantage of our enemies' folly as we do of their cowardice. And certainly war has many reasonable privileges not consonant with reason; and in this case the rule fails: *No one should so act as to profit by another's ignorance.*[5] But I am surprised at the extention which Xenophon gives these privileges,[6] both by his words and by divers deeds of his perfect Emperor—he being a writer of wonderful weight in such matters, as a great captain and as a philosopher among the first disciples of Socrates; and I do not accede to the measure of his dispensation in all things and everywhere.

When Monsieur d'Aubigny was besieging Capua,[7] and

The Hour of Parley is a Dangerous Time

after he had made a fierce assault, Signor Fabricio Colonna, commander of the city, having begun to discuss terms of surrender from the top of a bastion, and his soldiers having relaxed their watchfulness, ours took possession of the city, killing right and left. And in still more recent times, at Yvoy,[8] Signor Jullian Rommero, having adopted the blundering course[9] of going out to parley with the Constable, on his return found the place taken. But, that we might not go unpunished, when the Marquis of Pescara was besieging Genoa, where Duke Octaviano Fregoso commanded, under our protection, and when the accord between them had been carried so far that it was regarded as settled and on the point of being concluded, the Spaniards, having crept into the town, treated it as if they had won a complete victory.[10] And later, at Ligny en Barrois, where the Count of Brienne commanded, the Emperor in person having laid siege to the town, and Bertheville, the said count's lieutenant, having ventured forth to parley, during the parley the place was then taken.[11]

> It is always glorious to conquer, whether the victory be due to chance or to skill,[12]

they say. But the philosopher Chrysippus would not have been of that opinion, and I as little; for he said that they who run races ought to put forth all their powers of swiftness, but that it was in no wise allowable for them to put their hand on their opponent to stop him, or to thrust out their leg to trip him.[13] And even more magnanimously that great Alexander replied to Polypercon, who was urging him to make use of the advantage that the darkness of the night gave him to attack Darius: "No, far be it from me to seek victories by stealth; *I would rather have a misfortune to regret than a victory that should cause me shame.*"[14]

And he did not deign to attack Orodes as he fled, nor to wound him from behind with a throw of his lance; he ran in front of him, meeting him face to face, and fought man against man, conquering, not by stealth, but by force of arms.[15]

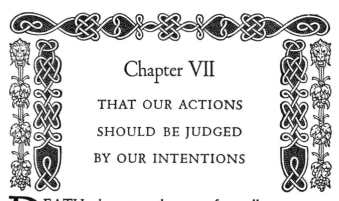

Chapter VII

THAT OUR ACTIONS
SHOULD BE JUDGED
BY OUR INTENTIONS

DEATH, they say, releases us from all our engagements; I know some who have regarded this differently. Henry the Seventh, King of England, made an
agreement with Dom Philip, son of the Emperor Maximilian,—or, to give him a position of higher honour, father
of the Emperor Charles the Fifth,—that the said Philip
should deliver into his hands his enemy, the Duke of Suf-
folk, of the White Rose party, who had fled from England
and retired to the Low Countries; while, on his side, he
promised to make no attempt on the life of the said duke;
but when dying, by his testament he expressly ordered his
son to put the duke to death as soon as he himself should
be dead.[1] Lately,[2] in the tragedy which the Duke of Alva
gave us to see at Brussels, of Count Horn and Count Egmont,[3] there were many noteworthy incidents, among
others, this: that the said Count Egmont, on the faith of
whose guaranty Count Horn had surrendered himself to
the Duke of Alva, demanded with great earnestness that he
should be put to death first, to the end that his death might
release him from his pledge to the said Count Horn. It
would seem that death did not discharge the former[4] from

his plighted faith, and that the latter[5] was released from his, even without dying. We cannot be held responsible beyond our strength and our resources; for this reason, that results and consequences are in no wise within our power, and that there is, in truth, nothing within our power but our will; upon that are necessarily based and established all the rules of the duty of man. Thus Count Egmont, holding his soul and his will pledged to his promise, although the power to put it into execution was not in his hands, was unquestionably absolved from his duty, even had he survived Count Horn. But the King of England, having by intention broken his word, cannot be excused because he postponed the execution of his faithlessness until after his death; any more than the mason in Herodotus,[6] who, having loyally kept while he lived the secret of the treasures of his master the King of Egypt, disclosed it to his children when dying.

I have known many persons of my own time, being convicted by their conscience of retaining what belonged to others, to attempt to set it right by their testament, and after their death. And the more irksomely and inconveniently they pay, the more just and meritorious is their atonement. They do even more who reserve the revelation of some feeling of hate against their neighbour for their last expression, having concealed it during their life; and they prove that they have but little regard for their own honour,—thus rousing the anger of the offended man against their memory, —and less for their conscience, being unable, even in the presence of death itself, to put an end to their ill-will, but prolonging its life beyond their own. I shall be on my guard, if I can, that my death may say nothing which my life has not previously said.

34

Chapter VIII

OF IDLENESS

AS we find fields that lie fallow, if they are rich and fertile, continue to abound in a hundred thousand kinds of wild and useless plants, and that, to keep them serviceable, we must bring them under subjection, and make them produce certain crops for our profit; and as we see that women, quite by themselves, produce shapeless masses and lumps of flesh, but that, to assure a sound and natural birth, we must fertilize them with other seed,[1] so it is with our minds: if we do not keep them occupied with a distinct subject, which curbs and restrains them, they run aimlessly to and fro, in the undefined field of imagination,—

> Like a dancing light from water within brazen vats, reflected from the sun or from the form of the radiant moon, that flits afar in every direction, and now rises in air and strikes the lofty fretted ceilings.[2]

And there is no folly or fantasy to which they do not give birth in this agitation.

> Unreal monsters are imagined, like a sick man's dreams.[3]

Of Idleness

The mind that has no fixed goal loses itself; for, as they say, to be everywhere is to be nowhere.

> He who dwells everywhere, Maximus, dwells nowhere.[4]

When, not long ago, I withdrew into my own house, determined, so far as it was in my power, to take no thought of any thing except to pass in peace and by myself the little of life that remains for me, it seemed to me that I could do my mind no greater service than to leave it in complete and idle liberty to commune with itself and to give itself pause and steady itself; which I hoped that it could do thenceforth the more easily, having become with time far more solid and more mature; but I find,—

> Leisure ever breeds an inconstant mind,[5]—

that, on the contrary, like a runaway horse, it is a hundred times more active for itself than it ever was for another, and presents me with so many chimeras and fanciful monsters, one after another, irregular and unmeaning, that, in order to consider at leisure their absurdity and strangeness, I have begun to put them on paper, hoping in time to make my mind ashamed of itself.

Chapter IX

OF LIARS

THERE is no man whom it becomes so ill to undertake to speak about memory as myself. For I recognize scarcely a trace of it in myself, and I do not believe that there can be another man in the world so horribly deficient in this respect. All my other faculties are mean and ordinary; but regarding this one, I think I am exceptional and most unusual, and worthy to win name and fame thereby. I could tell some wonderful stories about this, but for the present it is more worth while to pursue my subject.[1]

In addition to the natural troublesome consequences that I suffer because of this,—for surely, considering its indispensableness, Plato is justified in calling memory a great and powerful goddess,[2]—if, in my part of the world they mean that a man is lacking in intelligence, they say that he has no memory; and when I complain of the failure of mine, they correct me and disbelieve me, as if I accused myself of being unintelligent; they see no distinction between memory and understanding. This makes my case much worse. But they wrong me, for, quite to the contrary, experience shows that excellent memories are frequently found in conjunction with feeble powers of judgement. They wrong me also in this, that the same words which indicate my malady[3] stand for ingratitude—for I can do nothing else so well as be a friend. They lay the blame on my heart instead of on my memory, and of an involuntary defect they make a wilful one. "He forgets," they say, "this request or that promise; he does n't remember his friends; he did not remember to do this, or to say that, or to hold his tongue about the other, for my sake." Certainly, I can easily forget; but to be indifferent about the service my friend has asked of me, that I am not. Let them be content with my misfortune, without distorting it into a sort of ill-will, and of a kind so foreign to my disposition. I thus somewhat console myself: in the first place because it is an evil from which I have mainly derived the argument for ridding myself of a worse evil that would easily have taken root in me—namely, ambition; for it[4] is an infirmity unendurable for him who involves himself in public affairs; also, as many like examples of nature's action show us, it has fairly strengthened other faculties in me in proportion to its own weakness; and I might otherwise readily let my intelligence follow indolently in another's footsteps, as all the world does, without exerting its own power, if foreign ideas and opinions had presented themselves to me through the medium of the memory; also, my speech is consequently the briefer, for the storehouse of memory is easily better supplied with matter than is that of invention. If my memory had held good, I should have deafened all my friends with my chatter, as subjects that arouse the faculty, such as it is, that I have, of handling and making use of them, and warm me up and excite me in conversation. This is lamentable. I have tested

Of Liars

it by the case of some of my personal friends: as memory presents the thing to their minds completely and [as it were] before their eyes, they carry their tale so far back, and load it down with so many idle details, that, if the story be a good one, they stifle its goodness; if it be not so, you curse their good fortune in their memory or their ill-fortune in their judgement. It is a difficult thing to stop in talk, and cut it short when one has got started; and there is nothing in which a horse's strength is more manifest than in making a clean, quick stop. Even with pertinent talkers, I find some who would, but can not, stay their course: while they are seeking the effective way to conclude, they go trifling along and dragging the matter out, like men staggering from weakness. Above all, old men are in danger, who retain remembrance of past things and have lost remembrance of their twice-told stories. I have known some really amusing tales to become very tiresome in the mouth of a man of the world, every one present having heard them poured out a hundred times.

In the second place [I am consoled[5]] because I remember less the affronts I have received, as said an ancient writer.[6] I should have to keep a register of them; as Darius, in order not to forget the affront he had received from the Athenians, arranged that a page, every time he sat down to table, should come and repeat thrice in his ear: "Sire, remember the Athenians";[7] also, [I am consoled] because the places and books that I see for a second time always charm me with the freshness of novelty.

Not without reason is it said that he who does not know himself to be of sane memory should not meddle with lying. I am well aware that the grammarians[8] make a distinction between saying what is false and lying;[9] and they state that to say what is false is to say something which is untrue, but which one believes to be true, and that the definition in Latin of the word *mentiri*, from which our French word is derived, is equivalent to going against one's knowledge, and that, consequently, the word applies only to those who speak contrary to what they know; and it is to these that I refer. Now, they either invent the whole thing, or disguise and alter an actual fact. When they disguise and alter it, if they often recur to this same tale, they are likely to be embarrassed; because, the thing as it really is having been the first to become fixed in the memory, and having stamped itself there by force of outward and inward knowledge, it is very difficult not to let it present itself to the imagination, supplanting the false version, which cannot have so firm and assured a footing there; and the circumstances that one first learned about the thing, always slipping back into the mind, drive out recollection of the false, or modified, added details. When they invent altogether, inasmuch as there is no contrary impression to oppose their falsification, they seem to have so much the less reason to be afraid of making a mistake. Yet, even then, because it is a vague, bodiless thing, not easily held, it readily escapes the memory, unless it be very reliable. Whereof I have often seen amusing proof, at the expense of those who make it their business so to frame their speech as will best serve in their negotiations, and will be agreeable to those in high station with whom they are talking; for as these circumstances to which they choose to subordinate their faith and conscience are subject to frequent changes, their language must needs be changed likewise; from which it comes about that they call the same

Of Liars

thing now gray and now yellow; say this to one man and that to another; and if, by chance, these men bring together as common booty their so inconsistent pieces of information, what becomes of that noble art? Besides, they too often imprudently embarrass themselves; for what memory could suffice to keep in mind the multitude of different forms they have given to a single subject? I have known many of my contemporaries to envy the reputation for this noble kind of prudence, who do not see that, if there be the reputation, there cannot be the effect.

In truth, lying is an accursed vice.[10] We are men only by speech, and are only thereby bound to one another. If we understood the horribleness and the weight of it, we should drag it to the stake more justly than other crimes. I find that people ordinarily busy themselves most ill-advisedly with punishing children for harmless mistakes, and worry them about heedless acts which leave no trace or consequence. Lying alone, and in a less degree obstinacy, seem to me to be the faults whose birth and progress we should most insistently combat; they increase with the child's growth, and when the tongue has been given this false direction, it is wonderful how impossible it is to turn it. Whence it comes about that we see those who are otherwise excellent men subject to this fault and enslaved by it. I have a nice fellow of a tailor whom I never hear tell the truth, not even when it would be useful to him. If falsehood, like truth, had but one face, we should be better off, for we should take for certain the contrary of what the liar said. But the opposite of truth has a hundred thousand shapes and a limitless field. The Pythagoreans regard good as certain and definite, evil as indefinite and uncertain. A thousand roads

Of Liars

lead away from the goal, one leads to it. Certainly I am not sure that I could induce myself to ward off an obvious and extreme danger by a brazen and deliberate lie.

An ancient father says that we are better off in the company of a dog we know than in that of a man whose language is unknown.[11] *So that those of different nations do not regard each other as men.*[12] And how much less companionable is untruthful speech than silence! King Francis the First boasted of having completely bewildered[13] by means of this sort of performance, Francisco Taverna, ambassador of Francisco Sforza, Duke of Milan—a man of great reputation in the art of speechmaking. He had been despatched to carry his master's excuses to His Majesty in regard to a very important matter, which was this. The king, in order to have always some sources of information in Italy, whence he had recently been driven, especially in the Duchy of Milan, had arranged to keep at the duke's court a gentleman of his own, an ambassador in fact, but in appearance a private individual, who had the air of being there for his own affairs; all the more because the duke, who was much more bound to the emperor,—just then especially, when he was negotiating a marriage with his niece, the daughter of the King of Denmark, now Duchess Dowager of Lorraine,—could not openly have any relations or communication with us without prejudice to himself. For this office a Milanese gentleman was thought fit—one of the king's equerries, named Merveille. He, being despatched with secret credentials and instructions as ambassador, and with letters of recommendation to the duke bearing upon his private concerns,—as a cloak and for show,—remained so long at the ducal court that the emperor somewhat resented it, which, we believe, was the cause of what happened afterward, which was this: that, on the pretext of some murder or other, lo and behold, the duke had Merveille's head cut off one fine night, his trial having been carried through in two days. Messire Francisco, having come all primed with a long, distorted version of this affair (for the king, demanding satisfaction, had addressed himself to all the princes of Christendom, and especially to the duke), was received in audience one morning; and having prepared and laid down as the basis of his plea several plausible versions of the facts: that his master had never regarded our man as anything more than a private individual and a subject of his own, who had come to Milan for his private affairs and had never lived there in any other character; [the duke] denying even that he had been aware that he was of the king's household, or known to him—very far, indeed, from taking him to be an ambassador; the king, in his turn, pressing him[14] hard with objections and questions, and attacking him on all sides, cornered him at last on the point of the execution by night and in secret. To which the poor embarrassed man replied, to show courtesy, that out of respect for His Majesty, the duke would have been very sorry to have such an execution take place by day.[15] It can be imagined how he was brought to book, having so stupidly contradicted himself, and in presence of so keen a scent as King Francis had.

Pope Julius the Second having sent an ambassador to the King of England, to incite him against King Francis, when the ambassador had been heard concerning his mission, and the King of England in his reply had dwelt on the difficulties he should encounter in making the necessary preparations to go to war against so powerful a monarch, and had

Of Liars

alleged certain reasons [for these conditions], the ambassador ill-advisedly rejoined that he too had considered them and had stated them to the Pope. From this remark, so far removed from the original proposal, which was to urge him forthwith into war, the King of England derived the first hint of what he afterwards found to be the fact—that this ambassador was privily inclined to the side of France; and having advised his master of that fact, his property was confiscated and he was very near losing his life.[16]

Chapter X

OF READINESS
OR UNREADINESS
OF SPEECH

Never were all graces given to any man.[1]

THUS we see that, in the gift of eloquence, some have facility and readiness, and, as they say, the tongue so well oiled,[2] that they are ready at every turn; others, less ready, never say any thing they have not thought out and elaborated. As rules are given to ladies for pursuing those games and bodily exercises which give advantage to their finest points, so, if I had to advise on similar lines in respect to these two different merits of eloquence, to which it would seem, in our time, that preachers and lawyers principally lay claim, the unready man would make the better preacher, it seems to me, and the other the better lawyer; for the reason that the profession of the former gives him as much leisure as he desires to prepare himself, and, moreover, his discourse[3] flows smoothly on, without interruption; whereas the exigencies of the advocate's profession force him to enter the lists at any moment; and the unforeseen rejoinders of his opponent throw him out of his stride; so that he must needs take a new start on the instant. And yet, at the interview between Pope Clement and King Francis at Marseilles it happened, quite contrariwise, that Monsieur Poyet, a man who had passed his whole life at the bar and had a great reputation, having it in charge to make the harangue to the Pope, when he had long meditated upon it,—indeed, it was said that he had brought it from Paris all prepared,—the Pope, fearing lest something might be said to him which would offend the ambassadors of the other princes, who were in attendance upon him, sent to the king the argument which seemed to him most suited to the time and place. But it, by chance, was altogether different from that over which Monsieur Poyet had laboured; so that his harangue became useless, and it was necessary for him to compose another at once. But as he felt that he was incapable of doing this, Monsieur le Cardinal du Bellay had to undertake the duty.[4] The lawyer's art is more difficult than the preacher's, and yet we find, in my opinion, more passable lawyers than preachers, at least in France.

It would seem that it is more a characteristic of the wit to be ready and quick in operation, and more a characteristic of the judgement to be slow and sedate. But he who remains altogether dumb if he has no leisure to prepare himself, and he to whom leisure is of no help to better speech, are equally singular. It is said of Severus Cassius that he discoursed better without preparation; that he owed more to good fortune than to diligence; that it was an advantage to him to be disturbed when speaking, and that his opponents were afraid to harass him, lest wrath should increase his eloquence two-fold.[5] I know by experience that inborn disposition which cannot sustain eager and laborious premeditation; if it does not move joyously and freely, it does nothing that is worth while.[6] We say of some works that they smell of the oil and

Of Readiness or Unreadiness of Speech

the lamp, because of a certain harshness and roughness which labour imparts to those in which it has a large share; but, in addition to that, the anxiety to do well, and the struggling of the mind too constrained and too intent upon its undertaking, bewilder it, interrupt and impede it, as happens to water, which, by force of pressure from its violence and abundance, cannot vent itself in an open sluice. In this sort of nature of which I am speaking, there is also, at the same time, this peculiarity, that it demands not to be set in motion and spurred on by strong passions, like the anger of Cassius (for that impulsion would be too violent); it requires not to be shaken, but to be solicited; it requires to be kindled and aroused by outward circumstances, immediate and accidental. If it moves by itself, it does but drag along and hang fire. Excitement is its life and is favourable to it.

I do not well hold myself in my own possession and at my own disposition; chance has more to say therein than I. The occasion, the company, the very sound of my voice, draws from my mind more than I find there when I sound ✝ it and use it when alone. Thus my spoken words are worth more than my written ones, if there can be a choice where there is nothing of value. I may have thrown off some subtle concept in writing (I mean one that is pointless to others, but in my eyes well-sharpened; let us be permitted such sincerities; every one says such things according as he can); I have lost it so completely that I do not know what I meant to say; and sometimes an outsider has discovered the meaning before I have. If I should erase every thing where this happens to me, I should destroy all. Chance, at another time, will throw a light on it for me clearer than that of noon-day, and will make me wonder at my hesitation.

Chapter XI

OF

PROGNOSTICATIONS

AS to oracles, it is certain that a good while before the coming of Jesus Christ they had begun to be discredited; for we see Cicero trying to find out the cause of their failure. And these are his words: *Why is it that oracles of such a sort not only are not uttered at Delphi in our time, but have not been given out for some time past, so that nothing could be more contemptible?*[1] But as for the other prognostics which were derived at sacrifices from the anatomy of animals, to which Plato[2] ascribes in part the natural structure of their internal organs, from the quick motions[3] of chickens, or the flight of birds, *we hold that certain birds were purposely created to be used in the art of augury,*[4] from thunder and lightning, from the overflow of rivers; *many things the soothsayers discern; many the augurs foresee; many are announced by oracles, many by prophecies, many by dreams, many by portents;*[5] and other things upon which antiquity based most of its undertakings, both public and private—our religion has done away with them. And although there still remain among us certain methods of divination, by the stars, by spirits, by ghosts, by dreams, and otherwise,—a notable example of the senseless curiosity of our nature, occupying itself with future matters, as if it had not enough to do in digesting those at hand,—

> Why did it please thee, ruler of Olympus, to add another care to anxious mortals, that through boding omens they know the calamities that are to come?
> . . . Be it sudden, whatever thou dost prepare; let men's minds be blind to the future; let the timid man still hope,[6] —

It is no advantage to know the future; for it is a wretched thing to suffer suspense all to no purpose,[7] still, it[8] is of much less authority [than formerly]. This is why the instance of Francis, Marquis de Sallusse, has seemed to me worthy of note.[9] For while he was lieutenant of King Francis in his army on the other side of the mountains,[10] and was in highest favour at our court and indebted to the king for the marquisate, which had been confiscated from his brother, there being indeed no occasion for him to do this,"[11]—his inclination even pointing the other way,—he allowed himself to be so terrified, so it has been asserted, by the fine prognostications that were then current on all sides to the advantage of the Emperor Charles the Fifth and to our disadvantage (even in Italy, where those absurd prophecies had gained so much credence that in Rome a large sum of money changed hands on account of the belief in our downfall) that, after frequently lamenting with his intimates the disasters which he saw to be inevitably in store for the crown of France and for his friends there, he rebelled and changed his allegiance—to his great harm, however, whatever constellation was in the sky. But he behaved like a man torn by conflicting passions; for, having both cities and troops under his command, and the hostile army, under Antonio de Leyva, being close at hand (and we unsuspicious of what he was about), he might have done much worse than he did; for by his treachery we lost neither man nor town, except Fossan, and that only after a long struggle.

> A wise god conceals in thick darkness the outcome of the future, and laughs if some mortal is more alarmed than he should be. . . . He will be master of himself and happy, who can say each day, "I have lived; to-morrow let the father cover the heavens with a dark cloud or with pure sunshine."[12]

> The mind happy in the present shuns all thought of the future.[13]

And, on the other hand, they who believe the following statement, believe it mistakenly: *Thus the argument is converted: If there be an art of divination, there are gods; and if there be gods, there is an art of divination.*[14] Much more wisely Pacuvius says:—

> As for those who understand the language of birds and learn more from the liver of a beast than from their own thought, they should be heard, I think, rather than heeded.[15]

The Tuscans' celebrated art of divination originated thus: A ploughman, driving his plough deep, saw Tages rise out of the earth[16]—a demigod with the face of a child but an old man's wisdom. Every one hastened to the place, and his words and his learning, embodying the principles and processes of this art, were collected and preserved for many cen-

turies. An origin consonant with its growth. I should much
prefer to manage my affairs by the cast of the dice than by
such dreams. And, in truth, in all republics, a large share of
authority has always been ascribed to the drawing of lots.
Plato, in the laws of government which he makes as pleases
him, entrusts to it the decision of numerous matters of importance,[17] and decrees, among other things, that marriages
between the good shall be arranged by lot; and he attributes
so much weight to this chance selection, that he decrees that
children born from it shall be brought up within the country, and that those born from ill-assorted unions shall be sent
away; but if one of those banished[18] should by any chance,
as he grew up, manifest some hopeful indications of worth,
let him be recalled; and also let any one of those originally
retained be expelled who during his adolescence manifests
little that is hopeful.

I see some who study and annotate their almanacs, and
hold them up to us as authority about things that are taking
place. Saying so much, they must needs say what is truth
and what falsehood. *Who can shoot all day and not sometimes hit the mark?*[19] I think no better of them because I
see them sometimes make a lucky hit. There would be more
certainty and truth if it were the rule always to lie.[20] It may
be added that no one keeps a record of their miscalcula-
tions,[21] as they are of common occurrence and endless; and
every one ranks their true prognostics as remarkable, incredible, and prodigious. Witness the answer of Diagoras, to
whom, when he was in Samothrace, some one pointed out
in the temple many votive offerings and pictures of those
who had been rescued from shipwreck, saying: "Look, you
who believe that the gods are indifferent to human affairs

—what say you to so many men saved by their mercy?"
—"I say this," he replied: "those who have been drowned,
a far greater number, have not been painted."[22] Cicero says
that Xenophanes the Colophonian alone of all the philosophers who acknowledged the existence of the gods, tried to
uproot every kind of divination.[23] It is in so much the less
strange if we have seen sometimes, to their hurt, some of
our princely personages dally with these vanities.

I should greatly like to have beheld with my own eyes
those two marvels—the book of Joachim, the Calabrian ab-
bot,[24] who predicted all the popes to come, their names and
persons; and that of the Emperor Leo,[25] who predicted the
emperors and patriarchs of Greece. This I have seen with
my own eyes, that, in times of public confusion, men
amazed by what happens to them fall back, as into other
forms of superstition, into seeking in the heavens the causes
and past threatenings of their ill-fortune; and they are so
strangely lucky at it in my time that they have convinced
me that, inasmuch as it is an occupation for keen and idle
minds, those who are trained to this subtle art of knotting
and unknotting these signs would be capable of finding in
any writings whatever they sought therein. But what above
all helps them in this game is the obscure, ambiguous, and
fantastic language of the prophetical jargon, to which those
who use it give no clear sense, so that posterity may ascribe
to it any meaning it pleases.[26] The Demon of Socrates was,
perhaps, a certain impulse from the will, which moved him
without awaiting the concurrence of his reason. In a mind
so purified as his, and so prepared by the continuous practice of wisdom and virtue, it is probable that those impressions, although unexpected and formless, were always im-

Of Prognostications

portant and worthy of being followed. Every man feels within himself some likeness to such emotions, of a quick, vehement, and haphazard judgement.[27] I can but give these some weight, who give so little weight to our sagacity; and I have had some equally weak in common sense and vehement in persuasion,—or in dissuasion, which were more usual in Socrates,—by which I have allowed myself to be guided so profitably and fortunately, that they might be judged to contain something of divine inspiration.

Chapter XII

OF STEADINESS

THE rule of firmness and steadiness does not require that we should not protect ourselves, so far as is in our power, from the evils and misfortunes which threaten us, nor, consequently, from the fear of their taking us by surprise. On the contrary, all honourable means of securing ourselves from harm are not only permissible, but praiseworthy. And the character of steadiness is shown[1] mainly by bearing patiently and unshaken the misfortunes for which there is no remedy; so that there is no agility, no motion, which, when armed, we should think ill of, if it serves to ward off the blow about to crush us.

Many very warlike nations use flight in their encounters as their chief means of advantage, and show their backs with more danger to their enemies than their faces. The Turks retain something of this habit, and Socrates, in Plato,[2] makes sport of Laches, who had defined fortitude, "to stand fast in one's place against the foe."—"What," he says, "would it be cowardice, then, to beat them by giving way?" And he cites Homer, who praises Æneas for skill in flight. And because Laches, on further consideration, admits the existence of such a custom among the Scythians, and indeed generally

54

Of Steadiness

among all peoples that fight on horseback, he cites further the example of the Lacedæmonian foot-soldiers (the nation especially trained to fight shoulder to shoulder[3]), who, on the day of Platæa, being unable to break into the Persian phalanx, decided to scatter and fall back, so that, by having it believed that they had fled, they might cause that mass to break and melt away in pursuing; by which means they obtained the victory.

Regarding the Scythians, it is said that, when Darius set forth to subjugate them, he sent to their king many reproaches because he found him always falling back and avoiding an encounter. To which Indathyrses (for so he was named) replied, that it was not because he was afraid of him or of any man alive; but that it was his nation's way of fighting, as they had neither tilled fields, nor cities, nor houses to defend, and had not to fear that the enemy could make any profit from these; but if he was so hungry for a taste of them, let him come to look at their ancient places of burial, and he would find his fill of people to talk to.[4]

None the less, in a cannonade, when one is directly exposed to it, as the hazards of war often bring about, it is unbecoming to start at the threat of the shot, since, by reason of its impetus and speed, we know it to be inescapable; and there is many a man who, by lifting his hand or lowering his head, has at least given his comrades ground for laughter. Yet it is true that on the Emperor Charles the Fifth's expedition against us in Provence,[5] the Marquis de Gaust, having gone to reconnoitre the town of Arles, and having stepped out from the shelter of a windmill under cover of which he had approached, was espied by the Seigneur de Bonneval and the Seneschal of Agenois, who were walking on the walls of the amphitheatre.[6] They having pointed him out to the Seigneur de Villier, commissary of artillery, he aimed a culverin at him so exactly at the right moment that, if the said marquis, seeing him light the match, had not jumped aside, it was thought certain that he would have been hit. And likewise, a few years earlier, when Lorenzo de Medicis, Duke of Urbino, father of the Queen-Mother,[7] was besieging Mondolpho, a fortified place in Italy, in the region called the Vicariate, seeing the match touched to a gun aimed in his direction, it was well that he ducked,[8] for otherwise the ball, which merely grazed the top of his head, would doubtless have hit him in the stomach. To say the truth, I do not believe that such motions are made with intention; for what judgement can you form as to high or low aim in so sudden a matter? And it is much easier to believe that fortune smiled upon their fright, and that another time such action would be quite as likely to throw them in front of the blow as to avoid it. If the flashing report of a musket strikes my ears without warning, in a place where I have no reason to expect it, I can not help starting violently—which I have seen happen to others who are better men than I. Nor do the Stoics[9] hold that the soul of their sage can resist the first visions and fancies that occur to him; rather, they admit that from a natural subjection he may be affected by a loud noise in the sky, or of a falling building, for example, to the point of pallor and paralysis, as well as to other expressions of emotion, provided that his thought remains entrenched and whole, and that the seat of his judgement suffers no injury or change, and that he gives no countenance to his fright and suspense. With him who is no sage, it is the same as to the first point, but altogether different as to

Of Steadiness

the second. For in him the impression of perturbations is not superficial, but penetrates to the seat of his reason, infecting and corrupting it; he judges according to them and adapts himself to them. See the state of the Stoic sage well and fully set forth:—

His mind remains unshaken; useless are her flowing tears.[10]

The Peripatetic sage is not free from agitations, but he governs them.

Chapter XIII

THE CEREMONY

AT INTERVIEWS OF KINGS

THERE is no subject so trivial as not to deserve a place in this medley.[1] According to our ordinary conventions, it would be a signal discourtesy, both to an equal and even more to a great man, to fail to be at home when he had notified you that he was about to come to your house. Indeed, Queen Marguerite of Navarre went further and said, on this subject, that it is uncivil for a gentleman to leave his house, as is most often done, and go forth to meet the person who is coming to visit him, however great a man he may be; and that it is more respectful and civil to wait at home to receive him, were it only for fear of missing him on the road; and that it is enough to accompany him on his departure. For my own part, I often forget both one and the other of these idle civilities, as in my own house I do away with all ceremony so far as I can. If some one should take offence, what matters it to me? It is better to offend him once than myself every day: that would be a never-ending subjection. To what end do we shun the servitude of courts, if we bring it into our own lair?[2]

It is also a common rule in all gatherings that it is for the inferior persons to be first at the place appointed, since it is

58

The Ceremony at Interviews of Kings

more fitting that the greater should be waited for. And yet at the interview which was arranged between Pope Clement[3] and King Francis at Marseilles, the king, having ordered the necessary preparations, left the city and gave the Pope two or three days of leisure, to make his entry and recreate himself before meeting him. And in like manner, at the entry of the same Pope and the emperor[4] into Bologna, the emperor gave the Pope opportunity to be there first, and arrived after him. It is, they say, a common ceremonial at the conferences of princes, that the greatest should arrive before the others at the place assigned, even before him in whose country the meeting is held; and they look at it in this way:[5] that it is because this arrangement testifies that the inferiors go to find the greatest, and seek him, not he them.

Not only every country, but every city and every profession has its special code of manners. I was trained carefully enough in my childhood, and have lived in sufficiently good society, not to be ignorant of the laws of our French manners; and I might teach them. I like to follow them, but not so slavishly that my life is constrained by them. They have some troublesome forms, which if we forget discreetly and not erroneously, we suffer no loss of grace. I have often seen men uncivil through over-civility, and importunate out of courtesy. After all, the art of social tact[6] is a very useful art. Like grace and beauty, it conciliates the approaches of sociability and familiarity, and consequently opens the way for us to instruct ourselves by the examples of others, and to put into execution and make visible our own example, if there be in it any thing instructive and communicable.

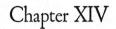

Chapter XIV

THAT THE SAVOUR
OF GOODS AND ILLS DEPENDS
IN LARGE PART ON THE IDEA
THAT WE HAVE OF THEM[1]

AN old Greek proverb says that men are afflicted by
their ideas of things, not by the things themselves.[2]
There would be a great point gained for the solace of our
miserable mortal state if some one could prove this proposition to be always true; for if the ills of life enter into us only
through our judgement, it would seem to be in our power to
despise them or to turn them to good. If things are surrendered to us, why should we not make use of them, or
adapt them to our benefit? If that which we call evil and
affliction is neither evil nor affliction in itself, but our imagination alone gives it that character, it is in our power to
change it; and having the choice, if nothing compels us,
we are strangely unwise to exert ourselves for the side which
is most painful for us,[3] and to give to disease, poverty, and
contumely a bitter and bad taste if we can give them a good
one, and if, fortune simply supplying matter, it is for us
to give it shape. Now, that what we call evil is not so in
itself, or, at least, whatever it may be, that it depends on us
to give it another savour and another aspect,—for it all
comes to the same thing,—let us see if this can be maintained.

60

The Savour of Goods and Ills

If the primal nature of these things that we dread had power to lodge in us of its own authority, it would have the same power in all; for men are all of one species, and, save as regards the more and the less, they are supplied with the same tools and instruments for conceiving and judging. But the diversity of our opinions concerning these things shows clearly that they enter into us only as we accept them:[4] one man, it may be, holds them in himself in their true character, but a thousand others give them in their minds a new and different character. We regard death, poverty, and pain as our chief enemies. Now this death, which some call the most horrible of horrible things—who does not know that others call it the only haven from the tempests of this life, the sovereign benefaction of nature, the sole stay of our liberty, and the universal and speedy remedy for all ills.[5] And as some await it in fear and trembling, others endure it more easily than life. This man laments its easy attainment:—

> O death, would that thou wert not willing to take life from the craven, and that valour alone could obtain thee![6]

Now let us have done with this vainglorious valour. Theodorus replied to Lysimachus who threatened to kill him: "You will perform a great feat to attain the strength of a fly."[7] Most philosophers are found either to have purposely anticipated, or to have hastened and aided, their deaths. How often we see common people, when led forth to death,—and not to a simple death, but to one accompanied by disgrace and sometimes by grievous suffering,—face it with such confidence, some from stubbornness and some from natural shallowness, that we can detect no change from their ordinary frame of mind: arranging their domestic affairs, commending themselves to their friends, singing, haranguing, and talking with the populace, nay, sometimes even cracking jokes, and drinking to their acquaintances, as if they were Socrates.[8] One man, who was being taken to the scaffold, told them not to go through a certain street, for there was danger that a tradesman would lay hands on him because of an old debt. Another told the hangman not to touch his throat, for fear of making him squirm with laughter, he was so ticklish. Another replied to his confessor, who promised him that he would sup that day with our Lord, "Go thither yourself; for my part, I am fasting." Another, having asked for a drink, and the hangman having drunk first, declared that he would not drink after him for fear of catching small-pox. Every one has heard the story of the Picard, to whom, when he was on the very steps of the scaffold, a wench was offered, whom if he chose to marry, they would spare his life (as our laws permit on occasion). Having looked at her for a moment, and perceived that she was lame, "Tie me up! tie me up!" he cried; "she limps!" And they say, likewise, that in Denmark a man who was sentenced to have his head cut off, being actually on the scaffold, when a similar alternative was given him, declined it because the girl they offered him had hanging cheeks and too sharp a nose.[9] A man-servant who was charged with heresy at Toulouse referred, for the ground of his belief, to that of his master, a young student who was a prisoner with him; and preferred to die rather than allow himself to be convinced that his master was in error.[10] We read of the citizens of Arras, when King Louis

62

The Savour of Goods and Ills

XI took the city, that there were a goodly number of them who submitted to be hanged rather than say, "Vive le roi!"[11] And of such narrow-minded clowns there have been some who would not abandon their pleasantries even in death. One whom the hangman was just turning off cried: "Let go, in God's name!"[12] which was his customary refrain. And that other who, at the point of death, had been laid on a mattress by the hearth, and being asked by the doctor where he felt pain, replied: "Between the bench and the fire"; and when the priest, in order to give him extreme unction, was feeling for his feet, which were drawn up and stiffened by pain, "You'll find them," he said, "at the end of my legs." He asked the man who exhorted him to commend himself to God, "Who is going thither?" and on the other's replying, "It will be you yourself very soon, if it is his pleasure," he rejoined: "Shall I surely be there to-morrow evening?"—"Just commend yourself to him," continued the other; "you'll be there very soon."—"It is better then," he retorted, "for me to carry Him my recommendations myself."[13]

In the kingdom of Narsinga,[14] to this day, the wives of the priests are buried alive with their deceased husbands. All other wives are burned at the obsequies of their husbands, not with fortitude simply, but gaily. And when the body of their deceased king is burned, all his wives and concubines, his favourites, and every sort of official and public servant, forming a great multitude, rush so light-heartedly to the fire, to throw themselves into it with the master, that they seem to regard it as a great honour to be his companions in death.[15] During our last wars in Milan, with so many captures and recaptures, the people, being made impatient by such perpetual alternations of fortune, so deliberately chose death, that I have heard my father say that he heard of as many as five-and-twenty heads of families who had made way with themselves in one week; an incident resembling that of the Xantians, who, besieged by Brutus, were seized pell-mell—men, women, and children—with so fierce a craving for death, that there is nothing done to escape death which they did not do to escape life; so that Brutus scarcely could save a very small number.[16]

Every belief is strong enough to cause men to espouse it at the cost of life. The first article of that fine oath that Greece took and kept to in the Median war was that every man should exchange life for death rather than their laws for those of the Persians.[17] In the war between the Greeks and the Turks, what numbers of them are seen accepting violent death rather than renounce their faith and be baptised! A test of which no form of religion is incapable.

The kings of Castile having banished the Jews from their realm, King Jan of Portugal[18] sold them, at eight crowns a head, refuge among his people, on condition that they should depart on a certain day; and he promised to supply them with vessels to take them across to Africa. The day came, of which he had said that, when it had passed, those who had not obeyed would remain as slaves. The vessels were scantily supplied to them, and those who embarked were roughly and villainously treated by the sailors, who, in addition to many other indignities, kept them wearily sailing about, sometimes going ahead, sometimes going back, until they had consumed all their own provisions and were compelled to buy food from them at such high prices, and for so long a time, that they were not set ashore till they

The Savour of Goods and Ills

had nothing left. News of this inhuman treatment being carried back to those still on land, the greater number made up their minds to servitude; some pretended to change their religion. Emmanuel,[19] having come to the throne, first set them at liberty, and then, changing his mind, gave them time to leave his dominions, assigning three ports for their embarkation. He hoped, says Bishop Osorio, the best Latin historian of our time, that, the grace of freedom which he had bestowed on them having failed to convert them to Christianity, their reluctance to expose themselves, like their companions, to the thievery of the seamen, to leave a country where they had lived in great prosperity and to cast their lot in an unknown and foreign land, would bring about this result. But finding his hope disappointed, and that they were all determined to depart, he cut off two of the ports he had promised them, in order that the length and discomfort of the passage might cause some to reconsider, or in order to pile them all up together in one place for greater facility of execution of what he purposed, which was this. He ordered that all the children under fourteen should be taken from the hands of their fathers and mothers and transported out of their sight and intercourse, to a place where they would be instructed in our religion. It is said that this action led to a horrible spectacle—the natural affection between the parents and their children and, moreover, their zeal for their ancient beliefs, contending against this violent decree. It was a common sight to see mothers and fathers taking their own lives, and—an even stronger testimony—for very love and pity throwing their young children into wells to evade the law. Finally, the time that had been fixed having expired, they returned, for lack of means, into slavery. Some became Christians—on whose faith or that of their race, even today, a hundred years after, few Portuguese rely, although habit and lapse of time are much stronger counsellors than all other pressure.

In the city of Castelnau-Darry, fifty Albigensian heretics suffered all at one time, courageously resolute to be burned alive in one fire rather than renounce their beliefs.[20] *How often have not only our generals but whole armies dashed forward to meet certain death!*[21] I have seen one of my intimate friends give hot chase to death, with a true longing rooted in his heart from various points of view,[22] which I could not diminish in him; and at the first shape of it that presented itself crowned with a halo of honour, he hastened to meet it, beyond all likelihood, with a sharp and eager hunger.

We have many examples in our own days of persons, even children, who, from dread of some slight disaster, have killed themselves. And in this connection, an ancient writer says: "What shall we not fear, if we fear what cowardice itself has chosen as a refuge?" Were I to enter here on a long list of those of all sexes and conditions and of all sects who, in happier ages, have either awaited death with steadiness or sought it voluntarily, and sought it, not only in order to fly from the ills of this life, but in some cases simply to fly from satiety of living, and in others in the hope of a better state elsewhere—I should never have done; and the number is so infinite that, in truth, it would be a better bargain for me to count up those who have feared it. This only will I note: Pyrrho the philosopher, being one day in a tempest at sea, pointed out to those about him whom he saw to be most frightened, a pig on board that was in no wise disturbed

The Savour of Goods and Ills

by this storm, and encouraged them by this example.[23]

Shall we venture then to say that this privilege of the power of reasoning, about which we so flatter ourselves, and because of which we regard ourselves as the masters and monarchs of the rest of creation, was given us for our torment? What profits the knowledge of things,[24] if we lose the tranquillity and repose in which we should be without it, and if it puts us in worse case than Pyrrho's pig? The intelligence that has been given us for our greater welfare—shall we employ it for our destruction, combatting the purpose of Nature and the universal order of things, which ordains that every one use his tools and resources for his own pleasure?[25]

"Very good," you will answer me, "your precept is well enough for death; but what will you say of poverty which Aristippus, Hieronymus, and most wise men considered the worst of evils?"[26] And they who denied it in words confessed it by their acts. Posidonius being in great suffering from a sharp and painful malady, Pompey went to see him and apologised for having come at so inopportune a time to hear him discourse on philosophy. "God forbid," said Posidonius, "that pain should so prevail over me as to prevent me from discoursing and talking of that!" and he threw himself into this very subject of contempt of pain. But meanwhile pain played its part and tormented him incessantly, whereupon he exclaimed: "Do what you will, pain: I still will not say that you are an evil thing!"[27] This tale that they make so much of—what meaning has it with respect to contempt of pain? It is only a quibble about the words; and meanwhile, if those twinges do not affect him, then why does he interrupt his talk? And why does he think that he does such a great thing in not calling it an evil?

Here it is not all imagination. We argue about other matters, here it is absolute knowledge that comes into play; our very senses are judges of it;

> Unless the senses be true, reason itself must be wholly deceived.[28]

Shall we persuade our skin that the blows of a stirrup-leather tickle it, and our palate that aloes is Bordeaux wine? Pyrrho's pig is of our company here: he is unterrified by death, but if he is beaten, he squeals and squirms. Shall we run counter to the universal law of Nature,—which is seen in every living thing under the sky,—of trembling under pain? The very trees seem to groan at the injuries we inflict on them. Death is felt only through the reason, as it is the action of an instant.

> [Death] either has come or is yet to come; there is nothing in it of the present,[29]

> And death itself is easier to endure than the awaiting death.[30]

A thousand beasts, a thousand men are dead unthreatened. And, in truth, we confess that what we chiefly dread in death is pain, its customary forerunner.

None the less, if we are to believe a holy father, *death is made an evil only by what follows death*.[31] And I will say even more plausibly that neither what precedes nor what follows death is an appurtenance of death. We excuse ourselves falsely; and I find by experience that it is chiefly the unendurableness of the thought of death that makes pain unendurable to us, and that we feel it as doubly grievous

The Savour of Goods and Ills

because it threatens us with death. But since reason accuses us of cowardice in dreading a thing so sudden, so inevitable, so imperceptible, we seize this other more defensible pretext. All those maladies which threaten no other danger than that of the malady itself we say are without danger. Toothache, or gout, however painful they may be, still, as they do not kill, who counts them as sicknesses? Now let us assume that in death we consider chiefly the pain. In like manner, poverty has nothing to fear but this—that it will throw us into the arms of pain through the thirst, the hunger, the cold, the heat, the vigils, which it makes us suffer.

Thus we have to do with pain alone. I grant that it is the worst mischance of our being, and I grant this readily, for there is no man on earth who regards it with such disfavour or who shuns it so much as I, because hitherto, thanks to God, I have not had much familiarity with it; but it is in our power, if not to annihilate it, at least to diminish it by patience; and even when the body is perturbed by it, to maintain none the less the soul and the reason in good condition. And if it were not so, what would have brought courage and valour and strength and greatness of soul and resolution into good repute? How should they play their part if there were no pain to defy? *Courage is eager for danger.*[32] If we have not to lie on the hard ground, to endure in complete armour the noon-day heat, to eat horse-flesh or that of an ass, to be hacked in pieces, to extract a bullet from among our bones, to be sewn up and cauterised and probed, whence shall we acquire the advantage that we desire to have over the common crowd? What the sages say, that of actions equally meritorious the one is most desirable to perform in which there is most difficulty, is a long way from avoiding evil and pain. *It is not from gaiety or sportiveness or laughter or jesting, companions of frivolity, that happiness is won; even austere men often achieve it by steadfastness and fortitude.*[33] And for this reason it was impossible to persuade our fathers that conquests made by the strong hand, at the hazard of war, were not more beneficial than those effected in all security by plots and stratagems.

The nobler the virtue, the more it costs us.[34]

Moreover, this ought to console us, that, in the nature of things, if pain is violent, it is short; if it lasts long, it is slight; *si gravis [dolor], brevis; si longus, levis.*[35] You will hardly feel it long if you feel it too much; it will put an end to itself or to you; the one or the other comes to the same thing.[36] If you do not bear it well, it will bear you off. *Remember that the greatest sufferings are ended by death; that the little ones have many intermittences; that of those that are moderate we are the masters; that, if they are tolerable, we can bear them, but if not, when life is not agreeable to us, we can make our exit from it as from a theatre.*[37]

What makes us suffer pain so intolerantly is the not being accustomed to take our chief satisfaction in the soul,[38] the not relying enough on her[39] who is the one sovereign mistress of our being and our behaviour. The body has for the most part but one mode of action and one kind of life; the soul changes into every variety of guise and brings into relation with herself and her condition, whatever that may be, the perceptions of the body and all other external things.[40] Therefore we must study her and question her and arouse her all-powerful springs. There is no argument, no tradition, no force, which is of any avail against her inclina-

70

The Savour of Goods and Ills

tion and her choice. Of the many thousand twists and turns she has at her command, let us make her take one conducive to our repose and preservation; then we are not only shielded from all harm, but even pleased and flattered, if it seems well to her, by hurts and ills. She turns every thing to her advantage, no matter what it is: error, dreams, are useful to her as legitimate material for making us secure and content.

It is easy to see that what gives an edge to pain and pleasure within us is our state of mind. The animals, who are unaffected by this,[41] feel in their bodies their unconstrained natural sensations, which consequently are almost invariable in each species, as we see by the conformity of their actions. If we did not disturb in our members their jurisdiction in this matter, it may be believed that we should be the better off, and nature has given them a just and moderate mingling of pleasure and of pain which cannot fail to be just, being equal and alike to all. But since we have cut loose from her rules, to abandon ourselves to the vagabond license of our imaginations, let us at least help to turn them in the most agreeable direction. Plato is displeased by our immitigable union with pain and pleasure, because it binds the soul to the body and attaches it too closely; I, on the contrary, am displeased by it, inasmuch as it detaches and separates them.[42] Just as the enemy becomes fiercer when we fly, so pain grows proud to see us tremble before it.[43] It will surrender on much better terms to the man who shows it a bold front; we must resist it and brace ourselves against it. By being cornered and falling back, we invite and attract the destruction that threatens us. As the body is steadier against the onset by stiffening its muscles, so is the soul.[44]

The Savour of Goods and Ills

But let us come to examples, which are proper game for the weak-loined like me: here we shall find that it is with pain as with stones, which take on a brighter or darker hue according to the foil on which we place them, and that it fills only so much room in us as we make for it. *They suffered the more, the more they gave themselves up to suffering.*[45] We feel a cut from the surgeon's knife more than ten sword-cuts in the heat of battle. The pains of childbirth, which are considered severe by the doctors and by God himself,[46] and which we carry through with so many observances—there are whole nations which make nothing at all of them. I say nothing of the Lacedæmonian women; but the Swiss women with our infantry—what change do you find in them, except that, trotting after their husbands, you see them to-day carrying in their arms the child that yesterday they carried in their womb? And these make-believe Egyptian women among us go themselves to wash their new-born babes, and take their own bath, in the nearest stream. Besides the multitude of wenches who every day conceal their children as well at their birth as at their conception, the virtuous wife of Sabinus, a Roman patrician, endured the birth of twins alone and unaided, without a word or a groan.[47] A simple lad of Lacedæmon, having stolen a fox, and having hidden it under his cloak, (for they dreaded the disgrace of their lack of skill in thieving even more than we dread the punishment),[48] endured having his bowels gnawed by it rather than betray himself.[49] And another, while offering incense at a sacrifice, allowed himself to be burned to the bone by a coal that dropped into his sleeve.[50] And a great many boys have been known who, at the age of seven, merely for a test of their courage, in ac-

The Savour of Goods and Ills

cordance with their education, have endured being whipped to death without change of countenance. And Cicero saw them fight in companies, with fists and feet and teeth, till they fainted, before admitting that they were beaten.[51] *Custom could never overcome nature, for she is invincible. But we have spoiled our minds with illusory pleasures and with the languor of idleness; we have weakened them with the charm of false belief in bad habits.*[52]

Every one knows the history of Scævola,[53] who, having slipped into the enemy's camp to kill their leader, and having failed of his purpose, in order to gain his end by a more extraordinary scheme, and to set his country free, not only confessed his design to Porsenna, who was the king he sought to kill, but added that in the king's camp there were a great number of such Romans as himself, who were accomplices in his undertaking; and, to show what manner of man he was, having caused a brazier to be brought, he saw and suffered his arm to be broiled and roasted until his very enemy, horror-struck, ordered the brazier removed. What can we say of him who did not condescend to interrupt his reading while he was under the surgeon's knife?[54] And of him who persisted in laughing at himself and gaily vying with the sufferings inflicted on him, so that the excited cruelty of the executioners who had him in their keeping, with all the contrivances of torture piled one upon another, confessed themselves to be powerless? But he was a philosopher. And what of Cæsar's gladiator, who endured having his wounds probed and cut open, laughing all the while?[55] *What ordinary gladiator ever uttered a groan? Which of them ever changed countenance? Which of them in fighting, or even in falling, shewed cowardice? Which, when he had fallen, and was to receive his death-stroke, turned away his head?*[56]

Now let us consider the women. Who has not heard in Paris of her who caused herself to be flayed, solely to acquire the fresher colouring of a new skin?[57] There are those who have had sound, living teeth pulled out, in order to make their pronunciation more flexible or more lisping, or to arrange the teeth more regularly. How many examples we have of this sort of contempt of pain! What can they not do? What do they fear, if in the doing there is any hope of enhancement of their beauty?

> They who are careful to pluck out by the roots their white hairs, and to make a new face by peeling off the skin.[58]

I have seen them swallow sand and ashes, and labour deliberately to destroy their stomachs, in order to acquire a pale complexion. To give themselves a Spanish slenderness,[59] what discomfort do they not endure, bound and girt, with great slashes on their sides, even to the quick—yes, and sometimes till these are fatal!

It is a common custom with many nations of our day to wound themselves purposely, to give credit to their word; and our king[60] relates noteworthy instances of what he saw of this in Poland, and in relation to himself. But besides what I have heard of as having been done, of this sort, by some persons in France, I myself saw a girl,[61] to testify to the ardour of her promises and also her firmness, give herself, with the bodkin she wore in her hair, four or five sharp blows on the arm, which tore the skin and brought blood in good earnest. The Turks make for themselves great scars in hon-

our of their mistresses; and, that the mark may remain,
they instantly apply fire to the wound and hold it there an
incredible time, to stop the bleeding and form the cicatrix.[62]
Men who have seen it have written of this and have sworn
to the truth of it to me. But any day there may be found
those among them who, for ten *aspers,*[63] will give themselves
a very deep slash on the arm or the thigh.

I am very glad that there are witnesses nearer to us, where
we are more concerned; for Christendom supplies us with
them more than sufficiently. After the example of our
blessed exemplar, there have been many who, from devotion, have chosen to suffer greatly.[64] We learn from a witness most worthy of belief,[65] that the King Saint Louis
wore a hair-shirt until, in his old age, his confessor dispensed
him from it; and that every Friday he had his priest scourge
his back with five small iron chains, which, for that purpose,
were always carried in a box with the other things that he
used at night. Guillaume, our last Duke of Guyenne, father
of that Alienor[66] who transmitted this duchy to the royal
houses of France and of England, constantly wore, by way
of penance, a corselet under the frock of a monk.[67] Fulke,
Count of Anjou, went all the way to Jerusalem, to be
scourged there by two of his servants, with a rope round his
neck, in front of our Lord's sepulchre.[68] But do we not still
see, on every Good Friday, in various places, a great number
of men and women scourge themselves even to the tearing
of their flesh and wounding to the bone?[69] This I have often
seen, and without delusion; and it is said (for they go
masked) that there are among them those who, for money,
undertake thereby to warrant another's religion by a contempt of pain so much the greater as the spurs of piety are

more potent than those of avarice. Quintus Maximus buried his son, of consular rank, Marcus Cato his, prætor elect, and Lucius Paulus his two within a few days of each other, with serene countenance and giving no sign of grief.[70] I once said of some one,[71] in jest, that he had cheated divine justice; for the deaths by violence of three noble sons having been sent in one day, by way, as may be believed, of a severe chastisement, it lacked little that he received it as a blessing.[72] I have lost, but in infancy, two or three children, if not without regret, at least without distress; nevertheless there are few misfortunes which touch men so to the quick. I see a good many other common occasions for sorrow which I should scarcely feel, should they come to me; and I have scorned, when they have come, some of those to which the world ascribes so baleful an aspect that I could not dare to boast publicly of this without blushing. *So it is evident that the scourge of discomfort is not in nature, but in the mind.*[73]

Opinion is a powerful auxiliary, confident and not to be measured. Who ever sought safety and repose with such longing as Alexander and Cæsar had for disquietude and difficulties? Teres, father of Sitalces, was wont to say that, when he was not making war, it seemed to him that there was no difference between him and his groom.[74] Cato, when consul, in order to make sure of certain cities in Spain, having merely forbidden their inhabitants to bear arms, a great number killed themselves: *a fierce people who could not conceive of a life of peace.*[75] How many men we know who have fled from the enjoyment of a quiet life in their own house, among their acquaintance, to seek the frightfulness of uninhabitable deserts, and who have cast themselves into abjection and degradation and the world's contempt, and

The Savour of Goods and Ills

have delighted therein, even in preference to all else. Cardinal Borromeo,[76] who died recently at Milan, maintained, in the midst of debauchery, to which his noble birth and his great wealth and the air of Italy and his youth all invited him, a mode of life so vigorous that he wore the same coat in winter as in summer, had nothing but straw for his bed, and passed what hours remained to him after discharging the duties of his office in constant study, resting on his knees, with a little bread and water beside his book, which was all that he had to eat and all the time that he gave to eating. I know some men who have derived both profit and advancement from cuckoldry, of which the mere name frightens so many persons. If sight be not the most necessary of our senses, it is certainly the most agreeable; but the most agreeable and useful of our members seem to be those which serve the purpose of generation; and yet many persons have held them in mortal hatred solely for the reason that they were too delightful, and have rejected them because of their value. So opined of his eyes the man who put them out.[77]

The greater number and most healthy-minded among men[78] consider it great good fortune to have an abundance of children; I and some others consider the lack of them equally good fortune. And when some one asks Thales why he does not marry, he replies that he does not desire to leave any descendants of himself.[79] That our opinion gives their value to things is seen by those, many in number, which we do not regard solely by themselves in estimating them, but with regard to ourselves. And we consider neither their qualities, nor their usefulness, but only what it costs us to obtain them, as if the cost were a part of their being; and we call value in them, not what they bring, but what we bring

to them. In this respect I think we are very thrifty in our
outlay; according to its weight it is of use, to the extent that
it has weight. Our opinion never lets it pass with false
freightage.[80] The purchase gives value to the diamond, as
resistance does to virtue, grief to devotion, and bitterness to
medicine.

A certain man,[81] in order to attain poverty, threw his
money into that same ocean which so many search in all
parts, seeking to fish up wealth. Epicurus says that to be
rich is not an alleviation, but simply a change of trouble.[82]
In truth, it is not want, but rather abundance, which gives
birth to avarice. I will tell my experience in regard to this
matter. I have lived in three different kinds of conditions
since I left childhood behind. The first period, which lasted
nearly twenty years, I passed with no other than haphazard
resources, depending on the arrangements and support of
others, with no established profession and without regulations. I spent my money the more easily and carelessly because it all lay in the turn of fortune. I was never better off.
It never happened to me to find my friends' purses closed,
for I had impressed upon myself the necessity, beyond every
other necessity, of never being in default at the end of the
term in which I had agreed to pay my debt, which term they
a thousand times prolonged, seeing the effort that I made to
satisfy them; so that I gained by my thrifty and somewhat
deceptive loyalty.[83] My nature is to feel some pleasure in
paying, as if I relieved my shoulders of an annoying burden
and of that semblance of servitude; as I feel a pleasure that
flatters me in doing a good action and pleasing another. I
except those payments about which one must needs haggle
and calculate; for if there is no one to whom I can give

The Savour of Goods and Ills

charge of them, I shamefully and unjustly postpone them as long as I can, in dread of this altercation with which both my disposition and my manner of talking are completely incompatible. There is nothing that I hate so much as haggling; it is a mere interchange of cheating and impudence. After an hour of wrangling and chaffering, one and the other side sacrifices his word and his oaths for a charge of five sous. Nevertheless I was at a disadvantage in borrowing; for, not having the courage to ask by word of mouth, I used to commit the chance to paper, which produces little effect, and which makes it very easy to refuse. I entrusted the conduct of my deeds to the stars more gaily and more freely than I have since done to my own providence and my good sense. Good managers think it horrible to be in such uncertainty, and do not consider, in the first place, that most of the world lives so. How many worthy men have thrown overboard all their assured well-being, and do it every day, to seek the wind of the favour of kings and of Fortune! Cæsar, to become Cæsar, incurred debts to the amount of a million in gold, besides using all he was worth;[84] and how many merchants begin their commerce by the sale of their farms, which they send to the Indies,

Across so many raging straits?[85]

In so great a drying-up of piety we have thousands and thousands of colleges[86] which go on easily, awaiting every day, from the liberality of Heaven, what they must have to dine. In the second place, they do not consider that this certainty on which they rely is scarcely less uncertain and matter of chance than chance itself. I see poverty as near, outside of[87] two thousand crowns a year, as if it were close at

79

hand. For besides the fact that fate has the power to open a hundred breaches for want to enter in through our riches, —there being often no mean between the highest and the lowest fortune,—

Fortune is as glass: when it is brilliant, it is fragile;[88]

and to turn topsy-turvy all our dikes and defences, I think that, from divers causes, indigence is as commonly seen to be domiciled with those who have wealth as with those who have none; and that perhaps it is somewhat less troublesome when it is alone than when it is in the company of riches, which come rather from good management than from income: *Each man is the forger of his own fortune.*[89] And an uneasy, timid rich man, full of affairs, seems to me more miserable than the man who is simply poor. *Poor amid riches, which is the hardest kind of poverty.*[90] The greatest and wealthiest princes are, by poverty and dearth, commonly driven to extreme need. For is there any more extreme than to become consequently tyrants and unjust usurpers of the property of their subjects?

My second condition was to have money, to which I so clung that I soon laid by a notable hoard, considering my position, deeming that a man has only so much as he possesses beyond his expenses and his ordinary outgo; and that he cannot rely upon the money which he is still only in hopes of receiving, however well-founded his hopes may be. For, I said to myself, what if I should be taken unaware by such or such an accident? And as the result of these futile and fallacious imaginings, I exerted my ingenuity to provide by these superfluous savings for all emergencies; and I could still reply to him who declared that the number of

The Savour of Goods and Ills

emergencies was too infinite, that, if it would not suffice
for all, it would for some, aye, for many. This did not go on
without painful solicitude. I kept it secret; and I, who dare
to talk so much about myself, spoke of my money only with
untruths, as others do who, when rich, have the air of being
poor, and, when poor, of being rich, and dispense their consciences from ever testifying honestly to what they have:
an absurd and shameful sort of prudence. Was I going on
a journey—it never seemed to me that I was sufficiently
provided; and the more I was laden with coin, the more also
was I laden with fear, sometimes as to the safety of the
roads, sometimes as to the fidelity of those who carried my
luggage, about which, like others I know, I was never sufficiently sure unless I had it under my eyes. Did I leave my
strong-box at home—what a multitude of suspicions, and
thorny thoughts, and, what is worse, incommunicable ones!
My mind was always turned in that direction. Considering
every thing, it is more trouble to keep money than to get
it. If I did not conduct myself exactly as I say, at least it
was difficult to prevent myself from doing so. I derived from
this state little or no ease: with more money to spend, expenditure weighed no less on me; for, as Bion said, "A man
with hair is as much displeased as a bald man, to have his
hair pulled out."[91] And when you are accustomed to a certain pile [of money] and have set your mind upon it, it is
no longer at your service; you would not dare to encroach
upon it. It is a structure which, so it seems to you, will
crumble if you touch it; necessity must take you by the
throat for it to be broken into. And I would have first
pawned my clothes, and sold a horse, with much less reluctance and less repining than I would then have made a

breach in that favored purse which I kept apart. But the danger lay in this, that with difficulty can one establish definite limits to this craving (they are hard to find in respect to things which one thinks good, and fix the moment to stop saving. One goes on ever and ever enlarging the heap, and raising it from one figure to another, to the point of churlishly depriving oneself of the enjoyment of one's own property, and of putting it all under lock and key and making no use of it. With this kind of use of money, the richest men in the world are those who guard the gates and walls of an important city. Every man who himself possesses money is avaricious, to my thinking. Plato marshals thus the goods belonging to the body or to external conditions: health, beauty, strength, wealth; and wealth, he says, is not blind, but very clear-sighted when it is enlightened by wisdom.[92] Dionysius the younger showed an excellent graciousness in this matter.[93] He was told that one of his Syracusan subjects had hidden a treasure in the earth; he ordered him to bring it to him, which he did, secretly keeping back a part of it with which he went to another city, where, having lost his appetite for hoarding, he began to live more liberally. Learning of this, Dionysius ordered the rest of his hoard returned to him, saying that since he had learned how to use it, he gladly gave it back.

I remained several years in this stage.[94] I know not what good spirit most beneficially drove me out of it, like the Syracusan, and sent all that habit of saving to the winds, the pleasure of a certain very expensive journey having trampled underfoot that foolish fancy. Whence I have fallen into a third sort of existence (I say what I feel about it), certainly much more agreeable and better regulated—which is, that

The Savour of Goods and Ills

I make my outgo run evenly with my income: sometimes one is in advance, sometimes the other, but they are never far apart. I live from day to day, and content myself with having the wherewithal to supply my present and ordinary needs; as for the extraordinary ones, all the providing in the world would not suffice for them. And it is madness to expect that Fortune herself ever arms us sufficiently against herself. It is with our own weapons that we must fight her. Haphazard weapons will betray us at the height of need. If I now save, it is only with the expectation of some speedy outlay; and not to buy lands, for which I have no use, but to buy pleasure. *Not to be covetous, is wealth; not to be spendthrift, is revenue.*[95] I have little fear that my means will give out, nor any desire that they shall increase. *The fruit of riches is abundance; contentment indicates abundance.*[96] And I am especially pleased that this change for the better came to me at an age that is naturally predisposed to avarice, and that I find myself quit of that malady so common to the old, and the most absurd of all human foibles.

Feraulez, who had known both sorts of fortune, and had found that increase of possessions was not increase of appetite for drinking, eating, sleeping, and embracing his wife, and who, on the other hand, felt the urgency of household cares as a burden on his shoulders, as it is on mine, took it into his head to gratify a poor young man, his faithful friend, who was longing for wealth, and made him a present of all his riches, exceedingly great, and also of all that he was in the way of accumulating every day through the liberality of Cyrus, his kind master, and through war: on condition that this young man should undertake to maintain and support him honourably, as his guest and his friend. They thus lived from that time very happily, and both equally glad of the change in their condition.[97] That is a course which I should very heartily imitate. And I praise highly the fortune of an elderly prelate whom I know to have resigned his purse so completely, as to both receipts and expenditures, sometimes to one chosen servant, sometimes to another, that he has glided through many years in as great ignorance of his household affairs of that nature as any stranger. Confidence in another's goodness is no slight testimony of one's own goodness, therefore God freely favours it. And respecting him,[98] I know of no household more worthily or more consistently managed than his. Happy is he who has regulated his needs so accurately that his means can supply them without his being anxious or kept busied about them, whilst the spending or collecting of them does not interrupt other occupations that he follows, more suitable, more tranquil, and more after his own heart.

Affluence, then, and indigence, depend on each man's opinion; and renown and health, no less than wealth, have just so much charm and pleasure-giving as he who possesses them attributes to them. Every one is in good or bad case according as he thinks himself to be so. Not he whom others believe to be well off, but he who believes it himself, is happy, and in that matter the belief alone creates essential truth. Fortune does us neither good nor harm; she simply offers us their material and seed, which our soul, more powerful than she,[99] turns and applies as it pleases, being the sole cause and controller of her own happy or unhappy state.[100] External circumstances[101] take savour and colour from the internal constitution, just as our garments warm us, not with their warmth, but with our own, which they are adapted to keep in and nourish;[102] who should cover with them a cold body would obtain from them the same service for its coldness: thus snow and ice are preserved.

Certainly just as study is torment to an indolent man and abstinence from wine to a drunkard, as frugality is abhorrent to the luxurious and exercise is distressful to an effeminate and slothful man, so it is with the rest. Things are neither so grievous nor so difficult in themselves, but our weakness and cowardice make them so. To judge of great and high things, one must have a mind of the same quality; otherwise we attribute to them the defect which is ours. A straight oar always looks crooked in the water. It does not matter that the thing simply is seen, but how it is seen.[103]

Now, amongst so many arguments which in divers ways urge men to despise death and to bear pain, do we not find one to serve us? And amongst all these varieties of ideas which have persuaded others, may not each man apply to himself the one most in accord with his nature? If he can not digest the cleansing purgative powerful to eradicate the evil, let him at least take a sedative to relieve it. *There is a certain effeminate and frivolous humour, common both to pleasure and to pain, which so softens and melts us that we can not bear the sting of a bee without crying out. . . . The whole matter turns on command of one's self.*[104] Moreover, we do not elude philosophy by exaggerating beyond measure the sharpness of sufferings and human weakness. For we coerce it to fall back upon unanswerable retorts: if it be unfortunate to live in need, at least there is no need to live in need.[105] No man is long in evil save by his own fault.[106] He who has not the courage to support either death or life, who will neither resist nor fly—what shall be done with him?

85

Chapter XV

UNREASONABLE PERSISTENCE
IN THE DEFENCE OF A STRONGHOLD
IS PUNISHED[1]

VALOUR, like other virtues, has its limits, which being overstepped, we find ourselves followers of vice; in such wise that, in its own region, a man may give way to rashness, obstinacy, and foolishness, if he does not well know their boundaries, the lines of which are, in truth, not easy to discover. From this consideration arises the custom we have in time of war, of punishing with death those who persist in defending a stronghold which, according to military rules, can not be held. Otherwise, with the hope of impunity, there would be no hovel that might not delay an army. The Constable de Montmorency, at the siege of Pavia,[2] having been appointed to cross the Ticino and establish himself in the Faubourg St. Antoine, being hindered by a tower at the end of a bridge which persisted in contesting the way, had every one in it hanged. And afterward, accompanying my lord the dauphin in his expedition beyond the Alps, having taken by force the castle of Villano, and all those in it having been torn to pieces by the fury of the soldiers, save only the captain[3] and the ensign, he caused them also to be hanged and strangled for the same reason. As Captain Martin du Bellay, when Governor of Turin in that same region, likewise did to Captain de St. Bony, all his soldiers having been massacred on the taking of that place.[4] But inasmuch as the judgement of the strength or weakness of the place is based on the estimate and counterpoise of the besieging forces (for a man might justifiably hold out against two culverins who would be mad to await the assault of thirty cannon), and even takes into the account the greatness of the victorious prince, his reputation, the respect due to him, there is danger that the scales may be weighted overmuch on this side. And it happens in these same conditions that some men have so high an opinion of themselves and their powers that, as it does not seem comprehensible to them that anything is worthy to make head against them, they put every one to the sword wherever they meet with resistance, so long as their good fortune lasts; as we see by the forms of summons and defiance which the Eastern princes, and their successors who still remain, are accustomed to use—proud and haughty and full of an unmannerly tone of command. And in the region where the Portuguese cut into the Indies, they found nations with this universal and inviolable law, that every enemy vanquished by the king in person, or by his lieutenant, is outside all terms of ransom or pardon.[5] Thus every one who can, must especially beware of falling into the hands of a hostile, victorious, well-armed judge.

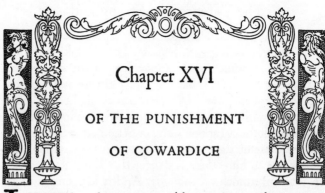

Chapter XVI

OF THE PUNISHMENT

OF COWARDICE

I ONCE heard it maintained by a prince and very great captain that a soldier could not be condemned to death for faint-heartedness; and at table he told the story of the Seigneur de Vervins, who was sentenced to death for surrendering Boulogne.[1] In truth, it is reasonable to make a great distinction between the faults which come from our weakness and those which come from our evil intent; for in the one case we have knowingly set ourselves against the laws of reason which nature has imprinted in us; and in the other case it seems that we could call upon that same nature to answer for having left us in such imperfection and feebleness. So that many people have thought that we could not be blamed except for what we do against our consciences; and on this rule is based in part the view of those who condemn capital punishment for heretics and unbelievers, and that which maintains that an advocate and a judge can not be held to account for having fallen short in the discharge of their duties through ignorance. But as for cowardice, it is certain that the most usual way is to chastise it by shame and ignominy. And it is said that this rule was first employed by the legislator Charondas,[2] and that before his

Of the Punishment of Cowardice

time the laws of Greece punished with death those who had run away from a battle, whereas he decreed only that they should be for three days seated in the public square, dressed in women's clothes, in the hope that they might still be made use of, their courage being restored by this disgrace. *Seek rather to bring a man's blood to his cheek than to shed it.*[3] It seems, too, that the Roman laws in old times condemned to death those who had run away; for Ammianus Marcellinus relates[4] that the Emperor Julian condemned ten of his soldiers, who had turned their backs during a charge against the Parthians, to be degraded and afterward to suffer death, according, as he says, to the ancient laws. But at another time, for a similar offence, he condemned others only to remain among the prisoners under the standard of the baggage.[5] The severe condemnation by the Roman people of the troops who escaped from Cannæ, and, in that same war, of those who were the companions of Cneius Fulvius in his defeat, did not go so far as death.[6] Yet it is to be feared that disgrace drives them to despair, and makes them not lukewarm simply, but foes.

In the time of our fathers, the Seigneur de Franget, formerly lieutenant of the maréchal de Chastillon's company, having been made governor of Fontarabia by the maréchal de Chabannes, in place of Monsieur de Lude, and having surrendered it to the Spaniards, was condemned to be deprived of his titles, and to be declared—and his posterity as well as himself—base-born, taxable, and incapable of bearing arms; and this harsh sentence was carried into effect at Lyons.[7] Later, a similar punishment was inflicted on all the gentlemen who were in Guise when the Comte de Nansau entered there,[8] and others still later.

Chapter XVII

A PROCEEDING OF

SOME AMBASSADORS

I OBSERVE in my travels this practice—in order always to learn something from intercourse with others, which is one of the best schools possible[1]—of always leading those with whom I am conversing to talk of the things they know best:

> Let the pilot be content to speak of the winds, the labourer of his bulls; and let the warrior tell of his wounds, the shepherd of his flocks.[2]

For it most frequently happens, on the contrary, that every one prefers to discourse of the occupations of another rather than his own, deeming that it is so much fresh reputation gained; witness Archidamus's rebuke to Periander, that he abandoned the fame of a good doctor to acquire that of a wretched poet.[3] See how diffusely Cæsar holds forth to make us understand his inventions for building bridges and engines of war,[4] and how concise he is, in comparison, when he is speaking of his professional functions, of his valour, and regarding the management of his troops. His exploits sufficiently prove him to be an excellent captain; he desires to make himself known as an excellent engineer, a somewhat

A Proceeding of Some Ambassadors

alien matter. A man of the legal profession, being taken
not long since to see a study supplied with all sorts of books
of his own calling and of every other kind, found there
nothing to talk about. But he paused to comment severely
and magisterially upon a barricade placed on the winding
staircase of the study, which a hundred officers and common
soldiers see every day without note and without displeasure.
The elder Dionysius was a very great commander in war, as
befitted his position;[5] but he laboured to obtain commendation chiefly for his poetry, which indeed he knew little
about.

> The slow ox desires saddle and bridle; the horse
> desires to plough.[6]

By such procedure you never attain any thing worth while.
Thus the architect, the painter, the shoemaker should always be thrown back, each on his own interests. And in this
connection, when reading history, which is everybody's
subject, I am wont to consider who the writers of it are: if
they are persons who practise no other profession than letters, I attend mainly to their style and language; if they are
physicians, I believe them more readily in what they tell us
of the temperature, of the health and constitution of princes,
of wounds and diseases; and, if jurists, there must be studied
in them the controversies about rights, the laws, the foundations of governments, and such matters; if theologians,
affairs of the church, ecclesiastical censures, dispensations,
and marriages; if courtiers, manners and ceremonial; if
military men, such things as pertain to their profession, and,
chiefly, accounts of the exploits in which they have personally taken part; if ambassadors, diplomatic practices,

private information, usages,[7] and the ways to carry them on.
ways be thrown back, each on his own interests. And in this
For this reason, that which I should have passed over in another without pausing, I have noted and weighed in the
history of the Seigneur de Langey,[8] who was very well informed in such matters. It is what follows his report of those
fine reasonings of the Emperor Charles the Fifth before the
consistory at Rome,[9] in the presence of the Bishop of Mâcon
and the Seigneur de Velly, our ambassadors, wherein he had
introduced many insulting remarks about us, and among
other things had said that, if his officers and soldiers had no
more loyalty and no more knowledge of military art than
those of the king[10] had, he would at once, with a rope about
his neck, go to him to ask mercy (and it seems that he
believed something of this: for two or three times later in
his life it chanced that he repeated these same words); and
he challenged the king to fight with him in their shirts,
with sword and dagger, on board a boat. The said Seigneur
de Langey, continuing his story, adds that the said ambassadors, in preparing a despatch to the king concerning
these matters, concealed the greater part of them from him,
and even said nothing of the two foregoing passages. Now,
I find it very strange that it should be in the power of an
ambassador to decide concerning the warnings he should
give to his master, even when they were of such consequence, coming from such a personage, and uttered in so
large an assembly. And it would have seemed to me the
duty of the servant to represent things faithfully, in their
entirety, just as they happened, so that the master should be
free to command, to judge, and to choose; for to twist or
conceal the truth, for fear lest he take it otherwise than he

A Proceeding of Some Ambassadors

ought and lest it drive him to some ill-advised course of action, and meanwhile to leave him in ignorance of his affairs—that would have seemed to me to belong to him who makes the law, not to him who receives it; to the administrator and master of discipline, not to him who ought to deem himself inferior, not in authority only, but in wisdom and good counsel. However this may be, I should not desire to be served in that fashion in my small concerns. We are so ready to withdraw ourselves from another's command on any pretext, and to encroach upon mastership; every one aspires so naturally to liberty and authority, that no benefit ought to be so dear to the superior, coming from those who serve him, as should be their simple and sincere obedience.

The function of command is perverted when one obeys from choice, not from subordination.[11] And P. Crassus, whom the Romans deemed five times happy,[12] when he was consul in Asia, having ordered a Greek engineer to bring him the larger of two beams[13] he had seen at Athens, for use in some battering ram which he proposed to make, the engineer, being entitled, he thought, by his own knowledge, took the liberty of choosing otherwise, and brought the smaller, which, by the judgement of his art, was the most suitable. Crassus, having listened patiently to his reasons, had him soundly whipped, considering the importance of discipline greater than the importance of the work.

But, on the other hand, it is to be considered that such hard-and-fast obedience is due only to precise and predetermined commands. Ambassadors have a freer office which, in several respects, is entirely at their disposal. They do not simply execute the will of their master, but they likewise,

93

by their advice, shape and direct it. I have seen in my time men in high command rebuked for having rather obeyed the words of the king's letters than the exigencies of the business they had in hand. Those who understand such matters still blame the custom of the kings of Persia in giving so short a span to the powers of their agents and lieutenants that for the merest trifles they had to recur to their instructions—the consequent delay, in so vast an extent of dominion, having often caused serious injury to affairs. And when Crassus wrote to a professional man, and informed him of the use he proposed to make of the beam, did he not seem to consult with him, and to invite him to give his own opinion?

Chapter XVIII

OF FEAR

I was stunned, my hair stood on end, and my voice stuck in my throat.[1]

I AM not a good natural philosopher,[2] as the term is, and I do not well know by what authority fear acts in us; but I know this, that it is a strange passion, and physicians say that there is none which more quickly sweeps our judgement from its due place. In truth, I have seen many persons beside themselves with fear; and in the calmest minds it is beyond question that, while the attack lasts, it causes terrible bewilderments. I leave aside the common people, to whom it sometimes presents its grandsires come from their graves wrapped in their winding-sheets, sometimes hobgoblins or imps or chimæras. But even among soldiers, where it should least of all find a place, how many times has it transformed a flock of sheep into a squadron of pikemen; reeds and rushes into men-at-arms and lancers; friends into foes, and the white cross into the red![3]

When Monsieur de Bourbon took Rome,[4] a standard-bearer, who was on guard at the gate of the quarter of St. Peter, was so terrified at the first alarum, that he rushed

95

through a breach in a ruined wall, standard in hand, out of the city and straight to the enemy, thinking that he was going into the city; and at last, seeing the troop of Monsieur de Bourbon preparing to meet him, still thinking that it was a sortie on the part of those within the city, he came to himself, and, turning about, reëntered by the same breach through which he had gone forth more than three hundred paces into the open fields. By no means so fortunate was the ensign of Captain Juille, when St. Pol was taken from us by the Comte de Bures and Monsieur du Reu; for being so beside himself with fright as to throw himself with his standard out of the city through a loop-hole, he was cut to pieces by the besiegers.[5] And in the same siege, that was a memorable fear which so seized and contracted and froze the heart of a gentleman, that he fell stark dead in the breach, without a wound.

Similar fear sometimes impels a whole multitude. In one of the encounters of Germanicus with the Germans, two large bodies took, from fright, opposite roads: one fled in the direction from which the other came.[6] Sometimes it gives wings to our heels, as in the first two cases; sometimes it stays our feet and hobbles them, as we read of the Emperor Theophilus, who, in a battle he lost against the Agarenes, was so astounded and stupefied that he could not decide to fly *(so greatly does fear dread even assistance)*[7] till Manuel, one of the principal officers of his army, having pulled and shaken him as if to awake him from a deep sleep, said to him: "If you don't come with me, I shall kill you; for it is better that you should lose your life than that, being a prisoner, you should destroy the Empire."[8]

Fear shows its supreme force when, in its own service, it

Of Fear

gives to us the courage which it has stolen from our duty and our honour. In the first regular[9] battle that the Romans lost against Hannibal, under the Consul Sempronius, a body of fully ten thousand foot, seized with panic, and seeing nowhere else to force a passage for their cowardice, rushed at the main body of the enemy, which they cut through by a superhuman effort, with great slaughter of the Carthaginians, purchasing a shameful flight at the same price at which they might have had a glorious victory.

The thing I am most afraid of is fear. And, indeed, it surpasses in sharpness all other calamities. Could there be a keener and more justified emotion than that of Pompey's friends, who were on his ship and were spectators of that horrible massacre?[10] And yet, fear of the Egyptian vessels which were beginning to draw near so stifled this emotion, that it was noticed that they were occupied only in urging the sailors to hasten, and in saving themselves by rowing, until, when they arrived at Tyre and were free from fear, they were at leisure to turn their thoughts to the loss they had met with, and to give free rein to the lamentations and tears which that other stronger passion had held in check.

Then fear expelled all feeling from my breast.[11]

Those who have been well thrashed in some encounter, and are still wounded and bleeding, can be led back to the charge the next day; but those who have conceived a sound fear of the foe, those you cannot make even look him in the face. Those who are in extreme dread of losing their property, of being exiled, of being enslaved, live in constant anguish, unable to eat or drink or sleep; while the poor, the exiled, the slaves, often live as happily as any others. And the many people who, finding unendurable the stings of fear, hang or drown themselves, or throw themselves from heights, teach us clearly that fear is more importunate and unbearable than is death. The Greeks recognise another variety of it, which is not due to the wandering of our reason, coming, they say, without apparent cause and by an impulse from above. Whole nations are often seen to be seized by it, and whole armies. Such was that which brought marvellous desolation upon Carthage.[12] Only shrieks and terrified voices were heard; the inhabitants were seen rushing from their houses as at an alarm, and attacking, wounding, and killing one another, as if they were enemies who had come to take possession of their city. Every thing was in confusion and tumult until they had appeased the anger of the gods by prayers and sacrifices. Such conditions were called "panic terrors."[13]

Chapter XIX

THAT OUR FORTUNE
MUST NOT BE JUDGED
UNTIL AFTER DEATH

For always the last day of a man must be awaited;
and no man should be called blessed before his death
and the last rites of his funeral.[1]

CHILDREN know the story of King Crœsus which regards this point: that, having been made prisoner by
Cyrus and condemned to death, he exclaimed at the moment
of his execution, "O Solon! Solon!" This being reported to
Cyrus, and he having asked what it meant, Crœsus informed
him that he was then, at his cost, verifying the warning
which Solon had given him in other days, that men, however much Fortune may seem to smile on them [whatever
riches and kingdoms and empires they may have on their
hands],[2] cannot be called fortunate until we have seen how
the last day of their lives went by, because of the uncertainty
and variableness of mortal things, which, at a very slight stirring, change from one condition to another wholly different.[3] And therefore Agesilaus, to some one who called the
King of Persia fortunate because he had come so young to
such a powerful estate, replied: "Yes, forsooth, but Priam
at the same age was not unfortunate."[4] Sometimes, of kings

of Macedonia, successors of the great Alexander, Fortune makes joiners and clerks at Rome;[5] of tyrants of Sicily, schoolmasters at Corinth;[6] and a conqueror of half the world and the ruler of countless armies, she renders a wretched suppliant of the base-born officials of the king of Egypt, so high a price did the great Pompey pay for the lengthening of his life by five or six months.[7] And in the time of our fathers that Ludovic Sforza, tenth duke of Milan, who had so long kept all Italy in a turmoil, was seen to die at Loches, but not till he had lived there ten years, which was the worst part of his catastrophe.[8] The loveliest of queens,[9] widow of the greatest king in all Christendom, has she not just died by the hand of an executioner? Shameful and barbarous cruelty?[10] And a thousand like examples; for it would seem that, as storms and tempests rage against the pride and loftiness of our buildings, so there are, on high, spirits envious of earthly grandeurs.

> So true it is that a hidden power tramples on human affairs, and seems as in sport to tread underfoot the fair rods and the cruel axes.[11]

And it would seem that Fortune precisely watches for the last day of our life, in order to show her power to overturn in an instant what she has built up in long years,[12] and makes us cry, like Laberius: *Surely I have lived to-day one day longer than I should have lived.*[13]

So that good judgement of Solon may wisely be accepted. But because by him, as a philosopher, the favours of Fortune are ranked neither as good luck nor as ill luck, and grandeur, wealth, and power are almost indifferent chances of condition, I think it very possible that he looked deeper,

Our Fortune after Death

and meant to say that this same good luck of our lives, which depends on the tranquillity of a lofty spirit,[14] and on the resolution and confidence of a well-ordered mind, should never be accredited to a man until we have seen him play the last and, doubtless, the most difficult act of his drama. In all the rest there may be disguise, whether it be that those fine reasonings of philosophy are in us only conventionally, or that the things that happen, not proving us to the quick, permit us to keep always a serene demeanour. But in this last scene between Death and ourselves, there is no more feigning, we must talk plainly,[15] we must show what there is good and unspotted in the bottom of the pot;

> For then at last words of truth come from the depths
> of the breast; the mask is torn off; reality remains.[16]

It is thus that all the other acts of our lives must be put to the touch and tested by this last stroke. It is the masterday, it is the day that is the judge of all other days. It is the day, says one of the ancients, which is to pass judgement on all my past years.[17] I postpone until death the trial of the fruit of my studies. We shall see then whether my words come from the lips or the heart.[18] I have known many men by the manner of their deaths to give to their whole life a good or evil esteem. Scipio, Pompey's father-in-law, amended, by dying nobly, the evil opinion that men had held of him up to that time.[19] Epaminondas, being asked which of the three he most valued, Chabrias, Iphicrates, or himself, replied: "It must first be seen how we die, before the question can be solved."[20] Verily, he[21] would be robbed of much were he weighed without the glory and grandeur of the end of his life. God hath willed it as it pleased him; but in my own days, three of the most execrable persons I have known, living in every sort of abomination, and the most infamous, have had well-ordered deaths and perfectly disposed in every detail.

There are noble and fortunate deaths. I have seen death cut short a wonderful upward progress in the springtime of its development,[22] by an end so glorious that, in my opinion, there was nothing in the man's ambitious and daring plans so exalted as was their interruption. He arrived without going thither at the place where he would be, more grandly and gloriously than had been his desire and hopes, and attained by his fall the power and the fame to which he aspired by his course in the race.

In judging another's life I observe always how its close has borne itself, and my chief endeavour regarding my own end is that it may carry itself well, that is to say, quietly and insensibly.[23]

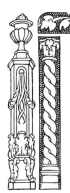

Chapter XX

THAT TO THINK

AS A PHILOSOPHER IS TO

LEARN TO DIE

CICERO says that to think as a philosopher is nothing else than to make ready for death.[1] This is inasmuch as study and contemplation to some degree withdraw our soul outside of us and set it at work apart from the body, which is a sort of apprenticeship and likeness to death; or, indeed, it is because all the wisdom and reasoning in the world finally comes at last to the point of teaching us not to be afraid to die.[2] In truth, either our reason fools itself,[3] or it must aim only at our satisfaction, and the sum of all its labour should tend to make us live rightly and at our ease, as says Holy Writ.[4] All the beliefs in the world agree in this, that pleasure is our goal, although they take divers means to attain it; otherwise we should reject them at once, for who would listen to that argument which should set our affliction and discomfort as its end?

The disagreements of the philosophical sects about this matter are verbal. *Let us pass quickly over these trifling subtleties.*[5] There is more opinionativeness and wrangling than befits so godly a calling. But whatever part in the world's drama a man undertakes to play, he always plays his own nature too.[6] Whatever they may say, in virtue her-

103

self the final object of our aim is delight.[7] It pleases me to belabour their ears with that word, which is so abhorrent to them; and if it signifies some supreme enjoyment and excessive satisfaction, it is due rather to the assistance of virtue than to any other assistance. This delight, because it is more lusty, vigorous, robust, and virile, is only the more completely delightful; and we should give it the name of pleasure,[8] which is more gracious, more gentle, and more according to its nature, and not that of vigour, by which we have denominated it. That other, baser delight, if it deserved that fair name, would do so only conjointly, not exceptionally. I find it less free from troubles and trammels than virtue is. Besides that its savour is more transitory, unstable, and unreliable, it has its vigils, its fastings, and its labours, and sweat and blood, and also, especially, its poignant sufferings of so many sorts, and, accompanying it, so heavy a satiety, that it is equivalent to a penance. We are in the wrong in thinking that its troubles serve as a spur and seasoning to its sweetness,—as in nature one contrary is vivified by another,—and in saying, when we come to virtue, that similar consequences and difficulties over-burden her and make her austere and inaccessible; whereas much more quickly than in earthly delight, they ennoble, intensify, and heighten the divine and perfect pleasure which she brings us. Surely very unworthy of her acquaintance is he who balances her cost against her fruit, and who knows neither her charms, nor her popular use. They who proceed to instruct us that her quest is hard and laborious, and her possession agreeable, what do they suggest by that, if not that she is always disagreeable? For what human power ever attained to her possession? The most perfect are well content to aspire to

To Think as a Philosopher

her and to approach her without possessing her; but they[9] are mistaken; for of all the pleasures that we know, the very pursuit of them is pleasant. The enterprise is affected by the quality of the thing with which it is concerned, for the quality is a large part of the deed, and is of the same substance.[10] The happiness and blessedness which shines in virtue fills all her avenues and approaches, even to the first entrance and the furthest gate. Now, among the chief benefactions of virtue is the contempt of death, a means of supplying our life with placid tranquillity and giving to it a pure and agreeable savour, without which all other delight is abolished.

That is why all doctrines meet and agree on this article;[11] and although they all with common accord lead us also to despise pain, poverty, and other calamities to which human life is liable, it is not with equal painstaking; not only because these calamities are not of the same necessity (the greater number of men pass their lives without a taste of poverty, and some even without feeling pain or illness, as Xenophilus the musician, who lived a hundred and six years in perfect health[12]), but also because, at the worst, death whenever we please can put an end to all other mishaps, and cut them short. But death itself is inevitable:

> We are all driven to the same end; for all of us our lot is shaken in the urn, and sooner or later will come forth to launch us on our everlasting exile.[13]

And consequently, if it terrifies us, it is a constant source of anguish, which can in no wise be allayed. It may come upon us from everywhere.[14] We may turn our heads incessantly this way and that, as in a suspicious country: *this, like the rock of Tantalus, ever hangs overhead.*[15] Our parliaments often send criminals back for execution to the place where the crime was committed; on the road, take them to fine houses, give them all the good cheer you please,—

> Not the banquets of Sicily will produce a sweet taste, nor will the songs of birds and of the lyre bring back sleep,[16]—

do you think that they could be gladdened by it, and that the final purpose of their journey, being all the time before their eyes, has not weakened and destroyed their taste for all those enjoyments?

> He asks about the route and counts the days, and measures his life by the length of the road; he is tortured by the coming calamity.[17]

The end of our career is death; it is the unavoidable object of our vision; if it terrifies us, how is it possible to go a step forward without trembling? The remedy of the common people is not to think about it. But from what brutish stupidity can they derive such gross blindness! It makes them put the bridle on the ass's tail,—

> Who places himself with the head where his feet should be.[18]

It is no wonder that they are so often caught in the trap. Such people are terrified by only hearing death named, and most of them cross themselves as at the name of the devil. And because it is mentioned in testaments, do not expect them to put their hand thereto until the doctor has pronounced their final doom; and then, betwixt pain and fear,

To Think as a Philosopher

God knows with what excellent judgement they cook it[19] up!

Because that syllable struck their ears too harshly, and that word seemed to them of evil omen, the Romans had learned to soften it, or to stretch it out by periphrases. Instead of saying, "He is dead," they said, "He has ceased to live," "He has lived."[20] So long as it is life, even past life, they are consoled. We have borrowed from them our *feu*[21] Master Jehan. Is it, perchance, that, as the saying goes, the delay is worth the money?

I was born between eleven o'clock and noon, on the last day of February one thousand five hundred thirty-three, as we reckon nowadays, beginning the year in January.[22] It was just fifteen days ago that I completed my thirty-ninth year; I need at least as many more. Meanwhile, to trouble oneself with thoughts of a thing so distant would be folly. But see how it is! the young and the old leave life in the same condition.[23] No one goes hence otherwise than as if he were to return forthwith. Moreover, there is no man so decrepit that, so long as he has Methuselah before him, he does not think that he still has twenty years in his body. Furthermore, poor fool that you are, who has fixed the limits of your life? You rely on the tales of doctors. Look rather at fact and experience. By the common run of things you have lived long already by extraordinary good fortune. You have passed the accustomed term of life; and that it is so, count up how many more of your acquaintance have died before your present age than have attained it. And even of those who have ennobled their lives by winning renown— make a list of them, and I wager that I shall find more who died before the age of thirty-five than after.[24] It is truly

reasonable and pious to take example even from the human
existence of Jesus Christ: now, his life ended at three-and-
thirty years. The greatest man who was a mere man, Alexander, also died at the same age.[25]

How many ways of surprising us Death has!

> What is to be avoided from hour to hour, man never
> sufficiently foresees.[26]

I say nothing of fevers and pleurisies. Who would ever have
thought that a duke of Bretaigne would be stifled by the
crowd, as he was at the entry into Lyons of Pope Clement,
my neighbour?[27] Have you not known of one of our kings
killed while jousting?[28] and did not one of his ancestors die
from being jostled by a hog?[29] To no purpose did Æschylus, when threatened with the fall of a house, remain out-
of-doors;[30] lo, he was killed by a tortoise-shell that fell from
the claws of an eagle in the air.[31] Another died from a grape-
seed;[32] an emperor from the scratch of a comb in dressing
his hair; Æmilius Lepidus from stumbling over his threshold, and Aufidius from hitting against the door of the council chamber as he went in.[33] And while lying with women,
Cornelius Gallus, prætor; Tigillinus, captain of the watch
at Rome; Ludovic, son of Guy de Gonzague, Marquis of
Mantua; and, of even worse example, Speusippus the Platonic philosopher, and one of our popes.[34] Poor Bebius, a
judge, was seized as he was granting an extension of bail,
his own [extension] of life having expired; and Caius Julius,
a physician, while he was anointing a patient's eyes, lo,
death closed his own.[35] And, if I must bring myself in, a
brother of mine, Captain St. Martin, twenty-three years of
age, who had already given good proof of his worth, while

To Think as a Philosopher

playing at tennis received a blow from a ball which struck
him just above the right ear, with no bruise or wound. He
did not sit down or stop playing; but five or six hours later
he died of a stroke of apoplexy caused by that blow. While
such examples as these occur so frequently and familiarly
before our eyes, is it possible that we can get rid of the
thought of death, and that it should not every moment seem
as if he may clutch us by the collar?[36] What does it matter,
you will say, how that may be, so long as we give ourselves
no trouble about it? I am of this opinion,[37] and in whatever
manner one can find shelter from blows, were it in the skin
of a calf, I am not the man to refuse it; for it suffices me to
hold my course in ease; and the best way that I can play my
cards, I use,[38] as little praiseworthy and exemplary it may be
as you please.

> I would rather appear foolish and feeble, provided
> that my weaknesses gave me pleasure, or, at least, that
> I were not aware of them, than be wise and uncom-
> fortable.[39]

But it is madness to think of arriving where one desires by
that road. Men go and come, they gad about and dance—
of death, no thought. That is all very fine; but when death
comes to them, or to their wives, children, or friends, surprising them suddenly[40] and defenceless, what anguish,
what shrieks, what frenzy, and what despair overwhelms
them! Saw you ever any thing so cast down, so changed, so
bewildered? We must provide against it earlier; and such
brutish thoughtlessness, if it could lodge in the head of a
man of intelligence,—which I deem altogether impossible,
—sells us its merchandise too dear. If it were an enemy that

To Think as a Philosopher

could be avoided, I would advise borrowing the arms of cowardice; but since it is such a one as can not be avoided, since it overtakes you running away and a coward, as it does a worthy man,—

> And assuredly it pursues the man who flees and does not spare the hamstrings and the timid back of cowardly young men;[41]

since the best cuirass does not protect you,—

> He may protect himself prudently with iron and bronze; none the less, death drags his head forth from its encasement,[42]—

let us learn to meet it firmly and to combat it; and, to begin by depriving it of its greatest advantage over us, let us adopt a course just contrary to the usual one. Let us deprive it of its unfamiliarity, let us live with it, let us habituate ourselves to it; let us think of nothing so often as of death; let us constantly place it before our imaginations and in all its aspects; at the stumbling of a horse, at the fall of a tile, at the slightest prick of a pin, let us immediately reflect: Well, what if this were death itself? and thereupon let us stiffen and strengthen ourselves.[43] Amid festivals and merry-making, let us be always restrained by the remembrance of our condition, and let us not be so carried away by pleasure but that at times our memory recalls in how many ways this lightheartedness of ours is exposed to death, and with how many modes of attack death threatens. So did the Egyptians, who, at the height of their festivals, and amid their best cheer, used to have the skeleton of a man brought in, as a warning to the guests.[44]

To Think as a Philosopher

Think of each day that shines upon you as your last; the unhoped-for hours will be welcome when they come.[45]

It is uncertain where death awaits us; let us await it everywhere.[46] Prevision of death is prevision of liberty. He who has learned to die has unlearned servitude. To know how to die frees us from all subjection and compulsion. There is nothing evil in life for him who clearly understands that the loss of life is not an evil.[47] Paulus Æmilius replied to the messenger whom that wretched king of Macedonia,[48] his prisoner, sent to him to beg that he would not carry him in his triumph, "Let him make the request to himself."

In truth, in all things, if Nature does not help a little, it is very hard for art and endeavour to go far. I am myself not melancholy, but given to serious dreaming;[49] there is nothing with which I have always been more occupied than with thoughts of death; yes, even in the most wanton season of my days,—

When my flowering life was in its pleasant spring,[50]

among ladies and in games it was thought that I was occupied in inwardly considering some suspicion, or an uncertain hope, when I was thinking about some one, whoever it might be, who had been lately seized upon by a high fever and by death, when leaving a similar festivity, and with his head full of trifles and love and gaiety, like myself; and that I had as much to answer for.[51]

Soon [the present] will be the past, never to be recalled.[52]

I no more scowled at that thought than at another. It is not possible that at the outset we should not feel stings from such thoughts; but by handling them and going over them again and again, we are sure to make them tractable in the long run; otherwise, for my part, I should be in a constant terror and frenzy; for never was man so distrustful of his life, never did man count less on its duration. My health, which has hitherto been very robust and infrequently interrupted, does not lengthen my expectation, nor do illnesses shorten it. Every moment it seems to me that I come through safely; and I reiterate to myself incessantly: "Whatever can happen another day, can happen to-day."[53] In truth, risks and perils bring us little, or not at all, nearer our end; and if we think how, besides the danger that seems most to threaten us, there are millions of others hanging over our heads, we shall find that, lusty or fever-stricken, at sea or in our houses, in battle or at rest, it is equally near to us.[54] *No man is more frail than another, no man more certain of his morrow.*[55] What I have to do before I die, any amount of leisure seems to me short to accomplish it, were it but an hour's work. Some one, turning over my tablets the other day, found a memorandum of something that I wished to have done after my death. I told him—and it was true—that, being only a league from my house, and sound and hearty, I had made haste to write that down because I was not sure of reaching home. As one who is constantly brooding over his thoughts, and imprinting them on his mind, I am at all hours prepared as much as I can be so; and the sudden coming of death will admonish me of nothing new. We must be always booted and ready to depart, so far as lies in us, and, above all, look to it that we have no business then except with ourselves.

To Think as a Philosopher

Why, in so short a life, make so many plans?[56]

For we shall have enough work then without surplusage. One man bewails, more than for death itself, that it breaks off the progress of a glorious victory; another, that he must leave his lodging before he has married his daughter or arranged for the education of his children. One deplores the loss of the company of his wife, another of that of his son, as chief pleasures of his existence. I am at this hour in such a state, God be praised, that I can dislodge whenever it may please him, without regret for anything whatsoever, if it be not for life itself, if its loss begins to be important to me.[57] I am untying myself from all things; my farewells are now said to every one save myself. Never did man prepare to leave this world more wholly and entirely, or to detach himself from it more completely, than I endeavour to do.[58]

"Oh, wretched, wretched man that I am!" they say; "one hostile day has taken everything from me— all that life has won."[59]

And the builder:—

The works remain broken off, and the great walls of threatening height.[60]

We must not plan any thing requiring so long a breath, or, at least, not with the idea of being distressed if we do not see the end of it.[61] We are born to act [and I am of opinion that not only an emperor, as Vespasian said, but every high-spirited man ought to die standing up].[62]

When I die, may I find my release in the midst of my work and surrounded by it.[63]

To Think as a Philosopher

I desire that a man should act, and prolong the employments of life as long as he can, and that death may find me planting my cabbages, but indifferent regarding it, and even more regarding my unfinished garden. I have seen a man die, who, when he was at the last gasp, incessantly complained because his fate cut the thread of the history he had in hand of the fifteenth or sixteenth of our kings.

> They do not add thereto: "Neither does there now remain in your mind any longing for these things."[64]

We must get rid of such ordinary and harmful ideas. Just as our cemeteries have been laid out adjoining the churches and in the most frequented part of the towns, in order, as Lycurgus said,[65] to accustom the lower classes, the women and children, not to take fright at the sight of a dead body, and that the constant spectacle of bones and tombs and funerals might warn us of our condition—

> Once it was the custom to enliven a banquet for the revellers by carnage, and to combine with the feast the horrible spectacle of fighting swordsmen, who often fell over the cups, and the tables were splashed with blood;[66]

and as the Egyptians, after their festivals, caused a great image of death to be exhibited to the guests by one who cried: "Drink and enjoy yourselves, for when dead you will be like this,"[67] so I have fallen into the habit of having death constantly, not in my mind alone, but on my lips; and there is nothing of which I enquire so eagerly as of the deaths of men, what words they said, what their expression was, and their bearing; nor are there any passages in histories which

To Think as a Philosopher

I read so carefully. This appears by my cramming these pages with examples; and that I have a special fondness for this sort of matter. Were I a maker of books, I should make an annotated record of different deaths.[68] He who should teach men how to die would teach them how to live. Dicearchus[69] made a book with a similar title, but with another and less useful purpose.

I shall be told that the thing itself goes so far beyond one's idea of it, that the best fencing is at a loss when one reaches that point. Let them say what they will: to think upon it beforehand unquestionably gives one a great advantage;[70] and then, too, is it nothing to go so far as that without emotion and without trembling? Yet more:[71] Nature herself lends us a hand and gives us courage. If it be a sudden and violent death, we have no time to dread it; if it be otherwise, I perceive that, in proportion as I become sick, I feel involuntarily some contempt of life.[72] I find that I have much more difficulty in swallowing the thought of death when I am in health than I have when I am sick, inasmuch as I no longer cling so closely to the pleasures of life, since I begin to lose the habit and enjoyment of them; then I look upon death with a much less terrified vision. This makes me hope that the further I shall draw away from life and the nearer I approach to death, the more easily I shall accept the exchange. Just as I have experienced on several occasions the truth of what Cæsar says,[73] that things often appear greater to us at a distance than close at hand, so I have found that when well I have had much more horror of maladies than when I have been touched by them. My lightheartedness, my enjoyment, and my vigour make the other condition[74] appear to me so utterly disproportionate to this, that in imagination I magnify its discomforts by half, and fancy them more burdensome than I find them when I have them on my shoulders; I hope that it will be so for me with death.

See how Nature, in the ordinary changes and impairments that we undergo, takes from us the perception of our loss and our waning powers. What is left to an old man of the vigour of his youth and his past years?

> Alas! how small a portion of life remains for the old![75]

To a worn-out and broken soldier of his guard who came to him in the street and asked his leave to kill himself, Cæsar, observing his decrepit aspect, replied jestingly: "Do you think then that you are living?"[76] Were we to fall into it suddenly, I do not think that we should be capable of enduring such a change; but, led by her[77] hand, down a gentle and, as it were, imperceptible descent, little by little, step by step, she impels us into that wretched state and enures us to it, so that we feel no shock when our youth dies in us, which is essentially and in truth a sterner death than is the utter death of a languishing life, and than is death in old age; because the leap from half-existence to non-existence is not so great as from a pleasant and flourishing existence to a painful and grievous one. The bent and bowed body has less strength to sustain a burden; so likewise our soul: we must train her and educate her to meet the force of this adversary. For, as it is impossible for her to be at ease while she stands in fear of death, on the other hand, if she be reassured, she can boast (which is something surpassing, as it were, the human state) that it is impossible that anxiety, anguish, fear, nay, even the least annoyance, should lodge with her:

To Think as a Philosopher

Neither the countenance of a threatening tyrant,
nor Auster, the boisterous ruler of the stormy Adriatic,
nor the mighty hand of thunder-hurling Jupiter can
shake his firm soul.[78]

She has made herself mistress of her passions and lusts,
mistress of destitution, shame, poverty, and all other buffets
of Fortune. Let those of us who can, gain this superiority:
here is the real and sovereign liberty, which gives us the
power to snap our fingers[79] at force and injustice, and to
laugh at prison-bars and fetters:[80]

"I will hold you captive in fetters and shackles,
under the eye of a pitiless jailer." "A god himself will
set me free as soon as I so desire." He means this, I
suppose: "I shall die. Death is the end and goal of all
things."[81]

Our religion has had no more solid human basis than contempt of life. Not only do reasonable considerations[82] lead
us to this: for why should we dread the loss of a thing which,
when lost, can not be regretted? And since we are threatened
by so many ways of dying, is there not more harm in dreading them all than in enduring one of them?[83] What does
it matter when it happens, since it is inevitable? To him
who said to Socrates, "The thirty tyrants have sentenced you
to death," he replied, "And Nature them."[84] What folly,
to distress ourselves on the subject of the passage to exemption from all distress! As our birth brought to us the birth of
all things, so will our death the death of all things. Wherefore it is no less foolish to weep because we shall not be
living a hundred years hence than to weep because we were

not living a hundred years ago.[85] Death is the beginning of another life. Thus we wept; thus it was painful for us to enter into this life, thus did we divest ourselves of our former veil on entering into it.[86] Nothing can be grievous which happens but once. Is it reasonable to fear so long a thing so brief? A long life and a short life are made quite the same by death, for long and short are not of things that have ceased to be. Aristotle says that there are tiny things on the river Hypanis that live only one day.[87] The one that dies at eight o'clock in the morning dies in youth; the one that dies at five in the evening dies in decrepitude. Who does not find it amusing to see this moment of duration considered as good or ill fortune? The greater or the less length of our lives, if we compare it to eternity, or even to the duration of mountains and rivers and stars and trees, and even of some animals, is no less absurd.

But Nature forces us to it.[88] "Go from this world," she says, "as you came into it. The same transition that you made from death to life, without suffering and without fear, make it again from life to death. Your death is one of the parts of the order of the universe; it is a part of the life of the world";

> Mortals live mutually dependent, and like runners
> pass on the torch of life.[89]

"Shall I change for you the admirable arrangement of things?[90] Death is the condition of your creation, it is a portion of yourself; you fly from yourself.[91] This existence of yours, which you have the enjoyment of, is equally divided between death and life. The day of your birth starts your steps toward dying as well as toward living."

To Think as a Philosopher

The first hour that gave us life shortened our life.[92]

From our birth we die, and our end hangs upon our beginning.[93]

All the time you live you purloin from life; it is at its expense. The continual work of your life is to build up death. You are in death while you are in life, for death has passed when you have ceased to be in life. Or, if you like it better in this way, you are dead after life; but during life you are dying; and death treats the dying much more roughly than the dead, and more acutely and essentially.[94]

If you have profited by your life, you have had enough of it;[95] go hence content.

Why do you not depart like a guest who has had enough of life?[96]

If you have not known how to make use of it, if it was useless to you, what does it matter to you to have lost it? wherefore do you still desire it?

Why desire to add to the length of that which will again come to an evil end and will altogether perish unavailingly?[97]

Life is in itself neither good nor evil: it is the seat of good and evil according as you dispose it.[98] And if you have lived one day, you have seen every thing: one day is equal to all days. There is no other light, there is no other darkness. This sun, this moon, these stars, the whole disposition of the heavens is the same which your ancestors enjoyed and which will be unchanged for your distant descendants.

To Think as a Philosopher

> Your fathers saw no other things, nor will your sons behold anything different.[99]

And, at the utmost, the division and variety of all the acts of my comedy are completed in a year. If you have taken heed to the movement of my four seasons, they embrace the childhood, the youth, the manhood, and the old age of the earth. It has played its game; it knows no other trick than to begin again; it will be always the same:—

> We turn, ever enclosed in the same circle,[100]
>
> And the year returns, circling in its own track.[101]

I have no intention of manufacturing new pastimes for you.

> For there is nothing else that I can devise or find that can please you: all things are the same always.[102]

Give place to others as others have done to you.

Equality is the chief part of equity.[103] Who can complain of being included where all are included? However long you may live, you will thereby subtract nothing from the time that you must be dead; it is all for naught; you will be as long in that state which you dread as if you had died in infancy.[104]

> Live as long as you will, conquering time; eternal death will yet no less remain.[105]

And truly I shall put you in such a condition that you will have no discontent:—

> Thou dost not see that in true death there will be no other self which, living and standing by thy prostrate

120

To Think as a Philosopher

body, can mourn to thyself thy extinction;[106]

neither will you desire the life which you so bewail.

> For then no man feels the want of his own life. Nor
> are we affected by any regard for ourselves.[107]

Death is less to be feared than nothing, if there be any thing
less than nothing:—

> We must account death to be much less to us, if in-
> deed there can be less than what we see to be noth-
> ing.[108]

It concerns you neither dead nor living: living, because you
are existing; dead, because you no longer are.[109] No man
dies before his hour; what amount of time you leave behind
was no more yours than what passed before you were
born,[110] and concerns you no more.

> For consider, how as nothing to us is the bygone
> antiquity of old times.[111]

Wherever your life ends, it is all there.[112] The usefulness
of living is not in length of time, but in its use.[113] A man
may have lived long who has lived little.[114] Look well to
life whilst you are in life. It depends on your will, not on the
number of your years, whether you have lived long
enough.[115] Did you think that you were never to arrive
where you were always going? There is no road that has not
its end.[116] And if companionship can comfort you, does not
all the world go the same way that you go?

> All things, when they have done with life, will fol-
> low thee.[117]

To Think as a Philosopher

Does not every thing dance your dance? Is there any thing which does not grow old with you? A thousand men, a thousand beasts, and a thousand other creatures die at the same instant that you die.[118]

> For night has never followed day, nor dawn night, without hearing the sound of lamentation and plaintive wailings, the companions of death and of the sad funeral rites.[119]

Wherefore do you recoil if you can not go back?[120] You have seen many men who have found it well to die, thus avoiding great calamities.[121] But any one who has found himself badly off from death—have you seen such a one? Surely it is great folly to condemn a thing that you have never experienced, either by yourself or by another. Why do you complain of me and of fate? Do we wrong you? Is it for you to govern us, or for us to govern you? Although your age may not be finished, your life is.[122] A small man is as whole a man as a large one. Neither men nor their lives are measured by the ell. Chiron refused immortality when informed of its conditions by the very god of time and duration, his father Saturn.[123] Imagine, in fact, how much less endurable and more toilsome to man an everlasting life would be, than the life that I have given him. If you had not death, you would incessantly curse me for having deprived you of it. I have purposely mingled something of bitterness with it, to prevent you, seeing how advantageous it is, from embracing it too greedily and unadvisedly. To establish you in this moderate course, of neither flying from life nor shunning death, which I demand of you, I have modified both with sweetness and with bitterness. I taught Thales, the first of your

To Think as a Philosopher

wise men, that to live or to die was indifferent; wherefore he replied very wisely to one who asked him why, then, he did not die, "Because it is a matter of indifference."[124] Water, earth, air, fire, and other elements of this edifice of mine, are no more instruments of your life than of your death.[125] Why do you fear your last day? It contributes no more to your death than does each of the other days. The last step does not cause lassitude: it manifests it. All days go toward death; the last day arrives there.[126]

Such are the good counsels of our mother Nature. I have often reflected why in war the face of death, whether we see it in ourselves or in others, seems incomparably less appalling than in our houses (otherwise the army would consist of physicians and wailers); and, death being always one and the same thing, why there is always much more composure among peasants and those of low estate than among others. I believe, truly, that it is the fear-inspiring visages and paraphernalia with which we surround death which frighten us more than the thing itself: a wholly new form of life, the outcries of mothers, wives, and children, the visits of surprised and grief-stricken friends, the presence of a number of pale-faced, weeping servants, a darkened room, lighted candles, our bedside besieged by physicians and preachers—in short, all about us horror and dismay. Lo, we are already shrouded and interred. Children are afraid even of their friends when they see them masked; so it is with us.[127] We must remove the mask from things as from persons. When it is removed, we shall find underneath only the selfsame death that a man-servant or mere chambermaid met but now without fear.[128] Fortunate is that death which allows no time for the preparation of such an array.

Chapter XXI

OF THE

POWER OF IMAGINATION

A STRONG *imagination begets the event,*[1] say the men of learning. I am one of those persons who feel a very great force in the imagination; every one is aware of the shock, but some are overthrown by it.[2] Its thrust transpierces me, and my art is to elude it, for lack of strength to resist it. I should live in the company only of healthy and joyous persons. The sight of another's anguish causes me physical anguish, and my own sensations have often usurped the sensations of a third person. A cougher constantly coughing irritates my lungs and my throat; I visit more reluctantly sick people in whom duty interests me, than those who less demand my attention, and whom I think of less. I catch the disease I study and give it to myself. I do not think it strange that it[3] brings fevers and death to those who let it have its way and who encourage it.[4]

Simon Thomas was a great physician in his time. I remember that I met him one day at Toulouse,[5] at the house of a rich old man whose lungs were affected; and that, while discussing with him[6] means of curing him, he told him that one method was to give me reason to enjoy myself in his company, and that, fixing his eyes on the freshness of my

124

Of the Power of Imagination

complexion, and his mind on the cheerfulness and vigour that flowed from my youth, and filling all his senses with the blooming state in which I then was, his condition might be improved; but he forgot to say that mine might grow worse at the same time. Gallus Vibius bent his mind so strongly to understand the essence and the actions of madness, that he dragged his judgement from its seat, so that he was never able to replace it there, and could boast of having become insane by wisdom.[7] There are some who, from terror, anticipate the hand of the executioner; and he who was unbound that his pardon might be read to him, was found stark dead on the scaffold solely from the stroke of his imagination. We sweat, we tremble, we turn pale, and we blush at the assaults of our imagination, and, sunk in a feather-bed, feel our bodies shaken by their commotion, sometimes even to death. And ebullient youth is so greatly excited[8] while sound asleep, that it satisfies in dreams its amorous desires.

> So that, with all the matter acted out,
> They pour forth a stream, and stain their garment.[9]

And although it may be no new thing to see horns grow in the night on one who had none when he went to bed, nevertheless the case of Cyppus, King of Italy, is noteworthy, who, after he had been present during the day, with great zest, at a bull-fight, and had dreamed all night of horns, produced them on his head by the force of imagination.[10] Passion gave to the son of Crœsus the voice that Nature had denied him.[11] And Antiochus was seized by a fever because of the beauty of Stratonice too vividly imprinted on his soul.[12] Pliny says that he saw Lucius Cossitius changed from a woman to a man on his wedding day.[13] Pontanus and

125

Of the Power of Imagination

others tell of similar metamorphoses having occurred in Italy in times past; and because of his own and his mother's vehement desire,

> As a boy Iphis paid the vows that as a girl he had made.[14]

Passing through Vitry le Francoys, I might have seen a man whom the Bishop of Soissons had christened Germain at his confirmation, and whom all the inhabitants of that place had seen and known as a girl, named Marie, up to the age of twenty-two. He was, when I was there, heavily bearded and old and unmarried. He says that, when making a certain effort in leaping, his virile parts appeared; and there is still current among the girls of that place a ballad in which they warn one another not to take long strides for fear of becoming boys, like Marie Germain.[15] It is not very marvellous that this sort of accident happens frequently; for, if the imagination has power in such matters, it is so continually and so strongly turned to this subject that, not to be obliged to fall back so often upon the same thought and keenness of desire, it does better to incorporate this virile part in young women once and for all.

Some attribute the scars of King Dagobert and St. Francis to the power of imagination. It is said that by it bodies are sometimes lifted from their places. And Celsus tells of a priest whose soul was ravished into such an ecstasy that his body remained a long time without breath and without feeling. St. Augustine[16] mentions another, who had only to hear[17] grief-stricken and plaintive outcries when he would suddenly lose consciousness and be so completely carried out of himself that it was of no avail to storm at him, and shout,

Of the Power of Imagination

and pinch him, and scorch him, until he had come to; then he would say that he had heard voices, but as if coming from far away; and he would perceive his burns and bruises. And that it was not a secret wilful persistence in opposition to his real sensations was shown by the fact that he had meanwhile neither pulse nor breath.

It is probable that the belief in miracles, enchantments, and such extraordinary matters, is due chiefly to the power of the imagination, acting principally on the minds of the common people, which are more easily impressed. Their credulity has been so strongly taken possession of, that they think they see what they do not see. I am also of this opinion, that these absurd marriage hindrances,[18] by which our society finds itself so embarrassed that it talks of nothing else, are easily impressions of apprehension and fear. For it is within my own knowledge that a certain man, for whom I can answer as for myself, on whom could fall no suspicion of weakness and as little of sorcery, having heard an acquaintance of his tell the story of an extraordinary loss of manhood, into which he had fallen at a moment when there was least occasion for it, he finding himself in a similar position, the horror of this tale suddenly struck his imagination so vividly that he incurred in consequence a similar misadventure; and thereafter was subject to relapses, the wretched memory of his impediment taunting him and tyrannising over him. For this fancy he found some remedy in another fancy. By himself confessing and declaring beforehand this tyranny he was subject to, the strain on his mind was relieved by the reflection that, his evil being expected, his duty was thereby diminished, and weighed less on his mind. When he was at leisure and could choose his time (his thoughts being free and unfettered, and his body in proper trim), to have it then first tried, seized, and taken unawares in the knowledge of the other party, he was completely cured of this infirmity.

When a man has once been capable with a person, he is not again incapable with her, except through an excusable weakness.

This disaster is not to be feared but in an enterprise where the mind is excited beyond measure by desire or diffidence, and especially when the opportunity is of an unforeseen and pressing nature; there is no way then of recovering from this trouble. I have known of one who found it of service to bring his body to it half-sated from elsewhere, to abate the ardour of his fury, and of one who, by reason of his age, is the less impotent for being less vigorous.

I know another to whom it was of service to be assured by a friend that he was supplied with a counter-battery of enchantments certain to shield him. It is worth while for me to tell how this came about. A count, highly esteemed, with whom I was very intimate, was marrying a fair lady who had been sought in marriage by one who was present at the nuptial feast; this caused great anxiety to his friends, and especially to an old lady, his kinswoman, who presided over the festivities and gave them at her house, and who was fearful of these enchantments—as she gave me to understand. I begged her to rely on me. I had by good luck, in my boxes, a certain small flat piece of gold on which were engraved some celestial signs, as a charm against sunstroke, and as a remedy for headache by placing it just on the suture of the skull; and, to keep it in place, it was sewn to a ribbon intended to be tied under the chin; an effect of the imagina-

Of the Power of Imagination

tion akin to that of which we are talking. Jacques Pelletier,[19] when staying at my house, had given me this odd present. I bethought myself now to make some use of it, and I told the count that he might have bad luck, like others, there being men in the company who would desire to give him trouble; but that he might go boldly to bed; that I would do him a friendly turn, and in his need would not withhold a miracle which was in my power, provided that he would promise on his honour to keep it absolutely secret; but when they came in the night to bring him refreshment,[20] if things had gone ill with him, he should make me a certain signal. He had had his mind and his ears so belaboured that he found himself shackled by the disturbance of his imagination, and he gave me the signal at the appointed time. I whispered to him then to get up, on the pretext of turning us out, and to take, as if in sport, the night-robe that I wore (we were nearly of the same size), and to put it on whilst he followed my instructions: which were that, when we had gone out, he should withdraw to make water; should say certain prayers and go through certain motions thrice; that at each of the three times he should tie round his waist the ribbon which I put in his hand, and should very carefully place on his kidneys the medal that was attached to it, with the figure in a certain position; that, when this was done, and he had finally drawn the ribbon so tight that it could not be untied or moved from its place, he should return to his business, and not forget to throw my robe on his bed in such a way as to cover them both. Such idle tricks are the chief cause of the effect, the mind not being able to free itself from the idea[21] that methods so strange are due to some abstruse knowledge; their inanity gives them weight and

129

honour. In short, my figures certainly proved more Venerian than Solor, more powerful for action than for prevention. It was a sudden and odd impulse that led me to such a proceeding, far removed from my nature. I am a foe to subtle and deceptive acts, and I hate cunning, for myself, not only in amusements, but when profitable; if the act be not vicious, the road to it is. Amasis, King of Egypt, married Laodice, a very beautiful Greek girl; and he, who showed himself a well-behaved gallant elsewhere,[22] found himself unable to enjoy her, and threatened to kill her, believing this to be some sorcery. As in things which exist only in the fancy, she urged him toward devotion; and having made his vows and promises to Venus, he found himself divinely restored the very first night after his oblations and sacrifices.[23]

Now they[24] do wrong to greet us with such coy, disagreeable, shrinking looks, which put out our fire while kindling it. The daughter-in-law of Pythagoras[25] said that the woman who lay with a man should put aside her modesty with her clothes and put it on again with her clothes. The mind of the assailant, disturbed by many several alarms, is easily dismayed, and if his imagination has once made him suffer this shame (he suffers it only at the first encounters, the more so as they are more fierce and impetuous, and also because in this first intimacy one is much more afraid of failure), having made a bad beginning, he falls into a fever of vexation at this mishap, which is apt to continue on the following occasions.

Married men, time being at their command, should not attempt or hasten the action if they are not ready; it is better to fail ingloriously to handsel the nuptial couch, which fills one with feverish agitation, and to await some other

Of the Power of Imagination

more intimate and less alarmed opportunity, than to fall into perpetual misery through being disturbed and made desperate by the first refusal. Before possession be taken, the patient should, by sallies and at different times, make light essays and overtures, without any pique and persistence in trying definitely to convince himself. Such as know their members to be naturally docile, let them only take care to counter-beguile their fancies.

One has reason to remark on the unruly liberty of this member that so importunately asserts itself when we have no need of it, and so inopportunely fails us when we have most need of it, so imperiously contesting in authority with our will, so proudly and obstinately refusing our solicitations, both mental and manual.

If, however, on being scolded for his rebellion and condemned on that score, he were to fee me to plead his cause, I might peradventure arraign our other members, his fellows, of having purposely got up this quarrel against him, out of pure envy of the importance and pleasure attached to his function, and of having plotted to arm the world against him, by maliciously charging him alone with their common offence. For I ask you to consider whether there is one of the parts of our body that does not often refuse to work at our will, and does not often exert itself contrary to our will. They all have passions of their own, which awaken them and put them to sleep without our permission. How often do the involuntary movements of our features testify to the thoughts that we hold secret, and betray us to those about us! The same cause that animates the male member animates also, without our choice, the heart, the lungs, and the pulse, the sight of a charming object imperceptibly diffusing within us the flame of a feverish emotion. Is it those muscles and those veins alone that rise and subside, without the consent, not only of our will, but even of our thought? We do not command our hair to stand on end and our skin to quiver with desire or with fear; the hand often goes where we do not send it; the tongue becomes tied and the voice choked at their own time; the appetite for food and drink, even when, having nothing to cook, we would gladly forbid it, does not fail to stir up those parts that are subject to it, neither more nor less than this other appetite, and it abandons us as unseasonably, whenever it pleases. The organs that serve to discharge the bowels have their own dilatations and compressions, outside of and contrary to our wishes, as those have that serve to discharge our kidneys. And although, to establish the supreme power of our will, St. Augustine declares that he had seen a man who obliged his hinder parts to break wind as often as he chose,—which fact Vivès, his commentator, caps with another case in his own day, of systematised explosions, following the measure of verses which were pronounced,[26]—this does not imply complete obedience in that organ; for is there one which is commonly more indiscreet and unruly? Moreover, I know one so turbulent and untractable that for forty years it has compelled its master to break wind at every breath,[27] and with a constant and unremitting constraint, and so brings him near to death. And would to God that I knew only by hearsay how often our belly, by a single refusal to break wind, carries us even to the gates of a very agonizing death; and would that the emperor who gave us leave to break wind everywhere, had given us the power.[28]

But our will, in behalf of whose claims we bring forward

Of the Power of Imagination

this reproach—with how much more semblance of truth can we charge her with rebellion and sedition, from her disorderliness and disobedience! Does she always desire what we would like her to desire? Does she not often desire, and to our evident injury, what we forbid her to desire? Does she allow herself to be guided by the conclusions of our judgement? To conclude, I will urge on behalf of Monsieur my client, that it please you to consider that though his cause, in this matter, is inseparably and indiscriminately joined to that of a consort, yet he alone is accused, and that by arguments and accusations which, seeing the conditions of the parties, cannot concern or be charged to his said consort. [For the latter may be said at times to invite inopportunely, but to refuse, never; and to invite, moreover, tacitly and quietly.] Wherefore the animosity and illegality of his accusers are manifest. However that may be, Nature, making it clear that lawyers and judges idly wrangle and pass sentence, will meanwhile go her way, who would have done no more than right had she endowed the male member with some peculiar privilege, the author of the sole immortal work of mortals. For this reason, procreation is a divine act according to Socrates;[29] and love, desire of immortality, and itself an immortal spirit. Perchance one man, by this effect of imagination, leaves here the king's evil that another carries back to Spain. We see, therefore, that in such matters we are wont to require an expectant mind. Why do physicians make use beforehand of the credulity of their patients by so many false promises of recovery, if not that the action of imagination may come to the aid of the imposture of their decoctions? They know that one of the masters of their profession[30] left them in writing the statement that there

133

have been men with whom the mere sight of a medicine did its work; and I have been led to take in hand this vagary by a tale told me by an apothecary in the household of my late father, a simple-minded man, a Swiss,—a nation not unintelligent and little given to lying,—of having, known for a long time a tradesman at Toulouse, a sickly man, and subject to the stone, who was often in need of injections, and had them differently prepared by physicians according to the phases of his disease. When they were brought, none of the usual forms was omitted: often he felt of them, to judge if they were too hot; and then he was to be seen on his stomach, every thing in readiness, but no injection was administered. The apothecary having withdrawn after this ceremony, the patient being arranged as if he had actually taken the injection, the same effect was produced as on those who take them. And if the physician found the operation insufficient, he would give him two or three more in the same way. My witness swears that, to save the expense (for he paid for them as if he had taken them), the sick man's wife having tried sometimes to do with only warm water, the result betrayed the imposture, and that sort being found to be useless, it was necessary to return to the first method.

A woman, thinking that she had swallowed a pin with her bread, cried out and bewailed herself as if she had an intolerable pain in her gullet where she thought she felt that it had lodged; but because there was neither swelling nor unusual appearance outside, a clever man, having concluded that it was only fancy, an idea suggested by a piece of crust that had pricked her as it went down, made her vomit, and stealthily tossed a bent pin into what she threw up. Believing that she had thrown it up, the woman immediately

Of the Power of Imagination

felt relieved of her pain. I know that a gentleman who had
entertained a large company at his house bragged three or
four days afterward—by way of jest, for there was no truth
in it—that he had made them eat a cat in a pasty; at which
a young lady of the party was so horror-struck that she fell
into such great weakness of the stomach and fever, that it
was impossible to save her.

The very beasts are seen to be subject, like ourselves, to
the power of the imagination: witness the dogs who die of
grief for the loss of their masters; we see that they, too,
bark and tremble when dreaming, and that horses whinny
and struggle.[31]

But all this may be attributed to the close connection between the mind and the body, interchanging their conditions. It is another matter that the imagination may sometimes act, not only against its own body, but against the
body of another; and just as one body passes a disease on
to its neighbour as is seen in the plague, in small-pox, and
sore eyes, which are communicated from one to another,—

> When eyes behold eyes in pain, they become pain-
> ful themselves; and many things harm our bodies by
> contagion,[32]—

so the imagination, being violently roused, launches shafts
which may hit a distant object. In ancient times it was believed that certain women in Scythia, being aroused and
angered against some one, killed him with a single look.[33]
Tortoises and ostriches hatch their eggs by only looking at
them[34]—a proof that they possess some ejaculatory power.
And as for magicians, they are said to have baleful and
malignant eyes:[35]

135

Of the Power of Imagination

> I know not whose evil eye bewitches my tender lambs.[36]

But to my mind magicians are poor creatures. However, we know by experience that women transmit to the bodies of children in their womb the marks of their fantasies—witness her who gave birth to the Moor.[37] And there was brought to Charles, King of Bohemia and Emperor, a girl from near Pisa, all hairy and rough, whom her mother declared to have been so conceived because of an image of St. John the Baptist that hung by her bed. With animals it is the same; witness Jacob's sheep,[38] and the partridges and hares turned white by the snow on the mountains.[39] Some one saw lately at my home[40] a cat watching a bird at the top of a tree; and after they had gazed fixedly at each other for some time, the bird let itself drop as if dead into the cat's paws, either bewildered by its own imagination, or drawn by some power of attraction in the cat. Those who like hawking have heard the story of the falconer who, fixing his eyes persistently on a kite in the air, wagered that he would bring it down simply by the power of his eyes, and did it, so they say.

For the anecdotes that I borrow, I refer them to the consciences of those from whom I receive them;[41] the inferences are my own, and are derived from the evidence of common sense, not of experience; every one can add his own examples, and let him who has none not fail to believe that there are plenty of them, because of the number and variety of the chances. If I do not rightly comment on them, let another comment for me.[42] In the study that I enter upon of our manners and acts, fabulous testimonies, provided that

Of the Power of Imagination

they are possible, serve as well as true ones. Whether it really happened or not, at Rome or at Paris, to Peter or to John, it is always an illustration of what is contained in men's minds,[43] of which I am advantageously informed by the tale. I see it and profit by it, whether it be a shadow or a solid body. And of the different forms that histories often contain, I make use of that which is most unusual and memorable. There are authors whose object it is to narrate real events. Mine, if I should be able to attain it, would be to tell of what is possible to happen. The schools are rightly permitted to imagine examples[44] when they have none. I do not do so, however, and in that respect I surpass in scrupulous conscientiousness all the fidelity of historians. In the examples which I here derive from what I have heard, done, or said, I have forbidden myself to venture to change even the most trivial and unimportant details. Consciously I do not falsify one iota; unconsciously, I can not say.

It sometimes comes into my mind about this matter, how it can be that it well befits a theologian, a philosopher, and such-like persons of delicate and accurate conscience and prudence, to write history. How can they rest their faith on a popular faith? how be responsible for the thoughts of unknown persons, and put forth their conjectures as of value? About actions with divers phases which take place in their presence, they would refuse to give evidence sworn to before a magistrate, and they know no man so intimately that they would be ready to answer fully regarding his intentions. I hold it less hazardous to write of past than of present matters, inasmuch as the writer then has only to produce a borrowed assertion. Some people urge me to write of the affairs of my own time, judging that I view them with eyes less impaired by passion than other men, and at closer quarters, because of the access which fortune has given me to the chiefs of different parties. But they do not recognise that I would not, for the fame of Sallust, take the trouble to do this, being a sworn foe to obligation, to assiduity, to perseverance; that there is nothing so contrary to my style as a long narrative, I am stopped short so often by lack of breath; I have no skill in composition or exposition; I am more ignorant than a child of the words and phrases used for the commonest things. Therefore I have undertaken to say what I know how to say, accommodating the matter to my powers; if I should take a subject to be followed up, my measure might fall short of my topic; and were my liberty so free, I might publish opinions which, even according to my own judgement and to reason, are unlawful and punishable. Plutarch would readily acknowledge, concerning what he wrote, that it is due to others if his examples are wholly and always true; if they are profitable to posterity and presented with a brilliancy that lights our way to virtue, that is due to him. It is not of importance in an ancient tale, as it is in a medicinal drug, that it should be thus or thus.

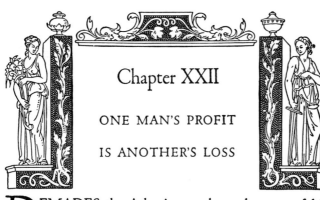

Chapter XXII

ONE MAN'S PROFIT

IS ANOTHER'S LOSS

DEMADES the Athenian condemned a man of his city, whose trade was selling the things necessary for burials, on the ground that he demanded too large a profit, and that this profit could not accrue to him without the death of many people.[1] This judgement seems to be ill-advised, because no profit is made save at a loss to some one else, and by such reckoning we should have to condemn every sort of gain. The merchant succeeds in his business only by the unthriftiness of the youth; the farmer, by the high price of grains; the architect, by the falling to pieces of houses; the officers of the law, by men's litigation and quarrels; the very honour and functions of the ministers of religion are derived from our deaths and from our vices. No physician takes pleasure in the good health even of his friends, said the old Greek comedy-writer,[2] nor any soldier in the peace of his city; and so with the rest. And, what is worse, let any man search his own heart, and he will find that our inmost desires are for the most part born and fed at another's expense. Nature does not herein belie her general policy; for physicists hold that the birth and increase of every thing is the change and decay of something else.

139

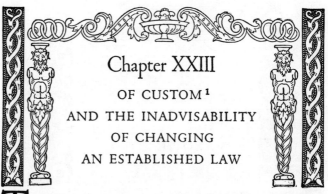

Chapter XXIII

OF CUSTOM [1]
AND THE INADVISABILITY
OF CHANGING
AN ESTABLISHED LAW

THAT man seems to me to have had a just conception of the power of habit who first invented this tale:[2] that a village woman, having been wont to fondle a calf and carry him in her arms from the moment of his birth, continuing always to do so, gained such power by habit, that she still carried him when he was a full-grown ox. For habit is truly a violent and deceitful school-mistress. Little by little, and stealthily, she establishes within us the footing of her authority; but having, by this mild and humble beginning, stayed and rooted it with the aid of time, she then displays a fierce and tyrannical countenance, in opposition to which we no longer have liberty even to lift up our eyes. We see her do violence constantly to the laws of nature. *Custom is the most powerful master of all things.*[3] I believe, about this, Plato's cavern in his "Republic,"[4] and I believe the physicians who so often relinquished to her authority the logic of their art; and that king who, by her means, trained his stomach to feed on poison;[5] and the girl who, as Albert tells, was wont to feed on spiders.[6] And in this new world of the Indies there were prosperous races, and in very different climates, who lived on them, and laid in supplies of them, and fed them;[7] and the same with grasshoppers, ants, lizards, bats; and a toad was sold for ten crowns when provisions were scarce. They cook them and dress them with different sauces. There were found there other peoples, to whom our meats and viands were poisonous and fatal. *Great is the power of custom; huntsmen pass the night in the snow and endure the sun's heat in the mountains; boxers, when bruised by the gloves, do not even utter a groan.*[8]

These foreign examples are not foreign to our comprehension, if we consider—a common experience—how accustomedness dulls our senses. We need not go in search of what is said about those who live near the cataracts of the Nile;[9] and what the philosophers think about celestial music, that the bodies in those spheres, being solid and polished, and slipping and rubbing against one another as they revolve, can not fail to produce harmonies by whose divisions and variations[10] the evolutions and changes in the dances of the stars are guided; but, as elsewhere in the universe, the ears of the beings of that region, benumbed, like those of the Egyptians, by the continuance of the sound, can not hear it, loud as it may be. Blacksmiths, millers, armourers, could not hold out against the noise that beats upon their ears, if they were dazed by it as we are. My perfumed doublet[11] is perceptible to my nose; but after I have worn it three successive days, it is perceived only by the noses of others. This [other fact] is even stranger—that, notwithstanding long intervals and breaks, accustomedness can span the gap and render permanent the effect of the impression on our senses, as they find who live near church-towers. I sleep at home in a tower in which every day, in the morning and evening, a very large bell rings for the Ave

Maria. The racket amazes[12] my whole tower, and whereas, when I am first there, it seems intolerable to me, in a short time it becomes so familiar that I hear it without annoyance, and often without waking.

Plato reproved a child who was gambling for nuts.[13] The child answered: "You reprove me for a small matter." "Habit," Plato replied, "is not a small matter." I find that our greatest vices are contracted in our earliest childhood, and that our chief guidance lies in the hands of our nurses. It is a pastime for a mother to see a child wring a chicken's neck, and amuse himself by hurting a dog or a cat; and a father may be foolish enough to take it for a good omen of a valorous spirit when he sees his son insulting by a blow a peasant or a servant who does not defend himself; and for a pretty wit when he sees him cheat his comrade by some crafty falsehood and fraud. These are, however, the true seeds and roots of cruelty and of tyranny and of treachery. They sprout there, and afterward grow lustily and greatly thrive at the hands of custom. And it is a very dangerous education to excuse such base tendencies by the feebleness of childhood and the trivial nature of the subject. Firstly, it is Nature who speaks, whose voice is purer and more piercing, as it is shriller.[14] Secondly, the ugliness of deceit does not consist in the difference between crowns and pins: it exists in itself. I find it much truer to argue thus: "Why would he not cheat about crowns, since he cheats about pins?" than, as they do: "It is only about pins; he would be careful not to do so about crowns." We must sedulously teach children to hate vices for their own texture, and must teach them their natural monstrosity, so that they may shun them, not in their actions only, but, above all, in their hearts; that the mere thought of them may be hateful, whatever mask they wear. I know well that, from having been taught[15] in boyhood to follow always my broad, straight road, and from having always had a repugnance to mingle trickery or cunning in my childish games (indeed, it should be noted that the games of children are not games, and must be judged as their most serious acts), there is no pastime so trivial that I do not bring to it inwardly, and by a natural and unstudied propensity, an extreme aversion to deceit. I play cards for doubles,[16] and keep count as carefully as if they were double doubloons, when gaining or losing against my wife and daughter is a matter of indifference to me, as when I am playing in earnest. In every thing and everywhere my eyes are enough to keep me straight; there are no others which watch me so closely or which I more respect.

I have just seen at my house a little man, a native of Nantes,[17] who was born without arms and who has so well trained his feet for the service which hands ought to perform, that they have in truth half forgotten their natural office. Furthermore, he calls them his hands; he carves, loads a pistol and fires it, threads his needle, sews, writes, takes off his cap, combs his hair, plays at cards and with dice, and handles them as dexterously as anybody else could do. The money that I gave him (for he earned his living by exhibiting himself)[18] he carried away in his foot as we do in our hand. I saw another who lost his arms when a child,[19] who wielded a two-handed sword and a halberd in the bend of the neck, for lack of hands, threw them in the air and caught them, cast a dagger, and cracked a whip as well as any carter in France.

Of Custom

But we discern her effects[20] much better in the strange impressions she makes on our minds, where she does not find so much resistance. What is impossible to her regarding our judgements and our beliefs? Is there any opinion so fantastical (I leave out of account the gross imposture of religious belief wherewith so many great nations and so many able personages are seen to be bewildered; for that matter being outside of our human reasonings, it is more excusable for him who is not extraordinarily enlightened by divine favour to lose himself therein)—but of other opinions are there any so strange which she has not planted and established by law in the countries where it has seemed to her well to do so? And that ancient exclamation is very true: *Is not the natural philosopher, that is, the explorer and the hunter of nature, ashamed to seek evidence of the truth from minds prejudiced by custom!*[21] I believe that no fancy, however extravagant, ever comes into the human imagination, which does not find example in some public custom, and which consequently our reason does not prop up and support. There are peoples who turn the back on the person saluted, and never look at one to whom they desire to do honour.[22] There are other nations where, when the king spits, the greatest favourite among the women of his court holds out her hand; and in still another the most eminent of those about his person stoop to take up his dirt in a cloth.

Let me find room here for an anecdote. A certain French gentleman always blew his nose with his hand (a thing altogether contrary to our custom). Defending this action of his,—and he was famous for keen sayings,—he asked me what distinction that dirty excrement had, that we should provide a fine piece of delicate linen to receive it in, and then,

Of Custom

what is more, fold it up and carry it about with us; that that
would seem naturally to cause us more disgust and sicken
us more than to see it dropped here or there, as we do our
other excrements. I found what he said not at all unreasonable; and that habit had prevented my marking this strange
act, which, however, we find so odious when it is told of
another country. Miracles exist from our ignorance of nature, not in nature herself. Habituation closes the eyes of
our judgement. Barbarians are in no wise more astonishing
to us than we are to them, nor with more reason, as every
one would admit if every one, after having gone through
these unfamiliar examples, would consider his own,[23] and
compare them judiciously. Our human reason is a dye,
infinite in quality, infinite in variety, infused in almost equal
degree in all our opinions and manners, of whatever form
they may be.

I resume. There are nations where no one save his wife
and children speaks to the king except through a speaking-
trumpet. In another, the maidens go with their private parts
uncovered, while the married women carefully cover and
conceal theirs; to which this other custom, found elsewhere,
bears some relation; chastity is valued only for the behoof
of the marriage tie, for unmarried women can abandon
themselves at their pleasure, and, being with child, can cause
themselves to abort by taking the proper drugs, in every
one's sight. And elsewhere, if it be a merchant who marries, all the merchants invited to the wedding lie with the
bride before he does, and the more of them there are, the
more she acquires of honour, and of reputation for endurance and capacity. If a man holding public office marries,
the same rule applies; so, if it be a noble; and the same with

others, unless it be a labouring man or any one of the common people; for in that case it is the lord's prerogative; and yet, in that country, they do not fail to enjoin strict fidelity during wedlock. There are other [peoples] where there are public brothels for males, and, actually, marriages; where the women go to war along with their husbands, and have their place, not in battle only, but also in command; where not only are rings worn in the nose, the lips, the cheeks, and the big toe, but rods of gold, very heavy, are thrust through the breasts and the buttocks; where, while eating, they wipe their fingers on their thighs, their private parts, and the soles of their feet; where children do not inherit, but brothers and nephews, and elsewhere nephews alone, except in succession to the prince; where, in order to regulate the community of goods which is customary there, certain magistrates with sovereign power have entire charge of the cultivation of the land and of the distribution of crops according to each one's need; where they weep over the deaths of children and make rejoicing over those of old men; where they lie ten or twelve in a bed with their wives; where women who lose their husbands by a violent death may remarry, but not others; where they think so ill of the condition of women that they kill all the female children who are born there, and buy from their neighbours women for breeding; where husbands can repudiate [their wives] without cause, but not wives [their husbands] for any cause whatsoever; where husbands can lawfully sell their wives if they be sterile; where they have the body of the dead boiled and then pounded until it is like a broth, which they mix with their wine, and drink; where the most desirable sepulture is to be eaten by dogs, elsewhere by birds;[24] where

Of Custom

they believe that the souls of the blessed live in perfect freedom, in delightful fields, supplied with all pleasures, and
that it is they who make the echo we hear; where they fight
in water, and discharge their arrows with sure aim while
swimming; where, in token of submission, a man must
raise his shoulders and hang his head, and remove his shoes
when he enters the king's palace; where the eunuchs who
have the nuns in their charge lack nose and lips as well, so
that they cannot be loved, and the priests put out their own
eyes in order to become acquainted with the demons and to
receive oracles; where every one makes a god of whatever he
chooses,—the hunter, of a lion or fox, the fisherman, of certain fish,—and idols of every human action or passion: the
sun, the moon, and the earth are the chief gods; the manner
of making oath is to touch the ground while looking at the
sun; and they eat flesh and fish raw. Where the most
binding oath is to swear by the name of some dead man who
bore a good reputation in the country, placing the hand on
his tomb;[25] where the annual gift that the king sends to the
princes his vassals is fire; when the ambassador who brings
it arrives, the old fire is everywhere put out in the house,
and all the people are required to come and supply themselves from this new fire, or be adjudged guilty of lèse-
majesté;[26] where, when the king, in order to give himself entirely to religion, as they often do, abdicates his sovereignty,
his next successor is obliged to do likewise, and the right of
kingship passes to the third in succession; where they vary
the form of government as circumstances require: they de-
pose the king when it seems well, and substitute for him
elders of the state, to take the helm, and sometimes, too,
leave it in the hands of the commonalty; where men and

women are circumcised, and likewise baptised; where the soldier who, in one or several battles, has succeeded in presenting to his king the heads of seven foes is ennobled.[27] Where men live under the unusual, uncivilized doctrine of the mortality of the soul; where the women lie in without complaint and without fear. Where the women wear copper rings on both legs, and, if a louse bites them, are bound by the duty of courage, to bite back, and dare not marry until they have offered their virginity to the king if he desires it.[28] Where men salute each other by putting the finger to the ground, then raising it toward heaven; where the men carry burdens on their heads, the women on their shoulders:[29] the latter make water standing, the men stooping; where they send some of their blood as a symbol of friendship, and burn incense, as to the gods, to the men whom they wish to honour; where kinship not only in the fourth, but in even more distant degrees, is a bar to marriage; where children are kept four years at nurse, and often twelve, and there too it is considered fatal to give a child the breast during the first day; where fathers have the duty of punishing the male children, and mothers, exclusively, the females; and the punishment is to smoke them while they are hung up by the feet; where the women are circumcised; where they eat all sorts of herbs, without other discrimination than that of refusing those which seem to them to have a bad odour; where every thing is open, and the houses, however beautiful and sumptuous they may be, have neither door nor window nor chest that can be locked, and thieves are punished twice as severely as elsewhere; where they kill lice with their teeth, as monkeys do, and think it horrible to see them crushed by the nails; where they never cut either

Of Custom

the hair or the nails during life; other places where they cut
the nails of the right hand only, those of the left hand being
kept long for prettiness. Where they let all the hair on the
right side of the body grow as long as it can, and shave the
left side clean;[30] and in neighbouring provinces, in one
they let the hair grow in front, in the other, behind, and
shave the front.[31] Where fathers lend their children, husbands their wives, to be enjoyed by their guests, for pay;
where a man can lawfully have children by his mother, and
where fathers forgather with their daughters, and mothers
with their sons; where, on festal occasions, they lend[32]
their children one to another. In one country human flesh
is eaten; in another it is a pious duty to kill your father at a
certain age; elsewhere, fathers decree, as to their still unborn
children, which one they wish brought up and preserved,
and which they wish to be cast out and killed; elsewhere,
aged husbands lend their wives to young men to be used,
and elsewhere they are blamelessly common;[33] indeed, in
one land they wear as a badge of honour as many rows of
fringe on the edge of their garments as they have known
men.[34] And has not custom even caused a separate state of
women[35] to exist? has she not put arms in their hands, and
caused them to train armies and fight battles? And that
which reason and all philosophy can not implant in the
heads of the wisest men, does not she teach, solely by her
decree, to the dullest of the common people? For we know
whole regions where death was not only scorned, but welcomed with rejoicing;[36] where children of seven endured to
be whipped to death without changing countenance; where
riches were held in such scorn that the meanest citizen in the
town would not have deigned to stoop to pick up a purse full

of gold. And we know places very fruitful in all sorts of provisions where, none the less, the most usual and most delicate dishes were bread, cresses, and water.[37]

Did not custom work even that miracle in Cio, that seven hundred years passed during which there was no remembrance that either maid or wife there had been false to her honour?[38] In fine, to my thinking, there is nothing which she does not do or could not do; and Pindar justly calls her, as I have been told, the Queen and Empress of the world.[39]

The man who was found beating his father declared that it was the custom of his family: that his father had thus beaten his grandfather, and his grandfather his great-grandfather; and, pointing to his son, he said: "He will beat me when he has reached my present age." And that father whose son haled him and tugged him through the street bade him stop at a certain door, for he himself had dragged his father only so far; that that was the limit of the hereditary humiliating treatment which, in their family, the children were accustomed to inflict on their fathers. From custom, says Aristotle,[40] as often as from sickness, women tear their hair, gnaw their nails, eat coals and earth; and more from custom than from nature, males cohabit with males. The laws of conscience, which we say are engendered by nature, are born of custom; every man, holding in inward veneration the opinions and fashions approved and received around him, can not depart from them without [self] upbraiding, or conform to them without [self] commendation.[41]

When the Cretans, in old days, wished to curse some one, they besought the gods to involve him in some evil cus-

Of Custom

tom.[42] But the principal effect of her authority is to seize and grip us in such wise that it is scarcely in our power to throw off her clutch, and to return into ourselves to reflect and reason about her decrees. In truth, because we suck these in with the milk of our birth, and because the face of the world presents itself in this guise to our earliest vision, we seem born necessarily to follow this course. And the common ideas that we find in credit around us, and infused in our minds by the seed of our fathers, seem to be universal and natural ideas. Whence it happens that whatever is unhinged from custom, we believe to be unhinged from reason,[43] God knows how unreasonably in most instances. If, as we who study ourselves have learned to do, every one who hears a wise thought should consider instantly how it applies to his own case, he would find that it was not so much an excellent saying as an excellent blow at the usual stupidity of his judgement. But we receive the warnings of truth and its precepts as addressed to the common people, never to ourselves; and every one, instead of applying them to his morals, impresses them on his memory, very foolishly and very uselessly.

Let us return to the authority of custom. Peoples brought up in liberty, and to rule themselves, consider every other form of government monstrous and contrary to nature. Those who are accustomed to monarchy think after the same fashion; and whatever facility for change fortune affords them, even when they have with great difficulty rid themselves of the burden of a master, they hasten to install a new one with the like difficulty, because they can not resolve to regard with detestation the being lorded over. It is through the intervention of custom that every one is content with the place where nature has planted him; and the savages of Scotland have no use for Touraine, nor the Scythians for Thessaly.[44]

Darius asked certain Greeks what would induce them to adopt the Indian custom of eating their deceased fathers (for that was their habit, deeming that they could give them no more propitious sepulture than within themselves); they replied that not for any thing in the world would they do it; but [Darius] having also tried to persuade the Indians to lay aside their custom and adopt that of the Greeks, which was to burn their fathers' bodies, he horrified them even more.[45] Each one of us acts in the same way, inasmuch as habit conceals from us the true aspect of things.

> There is nothing so great or so admirable at first,
> that we do not gradually admire it less.[46]

Having occasion once to show the value of some one of our regulations, accepted with settled authority on all sides of us; not desiring, as is commonly done, to establish it solely by the powers of law and example, but harking back to its origin, I found its basis so weak[47] that I was almost out of conceit with it—I who had to assert it to another.

It is by this remedy (which he considers the chief and most potent one) that Plato undertakes to expel the unnatural [and preposterous[48]] passions of his age: namely, that public opinion condemns them; that the poets, that every one speaks ill of them—a remedy by whose operation the fairest daughters no longer arouse the love of their fathers, nor the brothers who most excel in beauty the love of their sisters; the very legends of Thyestes, of Œdipus, and of Macareus having, with the charm of their music, in-

Of Custom

stilled this probable belief[49] in the tender brains of children.[50] In truth, chastity is an excellent virtue, whose utility is very well known; but to treat of it and show its value by natural conditions is as difficult as it is easy to show its value in custom, laws, and precepts. The fundamental and universal reasons for it are difficult of investigation, and our masters skim lightly over them, or, not daring even to touch them, throw themselves from the first into the sanctuary of custom, where they can strut and triumph easily. Those who do not choose to let themselves be carried away from the original source err even more, and are subjected to uncivilised opinions: witness Chrysippus, who scattered about in so many places in his writings the small importance he attributed to incestuous unions, of whatever nature they might be.[51] Whoever would make a similar attempt and rid himself of this violent pre-judgement of custom, will find several things to be accepted with unquestioning resolution, which have no support save in the gray beard and wrinkles of the wontedness that is associated with them. But when that mask is torn away, these things being brought into relation with truth and right, he will feel that his judgement has been turned topsy-turvy, but is consequently reestablished much more surely. For example, I will ask them what can be stranger than to see a people obliged to follow laws that it never understands; bound in all its domestic affairs—marriages, donations, testaments, sales, and purchases—by rules of which it can not have knowledge, as they are neither written nor proclaimed in its own language, and of which it must necessarily purchase the interpretation and the practice. Not according to the ingenious conception of Isocrates, who advised his king to make the traffic and negotiations of his subjects free, unrestrained, and lucrative, and their disputes and quarrels burdensome, loading them with heavy penalties,[52] but according to a monstrous conception that the right itself should be made a matter of traffic, and the laws treated as merchandise. I am grateful to fortune that, so our historians say, it was a Gascon gentleman, a countryman of mine, who first opposed Charlemagne when he desired to give us the laws of Rome and the Empire.[53] What is more barbarous than to see a nation where, by a legalised custom, the office of judge is sold, and judgements are bought for ready money, and where justice is legally denied to him who has not the means to pay for it; and where this traffic is in such great repute that there exists in a government a fourth estate of persons dealing in lawsuits, alongside the three ancient estates of the church, the nobility, and the common people; which fourth estate, having the administration of the laws and sovereign authority over property and lives, forms a body apart from that of the nobility. Whence it happens that there are two sorts of laws, in many respects very different—those of honour and those of justice: thus, the former condemn as strictly the lie tamely submitted to, as the latter do the lies revenged; by the decree of arms he is stripped of honour and nobility who submits to an insult, and by civil decree he who takes vengeance for it incurs a disgraceful punishment; he who appeals to the laws to obtain satisfaction for an offence to his honour, dishonours himself, and he who does not so appeal is punished and chastised by the laws. And of these two bodies,[54] so unlike yet connected under one head,[55] those represent peace, these war; those profit, these honour; those learning, these merit; those speech, these action: those jus-

Of Custom

tice, these valour; those reason, these force; those have the robe, these the sword for their portion.[56]

As for unimportant things, such as clothes, to whoever may desire to connect them with their true purpose, which is the service and pleasure of the body, upon which their charm and essential seemliness depend—I will suggest to him as, among others, the most fantastic that can be imagined, our square caps, that long tail of folded velvet, with its vari-coloured trimming, which hangs from the heads of our women, and that idle and useless covering of a member which we cannot decently even name, of which none the less we make show and parade in public. These considerations do not, however, turn a man of understanding aside from following the common custom. But, on the other hand, it seems to me that all unusual and peculiar fashions proceed rather from foolishness or ambitious affectation than from right reason; and that the wise man should inwardly withdraw his mind from the crowd and give it liberty and power to judge freely of things; but outwardly he should altogether follow the accepted fashions and forms. Society at large has no concern with our thoughts; but all the rest, as our acts, our work, our fortunes, and our lives, we must lend and abandon to its service and to public opinion: as the great and good Socrates refused to save his life by disobeying the magistrate, and verily a most unjust and most iniquitous magistrate.[57] For it is the rule of rules and the universal law of laws, that every one must obey those of the place where he is:—

It is noble to obey the laws of the country in which one dwells.[58]

Of Custom

Here is a consideration of another sort.[59] There is great doubt if there can be found as manifest advantage in altering an accepted law, whatever it may be, as there is harm in disturbing it; inasmuch as a system of government is like a structure of many parts so closely bound together that it is impossible to move one of them without the whole building feeling it. The law-maker of the Thurians[60] decreed that whoever should desire either to repeal an old law, or to introduce a new one, should present himself before the people with a rope about his neck, so that, if the innovation were not approved by every one, he might be instantly hanged. And he of Lacedæmon[61] spent his life in obtaining from his fellow citizens a firm promise not to violate any of his decrees. The ephor who so harshly cut the two strings that Phrynis had added to his lyre was not concerned as to whether it was bettered by them, or whether the chords were the richer; it was enough for their condemnation that they were a change from the old mode.[62] The same was signified by the rusted sword of justice at Marseilles.[63]

I am disgusted with novelty, whatever aspect it bears; and rightly so, for I have seen most harmful consequences of it. That which has been harrying us for so many years[64] has not seized upon every thing; but we can say with plausibility that incidentally it has produced and given birth to every thing, verily, even to the ills and destruction which in the meantime have taken place without it and in opposition to it; there is good reason for it to blame itself therefor.[65]

Alas! I suffer from wounds made by my own weapons.[66]

They who first shake a state are easily the first to be involved in its ruin. The profit of the disturbance seldom

156

Of Custom

falls to the lot of him who has stirred it up; he lashes and muddies the water for other fishers. The joints and framework of this monarchy, this great edifice, notably in its old age, having been displaced and loosened by novelty, afford all the opening and entrance you please to such outrages. The royal majesty is cast down with much more difficulty, says an ancient writer, from the summit to the halfway point, than hurled from that point into the depths. But if the inventors are the more harmful, the imitators are the more vicious in recklessly following examples of which they have perceived and punished the detestableness and the evil; and if there are degrees of honour, even in doing evil, the latter should accord to the others the glory of the invention and the courage of the first attempt.

All sorts of new disorders draw, by good luck, from this first and prolific source, devices and models for disturbing our government. We read in our very laws, designed to remedy this original evil, the training and excuse for all sorts of evil undertakings; and there happens to us what Thucydides says of the civil wars of his time—that, favouring the public vices, they created new and gentler words in their excuse, falsifying and softening their true names.[67] And this, howsoever, is to reform our consciences and our beliefs! *The pretext is honourable.*[68] But the best pretext for innovation is very hazardous. *Indeed, no change from ancient customs is worthy of approval.*[69] And it seems to me, to speak frankly, that there is great self-love and presumption in setting so high a value on one's opinions that, to establish them, it is necessary to upset public tranquillity and to introduce so many inevitable evils and such shocking corruption of morals as civil wars bring about, and the mutations in the state in a matter of such weight—and to introduce them into one's own country. Is it not bad management to bring to the front so many certain and known vices, to combat errors denied and debatable? Is there any worse sort of vice than those which offend one's own conscience and instinctive knowledge? The [Roman] Senate, in the dispute between it and the people as to the administration of their religion, ventured to give as satisfaction this excuse: *This matter concerned the gods more than it did them; the gods themselves would see to it that their sacred rites were not profaned,*[70] conformably to what the oracle replied to those of Delphi in the war against the Medes. Fearing the invasion of the Persians, they asked the god what they were to do with the sacred treasures of his temple—whether they should conceal them, or carry them away. He replied that they should move nothing; that they should care for themselves; that he was able to provide for what was his.[71]

The Christian religion has all the marks of the greatest rightness and usefulness; but none more evident than the explicit injunction of obedience to authority, and upholding of the forms of government. What a marvellous example of this, divine wisdom has given us, which, to ensure the salvation of the human race, and to conduct its glorious victory over death and sin, chose to do this only under sufferance of our political system, and subjected its progress and the guidance toward so high and so salutary a result to the blindness and injustice of our observances and usages, allowing the innocent blood to flow of so many of the elect, its beloved, and permitting the loss of long years in the ripening of this inestimable fruit! There is a vast difference

Of Custom

between his cause who follows the customs and laws of his country, and that of him who undertakes to govern them and change them. The first may plead in excuse single-mindedness, obedience, and precedent; whatever he may do, it cannot be from ill intent; at the worst, it is disastrous. *For who is not moved by antiquity, witnessed and attested by the most glorious monuments?*[72] Besides what Isocrates says, that falling short is more akin to moderation than excess is.[73]

The other is in a much worse posture; for he who meddles with choosing and changing usurps the authority of judging, and should be quite sure that he sees the error of what he rejects and the benefit of what he introduces. This commonplace consideration settled me in my seat, and kept even my more heedless youth in check from burdening my shoulders with so heavy a load as to make myself a surety for knowledge of such importance, and from venturing, in this matter, what in sound discretion I could not venture to do in the simplest of those matters in which I had been instructed, and in which rashness of judgement does no harm. For it seemed to me very wrong to seek to subject public and fixed constitutions and usages to the instability of a private opinion (private judgement has only a private jurisdiction), and to undertake with respect to divine laws what no government would suffer with respect to human laws, which, although human reason has much more connection with them, yet are they sovereign judges of their judges, and the greatest ability serves but to explain and extend the accepted use of them, not to divert it and innovate upon it. If sometimes divine providence has overridden the rules to which it has necessarily subjected us, it is not for us to dispense with them: those are strokes of the divine hand which we must not imitate, but admire; and extraordinary cases, marked with a designed and special warranting of the sort of miracles which it offers us as evidence of its omnipotence, far above our methods and our powers, and which it is folly and impiety to try to reproduce—paths, not for our feet, but for us to contemplate with amazement; acts belonging to the part it plays, not to us.[74] Cotta protests very fitly: *In religious matters I follow T. Coruncanius, P. Scipio, and P. Scævola, high pontiffs, and not Zeno, or Cleanthes, or Chrysippus.*[75]

God knows, in our present quarrel, in which there are a hundred points of dispute to be taken out and put back,—points of great and profound importance,—how many persons there are who can boast of having accurately grasped the arguments of one and the other party. It is a number, if a number there be, which would have no great power to disturb us. But all this other crowd—whither is it going? under what standard does it turn out of the road?[76] It happens with theirs as with other weak and ill-employed drugs: the humours of which it sought to purge us, it has heated and irritated and embittered by the conflict, and still it has remained in our body. It has failed to purge us because of its weakness, and yet it has weakened us so that we can no longer void it, and we get from its operation only intestinal pains long-continued. Yet, however, fortune, retaining always its authority over our judgements, sometimes presents us with so urgent a necessity that there is need for the laws to give way to it somewhat. And when we resist the growth of an innovation which has been introduced by violence, to hold ourselves in every thing and everywhere

Of Custom

in check and bound by rule, while our opponents have full liberty,[77] to whom every thing is permissible that can advance their purpose,—who have no other law or rule to follow than their own advantage,—imposes a hazardous obligation and disparity. *He who puts faith in a treacherous man gives entrance to harm.*[78] For the ordinary polity of a state in good health does not provide for such extraordinary accidents; it presupposes a body which is composed of its principal members and offices, and a common consent to respect and obey it. Lawful procedure is a cold, heavy, and constrained procedure, and is not fitted to make head against a lawless and unbridled procedure.

We know that it is still matter of reproach to those two great men, Octavius[79] and Cato, in the civil wars,—the first with Sylla, the other with Cæsar,—that they allowed their country to incur the utmost extremities rather than succour it at the expense of its laws and by changing any thing. For, in truth, in those extreme emergencies, where to hold one's ground is the most to be looked for, it would be perchance more wisely done to bow the head and give way a little to the blow, rather than, persisting beyond possibility in yielding nothing, to give violence opportunity to trample every thing underfoot; and it would be better to make the laws desire to do what they can, since they can not do what they desire. Thus did he who ordered that they [the laws] should sleep four-and-twenty hours;[80] and he who for that occasion took a day out of the calendar; and that other who of the month of June made a second May.[81] Even the Lacedæmonians, who observed so religiously the laws of their country, being hampered by that one which prohibited the election of the same person twice as admiral, and, on the other hand, their affairs rendering it absolutely necessary that Lysander should again assume that office—they made, indeed, one Aracus admiral, but Lysander superintendent of the navy.[82] And with the same sort of subtlety, one of their ambassadors being sent to the Athenians to secure a change in some decree,[83] and Pericles declaring to him that it was forbidden to take away the tablet on which a law had once been set down, he [the ambassador] advised him merely to turn it over, inasmuch as that was not forbidden. It is for this that Plutarch praises Philopœmen—that, being born to command, he knew, not only how to command according to the laws, but how to command the laws themselves when public necessity required it.[84]

Chapter XXIV

DIFFERENT RESULTS

OF THE

SAME COUNSEL

JACQUES AMYOT, grand almoner of France, told me one day this story to the honour of a prince of ours,[1] —and ours he was, by very good titles, although he was of foreign descent,—that, during our first troubles, at the siege of Rouen, that prince, having been warned by the queen-mother of a conspiracy against his life, and distinctly informed by her letters of the leader in its conduct, who was a gentleman of Anjou or Le Mans,—at that time, with this end in view, frequently with the prince's household,—he told no one of this warning, but the next day, walking on Mont Sainte-Catherine, from which our guns were trained on Rouen (for it was at the time that we were laying siege to it), having by his side the said lord almoner and another bishop, he descried the gentleman he had been told of, and had him summoned before him. When he was in his presence, observing that he was already turning pale and trembling from his conscience sounding the alarm, "Monsieur So-and-so," said the prince, "you suspect why I have sent for you, and your face shews it. You have nothing to conceal from me, for I am so fully acquainted with this affair of yours, that you would only make your plight the worse by trying to cover it. You are aware of this and that thing [which were points[2] of the most secret parts of the plot]; do not, on your life, fail to confess to me the truth about this whole project." When the unfortunate man found that he was caught and convicted,—for every thing had been revealed to the queen by one of the confederates,—he could only, with clasped hands, implore the prince's pardon and mercy, at whose feet he would have thrown himself; but he prevented him from so doing, and went on to say: "Look you—have I ever offended you? have I injured any of your associates by private enmity? It is not three weeks since I first knew you: what motive can have impelled you to undertake my death?" To this the gentleman replied, in a trembling voice, that no private reasons had moved him, but the general interest of his party's cause; and that certain persons had persuaded him that it would be a pious deed to make away with so powerful an enemy of their form of faith by any means whatsoever. "Now," pursued the prince, "I propose to shew you how much milder is the form of faith which I follow than that which you profess. Yours induced you to kill me without hearing me, having received no injury at my hands; and mine commands me to forgive you, convicted as you are of having desired, without cause, to kill me. Now go, take yourself off, and let me never see you here again; and, if you are wise, henceforth in your undertakings take better men than those for your advisers."

The Emperor Augustus, being in Gaul,[3] received reliable warning of a conspiracy that Lucius Cinna was brewing against him. He determined to be revenged, and to that end summoned a council of his friends for the next day. But the intervening night he passed in great disquiet, reflecting that

164

Different Results of Counsel

he was about to put to death a young man of good family and a nephew of the great Pompey; and in his dejection conceived several contrary arguments. "How then!" he exclaimed; "shall it be said that I live on in fear and alarm, and that I let my murderer go his way unharmed? Shall he go free, having aimed at my life, which I have brought safely through so many civil wars, so many battles by sea and land, and after I have established universal peace throughout the world? Shall he be absolved, when he had plotted, not simply to murder me, but to sacrifice me?" For the intention was to kill him as he was offering some sacrifice. Then, having been quiet for a time, he began again, in a louder voice, and apostrophised himself: "Why do you live, if it seems to so many people important that you should die? Is there to be no end to your vengeances and your cruelties? Is your life worth so much harm being done to preserve it?"

Livia, his wife, perceiving his perplexities, said to him: "Will feminine counsels be entertained? Do what physicians do: when the usual remedies are of no avail, they try contrary ones. By severity you have hitherto in no wise profited. Lepidus followed Salvidienus; Murena, Lepidus; Cæpio, Murena; Egnatius, Cæpio. Begin to try how mildness and clemency will succeed with you. Cinna is convicted —pardon him; henceforth he will be unable to injure you, and it will redound to your glory."

Augustus was well pleased to have found an advocate of his own inclination, and having thanked his wife and countermanded his friends whom he had summoned to take counsel, ordered that Cinna, quite alone, should be brought before him; and having sent every one from the room and given Cinna a seat, he addressed him thus: "In the first place, Cinna, I ask you to listen quietly: do not interrupt me; I will give you time to reply at your leisure. You know, Cinna, that, having found you in the camp of my enemies, —you not having simply made yourself my enemy, but being so by birth,—I protected you; I put all your property in your hands, and, in short, made you so well-to-do and so at ease, that the victors are envious of the situation of the vanquished. The office in the priesthood which you asked of me, I granted you, having refused it to others whose fathers had always fought by my side. After being so indebted to me, you have proposed to kill me." At these words Cinna exclaimed that such a wicked thought was far from him. "You are not keeping the promise that you made me, Cinna," Augustus continued; "you assured me that I should not be interrupted. Yes, you have proposed to kill me, at such a place, on such a day, with such companions, and in such a manner." Seeing that he was appalled by this information, and that he was silent, no longer because of his bargain to say nothing, but from his crowding thoughts, "Why," he added, "do you do it? Is it to be emperor? To-day it is ill with public affairs, if I am the only obstacle to your attaining supreme power. You can not even defend your own family, and you lately lost a lawsuit against a mere freedman.[4] What! have you no resources or power in any other matter than to attack the emperor? I renounce the office, if I alone stand in the way of your hopes. Do you think that Paulus or Fabius, that the Cossæans and the Servilians will tolerate you? and so great a throng of nobles —not noble in name alone, but who honour their nobility by their valour?" After many other remarks (for he talked

Different Results of Counsel

to him for more than two full hours), "Now go," he said; "I give to you, Cinna, a traitor and parricide, the life that I gave you before as a foe. Let friendship this day begin between us: let us see which of us is the more loyal, I who have given you your life, or you who have accepted it." And so he parted from him. Some time after, he gave him the consulship, lamenting that he [Cinna] had not dared to ask it of him. He was regarded by him [Augustus] thenceforth as a devoted friend, and was made by him his sole heir. Now, after this incident, which happened to Augustus in his fortieth year, there was never any conspiracy or enterprise against him, and he received the due reward of this clemency on his part. But our prince had not the same fortune; for his mildness was unable to protect him from falling afterward into the net of a similar treason.[5] So vain and idle a thing is human circumspection! and amid all our plans, our counsels and precautions, fortune always retains the control of events.

We call physicians lucky when they attain some good result, as if there were no art but theirs which can not sustain itself unaided, and whose bases are too weak to be leaned on with its whole weight, and as if it alone needed to have chance and fortune lend a hand in its operations. I believe the worst or the best of it that you choose, for we have, God be praised! no commerce together. I am different from other men: for I despise it heartily at all times; but when I am ill, instead of arranging a compromise, I begin still more to hate it and fear it, and I reply to those who urge me to take physic, that they may at least wait until I have recovered my health and my strength, and have more power to sustain the working and the hazards of their draught. I let Nature do her work, assuming that she is supplied with teeth and claws to defend herself from the assaults that are made upon her, and to maintain this contexture of which she dreads the dissolution. I fear lest in thus aiding her, when she is in close grapple, struggling with the disease, we aid her adversary instead, and burden her with new work.

Now I say that, not in medicine alone, but in many arts more certain, fortune plays a large part. The poetic impulses which carry away him who begets them, and snatch him out of himself—why shall we not ascribe them to his good luck, since he himself confesses that they surpass his ability and his powers, and recognises them as coming from elsewhere than himself, and as being in no wise under his control; just as orators say that they have not under their control those exceptional emotions and agitations which impel them beyond their purpose? It is the same in painting —that at times there escape from the painter's hand strokes surpassing his conception and his knowledge, which draw forth his own admiration and astonish him. But fortune shows even more clearly the share that she has in all these works by the charms and beauties which are found therein, not only without the intention, but even without the knowledge of the workman. A competent reader often discovers in another's writings other perfections than those which the author has consciously imparted to them,[6] and lends to them a richer meaning and aspect.

As for military undertakings, every one can see how large a part fortune has in them. Even in our councils and our deliberations, it is certain that there is an admixture of chance and good luck; for all that our wisdom can do does not amount to much; the more keen and more alert it is, the

Different Results of Counsel

more weakness it detects in itself, and distrusts itself so much the more. I am of Sylla's opinion,[7] and when I scrutinise closely the most glorious exploits of war, I see, so it seems to me, that those who conduct them employ in them deliberation and advice only as a matter of form, and the larger part of the enterprise they abandon to fortune; and from the trust they have in her aid, they often go beyond the bounds of all judgement. There result chance outbursts of energy and unlooked-for spasms of wrath[8] in their deliberations, which impel them most frequently to make the choice apparently least well founded, and which swell their courage beyond reason; whence it has happened that several great captains of old, in order to give weight to these rash counsels, declared to their soldiers that they were suggested by some inspiration, by some sign of prognostic. Here is the reason why, in this uncertainty and perplexity caused by our inability to see and choose what is most fitting for the difficulties that the varying casualties and circumstances of every event bring with them, the safest way, even if no other consideration suggested it to us, is, in my opinion, to throw oneself on the side on which are the most uprightness and justice; and when one is in doubt as to the shortest road, to take always the straight one;[9] just as in the two examples which I have set forth there is no doubt that it was nobler and more generous in him who had received the wrong to forgive it, than if he had done otherwise. If for the first[10] there was ill success, it should not be attributed to that good intent of his; and we do not know whether, had he taken the contrary course, he would have escaped the end to which his destiny summoned him; and then he would have lost the glory of such humane conduct.

Different Results of Counsel

We see in histories very many men moved by this sort of dread, of which the larger number have followed the method of forerunning, by vengeance and by punishments, the conspiracies against them; but I see very few to whom this remedy has been of use—witness so many Roman emperors. He who finds himself in this danger should not hope much either from his strength or from his vigilance; for how difficult is it to shield oneself against an enemy who wears the mask of the most assiduous friend we have, and to know the inward desires and thoughts of those who are about us. It avails him little to employ foreign soldiers for his guard, and to be constantly surrounded by a hedge of armed men —he who holds his own life cheap can always make himself master of another's.[11] And then this constant suspicion, which makes the prince doubt every one, must wonderfully torment him. For this reason, Dion, being warned that Callipus was watching for the means of bringing about his death, was never minded to search into the matter, saying that he liked better to die than to live in this wretched plight of having to guard himelf, not only against his foes, but against his friends as well.[12] A feeling which Alexander shewed forth much more vividly and more courageously by deed, when, having been warned by a letter from Parmenion that Philip, his favourite physician, had been bribed by Darius's money to poison him, at the same moment that he gave Philip the letter to read, he drank off the draught that he [Philip] had handed him.[13] Was not this giving expression to the determination that, if his friends wished to kill him, he consented to their doing so?[14] This prince is the supreme pattern of venturesome deeds; but I know not any feature in his life which shewed, from so many points of view, more firmness, or a more honourable beauty. They who teach princes such watchful distrust, under colour of teaching them [to regard only] their safety, teach them their ruin and their shame. Nothing noble is done without risk. I know a man of very valorous and enterprising spirit by nature, whose good fortune is marred every day by such arguments as this: "Let him be surrounded by his friends; let him listen to no reconciliation with his former foes; let him stand apart and not trust himself to stronger hands, whatever promise may be made to him, whatever advantage he may see therein." I know another who has forwarded his fortunes beyond all hope by having taken directly contrary advice. The courage of which they seek the glory so eagerly displays itself, when there is need, as nobly in a doublet as in armour; in the study as in camp; with the hand at the side as with hand upraised.[15]

Prudence, so sensitive and so circumspect, is the mortal enemy of lofty actions. Scipio, to discover the intentions of Syphax, ventured to leave his army, abandoning Spain, still insecure after his recent conquest, and crossed over to Africa in two small barks, trusting himself on hostile territory, to the power of a barbarian king, to an unknown faith, without any pledge, without hostage, under the sole security of the mightiness of his own courage, of his good fortune, and of the promise of his lofty hopes.[16] *Faith in another often makes reciprocal faith obligatory.*[17] On the other hand, an ambitious and distinguished life must give way little to suspicions, and must hold a tight rein on them;[18] fear and distrust attract crime and invite it. The most suspicious of our kings[19] assured his transactions chiefly through having voluntarily abandoned and entrusted his life and liberty to the hands of his enemies, showing that he had entire confidence in them, to the end that they might have the same in him. To his legions when they had mutinied and risen in arms against him, Cæsar opposed only the authority of his countenance and the haughtiness of his speech, and counted so fully on himself and his fortune that he did not fear to give himself up and entrust himself to a seditious and rebellious army.

> He stood firmly on a grassy mound, undaunted in bearing; and he deserved to be feared, for he feared nothing.[20]

But it is quite true that this stout self-assurance can not be exhibited to the full and sincerely except by those to whom the idea of death and of the worst that may after all happen causes no terror; for to shew it forth tremblingly, and, while in doubt and uncertainty, to aid in an important pacification, avails nothing. It is an excellent means of gaining the heart and good-will of another, to meet him with submission and trust, provided it be done freely and not compelled by any necessity, and with the obligatory condition that we bring thither a serene and pure confidence, our countenance at least clear of all sign of distrust. I saw in my boyhood a gentleman who governed a large city hard pressed by the commotion of a frenzied populace. To suppress the turmoil at the beginning, he decided to go out from a very safe place where he was, and to meet this rebellious mob, which turned out ill for him, and he was miserably killed; but it does not seem to me that his mistake lay so much in the having gone out, for which his memory is commonly reproached, as in the having adopted the course of submis-

sion and mildness, and in the having sought to soothe that
fury rather by flattering than by commanding, and by beseeching rather than by remonstrating; and I consider that
a gracious severity, with a military word of command full of
security and confidence, befitting his rank and the dignity
of his office, would have had better issue, at least, with
greater honour and becomingness. There is nothing less to
be hoped for from that monster when thus aroused than
humanity and tractableness;[21] it is much more accessible to[22]
respect and fear. I should blame him also because, having
formed a resolution, which was to my mind rather brave
than rash, of throwing himself, powerless and unarmed,[23]
into that tempestuous sea of madmen, he should have held
it to the end, and should not have dropped the character he
had assumed,[24] whereas when, on a closer view, he became
fainthearted,[25] and the submissive and flattering bearing he
had assumed was then exchanged even for an air of terror,
his voice and his eyes filled with consternation and repentance, and he, seeking to slink away and hide, inflamed their
passions and called them down upon himself.

It was proposed to hold a general muster of different
bodies of troops under arms[26] (it is the place for secret re-
vengements, and there is no place where they can be managed with greater security). There were public and notorious symptoms that it boded no good to some persons to
whom fell the principal and necessary duty of reviewing
them. Many different suggestions were put forward, it
being a difficult matter and one of much weight, on which
much depended. My opinion was that, above all things,
giving any indication of this suspicion should be avoided;
and that we should be there, and mingle with the rank and

file, with head erect and open countenance; and that, instead of cutting out anything (which the other opinions favoured most), we should, on the contrary, urge the officers to notify the troops to make their volleys full and gallant,[27] in honour of those present, and not to spare their powder. This served to gratify the suspected troops, and engendered thenceforth a mutual and useful confidence between us and them.[28]

The course that Julius Cæsar took appears to me the finest that can be. First, he tried, by clemency, to make himself beloved even by his enemies, contenting himself with regard to the conspiracies that were revealed to him by simply making it known that he had been warned about them. That done, he adopted the very noble resolution of awaiting, without dread and without solicitude, whatever might happen to him, taking no thought for himself, and committing himself to the keeping of the gods and of fortune; for surely, that was his frame of mind when he was killed.[29]

A stranger said and proclaimed everywhere that he could inform Dionysius, tyrant of Syracuse, of a way to scent out and discover with absolute certainty the schemes that his subjects hatched against him, if he would give him a round sum of money. Dionysius, having notice of this, had him brought before him, to enlighten him about an art so essential to his preservation. The stranger told him that there was no other art in it than that he should order a talent to be given him, and should boast of having learned an extraordinary secret from him. Dionysius thought this device excellent, and had six hundred crowns counted out to him. It was not likely that he had given so large a sum to an un-

Different Results of Counsel

known man except as recompense for very useful instruction;[30] and that repute served to keep his enemies in fear. For this reason, princes wisely make public the information they receive of secret plots devised against their lives, in order to have it believed that they are well warned, and that nothing can be undertaken without their smelling it.[31] The Duke of Athens did many foolish things in establishing his new tyranny over Florence; but the most notable was this: that, having received the first notice of the factious combinations which the people were forming against him from Mattheo di Morozo, one of the conspirators, he had him put to death, in order to suppress this information, and to avoid its being perceived that any one in the city was weary of his sway.[32]

I remember to have read at some time the story of some Roman, a person of rank, who, flying from the tyranny of the Triumvirate, had eluded innumerable times the grasp of his pursuers by his crafty devices. It happened one day that a troop of horse, who were commissioned to capture him, passed very close to a thicket in which he was lurking, and failed to discover him. But, at that juncture, reflecting upon the trouble and difficulties he had already endured so long, to save himself from the constant and careful search for him that was made in all directions, and [reflecting upon] the little pleasures that he could hope for in such a life, and how much better it would be for him to go once the way of all flesh,[33] than to live always in this extreme fear, he himself recalled them and betrayed his hiding-place, voluntarily abandoning himself to their cruelty, in order to relieve them and himself from further trouble.[34] To summon the hands of one's enemies is a somewhat fantastic step;[35] nevertheless do I believe that it would still be better to take it than to remain in perpetual feverish fear of a casualty which has no remedy. Also, since the preparations we can make for that are full of uneasiness and uncertainty, the better way is to make ourselves ready with becoming assurance for whatever may happen, and derive some consolation from the fact that we are not sure that it will happen.

Chapter XXV

OF PEDANTRY

I WAS often vexed in my boyhood by seeing, in the Italian comedies, a pedant[1] always the fool of the piece, and the title of schoolmaster[2] had a scarcely more honourable significance among us. For being under their control and care, how could I help being sensitive about their reputation? I tried hard to excuse them by the natural disparity there is between most people and persons of unusual judgement and learning, inasmuch as these and those pursue entirely different courses. But in this I wasted my pains,[3] for the men of widest experience were the ones who held them most in contempt; witness our worthy du Bellay: "But I detest above all things pedantic learning." And this habit is an ancient one; for Plutarch says that Greek and scholar were words of reproach and scorn among the Romans.[4] Afterward, as I grew older, I found that there was a very great reason for this, and that *the greatest scholars are not the wisest men.*[5] But how it can be that a mind rich in the knowledge of so many things does not thereby become more alive and more awake, and that an uncultivated and common-place intelligence can retain, without improvement, the arguments and opinions of the most excellent minds

Of Pedantry

that the world has produced, by this I am still perplexed.

"To receive so many alien brains and such great and powerful ones," said a daughter of France, the highest of our princesses,[6] to me, speaking of some one or other, "it must be that his own brain crowds itself into a corner, cramps, and diminishes itself, to make room for the others." I should be inclined to say that, as plants are choked by too much moisture, and lamps by too much oil, so the action of the mind, through an excess of study and of subjects, being seized and embarrassed by so great a diversity of things, would lose the power of freeing itself, and this burden would keep it bent and cowering.[7] But the fact is otherwise; for our mind expands the more, the more it is filled; and by the examples of old days, it may be seen, quite to the contrary, that men of competence in the handling of public matters, great captains, and eminent counsellors in state affairs, have been also very learned men.

And as to the philosophers, withdrawn from all public employment, they were, in truth, sometimes treated with contempt by the comic poets[8] of their day, their opinions and their manners making them ridiculous. Would you make them judges of the merits of a law-suit, of a man's acts? They are quite ready for it! they are even trying to find out whether there is life; whether there is motion; whether man is different from an ox; what it is to act and to suffer; what sort of animals the laws and justice are. Do they speak of the magistrate or to him? they do so with disrespectful and discourteous freedom. Do they hear a prince praised, or a king? to them he is a mere shepherd, lazy as a shepherd, occupied with milking and shearing his flock, but much more roughly than a shepherd. Do you think some

man the greater for possessing two thousand acres of land?
they scoff at that, accustomed to look upon the whole world
as their possession. Do you boast of your nobility because
you can reckon seven wealthy ancestors? they think slight-
ingly of you, as having no conception of the universal image
of nature, and of how many forbears each of us has had—
rich, poor, kings, servants, Greeks, and barbarians; and if
you are the fiftieth in descent from Hercules, they deem you
absurd to attach value to that gift of fortune.[9] So the vulgar
despised them as being ignorant of simple and most common
things, and as presumptuous and insolent. But this Platonic
description is far removed from what befits those whom we
speak of.

The ancient philosophers were condemned as being
above common customs, as holding in contempt public doings, as having assumed a special and inimitable manner
of life, conformed to certain lofty and unusual principles;
but these of our day are despised as being below common
customs, as incapable of public service, as leading, in the
eyes of the vulgar, a life of low and vile condition. *I hate
men of cowardly deeds and philosophical phrases*.[10] As for
those philosophers, say I, as they were great in learning,
they were even greater in all action. And just as it was told
of the geometrician of Syracuse that, when he was aroused
from his contemplation to do something practical for the defence of his country, he instantly set on foot terrible engines
and forces surpassing all human belief, yet, none the less,
himself despised all that handiwork of his, and thought that
he had thereby impaired the dignity of his art, of which his
works were only, as it were, experiments;[11] so they,[12] when
sometimes they were put to the test of action, were seen to

soar on so lofty a wing that it clearly appeared that their hearts and minds must be marvellously enlarged and enriched by their understanding of things. But some of them, seeing the seat of political government seized upon by incapable men, recoiled from it; and he who asked Crates how long it was necessary to study philosophy received this reply: "Until our armies are not led by donkey-drivers."[13] Heraclitus resigned the kingship to his brother; and when the Ephesians charged him with wasting his time playing with children in front of the temple, "Is not this better worth doing than to rule affairs of state in your companionship?" he asked.[14] Others, whose imaginations dwelt above fortune and the world, found the seats of justice, and even the thrones of kings, low and vile. And Empedocles refused the kingship which the Agrigentines offered him.[15] Thales, having sometimes blamed the care taken about domestic affairs, and to get rich, was charged with talking like the fox, since he himself could not succeed therein. The desire came to him to test this, as a pastime; and having, to that end, brought down his knowledge to the service of profit and gain, he set up a commerce which in a year drew in such wealth that those most experienced in that business could scarcely in their whole lives do the like.[16]

As to what Aristotle tells us of some persons who called both this man and Anaxagoras and their like, sages and not prudent men, since they did not pay enough heed to matters of more utility,[17]—though I do not clearly conceive this verbal distinction,—it offers no excuse for these persons;[18] and in view of the low and necessitous lot with which they content themselves, we should rather be justified in declaring them to be neither sages nor prudent men.

Of Pedantry

I leave this first reason,[19] and think it better worth while to say that this ill-repute comes from their wretched method in their studies, and that, considering the way in which we are instructed, it is no wonder that neither scholars nor masters become more able, although they may make themselves more learned. In truth, the care and outlay of our fathers aim only at furnishing our heads with learning; concerning good judgement and virtue there is little thought.[20] Cry out to our people, of one passer-by, "Oh, the learned man!" and of another, "Oh, the excellent man!" they will not fail to turn their eyes and their respect toward the first.[21] There should be a third exclamation: "Oh, the blockheads!" We readily ask ourselves: "Does he know Greek or Latin? Does he write in verse or in prose?" but whether he has become better or more thoughtful—that is the principal thing, and that is left in the background. The enquiry should be, who is the best learned, not who is the most learned.[22] We labour only to fill the memory, and we leave the understanding and the conscience empty. Just as birds go at times in quest of grain and carry it in their beaks without tasting it, to feed it to their little ones,[23] so our pedants go about picking up learning from books and take it only in their tongues, simply to void it and make parade of it.[24]

It is a wonder how nicely this folly finds an example in me. Is it not doing the same thing that I do in the greater part of this composition? I go about, here and there, carrying away from books sentences which please me, not to keep them in mind, for I have no memory,[25] but to transport them hither, where, to tell the truth, they are no more mine than when in their original place. We are, in my opinion, learned only through immediate knowledge, not through that of the past, as little as through that of the future. But, what is worse, their pupils and their little ones are in no wise nourished and fed by it: instead, it passes from hand to hand, for the sole purpose of making a show of it, of talking of it to others, and of telling stories from it, as it were false coin, useless for any other purpose and business than as counters and for calculation.[26] *They have learned to talk with others, not with themselves.*[27] *The important thing is not talk, but conduct*.[28] Nature, to show that there is nothing rude in what is guided by her, causes the birth, in nations least cultivated by art, of productions of the intelligence which often vie with the most artistic productions. On my present subject, how subtle is the Gascon proverb, derived from the bagpipe: "Bouha prou bouha, mas a remuda lous ditz qu'em" (Blow hard, blow; but we have still to move the fingers).[29] We learn to say: "Cicero so says; such is Plato's character; these are Aristotle's very words." But what do we ourselves say? what is our judgement?[30] A parrot could speak as wisely. This sort of thing reminds me of that wealthy Roman[31] who had taken pains to find, at very great expense, men competent in all branches of knowledge, whom he kept constantly about him, so that when, among his friends, the occasion should arise to talk of one thing or another, they should come to his assistance, and should be quite ready to furnish him, this one with a speech, that one with a line of Homer—each according to his studies;[32] and he believed this learning to be his own, because it was in the heads of his attendants; and as those also do,[33] whose learning resides in their costly libraries. I am acquainted with a man who, when I ask him what he knows, asks me for a book, that he may show me; and he would not venture to tell me that he had the itch on his rump, without first going to the lexicon,[34] to study about the itch and about the rump.

We take into our keeping the opinions and knowledge of others, and that is all; we should make them ours. We much resemble the man who, having need of fire, should go to his neighbour in search of it, and, having found a fine big blaze there, should stay to warm himself, quite forgetting to carry any home.[35] What does it avail us to have a stomach full of food, if it does not digest, if it does not become transformed within us, if it does not increase our size and strength? Do we think that Lucullus, whom letters made and fashioned into so great a captain, without experience,[36] regarded them as we do? We allow ourselves to lean so heavily on the shoulders of others, that we enfeeble our own powers. Do I desire to arm myself against the fear of death? It is from Seneca's storehouse. Do I desire to obtain consolation for myself or another? I borrow it from Cicero. I should have found it in myself if I had been practised in so doing. I do not like this derived and solicited competency. Even if we could be learned with another's learning, in any case we can be wise only with our own wisdom.

I hate the wise man who is not wise in his own affairs.[37]

As to which Ennius [says]: Fruitless is wisdom to the wise man if he himself can not profit by it.[38]

If greedy, false, and weaker than a Euganean lamb.[39]

For wisdom should not only be acquired by us, but be enjoyed.[40] Dionysius derided the grammarians who investigate so carefully the misfortunes of Ulysses and are ignorant of their own; the musicians who tune their flutes, but do not

Of Pedantry

tune their morals; the orators who study to speak justly but not so to act.[41]

If our minds do not go a livelier pace,[42] if we have not a sounder judgement, I would as lief that the student had passed his time playing at tennis; at least, his body would be the better for it. See him when he returns home after thus spending fifteen or sixteen years: there is nothing in the world so unfitted to be employed; all the gain you can see in him is that his Latin and Greek have made him prouder and more vain-glorious than when he left home. He should bring his mind back well filled; he does bring it back only swollen; he has merely inflated it instead of fattening it. These teachers, as Plato remarks of the Sophists,[43] who are closely akin to them, are of all men those who promise to be most useful to mankind; and alone of all men, they not only do not improve what is entrusted to them, as a carpenter does and a mason, but they injure it and exact payment for injuring it. If the rule were followed which Protagoras proposed to his disciples,[44] that they should either pay him his own price, or should swear in the temple what value they set on the profit they had received from his teaching, and according to that should recompense his painstaking—our pedagogues would find themselves disappointed, were they referred back to the asseveration of my own experience.

My Perigordian dialect very wittily calls these dullards[45] "Lettreferits"—to whom letters have dealt a sledgehammer blow, as they say. In truth, they seem in most cases to have sunk even below common sense. For you see the peasant and the cobbler go simply and naturally about their business, talking of what they know; these men, because they would exalt themselves and bluster with the knowledge

that floats on the surface of their brains, are always entang-
ling and encumbering themselves. They let fall fine words,
but that another may apply them; they are familiar with
Galen, but know nothing of disease; they have gone so far
as to fill their heads with laws, but none the more have they
apprehended the chief point of the case; they know the the-
oric of every thing—find one of them who can put it in practice. I have seen, in my house, a friend of mine, in intercourse
with such a man, concoct, by way of pastime, a farrago
of nonsense, incoherent sentences, made up of borrowed
phrases,—save that it was often interlarded with words appropriate to their discussion,—and thus keep this dunce
debating for a whole day, thinking always that he was answering the arguments which were brought against him.
None the less, he was a man of letters and of reputation and
one who had a high position.[46]

O you of patrician blood, whom nature has made
blind to all that lies behind you, turn and face the grimaces that are made behind your back.[47]

Whoever shall look closely at this class of persons, which
is very widespread, will find, as I have, that, for the most
part, they understand neither themselves nor others, and
that, while their memory is quite full, their judgement is
wholly empty, unless their nature has of itself fashioned
them otherwise; as I have seen with Adrianus Turnebus,
who, having no other profession but letters, in which he was,
in my opinion, the greatest man who had been for a thousand years, had nevertheless nothing pedantic about him
save the way he wore his gown, and something in his external manner which could never be formed into courtliness—

Of Pedantry

which are mere trifles. And I detest people who find it
harder to put up with a gown awry than with a soul awry,
and who see in a man's salutation, in his demeanour, and in
his boots, what sort of man he is. For within, his was the
most polite soul in the world. I have often purposely drawn
him into talk far removed from his experience: he was so
clear-sighted, his apprehension was so quick, his judgement
so sound, that it seemed as if he had never had other occupation than war and statecraft. Those are beautiful and
powerful natures—

> Whose hearts the Titan fashioned with kindly art
> and with better clay[48]

which carry themselves rightly in spite of a poor education.
Now it is not enough that our education should not spoil
us: it must change us for the better.[49]

There are some of our parliaments which, when they are
to admit magistrates, examine them only upon their learning; others add to this a test of their understanding, giving
them some case to pass judgement upon. These latter seem
to me to have much the better method; and while both these
qualities are necessary, and it is essential that both should
exist, yet in truth that of learning is less valuable than that
of judgement; the last can get along without the first, but
not the first without the last. For, as that Greek verse says,—

> I hate the wise man who is not wise in his own affairs.[50]

Of what use is learning, if understanding is lacking? Would
God that for the good of our judicature those companies
were found as well supplied with understanding and conscience as they are even now with learning. *We learn, not*

Of Pedantry

about life, but about matters of discussion.[51] Now we must
not fasten learning to the mind, but incorporate it therewith;[52] with it we must not sprinkle the mind—we must
colour it;[53] and if it does not change the mind and improve
its imperfect state, surely it is much better to leave it alone; it
is a dangerous weapon, which impedes and injures its master
if it is in a feeble hand which does not know how to use it,
so that it had been better not to have learned at all.[54] Perchance this is the reason that neither we nor the church demand much learning of women, and that Francis, Duke of
Brittany, son of Jean the Fifth, when they suggested to him
his marriage to Isabeau of Scotland, and added that she had
been brought up simply and without any instruction in letters, replied that he liked her the better for that, and that a
woman knew enough when she knew how to distinguish
between the shirt and the doublet of her husband.[55]

In truth, it is not so great a marvel as it is considered, that
our ancestors did not set great store by learning,[56] and that
now it is found only by accident in the chief councils of our
kings; and if this purpose of enriching ourselves,—which
alone is set before us to-day,[57]—by means of jurisprudence,
of medicine, of pedagogy, and even of divinity, did not keep
it in credit, you would find it doubtless in as wretched plight
as it ever was. Why not? if it teaches us neither to think
well nor to do well? *Since learned men have appeared, good
men are lacking.*[58]

All other knowledge is harmful to him who has not the
knowledge of goodness. But the reason I was seeking just
now,[59] would it not also come from this, that, since our
studies in France have no other aim than profit,—few whom
Nature has destined from birth for functions more noble

187

than lucrative devote themselves to letters, or for but a short time (being withdrawn, before they have taken a liking for them, to a vocation which has nothing in common with books),—there are ordinarily left to apply themselves to study only persons of small means who are therein seeking a livelihood? And the minds of those persons being, both by nature and by home training and example, of the poorest quality, make a false application of the fruit of knowledge; for it is not hers to give light to that mind which has none, or to make a blind man see; it is not her business to supply him with vision, but to train his vision, to direct its steps, provided that it has well-made and strong feet and legs of its own.

An excellent drug is learning, but no drug is powerful enough to keep itself from change and corruption if there are baneful qualities in the vessel that contains it. A man may have clearness of sight and not see straight;[60] and consequently he sees the good and does not follow it, sees knowledge and makes no use of it. The chief precept of Plato, in his *Republic*,[61] is to assign to its citizens their offices according to their natures. Nature can do and does every thing. The lame are ill adapted to bodily exercises, and lame minds to mental exercises; degenerate and common minds are unworthy of philosophy. When we see a man ill shod, we say it is no wonder, if he is a shoemaker; in like manner it seems to me that experience often shows to us a physician worse physicked, a divine less amended, a scholar less able, than any other. Aristo Chius had in old times grounds for saying that philosophers were harmful to their listeners, inasmuch as the greater number of minds are not adapted to profit by such instruction, which, if it does not lead to good, leads to

evil: *they go forth from the school of Aristippus de-
bauched, from that of Zeno soured.*[62]

In that excellent system of education which Xenophon
attributes to the Persians,[63] we find that they taught virtue
to their children as other nations teach letters. Plato says[64]
that, in their royal family, the oldest son was brought up
thus: after birth he was given over, not to women, but to
those eunuchs who had the highest reputation in the king's
household because of their virtue. They assumed the duty
of making his body beautiful and sound, and after seven
years they taught him to ride and to hunt. When he reached
his fourteenth year, they placed him in the hands of four
men: the wisest, the most upright, the most temperate, and
the bravest of the nation. The first taught him religion, the
second to be always truthful, the third to make himself
master of unworthy desires, the fourth to fear nothing.

It is a matter worthy of very serious consideration, that,
in that excellent form of government of Lycurgus,[65]—in
truth, it was a prodigy from its perfection,—although so
heedful of the bringing up of children as its principal office,
and in the very resting-place of the Muses, there is so little
mention made of scholarship; as if those noble-minded
youths, disdaining any other yoke than that of virtue, had to
be supplied only with masters in valour, discretion, and
justice, instead of masters in learning; an example which
Plato followed in his *Laws*.[66]

The manner of their[67] teaching was to put questions to
them of judgement of men and of actions; and if they condemned or praised this person or that act, they were required to give their reasons for what they said, and by this
method they, at one and the same time, sharpened their un-

derstanding and learned the law. Astyages, in Xenophon, asks Cyrus to tell him about his last lesson.[68] "In our school," he says, "there was a big boy who, having a small jacket, gave it to a schoolmate who was smaller than he, and took from him his jacket, which was larger. Our master having made me the judge of the disagreement, I decided that things should be left as they were, and that both boys seemed to be better provided for by this arrangement. Whereupon he pointed out to me that I had done wrong, for I had gone no further than to consider the suitableness, and justice ought before all else to have been satisfied, which demanded that no one should be constrained about what belonged to him." And he says that he was flogged for this, just as we are in our village [schools] for forgetting the aorist of τύπτω. A schoolmaster of to-day[69] might harangue me at length *in genere demonstrativo*, before he could convince me that his system is equal to that one. They chose to shorten the way; and since learning, even when it is taken in a direct manner,[70] can teach us only discretion, loyalty, and resolution, they chose to put their children from the beginning in the midst of facts,[71] and to instruct them, not by hearsay, but by the test of action, shaping and moulding them vigorously, not by precepts and words alone, but chiefly by examples and works, to the end that knowledge should not be a thing lodged in their mind,[72] but its complexion and habit; that it should not be an acquisition, but a natural endowment. Some one asked Agesilaus what in his opinion children should learn. "What they must do when they are men," he replied.[73] It is no wonder that such an education produced results so admirable.

Men used to go to the other cities of Greece, it is said,

Of Pedantry

in search of orators, painters, and musicians, but to Lacedæmon for legislators, magistrates, and generals; at Athens they learned to talk wisely, here to do wisely; there to extricate themselves from a sophistical argument and to frustrate the imposture of words craftily intertwined, here to extricate themselves from the allurements of pleasure and to frustrate with a high heart the threats of fortune and of death; there men were occupied about words, here about things; there there was continual exercising of the tongue, here continual exercising of the mind. Wherefore it is not strange that, when Antipater demanded of them fifty children as hostages, they replied, altogether contrary to what we should do, that they would rather give twice as many grown men, at so high a cost did they value the loss of the education of their country.[74] When Agesilaus invites Xenophon to send his children to Sparta to be educated, it is not to learn rhetoric or dialectics, but to learn, so he says, the noblest art that there is, namely, the art of obedience and of command.[75] It is very amusing to see how Socrates, after his fashion, laughs at Hippias[76] when he tells him how he has earned, chiefly in certain small hamlets in Sicily, a good sum of money by teaching, and that in Sparta he has not earned a farthing; that they are stupid folk, who can neither measure nor reckon, who make no account either of grammar or of rhythm, caring only to know the succession of their kings, the rise and fall of states, and such a jumble of idle stories. And at the end of it all, Socrates, forcing him to admit step by step the excellence of their form of public government, and the happiness and virtue of their private life, leaves him to divine, in conclusion, the uselessness of his occupation.

Of Pedantry

Examples teach us, both in the case of military concerns and in all others like them, that the study of letters more softens and weakens men's spirits than strengthens them and fits them for the fight.[77] The state which appears at the present time to be the most powerful in the world is that of the Turks, a people brought up to prize arms and to despise letters in equal measure. I find Rome to have been more valiant before she became learned.[78] In our day the most warlike nations are the most rude and ignorant: the Scythians, the Parthians, Tamburlaine, are examples that prove this. When the Goths ravaged Greece, what saved all the libraries from being burned was that one of the invaders spread abroad the idea that they had better leave that sort of article untouched to their enemies, as likely to divert them from military training and absorb them in sedentary and lazy pursuits. When our King Charles the Eighth found himself master of the Kingdom of Naples and of a large part of Tuscany, almost without drawing the sword from the scabbard, the noblemen of his suite ascribed this unhoped-for facility of conquest to the fact that the princes and nobles of Italy were more occupied in making themselves sharp-witted and learned, than sturdy and warlike.

Chapter XXVI

OF THE EDUCATION

OF CHILDREN

TO MADAME DIANE DE FOIX, COUNTESS OF GURSON[1]:

I NEVER knew a father who, however feeble or deformed his son might be, failed to acknowledge him; not, to
be sure (unless he be completely bewildered by this feeling),
that he does not perceive his defect; but, none the less, he
is his own. And I, too, I see better than any one else that
here are but the idle musings of a man who has conceived
in his childhood only the outer covering of learning,[2] and
has retained of it merely a general and shapeless impression;
a little of every thing and nothing thoroughly, after the
French fashion. For, in fine, I know that there is a science
of medicine, of jurisprudence, four divisions of mathematics,[3] and, roughly, what they aim at; and perchance I
know, also, the contribution of sciences in general to the
service of our lives. But as for pushing the matter further
and biting my nails over the study of Aristotle,[4] the monarch of modern learning, or persisting in any branch of
knowledge, I have never done it.[5] Nor is there any art of
which I can sketch so much as the first outlines. And there
is no child of the middle forms who may not think he knows

193

more than I, who have not the ability to examine him on his easiest lesson, at least, after its manner. And if I must do this, I am forced, ineptly enough, to draw from it some matter of common talk, with regard to which I examine his native judgement—a lesson that is as unfamiliar to him as his is to me. I have not been familiar with any solid book, except Plutarch and Seneca, from whom I draw like the Danaïdes, filling and emptying incessantly. So doing, something of theirs clings to this paper; to myself, so little that it is nothing.

History is my chief pursuit in the way of books; or poetry, which I love with a special inclination. For, as Cleanthes said,[6] just as the voice, when confined with the narrow channel of a trumpet, comes forth more penetratingly and more strongly, so it seems to me that the thought, being compressed within the various forms of verse, darts forth more briskly and strikes me with a livelier impact. As for the native faculties that are in me, whereof here is the trial flight, I feel them bend beneath the burden; my ideas and my judgement grope their way, staggering and stumbling and tripping; and when I have gone as far as I can, still I am in no wise content; I see, but with a disturbed and clouded vision, other regions beyond, which I can not clearly distinguish. And venturing to treat heedlessly of whatever comes into my head, and in this using only my own native resources, if it happens, as it often does, that I meet, in good authors, with the same topics that I have undertaken to discuss,—as I have but now done in Plutarch, in his discourse on the power of the imagination,[7]—on realising how weak and insignificant, how dull and lifeless I am, compared with those writers, I feel compassion or contempt for myself. But I solace myself with the fact that my opinions have the honour of often meeting with theirs, and that I follow after, although a long way behind them, saying that they are right.[8] Also I have this [quality], which not every one has, of recognising the extreme difference between them and me; and, notwithstanding, I let my conceptions go their way, as feeble and trivial as when I gave birth to them, without plastering and patching up the faults which this comparison has revealed to me. A man must have strong loins to attempt to march in the same line with such as these.[9] The indiscreet writers of our time, who intersperse in their worthless works whole passages from the ancient authors, to give themselves reputation, do just the opposite. For the infinite difference in brilliancy gives to their work an aspect so pallid, so dull, and so ugly, that by doing thus they lose much more than they gain.

There were [of old] two contrary humours. The philosopher Chrysippus scattered through his books, not passages simply, but whole works, of other authors, and in one the "Medea" of Euripides; and Apollodorus said that, if there were cut out of his work what was foreign to it, the paper would be blank.[10] Epicurus, on the other hand, in the three hundred volumes that he left, had not introduced a single alien citation.[11]

It happened the other day that I came upon such a passage.[12] I had dragged languidly along through French words so bloodless, so fleshless, and so void of substance and of sense, that they were really only French words. At the end of a long and wearisome road, I came upon a lofty, ornate fragment, rising to the clouds. Had I found the slope gradual and the ascent a little prolonged, the thing would have been pardonable; but it was a steep so sheer and abrupt that, from the first six words, I knew that I had escaped into heaven. Thence I discerned the pit from which I had come, so far below and so deep, that I have never since had the courage to go down again into it. If I should stuff out one of my discourses with these rich spoils,[13] it would throw too much light on the stupidity of the others.

To reprehend my own faults in another seems to me no more intolerant[14] than to reprehend, as I often do, those of another in myself. We must impeach them everywhere, and deprive them of every place of sanctuary. I know well how audaciously I myself often attempt to make myself equal to my purloinings, to march cheek by jowl with them, not without a rash hope that I can delude the eyes of the judges from distinguishing them; but as much by favour of my use of them, as by favour of my original ideas and my vigour. And again, I do not contend with those ancient champions all at once, hand to hand, but by repeated hits, trivial and slight touches. I do not persist, I simply examine them, and I do not go so far as I think of going. If I could keep even with them, I should do well, for I take them on only at their ablest.[15] To do what I have detected some in doing; to protect oneself with another's armour so completely as not to show even the ends of one's fingers; to clothe one's idea with old-time conceptions patched up here and there[16] (which is easy for men of learning on a subject common to all)—this, in those who seek to conceal them, and to make them seem their own, is, in the first place, wrongdoing and cowardice, because, having nothing in their own resources by which to bring themselves forward, they aim to present themselves by a purely alien value; and

Of the Education of Children

besides, it is great folly to be content with obtaining by fraud the ignorant approbation of the vulgar, while discrediting themselves in the eyes of intelligent persons whose praise alone has weight, and who turn up their noses at this borrowed veneer. For my part, there is nothing which I less desire to do. I do not quote others, save the more fully to express myself.[17] This does not concern the "centos" which are published as such; and I have seen some very ingenious ones, among others one under the name of Capilupus,[18] besides the ancient ones. There are minds which manifest themselves, both elsewise and in this wise, as Lipsius, in the learned and laborious structure of his "Politics."[19] I mean to say[20] that, however this may be, and of whatever worth these idle thoughts of mine,[21] I have not planned to conceal them, any more than a portrait of myself, bald and turning gray, in which the painter had drawn, not a perfect face, but mine.[22] For likewise these are the humours and opinions personal to me; I give them out as what I believe, not as what is to be believed; I aim here only at revealing myself, who may perchance be different to-morrow, if fresh experience changes me. I have no authority to be believed, nor do I desire to be so, feeling myself too poorly instructed to instruct another.

Some one who had read the preceding pages[23] said to me the other day, at my house, that I ought to have enlarged a little on the subject of the education of children. Well, madame, if I have any competence on that subject, I can make no better use of it than to make a present of it to the little man who threatens soon to make a happy exit from you (you are too noble by nature[24] to begin otherwise than with a boy); for, having had so large a part in the arrangement of your marriage,[25] I have some right and interest in the greatness and prosperity of all that comes from it; besides that, the long-standing claim that you have upon my service well constrains me to desire honour, good, and profit for whatever concerns you. But, really, I know nothing of this matter except that the greatest and most weighty difficulty in human knowledge seems to lie at that point where it deals with the nurture and education of children. Just as in agriculture the methods that precede planting are certain and easy, and the same with planting itself; but after what is planted has taken on life, there is a great variety of methods, and much difficulty in raising it; in like manner with men, there is little skill in planting them, but after they are born, we have a varied burden, full of toil and anxiety, in training and nurturing them.[26] The display of their inclinations is so slight and so obscure at that tender age, the promises so uncertain and so deceitful, that it is difficult to base on them sure judgements. Look at Cymon, look at Themistocles, and a thousand others, how inconsistent they were with themselves.[27] The young of bears and dogs show their native inclination; but men, being cast forthwith into the midst of usages, opinions, and laws, are easily changed or disguised.[28] Yet it is hard to overcome the natural propensities; whence it happens that, for lack of having fitly chosen their path, we often labour to no purpose, and employ much of our life in training children to things in which they can not find a footing. Howbeit, in this difficulty my judgement is to direct them always to the best and most profitable things, and that we should pay little heed to the slight conjectures and prognostications that we derive from the impulses of their childhood. Plato even, in his Republic,

Of the Education of Children

seems to me to let them enjoy far too much authority.[29]

Learning is a noble adornment, madame, and a marvellously useful tool, notably to persons raised to such a degree of fortune as you are. In fact, it is of no true use in mean and low hands. It is much more proud to lend its resources to conduct a war, to rule a people, to cultivate the friendship of a prince or a foreign nation, than to draft a dialectical argument, or to argue an appeal, or concoct a mixture for pills. And so, madame, because I believe that you will not forget this portion of the education of your children, you who have tasted its delights and who are of a lettered race,—for we have still the writings of those former Comtes de Foix from whom monsieur le comte, your husband, and you are both descended; and François, Monsieur de Candale, your uncle, gives birth every day to other writings which will extend the knowledge of this quality of your family to many ages,—I desire to tell you of one single idea of mine regarding this, which is contrary to the common wont; it is all that I can offer for your service in this matter.

The office of the tutor whom you will give him—upon the choice of whom the whole result of his education depends—has many other important duties; but I do not touch on those, because I am unable to contribute there any thing of value; and upon this one point, about which I take upon myself to give him advice, he will believe me so far as he shall see reason so to do. For a child of good family, who seeks letters and learning, not for profit (for so base an object is unworthy of the grace and favour of the Muses, and, too, it concerns and depends upon others), and not so much for external benefits as for those peculiar to himself, and to enrich and adorn himself inwardly,[30] being

199

Of the Education of Children

desirous to turn out a man of ability rather than a learned man, I should wish, moreover, that care should be taken to select a guide whose head is very sound rather than very full; and that, while both qualities should be required, good morals and understanding, rather than book-knowledge, should be the more so; and that he should carry himself in his office in a novel way. They[31] are always bawling into our ears as if pouring into a tunnel; and our business is simply to repeat what they tell us. I would have him amend this state of things, and that from the outset, according to the ability of the mind he has to deal with, he should begin to exercise it,[32] making it examine things, choose among them, and distinguish them by itself; sometimes breaking out the path for it, sometimes letting it break it out. I would not have him alone think and speak: I would have him listen while his pupil takes his turn at speaking. Socrates and, after him, Arcesilaus, first made their pupils talk, and then talked to them.[33] *The authority of those who teach is very often a hindrance to those who wish to learn.*[34] It is well that he make him trot before him, in order to judge of his paces, and to determine how far he must hold himself back to accommodate himself to his[35] powers. For lack of this proportion we mar all. And to learn how to attain it, and how to conduct oneself therein with due measure, is one of the most difficult tasks that I know; and it is a high and very strong character that knows how to stoop to his childish ways and to guide them. I walk more steadily and more sure-footedly up hill than down. Those who, as our custom is, undertake to direct several minds of such diverse measure and structure with the same lessons and similar rules of conduct—it is no wonder if, among a whole multitude of children, they find only two or three who produce any sound fruit from their teaching.

Let him not demand an account of the words of the lesson simply, but of its meaning and substance; and let him judge of the benefit that he[36] has derived, by the evidence, not of his memory, but of his life.[37] What he shall learn, make him look at it in a hundred aspects and apply it to as many different subjects, to see if he has fully apprehended it and made it his own, taking guidance for his[38] progress from the pedagogic method of Plato. It is evidence of indigestibleness and indigestion to throw up food as it has been swallowed: the stomach has not done its work if it has not changed the condition and character of what was given it to cook.

[39]Our minds act only from belief in others, tied and constrained by liking for another's opinions, enslaved and imprisoned under the authority of their instruction. We have been so subjected to trammels that we can no longer move freely; our energy and independence are lost; *they never become their own masters.*[40] I saw familiarly at Pisa an excellent man,[41] but such an Aristotelian that his strongest opinion[42] is that the touchstone and canon of all truth is conformity to the teachings of Aristotle; that outside of these there are nothing but chimeras and inanities;[43] that he saw every thing and said every thing. This position of his, because it was interpreted a little too broadly and maliciously, placed him in old times, and kept him for a long while, in great danger[44] from the Inquisition at Rome.

Let him make him sift every thing,[45] and lodge nothing in his brain on authority merely and on trust; let not Aristotle's principles be his principles, any more than those of the Stoics or Epicureans; let this diversity of opinions be put before him: he will choose if he can; if not, he will remain in doubt. None but a fool is sure and determined.[46]

For doubt, not less than knowledge, pleases me.[47]

For if he embraces the opinions of Xenophon and of Plato by his own judgement, they will no longer be their opinions, they will be his. He who follows another, follows nothing, finds nothing, nay, seeks nothing.[48] *We are not subject to a king; let each man claim his rights.*[49] Let him at least know what he knows. He must imbibe their ideas, not learn their precepts;[50] and let him boldly forget, if he will, whence he gets them, but let him learn to appropriate them to himself.[51] Every man may lay claim to truth and reason; they are no more his property who first uttered them than his who utters them later. It is no more according to Plato than according to me, since he and I understand it and see it alike. The bees pilfer from the flowers here and there,[52] but later of their booty they make honey, which is all their own; it is no longer thyme or marjoram. So with the parts borrowed from others: he will transform and blend them, to make from them a work all his own, namely, his judgement; his education, his labour, and study have no other aim than to fashion that.

Let him conceal all that by which he has been helped, and show forth only what he has made of it.[53] Plunderers and borrowers exhibit their buildings and their purchases, not what they derive from others. You do not see the fees of a parliament man, you see the alliances he has gained, and honours for his children. No one makes a public accounting of his receipts, every one of his profits. The profit of our

Of the Education of Children

study is to have become better and wiser thereby. It is the understanding which sees and hears, said Epicharmus; it is the understanding which turns every thing to profit, which makes use of every thing, which acts, which commands, and which reigns; all things else are blind and deaf and soulless.[54] Unquestionably we make it servile and cowardly when we do not leave it free to do aught of itself. Who ever asked his pupil what he thought of the rhetoric and the grammar of this or that sentence of Cicero? They fasten them tight to our memory,[55] like oracles, in which the letters and syllables are of the substance of the living. To know by heart is not to know: it is to possess what has been given into the keeping of one's memory. What we rightly know, we make use of without looking at the pattern, without turning our eyes toward the book.[56] A pitiful competence is a competence purely bookish! I look for it to serve as ornament, not as foundation, according to Plato's opinion, who said that firmness, trust, and sincerity were true philosophy; other kinds of knowledge, those which had a different aim, were but deceitful.

I should like to have Paluel or Pompey, those fine dancers of my time, teach their capers just by seeing them performed without our moving from our seats, as these persons seek to instruct our understanding without jogging it; or that we should be taught to manage a horse, or a pike, or a lute, or the voice, without practice, as these persons seek to teach us to think well and talk well, without practice in talking or thinking. Now, in this study, all that presents itself to our eyes serves as a book to learn from: the mischief of a page, the stupidity of a servant, a remark at table, are so many new subjects.[57]

Of the Education of Children

For this reason, intercourse with men is wonderfully proper for it,[58] and travel in foreign countries,[59] not simply to bring back, after the manner of our French nobility, the number of feet of the Santa Rotonda, or the elegance of Signora Livia's drawers; or, like others, how much longer or broader the face of Nero is in some old ruin, than it is on some equally old coin; but chiefly to bring back the characterstics of those nations and their manner of living, and to rub and file our wits against those of others. I would have him begin to be taken about in his tender years, and especially, to kill two birds with one stone, among the neighbouring nations whose languages are most unlike ours, to which the tongue can not be wonted unless you train it in good season. And also, it is an opinion accepted by every one that it is not well to bring up a child in the lap of his parents: their natural affection softens and relaxes them too much, even the wisest; they are capable neither of punishing his faults nor of allowing him to be nurtured roughly, as he should be, and at haphazard; they could not endure his returning sweating and dusty from his exercises, taking hot or cold drinks,[60] or to see him on a restive horse, or facing a skilful fencer, foil in hand, or his first arquebus. But there is no escape: he who would make of him a man of worth must doubtless not spare him in those early years, and must often run counter to the rules of medicine.

> Let him live under the open sky and amid dangers.[61]

It is not enough to strengthen his mind—we must strengthen his muscles also. The mind is too hard pressed if it be not supported,[62] and has too much to do to discharge alone

Of the Education of Children

two functions. I know how mine labours[63] in company with
so tender, so sensitive a body, which lets itself so greatly
depend upon it; and I often observe in my reading that my
masters, in their writings, pass off as due to magnanimity
and high spirit, examples which usually belong more to
thickness of skin and hardness of bone. I have seen men,
women, and children of such nature that a flogging is less
to them than a fillip to me; who neither cry out nor scowl
under the blows that are given to them. When athletes are
like philosophers in patience, it is strength of nerve rather
than of mind. Now, accustomedness to labour is accustomedness to pain: *Labor leads to insensibility to pain.*[64] He
must be practised in the discomfort and severity of action,
to train him for the discomfort and severity of dislocation,
of the colic, of the cautery, and of prison, and of torture. For
even he may fall into the clutches of these last, which, according to the times, seize upon good men as well as bad.
We are experiencing this. He who rebels against the laws
renders the best men liable to whippings and the rope.

And then,[65] too, the authority of the tutor over him,[66]
which should be sovereign, is interrupted and hindered by
the presence of parents. Besides which, the respect that
the household pays to him,[67] the knowledge of the wealth
and grandeur of his race, are in my opinion no slight disadvantages at that age. In this school of intercourse with men,
I have often observed this defect, that, instead of acquiring
knowledge from mothers, we strive only to give it of ourselves, and are more desirous to dispose of our wares than
to acquire new ones. Silence and modesty are very needful
qualities in social relations. This child will be trained to be
saving and thrifty with his store of knowledge when he shall

Of the Education of Children

have acquired it, and not to take exception to the follies and falsehoods that are uttered in his presence; for it is a discourteous unmannerliness to do battle with every thing that is not to our liking. Let him be content with correcting himself, and not seem to reprove in others all that he refuses to do, or to oppose public morals: *let him be wise without display and without ill-will;*[68] let him shun such discourteous conceits and the puerile ambition of desiring to appear more subtle by being different; and—as if reprehension and innovations were difficult matters—to seek to derive reputation of some special worth from them. As it befits only great poets to employ the licenses of the art, so it is tolerable only for great and illustrious minds to claim privileges above what is customary. *Because a Socrates and an Aristippus did something contrary to general usage and custom, let him not suppose that he has a similar license; for they acquired it by great and superhuman virtues.*[69]

He is to be taught not to enter into discussion or disputation except with a champion worthy of his steel, and even then not to employ all the methods that may be of service to him, but only those that will be most effective. Let him be trained to be nice in the selection and sifting out of his arguments, loving pertinency and, consequently, brevity. Let him be taught above all to surrender and lay down his arms to the truth,[70] just as soon as he discovers it, whether it be born in the hands of his opponent, or in himself on second thought. For he is not to be put in a high place of instruction,[71] to repeat a prescribed lesson. He is pledged to no cause save by the fact that he approves it; nor is to belong to the confraternity in which freedom to repent and reconsider is sold for ready money. *Nor is he obliged by*

Of the Education of Children

any necessity to defend all that is prescribed and enjoined.[72]

If his tutor be of my mind, he will train his will to be a most loyal and devoted and fearless servant of his prince; but he will blow cold upon the desire to attach himself to the prince otherwise than by a public service. Besides many other disadvantages which impair our liberty by these private obligations, the judgement of a man who is pledged and bought is either less sound and less free, or is marred by prudence and ingratitude. A courtier can have neither the right nor the desire to speak or think otherwise than favourably of a master who has chosen him from the many thousands of his subjects to foster and advance with his own hand. Such favour and benefit not unreasonably impair his freedom and bedazzle him. Wherefore we ordinarily find these persons[73] talking in a different tone from everybody else in a state, and that they are untrustworthy in such matters.[74] Let his conscience and his virtue shine forth even in his speech, and have only reason for their guide. Let him be made to understand that to avow the flaw that he finds in his own argument, although it be perceived only by himself, is an act of good judgement and sincerity, which are the qualities that he chiefly seeks; that obstinacy and pugnacity are vulgar conditions, seen oftenest in the meanest minds; that to reconsider and correct oneself, to abandon an ill-advised course at the height of one's ardour, are rare and strong and philosophical qualities.

He must be warned, when he is in company, to keep his eyes open in all directions; for I find that the highest positions are usually taken possession of by the least capable men, and that greatness of fortune is seldom combined with ability. I have seen, while, at the upper end of the

Of the Education of Children

table, they were discussing the beauty of a tapestry or the flavour of the malvoisie, many fine sayings wasted at the other end. He must prove the range of every man: a herdsman, a mason, a wayfarer—he must put them all under contribution, and borrow from each according to his wares, for every thing is of some use in a household; even the folly and weakness of other men will be instructive to him.[75] By observing the graces and manners of each individual, there will be born a longing for good, and contempt for bad, manners. Let his imagination be moved by a decent curiosity to inquire into every thing; he should see every thing that may be about him that is out of the ordinary: a building, a fountain, a man, the site of an old-time battle, a place where Cæsar passed, or Charlemagne.

> What land is benumbed with cold, what land is
> crumbling with heat, what fair wind drives the sails
> toward Italy.[76]

Let him investigate the morals, the resources, and the alliances of this prince and of that. These are things very interesting to learn, and very useful to know.

In this study of man I mean to include, and chiefly, those who live only in the memory of books. Let him study by means of histories those great minds of the best ages. It is a profitless study if you will;[77] also, if you will, it is a study of inestimable value, and the only study, as Plato says, which the Lacedæmonians for their part considered worth while.[78] What shall he not gain in this direction by reading the Lives of our Plutarch! But let my guide remember the object of his office, and let him impress upon his pupil not so much the date of the fall of Carthage as the qualities of Hannibal

Of the Education of Children

and Scipio, or not so much where Marcellus died as why it was inconsistent with his duty that he died there. Let him not be taught chronicles so much as taught to pass judgement on them. It is, to my mind, of all subjects that to which our minds apply themselves in the most widely variable measure. I have read in Livy a hundred things that another has not read there. Plutarch read there a hundred things over and above what I have been able to read, and perchance over and above what the author put there. To some it is a pure grammatical study; to others, the anatomy of philosophy, whereby the most obscure parts of our nature are searched. There are in Plutarch many lengthy reflections, most worthy to be known; for he is, in my opinion, the master craftsman in such work; but there are a thousand others which he has barely touched; he merely indicates with his finger the way we can go, if we please, and contents himself sometimes with giving only a hint at the heart of a subject. We must draw these[79] forth, and place them in full view;[80] as that remark of his, that the people of Asia were subject to one man because they did not know how to pronounce one syllable, which was "No,"[81] furnished La Boëtie, it may be, with the substance and the suggestion of his *Servitude Volontaire*. Even to see him cull out a trivial act in a man's life, or a remark which seems not of importance, is a dissertation. It is a pity that men of intelligence are so fond of brevity: doubtless their reputation is the better for it, but we are the worse off. Plutarch prefers that we should praise him for his judgement rather than for his learning; he prefers to leave us with an appetite for him rather than satiated. He knew that even on worth-while subjects too much can be said, and that Alexandridas justly reproved him who made an excellent speech, but too long a one, to the Ephors: "O stranger; you say what is meet, but in unmeet fashion."[82] They who have slender bodies stuff them out with padding; they who have slender substance, inflate it with words.

There results a wonderful enlightenment of the human judgement from frequentation with mankind. We are all confined and packed close within ourselves, and our sight is contracted to the length of our nose. Some one asked Socrates of what place he was. He did not reply, "Of Athens," but, "Of the world."[83] He, whose imagination was fuller and more widely extended, embraced the universe as his native place, cast his knowledge, his society, and his affections to all mankind—not like us, who look only beneath us. When the vines freeze in my village, my priest argues therefrom the wrath of God against the human race, and concludes that the pip already has the cannibals in its clutches. Looking upon our civil wars, who does not exclaim that this machine is overturned and that the day of judgement has us by the collar, not reflecting that many worse things have been seen, and that ten thousand parts of the world do not cease to make merry.[84] For my part, considering the license and impunity that attends them, I marvel to see them so mild and gentle. To a man in a hailstorm the whole hemisphere seems to be under a raging tempest. And the Savoyard said that if that fool of a king had known how to manage his fortune, he[85] might have been his duke's majordomo: his imagination could conceive no more exalted grandeur than his master's.[86] We all are unconsciously subject to this error—an error with important and prejudicial results. But he who sets before himself as in a picture this

Of the Education of Children

noble figure of our mother Nature in her full majesty; who
reads in her aspect a so universal and constant variety; who
perceives himself therein, and not himself alone but a whole
realm, as the smallest possible speck—he alone esteems
things according to their real proportions. This great world,
which some persons multiply further as species under one
genus, is the mirror in which we must look at ourselves in
order that we may know ourselves from the right point of
view. In short, I would have it my scholar's book. Such
a multitude of humours, of sects, of judgements, of opinions,
of laws, and of costumes teaches us to judge wisely of our
own, and teaches our judgement to recognise its imperfection and its natural weakness; which is no slight training.
So many civil commotions and changes of public fortune
teach us to make no great miracle of our own fortune. So
many names, so many victories and conquests buried in
oblivion make it ridiculous to hope to perpetuate our names
by the capture of ten insignificant troopers and an unimportant little fortress that is known only by its fall. The proud
pomp of so many foreign nations, the swollen majesty of so
many courts and stately mansions, steadies us and permits
our sight to endure the brilliancy of our own without blink-
ing. So many millions of men interred before ourselves encourage us not to fear going to join such good company in
the other world. And so with the rest.

Our life, said Pythagoras,[87] resembles the vast and populous assemblage of the Olympic games. Some exercise the
body to acquire glory in games; others carry merchandise
thither to sell for profit. There are those (and they are not
the worst) who seek there no other advantage than to observe how and why each thing is effected, and to be spec-

tators of the life of other men, in order to judge of it, and to regulate their own life. To examples can properly be joined all the most profitable teachings of philosophy, by which human actions should be tested as their canon. You will tell him,—

> What it is right to desire; what usefulness has newly coined money; how much it is fitting to bestow on thy country and on dear kindred; what sort of man God has commanded thee to be, and what is your post in the human commonwealth; what we are, and what the life we are born to lead,[88]—

what it is to know and not to know what should be the object of his study; what courage is, and temperance, and justice; what the difference is between ambition and cupidity, slavery and submission, license and liberty; by what signs genuine and solid contentment may be known; to what extent we should fear death, pain, and shame,—

> And how he may avoid or endure every kind of hardship;[89]—

what springs move us, and the occasion of so many different stirrings within us. For it seems to me that the first teachings in which the intelligence should be steeped should be those which may regulate his morals and his mind, and which will teach him to understand himself and to know how to die well and to live well.

Among the liberal arts, let us begin with the art that liberates us.[90] They all help somewhat in the instruction of our life and in its employment, as all other things help somewhat. But let us choose that one which helps directly

Of the Education of Children

and professedly. If we could confine the appurtenances of our lives within their due and natural limits, we should find that the greater number of the branches of knowledge that are in use are outside of our use, and that even in those which are [adapted to our use][91] there are breadths and depths which we should do well to let alone, and, following the teaching of Socrates,[92] limit our course of study in those branches where usefulness is lacking.

> Dare to be wise; set about it; the man who delays the hour of living rightly is like the rustic who waits for the river to pass away; but it flows on, and forever will it flow.[93]

It is great folly to teach our children

> What is the influence of Pisces, and of the constellation of bold Leo, and Capricornus bathed in the Hesperian Sea,[94]

the science of the stars, and the movement of the eighth sphere, before their own.

> What do the Pleiades matter to me, or the stars of Boötes?[95]

Anaximenes wrote to Pythagoras: "How can I meditate on the secrets of the stars, having death or slavery always before my eyes?"[96] (For at that time the kings of Persia were preparing to war against his country.) So every one might say: "Being beset by ambition, avarice, temerity, and superstition, and having so many other enemies of life within me, shall I attempt to think about the movement of the world?"

Of the Education of Children

After he has been taught what helps to make him wiser and better, then let his tutor enlighten him as to what logic is, and physics,[97] and geometry, and rhetoric; and the branch of learning that he shall choose when his judgement is formed, he will very soon master. Let his lesson be given sometimes by talk, sometimes by books; sometimes his tutor will supply him with the very author suitable for that part of his instruction; sometimes he will give him the marrow and substance of the book all prepared. And if he be not himself sufficiently familiar with books to find in them the many admirable passages they contain fit for his purpose, some man of letters can be joined with him, who, whenever there is need, can supply him with such provisions as he may require, to deal out and dispense to his nursling. And who can doubt that this method of instruction is easier and more natural than that of Gaza?[98] In that are thorny and disagreeable precepts and idle and bloodless words, in which there is nothing to catch hold of, nothing that awakens the mind.[99] In this other method the mind finds a place to browse and to pasture on. This fruit is incomparably greater, and yet it will be sooner ripe.

It is a remarkable fact that things have come to such a pass in our time that philosophy is, even to persons of intelligence, a vain and chimerical thing, of no use and no value, both in appearance and in reality. I think that these quibblings[100] which have blocked the approach to her[101] are the cause. It is a great mistake to describe her as inaccessible to children and of a lowering and frowning and terrifying aspect. Who has disguised her with that wan and hideous mask? There is nothing gayer, more jocund, more blithe, and, I might almost say, sportive. She exhorts always to

Of the Education of Children

holidaying and merry-making; a sad and spiritless air shows that not there is her abode. Demetrius the grammarian, finding a party of philosophers sitting together in the temple at Delphi, said to them: "Unless I am mistaken, seeing you so placid and gay in deportment, there is not very serious talk among you." To which one of them, Heracleon the Megarian, replied: "It is for them who seek to learn whether the future tense of βάλλω has the double λ, or who seek the derivation of the comparatives χεῖρον and βέλτιον, and of the superlatives χείριστον and βέλτιστον, to knit the brows while talking of their kind of knowledge; but, as for the discussions of philosophy, they are accustomed to enliven and exhilarate those who engage in them, and not to depress and sadden them."[102]

You may detect, hidden in a suffering body, mental pain, and likewise you may detect gladness; from both the face assumes an expression.[103]

The mind that harbours philosophy should by virtue of its soundness render sound the body likewise; it should make its tranquillity and gladness shine forth; should shape the outward bearing in its mould, and therefore arm it with a gracious pride, with an active and sprightly behaviour, and with a satisfied and courteous demeanour. The most express mark of wisdom is a constant gladness;[104] its state is like that of things beyond the moon—always serene. It is "Baroco" and "Baralipton" that make their adherents so dirty and smoke-begrimed, it is not she; they know her only by hearsay. What! it is her part to still the tempests of the soul and to teach hunger and fever to laugh, not by a few imaginary epicycles, but by natural and palpable arguments. Her purpose is virtue, which is not, as schoolmen say, established at the stop of a steep, rugged, and inaccessible mountain.[105] They who have approached her have, on the contrary, found her dwelling in a lovely plain, fertile and flower-strewn, whence she can see clearly beneath her all things; but yet one who knows the way can reach the place by shady, grassy, and sweetly blooming paths, pleasantly, and by an easy and smooth slope, like that of the heavenly vault. Those who have not frequented this sovereign Virtue, beautiful, triumphant, full of love, equally delicate and courageous, the professed and irreconcilable foe of bitterness and trouble and fear and constraint, who has Nature for her guide, and Good Fortune and Pleasure for her companions, have imagined according to their weakness this absurd, gloomy, contentious, grim, menacing, scornful image, and have placed it on a lonely rock amid brambles: a phantom to frighten folk.

My tutor, who knows that he ought to fill his pupil's heart with affection, as much as or more than with reverence for virtue, will not fail to tell him that the poets follow the common opinions, and to make him clearly to know[106] that the gods have placed toil in the approaches to the closets of Venus rather than to those of Pallas. And when he shall begin to be conscious of himself, putting before him, as a mistress to enjoy, Bradamante or Angelica,[107] and a natural, vigorous, noble beauty, not mannish but virile, in contrast to a soft, delicate, and artificial beauty,—the one attired as a boy, on her head a glittering helmet; the other dressed as a girl, on her head a tire trimmed with pearls,—he will judge his very love to be manly if he should choose quite differently from that effeminate Phrygian shepherd. He will teach him this new lesson, that the worth and eminence of true virtue lies in the ease and profit and pleasure of her employment, which is so far from being difficult that children can practise it as well as men, the simple as the crafty. Regulation, not force, is her instrument. Socrates, her prime favourite, intentionally lays aside his strength to slip into the naturalness and ease of her progression. She is the foster-mother of human joys. By making them honest, she makes them certain and pure; by moderating them, she keeps them in breath and in appetite; by cutting out those that she refuses us, she makes us the keener for those that she leaves us, and she leaves us in abundance all those that Nature approves, even to satiety, like a mother, if not to lassitude; unless perchance we choose to say that the authority which stops the toper before drunkenness, the glutton before indigestion, the lecher before baldness, is a foe to our pleasures. If ordinary fortune plays her false,[108] she escapes its blows; or does without it and makes for herself another all her own, no longer wavering and unsteady. She knows how to be rich and powerful and learned, and to sleep in perfumed beds; she loves life, she loves beauty, glory, and health. But her proper and especial function is to know how to make a disciplined use of these good things, and to know how to lose them unmoved: a function much more noble than grievous, without which the whole course of life is perverted, turbulent, and disfigured, and one may fairly attribute to it those rocks and bramble-bushes, and those monsters.[109] If the pupil proves to be of such a wayward humour that he prefers to listen to a fabulous story rather than to the narrative of an interesting journey or to a wise saying when he hears it; if, at the sound of the tabour that

awakens the youthful ardour of his comrades, he turns aside
to another note that invites him to the sports of the jugglers;
if in his heart he finds it no pleasanter and sweeter to return
dusty and victorious from a wrestling-match, with the prize
of that sport, than from the tennis court or from a ball,
then I can see no other remedy than that [in good season
his tutor strangle him, if he be without witnesses, or that][110]
he be set up as a pastry-cook in some big city, were he a
duke's son, according to the counsel of Plato, that children
should be disposed of,[111] not according to their father's
abilities, but according to the abilities of their minds.

Since it is philosophy that teaches us to live, and childhood, like other ages, has its lessons to learn from her, why
not make her known to childhood?

> The clay is moist and soft; now, now quickly
> fashion it with speed on the revolving wheel.[112]

They teach us to live when life is past. A hundred students
have caught the pox before they came to the reading of
Aristotle "On Temperance." Cicero said that, were he to
live the lives of two men, he would not take the time to
study the lyric poets;[113] and I consider these cavilling quib-
blers[114] even more deplorably futile. Our boy must be in
far greater haste: he owes to study only the first fifteen or
sixteen years of his life; the rest he owes to action. The time
being so short, let us devote it to necessary instruction. This
is waste.[115] Cut out all these thorny subtleties of dialectic—
by which our life can not be bettered; take the simple arguments of philosophy, learn how to select them and to discuss them pertinently; they are easier to understand than a
tale of Boccaccio; a child just weaned is more capable of it

Of the Education of Children

than of learning to read or write. Philosophy has teachings for men at their birth as well as in their decrepitude. I am of Plutarch's opinion, that Aristotle did not so much occupy the time of his famous pupil in the skill of constructing syllogisms, or in the principles of geometry, as in teaching him wise precepts concerning valour, prowess, nobleness of character, and temperance, and the courage to fear nothing; and with this preparation he sent him forth, when still a child, to subjugate the empiry of the world with only 30,000 foot-soldiers, 4000 horse, and 42,000 crowns.[116] The other arts and branches of knowledge,[117] he says, Alexander held in high esteem, and praised their excellence and charm; but, as for himself taking pleasure in them, it was not easy to surprise him in the desire to practise them.

> Take from this, young men and old, a fixed purpose for your minds, and make provision for the wretchedness of hoary old age.[118]

It is as Epicurus said at the beginning of his letter to Meniceus: "Let not the youngest shun philosophy, nor the oldest weary of it. He who does otherwise seems to say either that it is not yet the time to live happily, or that it is no longer the time."[119]

For all that, I would not have the boy confined.[120] I would not have him given over to the brooding melancholy of a passionate schoolmaster. I would not spoil his mind by keeping it in torture and at work, as others do, fourteen or fifteen hours a day, like a porter. Nor should I think it well, if, from an unsocial and pensive disposition, he were addicted to an unwise application to the study of books,[121] that he should be encouraged therein; it unfits boys for

219

Of the Education of Children

social intercourse and diverts them from better occupations. And how many men háve I seen in my time, stultified by a reckless greediness of learning! Carneades was so besotted with it that he had no time to attend to his hair and his nails.[122] Nor would I have his good manners spoilt by others' clownishness and rudeness. French discretion was long ago proverbial as a discretion which took root early but had little hold. In truth, we still see that there is nothing so charming as the young French children; but commonly they disappoint the hopes conceived of them, and as grown men, no excellence is seen in them. I have heard it maintained by men of understanding that it is these schools to which they are sent, of which there are so many, that brutify them thus.

To our pupil, a closet, a garden, table and bed, solitude, company, morning and evening—all hours will be alike to him, every place his study: for philosophy, which, as the moulder of opinions and manners, will be his principal lesson, has this privilege of entering into every thing. Isocrates the orator being urged at a banquet to talk about his art, every one thought he was right in replying: "It is not the time now for what I can do; and I can not do that for which it is now the time."[123] For to offer harangues or rhetorical discussions to a company assembled for merry-making and feasting would be too discordant a combination; and one might say as much of all the other kinds of learning. But, as for philosophy, in those parts where she treats of man, and of his duties and functions, it has been the universal opinion of all wise men that the charm of her conversation is such that she should not be denied admission to either banquets or games; and Plato, having bidden her to his Banquet,[124]

Of the Education of Children

we see how she discourses to the company in a pleasant
fashion, adapted to the time and place, although it is one of
his loftiest and most salutary treatises.

It equally profits the poor and the rich; and, neglected, will be equally harmful to boys and old men.[125]

Thus, doubtless, he will have not so many holidays[126] as the
others; but as the steps that we take in walking in a gallery
tire us less, although there may be three times as many,
than those we take on some highway, so our lessons, coming about as if by accident, without set obligation of time
and place, and being mingled with all our acts, will flow on
without making themselves felt. Even games and bodily
exercises will be a part of his study: running, wrestling,
music, dancing, hunting, the management of horses and
the use of weapons. I would have his exterior agreeableness
and social demeanour and his personal bearing shape themselves at the same time with his inner being. It is not a spirit,
it is not a body that we are training: it is a man; we must
not separate them.[127] And, as Plato says, we must not train
one of them without the other, but drive them side by side,
like a pair of horses fastened to the same pole.[128] And, listening to him, does he not seem to allot more time and care to
the exercises of the body, and to judge that the mind may be
exercised at the same time, and not the opposite?[129] Meanwhile, this instruction should be carried on with grave gentleness, not as it is. Instead of inviting children to study,
they bring them, in truth, nothing but fear and cruelty.
Away with violence and compulsion; there is nothing, in
my opinion, which so debases and stupefies a well-born
nature. If you wish him to fear disgrace and punishment, do

not harden him to them; harden him to sweat and cold, to the wind, to the sun, and to the chances which he ought to despise; take from him all sensitiveness and fastidiousness about his clothing and his bed, about eating and drinking; accustom him to every thing; let him not be a pretty boy and effeminate, but sturdy and vigorous. In youth, in middle age, and in old age, I have always believed and thought this. But, among other things, this method of government of the greater part of our schools has always offended me. Failure would perchance be less harmful in the direction of indulgence. They are veritable prisons of captive youth, whom they render disorderly by punishment beforehand. Go to one of them when the lessons are in progress: you hear nothing but outcries of children being punished and of masters drunk with anger. What a way of awakening an appetite for their lesson in those young and timid souls, to conduct them to it with a terrifying air and hands armed with whips! A wicked and pernicious fashion. It may be added, what Quintilian has very well observed, that such imperious authority leads to dangerous results, and especially our method of chastisement.[130] How much more seemly would it be if their classrooms were strewn with flowers and leaves rather than with bits of blood-stained switches! I would have joy and gladness pictured there, and Flora and the Graces, as the philosopher Speusippus had in his school.[131] Where their profit is, there let their pleasure be also. We should sweeten the food that is healthy for the child, and make bitter what is harmful to him. It is a marvel how solicitous Plato shows himself in his Laws, regarding the gaiety and pastimes of the youth of his city, and how he dwells upon their races, games, songs,

Of the Education of Children

jumpings, and dances, of which he says that the ancients attributed their ordering and patronage to the gods themselves—Apollo and the Muses and Minerva. He branches out in innumerable rules for his gymnasia; as for letters, he occupies himself very little with them, and seems especially to commend poetry only for music.[132]

All eccentricity and peculiarity in our manners and conditions is to be avoided as a foe to intercourse and companionship with others, and as unnatural. Who would not be astonished at the constitution of Demophon, Alexander's major-domo, who sweated in the dark and shivered in sunshine?[133] I have seen those who fled from the odour of apples more than from a volley of musketry, others frightened at a mouse, others sickened by the sight of cream, others by seeing a feather-bed shaken up; and Germanicus could not endure either the sight or the crowing of cocks.[134] There may perchance be some hidden property in this; but it could be got rid of, I think, if taken in good season. Training has accomplished this much with me,—not, to be sure, without some difficulty,—that, except beer, my stomach can accommodate itself indifferently to whatever is taken into it. While the body is still supple, we ought then to shape it to all fashions and customs; and, provided that a young man's desires and will can be held in check, let us boldly make him suited to all nations and all companionships, even to immoderateness and to excesses, if need be. Let his practice follow custom. Let him be able to do every thing, but enjoy doing only the best things. Even philosophers do not deem it praiseworthy in Callisthenes to have lost the favour of Alexander the Great, his master, by refusing to equal him in drinking.[135] Let him laugh and frolic and carouse with his prince; even in his debauches I would have him surpass his companions in vigour and persistency, and fail to do evil from lack neither of strength nor of knowledge, but from lack of inclination. *It makes a great difference whether a man does not wish to sin, or does not know how.*[136] I thought to do honour to a nobleman as far removed from such excesses as any man in France by asking him, in good company, how many times in his life he had got drunk in the interest of the king's affairs in Germany. He took it in that sense, and answered that it had happened three times, which he narrated. I know those who, lacking this faculty, have found themselves in sore straits, having to deal with that nation. I have often considered with great admiration the wonderful nature of Alcibiades, shaping himself so readily to customs so diverse, without injury to his health; sometimes surpassing the Persian sumptuousness and pomp, sometimes the Lacedæmonian austerity and frugality—being as much of an ascetic in Sparta as of a voluptuary in Ionia.[137]

> Every condition, every situation, every circumstance befitted Aristippus.[138]

Such a man I would train my pupil to be.

> He who patiently wraps himself in a patched garment will win my admiration if his new manner of life becomes him and he plays both parts without awkwardness.[139]

These are my precepts. He who practises them has profited more by them than he who simply knows them. If you see him, you hear him; if you hear him, you see him.

Of the Education of Children

Now, God forbid, says some one in Plato, that to philosophise is to learn many things and to discuss the arts![140] *This instruction in right living, the most liberal of all arts, they have sought more in life than in letters.*[141] Leo, prince of the Phalasians, inquiring of Heraclides Ponticus what science, what art he professed, "I know nothing," he said, "of either art or science, but I am a philosopher."[142] Some one reproved Diogenes because, being ignorant, he dealt with philosophy.[143] "I deal with it all the more fitly," he said. Hegesias begged him to read some book[144] to him. "You are queer," he replied; "you select real natural figs, not painted ones; why do you not select also natural and real things for the enrichment of the mind?"[145] Let him not so much say his lesson as do it; let him repeat it in his acts. We shall see if there be prudence in his undertakings, if there be sincerity and uprightness in his conduct, if there be good judgement and grace in his speech, courage in his sicknesses, modesty in his sports, temperance in his pleasures, indifference in his appetite,—whether it be flesh, fish, wine, or water,—good order in his expenditure. *Who regards his doctrine, not as a vain display of knowledge, but as a rule of life; who obeys himself and complies with his own precepts.*[146] The true mirror of our thought[147] is the course of our lives.

Zeuxidamus replied, to one who asked him why the Lacedæmonians did not reduce to writing the rules of valour and give them to their young men to read, that it was because they wished to accustom them to deeds, not to words.[148] Compare with such a one, after fifteen or sixteen years, one of those Latin-taught schoolboys, who will have spent as much time in simply learning to talk. The world is naught but chatter, and I never saw a man who did not talk

Of the Education of Children

rather more than less than he ought; and yet half of our lives is wasted over this. They keep us four or five years learning words and stringing them in sentences; as many more in shaping with them a great body divided in due proportion into four or five parts; and at least five more in learning to mingle and intertwine them concisely in some ingenious fashion. Let us leave this to those who make it their special business.

Going one day to Orleans, I met, in the open country this side of Clery, on their way to Bordeaux, two teachers[149] about fifty paces one from the other. Farther on behind them, I came upon a troop of horsemen with their master at their head—the late monsieur le comte de la Rochefoucaut. One of my people asked the foremost of the teachers who the gentleman behind him was. He, not having observed the retinue that was following and thinking that his own companion was referred to, replied amusingly: "He's not a gentleman: he's a grammarian and I am a logician." Now let us, who, on the other hand, are here seeking to fashion, not a grammarian or a logician, but a gentleman, leave them to waste their time; our concern is elsewhere. Let our pupil but be well supplied with things, and words will follow only too freely: he will draw them on, if they refuse to follow. I hear some people apologise for not being able to express themselves, and they have the air of having their heads full of fine things which, for lack of an eloquent tongue, can not be brought forth: 't is a delusion. Do you know how it is, in my opinion? They are shadows that fall upon their minds from some shapeless ideas which they can not disentangle and clarify inwardly, and consequently can not produce outwardly. They do not as yet understand them-

226

selves; and as you watch them a little, stammering on the point of giving birth, you conclude that their labour is not at the stage of delivery, but of conception, and that they are still simply nourishing this imperfect embryo. For my part, I maintain, and Socrates prescribes, that he who has in his mind a vivid and distinct idea should bring it forth, either in bergamesque, or by gestures if he be dumb.

> If the matter be clearly discerned, the words will follow unhesitatingly.[150]

And as this one said no less poetically in his prose, *when a matter occupies the mind, words offer themselves for your choice.*[151] And this other: *The subject itself seizes upon words.*[152] He knows not ablative, conjunctive, substantive or grammar; neither does his servant, or a fishwoman of the Petit Point; yet they will give you your fill of talk, and will perchance be as little embarrassed by the rules of their language as the best master of arts in France. He knows not rhetoric, nor how, by way of preface, to capture the gentle reader's good-will; nor does he care to know. In truth, all this fine painting is readily eclipsed by the brilliancy of a simple, artless truth; these refinements serve only to amuse the vulgar herd, who are incapable of swallowing solider and stronger food, as Afer shows very plainly in Tacitus.[153] The ambassadors from Samos had come to Cleomenes, King of Sparta, prepared with a fine and long speech, to incite him to war against the tyrant Polycrates. After he had heard them out, he replied: "As for your beginning and exordium, I no longer remember it; nor, consequently, the middle; and as for your conclusion, I do not desire to do any thing about it."[154] An excellent reply that, it seems to me, and haranguers well nonplussed. And what of this other? The Athenians had to choose one of two architects to build a great edifice: the first, being more wily, presented himself with a fine prepared speech on the subject of this undertaking and won favour in popular judgement; but the other, in three words, "Athenians, what this man has said, I will do."[155]

At the height of Cicero's eloquence many were moved to admiration; but Cato merely laughed at it. "We have," he said, "an entertaining consul."[156] Whether it come before or after, a profitable phase, a fine stroke of wit, is always in season. If it does not fit what goes before or what comes after, it is good in itself. I am not one of those who think that good rhythm makes a good poem: let him make a short syllable long if he will; about that it matters not;[157] if the conceptions are pleasing, if the mind and the judgement have played their parts well, "There's a good poet," I will say, "but a bad versifier,"—

> Of keen scent, but harsh in the composition of his verses.[158]

Let his work be divested, says Horace, of all its divisions[159] and measures,—

> [Take away] the rhythm and the metre, and change the order of the words, putting the first last and the last first, and you will find the dispersed limits of the poet,[160]—

it will not be changed in character by that; even its fragments will be beautiful. Menander, when he was taunted because, the day drawing near on which he had promised a comedy, he had not yet set hand to it, replied: "It is composed and ready; nothing remains to be done save to add the verses.[161] Having the subject and the details[162] arranged in his mind, he took small account of the rest. Since Ronsard and du Bellay have given reputation to our French poetry, every little beginner, it seems to me, uses as swelling words, and manages his cadences almost like them. *There is more sound than worth.*[163] In the opinion of the vulgar there were never so many poets; but while it has been very easy for them to reproduce their rhymes, they fall very far short in imitating the rich descriptions of the one and the delicate fancies of the other.

Aye, but how if he[164] be importuned by the sophistical artifice of some syllogism? Ham makes one drink, drink quenches thirst, therefore ham quenches thirst. Let him laugh them to scorn; there is more wit in so doing than in answering this.[165] Let him borrow from Aristippus this diverting counterstroke: "Why should I unloose it when, fettered, it impedes me?"[166] Some one propounding certain dialectical refinements against Cleanthes, Chrysippus said to him: "Play those tricks with children, and do not divert the serious thoughts of grown men to such things."[167] If these foolish quibbles, *involved and subtle fallacies,*[168] should lead him to believe what is false, that is dangerous; but if they remain without effect, and move him only to laughter, I see not why he should be on his guard against them. Some persons are so foolish that they will go far out of their way[169] to run after a witty remark; *or who do not fit words to their subject, but seek out irrelevant subjects for which their words may be suitable.*[170] And this other: *There are those who are drawn by the charm of some pleasing word to a subject they had not proposed to write about.*[171] I much more readily twist a fine saying in order to fasten it to me,[172] than I twist the thread of my own thought to go in search of it. On the contrary, it is for words to do service and to follow; and let Gascon come to the front if French can not get there. I would have the subject predominate and so fill the imagination of him who listens that he shall have no remembrance of the words. The way of speaking that I like is a simple and natural speech, the same on paper as on the lips; a style pithy, sinewy, brief, and concise, not so refined and smooth[173] as vehement and quick,—

That word is wise that strikes a blow,[174]—

more rough than tedious, far removed from affectation, free, loose, and bold: let each fragment have its own form; not pedant-like, not friar-like, not lawyer-like, but rather soldier-like, as Suetonius calls that of Julius Cæsar; but indeed I do not well understand why he calls it so.[175]

I have willingly imitated this disorderliness which we see in our young men in the manner of wearing their apparel—a mantle scarf-wise, the cloak over one shoulder, and wrinkled hose—which denotes a proud disdain of such outer trappings and indifference to rule. But this seems to me still better employed as regards the manner in talking. All affectation, especially in our French vivacity and freedom, is unbecoming to the courtier. And in a monarchy every gentleman should be trained to bear himself like a courtier; wherefore we do well to incline a little toward the artless and disdainful. I do not like a stuff in which the joinings and seemings are visible; just as in a beautiful body one should not be able to count the bones and veins. *Speech in the serv-*

Of the Education of Children

ice of truth should be unstudied and unadorned.[176] *Who speaks in a studied manner save him who chooses to speak affectedly?*[177] Eloquence which diverts our minds to itself is harmful to its subject.

Just as in habiliments it is a sign of weakness to wish to make oneself noticeable by some peculiar and unaccustomed fashion, so, in language, the quest of new-fangled phrases and little-known words comes from a puerile and pedantic ambition. Would that I could make use only of those that are used in the markets of Paris! Aristophanes the grammarian was all at sea[178] when he criticised in Epicurus the simplicity of his words and the aim of his oratorical art, which was solely perspicuity of language.[179] A whole people follows incontinently, by reason of its facility, the habit of imitating a mode of speech; not so quickly, a mode of judging or of thinking. Most readers, when they have found a like garment, think very mistakenly that they have hold of a like body. Strength and sinews can not be borrowed, but the attire and the cloak may be. Most of those who consort with me talk like the Essays, but I know not whether they think in the same way.

The Athenians, Plato says,[180] especially care for copiousness and elegance of language, the Lacedæmonians for brevity, and the Cretans for the fruitfulness of the ideas rather than for the language; these last are the best advised.[181] Zeno said that he had two kinds of disciples: one, whom he called φιλολόγους, who were eager to learn about things, and who were his favourites; the others, λογοφίλους, who cared for nothing but words.[182] This is not to say that it is not a fine and excellent thing to express oneself well; but it is not so excellent as it is made out to be; and it tries me that our life is wholly busied in that. I should want chiefly to know well my own language, and that of my neighbours with whom I have the most common intercourse. Greek and Latin are an admirable ornament, no doubt, but we buy it too dear. I will describe here a method of getting it more reasonably than is usually done, which was tried in my own case. Let him who will, make use of it.

My late father, having made all enquiry that a man can make, among scholars and men of intelligence, regarding the most excellent method of education, was apprised of the disadvantage of the method then in use;[183] and was told that the length of time we spend in learning languages, which cost the ancient Greeks and Romans nothing, is the only reason we can not attain their loftiness of character and of knowledge. I do not believe that this is the only reason. However that may be, the expedient that my father hit upon was this: while I was at nurse and before I could talk,[184] he gave me in charge to a German (who later died a famous doctor in France) wholly ignorant of our language and well versed in Latin. This man, whom he had summoned for this express purpose, and who was paid a very large stipend, had me constantly in his arms. He had also with him two others, less learned, to attend me and relieve him; they talked to me in no other language than the Latin. As for the rest of the household, it was an inviolable rule that neither my father nor my mother, nor manservant, nor maidservant should utter in my presence any thing except those Latin words that each of them had learned in order to talk blunderingly[185] with me. It was wonderful how much they all profited by this: my father and my mother thus learned enough Latin to understand it, and acquired the

Of the Education of Children

language sufficiently to use it at need, as did also the other members of the household most in attendance on me. In fact, we were so latinised that it overflowed to our neighbouring villages, where there are still divers Latin names, which have taken root by usage, for craftsmen and for tools. As for me, I was more than six years old before I understood French or Perigordin any more than Arabic; and without system, without books, without grammar or rules, without whipping and without tears, I had learned as pure Latin as my schoolmaster knew, for I could not have adulterated or changed it. If by way of test they desired to give me an exercise in composition after the fashion in colleges, given there in French,[186] to me they must needs give it in bad Latin, to be turned into good. And Nicolas Groucchi, who wrote *De comitiis Romanorum*, Guillaume Gerente, who commented Aristotle, George Buchanan, the great Scotch poet, and Marc-Antoine Muret, whom France and Italy recognise as the greatest orator of our day, who were my private tutors, have often told me that in my childhood I was so ready and so at ease in that language, that they themselves were shy in familiar talk with me. Buchanan, whom I met afterwards in the suite of the late maréchal de Brissac, told me that he was writing on the education of children, and that he was taking mine for a model; for he then had in his charge that comte de Brissac who showed himself later to be so courageous and gallant.[187]

As for Greek, of which I have scarcely any knowledge at all, my father proposed to have it taught me artificially but in a novel way, in the guise of pastime and exercise: we tossed our declensions to and fro after the fashion of those who learn arithmetic and geometry by certain table-games.

233

Of the Education of Children

For, among other things, he had been advised to make me relish learning and duty by unforced inclination and by my own desire, and to train my mind in all gentleness and liberty, without severity or compulsion. Let me say, he carried this to such an over-scrupulous degree that, because some people hold that it disturbs the delicate brains of children to waken them with a start in the morning, and to rouse them suddenly and violently from sleep (which is much deeper with them than with us), he caused me to be awakened by the sound of some instrument; and he was never without a man who performed that service for me.[188]

This example will suffice to judge of the rest, and to commend the circumspection and affection of so excellent a father, who is not to be discredited if the fruits he gathered did not correspond to such careful cultivation. Two things were the cause of this: in the first place, the sterile and unsuitable soil; for, although I had strong and sound health, and also a gentle and docile nature, I was withal so heavy and sluggish and sleepy that they could not rouse me from my slothfulness, even to make me play. What I saw, I saw clearly, and beneath that dull exterior I nourished bold fancies, and thoughts of a height above my age. My intellect was slow, and went only as far as it was led; my comprehension was tardy, my imagination weak; and on top of every thing I had an incredible lack of memory. From all this it is no wonder that he could draw forth nothing of value. In the second place, like those urged by a frantic desire for a cure who allow themselves to follow all sorts of advice, the good old man, being extremely afraid of failing in a thing that he had so much at heart, allowed himself at last to be led by the common opinion, which, like the cranes, al-

Of the Education of Children

ways follows those who go in front, and fell in with the general custom, no longer having about him the persons who had given him those first institutions, which he had brought from Italy; and he sent me at about six years of age to the college of Guienne, which was then very flourishing and the best in France. And there, it is not possible to have greater care than he took, both in the choice of competent private tutors and in all the other details of my training, in which he insisted upon certain peculiar methods contrary to the usage of colleges; but for all that, it was still a college. My Latin was corrupted forthwith, and since then, by unaccustomedness, I have entirely lost the use of it; and my unusual education was of no service to me except that it enabled me at the beginning to skip over the lower classes. For when I left the college, at thirteen, I had finished my course (as they call it), and in truth without any benefit that I can now put my hand on.

The first relish that I had for books came to me from pleasure in the fables of Ovid's *Metamorphoses*. For, at the age of about seven or eight, I stole away from every other pleasure to read them, inasmuch as their language was my mother-tongue, and it was the best suited, because of the subject, to my age, that I knew. For as to the *Lancelots du Lac,* the *Amadis,* the Huons de Bordeaux, and heaps of such trashy books on which childhood wastes its time, I did not even know their names, nor do I yet know their contents, so strict was the care given to my education. I became in consequence more indifferent to the study of my other prescribed lessons. It then happened to me most opportunely to have to do with a man of intelligence as a tutor, who dexterously connived at this irregularity of mine and

others of the same sort. For thus I ran through, in quick
succession, Virgil, in the *Æneid*, and then Terence, and
then Plautus, and Italian comedies, enticed always by the
charm of the subject. If he had been so foolish as to interrupt
that course, I believe that I should have brought away from
the college only a detestation of books, as almost all our
gentry do. He managed in this matter ingeniously, pre-
tending to see nothing of it; he sharpened my appetite by
allowing me only by stealth those books, and gently keeping
me to my duty in the other regular studies. For the principal
qualities that my father sought in those to whom he gave
me in charge were friendliness and natural approachable-
ness;[189] as my nature had no other fault than inertness and
idleness. The danger was, not that I should do wrong, but
that I should do nothing. No one prophesied that I should
become a bad man, but merely a useless one; they foresaw
distaste of work, not ill deeds.[190]

I am conscious that it has turned out so. The complaints
that sound in my ears are of this tenor: "Lazy; cold to the
duties of friendship and kinship, and to public duties; too
withdrawn." Even the most critical do not say: "Why has
he taken? Why has n't he paid?" but: "Why does n't he
renounce? Why does n't he give?" I ought to be thankful
that they ask of me only such acts of supererogation. But
they are unjust, to demand what I do not owe much more
strictly than they demand of themselves what they do owe.
By declaring this to be my duty they efface the gratification
of the act and the gratitude which should be due to me for
it: whereas active well-doing on my part ought to count for
more, from the consideration that there is nothing to constrain me to it. I am the more at liberty to dispose of my

Of the Education of Children

fortune as it is the more my own, [and of myself because I am more my own].[191] However, if I were a great blazoner[192] of my own actions, perchance I might confute these reproaches, and teach some people that they are not so much offended because I do not do enough as because I could do a good deal more than I do.

Yet for all this my soul did not fail, at the same time, to have secretly strong agitations, and assured and liberal judgements with regard to things with which it was acquainted; and it examined them alone without making them known to any one. And, among other things, I truly believe that it would have been altogether incapable of yielding to force and violence. Shall I take account of this faculty of my childhood—a command of countenance and a flexibility of voice and gesture in adapting myself to parts that I undertook to play? For before the age when

I had scarcely reached my twelfth year,[193]

I had acted the chief personages in the Latin tragedies of Buchanan, Guerente, and Muret, which were performed with dignity at our college of Guienne. In this Andreas Goveanus, our principal, as in all other branches of his office, was beyond comparison the greatest principal in France, and I was considered a master-workman. It is an amusement which I do not think ill of for children of good families; and I have since seen our princes addict themselves to it in person, after the example of some of the ancients, creditably and commendably. It was permissible, in fact, for men of honour to make it their trade in Greece: *He disclosed the matter to Ariston, the tragic actor, whose family and whose fortune were distinguished, and whose profession did not in-*

Of the Education of Children

jure his position; for among the Greeks it is not to be ashamed of.[194] For I have always accused of unreasonableness those who condemn such recreation, and of injustice those who deny admission to our big cities to actors who are worthy of it, and who grudge the common people these public pleasures. Wise administrations are careful to assemble the citizens and bring them together for exercises and sports no less than for the serious duties of religion; good-fellowship and friendship are enhanced thereby. Moreover, there could not be found for them pastimes more orderly than those which are carried on in every one's presence and before the very eyes of the magistrate. And it would seem to me reasonable that the magistrate, and that the prince at his own expense, should sometimes gratify the common people in this way from a quasi-paternal affection and kindness; and that in the populous cities there should be places set apart and arranged for such spectacles: some diversion from worse and hidden doings.

To return to my subject, there is nothing like tempting the appetite and the interest; otherwise, we make only asses laden with books; with strokes of the birch we give into their keeping their pocketfuls of learning, which, if it is so serve any purpose, we must not merely give lodging to— we must espouse it.

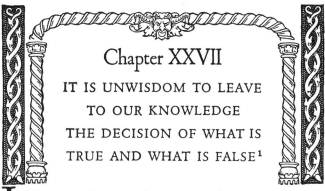

Chapter XXVII

IT IS UNWISDOM TO LEAVE
TO OUR KNOWLEDGE
THE DECISION OF WHAT IS
TRUE AND WHAT IS FALSE[1]

IT is not perchance without reason that we attribute to simple-mindedness and ignorance the readiness to believe and to be convinced; for it seems to me that I once learned that belief was, as it were, an impression that was made on our minds, and that, the softer and less resistant the mind, the easier it was to imprint something upon it. *As of necessity the scale of the balance must sink when weights are placed upon it, so the mind must yield to clear proof.*[2] The more empty and without counterpoise the mind is, the more readily the scale sinks under the weight of the first argument.

That is the reason why children, the common people, women, and sick persons are more subject to be led by the ears. But also, on the other hand, it is an absurd assumption to scorn and condemn as false what seems to us not probable: which is a common fault of those who think that they have more intelligence than the vulgar.[3] I used to be so minded myself, and if I heard some one talk of spirits returning, or of prognostications of future things, of enchantments, or sorceries, or tell some other tale of which I could make nothing,[4]—

Of what is True and what is False

Dreams, the terrors of magic, miracles, witches,
spectres of the night, and Thessalian prodigies,[5]—

I felt compassion for the poor people deceived by such
follies. And now I think that I was at least as much to be
pitied myself; not that experience has since then shown me
any thing beyond my former beliefs, and not certainly from
lack of interest; but reason has taught me that to condemn
a thing so positively as false and impossible is to assume the
advantage of knowing the boundaries and limits of the will
of God and of the power of our mother Nature; and that
there is no more notable foolishness in the world than to
measure these by our capacity and intelligence. If we call
contrary to reason, or miraculous, those things which our
reason can not grasp, how many are constantly offered to
our sight! When we consider through what mists and how
gropingly we are brought to acquaintance with most things
that are in our hands, surely we shall find that it is rather
familiarity than knowledge which takes away their strangeness,—

Now no man, weary and sated with seeing, deigns
to lift his eyes to the luminous spaces of the sky,[6]—

and that these same things, if they were presented to us
newly, we should find as incredible as any others, or more so.

If these things were for the first time unexpectedly
presented to mortals, or were suddenly thrown before
them, what more wonderful could be thought of, what
that previously the world would have less dared to believe possible?[7]

He who had never seen a river thought that the first he came

Of what is True and what is False

to was the ocean; and the largest things with which we are acquainted, we believe them to be the utmost that Nature can do in that kind.

To be sure, a river which is not very great seems so to a man who has not previously seen a greater one; and a tree appears huge, and so does a man; and an object of any kind, if it be greater than has been seen, is supposed to be large.[8]

Our minds become accustomed to things from the familiarity of our eyes with them, and feel no wonder, and ask no questions about the causes of things which they continually behold.[9] The novelty of things, more than their importance, spurs us on to seek the causes of them.

We must judge things with more reverence for this infinite power of Nature,[10] and with more recognition of our ignorance and weakness. How many improbable things there are, testified to by people worthy of credence, which, if we can not be convinced about them, should at least be left in suspense; for to condemn them as impossible is to pretend, by a rash assumption, to knowledge of the extent of possibility. If we understood clearly the difference there is between the impossible and the unusual, and between what is contrary to the order of the course of nature and what is contrary to the common opinion of mankind, neither believing hastily nor disbelieving lightly, we should observe the rule, "Nothing too much," enjoined by Chilo.[11]

When we find in Froissart[12] that the comte de Foix learned in Béarn of the defeat of King John of Castile at Juberoth the day after it happened, and the manner of this that he alleges, we may well smile; and so, too, when our

Of what is True and what is False

annals say that Pope Honorius, on the very day that King Philippe Auguste died at Mantes, had his obsequies publicly celebrated, and commanded them to be performed throughout Italy;[13] for the authority of these witnesses is not perhaps of sufficient weight to hold us in check. But when Plutarch, besides several examples which he alleges from ancient times, says that he knows with certain knowledge that, in the reign of Domitian, the news of the battle lost by Antonius in Germany, many days' journey from Rome, was made public there and dispersed through the world on the same day when the battle was lost;[14] and if Cæsar maintains that it has often happened that the report has forerun the event, shall we say[15] that these honest folk allowed themselves to be deceived like the common herd, and were not as clear-sighted as we? Is there any thing more delicate, more clear, and more keen than Pliny's judgement when it pleases him to bring it into play? any thing further removed from emptiness? I say nothing of the excellence of his learning, of which I make less account. In what part of these two qualities do we surpass him? And yet there is no meanest scholar who does not convict him of falsehood, and who does not undertake to instruct him concerning the movement of the works of nature.

When we read in Bouchet of the miracles wrought by the relics of St. Hilary,[16] we can pass on:[17] his credit is not great enough to deprive us of the liberty of gainsaying him; but to condemn altogether[18] all such stories seems to me singularly overbold. The great St. Augustine testifies to having seen, at Milan, a blind child recover its sight by the relics of Saints Gervais and Protaise;[19] at Carthage, a woman cured of a cancer by the sign of the cross that a woman lately

242

Of what is True and what is False

baptised made upon her; Hesperius, a familiar friend of his, had driven out the spirits that infested his house, with a little earth from our Lord's sepulchre, and this same earth having been taken afterward to the church, a paralytic brought thither was straightway cured; a woman in a procession, having touched the shrine of St. Stephen with a nosegay, and having with this nosegay rubbed her eyes, recovered her sight, lost long before; and several other miracles, at which he says that he was present. Of what shall we accuse him and two holy bishops, Aurelius and Maximinus, whom he summons for his witnesses? Shall it be of ignorance, lack of intelligence, credulity, or of evil intent and imposture? Is there a man in our day so bold as to think himself comparable to them, whether in virtue and piety, or in learning, judgement, and sufficiency? *Even though they adduced no reason, their mere authority would master me.*[20]

It is a dangerous audacity, and of moment, besides the unreasonable rashness that it carries with it, to despise what we do not understand. For when, by virtue of your eminent intelligence, you have established the boundaries of truth and falsehood, and you find that you have necessarily to believe things in which there is even more that is strange than in what you deny, you are immediately compelled to forego these boundaries. Now, what seems to me to bring so much confusion into our thoughts in our present religious troubles is the partial surrender that the Catholics make of their belief: it seems to them that they show themselves to be moderate and wise when they concede to their opponents some of the points in controversy. But, besides that they do not see what an advantage it is to him who attacks you for you to begin to give way to him and to draw back, and how greatly that encourages him to pursue his advantage, the very points that they select as the most trivial are sometimes very important. We must either submit altogether to the authority of our ecclesiastical government, or dispense with it altogether: it is not for us to fix how much obedience we owe it. And furthermore,—I can say this because I have tried it,—having formerly made use of this freedom in my own selection and sifting, regarding as of no importance certain points in the ceremonial of our Church, which seem to have an aspect more or less idle or strange, when I have come to confer about them with learned men, I have found that these things have a substantial and very solid foundation, and that it is only stupidity and ignorance which cause us to receive them with less reverence than the rest. Why do we not remember how much we are conscious of contradiction in our very judgement? how many things we regarded yesterday as articles of faith which are fables to us to-day? Vain-glory and curiosity are the scourges of our soul. The last leads us to put our noses into every thing, and the other forbids us to leave any thing unsettled and undecided.

Chapter XXVIII

OF FRIENDSHIP

OBSERVING the method of work of a painter in my employ, I have been tempted to imitate him. He chooses the best spot in the middle of each wall, to place there a picture worked out with all his skill; and the empty space all about it he fills with grotesques, which are fantastic paintings having no other charm than diversity and strangeness. And, in truth, what are these writings of mine but grotesques and monstrous bodies, botched up with divers members, without definite shape, having neither order, sequence, nor proportion, except by chance?

A beautiful woman above, ending in a fish.[1]

I go along with my painter in this second point, but I fall short in the other and better part; for my ability does not go so far as to venture to undertake a fine picture, of high finish and fashioned according to art. I have thought of borrowing such a one from Etienne de la Boëtie, which will do honour to all the rest of this work. It is a treatise to which he gave the name of *La Servitude Volontaire;* but those who did not know this have since very aptly rebaptised it *Le Contre-Un.* He wrote it by way of essay in his early youth,[2]

Of Friendship

in praise of liberty and against tyrants. It has for a long time been in the hands of men of understanding, not without very great and well-deserved commendation, for it is as noble and perfect as possible. Yet it is far from being the best that he could do; and if, in his maturer years, when I knew him, he had conceived such a plan as mine, of writing down his thoughts, we should now see many things of rare excellence which would bring us very near to the fame of antiquity; for especially in this portion of the gifts of Nature, I know no man who can be compared to him. But nothing of his has survived except this discourse—and that only by chance, and I believe that he never saw it after it left his hands— and some notes upon that edict of January,[3] famous in our civil wars, which also will perchance find their place elsewhere.

This is all that I have been able to recover of his (I whom, when death was at hand, he made, in his will, heir of his library and his papers, as a most loving remembrance of him), except the little volume of his works which I have had published;[4] and I am under special obligation to this treatise because it was the means of our first acquaintance. For it was shown to me a long while before I saw him, and gave me my first knowledge of his name, thus opening the way to the friendship between us, which we cherished as long as God willed, so absolute and so perfect that surely the like has seldom been read of, and among the men of our day[5] no trace is seen of any such. So many accidental circumstances must concur to build it up, that it is much if fortune attains that end once in three centuries. There is nothing to which nature seems more to have shown us the way than to companionship;[6] and Aristotle says that good legislators have

Of Friendship

given more thought to friendship than to justice.[7] Now the highest point of its perfection is this. For in general all those companionships which pleasure or profit, or public or private needs, beget and nourish, are in so far less beautiful and noble, and in so far less true friendships, as they introduce another cause and end and fruit into friendship than friendship itself. Nor do these four common kinds,[8]—natural, social, hospitable, sexual,—separately or conjointly, sort well with it.[9] The sentiment of children for their fathers is rather respect; friendship is nourished by familiar intercourse, which can not be between them on account of the too great difference in age, and might conflict with natural obligations; for neither can all the secret thoughts of fathers be communicated to their children, lest they give rise to an unseemly intimacy, nor can the warnings and reproofs which are among the first duties of friendship be administered by children to their fathers. Nations have been found where it was the custom for children to kill their fathers, and others where fathers killed their children, to avoid the burden they may sometimes become;[10] and by nature the one depends on the ruin of the other.[11] There have been philosophers who disdained this natural bond; witness Aristippus: when some one insisted upon the affection that he owed his children because they issued from him, he began to spit, saying that truly that also issued from him, that indeed we also engender lice and worms.[12] And that other whom Plutarch tried to induce to be reconciled to his brother: "I care no more for him," he said, "for having come out of the same hole."[13] In truth, the name of brother is a delightful name, and full of loving-kindness; and for that reason he and I made it the symbol of our union; but the commingling of property, the divisions, and the wealth of the one being the poverty of the other, wondrously weakens and relaxes the fraternal bond: brothers having to pursue their advancement in the same path and the same direction, it is inevitable that they often jostle and clash with one another. Moreover, why should the resemblance and relation which engenders true and perfect friendships exist between brothers? Father and son may be of entirely different dispositions, and brothers also: this is my son, this is my kinsman; but he is a barbarian, a villain, or a fool. And then, too, in proportion as these friendships are enjoined upon us by natural law and obligation, there is less of our own choice and free will in them; and our free will has no product which is more properly its own than affection and friendship. It is not that I have not had in this direction all possible experience, for I had the best father that ever lived and the most indulgent, even in his extreme old age, and being of a family famous and exemplary for generations in this matter of brotherly concord,—

One famed for fatherly affection toward his brothers.[14]

To compare with it the affection for women, although it proceeds from our own choice, is impossible; it can not be placed in the same category. Its flame, I admit,—

For I am not unknown to the goddess who mingles a sweet bitterness with the torments of love,[15]—

is more active, hotter, and fiercer; but it is a reckless and fickle flame, wavering and changing, fever-like, subject to risings and fallings; and it holds but a nook in us. In friendship there is a general and universal warmth, temperate, moreover, and uniform, a constant and settled warmth, all

Of Friendship

sweetness and smoothness, in which there is nothing of roughness or poignancy. What is more, in love there is but a mad craving for what eludes us.

> So the hunter follows the hare, in cold and in heat, on the mountain and by the shore; he no longer cares for it when it has become his prey, and he pursues only that which flees.[16]

As soon as it enters into the bounds of friendship, that is to say, into full agreement of desires, it languishes and weakens; enjoyment destroys it, as its object is fleshly and it is subject to satiety. Friendship, on the contrary, is enjoyed in the degree in which it is desired, nor does it spring up, become rooted, and grow, except by enjoyment as being of spiritual nature, and the soul being purified by the exercise of it. Subordinate to this perfect friendship, these ephemeral loves have in other days found lodging in me—not to speak of him[17] who reveals this only too clearly in his verses. So these two passions have entered into me, known to each other, but never in rivalry, the first holding its course with a lofty and proud flight, and disdainfully beholding the other go its way far below.

As for marriage, besides that it is a bargain of which the entrance only is free, its continuance being constrained and compelled, resting upon other things than our will,—and a bargain, too, which is ordinarily entered into for other objects,—there happen in it innumerable foreign complications to be disentangled, sufficient to break the thread and trouble the course of a lively affection; whereas in friendship there are no dealings or transactions save with itself. Moreover, to speak truly, the usual capacity of women is not equal to the demands of the communion and intercourse which is the sustenance of that sacred bond; nor do their minds seem firm enough to sustain the pressure of so hard and so lasting a knot. But surely, save for that, if there could be formed such a free and voluntary connection, wherein not only should the souls have this perfect employment, but the bodies too should have their share in the alliance, into which the whole man should enter, it is certain that the friendship would be more full and more complete; but there has never yet been an instance of this sex reaching that point, and by the common consent of the ancient schools this is denied. And by our morals that other Greek license is justly abhorred; which, moreover, from having necessarily, according to their custom, so great a disparity in age and difference in offices between the lovers, answered no better to the perfect union and harmony which in this we require. *What, after all, is this friendship-love? Why is it that an ugly youth or a handsome old man is never beloved?*[18] For the very picture that the Academy draws of it[19] will not, I think, disprove me, if I say this as coming from it:[20] that this first frenzy, inspired by the son of Venus in the lover's heart, for the possession of the flower of delicate youthfulness to which[21] they permit all the presumptuous and passionate efforts that an immoderate ardour can suggest, was based simply on external beauty, the deceitful design of corporeal generation; for it could not be based on the mind, which had not yet shown itself, which was but newly born and not yet blossoming. That, if this frenzy seized upon a mean heart, the instruments of its pursuit were riches, gifts, favour in promotion to places of dignity, and other such base trafficking which they[22] condemn. If it fell upon one of nobler temper, the means of pleasing adopted were noble likewise: philosophic instructions, teachings to reverence religion, to obey the laws, to die for the good of one's country—examples of valour, wisdom, justice; the lover studying how to make himself acceptable by the charm and beauty of his mind (that of his body being long since faded), and hoping, by this mental companionship, to make a stronger and more lasting contract. When this pursuit came to a result in due season (for while they did not require of the lover that he should take time and use discretion in his pursuit, they most strictly required this of the loved one, since he had to judge of an inward beauty difficult to recognise and hard to discover), then there was born in the loved one a desire for spiritual beauty. With him this was the principal thing, the bodily was fortuitous and secondary; with the lover it was just the opposite. For this reason they prefer the loved one, and aver that the gods too prefer him; and they find great fault with the poet Æschylus for having, in describing the love of Achilles and Patroclus,[23] given the lover's part to Achilles, who was in the first and beardless bloom of his youth, and the most beautiful of the Greeks. From this complete participation, its most commanding and worthiest part exercising its functions and predominating, they declare that there flowed results of great utility, private and public; that it was the strength of those countries which admitted the practice of it, and the chief bulwark of equity and of liberty; witness the salutary loves of Harmodius and Aristogeiton.[24] Therefore they call it sacred and divine, and to their thinking only the violence of tyrants and the weakness of peoples are opposed to it. In fine, all that we can concede in favour of the Academy is to say that this was a love that

Of Friendship

ended in friendship; which agrees not ill with the Stoic definition of love: *Love is the desire to win friendship from a beautiful being*.[25] I return to my description of a kind[26] more equitable and equable. *In general, friendships are not to be judged of until both the mind and the body have strength and maturity*.[27]

To continue—what we commonly call friends and friendships are only acquaintances and familiar relations formed by some chance or convenience, by means whereof our minds meet kindly. In the friendship of which I speak they are blended and melted one into another in a commingling so entire that they lose sight of that which first united them and can not again find it.[28] If I am urged to say why I loved him, I feel that it can not be expressed save by replying: "Because it was he, because it was I." There is, beyond all my reasoning and beyond all that I can say in detail about it, I know not what inexplicable and inevitable force that brought about this union. We sought each other before we had met, by reason of what we had heard of each other, which had more effect on our emotions than comports with hearsay reports, I believe, by some decree of Heaven. We embraced by our names. And at our first meeting, which was accidental, at a great festival and gathering in the city, we found ourselves so fast held, so well known, so bound to each other, that thereafter nothing was so close to either of us as each was to the other. He wrote an excellent Latin satire, which has been published,[29] wherein he excuses and explains the suddenness of our mutual understanding which so quickly reached its perfection. Having so short a time to last, and having begun so late (for we were both grown men and he a few years the elder),[30] it had no time to lose and to

Of Friendship

fashion itself on the model of weak and orderly friendships, which require so many precautions in the way of long preliminary intercourse. Such a one as this has no other type than itself and can resemble only itself. It was no one special consideration, nor two, nor three, nor four, nor a thousand; it was I know not what quintessence of all this blending which, having completely possessed itself of my will, led it to plunge into and lose itself in his; and having completely possessed itself of his will, led it to plunge into and lose itself in mine, by force of a like eagerness and impulse. I say "lose" with truth, for it left us nothing that was our own, or that was either his or mine.[31]

When Lælius, in presence of the Roman consuls who, after the condemnation of Tiberius Gracchus, proceeded against all those who had held intercourse with him, enquired of Caius Blosius—who was his[32] chief friend—how much he would have been willing to do for him, and he replied, "Every thing,"—"What, every thing?" rejoined Lælius. "But if he had ordered you to set fire to our temples?"— "He would never have ordered me to do that," replied Blosius.—"But if he had?" Lælius persisted.—"I would have obeyed," was the reply.[33] If he was so wholly the friend of Gracchus as the histories say, he had no occasion to offend the consuls by this last and audacious admission, and should not have deviated from the confidence he had in the mind of Gracchus.[34] But, moreover, they who blame this reply as treasonable do not well understand this mystery, and do not admit—as is the fact—that he held the mind of Gracchus in his hand, both through influence and through knowledge.[35] They were more friends than citizens, more friends than friends or enemies of their country, than friends

253

Of Friendship

of ambition and turmoil. Being completely pledged each to the other, each completely held the reins of the other's inclinations; and assuming this team[36] to be guided by virtue and governed by reason (as indeed it is quite impossible otherwise to conduct it), the reply of Blosius is what it should have been. If their acts did not mutually fit together, they were neither friends one of the other, nor friends to themselves, by my measure. Besides, that reply signifies nothing more than mine would, if, to one who should make this enquiry of me: "If your will bade you kill your daughter, would you kill her?" I should answer affirmatively. For that is no evidence of my readiness to do the deed, because I have no suspicion of my will, and as little of that of such a friend. It is not in the power of all the arguments in the world to dislodge me from my certainty of the intentions and judgements of my friend: no act of his could be presented to me, no matter what aspect it might wear, that I should not instantly discern its motive. Our souls journeyed together so in unison,[37] they regarded each other with such ardent affection, and with like affection revealed themselves one to the other, to their inmost depths, that not only did I know his soul as intimately as my own, but I would surely have trusted myself to him more freely than to myself.

Let no one place in the same rank those other everyday friendships; I have as much knowledge as any man of them, and of the most perfect in their kind; but I advise no one to confuse their rules: he would be deluded. In these other friendships one must walk, bridle in hand, with prudence and caution; the tie is not fastened in such wise that one has not reason to distrust it. "Love him," says Chilo, "as if you might some day come to hate him; hate him as if you might

Of Friendship

some day come to love him."[38] This precept, which is abominable in this sovereign and commanding friendship, is sound in the practice of ordinary, commonplace friendships, to which we should apply the frequent saying of Aristotle: "O my friends, there is no friend."[39]

In this noble intercourse, the services and benefactions that keep alive other friendships do not deserve to be taken at all into account, being occasioned by the complete blinding of our wills; for, just as the friendship that I have for myself is not augmented by the aid that I give myself at need,—whatever the Stoics may say,—and as I am no wise grateful to myself for the service that I render to myself; so, the union of two such friends being truly perfect, it causes them to lose the sense of such duties, and to detest and banish as between themselves those words implying separation and difference—benefit, obligation, gratitude, entreaty, thanks, and their like. Every thing being in fact common as between them,—will, thoughts, judgements, property, wives, children, honour, and life,—and their accord being that of one soul in two bodies, according to the very apt definition of Aristotle,[40]—they can not lend or give any thing to each other. That is why the lawmakers, in order to ennoble marriage by some fanciful resemblance to this divine union, forbid gifts between husband and wife, meaning by that to imply that every thing should belong to each of them, and that they have nothing to divide and part between them. If, in the sort of friendship of which I am speaking, one could give to the other, he who should receive the gift would be the one who conferred an obligation on his friend: for each seeking above all other things to confer a benefit on the other, he who affords the subject and the op-

Of Friendship

portunity is the one who plays the liberal part,[41] giving his friend the delight of accomplishing in regard to him what he[42] most desires. When Diogenes the philosopher had need of money, he used to say that he asked it back from his friends, not that he asked for it.[43] And to show how this may be put into effect, I will narrate a singular ancient example of it.

Eudamidas of Corinth had two friends: Charixenus a Sicyonian, and Aretheus a Corinthian. When he came to die, being a poor man and his two friends being rich, he made his will thus: "I bequeath to Arethus the support of my mother and the taking care of her in her old age; to Charixenus the finding a husband for my daughter and giving her as large a dowry as he can; and in case one of them shall die, I substitute for him the survivor." Those who were the first to see this will made sport of it; but his legatees,[44] having been informed of it, accepted it with extreme pleasure. And one of them, Charixenus, having died five days later, the substitution being carried out in favour of Aretheus, he took scrupulous care of the mother, and of five talents that he possessed he gave two and a half to his own only daughter on her marriage, and two and a half to the daughter of Eudamidas, and celebrated both nuptials on the same day.[45]

This example is very complete, except for one thing, namely, the multitude of friends: for this perfect friendship of which I speak is indivisible, each gives himself so entirely to his friend that he has nothing to dispose of elsewhere; on the contrary, he is grieved that he is not double, triple, or quadruple, and that he has not several souls and several wills, to bestow them all on that object. Ordinary friend-

Of Friendship

ships can be divided: one may love the beauty of this person, the courtesy of another, the liberality of another; the paternal affection of one man, the brotherly love of another, and so forth; but the friendship that possesses the soul and rules over it in full sovereignty—it is impossible that it should be double. If two friends should call for assistance at the same time, to which would you hasten? If they should require from you inconsistent services, what course would you pursue? If one entrusted to your secrecy a thing which it would be useful for the other to know, how would you extricate yourself? The sole and principal friendship dissolves all other obligations. The secret that I have sworn to disclose to no other, I may without perjury make known to him who is not another—he is myself. It is enough of a miracle to double oneself, and they do not know the greatness of it who talk of making themselves three. Nothing is the uttermost which has its like; and whoever imagines that of two persons I love one as dearly as the other, and that they love each other and me as much as I love them, he multiplies into a society the most single and indivisible of things,[46] of which a single instance is the hardest thing in the world to find.

The rest of this tale agrees entirely with what I was saying: for Eudamidas bestows upon his friends the boon and favour of using them for his need; he makes them inheritors of that liberality of his which consists in placing in their hands the means of benefitting him. And unquestionably the strength of friendship manifests itself much more abundantly in his act than in that of Aretheus. To conclude, these conditions are inconceivable to him who has never experienced them, and they lead me to praise exceedingly the

Of Friendship

reply of the young soldier to Cyrus, who asked him for how much he would sell a horse with which he had just won the prize of the race, and whether he would exchange him for a kingdom: "Surely not, sire; but I would readily part with him to gain thereby a friend, if I could find a man worthy of such fellowship."[47] Well did he say, "if I could find"; for one easily finds men fit for a superficial acquaintance; but in this other sort, in which one deals from the deepest depths of his heart, and without any reserve, certainly it is essential that all the parts that come into play[48] be perfectly spotless and reliable.

In those connections which hold by but one end we have only to take heed of the imperfections which particularly concern that end. It can not matter of what religion my physician is, and my lawyer; that consideration has nothing in common with the duties of the friendship which they owe me. And in the domestic relations which those who serve me form with me, I take the same position: I question little about a footman's chastity; I enquire if he is diligent; and am not so anxious about a gambling muleteer as about one wanting in strength, or about a profane cook as about an ignorant one. I do not busy myself with saying what should be done in the world,—enough other people busy themselves about that,—but what I do.

> Such is my custom; as for you, do as you have occasion.[49]

In the familiar intercourse of the table, I ask for the agreeable, not the discreet; in bed, beauty before virtue; in the companionship of thoughts, cleverness, even without integrity.[50]

258

Of Friendship

Just as he who was found bestriding a stick, in play with his children,[51] begged the man who caught him at it to say nothing about it until he was himself a father, thinking that the emotion which would then be born in his heart would make him a just judge of such an act, I also should desire to speak to people who have experienced what I describe; but knowing how far removed from the ordinary wont such a friendship is, and how rare it is, I do not expect to find any good judge of it. For the discourses that antiquity has left us on this subject seem to me cold[52] in comparison with the feeling that I have of it; and on this point the facts surpass the very precepts of philosophy:—

> So long as I am in my senses, I shall find nothing to compare with an agreeable friend.[53]

Old Menander called him happy who had met merely the ghost of a friend.[54] He was surely justified in saying this, even if he had made essay of it; for, in truth, if I compare all the rest of my life,—although by God's mercy I have found it sweet and easy, and, save for the loss of such a friend, exempt from any poignant grief, full of contentment and tranquillity of mind, having been satisfied with[55] my natural and original advantages, without seeking others,—if, I say, I compare it all with the four years that it was given to me to enjoy the sweet companionship and society of that lofty soul,[56] it is but smoke, it is but a dark and mournful night. Since the day I lost him,—

> [The day] which will ever be bitter to me, ever sacred; such, O Gods! has been your will,[57]—

I do but drag out a languishing existence, and even the

259

pleasures that offer themselves to me, instead of consoling me, redouble my regret for his loss. We halved every thing; it seems to me that I steal from him his share.

> I have resolved that here I may enjoy no pleasure while he, my comrade, is absent.[58]

I was formerly so enured and accustomed to be second in every thing, that it seems to me now that I am only half a man.

> If an untimely death has taken away the half of my life, what cause have I, the other half, to linger on, being not so dear, and itself impaired? That day struck down both of us.[59]

There is no act or thought of mine in which I do not miss him, even as it would have been with him for me; for even as he surpassed me infinitely in every other ability and power, so did he in the virtue of friendship.

> What shame, what bounds can there be in grief for so dear a head?[60]

> O brother, snatched from me to my grief! With thee have departed all the joys which in life thy sweet love nourished. Thou, O brother, thou hast destroyed by thy death all my comforts; with thee my whole soul is entombed. Since thy death I have wholly shunned the study of books and all delights of the mind.—Shall I speak with thee hereafter? Am I never again to hear thee talk? Shall I never again behold thee, O brother dearer than life? But surely I shall forever love thee.[61]

260

Of Friendship

But let us listen a while to this youth of sixteen.[62]

Because I have learned that this work has since been brought to light, and to an evil end, by those who seek to disturb and change the form of our government, heedless whether they will improve it, and that they have mixed it with other writings of their own make, I have given up placing it here. And that the author's memory may not by this [publication] be wronged in the minds of those who have not had the opportunity to know his opinions and his actions at close quarters, I inform them that this subject was treated by him in his boyhood, by way of practice only, as a familiar subject which had been travelled over a thousand times in books. I make no doubt that he believed what he wrote, for he was conscientious enough not to deceive, even carelessly; and I know furthermore that, if he had had his choice, he would have liked better to be born at Venice than at Sarlac, and with good reason. But he had another maxim, supremely imprinted on his mind—to obey, and submit most scrupulously to, the laws under which he was born. There was never a better citizen, or one more devoted to the repose of his country or more hostile to the commotions and innovations of his time: he would much rather have employed his ability in quieting them than in supplying the wherewithal to rouse them more. His mind was modelled on the pattern of other ages than this.

Now, in exchange for this serious work, I will substitute another, produced at the same period of his life, but more vivacious and blithe.[63]

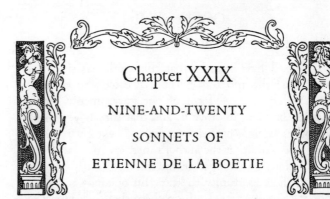

Chapter XXIX

NINE-AND-TWENTY
SONNETS OF
ETIENNE DE LA BOETIE

TO MADAME DE GRAMMONT, COMTESSE DE GUISSEN:

MADAME, I offer you nothing of my own, either because it is already yours, or because I find in it nothing worthy of you. But it is my desire that these verses, wheresoever they might find themselves, should have your name at their head, for the honour it will be to them to have the noble Corisande d'Andouins for their guide. This gift seems to me to be appropriate for you because there are few ladies in France who are better judges of poetry, or who make use of it more fitly than you; and since there is no one who can give it life and spirit as you do by those beautiful and rich tones with which among a million other charms, nature has endowed you. Madame, these verses deserve to be highly valued by you; for you will agree with me that none have come out of Gascony which had more originality and delightsomeness, and which testified to having come from a more opulent hand. And be not jealous because you have only the remainder of what some time ago I published[1] and dedicated to Monsieur de Foix, your honoured kinsman; for truly these have an indefinable something more

262

Sonnets of Etienne de la Boëtie

vivid and more ebullient, as he wrote them in his lustiest youth and inflamed by a fine and noble passion, about which some day, Madame, I will whisper in your ear. The others[2] were written later, for the love of his wife, when he was arranging his marriage, and they have already an indescribable touch of marital coolness. And I am one of those who maintain that poetry is never so charming as when treating a wanton and lawless subject.

These verses may be seen elsewhere.[3]

Chapter XXX

OF MODERATION

AS if our touch were infection, we by our handling corrupt things which in themselves are beautiful and
good. We can lay hold of virtue in such wise that it will become thereby vicious, if we embrace it with too eager and
violent a passion. Those who say that there is never excess
in virtue, because it is no longer virtue if there be excess,
play with words.

> The wise man would deserve to be called a fool,
> and the just man unjust, if he seek virtue itself to
> excess.[1]

This is a subtle consideration of philosophy. It is possible
both to love virtue overmuch, and to be excessive in a right
action. To this point of view are conformed the divine
words: Be no more virtuous than is needful, but be soberly
virtuous.[2]

I have known a man of high rank[3] to injure his reputation for devoutness by exhibiting himself as devout beyond all examples of men of his quality. I love temperate
and moderate natures. Lack of moderation, even in what is
right, while it does not offend me, amazes me, and it per-

Of Moderation

plexes me to give a name to it. Neither the mother of Pausanias, who gave the first directions and brought the first stone for her son's death,[4] nor the dictator Posthumius, who caused his son to be put to death, whom the ardour of youth had caused to dash successfully upon the enemy a little in advance of his time[5]—neither of the two seems to me so right as strange; and I prefer neither to counsel nor to follow a virtue so barbarous and which costs so dear. The archer who overshoots the mark fails equally with him who does not reach it; and my eyes trouble me as much in looking up suddenly toward a bright light as in looking down into the darkness. Callicles, in Plato, says[6] that philosophy carried to an extreme is harmful, and counsels us not to enter into it beyond the limits of profitableness; practised in moderation, it is agreeable and advantageous, but it makes a man uncivilised and unsound, scornful of common religions and laws, a foe to social intercourse, a foe to merely human pleasures, incapable of any political function and of giving aid to others or to himself—a man to be cuffed with impunity. He speaks the truth; for in its excess it enslaves our natural freedom, and turns us aside, by too great refinement, from the straight and level road that Nature has marked out for us.

Our friendship for our wives is most legitimate; yet theology does not fail to curb and restrain it. I think that I read long ago in St. Thomas,[7] in a passage where he condemns the marriage of kinsfolk in the prohibited degrees, this reason among others—that there is danger that the friendship that a man may have for such a wife may be extravagant; for if conjugal affection exists entire and perfect, as it ought, and if it be surcharged with the affection due to the blood-tie,[8] there is no doubt that that addition carries such a husband beyond the bounds of reason.

The branches of learning,[9] like theology and philosophy, which regulate the morals of mankind, enter into all things. There is no act so intimate and secret that it evades their knowledge and jurisdiction. Very ignorant are they who censure their liberty. They are like those women who expose their parts as much as you will in order to wanton; shame forbidding them to do so to the physician. I will then, in the name of philosophy and religion, teach husbands this, if there are yet any who are too eager: that even those pleasures they enjoy in knowing their wives are to be condemned, unless they observe moderation therein; and that in this connection there is as much scope for licentiousness and debauchery as in an illicit connection. Those shameless caresses which the first heat suggests to us in this sport, are not only indecently but detrimentally practised on our wives. If they must learn shamelessness let it be from others. They are always sufficiently lively for our need. I have always followed Nature's simple instructions.

Marriage is a religious and godly union; that is why the pleasure we derive from it should be a sustained, serious pleasure, combined with some austerity; it should be a somewhat prudent and conscientious pleasure. And because its chief end is generation, there are some who question whether, when we have no hope of such fruit, or when they are beyond the age or pregnant, it is permissible to seek their embraces. It is a homicide according to Plato. Certain nations, among others the Mohammedans, abominate any connection with a pregnant woman; many also with one who is in her courses. Zenobia received her husband but for

Of Moderation

one charge; that done, she let him go free during the whole time of her conception, only then giving him permission to recommence: a brave and generous example of marriage.

It was of some needy poet who was famished for this delight that Plato borrowed this story: That Jupiter one day attacked his wife so impetuously that, too impatient to wait till she had gained her couch, he threw her on the floor, and in the vehemence of his pleasure forgot the great and important resolutions he had but recently taken with the other gods in his celestial court; and be boasted that he found this encounter as good as when he first deflowered her by stealth and unknown to their parents.

The kings of Persia used to invite their wives to share in their banquets, but when the wine began to heat them in good earnest, and when they felt the need of giving an entirely loose rein to voluptuousness, they sent them back to their private apartments, that they might not participate in their immoderate appetites, sending for other women to take their places, to whom they were not obliged to show the same respect.

All kinds of pleasures and gratifications are not fitly bestowed on all sorts of men. Epaminondas had ordered a young debauchee to be imprisoned; Pelopidas begged that he might be set free, as a favour to himself; he[10] denied that to him, but granted it to a wench of his who also begged it, saying that it was a gratification due to a mistress, not to a captain. Sophocles, when associated with Pericles in the prætorship,[11] accidentally saw a handsome boy pass by. "Oh! what a handsome boy that is!" he said to Pericles. "That saying," said Pericles, "would be blameless for another than a prætor, who should have not only chaste hands, but chaste eyes." The Emperor Ælius Verus replied to his wife, when she complained of his allowing himself to love other women, that he did it from conscientious motives, because marriage was a title of honour and dignity, not of wanton and licentious concupiscence.[12] And our ancient religious authors[13] speak with all respect of a wife who repudiated her husband because she was unwilling to yield to his too licentious and immoderate passion. In short, there is no pleasure so lawful that excess and lack of moderation in it are not blameworthy. But speaking in good conscience, is not man a pitiful creature? It is hardly in his power, from his natural condition, to enjoy a single pure and unalloyed pleasure; yet he takes pains to lessen this power by precepts; he is not pitiable enough if he does not add to his wretchedness by craft and study.

> We artificially make worse the painful paths of fortune.[14]

Human wisdom plays the sage very foolishly[15] in exercising herself to diminish the number and the charm of the pleasures which belong to us, while she shows kindness and vigilance in employing her skill in smoothing and colouring our ills,[16] and lightening our perception of them. Had I been in command, I would have chosen a more natural path, and one more direct and godly; and perchance I might have made myself strong enough not to go too far.

What of the fact that our doctors, spiritual and corporeal, as if they had conspired together, find no road to a cure, nor any remedy for the ills of body and mind save by anguish, pain, and trouble. Vigils, fastings, hair-shirts, distant and solitary exile, perpetual imprisonment, scourgings, and other

Of Moderation

afflictions, were introduced for that purpose; and under such conditions that they are genuine afflictions, and are attended by poignant suffering; not as happened with one Gallio, who having been banished to the island of Lesbos, it became known at Rome that he was enjoying himself there, and that what had been alloted to him as a punishment had become a source of pleasure; wherefore they determined to recall him to his wife and his own house, and ordered him to remain there, so as to adapt his punishment to his state of mind.[17] For to him whose health and spirits were improved by fasting, or to whom fish was more appetising than meat, these would be no salutary prescriptions; no more than, in the other kind of medicine, drugs which have no effect on him who takes them with liking and pleasure. Bitterness and distaste are conditions that facilitate their operation. The constitution which welcomed rhubarb as familiar would vitiate its use; we must take something that offends our stomach, to cure it; and here the common rule fails, that things are cured by their opposites: for one ill cures another.[18] This belief is in some sort related to that other so ancient one, the thought that heaven and nature were gratified by our massacring and murdering, which was universally included in all religions. Even in our fathers' days Amurat,[19] at the taking of Isthmia, sacrificed six hundred Greek youths to his father's soul, that their blood might serve as propitiation, in expiation of the sins of the departed. And in the new regions discovered in our time, still pure and undefiled in comparison with our own, this custom is received everywhere to some extent: all their idols are sprinkled with human blood, not without divers instances of horrible cruelty. The victims are burned alive, and when half roasted, are taken from the bed of coals, in order to have their heart and entrails torn out. Others, even women, are flayed alive, and with their bloody skins others are clothed and disguised. And not less are there examples of endurance and resolution: for the poor creatures who are to be sacrificed, old men, women, and children, go about for some days beforehand, asking alms for the offering of their sacrifice,[20] and present themselves to be butchered, singing and dancing with the spectators. The ambassadors of the King of Mexico, impressing upon Ferdinand Cortez their master's greatness, after they had told him that he had thirty vassals, each of whom could assemble a hundred thousand fighting men, and that he dwelt in the most beautiful and strongest city under heaven, added that he had to sacrifice fifty thousand men to the gods each year. In truth, it is said, he waged constant war against certain great neighbouring nations, not only to train the youth of the country, but chiefly to have the wherewithal to supply his sacrifices with prisoners of war. Elsewhere, in a certain district, by way of welcome to this same Cortez, they sacrificed fifty men, all at once. I will tell this strange story also: some of these peoples, having been beaten by him,[21] sent to him by way of recognition, and to seek his friendship; the messengers presented him with gifts of three sorts, in this wise: "Lord, here are five slaves; if thou art a fierce god that dost feed on flesh and blood, eat them, and we will bring thee more; if thou art a kindly god, here are incense and feathers; if thou art a man, take these birds and fruits."[22]

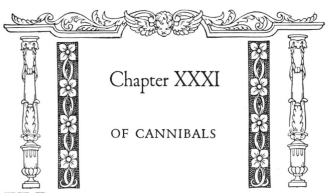

Chapter XXXI

OF CANNIBALS

WHEN King Pyrrhus invaded Italy, after he had surveyed the army that the Romans had sent out against him, drawn up in battle array, "I know not," he said "what barbarians these are" (for the Greeks so called all foreign nations), "but the disposition of this army that I see is in no wise barbarian."[1] The Greeks said the same of the army that Flaminius led into their country;[2] and Philip, when he saw from a little hill the order and arrangement of the Roman camp in his kingdom under Publius Sulpicius Galba.[3] Thus we see how we should beware of adhering to common opinions, and that we must weigh them by the test of reason, not by common report.[4]

I had with me for a long time a man who had lived ten or twelve years in that other world which has been discovered in our time in the region where Villegaignon made land, and which he christened Antarctic France. This discovery of a boundless country seems to be worth consideration. I do not know whether I can be assured that some other may not hereafter be found, so many greater personages having been deceived about this one. I fear that our eyes may be greater than our stomachs,[5] and that we have more curiosity than

Of Cannibals

capacity. We grasp at every thing, but clutch nothing but wind. Plato speaks of Solon narrating that he learned from the priests of the city of Sais in Egypt that in times past, and before the Deluge, there was a large island called Atlantidis, just at the mouth of the Strait of Gibraltar, which was of greater extent than Africa and Asia together, and that the kings of that country—who not only possessed that island, but had extended their dominion so far on the continent that they held the breadth of Africa as far as Egypt, and the length of Europe as far as Tuscany—undertook to stride into Asia and to subdue all the nations on the shores of the Mediterranean as far as the Euxine;[6] and to this end they traversed all Spain, Gaul, and Italy, even to Greece, where the Athenians resisted them; but, some time later, the Athenians and they and their island were swallowed up by the Deluge.[7] It is very probable that that immense inundation made strange changes in the inhabited places of the earth, as it is thought that the sea cut off Sicily from Italy,—

> They say that these lands were once torn violently asunder in a great convulsion; till then the two lands had been but one,[8]—

Cyprus from Syria, and the island of Negropont from the mainland of Bœotia; and elsewhere joined lands that were formerly separate, filling with mud and sand the channels between them,—

> Long a sterile fen, fit for the oar, it now feeds the neighbouring towns and feels the weight of the plough.[9]

Of Cannibals

But there is no great likelihood that this new world that we have just discovered is that island; for it almost touched Spain, and it would be an incredible effect of the inundation to have moved it away, as it is, more than twelve hundred leagues; besides which, the explorations of modern navigators have almost made sure that this is not an island, but mainland, connected with the East Indies on one side, and elsewhere with the countries that lie under the two poles; or, if divided from them, it is by so narrow a passage that it is not thereby entitled to be called an island. It seems as if there may be motions in those great bodies as in our own, some natural, others irregular. When I see the encroachment that my river Dordogne is making on its right bank, in my own day, and how much it has gained in twenty years, and has undermined the foundations of several buildings, I see clearly that it is an unusual disturbance; for if the river had always so done, or if it were always so to do, the face of the world would be subverted. But they[10] are subject to changes: sometimes they overflow on one side, sometimes on the other; sometimes they keep within their banks. I am not speaking of sudden inundations, of which we can lay our hand on the causes. In Medoc, along the seacoast, my brother, Sieur d'Arsac, saw an estate of his buried under the sand which the sea threw upon it; the roofs of some buildings are still visible; his revenues and domain are transformed into very poor pastures. The people of the place say that for some time past the sea pushes on so effectually toward them, that they have lost four leagues of land. These sands are her harbingers; and we see great moving sand dunes that march half a league before her and steadily advance.

Of Cannibals

The other assertion of ancient times with which it is attempted to connect this discovery, is in Aristotle—that is, if that little treatise of *Unheard-of Wonders*[11] be his. He there relates that certain Carthaginians, having started across the Atlantic Sea from the Strait of Gibraltar, and having sailed a long while, finally discovered a large, fertile island, well covered with forests, and watered by broad and deep rivers, far distant from any mainland; and that they, and others after them, attracted by the bounty and fertility of the soil, went thither with their wives and children, and set up their habitation there. The lords of Carthage, seeing that their country was being gradually depopulated, expressly forbade, upon pain of death, that any more of their people should go thither, and expelled these new settlers, fearing, so it is said, that, as time passed, they might so multiply that they would supplant themselves,[12] and ruin their state. This narrative of Aristotle's agrees no better[13] with our newly-discovered territories.

This man that I had[14] was a simple, plain fellow, which is a nature likely to give true testimony; for intelligent persons notice more things and scrutinise them more carefully; but they comment on them; and to make their interpretation of value and win belief for it, they can not refrain from altering the facts a little. They never represent things to you just as they are: they shape them and disguise them according to the aspect which they have seen them bear; and to win faith in their judgement and incline you to trust it, they readily help out the matter on one side, lengthen it, and amplify it. It needs a man either very truthful or so ignorant that he has no material wherewith to construct and give verisimilitude to false conceptions, and one who is wedded to nothing. My man was such a one; and, besides, he on divers occasions brought to me several sailors and traders whom he had known on his travels. So I am content with this information, without enquiring what the cosmographers say about it. We need topographers who would give us a detailed description of the places where they have been. But when they have the advantage over us of having seen Palestine, they desire to enjoy the privilege of telling us news about all the rest of the world. I could wish that every one would write what he knows and as much as he knows, not about one subject alone, but about all others; for one may have some special knowledge or experience as to the nature of a river or a fountain, who about other things knows only what every one knows. He will undertake, however, in order to give currency to that little scrap of knowledge, to write on the whole science of physics. From this fault spring many grave disadvantages.

Now, to return to what I was talking of, I think that there is nothing barbaric or uncivilised in that nation, according to what I have been told, except that every one calls "barbarism" whatever he is not accustomed to. As, indeed, it seems that we have no other criterion[15] of truth and of what is reasonable than the example and type of the opinions and customs of the country to which we belong: therein [to us] always is the perfect religion, the perfect political system, the perfect and achieved usage in all things. They are wild men,[16] just as we call those fruits wild[16] which Nature has produced unaided and in her usual course; whereas, in truth, it is those that we have altered by our skill and removed from the common kind which we ought rather to call wild. In the former the real and most useful and natural

275

virtues are alive and vigorous—we have vitiated them in the latter, adapting them to the gratification of our corrupt taste; and yet nevertheless the special savour and delicacy of divers uncultivated fruits of those regions seems excellent even to our taste in comparison with our own. It is not reasonable that art should gain the preëminence over our great and puissant mother Nature. We have so overloaded the beauty and richness of her works by our contrivances that we have altogether smothered her. Still, truly, whenever she shines forth unveiled,[17] she wonderfully shames our vain and trivial undertakings.

> The ivy grows best when wild, and the arbutus springs most beautifully in some lovely cave; birds sing most sweetly without teaching.[18]

All our efforts can not so much as reproduce the nest of the tiniest birdling, its contexture, its beauty, and its usefulness;[19] nay, nor the web of the little spider. All things, said Plato, are produced either by nature, or by chance, or by art; the greatest and most beautiful by one or other of the first two, the least and most imperfect by the last.[20]

These nations seem to me, then, wild in this sense, that they have received in very slight degree the external forms of human intelligence, and are still very near to their primitive simplicity. The laws of nature still govern them, very little corrupted by ours; even in such pureness that it sometimes grieves me that the knowledge of this did not come earlier, in the days when there were men who would have known better than we how to judge it. I am sorry that Lycurgus and Plato had not this knowledge; for it seems to me that what we see in intercourse with those nations sur-

276

passes not only all the paintings wherewith poetry has embellished the golden age, and all its conceptions in representing a happy condition of mankind, but also the idea and aspiration, even, of philosophy. They could not conceive so pure and simple an artlessness as we by experience know it to be; nor could they believe that human society could be carried on with so little artificiality and human unitedness.[21] It is a nation, I will say to Plato, in which there is no sort of traffic, no acquaintance with letters, no knowledge of numbers, no title of magistrate or of political eminence, no custom of service, of wealth, or of poverty, no contracts, no successions, no dividings of property, no occupations except leisurely ones, no respect for any kinship save in common, no clothing, no agriculture, no metals, no use of wine or grain. The very words that signify falsehood, treachery, dissimulation, avarice, envy, slander, forgiveness, are unheard of. How far from such perfection would he find the Republic he imagined: *men recently from the hands of the gods.*[22]

These are the first laws that nature gave.[23]

For the rest, they live in a country with a most agreeable and pleasant climate;[24] consequently, according to what my witnesses have told me, it is a rare thing to see a sick man there; and they have assured me that any one palsied, or blear-eyed, or toothless, or bent with old age is never to be seen. These people are settled on the sea-shore, and are shut in, landward, by a chain of high mountains, leaving a strip a hundred leagues or thereabouts in width. They have a great abundance of fish and meats, which bear no resemblance to ours, and they eat them without other elaboration[25] than cooking. The first man who rode a horse there, although he had been with them on several other voyages, so terrified them in that guise that they shot him to death with arrows before they could recognise him.

Their buildings are very long and can hold two or three hundred souls; they are built of the bark of large trees, fastened to the earth at one end and resting against and supporting one another at the ridge-pole, after the fashion of some of our barns, the roofing whereof falls to the ground and serves for side and end walls.[26] They have wood so hard that they cut with it and make swords of it, and gridirons for cooking their meat. Their beds are a cotton web, hung from the roof like those in our ships, each person having his own, for the women lie apart from their husbands. They rise with the sun and eat immediately after rising, for the whole day's need; for they have no other meal than this. They do not drink then, as Suidas[27] says of certain Oriental nations who drank when not eating; they drink many times during the day, and a great deal. Their beverage is made of some root, and is of the colour of our light wines; they drink it only luke-warm. This beverage will keep only two or three days; it is rather sharp in taste, not at all intoxicating, good for the stomach, and laxative for those who are not accustomed to it; it is a very pleasant drink for those wonted to it. Instead of bread they use a certain substance like preserved coriander. I have tasted it; its flavour is sweetish and rather insipid. The whole day is passed in dancing. The young men go hunting wild animals with bows. A part of the women employ themselves meanwhile in warming their drink, which is their chief duty. Some one of the old men, in the morning, before they begin to eat, counsels the whole

Of Cannibals

collected household,[28] walking from end to end of the building and repeating the same phrase many times, until he has completed the turn (for the buildings are fully a hundred paces in length). He enjoins upon them only two things—valour against the enemy and friendship for their wives. And they never fail, by way of response, to note the obligation that it is their wives who keep their drink warm and well-seasoned for them. There can be seen in many places, and, among others, in my house, the fashion of their beds, of their twisted ropes, of their wooden swords and the wooden armlets with which they protect their wrists in battle, and of the long staves, open at one end, by the sound of which they mark time in their dancing. They are clean-shaven, and they shave much more closely than we do, with no other razor than one of wood or stone.

They believe their souls to be immortal, and that they who have deserved well of the gods have their abode in that quarter of the heavens where the sun rises; the accursed, in the Occident. They have I know not what kinds of priests and prophets, who very rarely come among the people, having their abode in the mountains. On their arrival a great festival and solemn assemblage of several villages takes place. (Each building such as I have described is a village, and they are about a French league distant one from another.) The prophet speaks to them in public, inciting them to virtue and to their duty; but their whole moral teaching contains only these two articles: resoluteness in war and affection for their wives. He prophesies things to come and the results they may hope for from their undertakings; shows them the way toward war, or dissuades them from it; but all this is under the condition that, when he fails to prophesy truly, and if it chances them otherwise than he predicted to them, he is chopped into a thousand pieces if they catch him, and condemned as a false prophet. For this reason, he who has once erred is never seen again. Divination is a gift of God; that is why the misuse of it should be a punishable imposture. Among the *Scythians*, when the soothsayers failed in their venture, they were laid, loaded with chains, in carts filled with brushwood and drawn by oxen, in which they were burned alive.[29] Those who manage things subject to the guidance of human knowledge are excusable if they do with them what they can; but these others, who come cheating us with assurances of an extraordinary power which is beyond our ken—must not they be punished, both because they do not carry out the fact of their promise, and for the foolhardiness of their imposture?

They wage wars against the tribes that live on the other side of their mountains, farther inland, to which they go entirely naked, with no other weapons than bows, or wooden swords pointed at the end like the heads of our boar spears. The obstinacy of their combats is wonderful, and they never end save with slaughter and bloodshed; for as to routs and panic, they do not know what those are. Every man brings back as his trophy the head of the foe he has killed, and fastens it at the entrance of his abode. After they have for a long while treated their prisoners well and supplied them with all the comforts they can think of, the head man summons a great assemblage of his acquaintances. He ties a rope to one of the prisoner's arms, by the end of which he holds him at a distance of some paces, for fear of being injured by him; the other arm he gives to his dearest friend to hold in the same way; and they two, before the assembly, kill him with their swords. That done, they roast him, and all eat him in common and send portions to those of their friends who are absent. This is not, as some think, for sustenance, as the Scythians of old did, but to indicate an uttermost vengeance. And therefore,[30] having observed that the Portuguese, who had allied themselves with their adversaries, made use, when they captured them, of another sort of death for them, which was to bury them to the waist and cast many darts at the rest of their bodies, and hang them afterward, they thought that these people from the other part of the world, who had spread the knowledge of many villainies among their neighbours, and who were much more expert than they in all sorts of evil-doing, would not choose that sort of vengeance without good reason, and that it must be more painful than theirs; and they began to lay aside their old fashion and to follow this one.

I am not sorry that we note the savage horribleness there is in such an action; but indeed I am sorry that, while rightly judging their misdeeds, we are very blind to our own. I think there is more barbarism in eating a living man than a dead one, in rending by torture and racking a body still quick to feel, in slowly roasting it, in giving it to dogs and swine to be torn and eaten (as we have not only read but seen in recent days, not among long-time foes, but among neighbours and fellow citizens, and, what is worse, in the guise of piety and religion), than in roasting it and eating it after it is dead. Chrysippus and Zeno, heads of the Stoic school, did indeed think that there was no harm in using a dead body for any thing demanded by our need, and in deriving sustenance from it;[31] like our ancestors, who, being besieged by Cæsar in the town of Alexia, determined to relieve hunger during the siege by the bodies of old men, women, and other persons useless for fighting.[32]

The Gascons, it is said, prolonged life by the use of such food.[33]

And physicians do not fear to make use of it in every sort of way for our health, whether to be applied internally or externally; but there was never found an opinion so unreasonable as to excuse treachery, disloyalty, tyranny, and cruelty, which are our common faults.

We can, then, rightly call them barbarians with respect to the rules of reason, but not with respect to ourselves, who surpass them in every sort of barbarism. Their warfare is wholly noble and honourable, and has as much excuse and beauty as that malady of mankind can have. With them it has no other motive than simply eagerness of prowess.[34] They are not at strife for the conquest of new territories, for they still enjoy that natural fertility which supplies them, without labour and without trouble, with all things necessary, in such abundance that they have no reason to enlarge their boundaries. They are still at that fortunate point of desiring only so much as is ordained by their natural needs: every thing beyond that is superfluous for them. They generally call those of the same age brothers, those younger, children; and the old men are fathers to all the others. They leave to their heirs in common the undivided full possession of property,[35] without other title than that flawless one which Nature gives to her creatures on bringing them into the world.

If their neighbours come from beyond the mountains to attack them and win the victory over them, the victor's gain

282

is glory, and the advantage of having proved the superior in valour and prowess; for no otherwise do they give heed to the property of the vanquished; and they turn back to their own country, where they lack nothing that is necessary, nor do they lack that great gift of knowing how to enjoy their condition happily and to be content with it. When the turn of the others comes, they do the same; they ask no other ransom of their prisoners than the admission and acknowledgement that they are conquered; but there is not one found in a whole age who does not prefer death rather than to abate, either by manner or by word, a single jot of the grandeur of an invincible courage; not one is seen who does not prefer to be killed rather than merely to ask not to be. They give them every liberty, so that life may be all the dearer to them; and they entertain them usually with threats of their future death, of the torments they will have to suffer, of the preparations that are being made to that end, of the lopping off of their limbs, and of the feast there will be at their expense. All this is done for the sole purpose of extorting from their lips some faltering or downcast word, or of making them long for flight, in order to obtain this advantage of having frightened them and of having shaken their firmness. For, if rightly understood, true victory consists in this single point:—

> That only is victory which forces the foe in his own
> mind to acknowledge himself conquered.[36]

The Hungarians, very valorous fighters, did not formerly carry their point beyond reducing their enemy to their mercy; for, having extorted this admission from him, they let him go without injury and without ransom, save, at the most, forcing him to promise not henceforth to take arms against them.[37]

We obtain many advantages over our enemies, which are borrowed advantages, not our own. It is the quality of a porter, not of merit, to have stouter arms and legs; it is a lifeless and corporeal faculty to be always ready; it is a stroke of fortune to make our enemy stumble, and to dazzle his eyes by the glare of the sun; it is a trick of art and knowledge —which may fall to a dastardly and worthless person—to be skilled in fencing. A man's estimation and value depend upon his heart and his will; that is where his true honour lies; valour is strength, not of arms and legs, but of the mind and the soul; it does not depend upon the worth of our horse or of our armour, but upon our own. He who falls persistent in his will, *if he fall, he fights kneeling*.[38] He who abates no whit of his firmness and confidence for any danger from death not far away; he who, while yielding up his soul, still gazes at his foe with an unshrinking and disdainful eye—he is beaten, not by us, but by fortune; he is killed, not conquered.[39] The most valiant are sometimes the most unfortunate. So too there are defeats no less triumphant than victories. Nor did those four sister victories, the most splendid that the eyes of the sun can ever have seen,—of Salamis, Platæa, Mycale, and Sicily,—ever venture to compare all their combined glory to the glory of the defeat of King Leonidas and his men at Thermopylæ.

Who ever rushed with a more praiseworthy and more ambitious longing to the winning of a battle than did Captain Ischolas to the loss of one?[40] Who ever more skilfully and carefully assured himself of safety than he of his destruction? He was appointed to defend a certain pass in the

284

Of Cannibals

Peloponnesus against the Arcadians; finding himself wholly unable to do this because of the nature of the place and the inequality of the forces, and making up his mind that all who should meet the enemy would by necessity remain on the field; on the other hand, deeming it unworthy, both of his own valour and nobleness of spirit and of the Lacedæmonian name, to fail in his commission, he took a middle course between those two extremes, in this way: the youngest and most active of his force he preserved for the protection and service of their country, and sent them back to it; and with those who would be less missed, he decided to hold the pass, and by their deaths to make the enemy purchase the entrance thereto as dearly as possible. And so it fell out: for, being presently surrounded on all sides by the Arcadians, after he and his had made a great slaughter of them, they were all killed. Is there any trophy assigned to victors, which would not be more justly due to these vanquished? The real surmounting has for its part strife, not safety;[41] and the honour of courage consists in fighting, not in winning.

To return to our narrative, these prisoners, despite all that is done to them, are so far from yielding that, on the contrary, during the two or three months that they are kept in captivity, they bear themselves cheerfully; they urge their masters to make haste to put them to that test; they defy them, insult them, upbraid them with their cowardice and with the number of battles they have lost in mutual combat. I have a ballad written by a prisoner wherein is this taunt: Let them come boldly every one, and gather together to dine upon him; for they will at the same time eat their own fathers and grandfathers, who have served as food and nourishment for his body; "these muscles," he says, "this flesh, and these veins are your own, poor fools that you are; you do not recognise that the substance of your ancestors' limbs still clings to them. Taste them carefully, and you will find in them the flavour of your own flesh"—a conceit which has no smack of barbarism. Those who depict them when dying, and who describe the act of putting them to death, depict the prisoner as spitting in the faces of those who kill him and making mouths at them. Verily, in comparison with ourselves these men are savages indeed; for it must be that they are so, or else that we are so; there is a wonderful distance between their behaviour[42] and ours.

The men have several wives, and they have the larger number in proportion to their reputation for valour. A notably beautiful thing in their marriages is that the same eagerness that our wives have to keep us from the friendship and good-will of other women, theirs have to an equal degree to obtain this for their husbands. Being more solicitous for their husband's honour than for any other thing, they seek, and make it their care to have, as many companions as they can, forasmuch as it is a testimony to the husband's valour. Our wives will cry out on this as a miracle: it is not so; it is a properly matrimonial virtue, but of the highest type. And in the Bible, Leah, Rachel, Sarah, and the wives of Jacob gave their beautiful maidservants to their husbands;[43] and Livia seconded the appetites of Augustus, to her own detriment;[44] and the wife of King Dejotarus, Stratonica, not only lent to her husband for his use a very beautiful young maid in her service, but carefully brought up their children and gave them a helping hand[45] toward the succession to their father's estates. And, to the end that it

Of Cannibals

may not be thought that all this is done from simple and slavish compliance with usage, and by the influence of the authority of their ancient customs, without reflection and without judgement, and because their wits are so dull that they can not take any other course, some examples of their ability should be brought forward. Besides what I have just quoted from one of their warlike songs, I have another, an amorous one, which begins in this way: "Adder, stay thee; stay thee, adder, to the end that my sister may make, after the pattern of thy markings, the fashion and workmanship of a rich girdle,[46] which I may give to my love; so shall thy beauty and thy grace be for all time more highly esteemed than all other serpents." Now I have enough knowledge of poetry to form this judgement, that not only is there nothing barbaric in this conception, but that it is quite Anacreontic. Their language, moreover, has a soft and pleasant sound, and much resembles the Greek in its terminations.

Three of this people—not knowing how dear the knowledge of the corruption of this country will some day cost their peace of mind and their happiness, and that from this intercourse will be born their ruin, which conjecture may be already in process of confirmation;[47] most miserable in having allowed themselves to be tricked by the desire for things unknown, and in having left the sweetness of their own skies, to come to gaze at ours—were at Rouen at the time that the late King Charles the Ninth was there.[48] The king talked with them a long while; they were shown our modes of life, our magnificence, and the outward appearance of a beautiful city. Thereafter some one[49] asked them what they thought of all this, and wished to learn from them what had seemed to them most worthy of admiration. They mentioned in reply three things, of which I have forgotten the third, and am very sorry for it; but I remember two. They said that, in the first place, they thought it very strange that so many tall, bearded men, strong and well armed, who were about the king (they probably referred to the Swiss of the Guard), should humble themselves to obey a child, and that they did not rather choose some one of themselves to command them. Secondly (they have a fashion of speech of calling men halves of one another), they had perceived that there were among us some men gorged to the full with all sorts of possessions,[50] and that their other halves were beggars at their doors, gaunt with hunger and destitution; and they thought it strange that these poverty-stricken halves could suffer such injustice, and that they did not take the others by the throat or set fire to their houses. I talked with one of them a very long while; but I had an interpreter who followed me so badly, and who was so hindered by his stupidity from grasping my ideas, that I could not have any pleasure in it. When I asked what advantage he derived from his superior position among his people (for he was a captain and our seamen called him king), he said that it was the privilege of marching at their head in war. By how many men he was followed. He indicated a certain extent of ground, as if to signify that it was by as many men as that space would hold—perhaps four or five thousand. Whether, when there was no war, all his authority was at an end. He said that he still retained the right, when he visited the villages that were in his dependence, to have paths made for him through the thickets of their forests.

All this does not seem too much amiss; but then, they do not wear breeches!

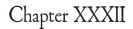

Chapter XXXII

THAT IT IS WITH SOBRIETY
THAT WE SHOULD UNDERTAKE
TO JUDGE OF
THE DIVINE DECREES

THINGS unknown are the chief field and subject of imposture, inasmuch as, in the first place, mere unfamiliarity gains attention; and secondly, the things unknown not being within the scope of our ordinary modes of thought, we are deprived of the means of disputing the imposture.[1] For this reason, said Plato,[2] it is much easier to give satisfaction when talking about the nature of the gods than when talking about the nature of men, because the ignorance of the hearers affords a free, wide course, and full liberty in the handling of an obscure subject. Thence it comes to pass that nothing is so firmly believed as that which we know least, nor any people so confident as those who tell us unlikely things, such as alchemists, seers, astrologers, palmists, doctors, *and all folk of that sort.*[3] To whom I should like to join, if I dared, a pack of people, interpreters and registrars in ordinary of the designs of God, who make it their business to discover the causes of every happening, and to see in the mysteries of the divine will the incomprehensible motives of his works; and although the continual variety and discordance of events drives them from corner to corner, from east to west, foolishly to pursue what eludes

To Judge of the Divine Decrees

them,[4] and to paint white and black with the same brush.

In an Indian nation there is this praiseworthy custom: when they are unsuccessful in any skirmish or battle, they publicly ask forgiveness for this from the Sun (who is their god), as for a wrong[5] action, laying their good or ill fortune before the divine intelligence, and submitting to it their judgement and opinion.[6]

For a Christian it is enough to believe that all things come from God, to receive them with recognition of his divine and inscrutable wisdom; therefore, to take them in good part under whatever aspect they be sent to him. But I think ill of what I see to be customary—the seeking to strengthen and support our religion by the prosperity of our undertakings. Our belief has enough other foundations, without giving authority to it by events; for if the people become accustomed to these arguments, which are plausible and suited to their taste, there is danger that when, in turn, adverse and disadvantageous events happen, their faith will be shaken by them. As when, in our present wars for religion, those who had the advantage in the fight at La Roche-labeille, boasting loudly of that circumstance, and making use of that good fortune as showing approval[7] of their party, when they come later to excuse their misfortunes at Moncontour and Jarnac, on the ground that these were paternal stripes and chastisements, if the people are not wholly under their control,[8] they[9] very quickly make them see that this is to take two grindings from one sack, and to blow hot and cold with the same mouth. It would be wiser to possess the people with the real bases of the truth.

That was a fine naval victory[10] that was won a few months ago against the Turks, under the leadership of Don John of

To Judge of the Divine Decrees

Austria; but it has well pleased God at other times to let us see other such victories at our expense. In fine, it is not easy to weigh divine things in our scales without their suffering diminution. And he who should desire to account for Arius and Leo his pope,[11] the chief heads of that [Arian] heresy, dying at different times in ways so alike and unusual—for each of them having withdrawn, because of a stomach-ache, from a debate to the closet, they there suddenly rendered up their souls; and who should exaggerate this divine vengeance by the accident of place, might well add the death of Heliogabalus, who also was killed in a privy.[12] But consider! Irenæus was involved in the same fortune.

God, desiring to teach us that the good have something else to hope for and the wicked something else to fear than the good fortunes or ill fortunes of this world, manages and allots these according to his occult will, and takes from us the means of unwisely counting on them.[13] And they who seek to prevail over them by human reasoning deceive themselves; they never give them one hit that they do not receive from them two. St. Augustine shows this clearly in his adversaries.[14] It is a contest that is decided by the weapons of memory rather than by those of reason. We must be content with the light that it may please the sun to shed upon us by his beams;[15] and he who shall raise his eyes to bring a brighter beam into his very body, let him not think it strange if, for the punishment of his audacity, he thus lose his sight. *For who among men is he that can know the counsel of God? or who can think what the will of God is?*[16]

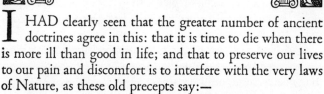

Chapter XXXIII

OF AVOIDING PLEASURES

AT THE COST OF LIFE

I HAD clearly seen that the greater number of ancient doctrines agree in this: that it is time to die when there is more ill than good in life; and that to preserve our lives to our pain and discomfort is to interfere with the very laws of Nature, as these old precepts say:—

> Either a tranquil life, or a fortunate death. It is well to die when life is a disgrace. It is better not to live than to live in wretchedness.[1]

But as for carrying contempt of death to such a degree as to make use of it to sever oneself from the honours, wealth, dignities, and other favours and possessions which we call good fortune,—as if reason had not difficulty enough to persuade us to abandon them, without the addition of this greater demand,—I had never seen it enjoined or practised until that passage of Seneca fell into my hands in which he advises Lucilius, a personage in power, and of great authority with those about the Emperor, to lay aside his life of pleasure and pomp, and to withdraw from worldly ambition to a solitary, tranquil, and philosophical mode of life; where-upon, Lucilius having put forward some difficulties, he

Of Avoiding Pleasures

said: "It is my opinion that you should either depart from this sort of life, or from life altogether; and I advise you to follow the easier path, and to untie rather than break that which you have unwisely knotted; provided that, if it can not be untied otherwise, you break it. There is no man so cowardly that he does not like better to fall once for all than to remain forever tottering."[2]

I should have thought this advice befitting the Stoic austerity; but it is the stranger because it is borrowed from Epicurus, who writes to Idomeneus on this subject with similar expressions.[3] And I think that I have observed a like feeling in men of the present day, but held with Christian moderation. St. Hilary, Bishop of Poitiers, that famous opponent of the Arian heresy, being in Syria, was informed that Abra, his only daughter, whom he had left behind with her mother, was sought in marriage by the most prominent nobles of the region, as a well-brought-up, beautiful, and wealthy maiden, in the bloom of youth. He wrote to her (as we see) that she should withdraw her inclination from all the pleasures and advantages offered her; that he had found in his journeying a much greater and worthier match for her, in a husband of far different power and magnificence, who would bestow upon her robes and jewels of inestimable value. His purpose was to cause her to lose the taste and habit of worldly pleasures, that she might be united wholly to God; but the shortest and surest means to that end seeming to him to be his daughter's death, he did not cease to implore God, by vows and prayers and supplications, to take her from this world and call her to Himself; as it came to pass; for very soon after his return she departed from him;[4] whereat he manifested a surpassing[5] joy. This seems to go

Of Avoiding Pleasures

further than the other examples, in that he resorts to this method at the outset, which they adopt only secondarily; and then, too, it concerned his only daughter. But let me not omit the end of this story, though it does not bear upon my subject. The wife of St. Hilary, having learned from him that their daughter's death had come about through his design and wish, and how much more fortunate it was for her to be removed from this world than to be in it, conceived so vividly the eternal and heavenly blessedness, that she besought her husband with extreme urgency to do as much for her. And God, at their united prayers, soon after taking her to himself, her death was welcomed by both with peculiar pleasure.[6]

Chapter XXXIV

THAT FORTUNE IS OFTEN

MET WITH

IN THE TRAIN OF REASON

FROM the inconstancy of the varying dance of fortune, she shows us every kind of aspect. Was there ever an action of justice more full of purpose than this? The Duke of Valentinois,[1] having determined to poison Adrian, Cardinal of Corneto, with whom his father, Pope Alexander VI, and himself were to sup at the Vatican, sent on beforehand a bottle of poisoned wine, and bade the butler keep it very carefully. The Pope arriving before his son and asking for something to drink, the butler, who thought that this wine had been specially committed to his care only because of its excellence, served it to the Pope; and the duke himself, arriving at the moment of the collation, and believing that his bottle had not been touched, in his turn drank from it; so it befell that the father instantly died, and the son, after having for a long time suffered greatly from illness, was preserved for another worse fate.[2]

Sometimes it seems that she of set purpose makes sport of us. The Seigneur d'Estrée, then ensign to Monsieur de Vendome, and the Seigneur de Liques, lieutenant in the company of the Duc d'Ascot, both being suitors to the sister of the Sieur de Foungueselles, although they were of different parties,—as often happens between neighbours on the frontier,—the Sieur de Liques was the winner; but, on the very day of the wedding, and, what is worse, before they were bedded, the husband, wishing to break a lance in honour of his new spouse, took part in the skirmish near Saint Omer, where the Sieur d'Estrée, being the stronger, made him his prisoner; and, to give value to his success, the maiden,—

> Compelled to release from her embrace her new
> spouse before two winters in succession, with their long
> nights, had sated her eager love,[3]—

must needs sue to him to render up to her, by way of courtesy, his prisoner; which thing he did, for the gentlemen of France never deny any thing to ladies.[4]

Does not this seem a purposed fate?[5] Constantine, son of Helen, was the first ruler of the empire of Constantinople; and, several centuries later, Constantine, son of Helen, was the last.[6]

Sometimes she[7] is pleased to vie with our miracles. It is believed that, when King Clovis was besieging Angoulême, the walls fell of themselves, by divine favour;[8] and Bouchet cites from some author that, when King Robert[9] was besieging a city, and had secretly left the siege to go to Orléans to celebrate the feast of Saint-Aignan, while he was at his devotions, at a certain point in the mass, the walls of the besieged city fell in ruins without any assault. She laid just the opposite in our Milanese wars; for when Captain Rense was besieging for us the city of Eronne, and had laid a mine under a great section of the wall, the wall, being suddenly lifted up from the ground, fell back nevertheless quite

whole,[10] and so exactly upon its foundation that the besieged were none the worse off.[11]

Sometimes she plays the physician. Jason Phereus, being
given up by the doctors because of an impostume in his
breast, and wishing to rid himself of it though it were by
death, rushed madly, in a battle, into the thick of the enemy,
where he was so fortunately wounded in the body that his
impostume broke, and he was cured.[12] Did she not excel the
painter Protogenes in the knowledge of his art? He, having
finished the picture of a tired and panting dog, to his satisfaction in all other respects save this, that he was unable to
represent as he desired the froth and slaver, greatly vexed
with his work, took his sponge, soaked as it was with divers
colours, and threw it at the painting, to efface it all; but
fortune opportunely guided the sponge to the place of the
dog's mouth, and there accomplished what art had been
unable to attain.[13]

Does she not sometimes show the best way to our decisions, and correct them? Isabel, Queen of England,[14] having to return from Zealand to her kingdom, with an army, in
support of her son against her husband, would have been
lost if she had arrived at the port she had selected, being
waited there by her enemies; but Fortune drove her, against
her will, to another place, where she landed in perfect safety.
And that ancient who, throwing a stone at a dog, struck
and killed his step-mother—was not he justified in uttering
this line:—

Fortune's plan is better than ours.[15]

Fortune is better advised than we.

Icetes had suborned two soldiers to kill Timolcon, then

tarrying at Adrans in Sicily. They chose the time when he was offering a sacrifice, and mixed with the multitude. As they were signalling to each other[16] that the moment was opportune for their business, lo, a third man who, with a great sword-cut, strikes one of them over the head and casts him dead to the ground, and then flees. The confederate, believing himself to be discovered and lost, ran to the altar and demanded sanctuary, promising to tell the whole truth. While he is giving account of the conspiracy, lo, the third man, who has been caught, and whom, as an assassin, the populace push and tug through the press, toward Timoleon and the eminent men of the assemblage. From them he cries for pardon, and declares that he had rightly killed the murderer of his father, proving on the spot, by witnesses whom his good luck opportunely supplied, that his father had in truth been killed, in the city of the Leontines, by him upon whom he had revenged himself. Ten Attic minæ were ordered to be given him for having had the hap, while taking satisfaction for his own father's death, to have saved from death the common father of the Sicilians.[17] This piece of fortune surpasses in guidance all the guidance of human prudence.[18]

To conclude: in the following fact is there not disclosed a very manifest expression of her favour, her kindness, and her singular compassion? The two Ignatii,—father and son, —proscribed by the triumvirs of Rome, resolved together on the virtuous action of giving their lives each to the other, and thus frustrating the cruelty of the tyrants. They rushed upon each other, sword in hand; she[19] guided the points and made the two thrusts alike mortal, and vouchsafed to them, in honour of so noble a friendship, that they should have just enough strength to withdraw their bloody weapons from the wounds,[20] in order to embrace each other, in that state, with so strong a clasp that the executioners cut off their two heads at the same time, leaving the bodies still clasped in that noble bond,[21] and the wounds, closely touching, sucking up the blood and what was left of life, one from the other.[22]

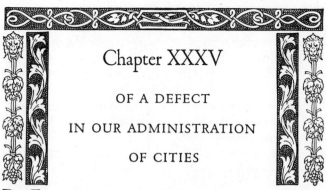

Chapter XXXV

OF A DEFECT

IN OUR ADMINISTRATION

OF CITIES

MY late father, a man of very sound judgement for one who had no other help than experience and his natural parts, told me in former days that[1] he had desired to arrange that there should be in cities a certain specified place to which those might go who had need of any thing, and have their business noted down by an official appointed for that purpose. As, for instance, I am trying to sell some pearls; I am looking for pearls for sale; So-and-so desires company in going to Paris; So-and-so is enquiring for a servant of such-and-such a sort, So-and-so for a master; So-and-so wants a workman; one this thing, and another that, each according to his needs. And it seems as if this method of mutual information would bring no slight convenience into public commerce; for at all times there are conditions which seek one another, and from not being able to come to an understanding, leave men in dire need. I learn, with great shame for our age, that before our eyes two men most eminent in learning have died in the condition of not having a sufficiency of food: Lilius Gregorius Geraldus[2] in Italy, and Sebastianus Castalio[3] in Germany; and I think that there are a thousand men who would have sent for them on most ad-

Of Our Administration of Cities

vantageous terms, or would have assisted them where they were, had they known the facts. The world is not so universally corrupted that I do not know a certain man who wishes with all his heart that the means which his forbears have put in his hands could be employed, so long as it pleases Fortune that he shall enjoy them, in placing beyond the reach of want those persons of rare and noteworthy merit of any sort whom ill-fortune sometimes forces to the wall—a man who would put them at least in such a condition that it would be unreasonable if they were not content.

In his household administration my father had a fashion which I can praise, but not at all follow. It was this: in addition to the register of the business transactions of the household, wherein are set down the small accounts, payments, bargains which do not require the hand of a notary, —which register a steward has in charge,—he ordered that one of his people who acted as his secretary to keep a daily record, and to set down in it, day after day, all the occurrences of any importance, and the chronicles of the life of his house: very pleasant to look over when time begins to efface the remembrance of these things, and often very convenient to save us trouble: when such a work was entered upon; when finished; what great personages came to us; how long they remained;[4] our journeys; our absences; marriages; deaths; the receipt of good or bad news; changings of the principal servants—such matters. An old custom which I think it a good plan to revive, each in his own house. And I think I am a fool for having failed to do so.

Chapter XXXVI

OF THE CUSTOM

OF WEARING CLOTHES

WHATEVER road I choose, I must needs break down some barrier set up by custom, so carefully has she blocked all our paths. I was questioning, in this chilly season, whether the fashion in these lately discovered nations of going entirely naked is a fashion compelled by the high temperature of the atmosphere, as we narrate of the Indians and Moors, or whether it is the original practice of mankind. Inasmuch as every thing under the heavens, as says Holy Writ,[1] is subject to the same laws, men of intelligence are accustomed, in matters like these, where the natural laws must be distinguished from those devised by man, to have recourse to the general administration of the world, in which there can be nothing irregular. Now, since all other creatures are perfectly supplied with what is needful to keep themselves alive,[2] it is truly incredible that we alone should be brought into the world in a defective and necessitous state, and in a state which can not be maintained without outside assistance. So I hold that, as plants, trees, animals, all living things, are furnished by nature with sufficient covering to protect themselves from the assaults of the weather,—

302

Of the Custom of Wearing Clothes

And for this reason almost all things are covered
with hide, or bristles, or shell, or hard skin, or bark,[3]—

so too were we; but, like those who quench by artificial light
the light of day, we have quenched our own means by borrowed means. And it is easy to see that it is custom which
makes, for us, impossible that which is not so in itself; for of
those nations which have no knowledge of clothing, some
there are, seated in much the same climate as ours;[4] and besides, our most tender parts are those which are always uncovered: the eyes, the mouth, the nose, the ears; and with
our peasants, as with our forefathers, the breast and the
belly. If we were born with the need of petticoats and
breeches, it is not to be doubted that nature would have
protected with a thicker skin the whole body exposed to the
battery of the seasons, as she has done the ends of the fingers
and the soles of the feet. Why does it seem difficult to believe? Between the way I am clothed and that of the peasant of my province I find far more difference than there is
between his way and that of a man who is clad only in his
skin. How many, especially in Turkey, go naked from
piety![5]

I know not who it was who asked one of our beggars,
whom he saw in his shirt in mid-winter as lusty as he who
goes muffled up to his ears in furs, how he could have such
endurance. "But you, sir," he replied, "have your face uncovered; now, as for me, I am all face." The Italians tell of
the fool of the Duke of Florence, I think, that, on his master's making enquiry how, so ill clad, he could bear the cold
wind by which he was himself much discomforted, "Follow my rule," he replied, "and pile on all your garments,

as I do mine; then you will suffer from the cold no more than I do." King Massinissa, even to extreme old age, could not be induced to cover his head, however cold or stormy or rainy it might be;[6] which is told also of the Emperor Severus. In the battles fought between the Egyptians and the Persians, Herodotus says that it was observed, both by others and by himself, that of those who fell, the skull of the Egyptians was incomparably harder than that of the Persians, by reason that the latter always covered their heads with biggins and afterwards with turbans, while the former were shaved close from childhood and went bareheaded.[7] And King Agesilaus, up to his days of decrepitude, continued to wear the same vesture in winter as in summer.[8] Cæsar, Suetonius says, always marched at the head of his forces, and oftenest on foot, with his head uncovered, rain or shine;[9] and the same is told of Hannibal:—

> With bare head he received the furious rain, and the torrents falling from heaven.[10]

A Venetian who has lived in the kingdom of Pegu a long while, and who has just come thence, writes that there both men and women, the other parts of their bodies being clothed, go always barefoot, even on horseback.[11] And Plato earnestly[12] advises, for the health of the whole body, that we give the feet and the head no other covering than that which nature has provided. He whom the Poles chose for their king[13] after the one of our nation,[14] and who is, in truth, one of the greatest princes of our time, never wears gloves, and does not change, in winter and whatever the weather [when he goes out of doors], the cap that he wears indoors.

Of the Custom of Wearing Clothes

While I can not bear to be unbuttoned and untied, the labouring men of my neighbourhood would feel as if in shackles were they otherwise. Varro holds that, when it was decreed that we should keep our heads uncovered in the presence of the gods or of a man high in authority, it was so decreed more for our health, and to strengthen us against the assaults of the weather, than as a token of respect.[15] And since we are on the subject of cold weather, and, being Frenchmen, are accustomed to array ourselves in many colours (not I, for I seldom wear other than black or white, following my father's fashion), let us add, on another subject,[16] what Captain Martin du Bellay narrates, that, in marching through Luxembourg, he knew frosts so severe that the wine provided for the army was broken with axe and hatchet, and distributed to the troops by weight, and that they carried it away in baskets.[17] And Ovid, to much the same effect,—

> The wine, frozen solid, keeps the form of the jar
> from which it has been removed; they do not drink it
> liquid, but doled out in lumps.[18]

The frosts are so hard at the mouth of the Palus Mœotides, that on the same ground where the lieutenant of Mithridates had given battle to the enemy on dry land, and had there defeated them, when summer had come, he won a battle at sea against them.[19] The Romans suffered great disadvantage in the engagement they had with the Carthaginians near Placentia, because they went into the fight with their blood congealed and their limbs stiffened by the cold; while Hannibal had had fires built everywhere in his army, to warm his soldiers, and oil distributed to the troops, in

305

Of the Custom of Wearing Clothes

order that, anointing themselves, they might make their muscles more limber and supple, and protect the pores against the blasts of the freezing wind that was blowing.[20] The retreat of the Greeks, from Babylon to their own country, is famous for the difficulties and discomforts that they had to overcome. One of them was this: that, being overtaken in the mountains of Armenia by a terrible snowstorm, they, in consequence, lost all knowledge of the country and the roads; and being suddenly beleaguered by it, they were a day and night without drinking or eating, the greater part of their animals and many of themselves dead, many blinded by the sleet and the glare of the snow, many maimed in their hands and feet, many stiff and benumbed and paralysed with the cold,[21] still in full possession of their senses. Alexander saw a nation among whom the fruit trees are buried in winter to protect them from the frost.[22]

On the subject of clothes, the king of Mexico changed his apparel four times a day, never wore any thing a second time, making use of his discarded garments in his constant liberalities and rewards; in like manner, no vessel, or dish, or kitchen or table utensil was put before him twice.[23]

Chapter XXXVII

OF THE

YOUNGER CATO

I DO not make that common mistake of judging another according to what I myself am. I readily believe that in others are things different from those that are in me.[1] While I feel that I am pledged to a certain manner of existence, I do not oblige every one to adopt it, as some men do; and I know and conceive a thousand contrary ways of life, and, unlike people in general, I perceive more easily the difference than the resemblance between us. I exempt another as much as you please from being of my conditions and principles, and consider him simply in himself, without connection, measuring him by his own model. While I am not continent, I do not fail fully to acknowledge the continence of the Feuillants and Capuchins, and to perceive clearly the character of their conduct. In imagination I enter very completely into their skin;[2] and I like and honour them all the more because they are different from me. I especially desire that we be judged each by himself, and that I be not depicted from common models.

My weakness in no wise changes the esteem that I ought to have of the strength and vigour of those who deserve it. *There are those who praise nothing save what they are con-*

Of the Younger Cato

fident they can themselves imitate.[3] Crawling on the muddy earth, I do not fail to observe the unattainable height, among the clouds, of some heroic souls. It is much for me to have my judgement well ordered, if my acts can not be, and to keep at least that sovereign part free from corruption; it is something to have my will right when my legs fail me. This age in which we live, at least so far as our region is concerned, is so leaden that I do not say the performance, but the very conception of virtue is lacking to it, and seems to be naught else than the chatter of schoolboys:—

> They think virtue is but a word, and the sacred
> grove a mere wood.[4]

Which they should revere even if they could not comprehend it.[5] It is a bauble to hang in a study, or on the tip of the tongue, like an ear-ring on the ear, for ornament.

There is no longer any recognition of virtuous[6] actions; those which bear that aspect have none the less not the essence of virtue; for gain, glory, fear, habit, and other such alien causes lead us to perform them. The justice, the valour, the kindliness which we then practise may be so styled from another's observation and from the aspect they wear to the public eye; but for the man himself[7] they are not virtues at all; he has had another end in view, there has been another moving cause. Now virtue accepts as her own nothing save what is done by her and for her alone.

In that great battle at Potidæa, which the Greeks under Pausanias won against Mardonius and the Persians, the victors, according to their custom, coming to apportion among themselves the glory of the exploit, attributed to the

308

Of the Younger Cato

Spartan nation the preëminence for valour in the conflict. The Spartans,—excellent judges of bravery,—when they came to decide to which individual the honour belonged of having done the best in this battle, found that Aristodemus had risked his life most fearlessly; but none the less they did not for this give him the prize, because his courage had been incited by the desire to clear himself from the blame he had incurred in the action at Thermopylæ, and by a longing to die courageously so that his past disgrace might be wiped out.[8]

Our judgements are now unsound, and follow the depravity of our morals. I see the greater number of the intelligent men of my time use their sharp-wittedness to dim the glory of the noble and generous acts of ancient times, giving them some base interpretation, and devising for them idle causes and occasions. Wonderful subtlety! Show me the most excellent act, of purest quality, and I will bring forward plausibly fifty vicious motives for it. God knows what a diversity of representations our secret will admits of, for him who is pleased to spread them out![9] They do not use their sharp-wittedness so craftily as clumsily and coarsely, in their detraction. The same trouble they take to belittle those great names, and the same license, I would gladly take to lend them a hand to boost them.[10] Those rare personages, culled out as examples to the world by the agreement of wise men—I should not hesitate to redouble their honour, so far as my imagination was capable, by interpretation and by favourable environment. But we must believe that the efforts of our imagination fall far short of their desert. It is the duty of men of worth to depict virtue with the utmost beauty; and it would not misbecome us if emotion should carry us out of ourselves with regard to such sacred figures. What they[11] do, on the contrary, they do, either from dissatisfaction, or from that fault of which I have just spoken, of adjusting their belief to their capacity, or, as I am more inclined to think, from their sight not being strong enough and clear enough, or trained to imagine and conceive the splendour of virtue in its native purity; as Plutarch says, that in his time some people attributed the cause of the death of the younger Cato to the fear he had had of Cæsar; whereat he[12] is justly offended; and we can judge from that how much more indignant he would have been with those who attributed it to ambition.[13] Fools! he would have done finely a fine thing, noble and rightful, with obloquy rather than for fame. This great man was in very truth a pattern that Nature chose, to show to how great a height human virtue and steadfastness could attain.

But this is not the place for me to treat this rich subject; I desire only to bring together in contention the expressions of five Latin poets in praise of Cato, both for Cato's sake, and, incidentally, for their own also. Now, the well-educated youth should find the first two, in comparison with the others, languid; the third more vigorous, but injured by the extravagance of his vehemence. He should perceive that there is room for one or two degrees of imagination before reaching the fourth, where he will clasp his hands in admiration. At the last, first by an interval,—but an interval which he will swear could not be filled by any human mind, —he will be amazed, he will be struck dumb. This is a marvel: we have many more poets than judges and interpreters of poetry; it is easier to create it than to know what it is. To a certain slight extent it can be judged of by max-

Of the Younger Cato

ims and by skill; but the excellent, the ineffable, the divine, is above rules and the power of judgement. Whoever discerns its beauty with a firm and steady vision, he does not see it any more than the splendour of a lightning-flash; it does not employ our judgement; it seizes it and sweeps it away.

The frenzy that possesses him who is able to understand it, is communicated to another from hearing him talk of it and recite it; as the magnet not only attracts a needle, but imparts to it its power to attract others. And it is seen more clearly at the theatre, how the sacred inspiration of the Muses—having first agitated the poet with anger, grief, hate, and carried him where they will, out of himself—enters, through the poet, into the actor, and consecutively, through the actor, into the whole audience: it is the chain of our needles, hanging one from another.[14] From my earliest childhood, poetry has had the power to pierce and transport me;[15] but that very keen emotion which is natural to me has been diversely touched by diversity of forms—not so much higher and lower forms, for they were always the highest of each kind, as difference in quality: first, a lively and fanciful fluidity; then, a keen and enhanced subtlety; lastly, a perfected and sure strength. Examples will express this better: Ovid, Lucan, Virgil. But behold our group on the race-track!

Grant that Cato, in his lifetime, was greater than Cæsar,[16]

says one.

And Cato, unconquerable, conquered death,[17]

311

Of the Younger Cato

says another. And another, speaking of the civil wars between Cæsar and Pompey,—

> The cause of the conqueror was approved by the gods, but that of the conquered by Cato.[18]

And the fourth, while praising Cæsar,—

> And the whole world was under subjection save the haughty spirit of Cato.[19]

And the leader of the choir, after having set forth in his verse the fames[20] of the greatest Romans, concludes thus:—

> These ruled by Cato.[21]

Chapter XXXVIII

HOW WE WEEP

AND LAUGH AT ONE

AND THE SAME THING

WHEN we learn in the histories that Antigonus was much displeased with his son for having brought to him the head of Pyrrhus, his foe, who had that very hour been slain while fighting against him, and that, when he looked upon it, he wept bitterly;[1] and that Duke René of Lorraine also lamented the death of Duke Charles of Burgundy,[2] whom he had just defeated, and wore mourning for him at his burial; and that, at the battle of Auroy,[3] which the Count of Montfort won against Charles of Blois, the victor, coming across the dead body of his enemy, greatly mourned over it, we must hastily exclaim:—

> And so it happens that every soul covers over its emotions with an unlike mantle, with a visage now bright, now dark.[4]

When Pompey's head was brought to Cæsar, it is told in histories that he turned his eyes away as from a hateful and unpleasant sight.[5] There had been between them so long-continued an understanding and association in the management of public affairs; so much community of fortune; so many reciprocal duties from their alliance, that it must

313

not be thought that Cæsar's bearing was wholly false and assumed, as this poet judges:—

> And now he thought he could with safety appear like a kind father-in-law; he shed tears that did not flow of themselves, and forced groans from a joyful heart.[6]

For, although in truth most of our acts are merely deceptive and of false colour,[7] and it may sometimes be true that

> The tears of an heir are smiles behind a mask,[8]

still, in judging of these incidents, we must consider how our souls are often agitated by diverse emotions. And just as there is, they say, in our bodies an assemblage of diverse humours, of which that one is sovereign which usually rules within us, according to our temperaments, so, in our souls, although there are diverse impulses which agitate them, yet it must be that one of these remains master of the field. But it is not with such complete advantage that, by reason of the volubility and activity of our souls, the weaker humours may not now and then regain the ground, and make a brief charge in their turn. Wherefore it is that not only do we see children, who artlessly follow nature, cry and laugh often at the same thing, but no man of us can boast—whatever journey he may be taking for his pleasure—that on leaving his family and friends he does not feel his heart tremble; and, if tears do not quite fall from his eyes, at least he puts foot in the stirrup with a pensive and saddened countenance. And despite the gentle flame that warms the hearts of well-born maids, they must be drawn unwillingly from their mothers' arms, to be given to their husbands,

314

How We Weep and Laugh

Is Venus really hateful to young brides, or do they check their parents' gladness with those feigned tears which they shed abundantly on the threshold of their chamber? Not true lamentations are these, so may the gods help me![9]

Likewise it is not a strange thing to lament when dead a man whom one would not call back to life.

When I chide my servant, I do it with the best heart I have; my imprecations are genuine and not feigned; but, that fit of anger blown over, let him have need of me, and I will gladly do him a kindness: I turn the leaf instanter. If it were not behaving like an idiot to talk when alone, there is scarcely a day or an hour when I might not be heard growling to myself: "Scum of a fool!"[10] And yet I do not mean that that is my exact description. The man who, seeing my manner toward my wife now cold and now loving, thinks that the one or the other deportment was feigned, is a fool. Nero, taking leave of his mother whom he was sending to be drowned, was none the less moved by that maternal farewell, and was stirred to horror and pity.[11]

'Tis said that the light of the sun is not continuous, but that it incessantly flashes its beams upon us so closely one after another that we can not detect the interval between them.

For the brilliant sun, the abundant fount of fluid light, continually bathes the sky with fresh radiance and furnishes light by ever-renewed light.[12]

In like manner the soul gives forth its rays diversely and imperceptibly.

315

How We Weep and Laugh

Artabanus took unawares Xerxes, his nephew, and chid him for the sudden change of his countenance. He was observing the immeasurable greatness of his forces crossing the Hellespont: at first he felt a thrill of joy to see so many thousands of men in his service, and manifested it by the cheerfulness and animation of his face; and all suddenly, in one instant, as it came into his mind that all those lives would be no more in a hundred years at furthest, he knitted his brow and was saddened even to tears.[13] We have sought with relentless determination revenge for an insult, and have been conscious of a peculiar satisfaction in our victory, and yet we weep over it. It is not for our victory that we weep; there is no change in that; but our soul regards the thing with a different eye, and represents it to itself in another aspect; for every thing has many sides and can be seen from many points of view. Kinship, former acquaintances, and friendships lay hold of our imagination and perturb it for the moment, according to their nature; but its[14] change of direction is so rapid that we do not perceive it.

> Nothing is seen to move so rapidly as the mind when it proposes and undertakes something. The mind is swifter than any visible thing that is seen by the eyes in nature.[15]

And consequently we deceive ourselves in attempting to make a continuous body of all this succession of ideas. When Timoleon weeps for the murder that he had committed after such mature and noble-hearted deliberation, he does not weep for the tyrant, but he weeps for his brother.[16] One half of his duty is performed; let us allow him to perform the other half.

Chapter XXXIX

OF SOLITUDE

ET us leave on one side this tedious comparison between a solitary and an active life; and as for that fine sentence under which ambition and avidity protect themselves, that "we are not born for ourselves alone, but for the public,"[1] let us boldly refer ourselves to those who are in the whirl, and let them beat their breasts[2] if, on the contrary, dignities, offices, and the needless toil of the world, are not sought chiefly to derive from the public a man's private profit. The evil methods by which men push themselves forward clearly indicate that the end is worth no more than the means. Let us answer on behalf of ambition that it is she herself who gives us the taste for solitude; for what does she avoid so much as society? what does she seek so much as elbow-room? Everywhere it is possible to do good and ill; none the less, if the saying of Bias be true, that the worst men are the greater number,[3] or what *Ecclesiasticus* says, that in a thousand there is not one good,[4]—

> For good men are rare; hardly are they more in number than the gates of Thebes or the mouths of the rich Nile,[5]—

Of Solitude

there is great danger of contagion in a crowd. We can not
help imitating the vicious or else hating them. There is danger, because they are numerous, of resembling them; and,
because they are unlike us, danger of hating them much.[6]
And the merchants who travel by sea are wise to look to it
that those who sail on the same ship are neither dissolute
nor blasphemers nor wicked men, esteeming such company
unlucky. Wherefore Bias jocosely said to those who incurred with him the perils of a great storm and called on the
gods for aid: "Hush! don't let them know that you are
here with me."[7] And, a more striking example, Albu-
querque, viceroy in India for King Emmanuel of Portugal,
being in extreme peril at sea, took a young boy on his
shoulders, with the sole object that, in the companionship
of their peril, his innocence might serve himself as warrant,
and as recommendation to the divine favour to put him in
safety.[8]

It is not that the wise man can not live content everywhere, aye, and alone, in the throng of a palace; but if he
has his choice, he will shun, he says, even the sight of a
crowd; he will endure the one, if need be; but if it rests with
him, he will choose the other.[9] It does not seem to him that
he is sufficiently purged of vices, if he must continue to
contend with those of others. Charondas punished as bad
men those who were convicted of frequenting bad company.[10] There is nothing so unsociable and so sociable as
man, in the one case by reason of his corruption, in the other
by his nature. And Antisthenes does not seem to me to have
answered satisfactorily him who blamed him for intercourse
with bad men, by saying that physicians live well among
the sick;[11] for if they are of benefit to the health of the sick,

Of Solitude

they impair their own by contagion, and by constantly seeing and dealing with diseases.

Now the object of all, so I believe, is the same—to live more at leisure and at ease. But we do not always intelligently seek the pathway to this end. Often we think that we have abandoned affairs when we have only changed them. There is little less trouble in the management of a family than of a great establishment; wherever the mind is busied, it is wholly so; and because domestic preoccupations are less important, they are not less importunate. Consequently, because we are quit of the court and the market-place, we are not quit of the chief torments of our life,—

It is reason and wisdom that banish care; not a place commanding a prospect of the widespread sea.[12]

Ambition, avarice, irresolution, fear, and all greedy desires do not desert us when we change our abiding-place:—

And gloomy care sits behind the rider.[13]

They often follow us even into cloisters and schools of philosophy. Neither deserts, nor caverns, nor fasting, rid us of them;

The deadly arrow remains fixed in her side.[14]

Socrates was told that a certain person had not changed for the better in his travels. "I must believe it," said he, "for he carried himself with him."[15]

Why seek we regions warmed by another sun? Who, departing from his native land, escapes from himself as well?[16]

Of Solitude

If a man do not first relieve himself and his soul from the burden that weighs it down, movement will cause it to press the more; as in a ship the cargo is less troublesome when it is stable.[17]

You do more harm than good to the man who is sick by making him change his place; you bottle up the disease[18] by moving it, as stakes are driven deeper and more firmly by wriggling and shaking them.[19] Therefore it is not enough to separate oneself from the common people; it is not enough to change one's place; we must separate ourselves from the common conditions that are within us; we must sequester ourselves and regain ourselves.

> "I have broken my chains," you will say. Yet the dog that, by straining, has broken the knot, drags at his neck, when he escapes, a long piece of his chain.[20]

We carry our fetters with us; it is not complete liberty; we still turn our eyes toward what we have left; our thoughts are full of it.

> If we do not purge our breasts, what battles and perils must then find their way thither in despite of us! What sharp anxiety rends the man who is agitated by lust! How many fears! What disasters are wrought by pride and uncleanliness and malice, by luxury and sloth?[21]

Our sickness is of the soul; now the soul can not escape from itself.

> The soul is at fault which never escapes from itself.[22]

Of Solitude

So we must bring it home and withdraw into ourselves.[23] That is true solitude, and it may be enjoyed in the midst of cities and of kings' courts; but it is enjoyed more fitly in private. Now, when we undertake to live alone and to do without companionship, let us see to it that our contentment depends on ourselves; let us cut loose from all ties that bind us to others; let us win from ourselves the power to live alone in good earnest and thus to live at our ease.

Stilpo having escaped from the conflagration of his city, in which he had lost wife, children, and substance, Demetrius Poliorcetes, seeing him with undaunted mien notwithstanding the utter ruin of his country, asked him if he had met with no loss. He answered no, and that, thanks to God, he had lost nothing belonging to him.[24] It was to the same effect that the philosopher Antisthenes said jestingly that men should supply themselves with provisions that would float on the water, and could thus escape from shipwreck with them.[25]

Surely the wise man has lost nothing if he has himself. When the city of Nola was ruined by the barbarians, Paulinus, who was bishop there, having lost every thing, and being their prisoner, prayed to God thus: "O Lord, preserve me from feeling this loss, for thou knowest that they have not indeed touched any thing that is mine."[26] The riches that made him rich, and the goods that made him good were still intact. See what it is to choose wisely the treasures which are guaranteed from harm, and to hide them in a place where no one may go, and which can not be betrayed but by ourselves. All of us who can must have wives, children, property, and, above all, health; but not be so attached to them that our happiness depends on them;

Of Solitude

we must reserve for ourselves a private room, all our own, subject to no one,[27] in which we may establish our true freedom and our principal retreat and solitude. Therein we must customarily converse with ourselves, and so inwardly that no outside commerce or communication may there find place; we must there examine things and make merry over them, as if without wife and children and wordly goods, without retinue and servants, so that, if the cause of their loss shall come to pass, it may be no new thing to us to do without them. We have a soul that can be turned to itself; it can be its own company; it has the means of attack and of defence, of giving and of receiving. Let us not fear the becoming dull in this solitude from wearisome inactivity;

in lonely places be to yourself a multitude.[28]

Virtue, says Antisthenes, is content by itself, without rules without words, without deeds.[29]

In our wonted actions there is not one in a thousand that concerns ourselves. He whom you see clambering up the ruins of yonder wall, frantic and beside himself, a target for so many gun-shots; and that other, all scarred, exhausted, and pale with hunger, resolved to be cut to pieces rather than open the gate—think you that they are there on their own account? It is for one, perhaps, whom they never saw and who gives himself no concern about their deeds, sunk meanwhile in inactivity and pleasures. That man, snuffling, snivelling, and blear-eyed,[30] whom you see come from a study after midnight—do you think that he is searching in books how he shall make himself a better man, happier and wiser? Nothing of the sort.[31] He will die at it, or will instruct posterity about the metre of the verses of Plautus

Of Solitude

and the true orthography of a Latin word. Who does not readily exchange health, tranquillity, and life for fame and glory, the most useless, hollow, and false coin that we use? Our own death not causing us enough fear, let us burden ourselves also with the death of our wives, our children, and our servants. Our own affairs not giving us trouble enough, let us take upon ourselves to worry and cudgel our brains over those of our neighbours and friends.

What! can any man take it into his head to hold any thing dearer than himself?[32]

Solitude seems to me to have most fitness and reasonableness for those who have given to the world their most active and vigorous years, after the example of Thales.[33] We have lived enough for others; let us live for ourselves at least this latter end of our life; let us bring our thoughts and our purposes home to ourselves, and for our full content.[34] It is no easy matter to effect our withdrawal completely; it gives us enough to do without mingling other undertakings with it. Since God gives us leisure to order our own flitting, let us prepare for it; let us pack our trunks, and let us take leave of society betimes; let us deliver ourselves from those violent seizures[35] which drag us elsewhere and carry us away from ourselves. We must cut loose from those strong bonds, and henceforth love this or that, but espouse nothing but ourselves; that is to say: all else may belong to us, but not so combined and united with us that it can not be detached without flaying us, and tearing off with it a part of our flesh.[36] The greatest thing in the world is to know how to belong to oneself.

It is time to cut loose from society when we can con-

Of Solitude

tribute nothing to it; let him who can not lend refrain from
borrowing. Our powers are failing; let us draw them in and
concentrate them in ourselves. He who can pour into himself and mingle together the duties of friendship and of society, let him do so. In this fallen estate, which makes him
useless and burdensome and troublesome to others, let him
beware that he be not to himself troublesome and burdensome and useless. Let him flatter and caress and, above all,
govern himself, respecting and fearing his reason and his
conscience, so that he can not without shame stumble in
their presence. *For it is a rare thing for a man to have sufficient deference for himself.*[37] Socrates says that young men
should seek instruction, grown men should practice doing
good, old men should withdraw from all civil and military
employments and live as they please, without being bound
to any definite duty.[38]

There are some temperaments better adapted than others
to these precepts of withdrawal from the world. They who
are weak and slow of apprehension,[39] and who have a fastidious disposition and will, which is not easily subjected
or made use of,—of whom I am one both by nature and
by judgement,—will better bend to this opinion than those
active and busy minds who grasp every thing and pledge
themselves on all sides; who are passionately interested in
all things; who offer themselves, who come forward and
give themselves at every opportunity. We should make
use of these accidental, outside pleasures, in so far as they
are agreeable to us, but should not make them our principal
support. They are not that; neither reason nor nature will
have it so. Why, then, should we, against their laws, subject our contentment to the authority of others? To antici-

Of Solitude

pate thus the accidents of fortune; to deprive ourselves of the pleasures that are in our hands, as many have done from religious zeal, and some philosophers from reasoning; to wait upon oneself; to sleep on a hard bed; to put out one's eyes;[40] to throw one's worldly goods into the river;[41] to seek pain (as some do, by means of suffering in this life, to acquire happiness in another; others, by placing themselves on the lowest step, to make themselves safe from an unlooked-for fall)—all these are the actions of excessive virtue. Stouter and stronger natures make their very withdrawal glorious and worthy of imitation.

> When possessions fail me, I praise quietness and humbleness, courageous enough among things of little value; but when there comes to me something better and more delicate, I, the very same man, say that those only are wise and live happily, whose fortune is seen to be well placed in fertile lands.[42]

I have enough to do without going so far; it suffices me, when favoured by fortune, to prepare myself for her disfavour; and, when at ease, to represent to myself the evil to come, so far as the imagination can attain thereto;[43] just as we train ourselves by jousts and tournaments, and make mimic war in time of perfect peace.

I do not think Arcesilaus the philosopher the less austere because I know that he used utensils of gold and silver as far as his means permitted; and I think more highly of him than if he had parted with them, since he used them unpretendingly and generously.[44] I see the full scope of the need arising from natural conditions;[45] and, as I consider the poor beggar at my door, often more jovial and healthier than myself, I set myself in his place, I try to put my soul into his shoes.[46] And running in like manner over other examples, although I imagine death, poverty, contempt, and sickness to be at my heels, I easily resolve not to be alarmed by what a lesser man than I take with such patience. And I can not believe that the inferiority of understanding avails more than strength, or that the effects of reasoning may not attain to the effects of accustomedness. And knowing how insecure these outside advantages are, I do not fail, in full enjoyment of them, to implore God, as my chief prayer, that he will make me satisfied with myself alone, and with the resources that are born within me. I see hale and hearty young men who never fail to carry in their boxes a quantity of pills to use when a cold lies heavy on them, which they fear the less, thinking that they have its remedy at hand. So it is well to do; and still more, if we feel subject to some more serious malady, to supply ourselves with those drugs which quiet and put to sleep the enemy.

The occupation to be chosen for such a life[47] should be an occupation neither laborious nor tedious; otherwise, it is for naught that we have undertaken to resort to it for repose. It depends on every man's individual taste; mine is in no wise inclined to household cares. They who like them should give themselves to them in moderation,—

> Let them strive to subordinate things to themselves,
> not themselves to things.[48]

The management of house and lands[49] is otherwise a servile business, as Sallust calls it;[50] it has some branches more justifiable than others, as the oversight of gardens, which Xenophon ascribes to Cyrus;[51] and there may be found

Of Solitude

a mean between that low and abject oversight, widely extended and full of perplexity, that we see in men who are wholly plunged in it, and that profound and extreme indifference, letting every thing go at random, that we see in others.

> Herds devour the fields and the harvests of Democritus, whilst his swift disembodied mind is far away.[52]

But let us hear the advice that the younger Pliny gives to his friend Cornelius Rufus on this subject of solitude: "I advise you, in that complete and idle seclusion[53] in which you live, to leave to your servants the base and sordid domestic cares, and to devote yourself to the study of letters, to derive therefrom something that will be all your own."[54] He means reputation: a thought akin to that of Cicero, who says that he desires to employ his solitude and his leisure from public affairs in acquiring immortality by means of his writings.[55]

> Is knowledge nothing to you, unless others know of your knowledge?[56]

It seems to me that it is wise, when one talks of withdrawing from the world, to look away from it. These men only half do this; they frame their arrangements very well for the time when they will be no longer there; but the profit of their determination they think still to draw from the world,—they themselves being absent,—by an absurd inconsistency. The conception those have who seek solitude from religious devotion, filling their hearts with the certainty of the divine promises in the other life, is much more sanely devised. They look forward to God—an object infinite both in goodness and in power. The soul has wherewith to satisfy its desires in entire liberty. To such, afflictions, sorrows are profitable, being employed in the acquisition of everlasting health and enjoyment; death is to be desired—the passage into a so perfect condition. The harshness of their rules is, as soon as may be, softened by accustomedness; and the carnal appetites repelled and dulled by their denial, for nothing maintains them but habit and exercise. This sole aim of another, happily immortal, life justly deserves that we should give up the satisfactions and charms of this life of ours and he who can in truth and constantly enkindle his soul with the flame of this living faith and hope creates for himself in solitude a life pleasurable and delicious beyond every other way of life.

Neither the end, therefore, nor the manner of this advice[57] pleases me: we go continually from bad to worse.[58] This occupation with books is as laborious as any other, and as great a foe to the health, which should be chiefly considered. And we must not let ourselves be deluded by the pleasure that we take in it; it is the same pleasure that ruins the administrator of domestic affairs,[59] the avaricious, the pleasure-loving, and the ambitious. Wise men sufficiently instruct us to beware of the treachery of our appetites, and to distinguish true and perfect pleasures from pleasures which are blended and diversified with more pain; for most pleasures, they say, touch us gently and embrace us, only to strangle us, as was the wont of those whom the Egyptians called Philistas.[60] If the headache came before drunkenness, we should beware of drinking too much; but enjoyment, to deceive us, goes in front and hides from us its companions.

328

Of Solitude

Books are agreeable, but if, by consorting with them, we end by losing vivacity and health, our best possessions, let us get rid of them. I am of those who think that their fruit can not counterbalance that loss. As men who have long felt themselves to be enfeebled by sickness place themselves at last at the mercy of medicine, and have determined for them by science certain rules of living not to be departed from, so he who withdraws, wearied and disgusted, from life in common, should shape his new life according to the rules of reason, should order and arrange it with premeditation and judgement. He should have taken leave of every sort of toil, whatever aspect it may wear, and should shun, in general, those passions which impede the tranquillity of the body and of the mind, and choose the path which is most in accordance with his judgement:—

Each man will choose to go his own way.[61]

In domestic affairs,[62] in study, in hunting, and every other pursuit, we must go to the very last limits of enjoyment, and must be on our guard against pledging ourselves further where trouble begins to be mingled with it. We must retain of busyness and occupation only so much as is needed to keep us in breath, and to guarantee us from the discomforts which the other extreme—a feeble and torpid idleness —brings in its train. There are sterile and thorny kinds of knowledge, devised mostly for the multitude; they must be left to those who are in the service of the world. I myself like, among books, only those that are amusing and easy, that move me with pleasure, or that comfort me and advise[63] me how to order my life and my death:—

Of Solitude

To stroll silently through health-giving woods, meditating on what is worthy a wise and virtuous man.[64]

Wiser men can create for themselves a wholly spiritual peace, having strong and vigorous souls; I, having a more ordinary one, must be helped by bodily comforts to sustain myself; and age having lately stolen from me those which were most to my liking, I train and whet my appetite for those remaining more adapted to this other time of life. We must hold on with all our strength[65] to the enjoyment of the pleasures of life, which our years tear from our grasp one after another:[66]—

> Let us pluck pleasures; life is all that is ours; soon you will be ashes, a shade, a mere name.[67]

Now, as for the goal of renown that Pliny and Cicero propose to us, it is very far from my reckoning. The humour most opposed to retirement is ambition: renown and repose are things that can not lodge in the same dwelling. In my eyes, they[68] have only their arms and legs unconstrained; their minds, their purposes are more than ever in bonds.

> Is it for you, old fool, to cater to the ears of assembled strangers?[69]

They have drawn back, only the better to leap, and by a more vigorous movement to make a livelier charge into the troop. Will you see how they shoot a trifle short? Let us weigh the advice of two philosophers,[70] belonging to two very different sects, writing to their friends, the one to Idomeneus, the other to Lucilius, to induce them to withdraw

Of Solitude

from the management of affairs, and from great positions, to solitude. You have (they say) lived swimming and floating until now—come into port to die; you have spent the rest of your life in the light, spend this in the shade.[71] It is impossible to abandon your occupations if you do not abandon their profits; for this reason put aside all care of fame and renown.[72] There is danger that the lustre of your past actions may throw only too much light upon you and follow you even into your cave; abandon, with other pleasures, that which comes from the approbation of others.[73] And as for your much learning,[74] take no thought of that; it will not lose its value if you profit better by it yourself.[75] Remember him who, when some one asked him to what end he in his art took such pains as could come to the knowledge of few persons, replied: "Few are enough for me; one is enough; not one is enough."[76] He spoke truly; you and a companion are theatre enough one for the other, or you alone for yourself.[77] Let all the world be to you as one person, and one person be to you as all the world.[78] It is a beggarly ambition to seek to derive renown from one's idleness and one's hiding-place; one must do like the animals, who efface their tracks at the mouth of their den.[79] It should no longer be your concern to make the world speak of you, but how you should speak to yourself.[80] Withdraw into yourself, but first prepare to receive yourself; it would be madness to trust yourself to yourself if you do not know how to govern yourself; it is possible to err in solitude no less than in society.[81] Until you have made yourself a man before whom you would not dare to stumble; and until you are bashful and respectful before yourself, *let noble images be present to your mind*,[82] keep always present in thought Cato, Pho-

Of Solitude

cion, and Aristides, in whose presence even fools would hide their faults, and make them the guides of all your purposes. If these go astray, your veneration for those men will put them in the path again; it will keep you in the way to be content with yourself, to detain and fix your mind upon certain definite reflections in which it can take pleasure; and having perceived the true blessings, which are enjoyed as soon as they are perceived, to content yourself with them, without desire for length of days or for fame. Such is the counsel of a true and sincere philosophy, not of an ostentatious and verbose philosophy as is that of the first two.[83]

Chapter XL

REFLECTION

CONCERNING CICERO

ONE word more in the comparison of these couples.[1] There may be drawn from the writings of Cicero and of this Pliny—who, in my opinion, bears little resemblance to the character of his uncle—innumerable proofs of natures ambitious beyond measure: among others, that before the whole world they entreat the historians of their time not to forget them in their chronicles;[2] and Fortune, as if in spite, has caused the vanity of those requests to endure to our day, and long ago consigned any such mention to oblivion.[3] But it goes beyond utter low-mindedness in persons of such standing to have desire to derive great glory from babble and prating, even to making use of private letters written to their friends; so that, some of them having failed to be sent in due season, the writers none the less have them published, with the noble excuse that they wish not to lose their work and their vigils. Does it not well become two Roman consuls, highest rulers of the republic that is empress of the world, to employ their leisure in devising and prettily composing an eloquent letter, to derive therefrom the reputation of being perfectly versed in their mother-tongue? What worse could a mere schoolmaster do, who might earn his living by it? If the deeds of Xenophon and Cæsar had not very far surpassed their eloquence, I do not believe that they would ever have written of them; they strove to turn attention, not to their sayings, but to their doings.[4] And if the perfection of writing well could confer any glory befitting a great man, surely Scipio and Lælius would not have resigned the credit for their comedies, and for all the daintinesses and delightfulnesses of the Latin language to an African bondman; for that this work was theirs, its beauty and its excellence sufficiently declare, and Terence himself admits it;[5] and I should be sorry if I were obliged to abandon that belief.

It is a sort of mockery and insult to seek to extol a man for qualities unbeseeming his station, although they be in other respects laudable; and also for qualities that ought not to be his most prominent ones: as if a king were praised for being a good painter, or a good architect, or even a good shot, or a good runner at the ring. Such praises confer no honour unless many of them are offered together, and after those that are appropriate to him, namely, justice and wisdom in guiding his people in peace and in war.[6] In this way agriculture does honour to Cyrus, and eloquence and knowledge of letters to Charlemagne. I have seen in my day, to put this more strongly, great persons, who derived both their titles and their station from writing, renounce their skill, debase their pens, and affect ignorance of so commonplace an acquirement,—and one which, our people hold, is seldom to be found in learned hands,—drawing attention to themselves by higher qualities.[7]

The companions of Demosthenes in the embassy to Philip praised that prince as being handsome and eloquent

334

Reflection Concerning Cicero

and a good drinker; Demosthenes said that those praises were more appropriate for a woman, a lawyer, and a sponge, than a king.[8]

> May he rule, superior to the warring enemy, merciful to the prostrate.[9]

It is not his main affair to know how to hunt well or to dance well.

> Others shall plead causes, and describe with the compass the movements of the heavens, and shall name the brilliant stars; let this man learn to rule nations.[10]

Plutarch says further that to appear so proficient in these less essential matters is to produce against oneself the proof of having ill spent one's leisure and the study which should have been employed in more necessary and useful things. So that when Philip, King of Macedonia, heard the great Alexander, his son, sing at a banquet and vie with the best musicians, "Are you not ashamed," he said to him, "to sing so well?"[11] And to this same Philip a musician with whom he was disputing about his art said: "God grant, sire, that such ill luck may never happen to you that you should understand these matters better than I do!"[12] A king should be able to reply as Iphicrates replied to an orator who importuned him in his opprobrious discourse in this wise: "Now, who are you that you so play the braggart? Are you an armoured horseman? Are you an archer? Are you a pikeman?"—"I am nothing like that," he replied, "but I am one who knows how to command all those."[13] And Antisthenes took it for an indication of small merit in Ismenias that he was vaunted as an excellent flute-player.[14]

Reflection Concerning Cicero

I know very well that, when I hear some one dwell on the language of these Essays, I should prefer that he were silent; it does not so much lift up the words, as it abuses the sense—and the more indirect it is, the more it stings.[15] For I am mistaken, if many others give more to lay hold of in the matter itself; and, however it may be, whether well or ill, if any writer has sowed his paper with more fruitful, or at least with more plenteous seed. In order to include more, I heap together only the heads; did I add their sequel, I should multiply this volume many times. And how many anecdotes have I scattered everywhere, themselves silent, from which he who inclines to examine them a little more thoughtfully may produce countless essays! Nor do these anecdotes or my quotations always serve merely for example or authority or ornament. I do not consider them solely for the use I make of them. They often bear, beyond the scope of my subject, the seeds of an ampler and bolder theme, and give forth on another side a more exquisite note, both to me, who do not choose to express it more fully, and to those who may fall in with my way of thinking. Recurring to the talent for words, I do not find much to choose between not knowing how to express any thing except badly, and not knowing any thing except how to express oneself well. *Elaborate ornamentation is not manly.*[16]

The wise men say that, with respect to knowledge, there is only philosophy, and with respect to actions, only courage,[17] which, in general, is appropriate for all degrees and all ranks. There is something of the same sort in those other two philosophers;[18] for they also promise immortality for the letters they write to their friends; but it is done in a different way, adapting itself for a good effect to the vanity of

336

others. For they tell them that if it be the desire to make themselves known to future ages and to fame that keeps them still engaged in affairs, and leads them to shrink from the solitude and retirement to which they[19] seek to attract them, they need give themselves no further anxiety, forasmuch as they[20] have sufficient credit with posterity to assure them that, if it be only by the letters they write to them, they will make their names as well known and as illustrious as their own public acts could do. And, besides this difference, these are no empty, fleshless letters, upheld only by a fastidious choice of words brought together in heaps and arranged in smooth cadence,[21] but are stuffed full of noble precepts of wisdom, by which we are made, not more eloquent, but wiser, and which teach us, not to use language well, but to act well. A fig for the eloquence which leaves us longing for it and not for things![22] unless we may say that Cicero's, being of such supreme perfection, is in itself substance.[23] I will add here, in this connection, an anecdote that we have of him, so that we may perceive his inborn disposition.[24] He had to make a public speech, and was a little pressed for time to prepare himself at leisure. Eros, one of his bondmen, came to tell him that the hearing was postponed to the following day. He was so overjoyed that he gave him his freedom for this good news.[25]

About this matter of letters I will say this, that it is a work in which my friends think that I have some facility. And I would more readily have adopted that form for publishing my thoughts, if I had had some one to address. There would have been needful for me what once I had— a certain intercourse which would lead me on, which would uphold me and lift me up.[26] For, as for dealing with a void,[27] as others do, I should not know how, except in dreams, nor how to create unreal persons to discourse with on serious matters, being a sworn foe of every sort of falsification. I should have been more careful and more assured had I had a sturdy and friendly person to whom to address myself, than I am in looking at the diverse aspects of a whole people; and I am mistaken if it would not have given me more success. I have naturally a free and familiar style,[28] but it is of a kind peculiar to myself, unsuitable for public employment, as in all respects is my language: too concise, irregular, abrupt, individual; and I possess no skill in formal letters, which have no other substance than that of a fine string of courteous words. I have neither faculty nor liking for those long-winded proffers of affection and service; I do not much believe in them, and I dislike to use them beyond the limits of my belief. This is a long way from the present custom, for never was there so abject and slavish a prostitution of polite formulas:[29] my life, my soul, devotion, adoration, servant, slave—all these words are in such common use that, when it is desired to make evident a more special and more reciprocal emotion,[30] there is no longer any way of expressing it. I hate mortally the air of flattery, which makes me naturally fall into a dry, blunt, unpolished mode of speech, which tends, to one who does not know me elsewhere, somewhat toward the contemptuous. I honour most those whom I honour least;[31] and where my soul moves with great gladness, there I forget the gait of ceremony; and I offer myself charily and coldly to those whose servant I am, and with least politeness to him to whom I am most devoted. It seems to me that they ought to read in my heart, and that what my words say does injustice to my ideas. In

Reflection Concerning Cicero

bidding welcome, in taking leave, in thanking, in salutation, in offering my services, and in other such verbal courtesies belonging to the ceremonial laws of our conventions, I know no one so stupidly barren of words as I am. And I have never been made use of to write letters of good-will and recommendation, that he for whom it was done has not found it dry and cold.

The Italians are great publishers of letters. I possess, I think, a hundred different volumes of them; those of Annibale Caro[32] seem to me the best. If all the paper which, in former days, I have hastily scrawled over to ladies when my hand was truly moved by passion, were in existence, there might perchance be found there some page worthy of being transmitted to languishing youths deluded by that madness. I always write my letters post-haste, and so hurriedly that, although my scrawl is intolerably bad, I prefer to write with my own hand rather than make use of another for this; for I find none who can follow me, and I never copy them. I have accustomed the great men who know me to put up with erasures in them, and words written over others, and with paper without folds and with no margin. Those which cost me most are those of the least value; when they drag, it is a sign that I am not there. I begin generally without any plan; the first sentence gives birth to the second. The letters of the present day consist more of extraneous matter[33] and preambles, than of substance. Just as I would rather compose two letters than close and fold one, and always hand over this business to another, so, when the subject-matter is finished, I would willingly give some one else the trouble of adding to it those long set speeches, offers of services, and prayers that we place at the end; and I wish that

339

some new custom would relieve us of them; as also of super-scribing our letters with a string of functions and titles which, for fear of tripping up in them, have many a time prevented me from writing, especially to kings' councillors and treasurers. So many new offices, such a difficult ar-rangement and ordering of various terms of honour, can not, being so dearly bought, be transposed or forgotten without offence. I find it likewise unseemly to burden with them the title-pages and dedications of the books we print.[34]

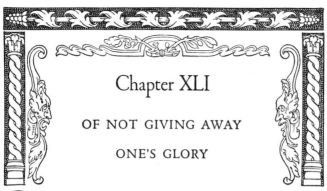

Chapter XLI

OF NOT GIVING AWAY
ONE'S GLORY

OF all the delusions in the world, the most fully accepted and most universal is the seeking for fame and glory, which we espouse to the point of giving up wealth, repose, life, and health, which are real and substantial goods, to follow that airy phantom and that mere voice which has neither body nor the wherewithal to clutch it.

> Fame, who by her sweet voice charms you, O proud mortals, and seems so fair, is an echo, a dream, nay, a shadow of a dream, which every mind scatters and blows away.[1]

And among the unreasonable foibles of mankind, it seems that even the philosophers divest themselves more tardily and more reluctantly of this than of any other. It is the most intractable and obstinate; *because it does not cease to tempt even those souls that are advancing well.*[2] There is scarcely one of which reason so clearly proves the hollowness; but its roots in us are so alive that I know not whether any man has ever been able to rid himself of them completely. After you have said every thing and believed every thing to discredit it, it exhibits, contrary to your argument, an inclination so innate that you can hardly resist it.[3] For, as Cicero says, those even who fight against it desire none the less that the books they write about it shall bear their names on the title-page, and desire to make themselves famous for having despised fame.[4] All other things fall within the field of communication; we give our property and lives to meet the need of our friends; but to part with what does one honour and to bestow on another one's glory —that is seldom seen. Catulus Luctatius, in the war against the Cymbri, having done his utmost to stop his soldiers who were flying before the foe, placed himself among the fugitives and played the coward, in order that they should seem rather to follow their captain than to fly from the enemy; thereby he sacrificed his own good name to conceal the disgrace of others.[5] When the Emperor Charles the Fifth went into Provence, in the year fifteen hundred thirty-seven [1536], it is believed that Antoine de Leve, seeing the emperor bent upon that expedition, and he himself thinking that it would add wonderfully to his renown, constantly maintained opposition to it and advised against it, to the end that all the glory and honour of this decision should be attributed to his master, and that it should be said that his good judgement and foresight had been such that, against every one's advice, he had carried through so fine an undertaking; this was doing him[6] honour at his own expense.[7] When the Thracian ambassadors consoled Archileonide, the mother of Brasidas, for the death of her son, and highly praised him, going even so far as to say that he had not left his like, she refused that private and personal praise, to give it to the public. "Do not tell me that," she said; "I know that the city of Sparta has many greater and more valiant

Of Not Giving Away One's Glory

citizens than he was."[8] In the battle of Crécy, the Prince of Wales, still very young, had command of the vanguard. The principal brunt of the conflict was at that spot. The lords who accompanied him, finding that they were in sore straits, sent to King Edward to come to their assistance. He enquired about his son's plight, and having been told that he was alive and on horseback, "I should wrong him," he said, "to go now and rob him of the honour of victory in this fight that he has sustained so long; whatever chance he may have in it, it shall be all his." And he would neither go nor send thither, knowing that, if he went, it would be said that all had been lost but for his assistance, and that to him would be attributed the success of this exploit;[9] *for the last comers always seem to be those who effect the whole.*[10]

At Rome many people thought, and it was commonly said, that the noble deeds of Scipio were due in part to Lælius, who besides was always promoting and aiding the greatness and glory of Scipio without any thought of his own.[11] And Theopompus, King of Sparta, when some one said to him that the commonwealth stood firm,[12] because he knew well how to rule, "It is rather," he said, "because the people know well how to obey."[13]

As women who succeeded to peerages had, notwithstanding their sex, the right to be present and to declare their opinion in law-suits within the jurisdiction of peers,[14] so the ecclesiastical peers, notwithstanding their profession, were bound to assist our kings in their wars, not only by their friends and retainers, but in their own persons. Thus the Bishop of Beauvais, being present with Philip Augustus in the battle of Bouvines, participated very bravely in the desired result; but it seemed to him that he ought not to obtain any fruit and glory from his fierce and bloody exertions. He overcame many of the enemy with his own hand that day, and turned them over to the first gentleman he met, to have their throats cut or to be made prisoners, leaving to him the whole execution of the thing. And thus he did with William, Earl of Salisbury, delivering him to Messire Jean de Nesle. From a like refinement of conscience, he was willing to strike down, but not to wound, and therefore he fought only with a club.[15] Some one in my time, being accused by the king of having laid hands on a priest, denied it stoutly and steadily; the fact was that he had battered and trampled him with his feet.

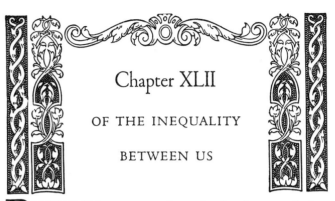

Chapter XLII

OF THE INEQUALITY

BETWEEN US

PLUTARCH says somewhere that he does not find so great a distance between beast and beast as between man and man.[1] He means regarding the worth of the soul and the inner qualities.[2] In truth, I find it so far from Epaminondas, as I imagine him to have been, to some that I know,—I mean, possessing common sense,—that I would readily go further than Plutarch, and say that there is a greater distance between such and such a man than there is between such a man and such a beast;

ah! how one man excels another![3]

and that there are as innumerable ranks of intelligences as there are arm's lengths between here and heaven.[4]

But, speaking of the valuation of men, it is extraordinary that, except ourselves, nothing is valued save for its own qualities.[5] We praise a horse because he is strong and active,—

Thus we praise the swift horse, who is animated by many applauding hands, and bounds triumphantly in the resounding circus,[6]—

345

not for his caparison; a greyhound for his speed, not for his
collar; a bird for his flight, not for his leash and bells. Why
do we not likewise judge a man by what is his own? He
has a great retinue, a fine palace, so much renown, so much
income: all these things are roundabout him, not in him.[7]
You do not buy a pig in a poke.[8] If you are bargaining for
a horse, you take off his trappings and look at him bare
and uncovered;[9] or, if he be covered,—as used to be the case
when they were offered to princes for sale,—it is only as to
the less essential parts, so that you may not waste your time
over the beauty of his coat or the breadth of his croup, but
give your attention principally to observing his legs and eyes
and feet, which are the most useful members.

> The great have this custom: when they buy horses,
> they inspect them covered, so that if, as often happens,
> a fine shape is united with bad feet, the eager buyer
> may not be seduced by the admirable quarters, the
> short head, and the shapely neck.[10]

Why, when you judge a man, do you judge him all swathed
and bundled up?[11] He exhibits to us only the parts which
are in no wise his, and hides from us those by which alone we
can judge truly of his value: it is the worth of the sword
that you are seeking, not of the scabbard.[12] You would not
perchance give a farthing for him had you stripped him.
He must be judged by himself, not by his adornments.
And, as an ancient writer very wittily says, "Do you know
why you think him tall? You take in the height of his
pattens."[13] The pedestal is not part of the statue. Measure him without his stilts; let him put aside his riches and
honours; let him stand forth in his shirt.[14] Is his body fit-

Of the Inequality between Us

ted for its functions—sound and active? What sort of soul
has he? Is it noble, large, and happily supplied with all its
faculties? Is it rich in its own right or another's? Has chance
no hand therein?[15] Whether, open-eyed, it awaits drawn
swords; whether it cares how life departs—through the
mouth or through the throat; whether it be a serene, equable, and contented soul—these are the things we must
observe, and discern therefrom the extreme differences that
exist among us.[16] Is he

> a wise man and master of himself, terrified neither
> by poverty, nor death, nor chains, strong in resist-
> ing passions and disdaining honours, self-contained,
> rounded and compact, whose polished surface nothing
> external can impede; with whom the assaults of for-
> tune can seize upon nothing?[17]

Such a man is five hundred arm's-lengths above kingdoms
and duchies: he is his own empire.

> The wise man, by Pollux! himself forges his for-
> tune.[18]

What is left for him to wish for?

> Do we not see that nature claims for herself no more
> than that pain hold aloof from the body, and that she
> enjoy in her mind a feeling of pleasure without care
> or fear?[19]

Compare with him the rabble of mankind, stupid, mean,
servile, unstable,[20] forever tossed about in the sea of the conflicting passions which drive the multitude back and forth,
wholly dependent on external conditions: there is a greater

347

distance than from heaven to earth. And yet we are so
blinded by custom that we make little or no account of it;
so that, if we regard a peasant and a king, a noble and a
boor, a man high in office and a private man, a rich man and
a poor man, there instantly appears to our eyes an extreme
disparity; yet they are different, so to speak, only in their
breeches.

In Thrace the king was distinguished from his people in
an amusing way, and one that seemed of much more value
than it was.[21] He had a religion of his own, a god all to
himself, whom his subjects were not entitled to worship,—
it was Mercury,—and he himself disdained their gods—
Mars, Bacchus, and Diana.[22] Yet these are but paintings
in which there is no essential dissimilarity. For, like actors,
you see them on the stage, assuming the mien of duke and
emperor; but, immediately after, lo, they are but wretched
varlets and porters, which is their genuine and original condition.[23]

So with the emperor, whose magnificence in public daz-
zles you,—

> Wearing great emeralds whose translucent green
> is set in gold, and garments of the color of the sea,
> which are defiled by the sweat of his debauches,[24]—

see him behind the curtain and he is but an ordinary man,
and, it may be, more worthless than the meanest of his subjects. *The one contains his own happiness; the other wears
it like gilt.*[25] Cowardice, irresolution, ambition, anger, and
envy agitate him like other men,—

> For neither treasures nor the consul's lictor can

Of the Inequality between Us

drive away the tumultuous troubles of the soul and the
cares that flit beneath panelled ceilings,[26]—

and anxiety and fear hold him by the throat in the midst
of his armies;

> In truth, the fears and cares that haunt men are not
> afraid of the sound of arms or of savage darts; they fre-
> quent kings and potentates, unabashed by the gleam
> of gold.[27]

Do fever and headache and gout spare him any more than
us? When old age falls upon his shoulders, will the archers
of his guard disburden him of it? When terror of death
appalls him, will he be reassured by the presence of his
gentlemen of the chamber? When he is full of distrust and
idle thoughts, will our salutations[28] bring him to himself?
That canopy over his bed, all stiff with gold and pearls, has
no virtue to ease the gripes of a sharp attack of colic.[29]

> Nor does feverish heat leave your body the sooner
> if you toss about on brocades and purple, than if you
> must lie on a poor man's bed.[30]

The flatterers of the great Alexander declared to him that
he was the son of Jupiter. One day, being wounded, he said,
as he looked at the blood flowing from his wound, "Well,
what do you say about this? is not this blood red and purely
human? It is not of the quality that Homer describes as
flowing from the wounds of the gods."[31] Hermodorus the
poet had written verses in honour of Antigonus, calling him
the son of the Sun; but he retorted: "He who empties my
close stool knows very well that that's not so."[32] He is noth-

ing, when all comes to all, but a man;[33] and if he is base by
nature, the sovereignty of the universe would not better him.

> May the girls seize upon him; on the ground he
> treads upon, may roses spring.[34]

What avails, if his be a coarse and stupid soul? Even pleasure and good fortune are never seen without strength and
intelligence.

> These things depend for their value on their pos-
> sessor; for him who knows how to use them well, they
> are good; for him who uses them ill, they are bad.[35]

We must have a sense that can relish the benefits of fortune, whatever they may be; it is the enjoying, not the possessing, that makes us happy.

> Not a mansion and an estate, nor a store of silver
> and gold can drive fever from the sick body of their
> possessor, or cares from his mind. He must be in good
> health if he hopes to enjoy his heaped-up riches. Man-
> sions and treasures give as little delight to the man who
> is full of desires and fears as paintings to the blear-eyed
> or fomentations to the gouty.[36]

If he be a fool, his perception is sluggish and deadened; he
enjoys nothing, any more than one with a cold in his head
does the savour of Greek wine, or than a horse does the costliness of the trappings with which he is bedecked. It is as
Plato says, that health, beauty, strength, wealth, and every
thing that is called good, are to the unjust no less evil than
good to the just, and what is evil, contrariwise.[37]

Furthermore, when body and soul are in poor condi-

Of the Inequality between Us

tion, of what use are these external advantages, inasmuch as the slightest prick of a pin and spiritual perturbation[38] suffices to take from us the pleasure of being monarch of the world? At the first twinge that gout gives him, to no purpose is he "Sire" and "Your Majesty,"—

All decked with silver, all decked with gold,[39]—

does he not lose all remembrance of his palaces and his grandeurs? If he is angry, does his high estate save him from flushing, from turning pale, from gnashing his teeth like a madman? And if he is a man of ability and of natural worth, royalty adds little to his happiness,—

If your stomach and lungs and legs are sound, the wealth of kings can give you no greater thing,[40]—

he sees that it is all illusion and deception; yes, perhaps he will be of the opinion of King Seleucus, that "he who knows the weight of a sceptre would not stoop to pick it up if he found it lying on the ground."[41] He said it thinking of the heavy and painful duties which are incumbent on a good king. Surely it is no small matter to have to govern others, when so many difficulties present themselves in governing ourselves. In this matter of commanding, which seems so delightsome, I am strongly of the opinion,—in view of the frailty of man's judgement and the difficulty of choice among novel and doubtful things,—that it is much easier and pleasanter to follow than to lead, and that it is great peace for the mind to have simply to pursue a beaten track and to be responsible for oneself alone.

Far better it is, quietly to obey, than to wish to rule with supreme power.[42]

351

Of the Inequality between Us

Moreover, Cyrus said that it belonged to no man to command who was not worth more than those whom he commanded.[43] But King Hiero, in Xenophon, says further that even with regard to the enjoyment of pleasures, kings are worse off than private persons, because easiness and facility take from pleasures the bitter-sweet relish that we find therein.[44]

> An over-abundant and over-mastering love becomes cloying and harmful to us, as sweet food to the stomach.[45]

Do we suppose that choir-boys greatly enjoy music? Rather, surfeit makes it distasteful to them. Festivals, dances, masquerades, joustings delight those who do not see them often, and who have desire to see them; but to him whose ordinary fare they are, their taste becomes insipid and unpleasant; nor do women charm him who with a cloyed heart possesses them. He who does not permit himself to be thirsty can not take pleasure in drinking.[46] The farces of strolling actors amuse us; but to the performers themselves they are a hard day's work. And that this is so, witness that it is the pastime of princes, it is their holiday, to be able sometimes to disguise themselves and descend to the low, plebeian manner of living.

> Often a change is agreeable to the great, and a single repast under the humble roof of a poor man, without a high table and purple hangings, has smoothed the careworn brow.[47]

There is nothing so burdensome, so hard to please as abundance. What appetite would not be repelled by the

352

Of the Inequality between Us

sight of three hundred women at his discretion, as the Grand Turk has in his seraglio?[48] And what an appetite and countenance for sport did that one of his ancestors provide for himself, who never went hawking without seven thousand falconers?[49] And, besides that, I believe that this effulgence of grandeur brings no slight impediments to the enjoyment of the sweeter pleasures; they[50] are too brightly lighted and too much in view. And I know not why it is that we require them the more to conceal and cover up their fault. For what in us is unguarded conduct, in them the people considers to be tyranny, and contempt and scorn for the laws; and over and above the inclination to vice, they seem to add to it also the pleasure of insulting and trampling under foot public laws. Indeed, Plato, in his *Gorgias,* defines a tyrant as one who has the power in a city[51] to do whatever he pleases. And often, for this reason, the display and publicity of their vice hurts more than the vice itself. Every one dreads being spied upon and criticised; they are so, even to their looks and thoughts, all the people considering that it is their right and for their interest to judge of them; besides which, blemishes are more obvious, in the degree in which the place they occupy is more in view and more brightly lighted,[52] and a mole and a wart on the face are more apparent than a scar is elsewhere.[53] This is why the poets represent the amours of Jupiter as carried on under other forms than his own; and of all the many amorous exploits which they attribute to him, there is but one, I think, in which he appears in his grandeur and majesty.

But let us return to Hiero: he tells, too, how many incommodities he feels in his kingship, not being able to go about freely and travel, being, as it were, a prisoner within

353

the boundaries of his kingdom; and that in all his acts he finds himself surrounded by an annoying crowd.[54] In truth, seeing our own[55] seated by themselves at table, beset by so many chattering and staring strangers, I have often felt more pity than envy of them. King Alphonso said that, in this respect, asses were better off than kings: their masters allow them to feed at their ease, whereas kings can not obtain that from their attendants. And it has never appeared to me that it was any great convenience in the life of a man of intelligence to have a score of onlookers about his close stool, or that the services of a man who has ten thousand livres a year, or who has taken Casal,[56] or defended Siena,[57] are more convenient and acceptable to him than those of a good and experienced body-servant.

Princely advantages are, as it were, imaginary: every degree of fortune has some image of principality. Cæsar calls all the lords who administered justice in France in his day petty kings.[58] In truth, except for the title of Sire, we are not far behind our kings. Observe, in the provinces remote from court,—say, Brittany, for example,—the retinue, the vassals, the officers, the occupations, the service and ceremonial of a retired and home-keeping nobleman brought up among his servants; and observe too the flight of his imagination—nothing is more royal; he hears talk of his master once a year, as he does of the King of Persia, and recognises him only by some old kinship which his secretary keeps on record. Truly our laws are liberal enough, and the burden of sovereignty is felt by a French gentleman scarcely twice in his life. Real and effectual subjection concerns only those among us who assent to it, and who like to obtain honours and riches by such service; for he who chooses to

Of the Inequality between Us

keep close to his own hearth-stone, and knows how to manage his house without quarrels and without law-suits, he is as free as the Duke of Venice. *Few are enslaved; many enslave themselves.*[59]

But, above all, Hiero lays stress on the point that he finds himself deprived of all friendship and companionship, wherein consists the most perfect and sweetest fruit of human life. For what testimony of affection and good-will can I derive from him who, will he or nill he, owes to me all that he can do? Can I make account of his humble speech and courteous homage, seeing that it is not in his power to refuse them to me? The honour that we receive from those who fear us is not honour; this homage is paid to my sovereignty, not to me.

> The chief advantage of royalty is this, that the subjects are compelled, not only to endure, but to praise the deeds of their ruler.[60]

Do I not see that the bad king and the good, he who is hated and he who is beloved, the one has as much honour as the other? The same manifestations, the same ceremonies were observed for my predecessor and will be for my successor. If my subjects do not harm me, that is not a proof of any great affection; why should I take it as such, since they could not if they would. No one becomes my companion for the friendship that may exist between him and me, for it would not be possible to knit friendship where there is so little connection and correspondence. My eminence has set me apart from intercourse with men; there is too great disparity and disproportion. They accompany me as a matter of form, and from habit; or rather my fortune

355

than me, thereby to add to their own. All that they say to me and do is mere outer show, their freedom being held under on all sides by the great power I have over them. I see about me nothing that is not covered over and disguised. His courtiers praised the Emperor Julian one day for his just judgements. "I should readily take pride in these praises," he said, "if they came from persons who would dare to accuse or blame my acts when they were the opposite."[61]

All the real advantages that princes have are common to them and men of moderate fortune; it is for the gods to ride winged horses and feed on ambrosia. They have no different sleep and no different appetites from ours; their steel is of no better temper than that with which we arm ourselves; their crown shelters them from neither the sun nor the rain. Diocletian, who wore one so revered and so prosperous, resigned it, to withdraw to the enjoyment of private life; and some time after, the exigencies of public affairs requiring that he should return to take charge of them, he answered them who besought him to do so: "You would not undertake to persuade me to this, if you had seen the beautiful rows of trees that I have planted with my own hands on my estate, and the fine melons I have sown there."[62] In the opinion of Anacharsis, the most fortunate form of government would be one in which, all other things being equal, precedence should be meted out to virtue, and the leavings[63] to vice. When King Pyrrhus undertook to go into Italy, Cyneas, his wise counsellor, wishing to make him perceive the emptiness of his ambition, "Well, Sire," he asked him, "for what end are you preparing this great enterprise?"— "To make myself master of Italy," he quickly replied.

Of the Inequality between Us

—"And then," continued Cyneas, "when that is done?"—
"I shall pass on," said the other, "into Gaul and into
Spain."—"And then?"—"Then I shall go on to conquer
Africa; and at last, when I have made the whole world subject to me, I will rest, and live in content and at my ease."—
"For God's sake, Sire," Cyneas thereupon retorted, "tell
me what prevents you from being now, if you choose, in that
condition? Why do you not from this hour take up your
quarters where you say that you aspire to be, and spare
yourself all the effort and risks that you interpose?"[64]

Surely it was because he did not well know what
should be the limit of getting, or, in general, what increases true pleasure.[65]

I will conclude[66] with an old verse, which I consider singularly appropriate to this subject: *A man's character fashions
his fortune.*[67]

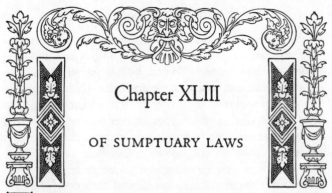

Chapter XLIII

OF SUMPTUARY LAWS

THE way in which our laws attempt to regulate the foolish and idle expenses of the table and of apparel seems to run counter to their object. The true method would be to engender in men a contempt for gold and silk as being idle and useless things; and we enhance their honour and their value, which is a very foolish way to disgust men with them; for to say that it is only princes who eat turbot and who may wear velvet and gold lace,[1] and to forbid common people to do so—what is that but making such things to be valued, and increasing every one's desire to use them? Let kings boldly lay aside these marks of grandeur; they have enough others; such extravagances are more pardonable in any other man than in a prince. By the example of several nations we can learn many better ways of externally distinguishing ourselves and our ranks (which, in truth, I consider to be most essential in a state), without fostering, to that end, this so manifest corruption and unfitness. It is astonishing how easily and how quickly custom establishes the footing of her authority in these indifferent matters. It is certain that barely a year had we worn broadcloth at court, in mourning for King Henry the

Of Sumptuary Laws

Second, when already, in every one's opinion, silks had fallen into such contempt[2] that, if you saw a person dressed in them, you at once set him down as a citizen.[3] They remained the portion of physicians and surgeons; and although every one was dressed almost alike, still there were elsewise enough manifest differences in the degrees of men. How suddenly in our armies did the dirty doublets of chamois skin and linen come into honour, and well-cared-for and costly garments into blame and contempt!

Let kings begin to do without these expenditures—the end will be gained in a month, without edict or decree: we shall all follow after. The law should declare, on the contrary, that crimson and goldsmith's work are forbidden to all conditions of men save mountebanks and courtesans. By such a device Zeleucus reformed the corrupt customs of the Locrians. His decrees were to this effect: that a free woman may not have more than one maidservant follow her, except when she is intoxicated; nor can she go out of the city at night, or wear gold ornaments about her person, or a richly embroidered garment, unless she be a common whore; that, except panders, no man is permitted to wear a gold ring on his finger, or a garment of fine stuff, like those of the cloths woven in the city of Miletus. And thus, by these shameful exceptions, he skilfully turned his citizens away from harmful superfluities and luxuries.[4] It was a very effective means of leading men to obedience by the way of honour and ambition.

Our kings are all-powerful in such external reforms; their inclination acts in these matters as law. *Whatever princes do is regarded as prescribed by them.*[5] The rest of France takes for its fashion the fashion of the court. Would that offence might be taken at those disgusting breeches which display so openly our private parts; at that thick padding-out of doublets, which makes us quite other than we are, so inconvenient in putting on armour; at those long effeminate tresses; at that fashion of kissing what we give to our friends, and our hands in saluting them—an act of homage formerly due to princes alone; and that a gentleman should appear in a place of ceremony without his sword at his side, all unbuttoned and untrussed, as if he were just from the house of office;[6] and that, contrary to the usage of our fathers and to the peculiar freedom of the nobility of this kingdom, wherever they[7] may be, we keep our heads uncovered even at a great distance from them; and, as with them, with a hundred others likewise, we have so many petty kings;[8] and also at other new and erroneous[9] innovations, which will find themselves incontinently banished and decried. These are superficial errors, but none the less of evil omen.

Plato, in his Laws, considers no calamity in the world more harmful to his city than to let the youth have liberty to change from one form to another in their apparel, their behaviour, their dances, their exercises, and their songs, shifting their opinions, now in this disposition of the mind, now in that; running after novelties, honouring their inventors; whereby morals are corrupted and all old forms of education are brought into scorn and contempt. In all things, save only those that are evil, change is to be dreaded —the change of seasons, of winds, of diet, of moods. And no laws have their due honour save those to which God has given such long continuance that no one knows their origin, nor that they have ever been different.[10]

Chapter XLIV

OF SLEEP

REASON bids us, indeed, to travel always the same road, but not always at the same speed;[1] and, while the wise man should not allow human passions to cause him to wander from the straight path, he can, without prejudice to his duty, leave it to them to hasten or slacken his pace, and not plant himself like an immovable and impassive Colossus. Were Virtue herself incarnate, I believe that her pulse would beat faster going to an assault than going to dinner; truly it is needful that she be heated and aroused.

For this reason, I have remarked as an unusual thing the having sometimes seen great personages, in the midst of the highest undertakings and most important affairs, remain so wholly themselves as not even to curtail their sleep. Alexander the Great, on the day appointed for that fierce battle against Darius, slept so soundly and so far into the morning that Parmenion was obliged to enter his chamber and, going to his bedside, to call him by his name twice or thrice, to wake him, the hour for going out to fight compelling him to do so.[2] The Emperor Otho being resolved to kill himself, that very night, having put his private affairs in order, divided his money among his servants, and sharp-

ened the edge of a sword with which he proposed to make
way with himself, waiting only to know whether every one
of his friends had retired in safety, he fell into so profound
a slumber that his attendants heard him snore.[3] The death
of this emperor has many points of resemblance to that of
the great Cato, and even in this respect: for Cato, being
prepared to kill himself, while he was waiting for information to be brought him whether the senators whom he
had sent away had put out from the harbour of Utica, fell
so sound asleep that those in the next room heard him
breathing; and he whom he had sent to the harbour having
waked him to say that a gale prevented the senators from
making sail at their leisure, he despatched thither still another, and, sinking back into bed, slumbered again until
his last messenger assured him of their departure.[4] We can
compare him with the case of Alexander also, in the great
and dangerous storm that threatened him, at the time of
the conspiracy of Catiline, from the sedition of the tribune
Metellus, who desired to publish a decree for the recall to
the city of Pompey with his army; against which decree
Cato alone protested; and he and Metellus had had harsh
words about it, and violent threats, in the Senate. But it was
the next day, in the public place, that it was necessary to
come to its carrying out; where Metellus, besides the favour
of the people and of Cæsar (then conspiring for the benefit
of Pompey), would be accompanied by many foreign slaves
and peculiarly devoted gladiators,[5] while Cato was strong
only in his own firmness; so that his kinsmen and household and many worthy people were in great anxiety about
him, and there were some of them who passed the night
together, unwilling to lie down or eat or drink, because of

Of Sleep

the danger they saw to be prepared for him. Likewise, his
wife and his sisters did nothing but weep and greatly grieve
in his house, where he, on the contrary, encouraged them
all, and after having supped as usual, went to bed and
slept a deep sleep until morning, when one of his colleagues
in the tribuneship came to wake him to go forth to the
affray.[6] The knowledge that we have, from the rest of his
life, of this man's high courage,[7] enables us to conclude with
full certainty that this condition arose from his soul being
lifted so far above such circumstances that he would not
vouchsafe to be moved by them more than by everyday
circumstances. In the naval battle that Augustus won
against Sextus Pompey in Sicily, as he was on the point of
beginning the fight, he was overcome with such deep sleep
that his friends were obliged to wake him to give the signal
for the battle. This afterwards furnished M. Antonius with
a pretext for the accusation that he had not had the courage
even to look with open eyes at the disposition of his army,
and had not dared to present himself to the soldiers until
Agrippa came and announced to him the news of the victory he had won over his enemies.[8] But as for young Marius,
who did even worse (for the day of his last fight against
Sylla, after he had disposed his army and given the word and
signal for battle, he lay down under a tree in the shade, to
rest, and fell into so dead a sleep that he hardly could be
awakened by the rout and flight of his men, having seen
nothing of the conflict), they say that it was because he was
so extremely exhausted by labour and by lack of sleep that
Nature had done her utmost.[9]

And in this connection let physicians decide whether
sleep is so essential that our lives depend on it; for we read

Of Sleep

that they killed King Perseus of Macedonia, when prisoner at Rome, by depriving him of sleep;[10] but Pliny cites persons who have lived a long time without sleep.[11] In Herodotus, we read of nations in which the men sleep and stay awake by half-years.[12] And they who write the life of Epimenides the sage say that he slept fifty-seven years without waking.[13]

Chapter XLV

OF THE

BATTLE OF DREUX

OUR battle of Dreux was all full of unusual incidents;
but those who do not greatly favour the renown of
monsieur de Guise readily declare that he can not be excused for having halted and delayed with the forces under
his command, while monsieur le connétable,[1] the head of
the army, was being driven back, with the artillery; and
that he would have done better to take the risk of attacking
the enemy's flank, rather than, by awaiting the advantage
of bringing up the rearguard,[2] to suffer so serious a loss. But
besides the proof afforded by the result in this case, whoever
will argue the matter dispassionately will, I believe, readily
admit that the end and aim, not only of a commander but
of every soldier, should be to consider victory as a whole;
and that no special occurrences, whatever their importance
may be, should divert him from that point.

Philopœmen, in an encounter with Machanidas, sent in
advance a large troop of archers and slingers to begin the
skirmish; and the enemy, after routing them, wasted their
time in hotly pursuing them, passing, after their victory, by
the squadron where Philopœmen was; he, although his men
were excited by this, thought it best not to budge from his

place, or confront the enemy, to succour his troops. Instead, having let them be pursued and cut to pieces in his sight, he began his attack on his foes by charging their infantry battalion when he saw them to be wholly deserted by their cavalry; and although they were Lacedæmonians, because he fell upon them at the moment when, thinking that the victory was won, they were beginning to fall into disarray, he easily compassed his end, and, that done, pursued Machanidas.[3] This case is germane to that of monsieur de Guise.

In that fierce battle of Agesilaus against the Bœotians which Xenophon, who was present, calls the most sanguinary that he ever saw, Agesilaus rejected the advantage that fortune offered him of allowing the battalion of the Bœotians to pass and setting upon them in the rear, however certain a victory he foresaw therefrom, thinking that it showed more skill than valour; and, to display his prowess, he chose rather, with a marvellous ardour of courage, to attack them in front. But so he was well beaten, and wounded, and obliged after all to extricate himself and adopt the course he had rejected at the outset—making his soldiers open their ranks to give passage to the torrent of Bœotians; then, when they had passed, observing that they were marching in disorder, like men who believed themselves out of all danger, he had them pursued and attacked in flank; but for all that, he could not turn their flight into a rout, for they retreated slowly, always showing their teeth, until they had reached safety.[4]

Chapter XLVI

OF NAMES

WHATEVER diversity of herbs there may be, the name salad covers them all. In like manner, in considering names, I am going to make here a gallimaufry of diverse articles.

Every nation has some names which, I know not why, are in ill-repute; and with us, Jehan, Guillaume, Benoît. Item, there seem to be, in the genealogy of princes, certain names that are inevitably assigned to them: as the Ptolemys in Egypt, the Henrys in England, the Charleses in France, the Baudoins [Baldwins] in Flanders, and in our old Aquitaine the Guillaumes, whence, they say, the name of Guienne is derived[1]—a stupid surmise,[2] were there not some quite as crude in Plato himself. Item, it is a trivial thing, but worth mention for its oddity, and written of by an eye-witness, that when Henry, Duke of Normandy, son of Henry the Second, King of England, gave a great banquet in France, the assemblage of the nobility was so great that, having for pastime assorted themselves in companies by similarity of names, there were in the first group, which was Guillaumes, a hundred and ten knights of that name seated at table, besides the simple gentlemen and retainers.[3] It is as

367

diverting to arrange the tables according to the names of the guests as it was to the Emperor Geta to arrange the service of his courses according to the first letters of the names of the viands: those were served together which began with M: mouton, marcassin,[4] merlus,[5] and marsouin,[6] and so with the others.[7]

Item, it is said that it is a good thing to have a good name, that is to say, honour and reputation; but beyond that, in truth it is an advantage to have a name that can easily be pronounced and remembered; for so kings and great folk recognise us more easily and forget us less readily; and even of our servants, we more commonly employ and give our orders to those whose names come most readily to our lips. I have seen King Henry the Second never able to call by his right name a gentleman from this province of Gascony; and he was fain to call a lady-in-waiting of the queen by the generic name of her family, because that of her father's house seemed too uncouth. And Socrates thinks it a matter worthy a father's attention to give well-sounding names to his children.

Item, it is said that the foundation of Notre Dame la Grand' at Poitiers had its origin from this: that a dissolute youth who lived in that place, having procured a wench, and having, on coming to her, asked her name, which was Marie, felt himself so ardently kindled with devotion and with respect for that sacrosanct name of the Virgin, mother of our Saviour, that he not only sent her away immediately, but thenceforth reformed the remainder of his life; and in consideration of that miracle, there was built, on the spot where that young man's house stood, a chapel dedicated to the name of Our Lady, and later the church that we see

Of Names

there.[8] That reformation, vocal and auricular, inspiring devoutness, went straight to the soul. This other, of the same sort, found its way through the bodily senses: Pythagoras, being in company with some young men whom, heated by merry-making, he heard planning to misuse an honest household, ordered the female musician to change the tune, and by means of slow and solemn and spondaic music gently charmed their excitement and put it to sleep.

Item, will not posterity say that our reformation of to-day may have been fastidious and vigorous for having not only combatted errors and vices, and filled the world with devoutness, humility, obedience, peace, and every kind of virtue, but for having gone so far as to combat our old baptismal names,—Charles, Louis, François,—to people the world with Methuselahs, Ezekiels, and Malachis, much more redolent of the true faith? A gentleman, a neighbour of mine, reckoning up the advantages of the olden time in comparison with ours, did not forget to take into account the stateliness and magnificence of the names of the nobility of those days—Don Grumedan, Quedragan, Agesilan, and [to say] that simply from hearing the names ring out, he felt that they had been very different men from Pierre and Guillot and Michel.

Item, I am grateful to Jacques Amyot for having left (in the course of a French work[9]) the Latin names in full, without disguising and changing them to give them a French cadence. It seemed a little unpolished at first; but already accustomedness, from the world's high opinion of his Plutarch, has freed us from all the strangeness. I have often wished that they who write histories in Latin would leave us our names just as they are; for when they turn Vaudemont

369

into Vallemontanus, and transform them to set them forth
in Greek or Roman fashion, we know not where we are and
lose knowledge of them.

To close our account, it is an ill custom, and with very evil
consequences in our France, to call each one by the name of
his estate and lordship, and the thing in all the world that
causes most confusion and mistake regarding families. A
younger son of good house, having received for his share[10]
an estate by the name of which he has been known and honoured, can not honourably relinquish it; ten years after his
death the estate goes to a stranger, who does the same with
it; fancy where we are as to knowledge of those two men.
We need not go in search of other examples than that of our
own royal house, where the surnames are as many as the
branches;[11] meanwhile the origin of the stock has escaped us.

There is so much license in these changes that in my day
I have seen no one raised by fortune to some extraordinary
height, to whom were not incontinently attached genea-
logical dignities new and unknown to his father, and who
was not grafted on some illustrious stock; and by good luck
the most obscure families are most meet for falsification.
How many gentlemen have we in France who are of royal
descent by their own account? More, I believe, than of
others. Was not this wittily shown by one of my friends?
Several of them had assembled about a quarrel of one lord
with another, which other had, in truth some preëminence
in the way of titles and alliances above the ordinary nobility. Discussing this preëminence, each one, striving to
make himself equal to him, brought forward, this man one
pedigree, that one another; this one a similarity of name,
that one, of arms, and another, an old family chart; and the

Of Names

humblest discovered himself to be the great-grandson of some king oversea. When they were going to dinner, this man,[12] instead of taking his seat, drew back with profound genuflections, begging the company to excuse him for having hitherto had the indiscretion to live with them in fellowship; but that, having been but now informed of their ancient privileges, he would begin to do them honour according to their rank; and that it was not for him to be seated amongst so many princes. After his jest, he heaped rebukes upon them: "In God's name be content with what our fathers were content with and with what we are; we are great enough if we know how to maintain our position; let us not disavow the fortune and rank of our ancestors, and let us cast aside these foolish fancies which can not be lacking to any one who has the effrontery to allege them."

Coats of arms are no more certain than surnames. I bear azure powdered with trefoils or, with a lion's claw of the same, armed gules, fesse. What license has this coat to remain especially in my house? A son-in-law will transport it into another family; some base-born purchaser will make his first coat of arms of it; there is nothing in which there is found more mutation and confusion. Let us search wellnigh to the bottom, and in God's name let us consider upon what foundation we establish that glory and repute for which the world turns itself topsy-turvy. Where do we fix this renown which we seek with such great pains? It is, finally, Pierre or Guillaume who bears it, who takes charge of it, and whom it concerns. Oh, what a bold faculty is hope, which, in a mortal man and in a moment, usurps infinity, immensity, eternity, and endows its possessor's poverty with all the things he can conceive of and desire, to such extent as she chooses.[13] Nature has given us therein a pleasing plaything. And this Pierre or Guillaume, what is it, after all, but a name for all sorts of people?[14] or three or four strokes of a pen, in the first place so easily varied that I should like to ask to whom is due the honour of so many victories—to Guesquin, to Glesquin, or to Gueaquin? There would be much more reason here than in Lucian for Σ to bring suit against T,[15] for

> the prizes sought are not small, not those awarded
> in games;[16]

this is a serious matter; it is a question which of these letters should be rewarded for the many sieges, battles, wounds, imprisonments, and services done and suffered[17] for the crown of France by this famous constable of hers. Nicolas Denisot paid heed only to the letters of his name, and changed their whole arrangement to fashion from them the "conte d'Alsinois," to whom he presented the renown of his poetry and painting. And the historian Suetonius cared only for the meaning of his name, and having taken from it Lenis, which was the surname of his father, left Tranquillus successor to the fame of his writings.[18] Who would believe that Captain Bayard had only the honour that he borrowed from the deeds of Pierre Terrail; and that Antoine Escalin should allow so many voyages and exploits on sea and land to be stolen from him before his eyes by Captain Poulin and the baron de la Garde?

In the second place, there are strokes of the pen common to a thousand men. How many persons are there, in every family, of the same name and surname? And in different families, times, and countries, how many? History has

Of Names

known three Socrates, five Platos, eight Aristotles, seven
Xenophons, twenty Demetrius, twenty Theodores; and
fancy how many it has not known! Who hinders my groom
from calling himself Pompey the Great? But, yet worse,
by what reasons, by what authority, are attached to, and
fastened upon, my groom when dead, that renowned word
and those so highly honoured strokes of the pen, that they
may be benefitted by them?

Dost thou believe that the buried ashes and manes
care for this?[19]

What perception have the two companions in highest esteem among men—Epaminondas, of that glorious line
which is upon our lips in his honour,—

My deeds have destroyed the fame of the Lacedæmonians;[20]

and Africanus, of this other,—

From the place of the rising to that of the setting
sun there is no one whose deeds can be deemed equal
to mine?[21]

The now living take delight in the sweetness of these words,
and, excited by zeal and desire, individually transmit in
imagination to dead men their own feelings, and by a deceitful hope make themselves believe that they in their turn
are as capable.[22] God knows! But

by this were the Roman, the Greek, and the barbarian generals excited; this was because of their inducement to meet danger and toil—so much greater is
the thirst for fame than for virtue.[23]

Chapter XLVII

OF THE UNCERTAINTY OF

OUR JUDGEMENT

WHAT this line says is well said:—

Wide is the range of man's speech hither and thither.[1]

It is entirely permissible to speak everywhere, both for and against. For example,—

Hannibal conquers and does not know how rightly to employ his victorious fortune.[2]

Whoever may choose to stand on this side,[3] and to lay stress, with men of our day, on the error of not having lately followed up our gain at Montcontour;[4] or whoever may choose to blame the King of Spain for not having known enough to make the most of his advantage over us at Saint-Quentin,[5] it may be said that that error proceeded from a soul intoxicated with its good fortune, and from that spirit in which a man filled to repletion with the beginning of good luck, loses the appetite to add to it, already finding difficult of digestion all he has; he has his arms full of it, he can grasp no more of it, unworthy that fortune should place such a boon in his hands. For what benefit does he derive from it, if none the less he gives his enemy the means

374

of recovering himself? What hope can there be that he may dare another time to attack those forces rallied and reformed, and armed anew with anger and revenge, since he dared not, or knew not enough to, pursue them all broken and terrified?

When fortune is animated, and terror subdues all things.[6]

But, in fine, what better can he expect than what he has just lost? It is not as in fencing, when the number of hits decides the winning; so long as the enemy is on his feet, it is all to be done over again; a victory is no victory if it does not end the war. In that encounter in which Cæsar was worsted, near the town of Oricum, he cast it in the teeth of Pompey's soldiers that he would have been lost if their leader had known how to win a fight; and he followed on Pompey's heels in very different fashion when it came his turn.[7] But why shall we not also say, on the contrary, that it is the effect of an impetuous and insatiable spirit not to know how to make an end of its avidity; and it is abusing the favours of God to seek to make them exceed the measure he has prescribed for them; and that to rush back into danger after victory is to place victory once more in the lap of fortune; that one of the greatest signs of wisdom in the art of war is not to drive one's enemy to despair.[8]

Sylla and Marius, in the Social War, having defeated the Marsæ, seeing still a remnant returning in despair to throw themselves upon them like wild beasts, did not think it well to await them. Had not the ardour of monsieur de Foix led him to pursue too closely the stragglers from the victory at Ravenna,[9] he would not have marred it by his death. But yet the remembrance of his recent example served to save monsieur d'Anguien from a similar disaster at Serisoles.[10]

It is dangerous to attack a man whom you have deprived of any other means of escape than fighting; for an impetuous schoolmistress is necessity. *The most grievous stings are those of angered necessity.*[11]

He is not vanquished without cost who offers his throat to the enemy:[12]

That is why Pharax prevented the King of Lacedæmon, who had just won the day against the Mantinæans, from assaulting a thousand Argives who had escaped in a body from the rout; instead, he made him let them slip away unhindered, in order not to put to the test valour spurred on and angered by ill-fortune.[13] Clodomire, King of Aquitaine, after his victory, pursuing Gondemar, King of Bourgogne, conquered and fleeing, forced him to turn about; and this persistence deprived him of the fruit of his victory, for he died on the field.[14]

In like manner, to him who should have to choose whether to keep his soldiers richly and sumptuously armed, or, simply, armed as need requires, it would appear in support of the first side,—on which were Sertorius, Philopœmen, Brutus,[15] Cæsar,[16] and others,—that it is always a spur to honour and pride for the soldier to find himself handsomely arrayed, and a reason for more stubbornness in battle, having his arms to save as being his riches and his possessions. Xenophon says that this is the reason why the Asiatics took with them in their wars their wives and concubines, with their most valuable jewels and treasures.[17] But it could be alleged on the other side that the care of

Of the uncertainty of our Judgement

self-preservation should rather be lessened for the soldier than increased; that by this course[18] he will doubly dread risking his safety; moreover, that the desire of the enemy for victory is heightened by such rich spoils; and it has been observed that in former days this wonderfully emboldened the Romans when encountering the Samnites.[19] Antiochus showing to Hannibal the army that he had prepared against them,[20] sumptuous and magnificent with every sort of equipment, and asking him, "Will the Romans be satisfied with this army?"—"Will they be satisfied with it?" he replied; "indeed, yes, however great their avarice."[21] Lycurgus not only forbade his troops all richness in their equipment, but also forbade them to despoil their conquered foes, desiring, he said, that poverty and frugality should shine forth with all else of the battle.[22]

In sieges and elsewhere, when occasion brings us near the enemy, we readily allow the soldiers to defy them, to show contempt and to insult them with all manners of taunts. And this is not without apparent reason; for it is no small advantage to take from them all hope of mercy and accord by making clear to them that there is no longer any possibility of expecting it from him whom they have so grossly outraged, and that there remains no help but in victory. Yet Vitellius had a contrary experience; for, having to deal with Otho, whose soldiers—long unaccustomed to active war and enervated by city pleasures—were weaker in courage, he so angered them at last by his cutting words, upbraiding them with pusillanimity and with desire for the ladies and the merrymakings they had left at Rome, that he thus restored their hearts to their bodies,[23] which no exhortations had availed to do, and himself drew them on to fall upon him, where they could not be driven.[24] And, in truth, when they are insults that cut to the quick, they can easily bring it about that he who was working sluggishly in his king's quarrel will enter with a different spirit into his own.

When we consider of how much importance is the safety of the commander of an army, and that the enemy's aim is directed chiefly at that head which all the others cling to and depend upon, it would seem that we can not question the plan, which we see to have been followed by many great commanders, of impersonating some one else and disguising themselves on going into the fight; but the disadvantage incurred by this means is no less than that which it is thought to avoid; for, the commander not being recognised by his own troops, the courage that they derive from his example and his presence fails them forthwith, and, losing sight of his usual insignia and standards, they suppose him either to be dead, or to have fled despairing of success. And as a matter of experience, we see that it[25] sometimes favours the one side and sometimes the other. The hap of Pyrrhus in his battle against the Consul Levinus in Italy supports both aspects: for having chosen to disguise himself in the armour of Demogacles, and having given him his own, he indeed undoubtedly saved his life, but he came near the other disaster[26] of losing the day. Alexander,[27] Cæsar, Lucullus liked to make themselves conspicuous in battle by rich accoutrements and armour of brilliant and unusual colours; Agis,[28] Agesilaus, and that great Gylippus, contrariwise, went to the war inconspicuous in appearance and without imperial array.

Among the criticisms of Pompey's conduct of the battle of Pharsalia is that he kept his army without moving,[29]

378

Of the uncertainty of our Judgement

awaiting the enemy: "because" (I shall here borrow Plutarch's very words, which are better than mine) "that loses the force which the act of running imparts to the first blows, and likewise prevents the leaping of the combatants upon one another, which is wont, more than any thing else, to fill them with impetuosity and fury when they rush violently against one another, inflaming their courage by outcries and by speed; and, so to speak, makes the hot blood of the soldiers cold and sluggish."[30] This is what he says about this class of facts.[31] But if Cæsar had been worsted, might it not have been as well said that, on the contrary, the strongest and steadiest position is that where they stand fixed without budging, and that those who come to a halt, confining their strength within themselves and saving it for the time of need, have a great advantage over those who have bestirred themselves[32] and have already spent half their breath in their onrush? Besides, an army being a body of so many different parts, it is impossible that it should move, under this excitement, with such accuracy of movement as not to change or break its due marshalling, and that the most active should not be at grips with the enemy before his comrade can aid him. In that deplorable battle between the two Persian brothers,[33] the Lacedæmonian Clearchus, who commanded the Greeks of Cyrus's party, led them very quietly[34] to the attack, without haste; but, when within about fifty paces, he started running, hoping, for the short distance, to keep their order and husband their breath, giving them at the same time the advantage, both for their persons and their shooting,[35] of impetuosity. There are others who, with regard to their armies, have decided this question thus: "If your enemies rush upon you, await them without moving; if they await you without moving, rush upon them."[36]

At the time of the entry of the Emperor Charles the Fifth into Provence, King Francis was in a position to choose whether to go to meet him in Italy or to await him on his own territory; and although he considered how great an advantage it is to keep one's land[37] clean and undefiled by the troubles of war, to the end that, its strength being unimpaired, it may successfully supply funds and furtherance at need; that the necessities of war lead to devastation at every turn, which it is hard to have inflicted upon us in our own domains, and that the peasant does not endure such spoliation so patiently from those of his own side as from the enemy, so that it may very readily kindle sedition and troubles among us; that the liberty to steal and to pillage, which can not be allowed in one's own country, is a great relief to the tedium of war; and that it is difficult to keep him to his duty who has no hope of profit beyond his pay, when he is only two steps from his wife and his house; that the expenses always fall on the host;[38] that there is more excitement in attacking than in defending; and that the shock of a battle in our midst[39] is so violent that it is difficult to prevent its shaking the whole body, seeing there is no passion so contagious as fear, and none that is so easily taken on trust, or that spreads more rapidly; and that there is danger that the cities which have heard the crash of the tempest at their gates, which have gathered in their officers and soldiers still trembling and breathless, will in the heat of the moment fall into some evil course—yet, notwithstanding, he chose to recall the forces which he had beyond the mountains and to let the enemy come to him. For it may be thought, on the other hand, that, being at home and among

his friends, he could not fail to have all manner of resources:
the rivers and passes, being under his control, would bring
him both provisions and funds in all security and without
need of an escort; that he would find his subjects the more
devoted to him as the danger was nearer to them; that, having so many towns and barriers to safeguard him, it would
be for him to give permission for the battle[40] according to his
opportunity and advantage; and that, if it pleased him to
temporise, he could, under cover and at his ease, see his
enemy dance attendance in the cold, and find defeat through
the difficulties which would beset him, engaged in a hostile
country, where neither before nor behind him nor on either
side would there be any thing which did not oppose him; no
means of refreshing or of increasing his army if attacked by
disease, or of lodging his wounded under cover; no money,
no provisions, save at the spear-point; no leisure to rest or
take breath; no knowledge of localities or of regions which
could protect him from ambuscades and surprises; and, if
he should lose a battle, no way to save the remains of his
army.[41] And there was no lack of examples on either side.
Scipio thought it much better to attack his enemy's territory in Africa than to defend his own and fight him in Italy
where he was, and it turned out well for him;[42] but, on the
other hand, Hannibal, in that same war, ruined himself by
having abandoned the conquest of a foreign country to go
back and defend his own.[43] The Athenians, having allowed
the enemy to enter upon their territory to go into Sicily,
had the opposite fortune; but Agathocles, King of Syracuse, had fortune on his side, when he went into Africa and
deserted the war in his own land. So we are wont often to
say, with good reason, that events and results depend for

Of the uncertainty of our Judgement

the most part, notably in war, upon fortune, which will not arrange itself and subject itself to our judgement and foresight, as these lines say:—

> And bad advice is of value; prudence is deceptive; fortune neither examines into causes nor accompanies the deserving, but wanders among all men, moved by no discrimination. There is indeed a stronger power which constrains us and guides us, and conducts earthly things by its own laws.[44]

Indeed, taking it rightly, it seems that our opinions and determinations depend quite as much upon fortune, and that it involves our judgement also in its confusion and uncertainty. We reason at random and rashly, as Timæus says in Plato, because our judgements, like ourselves, partake largely of chance.[45]

Chapter XLVIII

OF STEEDS[1]

HERE have I become a grammarian, I who never learned any language but by rote, and who do not yet know what adjective and conjunctive and ablative mean.[2] It seems to me that I have heard that the Romans had horses which they called *funales* or *dextrarios*,[3] which were led on the right,[4] or stationed in relays, so as to be quite fresh when needed; and hence it is that we call war-horses *destriers*. And our romances commonly say *adestrer* instead of *accompagner*. They also called *desulterios equos* those horses which were so trained that, as they ran at utmost speed, side by side, without bridle, without saddle, the Roman nobles, even when in complete armour, leaped in full course back and forth from one to the other. The Numidian men-at-arms led each a second horse, to change in the hottest of the conflict: *who, like vaulters in the circus, took with them two horses; and often when the battle was hottest were accustomed to leap in full armour from a tired horse to a fresh one; so agile were they, and so docile their breed of horses.*[5]

Horses are frequently to be found trained to succour their masters, to attack any one who shows them a naked sword, to throw themselves with feet and teeth upon those who attack and defy them; but it happens often that they are more harmful to friends than to enemies; moreover, you can not part them at will when they once feel themselves grappled, and you remain at the mercy of their fight. It was a rude mischance for Artibius, general of the Persian army, fighting against Onesilus, King of Salamis, man to man, that he was mounted on a horse trained in this school, for it was the cause of his death; the squire[6] of Onesilus having struck[7] him with a scythe between the shoulders as he reared up before his master.[8] And what the Italians report, that in the battle of Fornova the king's[9] horse freed himself by plunging and kicking from the enemies who pressed upon him, and that, but for that, he[10] was lost—if it is true, it was a great piece of luck. The Mamelukes boast that they have the most nimble war-horses in the world; that by nature and by habit they are trained to know and to recognise and discern the enemy whom they must throw themselves upon with teeth and feet, according to the word or sign given them, and likewise to pick up with their mouths the lances and darts on the field and give them to their riders when they so command.[11] It is said of Cæsar and also of the great Pompey that, among their other eminent qualities, they were very skilful horsemen;[12] and of Cæsar that, in his youth, mounted on a horse bareback and without bridle, he, with his hands behind his back, made him go where he wished.[13] While Nature chose to make of this personage and of Alexander two miracles of military achievement, you might say that she also did her best in arming them beyond the ordinary: for every one knows of Alexander's horse, Bucephalus, that he had a head resembling that of a bull;

Of Steeds

that he would not suffer himself to be mounted by any one but his master, could be trained by nobody else, was honoured after his death, and had a city named for him.[14] Cæsar, too, had another whose forefeet were like those of a man, the hoofs being divided like toes; he could be neither ridden nor trained by anybody but Cæsar, who dedicated his statue, after his death, to the goddess Venus.[15]

I am never ready to dismount when I am on horseback, for it is the place in which I find myself best off, whether well or sick. Plato recommends it for the health;[16] Pliny, too, says that it is salutary for the stomach and the joints.[17] Let us go on with this, since we are here. We read in Xenophon a law[18] forbidding a man who had a horse to travel on foot.[19] Trogus and Justinus say that the Parthians were accustomed, not only to make war on horseback, but also to transact all their public and private affairs, to bargain and parley, converse and take the air;[20] and that, among them, the most marked difference between free men and slaves was that the former went on horseback, the latter on foot:[21] an ordinance established by King Cyrus. There are many instances in Roman history (and Suetonius remarks it more especially of Cæsar[22]) of captains who, on finding themselves hard pressed, ordered their cavalry to dismount, to deprive the soldiers of all hope of flight, and for the advantage that they anticipated in that sort of fighting, *in which doubtless the Roman excels,*[23] says Livy. Therefore it was that the first provision they[24] made use of to bridle rebellion among newly conquered nations was to deprive them of arms and horses. It is because of this that we see so frequently in Cæsar: *he commands their arms to be brought forth, their horses to be led out, and hostages to be given.*[25]

Of Steeds

The Great Turk[26] does not to-day allow either Christian or Jew—of those who are under his rule—to have a horse of his own. Our ancestors, notably at the time of the English war, in serious engagements and pitched battles, fought dismounted most of the time, entrusting to nothing but their own strength, and the force of their courage and of their bodies, matters so dear as honour and life. Whatever Chrysanthes, in Xenophon, may say about it,[27] you blend your worth and your fortunes with those of your horse: his wounds and his death involve your own; his terror or his impetuosity makes you either rash or cowardly; if he is hard-mouthed or needs the spur, it is your honour that answers for it. For this reason it does not seem strange to me that such combats[28] should be more stubborn and fiercer than those fought on horseback.

> The victors and the vanquished equally succeeded
> and equally failed; for neither the one nor the other
> knew flight.[29]

Their battles we see to have been much better contested; to-day there are only routs: *the first shout and onset decides the issue.*[30] And whatever we bring into cooperation with ourselves in so great a risk should be as much as possible under our control; as I should advise choosing the shortest weapons and those we can best answer for. It is much more in conformity with reason to make sure of a sword that we hold in our hand than of a bullet that escapes from our pistol, in which there are several parts,—the powder, the flint, the lock,—the least of which, if it fail, will make your fortune fail. The hit that the air directs has little certainty.

Of Steeds

And to leave to the wind the direction of the blows:
the sword has force, and all manly nations fight with
the sword.[31]

But as for this weapon,[32] I shall speak of it more fully when
I compare ancient weapons with ours; and save for the
startlingness of the sound, with which now every one has
become familiar, I consider it a weapon of little effect, and
hope that some day we shall give up the use of it. That
which the Italians[33] used, as a missile and with flame, was
more terrifying. They called *phalarica* a certain kind of
javelin armed at the end with an iron head three feet long,
so that it could pierce through and through a man in armour; and it was sometimes thrown by the hand in the
field, sometimes by machines in defence of besieged places;
the shaft, wrapped in tow tarred and oiled, took fire in its
flight, and attaching itself to the body or the shield, took
away all use of weapons and of limbs. It seems to me, however, that, in coming to close quarters, it might be equally a
hindrance to the assailant, and that the field, strewn with
those burning bits, would cause in the fray like damage to
both sides.

The hurled phalaric came with a loud whistle,
thrown like a thunderbolt.[34]

They had other fashions in which usage directed them,—
and which seem to us, from inexperience, incredible,—by
which they made up for the lack of our powder and bul-
lets. They threw their javelins with such force that often
they pierced with them two shields and two men in armour,
and fastened them together. Nor were the shots from their
slings less accurate and far-reaching: *practised to throw*

from slings round stones into the open sea, and to hit circles of moderate size from a great distance, they wounded not merely their enemies' heads, but the exact part they aimed at.[35] Their battering-pieces resembled ours, not only in effect, but also in the horrible din: *when the blows on the walls resounded with a terrible din, terror and agitation followed.*[36] The Gauls, our cousins in Asia, hated those treacherous flying weapons: they used to fight with greater courage hand to hand. *They are not so much perturbed by visible wounds; when the wound is broader than deep, they even think to fight the more gloriously; but when they are wounded by the point of an arrow or by a ball that has hidden itself within with a wound slight in appearance, then, in rage and shame to die of so slight a hurt, they throw themselves on the ground;*[37] a picture very like that of a harquebus shot. The ten thousand Greeks, in their long and famous retreat, encountered a nation that marvellously endamaged them with great and strong bows, and such long arrows that, taking them in the hand, one could throw them like a dart, and they would pierce a shield and a man in armour from front to back.[38] The machines that Dionysius invented, at Syracuse, for firing large, heavy arrows and stones of terrifying size, with such a long flight and force, very closely resembled our inventions.[39]

Also must not be forgotten the amusing attitude on his mule of one Maître Pierre Pol, doctor of theology, who, Monstrelet reports, was accustomed to ride through the streets of Paris sidewise, as women do.[40] He says also, in another place, that the Gascons had terrible horses, accustomed to turn while running, of which the French, Picards, Flemings, and Brabantins made a great miracle because

Of Steeds

they were not used to seeing the like; these are his words.[41] Cæsar, speaking of the Suevi, says: "In the encounters which take place on horseback, they very often leap to the ground, to fight on foot, having schooled their horses not to stir meanwhile, having recourse to them again quickly, if there is occasion; and, in accordance with their custom, there is nothing so base and effeminate as to use saddles of any sort;[42] and they despise those who use them; so that, when themselves very few in number, they do not fear to attack many such."[43]

A thing that I was used to marvel at—to see a horse trained to be guided in all ways by a riding-rod, the reins dropped over his ears—was common among the Massilians, who used their horses without saddle and without bridle.

And the Massilian people who, sitting bare-back, ignorant of reins, manage their horses with a light rod.[44]

And the Numidians, who ride without bridles, surround [thy country].[45]

Their horses are without bridles; their gait is awkward, their necks are stiff, and they run with their heads stretched out.[46]

King Alphonso,[47] he who created in Spain the order of Knights of the Band, or the Scarf, gave them this among other rules, that they should not ride a mule, under penalty of a fine of a silver marc, as I have lately learned from the Letters of Guevara, of which they who have called them "golden" have formed a judgement very different from mine.[48] *The Courtier*[49] says that before his time it was a disgrace for a nobleman to ride a mule. The Abyssinians, on the contrary, the higher they are in rank and the nearer to Prester John, their master, affect riding mules as a mark of dignity.[50] Xenophon says that the Assyrians always kept their horses hobbled in their stables, they were so vicious and untractable; and that it took so much time to unloose them and put their trappings on that, since this delay would be harmful in war if they were suddenly surprised by their enemies, they never established themselves in a camp that was not entrenched and fortified.[51] His Cyrus, so great a master in the knowledge of horses, made his horses pay for their food,[52] and gave them nothing to eat until they had earned it by sweating at some exercise.[53] The Scythians, when necessity pressed them in war, drew blood from their horses and drank it and were nourished by it.

> And the Sarmatian comes, who drinks the blood of
> horses.[54]

The people of Crete, besieged by Metellus, found themselves in such dearth of all other beverages, that they had to avail themselves of the urine of their horses.[55] To show how much more economically the Turkish armies are managed and maintained than ours, they say that not only do the soldiers drink nothing but water and eat only rice and pulverised salted meat, of which each man easily carries upon himself a month's supply, but that they can live also on the blood of their horses, like the Tartars and Muscovites; and they salt it.[56]

These newly discovered peoples of the Indies, when the Spaniards arrived there, thought that they, men and horses alike, were either gods, or beings superior to their own nature in nobleness. Some of them, after having been conquered, coming to the men to sue for peace and pardon,

Of Steeds

and to bring them gold and provisions, did not fail to go to the horses to offer them as much, with a set speech exactly like that to the men, taking their neighing for words of accord and truce.[57] In the nearer Indies,[58] it was formerly the chief and royal honour to bestride an elephant; the next, to go in a coach drawn by four horses; the third, to be mounted on a camel; the last and lowest degree, to be carried or drawn by a single horse.[59] Some one in our day writes that he saw in that region countries where they ride oxen with pack-saddles, stirrups, and bridles, and think themselves well mounted. Quintus Fabius Maximus Rutilianus,[60] in battle against the Samnites, seeing that his horsemen, in three or four charges, had failed to break through the enemy's forces, decided that they should unbridle their horses, and spur their hardest; so that, nothing being of avail to stop them, overthrowing weapons and men, they opened the way for their foot-soldiers, who completed a most bloody defeat.[61] Quintus Fulvius Flaccus commanded the like against the Celtiberians: *"You will make the charge with greater force if you urge your horses unbridled against the foe. That the Roman cavalry often did this to their advantage is made known by history." They took off the bridles and passed in full career, back and forth, with great slaughter of the enemy and breaking all their spears to pieces.*[62]

The Duke of Muscovy formerly owed to the Tartars this act of homage,[63] that, when they sent ambassadors to him, he went out to meet them on foot, and offered them a goblet of mare's milk (a beverage which they delight in); and if, while drinking, a single drop fell on the manes of their horses, he was bound to lick it off with his tongue.[64]

Of Steeds

In Russia, the army that the Emperor Bajazet had sent thither was overwhelmed with such a terrible tempest of snow that, to shelter themselves from it and escape the cold, many of them thought it well to kill and disembowel their horses, in order to crawl inside them and enjoy that vital warmth.[65] Bajazet, after the fierce fight wherein he was cut to pieces by Tamburlane, would have escaped swiftly on an Arabian mare, had he not been obliged to let her drink her fill on crossing a stream; which made her so weak and chilled that he was afterward very easily overtaken by those who pursued him.[66] It is said truly that it lessens their speed to let them make water; but as for drinking, I should have supposed that it would have refreshed and strengthened her. Crœsus, while marching near the city of Sardis, found waste lands where there was a great quantity of serpents, which the horses in his army ate with good appetite; which was an evil omen for his affairs, says Herodotus.[67]

We call a horse entire[68] which has mane and ears; and no others will pass muster. The Lacedæmonians, having, defeated the Athenians in Sicily, on returning from the victory in state to the city of Syracuse, among other bravadoes caused the horses to be shaved, and led them thus in triumph.[69] Alexander fought a nation, the Dahas, who went to the war, two together, armed, on horseback; but in the fray one dismounted in turn, and fought now on foot, now mounted.[70]

I think that in skill and grace on horseback no nation excels us. "A good horseman," in our customary speech, seems to refer more to courage than to skill. The most expert man, the most assured and most graceful in training a horse properly[71] that I have known, was, in my opinion,

Of Steeds

monsieur de Carnevalet, who performed this service for our King Henry the Second. I have seen a man gallop standing on his saddle, take off his saddle, and, on returning, lift it up, readjust it, and resume his seat on it, going all the time at full speed; and having passed beyond a cap, make good shots at it with his bow behind his back; pick up whatever he chose, throwing himself to the ground with one foot and keeping the other in the stirrup; and other like tricks, by which he made his living. There have been seen in my time, at Constantinople, two men on one horse, who, at his fastest, threw themselves alternately to the ground and into the saddle; and one who bridled and completely accoutred his horse with his teeth alone; another who rode at full speed between two horses, with one foot on one saddle and one on the other, carrying a second man on his shoulders; this second man, standing erect upon him, making as they ran very good shots with his bow; several who galloped with the legs in the air, and the head resting on the saddle between the blades of scimitars fastened to the trappings.[72] In my youth the Prince of Sulmone, at Naples, while disciplining an untrained horse with all sorts of disciplines, held reals[73] under his knees and under his toes as if they were nailed there, to show the firmness of his seat.

Chapter XLIX

OF ANCIENT CUSTOMS

I SHOULD readily excuse in our people the having no other pattern and rule of perfection than their own manners and customs; for it is a common fault, not of the vulgar only, but of almost all men, to aim at and abide in the manner of life to which they are born. I am willing that, when they see Fabritius or Lælius, they shall deem their appearance or bearing barbarous, because they are neither dressed nor bred according to our fashion.[1] But I complain of their special lack of discernment in allowing themselves to be so cheated and blinded by the authority of present usage, that they are capable of changing their opinions and judgements every month, if custom so pleases, and that they form such diverse judgements about themselves. When they wore the busk of the doublet between the breasts, they maintained by vigorous arguments that it was in its proper place. Some years later, lo, it has dropped down to between the thighs; they jeer at the former fashion, declare it unbecoming and unbearable. The present style of dressing makes them incontinently condemn the earlier style, with so great a determination and so universal an accord, that you would say that it is some sort of mania that turns their

Of Ancient Customs

understanding about. Because our changing is so sudden and so swift in this respect, that the inventive powers of all the tailors in the world could not supply enough novelties, it is inevitable that the despised styles should often come again into fashion, and the others themselves soon after fall into disrepute; and that the same judgement may, in the course of fifteen or twenty years, adopt two or three, not simply different, but quite contrary, opinions with an incredible inconsistency and fickleness. There is no one of us so keen of wit that he does not allow himself to be fooled by this contradiction, and his inner as well as his outer eyes to be unconsciously dazzled. I propose to put together here some ancient customs which I remember, some like our own and others different, to the end that, having in our minds this continual variation of human things, we may have a more enlightened and stable judgement concerning them.

What we call fighting with sword and cape was in use among the Romans, according to Cæsar: *They wrap their left arms in their capes and draw their swords*.[2] And he remarks even then the objectionable habit in our nation of stopping travellers whom we meet on the way, and forcing them to tell us who they are, and taking it as an insult and cause of quarrel if they refuse to answer us.[3]

In their baths, which the ancients took every day before meals as regularly as we take water to wash our hands, they washed at first only their arms and legs; but later, and by a custom that lasted for several centuries, and in most of the nations of the world, they washed all over with prepared and perfumed water, so that they put it forward as evidence of great simplicity to wash in pure water.[4] The most delicate and refined perfumed the whole body several times a day.[5] They often had all the hair plucked out, as French women have for some time past taken up the habit of doing on their foreheads,—

> You pluck hairs from your chest, legs and arms,[6]—

although they had unguents available for that purpose.

> Her skin shines with psilotrum [a depilatory unguent] or is hidden by chalk dissolved in vinegar.[7]

They liked to lie in soft beds, and alleged as a proof of endurance their sleeping on mattresses.[8] They ate reclining on couches, almost in the same position as Turks of our day.

> Then from his high couch father Æneas thus began.[9]

And they tell of the younger Cato that, after the battle of Pharsalia, mourning for the evil state of public affairs, he always ate sitting up, adopting a more severe course of life.[10] They kissed their own hands to show respect to grandees and to make much of them; and, among friends, kissed one another on meeting, as the Venetians do;

> I should give you kisses with sweet words in congratulation.[11]

And touched the knees in petitioning or saluting a great person. Pasicles the philosopher, brother of Crates, laid his hands on the genitals instead of the knee. When a man he was addressing rudely repelled him he replied: "What, is not this yours as well as the knees?"

They ended their meals with fruit, as we do.

Of Ancient Customs

In the privy (that foolish squeamishness about words may be left to the women) they used a sponge; for which reason *spongia* is an indecent word in Latin; and this sponge was fastened to the end of a stick, as evidenced by the story of the man who, as he was being led along to be thrown to the beasts in presence of the people, asked permission to go and do his business, and, finding no other means of killing himself, thrust this stick and sponge down his throat and choked himself. After doing they used a piece of perfumed flannel:

I will bring thee nothing but washed wool.[12]

Where the streets met in Rome they placed vessels and small tubs for urinals:

Oft the young by sleep o'ermastered,
Think they lift their dress by pail or public jordan.[13]

They took a collation between their meals. And in summer there were venders of snow to cool the wine; and there were some persons who used snow in winter, finding the wine not cold enough even then. Men of high rank had their cup-bearers and carvers, and their fools to amuse them. In winter they were served with meat on hot stones, which were brought to the table; and they had portable kitchens—I have seen some—in which all the needed utensils were carried about with them.[14]

Keep these bouquets for yourselves, O ye sumptuous; these dinners of changing dishes displease me.[15]

And in summer, in their lower rooms, they often had fresh and clear water flow beneath them in open pipes, wherein there was a store of living fish from which the guests selected and caught by hand, to have them cooked, each man as he liked. Fish has always had this prerogative,—as it still has, —that grandees have a hand in the art of dressing it; also, the taste of it is much more exquisite than that of flesh, at least to my thinking. But in every sort of magnificence, of debauchery, and of voluptuous conceits, of effeminacy, and of costliness, verily we do what we can to equal them, for our wills are quite as corrupted as theirs, but our ability can not attain to it; our powers are no more able to overtake them in these vicious qualities than in the virtuous ones; for both are derived from a vigour of mind which was incomparably greater in them than in us; and souls, in proportion as they are less strong, have less means to do very well or very ill.

Among them the seat of honour was the middle.[16] The first and last had in writing and speaking no indication of eminence, as is plainly seen by their writings; they will say "Oppius and Cæsar" as readily as "Cæsar and Oppius," and "I and you" or "you and I," indifferently. This is the reason why I noticed some time ago, in the life of Flaminius, in the French Plutarch, a passage where it seems that the author, speaking of the jealousy between the Ætolians and the Romans about the glory of having won a battle which they had gained in common, gives some weight to the fact that in the Greek ballads the Ætolians were named before the Romans, if there is no amphibology in the French words.[17]

The ladies, when in hot baths, received men there, and made use of their men-servants to rub and anoint them.

A slave girt around the hips with a black leather

apron stands near you when, naked, you bathe in warm
water.[18]

They besprinkled themselves with some sort of powder to
keep down their sweat. The ancient Gauls, says Sidonius
Apollinaris, wore their hair long in front, and at the back
of the head had it clipped[19]—the same fashion that has
been revived by the effeminate and foolish usage of this age.
The Romans paid boatmen for passage on entering the boat;
which we do after we have reached the landing:

> In collecting the passage-money and harnessing
> the mule, a whole hour passes.[20]

The women lay in bed on the side next the wall: that is why
Cæsar was called "spondam Regis Nicomedis."[21]
　　They took breath while drinking. They baptised their
wine:[22]

> what slave will quickly cool the cups of fiery Fal-
> ernian in the neighboring brook?[23]

And our lackeys, with their independent ways,[24] were there
also:

> O Janus, behind whose back no mocking hand
> imitates a stork's bill or the white ears [of an ass], no
> tongue is thrust out as far as that of a thirsty Apulian
> dog![25]

The Argive and Roman ladies wore white for mourning,[26]
as ours were wont to do, and as they should continue to do,
if my advice were followed.

Chapter L

OF DEMOCRITUS
AND HERACLITUS

THE judgement is a tool for all subjects, and enters into every thing. For this reason, in the essays I here make of it, I employ it on every sort of occasion. If a subject is unfamiliar to me, for that very reason I essay it, measuring the depth of the ford from afar; and when I find it too deep for my stature, I remain on the shore; and this recognition of my inability to cross over is a form of its action,[1] aye, one of those of which it is most proud. Sometimes, with a hollow and empty subject, I essay to see if it[2] can find any thing to give it substance and with which to support it and prop it up. Sometimes I direct it to a famous and much-travelled subject about which it can find nothing original, there being such a beaten way that it must needs travel in the track of others. There it plays its game in selecting the road which seems to it the best, and of a thousand paths it says that this one or that one has been the better choice.

I take by chance the opening theme, since one is as good as another in my eyes, and I never plan to produce them completely. For I do not see the whole of any thing; nor do those who promise to make us see it. Of a hundred members

Of Democritus and Heraclitus

and aspects that every thing has, I take one, sometimes to taste it, sometimes to skim it,[3] and sometimes to squeeze it even to the bone. I stab into them, not as widely, but as deeply, as I know how. And I like in most cases to seize them by some unfamiliar side. I might venture to go to the bottom of some subject, if I knew myself less well.[4] Scattering a word here, another there, bits taken from the whole, set by themselves, without plan and without pledge, I am not responsible for them, nor bound to hold to them without changing if I so please, nor to refrain from giving myself up to hesitation and uncertainty, and to my dominant characteristic, which is ignorance.

Every motion reveals us. That same mind of Cæsar's which manifests itself in organising and arranging the battle of Pharsalia, manifests itself also in arranging idle and amorous matters. We judge a horse, not merely by seeing him when racing, but also by seeing him walk, aye, and by seeing him at rest in the stable.

Among the offices of the soul there are some that are inferior. He who does not see her in that wise does not know her wholly; and perchance we observe her best when she is jogging quietly along. The gusts of passion affect her more on her higher planes; moreover, she gives herself wholly to every matter and wholly busies herself in it; and she never treats more than one subject at a time, and treats it, not in accordance with its qualities, but in accordance with her own. Things by themselves have, it may be, their weights and measures and conditions; but within us, she fashions them as she thinks best. Death is terrifying to Cicero, desirable to Cato, indifferent to Socrates. Health, conscience, authority, learning, wealth, beauty, and their opposites, are stripped on entering, and receive from the soul new apparel and such colouring as pleases her—dark, light, dim, glaring, soft, deep, superficial—and as pleases each of our souls; for they have not agreed in common upon the titles, laws, and nature of their qualities; each soul is queen in her own domain.[5]

Wherefore let us no more find excuse in the external qualities of things; it is for us to estimate their value to ourselves. What is well and bad for us depends wholly on ourselves. Let us offer our gifts and our prayers to ourselves, not to Fortune: she can not affect our moral nature; on the contrary, that draws her in its train and moulds her to its likeness. Why shall I not judge of Alexander at table, talking and drinking heavily? or, when he played chess, what chord of the mind does not that foolish and puerile game touch and employ? I dislike it and shun it, because it is not play enough, and it is too serious a pastime; I feel ashamed to give to it the attention which would suffice for some worthy thing. He was no more completely engrossed in preparing for his glorious expedition to the Indies; nor is another man in solving the difficulties of a passage on which the salvation of the human race depends. See how heavy and compressed that absurd amusement makes our mind, if all her sinews do not stiffen themselves; how amply it permits every one to know himself and to judge himself rightly. I do not behold myself and feel myself more completely in any other situation.[6] What passion does not therein play upon us? anger, vexation, hatred, impatience, and a vehement ambition to conquer in a matter in which it would be more excusable to be ambitious of being conquered; for rare excellence, above the common, in frivolous things is unbe-

Of Democritus and Heraclitus

coming for a man of high standing. What I say regarding this example may be said of all others. Every particle, every occupation of a man betrays and displays him equally with every other.

Democritus and Heraclitus were two philosophers, the former of whom, deeming the human state vain and ridiculous, never appeared in public but with a mocking and laughing countenance; Heraclitus, having pity and sympathy for that same state of ours, wore an unchangeably sad visage, and his eyes were full of tears.

> The one laughed every time he stepped over the threshold; the other, on the contrary, wept.[7]

I like best the first humour, not because it is more agreeable to laugh than to weep, but because it is more contemptuous and condemns us more than the other; and it seems to me that we can never be despised as much as we deserve. Lamentation and commiseration are commingled with some estimation of that which we lament; the things we laugh at we esteem valueless. I do not think that we have so much ill fortune as inconstancy, or so much bad purpose as folly; we are not so full of evil as we are of inanity; we are not so wretched as we are base. Thus Diogenes, who in idle solitude passed his time rolling himself about in his tub, and flouting the great Alexander,[8] esteeming us as but flies or bladders full of wind, was a judge much more bitter and sharp-tongued, and consequently, to my feeling, more just, than Timon—he who was called the hater of men; for what we hate we take seriously. This man wished us ill, was passionately desirous of our destruction, shunned intercourse with us as dangerous, we being wicked and depraved;

the other thought so little of us that we could neither disturb him nor by our contagion harm him; he forsook our company, not from fear, but from contempt for our society; he thought us capable of doing neither well nor ill.

Of the same stamp was the reply of Statilius, when Brutus spoke to him to secure his aid in the conspiracy against Cæsar; he thought the enterprise a just one, but did not think that men deserved that any trouble should be taken for them.[9] This conforms to the rule of Hegesias, who said: "The wise man should do nothing except for himself, inasmuch as he alone deserves to have things done for him";[10] and that of Theodorus: "It is unreasonable that the wise man should risk his life for the good of his country, and that he should imperil wisdom for fools."[11] Our peculiar condition is as ridiculous as risible.

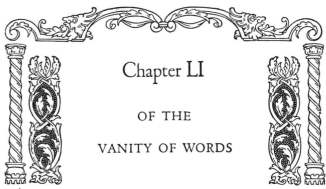

Chapter LI

OF THE

VANITY OF WORDS

A RHETORICIAN of past times said that his trade was to make small things appear great and be thought so. He is a cobbler who makes a big shoe for a little foot.[1] In Sparta they would have whipped him for professing a cheating and lying art. And I think that Archidamus, who was king there, did not hear without surprise the reply of Thucydides, of whom he inquired which was the more able in wrestling, Pericles or he. "That," he said, "would be difficult to say positively; for, when I throw him in wrestling, he persuades those who saw it that he was not thrown, and he wins."[2] Those who mask and paint women do less harm; for it is a small loss not to see them in their natural state; whereas these[3] make it their business to deceive, not our eyes, but our judgement, and to debase and corrupt the very essence of things.

Those commonwealths which maintained themselves in an orderly and well-governed condition—like the Cretan or the Lacedæmonian—made no great account of orators. Ariston sagely defines rhetoric: "The science of persuading the people";[4] Socrates, Plato: "The art of deceiving and flattering";[5] and they who deny this as a general description verify it everywhere in their precepts. The Mohammedans forbid their children to be taught it because of its uselessness;[6] and the Athenians, perceiving how pernicious was its use, which had great vogue in their city, decreed that its principal element, which is to stir the emotions, should be laid aside, together with exordiums and perorations.[7] It is an instrument invented to manage and excite a mob and a disorderly commonalty, and is an instrument that is employed only in diseased states, like medicine; in those where the common people, where the ignorant, where all had universal power,[8] like those of Athens, Rhodes, and Rome, and where things were in a continual turmoil—their orators swarmed. And, indeed, there were few persons in those commonwealths who attained to great influence without the help of eloquence: Pompey, Cæsar, Crassus, Lucullus, Lentulus, Metellus found in it their main support in rising to that height of authority at which they finally arrived, and were more effectively assisted by it than by arms; contrary to the opinion of more enlightened times. For L. Volumnius, speaking in public in favour of the election to the consulship of Q. Fabius and P. Decius, said: "They are men born for war; great in deeds; unpractised in the strife of words; minds truly consular; the subtle and eloquent and learned are good for the city, as prætors to administer justice."[9]

Eloquence was most flourishing at Rome when affairs were in the worst state, and the storm of civil war agitated them, as an open and uncultivated field bears the lustiest weeds. By which it would seem that the governments that are subject to a monarch have less need of it than the others; for the stupidity and credulity which are found in the com-

Of the Vanity of Words

mon people and which make them liable to be managed and led by the ears at the sweet sound of this harmony, without seeking to weigh and discover the truth about things by the power of reason—this credulity, I say, is not found so easily in a single person; and it is more easy to defend him by good instruction and good advice from the effect of that poison. There was never known to come from Macedonia or Persia any orator of renown.

I have quoted this saying[10] in connection with an Italian with whom I have just been talking, who was in the service of the late Cardinal Caraffa, as his steward, until his death. I made him tell me about his office. He discoursed to me on this science of the gullet with a magisterial gravity and demeanour, as if he were speaking to me of some great point in theology. He expounded to me a distinction in appetites: that which exists before eating, that after the second and third courses; how sometimes simply to gratify it, sometimes to arouse and stimulate it; the care of his sauces, first in general, and then going into particulars as to the qualities of the ingredients and their effect; the differences in salads according to their seasons—what ones should be heated, what ones require to be served cold; the way to decorate and embellish them to make them attractive even to the eyes. After that, he entered upon the order of courses, full of fine and important considerations.

> He announces that it is certainly not a thing that makes little difference, in what manner a hare or a hen is carved.[11]

And all this inflated with rich and magnificent words and even such as are used in discoursing about the government

Of the Vanity of Words

of an empire. There came to my mind what this man says:

> This is too salt, this is burned, this has not enough
> flavour; this one is very good; remember another time
> to have it the same. I carefully teach them what I can
> out of my wisdom. Finally, Demea, I bid them look
> into the dishes as into a looking-glass, and I advise
> them what it is profitable to do.[12]

Yet the Greeks themselves highly praised the order and
arrangement that Paulus Æmilius observed in the feast
that he gave them on his return from Macedonia.[13] But I
am not talking here of facts, I am talking of words. I know
not whether it is with others as it is with me, but when I
hear our architects puff themselves out with those big words,
pilasters, architraves, cornices, Corinthian and Doric work,
and other like ones of their jargon, I can not prevent my
imagination from being possessed instantly by the palace of
Apolidon;[14] and, in reality, I find that they are but the
paltry parts of my kitchen door. When we hear the words
metonomy, metaphor, allegory, and other such terms of
grammar, does it not seem that they betoken some rare and
foreign[15] form of language? They are names that describe
the chatter of your chambermaid. It is a deception akin to
this to call the dignitaries of our kingdom by the proud titles
of the Romans, since they have no resemblance in function,
and also less authority and power. And this, too, which, in
my opinion, will be matter of reproach some day to our age
—the employing unworthily, for whomsoever we please,
the most glorious titles wherewith antiquity honoured one
or two personages in several ages. Plato carried away the
surname Divine by a consent so universal that no one bore

Of the Vanity of Words

him a grudge; and the Italians, who pride themselves, and justly, upon having commonly more alert wits and saner judgement than the other nations of their time, have lately endowed with that title Aretino, in whom, save for a bombastic style, padded with witticisms, ingenious, in truth, but far-fetched and fanciful, and besides his eloquence, such as it is, I do not see that there is any thing superior to the common authors of his age; so far is he from approaching that ancient divinity. And the surname Great we fasten upon princes who have nothing in them above the ordinary.

Chapter LII

OF THE PARSIMONY OF

THE ANCIENTS

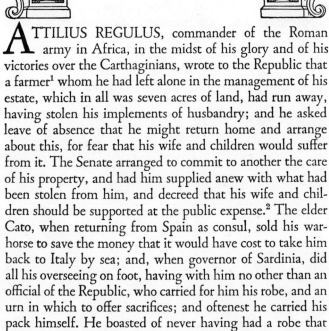

ATTILIUS REGULUS, commander of the Roman army in Africa, in the midst of his glory and of his victories over the Carthaginians, wrote to the Republic that a farmer[1] whom he had left alone in the management of his estate, which in all was seven acres of land, had run away, having stolen his implements of husbandry; and he asked leave of absence that he might return home and arrange about this, for fear that his wife and children would suffer from it. The Senate arranged to commit to another the care of his property, and had him supplied anew with what had been stolen from him, and decreed that his wife and children should be supported at the public expense.[2] The elder Cato, when returning from Spain as consul, sold his war-horse to save the money that it would have cost to take him back to Italy by sea; and, when governor of Sardinia, did all his overseeing on foot, having with him no other than an official of the Republic, who carried for him his robe, and an urn in which to offer sacrifices; and oftenest he carried his pack himself. He boasted of never having had a robe that had cost more than ten crowns, and of never having sent to market more than ten sous for a day's provisions; and that,

Of the Parsimony of the Ancients

as to his country houses, there was not one that was rough-cast and plastered outside.[3] Scipio Æmilianus, after two triumphs and two consulships, went on an embassy with a train of only seven slaves.[4] It is believed that Homer had never more than one; Plato three; Zeno, head of the Stoic sect, not one.[5] But five and a half sous a day were allowed Tiberius Gracchus when he went on a mission for the Republic, although he was then the first man among the Romans.[6]

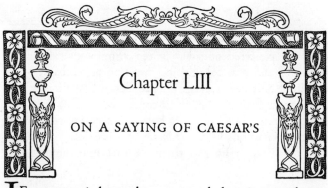

Chapter LIII

ON A SAYING OF CAESAR'S

IF we occupied ourselves now and then in considering ourselves, and employed the time that we spend in criticising others, and in learning about things with which we have no concern, in sounding our own depths, we should easily perceive that all this our structure is framed of weak and defective parts. Is it not a strange proof of imperfection, to be unable to have settled pleasure in any thing, and that even by desire and imagination it is beyond our power to decide what is needed for us? To this, strong testimony is borne by the great discussion which there has always been among philosophers, to discover the sovereign good of mankind, and which still goes on and will go on forever, without decision and without agreement.

> Whilst what we crave is wanting, it seems to transcend all other things; later, when that has been attained, we crave some thing else, and an equal thirst possesses us.[1]

Whatever may fall within our knowledge and our enjoyment, we feel that it does not satisfy us, and we go gaping after things to come, and unknown, because those of the present do not suffice us; not, to my thinking, that they have not the wherewithal to suffice us, but that we hold them with a sickly and senseless grasp.

> For when he [Epicurus] saw that all the things needed for the support of life we already have; more powerful by honour and reputation, overflowing with riches, and uplifted by the good name of their children; and yet the heart of every man was not the less inwardly uneasy, and life tormented by the discontent of the spirit; he perceived the cause of the violence of these threatening lamentations to lie here: it is in the vessel itself [the soul], and all the things, whatever they may be, brought to it from without, however agreeable, are corrupted by fault of this vessel.[2]

Our appetite is hesitating and uncertain; it can neither hold to any thing nor enjoy any thing in a worthy way. Man, thinking it to be the fault of these things, supplies himself with, and feeds upon, other things which he knows not, and which he understands not; on which he fixes his desires and his hopes, and holds them in honour and veneration; as Cæsar says: *It happens by a common natural weakness that we both trust more, and fear more violently, things that we have not seen, and that are hidden and unknown.*[3]

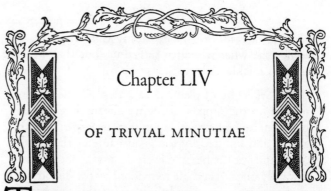

Chapter LIV

OF TRIVIAL MINUTIAE

THERE are certain frivolous and trivial minutiæ, by means of which men sometimes seek commendation; like those poets who make whole works of lines beginning with one and the same letter. We see eggs, bowls, wings, axes, designed in old times by the Greeks, with the measure of their lines, by lengthening them or shortening them in such wise that they came to represent this or that figure. Such was the art of the man who occupied himself in calculating in how many ways the letters of the alphabet could be arranged, and found the incredible number mentioned by Plutarch.[1] I agree with the opinion of him to whom a man was brought able to throw with his hand a grain of millet with such skill that he never failed to pass it through the eye of a needle, and from whom was asked some present to reward such rare ability; whereupon he jestingly, and justly in my opinion, ordered given to this artist two or three bushels of millet, so that such a fine accomplishment should not remain unexercised? It is evidence of the weakness of our judgement that it commends things by reason of their rarity or novelty, or even of their difficulty, if worth and usefulness be not combined.

Of Trivial Minutiæ

We have just been playing in my family the game of see-ing who could point out the most things of which the two extremes are opposed; as "Sire" is a title which is given to the highest personage of our State, who is the king, and is given also to the common people, as to tradesmen, and is never applied to those between the two. Women of quality we call "Dames," those of the middle class "Damoiselles," and "Dames" again, those of the lowest order. The can-opies that are placed over tables are permitted only in the houses of princes and in taverns. Democritus said that the gods and the beasts had more acute senses than men, who are on a plane between.[3] The Romans wore the same attire on days of mourning and on festal days. It is certain that extreme fear and extreme eagerness of valour[4] equally dis-turb the bowels and relax them. The nickname of "Trem-bler," which was given to Sancho, the twelfth King of Navarre,[5] shows that bravery as well as fear causes our limbs to tremble. And when his people, who were arming him, seeing his skin quiver, tried to reassure him by belit-tling the danger into which he was about to plunge, he said: "You know me ill; if my flesh were aware how far my courage will soon carry it, it would be thoroughly chilled."[6] That impotence which is the result of coolness or disgust in the exercises of Venus, is also occasioned by too vehe-ment a desire and an inordinate heat. Extreme cold and ex-treme heat boil and bake. Aristotle says that masses of lead melt and liquefy with cold and the severe temperature of winter as well as with fierce heat.[7] Desire and satiety fill with distress the regions above and below pleasure. Stupid-ity and wisdom in the endurance of human conditions meet at the same point of discernment and steadiness.[8] The wise

415

curb and command evil, and the others do not recognise it; the latter are, so to speak, on this side of conditions; the former beyond them, who,[9] having well weighed and considered the circumstances, and having measured them and judged them for what they are, fling themselves on them, with lusty courage; they scorn them and trample upon them, having a strong and stout soul, against which the shafts of fortune striking must of necessity rebound, blunted, meeting a body on which they can make no impression. The ordinary, average disposition of man is found between these two extremes: it is that of those who perceive evils, discern them, and can not endure them. Infancy and decrepitude are alike in feebleness of brain; avarice and lavishness, in a similar desire to attract and to obtain.

It may be said with reason that there is an abecedarian ignorance that goes before learning; another, belonging to teachers,[10] that comes after learning; an ignorance which learning makes and engenders, just as she unmakes and destroys the first. Of simple souls, less heedful and less instructed, there are made good Christians, who, from reverence and obedience, simply believe and keep themselves within the laws. In minds of medium strength and medium capacity mistaken opinions are engendered; they follow the suggestion of the first impression and have some right to interpret it as shallowness and stupidity that we have stayed in the old ways, those of us who are not therein instructed by study. Great minds, being more stable and clear-sighted, make another sort of true believers; who, by long and devout investigation, discern a deeper and more hidden light in the Scripture, and perceive the mysterious and divine secret of our ecclesiastical polity. But we see that some of

Of Trivial Minutiæ

these have arrived at this last stage by way of the second, with marvellous profit and strengthening, as the extreme limit of Christian understanding, and that they enjoy their victory with solace, thanksgiving, reformation of morals, and great modesty. And in this category I do not propose to place those others who, to clear themselves from the distrust due to their past error, and to give us confidence in them, become extreme, indiscreet, and unreasonable in the handling of our cause, and mar it with endless reproaches of violence.

The simple peasants are worthy people, and worthy people the philosophers, or, as our age calls them, naturally strong and clear in mind, enriched by wide education in useful knowledge. The mongrels (of whom I am one, and so many others) who are above the first condition, of ignorance of letters, and have not been able to reach the other, sitting between two stools, are dangerous, useless, troublesome; these disturb the world. Therefore, for my part, I draw back as far as I can to the first and natural condition, whence I have to no avail tried to depart. Popular and purely natural poetry has simplicities and graces by which it rivals the main beauty of poetry excellent in art;[11] as may be seen in the *villanelles* of Gascony and in the songs that are brought to us from nations that have no knowledge of learning, or even of writing. Mediocre poetry, which halts between the two, is despised without honour and without value.

But since, after the way was opened to the mind, I found, as commonly happens, that we had regarded as a difficult exercise, and concerning a rare subject, one that is not at all so; and that, after our searching power has been aroused, it discovers an infinite number of similar examples, I will add only this one: that, if these essays were worthy to be pronounced upon, it might well happen, in my opinion, that they would scarcely please common and ignorant minds or rare and learned ones;[12] the former would not understand them well enough, the latter would understand them too well; they might make shift to live in the middle region.

Chapter LV

OF ODOURS

IT is said of some persons, for example, of Alexander the Great, that their sweat gave forth sweet odours, by virtue of some rare and extraordinary constitution of the body; of which Plutarch[1] and others seek the cause. But the usual bodily habit is different; and the best possible condition is to be odourless. The sweetness of the purest breath can have no greater excellence than to be without any odour that offends us, as are the breaths of very healthy children. That, says Plautus, is why

> A woman then smells most agreeably when she does not smell at all:[2]

the most exquisite odour for a woman is to have no odour; as we say that the best odour of her acts is when they are impalpable and noiseless.[3] And we are justified in regarding the pleasant external odours as laying open to suspicion those who use them, and in thinking that they may be employed to conceal some natural defect in that direction. Whence are derived the quips of the ancient poets: "To smell sweet is to stink."

> You laugh at me, Coracinus, for not being scented;

Of Odours

I prefer not to smell at all rather than to smell sweet.[4]

And elsewhere,—

> Posthumus, he does not smell agreeably, who always smells agreeably.[5]

I like very much, none the less, to be surrounded[6] with pleasant odours, and I hate beyond measure bad smells, which I perceive at a greater distance than any one else.

> For my nose detects more acutely a cancer or a rank arm-pit than does a keen hound where lurks the boar.[7]

The most simple and natural odours seem to me the most agreeable; and this matter chiefly concerns the ladies. In the densest barbarism, the Scythian women, after bathing, powder and anoint the whole body and the face with a certain odoriferous plant which grows in their country, and having removed that fard, preparatory to rejoining their mates, their skin is softened and perfumed by it.[8] Whatever the odour may be, it is wonderful how it clings to me, and how adapted my skin is to absorb it. He who complains of Nature because she has left man with no instrument to carry odours to his nose is in error: for they carry themselves. But particularly in my case, my moustaches, which are thick, do that for me: if I put my glove or my handkerchief to them, the smell will last a whole day; they reveal the place I have come from. The warm kisses of youth, sweet and greedy and cloying, used in old times to cling to them, and remain for several hours. And yet I find myself but little subject to the common diseases which are taken by communication, and which arise from the contagion of the

Of Odours

air; and I have escaped those of my time, of which there have been several varieties in our towns and in our armies. We read of Socrates that, although he never left Athens during several returns of the plague which so many times cruelly afflicted her, he alone was never the worse for it.[9]

The doctors might, so I think, derive more profit from odours than they do; for I have often noticed that they affect me and act on my spirits according to their nature; which makes me think well of what is said, that the use of incense and perfumes in churches, so ancient and so widespread among all nations and religions, is to delight us and to arouse and purify our sense, the better to fit us for profound meditation.

I should well like, in order to judge of it, to have had personal knowledge of the art[10] of those cooks who knew how to unite foreign odours with the flavour of the meats, as was observed particularly in the service of that king of Tunis who, in our day, came to Naples to speak face to face with the Emperor Charles. His meats were stuffed with odoriferous ingredients so expensively that one peacock and two pheasants cost a hundred ducats to prepare in their way; and when they were carved, not only the banquet hall, but all the rooms in the palace and even in the neighboring houses were filled with a very sweet vapour which did not immediately pass away.[11]

My chief care in selecting my lodging is to avoid ill-smelling and heavy air. Those beautiful cities Venice and Paris impair the good opinion I have of them by the offensive smell, in the one, of her marshes, in the other, of her mud.

Chapter LVI

OF PRAYERS

I PUT forth formless and undetermined ideas, as those do who propound doubtful questions for discussion in the schools, not in order to establish the truth, but to search for it; and I submit them to the judgement of those to whom it belongs to regulate, not only my acts and my writings, but my thoughts as well. Condemnation of them will be as acceptable and useful to me as approval, as I hold it execrable if any thing be found ignorantly or inadvertently set down by me contrary to the sacred prescriptions of the Catholic, Apostolic, and Roman Church, in which I shall die and in which I was born. And therefore, submitting always to the authority of their judgement who have full power over me, I thus deal rashly with all sorts of subjects, as now.[1] I know not if I am mistaken; but since by a special favour of the divine goodness, a certain form of prayer has been prescribed and dictated word for word by the mouth of God, it has always seemed to me that we ought to make use of it more commonly than we do; and if my advice were followed, on sitting down at table and on leaving it, on rising and on going to bed, and on all special actions for which we are in the habit of offering prayers, I should desire

Of Prayers

that it might be the paternoster which all Christians repeat, if not by itself, at least always. The Church can amplify and diversify prayers according to the needs of our instructions; for I know well that it is always the same substance and the same thing; but we should give to this one the prerogative that the people should have it constantly in their mouths; for it is certain that it says all that is necessary, and that it is well adapted for all occasions. It is the only prayer that I use constantly, and I repeat it instead of changing it; whence it comes to pass that I remember no other so well as this.

I was reflecting just now on whence comes this error of ours of having recourse to God in all our schemes and undertakings, and of calling upon him in every sort of necessity and in whatsoever place our weakness desires aid, without considering whether the occasion be reasonable or unreasonable; and of invoking his name and his power, whatever condition and action we may be in, vicious though it may be. He is indeed our sole and only protector, and all things are possible to him to help us; but although he deigns to honour us with this gracious fatherly relationship, he is meanwhile as just as he is kind, and as he is powerful; but he employs his justice much more often than his power, and favours us in accordance with its dictates, not according to our petitions.

Plato, in his Laws, defines three varieties of harmful belief concerning the gods: That there are none; that they do not concern themselves with our affairs; that they deny nothing to our vows, offerings, and sacrifices. The first error, in his opinion, never remains unchanged in man from his childhood to his old age; the other two may obstinately persist.[2] His justice and his power are inseparable. To no purpose do we implore his might in a bad cause. Our souls must be clean—at all events at the moment when we pray to him—and free from evil passions; otherwise we ourselves present to him the rods wherewith to chastise us. Instead of redressing our offense, we redouble it, offering to him whose forgiveness we have to ask, a heart full of irreverence and hatred. This is why I do not readily praise those whom I see praying to God most frequently and most commonly, if their actions following the prayer do not witness to me some amendment and reformation;

> if, in your adultery by night, you veil your head
> with a Santonic cowl.[3]

And the state of mind of a man mingling religion with an execrable life seems to be in some sort more blameworthy than that of a man consistent with himself and depraved throughout. However, our church every day refuses to men persistent in any notorious wickedness the favour of entrance into communion with her.

We pray from habit and custom, or, to speak more truly, we read or utter our prayers; it is, indeed, only show. And it offends me to see the sign of the Cross made three times at the *Benedicite,* as many at Grace (and it offends me the more because it is a sign which I reverence and constantly use, even when yawning), and during all the other hours of the day see them occupied with hate, avarice, and injustice. To the vices their hour, to God his hour, as if by way of compensation and compromise. It is marvellous to see actions so different continue with such like tenor that there is no perceptible interruption or change, even on their con-

Of Prayers

fines and in the transition from one to the other. What unnatural conscience can find peace when harbouring in the
same lodging, in such harmonious and peaceful companionship, the crime and the judge? What does a man say whose
licentiousness controls his thoughts, and who knows it to be
most odious in the divine sight—what does he say to God
when he speaks of it to him? He summons his wits, but
soon falls back.[4] If the image of the divine justice and its
presence did, as he declares, strike and chastise his soul,
however short-lived might be his repentance, mere dread
would so often turn his thoughts that way that he would
speedily find himself master of those vices which have become habitual and enfleshed in him.

But what of those who base a whole life upon the fruits
and emoluments of sin which they know to be mortal? How
many accepted trades and vocations we have, of which the
essence is vicious! And he who, confessing himself to me,
told me that he had all his life professed and acted upon a
religion damnable in his opinion and opposed to that which
he had in his heart,—in order not to lose his reputation and
the honour of his high affairs,—how could he shape this
discourse in his mind?[5] In what language do they speak to
the divine justice on this subject? Since for them repentance would consist in a manifest and palpable amendment,
they lose both before God and before us the means of evidencing it. Are they so bold as to ask forgiveness without
making satisfaction and without repentance? I maintain
that the case is the same with the first as with the last; but
persistency is not so easy to prove in the wrong. This contrariety and changeableness of mind, so sudden and so violent which they pretend to us, has to me a flavour of the

425

miraculous. They represent to us a condition of interminable struggle.[6] How irrational seemed to me the opinion of those who, in these late years, were wont to charge every one in whom there was evident any clearness of mind, who professed the Catholic religion, that his profession was a pretence; and they maintained even, to do him honour, that, whatever he might say to save appearances, he could not fail inwardly to have his belief reformed on their foundation. It is a harmful disease to hold one's belief so strongly as to be persuaded that the contrary can not be believed; and even more harmful to be persuaded, with regard to such a mind, that it prefers I know not what superiority[7] of present fortune to the hopes and threats of eternal life. They may believe me: if any thing could have tempted my youth, strong desire for the hazard and difficulty which accompanied that recent enterprise would have had a large share in it.

It is not without much reason, it seems to me, that the Church forbids the promiscuous, inconsiderate, and indiscreet use of the sacred and divine songs which the Holy Spirit dictated to David. We must not bring God into our acts save with reverence and heedfulness full of honour and respect. Those words are too divine to have no other use than to exercise our lungs and please our ears. It is from the inmost thought[8] that they should be brought forth, and not from the tongue. It is not right to allow a shop-boy, among his empty and frivolous thoughts, to entertain and amuse himself with them. Nor surely is it right to see the holy book of the sacred mysteries of our faith tossed about in the hall and the kitchen. They were formerly mysteries; now they serve for recreation and pastime. Not casually and

426

Of Prayers

hastily ought so serious and reverend a study to be handled. It should be a purposed, sober action, to which we should always add this exordium of our divine service: "Sursum corda," and should bring to it even the body so disposed in its bearing as to evidence a peculiar attention and reverence. It is not a study for every body; it is a study for those persons who are consecrated to it, whom God calls to it. The wicked and the ignorant are the worse for it. It is not a story to tell; it is a story to revere, to fear, and to adore. Singular folk are they who think that they have brought it within the grasp of the people by putting it into the language of the people! Is it due to the words alone that they do not understand all that they find written? Shall I say more? by being brought this little nearer to it, they[9] are further removed from it. Pure ignorance, relying wholly on others, was much more salutary and wiser than is this verbal and futile knowledge, the nurse of presumption and rashness. I believe also that the liberty every one has, to scatter abroad in so many different languages sayings so sacred and important, has in it much more of danger than of utility. The Jews, the Mohammedans, and nearly all others are wedded to and revere the tongue in which their mysteries were originally conceived; and it is forbidden, not unreasonably, to modify or change them. Are we sure that in the Basque country and in Brittany there are enough judges to confirm the translation made into their language? The universal Church has no decision to make more difficult or more important. In preaching and speaking, the interpretation is vague, free, changeable, and of but a part; this is different.

One of our Greek historians justly blames his age in that the secrets of the Christian religion were scattered about the market-place, in the hands of the humblest artisans; that every one could discuss them and talk of them according to his own understanding; and that we ought to be greatly ashamed—we who, by God's grace, enjoy the pure mysteries of piety—to allow them to be profaned in the mouths of ignorant and vulgar persons, seeing that the Gentiles forbade Socrates, Plato, and the wisest men to examine and talk of the matters entrusted to the priests of Delphi. He says also that the factions of those of chief authority in the matter of theology[10] are armed, not with true zeal, but with anger; that zeal is connected with divine reason and justice, and governs itself in an orderly and temperate way; but when it is governed by human passion, it changes to hatred and envy, and brings forth, instead of corn and grapes, tares and nettles.[11] And, justly too, that other,[12] counselling the Emperor Theodosius, said that disputations did not so much put to sleep schisms in the Church as awaken them, and animate heresies; that consequently it was needful to avoid all disputes and dialectical argumentations, and to rely solely upon the rules and formulas of the faith as established by the fathers. And the Emperor Androdicus,[13] having found in his palace some principal men contending with Lopadius[14] concerning a point that we consider of great importance, reprimanded them so severely as to threaten to throw them into the river if they continued.

Our young men and our women, in these days, undertake to instruct older and experienced persons in the matter of ecclesiastical laws; whereas the first of Plato's laws forbids them to enquire regarding the rightness of even the civil laws, which ought to hold the same place as divine commands; and while allowing old men to discuss them among

Of Prayers

themselves and with a ruler, he adds: "Provided that it be not in the presence of young and light-minded[15] persons." A bishop has written that there is, at the other side of the world, an island that the ancients called Discorides, pleasant from its fertility in all sorts of trees and fruits, and from the salubrity of the air, of which the inhabitants are a Christian people, having churches and altars which are graced with crosses only, without other images; very observant of fasts and feasts, careful in paying tithes to the priests, and so chaste that none of them is allowed to know more than one woman during his life; and, moreover, so content with fortune that, in the midst of the sea, the use of ships is unknown to them; and so ignorant that of the religion which they so carefully observe they do not understand a single word[16]—an incredible thing to one unaware that the heathen, devout idolaters as they are, know naught of their gods but their names and images. The old beginning of *Menalippus,* a tragedy of Euripides, read thus: "O Jupiter —for of thee I know nothing save the name alone."[17]

I have known, too, in my own time, fault to be found with certain writings because they are purely humane and philosophical, with no mixture of theology. He would not be without justification who should say, on the contrary: that the divine doctrine better keeps a place apart, as queen and supreme mistress; that it should be everywhere sovereign, not subordinate and subsidiary; and that peradventure examples in grammar, rhetoric, logic might more fitly be drawn from elsewhere than from so sacred a source, as also the subjects of plays, games, and public spectacles; that the divine statements,[18] when alone and in their own order, are considered with more veneration and reverence than when conjoined with human conceptions; that we more often see the error of theologians writing too much of human matters, than the other error, of humanists writing too little of theology: philosophy, says St. Chrysostom, has been long banished from the school of religion as a useless servant, and esteemed unworthy to see, even from the doorway in passing by, the tabernacle of the sacred treasures of the celestial doctrine; that human speech is lower in its forms, and should not be employed for the dignity, majesty, and teaching of divine communication. For my part I let him[19] say, *in unconsidered words*,[20] fortune, destiny, chance, good luck, ill luck, and the gods, and other phrases, after his manner.

I set forth ideas which are human and my own, simply as human ideas, considered by themselves, and not as if decreed and ordained by divine edict, incapable of doubt or debate; matters of opinion, not matters of faith; what I judge from my own faculties, not what I believe from God; as children display their attempts, that they may be instructed, not to instruct; in a laical, not a clerical manner, but always very religious. And might not one say too, not unreasonably, that an edict forbidding all others than those who make express profession of it to undertake, except very sparingly, to write of the Religion would not lack some appearance of usefulness and justice, and would force me withal, perhaps, to be silent?[21]

I have been told that even those who are not of our church none the less prohibit among themselves the use of the name of God in their common talk; they will not have it employed by way of interjection or of exclamation, or for asseveration or for comparison; wherein I think they are

Of Prayers

right. And in whatsoever way we call upon God for aid and company,[22] it must be seriously and devoutly. There is, it seems to me, an argument of this sort in Xenophon, where he shows that we should pray to God more rarely, inasmuch as we can not easily bring our souls often into that controlled, amended, and devout state in which they should be for this act; otherwise our prayers are not only idle and useless, but sinful. "Forgive us," we say, "as we forgive those who have wronged us." What do we mean by that, if not that we offer to him our souls freed from revenge and rancour? Yet we invoke God and his assistance in plotting our iniquities, and invite him to our wrongdoing,

> Which you can confide to the gods only in private.[23]

The avaricious man prays to him for the vain and superfluous preservation of his riches; the ambitious man for his triumphs and the guidance of his passion; the thief employs him for aid in overcoming the risks which impede his evil enterprises, or thanks him for the ease with which a traveller has had his throat cut. At the wall of the house they are about to scale or blow up, they say their prayers, their purpose and hope being full of cruelty, lust, greed.

> Come, then, tell, Staius, what you seek to utter in the ear of Jupiter. "Jupiter," he will cry, "gracious Jupiter!" But will not Jupiter exclaim in like manner?[24]

Marguerite, the Queen of Navarre, tells of a young prince, —and, though she does not give his name, his high rank makes him easily recognisable,—that, when going to an amorous assignation, and to lie with the wife of an advocate of Paris, his road being through a church, he never went into this holy place, either going to or returning from his enterprise, that he did not make his prayers and petitions. I leave you to judge to what end he employed the divine favour, his mind filled with that delightful meditation; none the less she alleges this as evidence of peculiar devoutness.[25] But this is not the only proof by which we could verify that women are scarcely fit to treat of matters of theology. A true prayer and a pious communion[26] with God can not befall a soul impure and submissive at that very time to the sway of Satan. He who calls God to his assistance whilst he is in vicious courses is like a cut-purse who should call the law to his aid, or like those who bring forward the name of God as witness to a lie.

We softly murmur guilty prayers.[27]

There are few men who would dare to exhibit openly the secret petitions which they make to God.

It would not be easy to every man to bring his murmured and humble whispers outside the temple, and to live in accordance with a vow publicly known.[28]

This is why the Pythagoreans wished them to be public and heard by every one, so that no one should ask of him an unfit and unreasonable thing, like this man:—

When he has called aloud: "Apollo!" he moves his lips, fearing to be heard, and adds: "Fair Laverna, grant to me to deceive all eyes; grant to me to seem just and pious; cast night over my sins and a cloud over my frauds.[29]

Of Prayers

The gods punished severely the wicked prayers of Œdipus by granting them to him: he had prayed that his children should determine between themselves by arms the succession to his throne; he was so unhappy as to see himself taken at his word.[30] We must not ask that all things be in accordance with our will, but that they be in accordance with what is best.[31]

It seems, in truth, that we make use of our prayers like a jargon and like those who employ the sacred and divine words in sorceries and doings of magicians; and as if we reckoned that it is on the shaping,[32] or the sound, or the order of the words, or on our bearing, that the effect depends. For, having our minds filled with concupiscence, untouched by repentance or by any fresh communion with God, we go offering him those words which memory lends to our tongues, and hope to derive therefrom expiation of our sins. There is nothing so pleasant, so gentle, and so gracious as the divine law; she calls us to herself, blameworthy and detestable as we are; she holds out her arms to us and receives us into her bosom, however wicked, polluted, and begrimed we be and may have to be hereafter. But still, in return, we must look upon her with affectionate eyes; we must receive this pardon with thanksgiving; and during the moment, at least, that we address ourselves to her, the mind must be displeased with its sins and at enmity with the passions which have driven us to offend her. Neither the gods, nor good men, says Plato, will accept a gift from a sinner.[33]

If a guiltless hand has touched the altar, it has softened the irritated Penates with piously offered meal and sparkling salt quite as well as with a costly victim.[34]

Chapter LVII

OF AGE

I CAN NOT accept the way in which we fix the duration of our life. I see that the sages shorten it very much in comparison with common opinion. "What," said the younger Cato, to those who desired to prevent him from killing himself, "am I now at an age when I can be reproached with giving up life too soon?"[1] Yet he was only forty-eight. He considered that to be a very mature and very advanced age, considering how few men reach it; and they who declare that I know not what length of life,[2] which they call "natural," promises some years more, they might do so if they had a privilege that exempted them from the great number of accidents to which every one of us stands exposed by natural subjection, which may break off in the middle that length of life which they promise themselves. What folly it is to expect to die of the failure of strength which old age brings, and to set before ourselves that end to our duration, seeing that it is the rarest kind of all deaths and the least often experienced.[3] We call that alone natural, as if it were contrary to nature to see a man break his neck by a fall, suffocate in a shipwreck, be surprised by the plague or by a pleurisy; and as if our usual condition did not expose

434

Of Age

us to all these mishaps. Let us not flatter ourselves with fine words; we should rather, perchance, call natural what is general, common, and universal. To die of old age is a rare, peculiar, and extraordinary death, and in so much less natural than others; it is the last and uttermost sort of dying; the further removed it is from us, so much the less is it to be hoped for. It is, indeed, the bound beyond which we shall not go, and which the law of nature has prescribed as not to be overpassed; but it is a rare privilege from her to cause us to last till then. It is an exemption which she bestows by special favour upon a single person in the course of two or three centuries, relieving him from the obstacles and difficulties which she has strewn throughout that long career.

Therefore my judgement is that we should consider that the age we have reached is an age which few reach. Since, in ordinary progress, men do not go so far, it is a sign that we are well ahead; and since we have passed the usual limits, which is the true measure of our life, we ought not to hope to go much further. Having escaped so many causes of death, into which we see all the world stumble, we ought to recognise that such extraordinary fortune, outside of the common experience, as that which keeps us alive, is not likely to last much longer. It is an error in the very laws that they have this false idea: they declare that a man is not capable of managing his property until he is twenty-five years of age; and scarcely will he retain until then the management of his life. Augustus cut five years from the old Roman decrees, and declared that for those who held the place of judge it sufficed to be thirty years old.[4] Servius Tullius exempted from service in war those knights who had passed the age of forty-seven;[5] Augustus released them at

435

Of Age

forty-five. To send men to an easy life before fifty-five or sixty years seems to me not very reasonable.

I am of opinion that our employment[6] and occupation should for the public good be lengthened as far as possible; but I find the great mistake to be at the other end, in not putting us at work early enough. That man[7] had been the law-giver of the whole world at nineteen, and he decreed that to judge of the placing of a gutter a man must be thirty years old! For my part, I think that at twenty years our minds have manifested whatever they are to be, and that they promise all that they will be able to do. Never did a mind which had not at that age given a very evident pledge of its power give proof of it afterwards. The natural qualities and virtues produce by that time or never all that is in them of strength and beauty. If the thorn pricks not when 't is born, then 't will never prick at all, they say in Dauphiné. Of all the noble deeds of men that have come to my knowledge, of whatever sort they may be, I believe that a greater portion of them, both in old times and in our own, would be numbered among those that were performed before the age of thirty than after, yes, often in the lives of the same men. Can I not say this confidently of those of Hannibal, and of Scipio, his great adversary? Full half of their lives they lived on the glory acquired in their youth; great men afterward in comparison with all others, but not in comparison with themselves.

As for myself, I hold it for certain that since that age[8] both my mind and my body have rather diminished than amplified, and have gone back rather than forward. It is possible that, with those who employ their time well, knowledge and experience increase with years; but activity,

Of Age

promptitude, vigour, and other qualities much more a part of ourselves, more important and essential, languish and wither away.[9]

> When the body has already been enfeebled by the powerful weight of time, and the limbs have weakened, and all strength has been dulled, the intelligence staggers and the tongue and mind wander.[10]

Sometimes it is the body that yields first to old age, sometimes again it is the mind; and I have seen many whose brains have become enfeebled before their stomachs and their legs; and because it is a disease little perceptible to him who suffers from it, and obscure in its manifestations, so much the more is it dangerous. At this time I complain of the laws, not because they leave us at work too late, but because they set us at work too late. It seems to me that, considering the frailty of our life, and to how many common and natural dangers it is exposed, we ought not to give so large a share in our early years to idleness and learning to live.

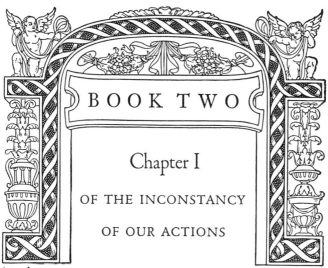

BOOK TWO

Chapter I

OF THE INCONSTANCY

OF OUR ACTIONS

THOSE who employ themselves in observing the actions of men find themselves nowhere so embarrassed as in piecing them together and placing them in the same light; for they are wont to contradict one another in such strange fashion that it seems impossible that they should come from the same person.[1] We find the younger Marius sometimes a son of Mars, sometimes of Venus.[2] Pope Boniface VIII, they say, entered into his dignity like a fox, bore himself therein like a lion, and died like a dog.[3] And who would believe that it could be Nero, that true embodiment of cruelty, who exclaimed, when they presented to him, according to custom, the sentence of a condemned criminal to sign: "Would God I had never learned to write!"[4] his heart was so pained at condemning a man to death! Such instances are so abundant, in truth, every one can supply so many for himself, that I find it strange to see, sometimes, intelligent people take the trouble to make these differences agree, since vacillation seems to me the most common and visible defect of our nature—witness this famous line of Publius, the comedian:—

That purpose is bad that can not be changed.[5]

There is some reason for forming judgement of a man from the most usual features of his life; but, considering the natural instability of our customs and opinions, it has often seemed to me that even good writers mistake when they persist in representing us as of a changeless and unyielding contexture. They select a prevailing characteristic of a man, and adapt and interpret all his actions in accordance with that image; and if they can not sufficiently bend them, they attribute them to dissimulation. Augustus has eluded them; for there was in that man's actions, throughout his whole life, a diversity so manifest, sudden, and continual, that he has been let go entirely, and without decision, by the boldest judges.[6] I find it more difficult to believe in the steadfastness of men than in any other thing; and in nothing do I more easily believe than in their unsteadfastness. He who should judge a man in details and severally, part by part, would chance oftenest to speak the truth. In all antiquity it is difficult to select a dozen men who have ordered their lives in a fixed and constant course, which is the chief aim of wisdom; for, to comprehend it all in a word, says an ancient writer, and to include in one rule all the rules of our life, "It is to wish and not to wish always the same thing; I would not deign," he says, "to add, provided that the wish be reasonable; for, if it be not reasonable, it is impossible that it should be always the same."[7] Truly I learned long

Of the Inconstancy of our Actions

ago that vice is only irregularity and lack of moderation, and consequently it is impossible to link constancy to it. It was a remark of Demosthenes, they say, that "the beginning of all virtue is reflection and deliberation, and its end and perfection, constancy."[8] If by our judgement we should take a certain road, we should choose the best; but no one has ever thought of that.

> What he sought, he disdains; he seeks again what just now he abandoned; he fluctuates, and contradicts himself throughout the whole course of his life.[9]

Our usual practice is to follow the inclinations of our appetite, to the left, to the right, up-hill, down-hill, according as the wind of opportunity carries us; we think of what we desire only at the instant that we desire it,[10] and we change like that animal who takes on the colour of the spot on which he is placed. What we proposed a moment since, we soon change, and soon again retrace our steps; it is nothing but wavering and inconstancy.

> We are dragged about like a puppet moved by outside strings.[11]

We do not of ourselves advance; we are swept along, like things that float, now gently, now with violence, according as the water is rough or smooth.[12]

> Do we not see that men know not what they wish, and are always seeking and changing place, as if they could lay down their burdens?[13]

Each day a new whim, and our moods shift with the shiftings of the weather.

Of the Inconstancy of our Actions

Men's minds vary like the daylight that Father
Jupiter sends upon the fruitful lands.[14]

We fluctuate between different minds: we desire nothing
freely, nothing absolutely, nothing constantly.[15] In him
who had prescribed and established in his mind definite laws
and a definite policy, we should see shining brightly everywhere throughout his life a uniformity of conditions, an
order, and an infallible connection between one thing and
another. Empedocles noticed this imperfection in the Agrigentines, that they abandoned themselves to pleasures as
if they were to die the next day, and built as if they were
never to die.[16] Their description[17] would be very easy to
make, as we see in the case of the younger Cato: he who has
sounded one note of such a mind has sounded the whole; it
is a harmony of perfectly concordant notes, which can not
be untrue.[18] For us, on the contrary, there must be as many
special judgements as there are actions. The safest way, in
my opinion, would be to refer them to the surrounding
circumstances, without entering upon a longer search, and
without drawing other conclusions from them.

During the disorders of our unfortunate kingdom I was
told that a young woman of my near neighbourhood had
thrown herself out of a window, to escape the violence of a
rascally soldier, who was quartered in her house; she did not
kill herself by the fall, and, to carry out her undertaking, had
tried to cut her throat with a knife, but was prevented; not,
however, until she had severely wounded herself. She voluntarily confessed that the soldier had only urged her with
requests and entreaties and presents, but that she had feared
that he would finally come to compulsion; and thence arose

442

Of the Inconstancy of our Actions

the words and behaviour and blood that bore witness to her virtue, after the very fashion of another Lucrece. Now I have learned that, in fact, both before and since, she was a wench of not so unrelenting a temper. As the story goes: However fine and virtuous you be, when you have failed in your design, do not hastily conclude that your mistress is inviolably chaste: it does not follow that the muleteer will not have his chance.

Antigonus, having become attached to one of his soldiers for his courage and valour, ordered his physicians to treat him for a persistent internal disease which had long tormented him; and, after he was cured, perceiving that he went much more listlessly about his duties, asked him what had thus changed and unmanned him. "You yourself, sire," he replied, "having relieved me from sufferings because of which I made no account of my life."[19] One of the soldiers of Lucullus, having been despoiled by the foe, made a brilliant attack upon them, to avenge himself. When he had made good his loss, Lucullus, having conceived a high opinion of him, was sending him, with all the kindest words he could think of, on some hazardous exploit,

> In language that might give courage even to a timid man.[20]

"Send some unfortunate despoiled soldier," he said;

> Rustic though he was, he replied: "He who has lost his purse will go—he will go wherever you choose;"[21]

and flatly refused to go.

When we read that, Mechmet[22] having outrageously

443

berated Chasan, the leader of his janissaries, because he saw his troop broken into by the Hungarians, and that he bore himself remissly in the battle, Chasan, for all reply, rushed madly, alone, just as he was, arms in hand, upon the first body of the enemy that appeared, in which he was instantly engulfed[23]—this was not, perchance, so much self-justification as change of mood; not so much natural valour as new-born anger. He whom you saw but yesterday so daring, think it not strange if you find him to-morrow as cowardly: either anger, or necessity, or company, or wine, or the sound of a trumpet had put the courage into him; it is not courage created by thought—these circumstances have fastened it on him;[24] it is no wonder if he becomes different in other contrary circumstances. This so swift variation and contradiction that is observable in us has caused some[25] to imagine that we have two souls; others, two powers, which accompany and move us, each in its own way, one toward good, the other toward evil, it not being possible to attribute such sudden diversity to one sole source.

Not only do chance winds sway me according to their direction, but I am also swayed and confused by the instability of my footing;[26] and he who closely observes about this finds himself scarcely twice in the same state. I give to my soul sometimes one point of view, sometimes another, according to the side to which I turn her. If I speak diversely about myself, it is because I see myself diversely. All contradictions exist in me at some moment and in some fashion. Shamefaced, insolent; chaste, licentious; talkative, taciturn; hardy,[27] effeminate; sharp-witted,[28] stupid; ill-humoured, courteous; a liar, truthful; learned, ignorant; and openhanded and avaricious and prodigal—all these things I

Of the Inconstancy of our Actions

see in myself in some degree, according as I turn myself about; and whoever studies himself very carefully finds in himself, aye, and in his very judgement, this same volubility and discordance. I have nothing to say of myself in complete, simple, and sound terms, without confusion and intermixture, or in a single word. *Distinguo* is the most universal part of my logic.

Although I am always inclined to speak well of what is well, and to interpret favorably rather than otherwise those things which can be so interpreted, yet such is the strangeness of our condition that we are often impelled by vice itself to do well, if the doing well be not judged by the intention alone. Therefore one courageous deed should not be held to prove a man brave; he who would be so to good purpose must be so always and on all occasions. If it were a habit of courage and not a violent outburst, it would make a man equally valiant in all circumstances, the same alone as in company, the same in single combat as in a battle; for, whatever they may say, there is not one valour for the street and another for the camp; he would bear a sickness in his bed as bravely as a wound on the field, and would fear death no more in his house than in an assault. We ought not to see the same man charge into the breach with brave confidence, and, later, lament like a woman over the loss of a lawsuit or of a son. When, being faint-hearted with regard to obloquy, he is undaunted in poverty; when, shrinking from the barber's razor, he is bold before the swords of his foes, the act is laudable, not the man.[29] Many Greeks, says Cicero, can not look upon the enemy, but are stouthearted in sickness; as to the Cimbri and Celtiberians, just the reverse; *nothing can be uniform that does not proceed*

Of the Inconstancy of our Actions

from a fixed principle.[30] There is no courage more extreme of its kind than that of Alexander; but it is of only one kind, nor is it perfect everywhere, and universal; incomparable as it is, it still has its blemishes; which is the reason that we see him so violently disturbed by the flitting suspicions that he conceives of the machinations of those about him against his life, and carrying himself in his investigations with such vehement and rash injustice, and with a fear that subverts his natural good sense. The superstition, too, with which he was so strongly infected[31] bears some likeness to pusillanimity; and the excess of his repentance for the murder of Clytus is also evidence of the irregularity of his mind.[32] Our doings are but borrowed fragments: *pleasure they despise, but in suffering they are weak; about fame they are indifferent, but by ill-repute they are cast down;*[33] and we seek to acquire honour falsely. Virtue will not be followed but for herself; and if we sometimes borrow her mask for other use, she soon tears it from our face. It is a bright and strong dye when the soul is once steeped in it, and it does not depart without taking the substance with it.[34] Therefore, to judge a man, we must long and carefully follow his path; if unchangeableness does not maintain itself throughout on its own base; [*If*] *his way of life has been considered and planned in advance;*[35] if the variety of events makes him change his pace (I will say his road, for the pace may be hastened or slackened by them),[36] let him go—such a one is driven by the wind, as the motto of our Talebot declares.

It is no wonder, says an ancient writer, that chance has such power over us, since it is by chance that we live.[37] He who has not directed his life in general to a certain end, for him it is impossible to adjust the separate acts;[38] for him it

446

Of the Inconstancy of our Actions

is impossible to arrange the pieces, who has not a figure of the whole in his head. Of what use is it to him who knows not what he has to paint, to provide himself with colours? No one makes a definite plan of his life, and we reflect upon it only by little and little. The archer must first know at what he aims, and then adapt his hand, the bow, the string, the arrow, and his emotions accordingly. Our judgements go astray because they have no direction and no aim.[39] No wind is fair for him who has no purposed port.[40] I do not agree with the judgement that was pronounced regarding Sophocles, against the complaint of his son, from seeing one of his tragedies, that he was competent to manage his domestic affairs.[41] Nor do I find the surmise of the Parians, who were sent to correct the condition of the Milesians, sufficiently well founded for the consequence they drew from it: in visiting the island, they noted the estates that were best cultivated and the country houses that were managed best; and having recorded the names of their owners, when they had assembled the citizens of the town, they appointed those owners as the new governors and magistrates, considering that, being careful about their private affairs, they would be so about public matters.[42]

We are all odds and ends, and of a contexture so shapeless and various that each part every moment plays its own game, and there is as much difference between us and ourselves as between us and another. *Consider it to be a great thing to be always one and the same man.*[43] Since ambition can teach men valour and temperance and liberality, aye, and justice; since greed can implant in the heart of a shopboy, brought up in obscurity and idleness, the boldness to throw himself far from his domestic fireside into a fragile

447

skiff, at the mercy of the waves and of angry Neptune; and since it also teaches discretion and prudence; and since Venus herself gives resolution and confidence to the youth still subject to discipline and the rod, and inspires with courage the tender hearts of maidens in their mothers' arms,—

> Under her guidance the maiden, furtively evading the watchers at the door, comes alone, in the dark, to her lover,[44]

it is not the work of a well-tempered mind to judge us simply by our outward actions; we must search the inward parts, and see by what springs the impulse is given; but, inasmuch as this is a high and hazardous undertaking, I would that fewer persons dealt with it.

Chapter II

OF DRUNKENNESS

THE world is all variety and dissimilarity. The vices are all alike in this—that they are all vices; and this perchance is the meaning of the Stoics;[1] but, although they are equally vices, they are not equal vices; and that he who has gone a hundred paces beyond the limits,—

> On either side [of those limits] the right can not exist.[2]

is in no worse plight than he who is only ten paces beyond, is not believable; and that sacrilege is no worse than the theft of a cabbage from a garden.

> Nor can reason prove that he who breaks down the tender cabbages of another's garden and he who by night steals objects consecrated to the gods sin equally and alike.[3]

There is in this as much difference as in any thing else. The confusion of the rank and measure of sins is dangerous; murderers, traitors, tyrants gain too much by it. It is not reasonable that their conscience should find comfort in the fact that another man is idle, or lewd, or less assiduous in

Of Drunkenness

piety. Every one lays weight on his fellow's sin and makes light of his own.[4] Our instructors even arrange them often wrongly, to my thinking. As Socrates said that the chief office of wisdom was to distinguish between goods and evils,[5] so we, in the best of whom is always something vicious,[6] ought to say the same of the art of distinguishing between vices, without which, and that very exact, the virtuous and the wicked remain confounded together and unknown.

Now drunkenness, among the others, seems to me a gross and brutish vice. In others the mind plays a greater part; and there are vices which have I know not what of high quality,[7] if I may say so. There are some with which are mingled knowledge, diligence, valour, prudence, skill, and adroitness; but this one is altogether corporeal and earthly. And so the grossest of all the nations that exist to-day is the only one which holds it in esteem. The other vices modify the understanding; this one overturns it and dulls the bodily senses.

> When the potency of wine has penetrated a man
> . . . there follows a heaviness of the limbs; his legs are
> hampered and he reels; his tongue stammers, his mind
> is besotted, his eyes swim; shouts, hiccoughs, wrang-
> lings arise.[8]

The worst state of man is that wherein he loses knowledge and control of himself. And they say of it, among other things, that, as the must fermenting in a vessel drives to the surface all that there is at the bottom, so wine causes the most intimate secrets to flow forth from those who have taken it to excess.[9]

450

Of Drunkenness

The troubles of wise men and their secret thoughts
thou dost unveil by the aid of Lyæus [Bacchus].[10]

Josephus narrates that he wormed much[11] from a certain
ambassador whom the enemy had sent him, by making him
drink all he could carry.[12] But Augustus, having entrusted
to Lucius Piso, who conquered Thrace, his most private
affairs, never found that he had misreckoned; nor did Tiberius with Cossus, to whom he unburdened himself of all
his thoughts, though we know them to have been so intemperate that it was often necessary to carry them both drunk
from the Senate,[13]—

With veins inflated as usual by Lyæus yesterday.[14]

And the plot to kill Cæsar was made known as trustfully as
to Cassius, a water-drinker, to Cimber, although he was
often drunk; wherefore he remarked jestingly: "How
should I carry a tryant, who can not carry wine!"[15] We see
our Germans, when drowned in wine, remember their
quarters, the pass-word, and their rank:—

nor is victory easy over men besotted and stammering and staggering from strong wine.[16]

I could not have believed in a drunkenness so profound,
so dead and senseless, if I had not read the following in
history: that Attalus, having invited to supper, with intent
to put a singular indignity upon him, that same Pausanias
who, for the same reason afterwards killed Philip, King of
Macedon (a king whose fine qualities testified to his up-
bringing in the house and company of Epaminondas), made
him drink so much that he could senselessly abandon his
beauty, as any hedge-side drab might do her body, to the

muleteers and a number of low-born slaves of his household.

And I have been told by a lady whom I hold in singular honour and esteem, that near Bordeaux, towards Castres, where she has her house, a woman of the village, a widow of chaste repute, feeling the first inklings of pregnancy, told her neighbours that she might think she was with child if she had a husband; but when from day to day her suspicion grew into evident certainty, she went so far as to authorize the priest to announce from the pulpit that, if any man should avow himself privy to the deed, she promised to pardon and, if he approved, marry him. A young labourer in her service, emboldened by this proclamation, declared that he had found her one holiday so much under the influence of wine, so fast asleep, and in so indecent a posture by her fireside, that he had been able to ravish without awakening her. They are still living as man and wife.

It is certain that antiquity did not greatly decry this vice; indeed, the writings of several philosophers speak very mildly of it; and even among the Stoics there are those who advise taking the liberty sometimes to drink one's utmost, and intoxicate one's self, to cheer the soul.

Also on this contest of ability, they say that the great Socrates sometimes won the palm.[17]

And that censor and corrector of others, Cato, has been charged with drinking too much.[18]

It is told that the strength of old Cato was often warmed with wine.[19]

452

Of Drunkenness

Cyrus, a king so renowned, alleges, among his other praise-worthy qualities, showing his superiority to his brother Artaxerxes, that he was the better drinker.[20] And in the nations that were best ordered and governed, this habit of drinking hard was very common. I have heard Silvius, an excellent physician of Paris, say that to guard against the faculties of our stomach becoming sluggish, it is well to rouse them up once a month by this excess, and to spur them, to prevent them from becoming dull;[21] and some one has written that the Persians, after drinking, took counsel concerning their most important affairs.[22]

My taste and my constitution are more hostile to this vice than my judgement; for besides that I readily submit my beliefs to the authority of ancient opinions, I consider this indeed a worthless and senseless vice, yet less deceitful and harmful than the others, all of which more directly injure the body of society.[23] And if we can not give ourselves pleasure without its costing us something, as they maintain, I think that this vice costs our conscience less than the others; besides which it is not of difficult preparation or hard to find; a consideration not to be despised. A man advanced in station and in years reckoned this among three principal enjoyments which he told me remained to him in life; and where can one look for them more properly than among the natural ones? But he had the wrong idea of it.[24] Fastidiousness is to be avoided, and careful selection of the wine. If you base your enjoyment on drinking delicate wines, you oblige yourself to suffer in drinking the other kinds. The taste must be wider and freer; to be a good drinker, the palate must not be so dainty. The Germans drink almost every kind of wine with equal pleasure. Their

Of Drunkenness

object is to swallow it rather than to taste it. They have thus the better bargain; their enjoyment is more abundant and nearer at hand. Secondly, to drink in the French fashion at two meals, and moderately, is to restrict too much the favours of this god; more time and persistency are necessary. The ancients used to pass whole nights at this business, and often joined the days to them; and, indeed, we should make our regular allowance more liberal and more fixed. I have seen a great nobleman of my time, a personage of eminent undertakings and famous triumphs, who, without effort and in the course of his regular meals, rarely drank less than five pottles[25] of wine, and afterward appeared only too wise and shrewd, at the expense of our affairs. The pleasure which we wish to count on throughout our life should occupy more space in it. Like shop-boys and workingmen, we should never refuse an opportunity to drink, and should have that desire always in our minds. It seems as if we abridge the use of wine every day, and as if in our houses, as I saw in my childhood, breakfasts and luncheons and suppers were more frequent and usual than now. Does this mean that in some respect we are moving toward reform? Truly, no; but it may mean that we are much more given over to lechery than our fathers were. These are two occupations which in their full strength hinder one another. On the one hand this latter[26] has weakened our stomachs, and on the other hand sobriety serves to make us more brisk and more ardent[27] in the practice of love.

It is wonderful what tales I have heard my father tell of the chastity of his time. It was for him to talk of this, being well fitted, both by art and nature, for intercourse with ladies. He talked little and agreeably, and was wont to

454

bring into his conversation ornaments from books in the vulgar tongue,[28] especially in Spanish; and among Spanish books, the one that they called *Marcus Aurelius*[29] was familiar to him. His manner was marked by a gentle, humble, and very courteous gravity; he took peculiar care of the niceness and propriety of his person and of his clothes, whether on foot or on horseback; he had an unheard-of faithfulness to his word, and a conscientiousness and piety leaning in general rather toward superstition than toward the other extreme. For a man of small stature he was abounding in strength, and of an upright and well-proportioned figure, with an agreeable face, of rather dark complexion; skilful and graceful in all gentlemanly exercises. I have seen lately canes loaded with lead with which they say he exercised his arms to prepare to throw the bar or the stone, or for fencing; and shoes with leaded soles to make him the lighter in running and jumping. In vaulting,[30] he has left a memory of little miracles. I have seen him at past sixty laugh at our agility, throw himself in his furred gown on a horse, make the circuit of the table on his thumbs, and scarcely ever go up to his chamber without springing over three or four stairs at a time. Regarding my subject, he said that, in a whole province, there was hardly a woman of quality who had an ill name; he told of strange private relations—particularly of his own—with virtuous women, free from any suspicion; and for his own part, he swore solemnly that he came pure to his marriage, and yet it was after he had served a very long time in the wars on the other side of the mountains, of which he left us a manuscript journal written by his own hand, following point by point what took place, both as to public affairs and as to his own private concerns.

Of Drunkenness

Moreover, he was married when well advanced in years, in the year 1528, which was his thirty-third, as he was returning from Italy.

Let us return to our bottles. The discomforts of old age, which have need of some support and invigoration, might reasonably create in me a desire for this license, for it is almost the last pleasure that the passage of years steals from us. The natural warmth, say boon companions, is at first in the feet; that belongs to childhood. Thence it ascends to the middle region, where it is fixed for a long time, and where it produces, in my opinion, the only true pleasures of bodily life. All other pleasures are dull in comparison. Finally, like a vapour which keeps ascending and spreading, it reaches the throat, where it makes its last stop. I can not, however, understand how a man can prolong the pleasure of drinking beyond thirst, and forge by his imagination an artificial and unnatural appetite. My stomach would not go so far; it has enough to do to manage what it takes for its need.

My natural inclination is not to care for drinking except after eating; and for this reason, my last drink is always the longest.[31] Anacharsis was amazed that the Greeks drank from larger glasses at the end of the meal than at the beginning.[32] It is, to my thinking, for the same reasons that the Germans do so, who begin then their contention of drinking as much as they can. Plato forbids children to drink wine before they are eighteen, and to get drunk before forty; but those who are past forty, them he directs to take pleasure in it, and to blend rather freely with their feasts the influence of Dionysus, that kindly god who restores gaiety to men, and youth to graybeards; who tempers and softens

Of Drunkenness

the passions of the soul as iron is softened by fire; and in his Laws he considers such drinking meetings useful, provided that there is a leader to restrain and rule them, drunkenness being a good test and sure of any man's nature, and at the same time to give to persons of mature age the spirit to make merry with dances and music, things useful which they dare not undertake in their sober senses; that wine is capable of giving discipline to the soul, and health to the body. But certain restrictions, borrowed in part from the Carthaginians, please him: that it should be used sparingly on warlike expeditions; that every ruler and every judge should abstain from it when about to execute his charge or to consult on public affairs; that we should never give the day to it, the time due to other occupations, nor that night when a man proposes to get children.[33] It is said that the philosopher Stilpo, weakened by old age, purposely hastened his end by drinking pure wine.[34] The same cause, but not designed, stifled the strength, broken down by years, of the philosopher Arcesilaus.[35]

But it is an old and odd question whether the soul of a wise man is of a nature to be overcome by the power of wine,[36]

If to fortified nature it does violence.[37]

To what vanity does the good opinion we have of ourselves carry us! The best-governed soul in the world and the most perfect has only too much to do to keep on her feet and to guard herself from falling, through her own weakness. Of a thousand there is not one soul that is upright and stable during an instant of her life; and it may be doubted whether, in consequence of her natural condition, she can ever be so.

Of Drunkenness

But to associate constancy with this—that is her supreme perfection; I mean, when nothing should stand in her way, which a thousand casualties may do. It is all very well for Lucretius, that great poet, to philosophise and brace himself—behold, he is driven mad by a love-philter.[38] Is it thought that apoplexy would not trouble the brains of Socrates as well as of a porter? Some persons have forgotten their own names by dint of illness, and a slight wound has overturned the judgement of others. However much of a sage he may be, after all, he is a man; what is there more unable to support itself, more miserable, more nearly nothing? Wisdom does not overcome our natural conditions.

> The whole body sweats and is pallid; the tongue falters and the voice dies away; the eyes are clouded, the ears ring, and the limbs fail; in short, from the soul's terror we see them succumb.[39]

He[40] must involuntarily close his eyes before the blow that threatens him; he must involuntarily tremble, standing on the edge of a precipice, like a child, Nature having willed to keep in her own hands these slight tokens of her authority, inexpugnable by our reason or by Stoic courage—to teach him his mortality and our lack of spirit. He turns pale with fear, he reddens with shame, he groans with the colic, if not despairingly and noisily, at least in broken and hoarse tones,—

> He finds himself no stranger to what belongs to humanity.[41]

The poets, who imagine all things at pleasure, dare not free from tears even their heroes:—

458

Of Drunkenness

So he spoke, weeping, and set sail with his fleet.[42]

Let it suffice him to bridle and moderate his inclinations, for it is not in him to overcome them. Even our Plutarch himself, so perfect and excellent a judge of human actions, at the thought of Brutus and Torquatus putting their sons to death, can but doubt whether virtue could go so far, and whether those personages had not rather been moved by some other passion.[43] All actions outside the ordinary limits are subject to a sinister interpretation, because our insight no more reaches to what is above it than to what is beneath.

Let us leave on one side that other sect which makes express profession of scorn.[44] But when, in the very sect which is considered the most submissive,[45] we hear these boastful words of Metrodorus: *I have anticipated thee and mastered thee, O Fortune; and I have closed all the avenues by which thou couldst approach me;*[46] when Anaxarchus, placed, by the command of Nicocres, tyrant of Cyprus, in a stone trough,[47] and beaten with an iron mallet, incessantly exclaims: "Strike, crush! 'T is not Anaxarchus, 't is his outer shell that you make havoc of!"[48] when we hear our martyrs cry out to the tyrant from the midst of the flame: "This side is roasted enough; chop it up, eat it, it is cooked; now begin on the other";[49] when, in Josephus, we hear of that child all torn with biting pincers and pierced by the awls of Antiochus, who continued to defy him, crying in a steady and resolute voice: "Tyrant, you waste your time; behold I am at ease; where is the pain, where the torments with which you threatened me? Do you know no more than this of them? My steadfastness causes you more torment than I feel from your cruelty. O cowardly scoundrel![50] you

459

give way and I take on new strength; make me bewail myself, make me bow the knee, make me yield, if you can;
give courage to your satellites and your executioners; see
how their heart fails them—they can do now no more; arm
them, egg them on!"[51] surely we must admit that in those
souls there was some disorder, some madness, however holy
it may have been. When we come to those Stoic sallies: "I
would rather be mad than pleasure-loving;"[52] when Sextius
tells us that he would rather be shackled by pain than by
pleasure; when Epicurus pretends to be fondled by the
gout,[53] and, refusing ease and health, light-heartedly defies
all ills, and, despising the less bitter sufferings, scorning to
struggle against them and fight with them, calls for and
desires great torments—piercing torments and worthy of
him,—

> He prays that a foaming boar may come amid these
> tame herds, or a tawny lion descend from the moun-
> tain,[54]—

who does not judge that these are outbursts of a courage
that has thrown itself out of its natural place? Our soul
could not attain to such a height from her seat; she must
needs leave it, and raise herself up, and, taking the bit in her
teeth, forcibly carry her man so far that afterward he is
himself astonished at what he has done; as in the feats of
war the heat of the combat often impels gallant soldiers to
venture upon matters of such peril that, when they have
come to themselves, they are the first to be struck with astonishment; as also poets are often surprised by admiration
for their own works and can not again find the track along
which they have run so fine a career; it is what is called, in

Of Drunkenness

them also, passion and madness.[55] And as Plato says that a man whose mind is at rest knocks in vain at the door of poetry, so Aristotle says that no surpassing soul is exempt from a mixture of madness;[56] and he is right in calling madness every outburst of feeling, however laudable it may be, which goes beyond our proper judgement and reason, inasmuch as wisdom is a steady control of our soul, which she guides with regularity and equableness, and makes herself surety for it.

Plato reasons thus: that the faculty of prophesying is beyond our nature; that we must be outside of ourselves when we use it; our knowledge must needs be befogged either by sleep or by some malady, or be conveyed from its place by a divine ravishment.[57]

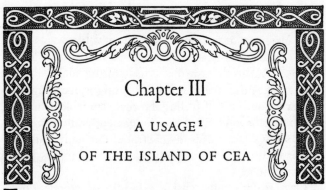

Chapter III

A USAGE[1]

OF THE ISLAND OF CEA

IF to philosophise be to doubt, as they say, then with stronger reason to treat matters ignorantly and fancifully,[2] as I do, must be to doubt. For it belongs to scholars to examine and discuss, and to the rightful judge[3] to determine. My rightful judge is the authority of the divine will, which rules us without gainsaying, and which has its place above these human and vain disputations.

Philip having entered the Peloponnesus with an armed force, some one said to Damidas that the Lacedæmonians would have much to suffer if they did not obtain his favour. "O dullard," he replied, "what can those suffer who fear not death?"[4] Agis was asked how a man could live free. "By making light of dying," he said.[5] These sayings, and a thousand similar ones that we find on this subject, evidently signify something beyond the mere waiting patiently for death to come to us. For there are in life many worse casualties than death. Witness the Lacedæmonian child captured by Antigonus, and sold as a slave, who, being constrained by his master to perform some menial service, "You shall see," he said, "whom you have bought; it would shame me to serve, having liberty so close at hand"; and so

A Usage of the Island of Cea

saying, he threw himself from the top of the house.[6] Antipater harshly threatening the Lacedæmonians to make them submit to a demand of his, "If you threaten us with worse than death," they replied, "we shall rather die."[7] And to Philip, who had written to them that he would hinder all their undertakings, "What! you will hinder us also from dying?"[8] It is as is said, that the wise man lives as long as he should, not as long as he can;[9] and that the kindest gift that Nature has given us, and that deprives us of all excuse for complaining of our condition, is the having left us the means of exit.[10] She has ordained but one entrance into life and a hundred thousand ways out.[11] We may lack land to live on, but land to die on we can never lack, as Boiocatus answered the Romans.[12] Why do you complain of this world? It does not hold you fast; if you live in sorrow, your cowardice is to blame; to die needs only the desire.[13]

Death is everywhere; this the god benevolently makes certain. Any one can take life from a man, but no one death; a thousand avenues are open to that.[14]

And this is not the remedy for a single sickness; death is the remedy for all ills.[15] It is a very certain haven, which is never to be feared and often to be sought. It all comes to the same thing, whether a man bring his end upon himself, or whether he suffer it; whether he run to meet his day, or whether he await it;[16] whencesoever it may come, it is always his;[17] at whatever place the thread breaks, it is all broken off, it is the last of the spindleful.[18] The most willing death is the noblest.[19] Life depends on the will of another, death on our own. In nothing should we so much adjust ourselves to our inclinations as in this. Reputation has noth-

ing to do with such an undertaking; it is folly to have regard for it.[20] To live is slavery if liberty to die is lacking.[21]
The common course of cure is carried on at the expense of
life; they cut us, they cauterise us, they lop off our limbs,
they deprive us of nourishment and blood; one step further,
and behold, we are cured altogether. Why is not the vein of
the throat as much at our command as that of the arm? For
the strongest diseases, the strongest remedies. Servius the
grammarian, having the gout, found for it no better remedy
than to apply poison to his legs and kill them;[22] they might
be as gouty as they chose, provided they had no feeling.
God gives us leave enough to depart when he puts us in
such a condition that life is worse than death to us.

It is weakness to yield to ills, but it is madness to nourish
them.[23] The Stoics say that, for the wise man, it is living in
conformity with nature to depart from life, even though
he be at the height of good fortune, if he does it opportunely; and, for the fool, to cling to his life, although he
is in miserable plight, provided that he has the greater
part of those things which they say are according to nature.[24]

As I do not break laws against thieves when I take what
is my own and rob my own purse, or those against incen-
diaries, when I burn my own wood, in like manner, I am not
subject, for having taken my own life, to the laws against
murder. Hegesias said that, as the conditions of life depend
upon our choice, so should the conditions of death.[25] And
Diogenes, meeting the philosopher Speusippus who, long
suffering with dropsy, had himself carried in a litter, and
who called out to him, "Good wishes, Diogenes!"—"No
wishes for you," he replied, "who being in such a state, en-

A Usage of the Island of Cea

dure life." In truth, some time afterward, Speusippus killed himself, being weary of such a painful condition of life.[26] But this does not pass uncontradicted; for many maintain that we can not quit this garrison of the world without the express command of him who stationed us in it; and that it is for God, who has sent us here, not for ourselves alone, but rather for his glory and the service of others, to give us leave to depart when it may please him, not for us to take it;[27] that we are not born for ourselves, but also for our country; the laws require from us an accounting of ourselves in their own interest; and have an action for homicide against us; otherwise we are punished in the other world as deserters from our post.

> The next region is inhabited by those melancholy beings who, though innocent, have given themselves death by their own hands, and hating the light of day, have rejected their souls.[28]

There is much more steadfastness in wearing away the chain that holds us than in breaking it, and more proof of firmness in Regulus than in Cato. It is lack of discretion and of patience that hastens our steps. No chance events can make live courage turn her back; she seeks misfortune and pain as her sustenance. The menaces of tyrants, racks, and executioners animate and vivify her;

> As the oak in the dark forests on Algidus, lopped by pitiless axes, derives power and vigour from its losses, from its wounds, from the steel itself.[29]

And, as this other says,—

> Valour consists not, my father, as you believe, in

fearing life, but in withstanding great troubles, not avoiding them and turning one's back on them.[30]

In adverse days it is easy to despise death; more courageous is he who can be wretched.[31]

It is the part of cowardice, not of courage, to go and crouch in a hole under a massive tomb, to avoid the blows of fortune. She[32] does not break off her journey and her course, however violent the storm may be.

Though the shattered heavens crumble, the ruins will strike her [courage] unterrified.[33]

Most frequently the avoidance of other mishaps drives us into this one; truly, sometimes the avoidance of death causes us to rush upon it:—

Is not this, I ask, madness, to die for fear of dying?[34]

like those who, from fear of the precipice throw themselves into it.

Many have been driven into the greatest peril from the very fear of coming ills; most courageous is he who, if they be near at hand, resolutely meets things to be feared, and is able to disperse them.[35]

From the dread of death, such a hatred of life and of the sight of daylight seizes upon mortals, that with mournful heart they kill themselves, forgetting that this fear is the source of their uneasiness.[36]

Plato, in his Laws, decrees ignominious burial for him who has deprived his nearest and best friend—namely himself—of life and of what destiny has in store, when not constrained

A Usage of the Island of Cea

by public sentence, or by some sad and inevitable accident of fortune, or by intolerable disgrace, but by the cowardice and weakness of a shrinking soul.[37] And the opinion that despises our life—that is ridiculous. For, when all is said, it is our existence, it is our all. Things which have a nobler and ampler existence may decry ours; but it is against nature that we should despise ourselves and set ourselves at naught; it is a disease peculiar to man, and found in no other creature, to hate and disdain himself. It is a like folly, that we desire to be other than we are. The result of such a desire does not reach us, inasmuch as it contradicts itself and is its own hindrance. He who desires to be changed from man to angel in no wise advantages himself; he would be not a whit the better for it. For when he no longer exists, who will perceive and be rejoiced by that promotion for him?

> For he whom evil is to befall must still exist at that time, when haply there is to be misery and suffering for him.[38]

The security, the insensibility, the impassibility, the absence of the ills of this life, which we purchase at the price of death, brings us no advantage. To no purpose does he avoid war who can not enjoy peace; and to no purpose does he fly from toil who has not the means of relishing repose.

Among those who take the first-mentioned view,[39] there has been much uncertainty on this point: what occasions are of sufficient weight to justify man in the decision of killing himself? They call this *a reasonable exit*.[40] For, although they say that men must often die for trivial causes, since those that detain us in life are not very powerful,[41] yet there must be some measure in this. There have been fan-

467

tastic and unreasonable humours which have driven, not single individuals only, but communities, to make way with themselves. I have already alleged some examples of this;[42] and we also read of the Milesian virgins that, in pursuance of a mad agreement, they hanged themselves one after another, until the magistrate took heed to it, ordering that those who should be found thus hanged should be dragged through the city, naked, by the rope.[43] When Threicion exhorts Cleomenes to kill himself on account of the bad state of his affairs, and, since he had shunned the most honourable death in the battle he had just lost, to accept this other kind which ranks next to that in honour, and not permit the victor to make him endure either a shameful death or a shameful life, Cleomenes, with the courage of a Lacedæmonian and a Stoic, refused that advice as cowardly and weak. "It is a remedy," he said, "which can never be lacking to me, and which should not be used while there remains one inch of hope"; adding that to live is sometimes firmness and valour; that he desires that even his death may be of service to his country and desires to make it an act of honour and desert. Threicion thought himself in the right, and killed himself. Cleomenes afterward did the same; but not until he had experienced the lowest point of fortune.[44] All possible misfortunes are not of so much weight that a man should wish to die to avoid them. Moreover, there being so many sudden changes in human affairs, it is difficult to judge at what point we are really at the end of our hope.

> The conquered gladiator in the savage arena has hopes, despite the hostile thumbs of the menacing crowd.[45]

A Usage of the Island of Cea

All things, according to an ancient saying, may justly be hoped for by a man as long as he lives. "True," rejoins Seneca, "but why should I have this in my head: that fortune is all-powerful regarding him who is living, rather than this: that fortune is powerless regarding him who is ready to die?"[46] We find Josephus involved in a peril so manifest and near at hand, a whole people having risen against him, that in reason he had no refuge; none the less, though advised, as he says, by one of his friends at this crisis, to make way with himself, it was well for him that he still persisted in hoping: for, beyond all human foresight, fortune turned aside the disaster in such a way that he found himself delivered from it without any mishap.[47] And Cassius and Brutus, on the contrary, destroyed the last remnants of Roman freedom, of which they were the protectors, by the headlong haste and rashness with which they killed themselves before the due time and occasion.

In the battle of Serisolles,[48] Monsieur d'Anguien tried twice to run his sword into his throat, despairing of the result of the battle, which was turning ill at the spot where he was; and by his precipitation was like to have deprived himself of the enjoyment of so fine a victory.[49] I have seen a hundred hares save themselves in the very teeth of the hounds. *There was a man who survived his executioner.*[50]

> Many things have been improved by time and the varying travail of the years; revisiting them, fortune has made sport of many men, again placing them on solid ground.[51]

Pliny says that there are only three kinds of malady to avoid which one may have the right to kill one's self: the most painful of all is the stone in the bladder, when the urine is checked.[52] Seneca, those only which deranged for a long time the functions of the mind.[53] There are those who believe that, to avoid a worse death, they may take their life when they please. Democritus, leader of the Ætolians, when taken to Rome a prisoner, found a means to escape by night. But, being pursued by his guards, rather than allow himself to be retaken, he ran his sword through his body.[54] Antinous and Theodotus, their city in Epirus being reduced to extremity by the Romans, advised the people to kill themselves, one and all; but the counsel rather to surrender having prevailed, they too went forth to seek death, throwing themselves upon the foe, to strike, not to protect themselves.[55] The island of Goza being violently entered by the Turks some years ago, a Sicilian who had two beautiful daughters of marriageable age killed them with his own hand, and afterward their mother, who came running to them as they died. This done, going into a street with a cross-bow and a harquebus, with two shots he killed the first two Turks who approached his door; and then, taking his sword in his hand, rushed madly among them, when he was instantly surrounded and cut to pieces, thus saving himself from slavery, after he had rescued his children from it.[56] The Jewish women, after they had had their children circumcised, precipitately killed themselves with them, flying from the cruelty of Antiochus.[57] I have been told that, a prisoner of good family being in one of our prisons, his kindred, being warned that he would surely be condemned, to avert the disgrace of such a death, secretly induced[58] a priest to tell him that the sovereign aid toward his deliverance was to commend himself to some saint, under

A Usage of the Island of Cea

such and such a vow, and to pass eight days without taking any sustenance, however faint and weak he might feel. He believed this, and by that means unwittingly rid himself of his life and of the danger. Scribonia, advising Libo, her nephew, to kill himself rather than to await the hand of justice, told him that it was really doing another man's work, to preserve his life in order to give it over to the hands of those who would come to take it two or three days later; and that it was to serve his enemies, to save his blood for them to glut themselves on it.[59]

We read in the Bible that Nicanor, the assailant of the law of God, having sent his satellites to seize the good old Rasias, surnamed in honour of his virtue the Father of the Jews, when that worthy man saw nothing but disorder, —his gate burned and his enemies ready to seize him,— choosing to die nobly rather than to fall into the hands of the miscreants to be cruelly dealt with, to the dishonour of his rank, he stabbed himself with his sword; but the blow, because of his haste, not reaching home, he ran and threw himself from the top of the wall into the midst of the soldiery; and they drawing apart and giving place, he pitched directly on his head. Notwithstanding this, finding that there was still some life left in him, he rekindled his courage, and rising to his feet, all bleeding and covered with wounds, breaking through the throng, he made his way to a certain craggy precipitous cliff, where, unable to do more, he seized his entrails with both hands through one of his wounds, tearing and rending them, and threw them among his pursuers, calling down upon them and affirming the divine vengeance.[60]

Of the outrages that are inflicted upon the conscience, the

A Usage of the Island of Cea

one to be most carefully avoided, in my opinion, is the violation of the chastity of women, inasmuch as there is by nature some bodily pleasure intermixed with it; and for this
reason the repugnance can not in this be complete, and it
seems that with the compulsion may be intermixed some
consent. Pelagia and Sophronia, both canonised—the one
threw herself into the river with her mother and sisters to
escape the compulsion of certain soldiers, and the other
likewise killed herself to escape the compulsion of the Emperor Maxentius.[61] Ecclesiastical history holds in veneration several like examples of devout persons who appealed
to death as a protection against the outrages that tyrants prepared against their conscience. It will, peradventure, be
creditable to us, in ages to come, that a learned author
of these days, especially as he was a Parisian, did his utmost
to persuade the ladies of our epoch to follow almost any
other course rather than to adopt so shocking a counsel of
despair. I much regret that he had not heard—that he might
include it in his arguments—of the pleasant remark, which
I learned at Toulouse, of a peasant woman who had passed
through the hands of several soldiers: "God be praised," she
said, "that at least once in my life I have been sullied without sinning!" In truth, such barbarities are unworthy of
our French amenity. Thank God, our air has been thoroughly purged of them since that pleasant caution: it is
enough that they say "Nay, nay!" while yielding, according to the rule of our excellent Marot.[62]

History is crowded with the persons who have exchanged
a life of dismay for death. Lucius Aruntius killed himself,
he said, to escape from both the future and the past.[63]
Granius Silvanus and Statius Proximus, after being par-

472

A Usage of the Island of Cea

doned by Nero, killed themselves, either to avoid living by the favour of so wicked a man, or to avoid the need another time of a second pardon, considering his readiness to suspect and accuse men of worth.[64] Spargapises, son of Queen Tomiris, and a prisoner of war of Cyrus, made use of the first favour shown him by Cyrus,—the leaving him unfettered,—to kill himself; having sought no other benefit from his liberty than to avenge upon himself the disgrace of his capture. [65] Boges, Governor in Eion under King Xerxes, being besieged by the army of the Athenians under the command of Cimon, refused the proposal to return in safety to Asia with all his substance, being unable to endure surviving the loss of what his master had entrusted to his keeping; and, after he had defended his city to the last extremity, there being nothing left to eat, he first threw into the river Strymon all the gold and every thing which it seemed to him that the enemy could make booty of; and then, having ordered a great pile to be kindled and his wives', children's, concubines', and servants' throats to be cut, he threw them into the fire, and then himself.[66] Ninachetuen, an Indian lord, having got wind of the intention of the Portuguese viceroy to dispossess him, without any visible cause, from his high office in Malacca, to give it to the King of Campar, privately formed this resolution: he caused a staging to be built, longer than broad, supported on columns, royally carpeted, and bedecked with flowers and perfumes in abundance; and then, having arrayed himself in a robe of cloth of gold loaded with precious stones of great value, he went out into the street and ascended the steps of the staging, in one corner of which a pile of aromatic woods was burning. All the people flocked to see for what end these unwonted prep-

473

arations were made. Ninachetuen, with a bold and displeased bearing, set forth the indebtedness of the Portuguese nation to him: how loyally lavish he had been in his
high office; that having so often testified in behalf of another, arms in hand, that honour was much dearer to him
than life, he was not the man to abandon the care of it in
his own behalf; that, since fortune denied him all means of
resisting the affront it was proposed to put upon him, his
heart bade him at least to free himself from perception of
it, and not to serve for a laughing-stock to the people and
for triumph to men who were worth less than he. So saying,
he cast himself into the flames.[67] Sextilia, wife of Scaurus,
and Paxea, wife of Labeo, to encourage their husbands to
escape from the perils that were hanging over them, in
which they had no share save by right of conjugal affection,
willingly forfeited life, to be examples and companions to
them in their extreme need.[68] What they did for their husbands Cocceius Nerva did for his country, less usefully, but
with equal affection. That great jurist, flourishing in health,
in riches, in reputation, and in influence with the emperor,
had no other reason to kill himself than community of suffering with the wretched state of the public affairs of
Rome.[69] Nothing can add to the fineness of feeling of the
death of the wife of that Fulvius who was in frequent intercourse with Augustus. Augustus, having discovered that he
had divulged an important secret which he had entrusted
to him, received him coldly one morning when he came to
visit him. He returned to his house, full of despair, and rue-
fully told his wife that, having fallen into this misfortune,
he had resolved to kill himself. She outspokenly replied:
"You will do but what is wise, seeing that, having often

A Usage of the Island of Cea

enough experienced the incontinence of my tongue, you have not been on your guard against it. But wait, that I may kill myself first." And without further parley she ran herself through the body with a sword.[70] Vibius Virius, despairing of the preservation of his city,[71] which was besieged by the Romans, and of their mercy, declared in the last deliberation of their[72] Senate that the noblest course was to escape from fortune by their own hands. The enemy would hold them in honour, and Hannibal would perceive what loyal friends he had abandoned. He invited those who were of his mind to partake of a good supper that was prepared at his house, where, after enjoying the good cheer, they would drink together what should be offered them: "A beverage which will deliver our bodies from torture, our souls from insult, our eyes and our ears from the consciousness of the many hateful wrongs which the vanquished have to suffer from victors most cruel and angered. I have given orders," he said, "that there shall be persons ready to throw us on a funeral pile before my door, when we have expired." Many approved his high resolution, but few imitated him. Twenty-seven senators followed him, and having tried to drown in wine that painful thought, ended their repast with the mortal potion brought to them; and embracing one another, after having deplored in common the ill-fortune of their country, some withdrew to their own houses, and others remained to be thrown with Virius into the flames. And they were all so long in dying, the fumes of the wine having filled their veins and retarding the effect of the poison, that some were within an hour of seeing the enemy in Capua, which was carried by storm next day, and of incurring the suffering that they had fled from at such cost.[73] Taurea Jubellius,

475

another citizen of that city, when the Consul Fulvius returned from the shameful slaughter that he had made of two
hundred and twenty-five senators, called to him haughtily
by his name, and having stopped him, said: "Command
that I too be murdered after all those others, so that you may
boast of having killed a much more valiant man than yourself." Fulvius making no account of him, as insane (and,
too, he had just received letters from Rome adverse to the
inhumanity of what he had done, which bound his hands),
Jubellius continued: "Since my country is captured, my
friends dead, and having with my own hands slain my wife
and children, to deliver them from the desolation of this
downfall, it is forbidden me to die by the same death with
my fellow citizens; let me borrow from courage vengeance
on this hateful life." And, drawing a blade that he had hidden, he thrust it into his breast, falling headlong, dying,
at the consul's feet.[74] Alexander was besieging a city in the
Indies; those within the walls, finding themselves hard
pressed, sturdily resolved to deprive him of the pleasure of
the victory; and setting fire to their city, all together burned
themselves with it, in despite of his humanity. A novel kind
of warfare was seen: the enemy fought to save them, they
to destroy themselves; and to ensure their death, they did
every thing that men do to ensure their lives.[75]

Astapa, a city in Spain, finding itself weak in walls and
defences to withstand the Romans, the inhabitants made a
pile of their valuables and household stuff in the public
square; and having placed their wives and children on the
top of the heap, and having surrounded it with wood and
materials that would take fire instantly, and left fifty of
their young men to execute their determination, they made a

A Usage of the Island of Cea

sally in which, in accordance with their vow, for lack of
being able to conquer, they caused themselves all to be
killed. The fifty, after having massacred every living soul
scattered through the town, and set fire to that heap, threw
themselves also upon it, ending their noble-hearted liberty
in a state without feeling rather than grievous and shameful, and showing their enemies that, had fortune so willed,
they would have had the spirit to snatch the victory from
them, as they had had to make it vain and ghastly, aye, and
fatal to those who, lured by the gleam of the gold melting in
the flame, having drawn near to it in large numbers, were
suffocated and burned by it, being prevented from turning
back by the crowd that followed them.[76] The Abideans,
hard pressed by Philip, formed the same resolution. But,
being short of time, the king, who was horrified in seeing
the reckless haste of their doings, having seized upon the
treasures and household articles which they were destroying
either by fire or in the sea,[77] withdrew his troops and
granted them three days to kill themselves in a more orderly
fashion, which days they filled with bloodshed and murder, exceeding the cruelty of any foe; and not a single person fled who might have done so.[78] There are numberless
examples of like popular decisions, which seem the more
severe in proportion as the result is more nearly universal.
They are less so than when formed separately. That which
reasoning would not do in each individual, it does in the
mass, the ardour of fellowship overpowering private judgement. In the time of Tiberius, those condemned persons who
awaited execution lost their property and were deprived of
sepulture; those who anticipated it by killing themselves
were buried and might make a will.[79]

A Usage of the Island of Cea

But death is sometimes, too, desired in the hope of a greater good. "I desire," says St. Paul, "to be released from life in order to be with Jesus Christ";[80] and, "who shall loose me from these bonds?"[81] Cleombrotus Ambraciota, having read the *Phædo* of Plato, felt so great a craving for the life to come that, without other cause, he threw himself in the sea.[82] Whence it appears how unfitly we give the name of despair to that voluntary departure from life to which the eagerness of hope often carries us, and often, too, a calm and deliberate inclination of the judgement. Jacques du Chastel, Bishop of Soissons, in the expedition that St. Louis made beyond the seas, seeing the king and the whole army on the point of returning to France, leaving religious matters unfinished, resolved rather to go to Paradise. And having bade his friends adieu, he charged alone, before the eyes of all, into the enemy's army, where he was cut to pieces.[83] In a certain kingdom of those newly discovered countries, on the day of a solemn procession, when the idol they worship is drawn in public on a car of wonderful size, besides many persons who are seen cutting off bits of their living flesh to present to it, many others prostrate themselves on the road, who are ground and crushed under the wheels, in order thus to acquire, after their death, veneration for sanctity, which is rendered to them.[84] The death of this bishop, arms in hand, has more nobility and less physical sensation, the ardour of combat doing away in part with that.[85]

There are governments which have undertaken to regulate the propriety and fitness of voluntary death. In our Marseilles there was kept in former times, at public cost, poison prepared from hemlock for those who wished to

A Usage of the Island of Cea

shorten their days, having first avowed to the Six Hundred, which was their Senate, the reasons for their action; and it was not allowable otherwise than by permission of the magistrate, and for legitimate reasons, to lay hand upon oneself.[86] This law existed also elsewhere.

Sextus Pompeius, on his way to Asia, touched at the island of Cea in Negropontis. It chanced while he was there, as we learn from one of those who were with him, that a woman of great authority, having explained to her fellow citizens why she had determined to end her life, invited Pompeius to be present at her death, to make it more honourable; which he was; and having long vainly endeavoured by the power of eloquence, which was wonderfully at his service, and of persuasion, to turn her from her purpose, at last consented that she should do her will. She had passed ninety years in a very fortunate condition of mind and body; but now, lying on her bed, which was more richly adorned than usual, and leaning on her elbow, "The gods, O Sextus Pompeius," she said, "and rather those I leave than those I go to seek, are grateful to you for that you have not disdained to be both a counsellor of my life and a witness of my death. For my part, having always beheld the favourable face of fortune, lest too great love of life should cause me to see another aspect of it, I purpose by a happy ending to dismiss the remnant of my soul, leaving behind me two daughters and a legion of nephews." This said, having exhorted and encouraged her family to live in unity and concord, having divided her property among them and commended the household gods to the care of her eldest daughter, she took with a steady hand the cup in which was the poison; and having made her vows to Mercury and prayed him to conduct her to some happy abode in the other world, she quickly swallowed that mortal draught. Now she informs the company of the progress of its operation, and how the parts of her body feel themselves becoming cold one after another; until, having said at the last that it had reached the heart and the bowels, she called her daughters to perform for her the last duties and to close her eyes.[87] Pliny narrates concerning a certain hyperborean nation that, on account of the mild temperature of the air, the lives of the people there commonly end only by their own will; but that, being weary and sated with living, they are accustomed, after long years, having made good cheer, to throw themselves into the sea from the top of a certain cliff appointed for that purpose.[88] Unbearable physical pain and the fear of a worse death seem to me the most excusable incitements.

Chapter IV

BUSINESS TO-MORROW

I GIVE, and, it seems to me, with good reason, the palm to Jacques Amyot over all our French authors, not only for simplicity and purity of language, wherein he surpasses all others, nor for his persistence in so prolonged a task, nor for the depth of his learning, which has made him able to interpret so happily an author so pathless and sure-footed[1] (for, say what you please, I know no Greek, but I find everywhere in his translation a significance so fine, so well combined and maintained throughout, that either he has certainly grasped the author's true thought, or having by long study rooted vividly in his mind a general idea of Plutarch's mind, he has at all events attributed to him nothing that belies or contradicts him); but above all I am grateful to him for having culled out and chosen a book so worthy and so opportune, to make a present of it to his country. We ignoramuses had been lost if that book had not lifted us out of the mire; thanks to it, we dare now to speak and write; the ladies lord it over the schoolmasters; it is our breviary. If this good man should live, I point out to him Xenophon to do as much by:[2] it is an easier task and one better fitted to his old age; and then, I know not why, it seems to

481

me that, although he gets clear quickly and completely from a difficult passage, nevertheless his style is more at home[3] when it is not constrained and flows leisurely along. I was but now reading the passage where Plutarch, speaking of himself, says that Rusticus, being present at a declamation of his at Rome, received a missive from the emperor, and delayed opening it until all was done; for which, he says, the whole audience peculiarly praised the composure of this personage.[4] Truly, as he was treating of curiosity, and of that passion, eager and greedy for news, that makes us so inconsiderately and impatiently drop every thing to talk to a newcomer, and throw aside all respect and decorum to open instantly, wherever we may be, the letters that are brought us, he had reason to praise the composure of Rusticus; and might have added a word of praise of his civility and courtesy in wishing not to interrupt the course of the declamation. But I am in doubt whether he can be praised for discretion, since, receiving letters unexpectedly, especially from an emperor, it might well happen that to defer reading them would cause great harm.

The opposite vice to curiosity is indifference, to which I am evidently inclined by temperament, and which I have seen so extreme in many men, that three or four days afterward there would be found in their pockets, still sealed, letters that had been sent to them. I never open any, not only of those that have been entrusted to me, but also of those that chance causes to fall into my hands; and I feel remorse if my eyes heedlessly steal some knowledge of important letters that a great man is reading when I am at his side.

Never was there any man less inquisitive about the affairs of others, or who pried less into them. In the time of our fathers Monsieur de Boutières almost lost Turin because, being at supper with pleasant company, he put off reading a warning that was brought him of treachery that was being contrived against that city, where he was in command; and I am informed by this same Plutarch that Julius Cæsar would have been saved if, on his way to the Senate the day when he was killed by the conspirators, he had read a letter that was handed him.[5] And he tells also this story of Archias, Tyrant of Thebes, that on the evening before the execution of the plot formed by Pelopidas to kill him in order to give back liberty to his country, another Archias, an Athenian, wrote to him what was in store for him, point by point; and this missive being given to him while he was at supper, he delayed opening it, saying this, which afterward became a proverb in Greece: "Business to-morrow."[6]

A wise man may, in my opinion, in the interest of others, —as, for instance, like Rusticus, in order not to disturb uncivilly those whom he is with, or not to break off another affair of importance,—postpone listening to new matters; but in his own personal interest or pleasure, especially if he be a man holding public office, not to break off his dinner, or even his sleep, is inexcusable. And in ancient times, at Rome, the most honourable place at the table was called the consular seat, because it was freer and more accessible to those who might come on a sudden to have speech with him who was seated there.[7] Which witnesses that, because they were at table, they did not desist from managing other affairs and occurrences. But when all is said, it is difficult in human actions to make, by exercise of the reason, so complete a rule that chance will not maintain her rights in them.

Chapter V

OF THE CONSCIENCE

AS my brother, the Sieur de la Brousse, and I were journeying once during our civil war, we met a gentleman of agreeable demeanour; he was of the party opposed to ours, but I knew nothing of that, for he pretended otherwise; and the worst of such wars is that the cards are so mixed, your enemy being distinguished from you by no apparent sign, either of language or of bearing, brought up under the same laws and customs and the same conditions of life, that it is difficult to avoid confusion and disorder. This made me myself dread meeting our troops in some place where I might not be recognised and might have difficulty in making myself known, and, perchance, worse than that. As it happened to me at another time; for through being mistaken, I lost both men and horses, and there was grievously killed, among others, a page, an Italian of gentle birth, whom I was bringing up with great care, and in him was extinguished a delightful youth full of great hope. But this gentleman was in this respect so far gone in fear, and I saw that he was so nearly dead at every meeting with mounted men, and when we passed through places that were loyal to the king, that I divined at last that they were

484

Of the Conscience

terrors which his conscience caused in him. It seemed to this poor man as if, through his mask and the crosses on his coat,[1] could be read in his heart his secret thoughts. So wonderful is the force of conscience! It makes us betray, accuse, and contend with ourselves, and in default of other testimony, it brings us forward against ourselves;

> With the soul of a torturer, brandishing an invisible scourge.[2]

This tale is in the mouths of children. Bessus, a Pæonian, blamed for having in sport[3] pulled down a nest of sparrows and killed them, said that he had reason to do so because those little birds incessantly accused him falsely as the murderer of his father. Until then that parricide had been hidden and unknown; but the furies, avengers of the conscience, caused him himself to disclose who was to do penance for it.[4] Hesiod corrects the remark of Plato, that the punishment follows close upon the sin; for he says that it is born instantly, and at the same time with the sin.[5]

Whoever expects punishment suffers it; and whoever has deserved it expects it.[6] Wickedness frames torments for itself;

> Bad counsel is worst for him that gives it;[7]

as the wasp stings and hurts others, but itself more, for it thus loses its sting and its power for ever:[8]

> They put their lives into the sting.[9]

Cantharides have in themselves something which acts as an antidote to their poison by an opposition of nature. In like manner, when we take pleasure in vice, there is engendered

Of the Conscience

an opposing displeasure in the conscience, which torments us with many painful fancies, waking and sleeping.[10]

Many criminals are said to have betrayed themselves by often talking in their sleep or in the delirium of fever, and to have revealed long-hidden crimes.[11]

Apollodorus dreamed that he saw himself flayed by the Scythians and then boiled in a cauldron, and that his heart muttered these words: "I have caused you all these ills."[12] No hiding-place avails the wicked, said Epicurus, because they can not feel assured that they are hidden, conscience revealing them to themselves.[13]

The punishment beyond all other is that no guilty man is absolved by his own judgement.[14]

Even as conscience fills us with fear, so it fills us with assurance and confidence. And I can say that I have walked through many perils with a much firmer step because of the secret knowledge I had of my desires and of the innocence of my intentions.

According to the testimony of each man's mind, so he conceives in his breast hope or fear from his deed.[15]

There are a thousand examples; it will suffice to instance three of the same person. Scipio, being accused one day before the Roman people with a weighty accusation, instead of excusing himself or flattering his judges, said: "It will become you well to undertake to pass judgement on one by whose means you have the authority to pass judgement on all the world."[16] And at another time, for all reply to the imputations which a tribune of the people laid upon him, in-

Of the Conscience

stead of pleading his cause, "Come, my fellow citizens," he cried, "let us go and render thanks to the gods for the victory they gave me over the Carthaginians on the same day as this"; and as he started toward the temple, the whole assembly, and even his accuser, were seen following him.[17] And Petilius having been incited by Cato to demand from him an accounting of the money used in the province of Antioch, Scipio, having come to the Senate because of this, produced the book of accounts which he had under his gown, and said that this book contained a true statement of receipts and expenditures; but as it had been demanded of him to deposit it in the registry,[18] he refused to give it up, saying that he did not choose to do that indignity to himself; and with his own hand, in the presence of the Senate, he destroyed the book, tearing it in pieces.[19] I do not believe that a seared[20] soul could feign such assurance. Livy says that his spirit was too great, and by nature accustomed to too high a position, for him to comport himself as a criminal and to stoop to the degradation of defending his innocence.[21]

The invention of instruments of torture is a dangerous one, and it seems as if they were a test of endurance rather than of truth. Both he who can endure them and he who can not endure them conceal the truth. For why shall pain make me confess what is true rather than force me to say what is not true? And, contrariwise, if he who has not done that of which he is accused has fortitude enough to endure those torments, why shall not he who has been guilty do the same, so precious a meed as life being proposed to him? I think that the foundation of that invention is based upon consideration of the force of conscience. For, in the case of the guilty man, it seems that conscience assists the torture to make him confess his wrongdoing, and that it weakens him; and on the other hand, that it gives the innocent man strength to endure the torture. To tell the truth, it is a method full of uncertainty and danger. What would one not say, what would one not do, to avoid such grievous pains?

> Pain forces even the innocent to lie.[22]

Whence it happens that the man whom the judge has tortured, in order not to put him to death if innocent, he puts to death both innocent and tortured.[23] Very many have taken upon themselves[24] false confessions. Among whom I place Philotas, when I consider the circumstances of the indictment that Alexander brought against him, and the course of his torture.[25]

But when all this is summed up, it is, they say, the least evil that human inability has ever been able to devise. Very inhumanly, however, and very uselessly, in my opinion. Many nations, less barbarous in this respect than the Greeks and the Romans, who called them barbarous, think it horrible and cruel to torture and dismember a man with regard to whose crime you still are in doubt. What can he do about your ignorance? Are not you unjust, who, in order not to kill him without reason, do worse than kill him? That this is so, observe how often he prefers to die without cause rather than go through that inquisition more painful than the condemnation, and which often by its severity anticipates the condemnation and executes it. I know not whence I take the following tale, but it represents precisely the character of our judicial procedure. A village

Of the Conscience

woman laid an accusation before a general, a great lover of justice, against a soldier, for having snatched from her living children the small amount of broth she had left to sustain them, the army having despoiled all the villages of the neighbourhood. As to proof, there was none. The general, after he had cautioned the woman to look well to what she said, since she would be found guilty of a false accusation[26] if she lied, as she persisted, ordered the soldier's stomach to be opened to throw light on the truth of the matter. And the woman was found to be in the right.[27] An instructive condemnation.

Chapter VI

OF EXPERIENCE[1]

IT is not easy for argument and instruction, although we readily give credence to them, to be powerful enough to carry us to action, if, in addition, we do not exercise and train our mind by experience in the course that we wish her to follow: otherwise, when she is in a position to act, she will doubtless find herself impeded. This is the reason why those among the philosophers who have desired to attain the highest excellence have not been content to await in safety and repose the rigours of Fortune, lest she should surprise them while untried and new to the combat; rather, they have gone to meet her, and have knowingly subjected themselves to the test of difficulties. Some have abandoned wealth, to exercise themselves in voluntary poverty;[2] others have sought toil and a painfully austere life, to enure themselves to suffering and to labour; others have deprived themselves of the most cherished parts of the body, as the eyes and the organs of generation, for fear that their use, too agreeable and too easy, would relax and enfeeble the constancy of the soul.[3] But to die, which is the greatest affair we have to achieve, practice can not aid us. We can, by habit and experience, fortify ourselves against pain, dis-

Of Experience

grace, indigence, and other like misfortunes; but as for death, we can essay it but once; we are all novices when we come to it.

In old days, there were men who were such excellent husbands of time that they tried, at the moment of death, to taste and savour it, and strained their wits to discover what that transition is; but they have not returned to tell us of it:—

no one wakes upon whom the chill cessation of life has once come.[4]

Canius Julius, a noble Roman of singular courage and steadiness, having been condemned to death by that scoundrel[5] Caligula, over and above many marvellous proofs that he gave of his firmness when he was on the point of feeling the hand of the executioner, a philosopher, his friend, having asked him: "Well, Canius, in what frame is your mind at this moment?" he replied: "I am occupied in holding myself ready and intent with all my strength, to see whether, at the moment of death, so short and so soon past, I shall be able to perceive any flitting of the soul, and whether it will have any consciousness of its departure; so that, if I learn any thing about this, I may return thence, to give information afterward, if I can, to my friends."[6] This man philosophises, not only till death, but in death itself. What confidence was that, and what a proud spirit, to wish that his death should serve him as a lesson, and to be at liberty to think of other things in so momentous a business!

This power over his mind he had when dying.[7]

Yet it seems to me that there is some way of familiarising

ourselves with her,[8] and, in some sort, of making trial of her. We may have experience of her, if not complete and perfect, at least to such a degree that it may not be useless, and which may make us better prepared and more confident. If we can not overtake her, we can recognise her; and if we do not quite enter into her stronghold, at least we shall see and become familiar with its avenues. It is not without reason that we are taught to take heed to our very sleep, for the resemblance it bears to death.

How easily we pass from waking to sleeping! With how little concern we lose consciousness of the light and of ourselves![9] Perchance the faculty of sleep, which deprives us of all action and all feeling, might seem useless and contrary to nature, were it not that, by this means, Nature teaches us that she has created us to die, as to live, and from our birth she shows us the eternal state which she has in store for us hereafter, to accustom us to it, and to take from us the fear of it. But they who, by reason of some violent accident, have swooned and have thus lost all consciousness, they have, in my opinion, been very near to seeing her[10] true and natural visage; for, as to the instant and the point of transition, it is not to be feared that she brings with her any travail or discomfort, inasmuch as we can have no feeling without leisure. Our sufferings require time, which, for death, is so brief and so headlong, that she must necessarily be imperceptible. It is the paths that lead to her that we have to fear; and these may fall within our experience.

Many things seem to us more important in imagination than in fact. I passed a large part of my life in sound and perfect health: I mean, not sound simply, but joyful and ardent.[11] That condition, full of vigour and gaiety, made the

Of Experience

thought of sickness so horrible to me that, when I came to experience it, I found these attacks mild and feeble compared with my fear.[12] This is what I put to the proof every day: if I am sheltered in a comfortable room during a stormy and tempestuous night, I am dismayed and distressed for those who are out in the fields; if I am there myself, I do not even desire to be elsewhere. The mere fact of being always confined to one room seemed intolerable to me. I was very soon used to staying there a week and a month, feverish and thirsty and weak; and I found that, when I was in health, I pitied the sick much more than I find myself an object of pity when I am one of them; and that the strength of my apprehension magnified almost by half the essence and truth of the thing. I hope that it will be the same with me about death, and that it is not worth the trouble I take in making so many preparations, in summoning and collecting so much assistance to sustain its assault; but, in any case, we can not give ourselves too much advantage.

During our third disturbances, or the second (I do not well remember which), having gone to ride one day a league or so from my house,—I am planted in the midst of all the turmoil of the civil wars in France,—thinking that I was in perfect safety, and so near my abode that I needed no better steed, I had taken a very easy-gaited, sure-footed horse. As I was returning, a sudden occasion having arisen for me to make use of this horse in a way that was not habitual for him, one of my people, a tall, strong fellow, mounted on a powerful roan[13] with a desperately hard mouth, fresh and mettlesome, to show spirit and outstrip his comrades, came at full speed directly in my path, and rushed like a colossus on the little man and his little horse, and bore them down with his impetus and his weight, sending both of us heels over head; so that there the horse lay, thrown down, quite stunned, and I ten or twelve steps[14] farther on, like one dead, stretched out on my back, my face all bruised and skinned, my sword, which I had had in my hand, more than ten steps away, my belt broken, with no more movement or feeling than a log. It is the only time, to this hour, that I have ever been unconscious. They who were with me, after they had tried by every means in their power to bring me to, thinking me dead, took me in their arms and carried me, with much difficulty, to my house, which was about half a French league distant. On the way, and after I had, for more than two long hours, been supposed to be dead, I began to move and breathe; for so great a quantity of blood had gone into my stomach, that, to be rid of it, nature had need to revive her powers. They stood me on my feet, and I then threw up a pailful of clots of pure blood; and several times on the road I had to do the same thing. With that I began to recover a little life, but it was by such slow degrees that for a long stretch of time my feelings were much nearer death than life.

> Because, still doubtful of its return, the astonished mind is not assured.[15]

This recollection, which is very strongly impressed on my mind, presenting to me her image and idea almost in its actual nature,[16] reconciles me to her in some sort. When I there began to see, it was with a vision so confused, so weak, and so lifeless, that I could at first discern nothing but the light;

494

Of Experience

as he who now opens, now shuts his eyes, half way
between sleep and waking.[17]

As for the functions of the mind, they came to life at the
same rate of progress with those of the body. I saw myself
all covered with blood, for my doublet was stained everywhere with that that I had thrown up. The first thought
that came to me was that I had been shot in the head; in
truth, there was a good deal of firing in our neighborhood
at that time. It seemed to me as if my life hung only on the
end of my tongue; I closed my eyes, to assist, so it seemed
to me, in expelling it, and I took pleasure in languishing and
letting myself go. It was a fancy that did no more than
float on the surface of my mind, as gentle and as weak as all
the rest, but, in truth, not only exempt from trouble, but indeed with a mingling of that pleasure which we feel when
gliding gently into sleep.

I believe that those whom we see fainting from weakness
in the death-agony find themselves in this same state; and
I hold that we pity them without cause, deeming that they
are distressed by severe sufferings, or that the soul is beset
by painful cogitations. It has always been my judgement,
contrary to the opinion of many others, and especially of
Etienne de la Boëtie, that they whom we see to be thus overthrown and deadened, as they draw near their end, or worn
out by the length of their sickness, or by the occurrence of
apoplexy or of the falling sickness,—

often a man, constrained by the violence of a disease, falls before our eyes, as if struck by a thunderbolt, and foams at the mouth, and groans; and his
body trembles; he loses his reason, his sinews stiffen,

495

he is racked, he pants fitfully, and wearies his limbs
with tossing,[18]

or of a wound in the head, whom we hear groaning and
sometimes exhaling sharp sighs, though we derive therefrom, and from some motions that we see them make with
the body, indications from which it seems that they still retain consciousness,—I have always thought, I say, that both
the soul and the body were buried and asleep;

He lives, but is not conscious of his own life;[19]

and I could not believe that, with such complete powerlessness of the limbs and so great a failure of the senses, the
soul can maintain any inward power to take cognisance of
itself; and consequently [I believed], that they had no reasoning faculty which tormented them, and could make
them estimate and feel the wretchedness of their condition;
and, therefore, that they were not greatly to be pitied.

I can conceive for myself no state so insupportable and
horrible as to have the soul living and in trouble, without
means of manifesting itself; as I would say of those who
are sent to execution, having had their tongues cut out, if it
were not that, in that sort of death, the most mute seems to
me the most fitting, if it is accompanied by a composed and
serious face; and like those wretched prisoners who fall into
the hands of the villainous, brutal soldiers of these days, by
whom they are tortured with every kind of cruel treatment,
to extort from them some excessive and impossible ransom,
held meanwhile in such conditions and in such a place that
they have no means whatever of expressing and indicating
their thoughts and their wretchedness.[20]

Of Experience

The poets have imagined some gods favourable to the deliverance of those thus dragging out a lingering death,—

> I am commanded to carry to Pluto this sacred [lock of hair], and I release thee from this body.[21]

And the short and meaningless words and replies that are sometimes forced from them by dint of screaming in their ears and harrying them, or the movements that seem to bear some relation to what one asks of them, are no evidence that they are yet living—at least, a complete life. In the same way it happens to us, when we are stumbling into sleep, before it has wholly possessed us, to perceive as in a dream what is going on about us, and to follow the voices with a confused and uncertain hearing, which seems to reach only the borders of the mind; and we make replies, to the last words addressed to us, which have more chance than meaning.

Now, since I have actually experienced this, I have no doubt that I have judged rightly about it hitherto; for, in the first place, though wholly unconscious, I laboured to open my doublet as best I could[22] (for I was unarmed); and yet I know that I was not aware in my mind of any thing that hurt me; for there are many motions we make which do not proceed from our will:—

> The half-dead fingers contract and seek to grasp the sword.[23]

Those who fall throw out their arms in advance of their fall, by a natural impulse which causes our limbs to assume functions and to be stirred apart from our reason.

> They tell how scythed chariots cut off limbs, yet

the part cut from the mutilated body is seen to quiver
on the ground; whilst, from the suddenness of the
mischief, the mind and faculties of the men do not
even feel pain.[24]

My stomach was oppressed by that clotted blood, my hands
went thither of themselves, as they often do to a place that
itches, against the counsel of our will. There are many
animals, and likewise men, whose muscles are seen to contract and move after they are dead. Every one of us knows
by experience that there are parts which often stir, rise up
and lie down, without his leave. Now, those painful sensations which touch us only externally[25] can not be said to
belong to us. To make them ours a man must needs be completely engaged in them; and the pains that the foot or the
hand feels while we are asleep are not our own. As I drew
near my house, where the alarm of my fall had already arrived, and members of my household met me with the outcries usual in such cases, not only did I make some answer
to the questions they asked me, but also they say that I bethought me to order that a horse should be given to my wife,
whom I saw stumbling and toiling along the road, which is
hilly and rough. It would seem as if that solicitude must
have come from a heedful mind; but the fact is that I was
not really conscious of it: they were idle thoughts, be-
clouded, which were excited by the senses of sight and hearing, but did not come from my real self.[26] I did not even
know either whence I came, or whither I was going, nor
could I weigh and consider what they asked me. These
were trifling matters, which the senses produced of themselves, as by habit; what the mind contributed to them was

Of Experience

as in a dream, it being very lightly touched and, as it were, merely shaped[27] and fashioned by the gentle pressure of the senses. Meanwhile, my condition was, in truth, very agreeable and placid: I had no distress either for others or for myself; it was languor and extreme weakness, without pain. I saw my house without recognising it. When they had put me to bed, I had a sense of infinite comfort in that repose, for I had been villainously pulled and hauled by those poor men, who had taken the trouble to carry me in their arms over a long and very bad road, and had tired themselves out several times, taking turns. They offered me many remedies, none of which I would take, holding it for certain that I was mortally wounded in the head. To say truth, it would have been a very happy death, for the weakness of my reason prevented me from thinking any thing at all about it, and that of the body from feeling any thing at all of it. I let myself slide along so gently, and in so soft and easy a fashion, that I know of hardly any other act less burdensome than that was. When I began to come to life again, and to recover my faculties,—

When at length my senses regained their powers,[28]—

which was two or three hours later, I found myself entirely possessed with pain, my limbs being all bruised and jarred by my fall; and I was so ill, in consequence, two or three nights after that, that I believed again I was dying, but by a more painful death; and I still feel the shock of that crash.[29] I must not forget this—that the last thing I could return to was the memory of this accident; and I made them tell me over and over again where I was going, where I was coming from, at what time it happened to me, before I could conceive it. As for the manner of my fall, they concealed it from me, for the sake of him who was the cause of it, and invented for me other accounts. But a long time after, and the first day when my memory had half opened and put before me the state I was in when I saw that horse rushing upon me (for I had seen him at my heels, and looked upon myself as a dead man; but this thought was so sudden that it did not permit the birth of fear), it seemed to me that it was a lightning flash that struck and shook my soul, and that I was returning from the other world. This tale of so trivial an event is of little moment, were it not for the instruction I have drawn from it for myself; since, truly, I find that, to familiarise oneself with death, one need only be near it. Now, as Pliny says, every man is a most excellent source of instruction for himself, provided that he has the ability to examine himself closely.[30] This that I set down here is not my teaching, it is my study; and it is not the lesson for another, it is for myself;[31] and yet I should not be blamed if I impart it. That which is of service to me may perchance be of service to another. Moreover, I mar nothing, I make use only of what belongs to me. And if I play the fool, it is at my own expense, and does no harm to any one. For it is a kind of foolishness that dies within me, and has no consequences. We have heard of but two or three of the ancients who travelled this road, and, even so, we can not say whether it was in quite the same manner as this, knowing only their names. No one since has followed in their footsteps. It is a difficult undertaking, and more so than it appears, to follow so vagrant a course as that of our mind; to penetrate the dim depths of its inmost folds; to select and note so many slight evidences[32] of its emotions.

Of Experience

And it is a novel and unusual employment, which withdraws us from the common occupations of the world, aye, and from those most commended.

It is many years that I have had only myself for the target of my thoughts, that I have observed and studied myself alone; truly, if I do study any thing else, it is only to fit it immediately upon myself, or, to say better, within myself. And it does not seem to me that I make a mistake if, as is done in other branches of learning, unquestionably less useful, I share with others what I have learned in this direction; although I am scarcely content with the progress I have made in it. There is no description equal in difficulty to the description of oneself, nor certainly in usefulness. Moreover, one must dress oneself carefully,[33] and also dispose and control oneself to appear in public. Now, I constantly trim myself up, for I constantly describe myself. Custom has made speaking of oneself blameworthy, and resolutely prohibits it, in detestation of the boastfulness which seems always to be connected with testimony about oneself. Instead of wiping the child's nose, this may be called wiping it off.[34]

Instead of an error, a fault is committed.[35]

I find more harm than good in this remedy. But if it were true that it is, of necessity, presumption to talk to the public about oneself, I must not, according to my general plan, refuse to take the step that makes known this unseemly quality, since it is a part of me; and I must not conceal this fault, which I not only practise, but preach. Moreover, to say what I believe about it, this same custom is wrong in condemning wine because many intoxicate themselves with it. One can misuse only things which are in themselves good. And I think concerning this rule[36] that it concerns only the general weakness. Such rules are to no purpose: neither the saints, whom we hear speak so approvingly of them, nor the philosophers, nor the theologians, are restrained by them.[37] Nor am I, although I am as little the one as the other. If they do not arrange to write of themselves,[38] at all events, when the occasion leads them to it, they do not hesitate to exhibit themselves in public.[39]

Of what does Socrates treat more fully than of himself? To what does he more frequently direct the discourse of his disciples than to talk of themselves—not of the lesson in their book, but of the existence and movement of their souls? We speak of ourselves devoutly to God and to our confessor, as our neighbours[40] do to all the people. But, some one will reply, we speak only of our sins. Then we speak of every thing; for our very virtue is faulty and to be repented of. My profession and my art is living. Whoever forbids me to speak of this according to my perceptions, experience, and habit, let him bid the architect talk about buildings, not according to his own ideas, but according to those of his neighbour; according to another's knowledge, not according to his own. If it is vain glory to proclaim one's own merits, why does not Cicero extol the eloquence of Hortensius, Hortensius that of Cicero? Perchance they mean that I should give witness of myself by works and deeds, not barely by words. I depict chiefly my thoughts, a shapeless subject, which can not be seen in material form;[41] only with great difficulty can I enclose it in this unsubstantial body of words. The wisest and most devout men have shunned throughout their lives all visible deeds. Deeds would speak more of chance than of me. They witness to their own character, not to mine, unless it be conjecturally and vaguely; specimens of a special exhibition.[42] I expose myself completely to view:[43] it is a *skeletos* in which, all together, the veins, the muscles, the tendons appear, each part in its place. The effect of a cough is apparent in one part of them, the effect of pallor or beating of the heart in another part, and doubtfully.[44] It is not what I do that I describe; it is myself, it is my essence.

I maintain that a man must be prudent in estimating himself, and equally conscientious in declaring his estimation, be it high or low, indifferently. If I seemed to myself good and wise, or nearly so, I should proclaim it at the top of my voice. To speak of yourself as less than you really are is folly, not modesty. To account yourself as less than you are worth is cowardice and pusillanimity, according to Aristotle.[45] No virtue is helped by falseness, and truth never mistakes. To speak of yourself as more than you really are is not always presumption, but, again, it is often folly. To be pleased to excess with what one is, to be possessed by unreasonable self-love, is, in my opinion, the root of that vice.[46] The best remedy for its cure is to do just the opposite of what they advise who, by forbidding a man to speak of himself, thereby forbid him yet more to think of himself. Pride lies in thought. The tongue can have but a very small part in it. It seems to them that to occupy yourself about yourself is to take pleasure in yourself; to frequent and be on intimate terms with yourself is to hold yourself too dear. It may be so. But such excess[47] is found only in those who know their own selves but superficially; who are intent upon their external affairs; who call it dreaming and idle-

Of Experience

ness for a man to converse with himself; to fashion and build himself up is to construct castles in Spain; regarding themselves as matters of indifference and strangers to themselves. If any man be excited about his learning, looking at those below him, let him turn his eyes upward to past ages: he will lower his horns, finding there so many thousand spirits that tread him under foot. If he conceives a flattering opinion of his own valour, let him remember the lives of Scipio, of Epaminondas, of so many armies, so many nations, who leave him very far behind them. No special quality will make that man proud, who shall at the same time take into account so many other imperfect and weak qualities in him, and, at last, the nullity of the human condition. Because Socrates alone had seriously digested the precept of his God, to know himself, and through this study had come to despise himself, he alone was deemed worthy of the title of Sage. He who shall know himself thus, let him boldly make himself known by his mouth.

Chapter VII

MARKS OF HONOUR [1]

THEY who write the life of Augustus Cæsar notice this in his training of his troops, that he was wonderfully liberal in gifts to those who deserved them, but that he was equally sparing of purely honourable guerdons.[2] Yet he himself had been gratified by his uncle with all the military symbols[3] before ever he had been to the wars. A happy idea it was, and one accepted by most of the governments in the world, to establish certain idle and valueless signs to honour and reward valour, like wreaths of laurel, of oak, of myrtle, the shape of some garment, the privilege of riding in a coach in the city, or at night with a torch, some special seat at public assemblies, the prerogative of bearing divers surnames and titles, certain arrangements on coats-of-arms, and such matters, the use of which has been variously accepted, according to the judgement of different nations, and still continues. We, for our part, and many of our neighbours, have orders of knighthood which were instituted to this end.

It is, in truth, a very good and profitable custom to find means of recognising the worth of rare and excellent men, and of pleasing and satisfying them, by rewards which in no wise burden the public and which cost the prince nothing.

What had always been known from ancient experience, and what we too could formerly observe among ourselves,—that men of high rank[4] were more eager for such rewards than for those in which there was gain and profit,—is not without reason and much justification.[5] If with the prize, which should be simply one of honour, we mingle other advantages and riches, that commixture, instead of increasing its estimation, diminishes and detracts from it. The Order of Saint-Michel, which was so long in credit among us, had no greater advantage than this, that it had no connection with any other advantage. The result was that formerly there was no office or position, whatever it might be, to which the nobility laid claim with such desire and longing as to the Order, nor any rank which brought with it more respect and eminence; since valour eagerly embraces, and ardently aspires to, a reward that belongs solely to itself, rather glorious than useful. For, in truth, other gifts have not so worthy an employment, since they are employed on every sort of occasion.[6] With money we recompense the service of a valet, the diligence of a courier, and dancing, tumbling, speaking,[7] and the basest services that we receive; aye, and with money vice is paid—flattery, pandering, treachery; it is no wonder that valour accepts and desires less readily that sort of common coin than that which is proper and peculiar to it, altogether noble and of the right stamp. Augustus was wise in being much more careful and sparing of this than of the other sort, inasmuch as honour is a prerogative which derives its very essence from its rarity; and it is the same with virtue:

506

Marks of Honour

How can he who finds no man bad find any man good?[8]

We do not remark in commendation of a man that he takes care of the bringing up of his children, inasmuch as it is a common action, however right it may be; any more than[9] a tall tree where the whole forest is alike. I do not think that any citizen of Sparta prided himself upon his valour,— for it was a universal virtue in that nation,—and as little upon loyalty and contempt for riches. No reward is due to any virtue, however great, which has passed into a custom; and indeed I know not if we should ever call it great when it is universal.

Since, then, these remunerations of honour have no other value and estimation than that few enjoy them, to make them worth nothing, it needs only to be lavish of them. If there are more persons now than in the past who deserve our Order, yet we must not debase its estimation. And it may easily happen that more deserve it, for no one of the virtues spreads so easily as military valour. There is another,[10] true, perfect, and wise, of which I am not speaking (and I use this word[11] according to our usage), much nobler than this one and more complete, which is a power and as-surance of the soul, despising equally every sort of adverse accident: equitable, uniform, and constant, of which ours is but a very little ray. Usage, education, example, and cus-tom can do whatever they will in the establishing of this one[12] of which I speak, and can easily make it common; as it is very easy to see by the experience which our civil wars afford us. Let some one now bring us together and excite our whole nation to join in a common enterprise—we should make our former military renown to flourish anew.

Marks of Honour

It is most certain that the bestowal of the Order did not in the past consider valour only; it looked further. It was never the remuneration of a gallant soldier, but of a famous captain. The knowing how to obey did not merit so honourable a guerdon. Formerly for this honour there was required a more universal skill in the art of war, which included the greater part of the qualities, and the most important ones, of a military man, *for the trade of a soldier and of a general are not the same,*[13]—who was also of a rank suited to such a dignity. But as I was saying, even if there are now more men deserving of it than there were found to be formerly, it is not well therefore to make it more general; and it would have been better to fail to endow with it all those to whom it was due than to lose forever, as we have done, the benefit of so useful a conception. No man of spirit prides himself on what he possesses in common with many others; and to-day those persons who have least merited this recompense make most show of disdaining it, to place themselves thereby on the level of those who have been wronged by the scattering broadcast and the debasing of this honour, which was due more especially to them.

Now to expect, by wiping out and abolishing this Order, to be able instantly to restore to favour and renew a similar custom, is not an undertaking suited to a time so lawless and unsound as that in which we now find ourselves; and it will consequently happen that the later one[14] will incur from its birth the penalties which have ruined the other. The rules for dispensing this new Order would need to be extremely stiff and contracted to give it any authority; and this tumultuous time is not able to bear a tight and firm rein; besides which, before we can have faith in this, we must have lost the memory of the first one, and of the contempt into which it has fallen. This place might admit some discourse on the high estimation of valour and the difference between this and other virtues; but Plutarch having often recurred to that subject,[15] it would be idle for me to deal with it by reporting here what he says about it. This is worth considering, that our nation give to vaillance the first rank among the virtues, as its name shews, which comes from *valeur;* and that, according to our custom, when we say a man of much worth or an excellent man,[16] in the phrase of our court and our nobility, it means nothing more than a valiant man after the Roman fashion. For among the Romans the general appellation *virtue* takes its etymology from strength.[17] The peculiar, sole, and essential characteristic of the nobility in France is the military vocation. It is probable that the first virtue that made itself manifest among men, and gave advantage to some over others, was this one, whereby the strongest and bravest made themselves masters of the weakest, and acquired preëminence and particular renown; whence this honour and dignity in speech remained with it; or else, that those nations, being very warlike, gave the palm to that one of the virtues which was most familiar to them, and the most suitable appellation. Just as our disposition, combined with the feverish solicitude that we have regarding the chastity of women, has in the same way this result, that to say a good woman, a worthy woman, a woman of honour and virtue, really means to us nothing more than a chaste woman; as if, to bind them to this duty, we made all others a matter of indifference, and let them have a loose rein for every other vice, thus bargaining to induce them to give up this one.

Chapter VIII

OF THE AFFECTION OF FATHERS

FOR THEIR CHILDREN

TO MADAME D'ESTISSAC:

MADAME, if the strangeness and the novelty of this foolish enterprise, which are wont to give value to things, do not save me, I shall never come forth with honour from it; and it is so fantastical and has an aspect so far removed from common custom, that that may make it pass. It was a melancholy mood, and consequently one much opposed to my natural disposition, brought about by weariness of the solitude in which a few years ago I buried myself, which first put into my head this idle thought of writing. And then, finding myself entirely unprovided and empty of all other matters, I proposed myself to myself for argument and for subject. It is the only book in the world of its kind[1] and is of an odd and extravagant design. Thus there is nothing in this work worthy to be noticed except that singularity; for to a subject so futile the best of draftsmen could not have given a shape deserving consideration.

Now, Madame, having to portray myself to the life, I should have forgotten one point of importance therein, had I not there set forth the honour[2] in which I have always

Of the Affection of Fathers

held your merit. And I desire to say this, especially at the beginning of this chapter, because, among your other good qualities, that of the affection which you have bestowed on your children holds one of the highest places. Whoever may know the age at which Monsieur d'Estissac, your husband, left you a widow; the great and honourable alliances that had been proposed to you—as many as to any lady in France of your rank; the courage and strength with which you have supported, during so many years and amid so many thorny obstacles, the burden and guidance of affairs which have carried you into every corner of France and which keep you still besieged; the fortunate direction of them which you have made by your unaided prudence or good fortune, he will readily say with me that we have no example of maternal affection in our days more manifest than yours. I praise God, Madame, that it has been so well employed; for the good hopes which Monsieur d'Estissac, your son, gives of himself are a sufficient assurance that, when he is grown up, you will receive from him the obedience and gratitude of a very good child. But since, by reason of his youth, he has been unable to remark the services of exceeding value which he has received from you in so great number, I desire—if these lines shall some day fall into his hands, when I shall have neither lips nor voice to speak to him—that he may receive from me this testimony in all verity, which will be even more vividly affirmed to him by the good results which, please God, he will be conscious of: that there is no gentleman in France who owes more to his mother than he does, and that he can give in the future no more certain proof of his uprightness and his virtue than by recognising you as such.[3]

Of the Affection of Fathers

If there be any truly natural law, that is to say, any instinct which is seen to be universally and unchangeably implanted in beasts and in ourselves (a matter not beyond dispute), I may say that, in my opinion, after the solicitude that every animal has for its own preservation, and to fly from whatever is harmful, the affection that the begetter bears to the begotten holds the second place in this class. And because Nature seems to have made this acceptable to us, having regard to the extension and forward movement of the successive parts of this structure of hers, it is no wonder if, in the other direction, from children to their parents, it is not so great. We may add this other Aristotelian reflection, that he who has done a good deed for some one loves him more than he is loved by him; and he to whom aught is owed loves more than he who owes; and every workman loves his work more than he would be loved by it if that work had feeling. Because what we hold dear is existence; and existence consists of movement and action. Consequently every one exists, in some sort, in his work. He who confers a benefit performs a noble and honourable action; while he who receives it performs a useful one only; now the useful is less lovable than the honourable. The honourable is stable and permanent, affording constant gratification to him who has done such an action. The useful easily disappears and slips away; and the memory of it is neither so vivid nor so agreeable. The things are dearest to us which have cost us most; and it costs more to give than to take.[4]

Since it has pleased God to endow us with some capacity for reasoning, so that we should not be, like the beasts, in slavish subjection to general laws, but should bend to them with judgement and of our free will, we may well yield a

Of the Affection of Fathers

little to the simple authority of Nature, but not allow ourselves to be tyrannically carried away by it; reason alone should have the guidance of our inclinations. For my part, my feeling is strangely insensible to those inclinations which spring up in us without the intervention and bidding of our judgement. As, for instance, touching the subject of which I am talking, I can not accept the ardour with which some people caress children scarcely born, who have neither any mental action nor any distinguishable bodily shape whereby they can make themselves loveable; and I have never willingly allowed them to be nurtured near me. A true and reasonable affection should be born and should increase with the knowledge that they give us of themselves; and then, if they deserve it, our natural inclination keeping step with our reason, it should cherish them with a truly paternal regard, and it should likewise judge them if they are aught else,[5] always yielding to reason, notwithstanding the force of nature. Very often it is the reverse; and most commonly we feel more moved by the frolickings and games and puerile nonsense of our children than we are later by their mature acts, as if we had loved them for our pastime, like monkeys, not like human beings.[6] And a parent may be very liberal in supplying playthings in their childhood, who becomes close-fisted at the slightest outlay necessary when they are grown up. Indeed, it seems that our jealousy at seeing them come forward and enjoy the world when we are not far from leaving it makes us more sparing and niggardly to them; it annoys us that they tread on our heels as if to urge us to depart; and yet, if this were to be feared, since the order of things decrees that they can not, to speak plainly, exist or live save at the expense of our existence and

Of the Affection of Fathers

of our life, we ought not to undertake to be fathers. For my part, I think that it is cruelty and injustice not to welcome them to a share and partnership in our property, and as associates in the knowledge of our domestic affairs, when they are capable of this, and not to diminish and restrict our pleasures to provide for theirs, since we engendered them to this end. It is an injustice that a father, old, used-up, and half-dead, should enjoy alone, in the chimney-corner, wealth which would suffice for the advancement and support of many children, and should let them in the meantime, for lack of means, lose their best years without being brought into public service and to men's knowledge. They are driven in desperation to seek by some way, however dishonourable it may be, to provide for their needs; as I have seen in my days many young men of good families so addicted to stealing that no correction could turn them from it. I know one, very well connected, to whom, at the request of a brother of his, a most honourable and gallant man, I spoke once on a time for that purpose. He answered me and confessed frankly that he had been driven to this foul course by the severity and avarice of his father; but that he now was so accustomed to it that he could not refrain from it; and just then he had been caught stealing the rings of a lady at whose morning reception he had been, with many others. This made me remember the tale I had heard of another gentleman so shaped and fashioned by this noble art in the days of his youth, that afterwards, when he was master of his property, having determined to abandon this trade, he still could not, if he passed a shop where there was any thing of which he had need, prevent himself from stealing it, with the penalty of sending afterward to pay for

Of the Affection of Fathers

it. I have seen many so trained and wonted to this, that even among their comrades they usually stole what they intended to return.

I am a Gascon, and yet there is no vice of which I have less comprehension. I detest it a little more by instinct than I blame it by reason; even in desire I would not rob any one of any thing. This province is, in truth, a little more discredited in this particular than the others of the French nation; yet we have seen in our day, at divers times, men of good families, of other provinces, in the hands of justice, convicted of many shocking robberies. I fear that we must, in some degree, attribute this disorder to that vice[7] of the fathers. And if one should answer me, as did one day a nobleman of excellent sense, that he was sparing of his wealth, not to derive from it any other profit and use than to make himself honoured and sought after by his kindred; and that, years having deprived him of all other powers, it was the sole resource left him to maintain himself in authority in his family, and to avoid being despised and scorned by all the world (truly, not old age alone, but every weakness according to Aristotle, fosters avarice[8]), that has some force; but it is a remedy for a disease of which we should eschew the birth. That father is much to be pitied who retains the affection of his children only by the need they have of his assistance, if that can be called affection. We must make ourselves respected by our virtue and our ability, and loveable by our kindness and the gentleness of our manner. Even the ashes of a rich substance have their value; and the bones and relics of honourable persons we are accustomed to hold in respect and veneration. Old age can never be so feeble and distasteful in one who has lived an honourable

Of the Affection of Fathers

life that it is not venerable, especially to his children, whose hearts should be schooled to their duties by reason, not by necessity and want, or by harshness and force.

And he greatly errs, in my opinion, who believes that authority to be stronger or more stable that acts by violence, than that which is united with friendship.[9]

I blame all violence in the education of a tender soul who is trained for honour and liberty. There is I know not what that is servile in harshness and constraint; and I hold that what can not be accomplished by reasoning and by discretion and skill is never accomplished by force. I was thus brought up. They say that in all my early years I felt the rod only twice, and then very mildly. I owed the like treatment to my own children; they have all died at nurse; but Leonor, one sole daughter who has escaped that ill hap, has arrived at six years or more of age without any thing other than words, and very gentle words, being employed in her guidance and for punishment of her childish faults, her mother's indulgence readily adapting itself to this. And even if my hopes should be here frustrated, there are enough other causes that can be assigned without laying the blame on my methods, which I know to be reasonable and according to nature. I should have been much more scrupulous in this matter with regard to male children, who are less born to subjection and of more free condition; I should have loved to enlarge their hearts with ingenuousness and frankness. I have seen no other effect from the rod than to make the soul more cowardly or more deceitfully wilful.[10]

Do we wish to be loved by our children? Do we wish to

Of the Affection of Fathers

take from them all occasion to desire our death[11]—albeit in truth no occasion for so shocking a desire can be either just or pardonable; *no wickedness is justifiable*[12]? Then let us arrange their lives reasonably, as far as is in our power. To do this, we should not marry so young that our mature years will, as it were, seem the same as theirs. For that undesirable condition casts us into many great difficulties. I am thinking of the nobility, whose condition is unlaborious, and who live, as the phrase is, wholly on their revenue. For, with others, the object of whose life is gain, the number and fellowship of children is an advantage for the family:[13] they are so many additional tools and instruments for getting rich.

I married at thirty-three,[14] and approve the judgement of thirty-five, said to be Aristotle's.[15] Plato would have no one marry before thirty; but he has reason to scoff at those who do the works of marriage after fifty-five; and he considers their offspring to be unworthy of sustenance and life.[16] Thales set the truest limits, who, when he was young, replied to his mother, who urged him to marry, that it was not yet time; and having reached maturity, that it was no longer time.[17] We must deny opportunity to every inopportune action. The ancient Gauls thought it a matter for extreme blame to have to do with a woman before twenty years of age, and especially urged men who desired to be trained for war to preserve their virginity till well advanced in years; because valour is enfeebled and driven away by commerce with women.[18]

> But now united to a young wife, and happy now in children, the affections of a father and husband had weakened him.[19]

Of the Affection of Fathers

Greek history remarks of Iecus Tarentinus, Chryso, Astylus, Diopompus, and others, that to keep their bodies strong for use in the races of the Olympic games, in wrestling and other exercises, they abstained from any sort of sexual intercourse so long as the need lasted.[20] Muleasses,[21] King of Tunis, he to whom the Emperor Charles V restored his kingdom, upbraided the memory of his father [Mahomet] for his frequentation of women, and called him weak, effeminate, a begetter of children.[22] In a certain part of the Spanish Indies, men were not allowed to marry until past forty, and yet girls were permitted to do so at ten years of age.[23] When a gentleman is thirty-five years old, it is not time for him to give place to the son who is twenty: he is himself in the way to appear both in expeditions of war and at the court of his Prince; he has need of all he has; and he ought certainly to share his means, but in such wise that he does not forget himself for another. And he may fairly make use of that saying which fathers have commonly at their tongues' end: "I do not choose to undress before going to bed."

But a father weighed down by years and ills, bereft by his weakness and lack of health of common association with men, wrongs himself and his kindred by fruitlessly sitting on a great heap of riches. He is in quite the condition, if he be wise, to desire to undress before going to bed, not quite to his shirt, but to a very warm dressing-gown; the surplusage of luxury[24] of which he has no longer need, he ought readily to bestow on those to whom, in the natural order of things, it should belong. It is reasonable that he should leave to them the use of it, since Nature deprives him of that; otherwise without doubt there is spite and envy. The finest ac-

Of the Affection of Fathers

tion of the Emperor Charles V was this, in imitation of certain ancients of his calibre—his recognising that reason bids us plainly enough to undress when our clothes burden and impede us; and go to bed when our legs fail us. He resigned his resources, his grandeur, and his power to his son, when he felt the enfeeblement of his firmness and strength for conducting affairs with the same renown that he had acquired therein.

> Wise betimes, unharness the ageing horse, lest in the end he ridiculously fail and become broken-winded.[25]

This mistake of not being able to recognise betimes, and of not perceiving, the lack of power, and the very great change that age naturally causes both in body and in mind, which in my opinion is equal (if it be not that the mind has more than the half of it),[26] has destroyed the reputation of the larger number of the great men of the world. I have seen and known intimately persons of my time, high in authority, who, it was very easy to see, had wonderfully fallen away from their former ability, of which I knew by the reputation they had thereby gained in their better years. For their honour's sake I could have heartily wished that they had retired comfortably into their houses and been relieved of public and military employments which were no longer for their shoulders. I was at one time familiar in the house of a gentleman, a widower and very old, but yet in a green old age. He had several marriageable daughters and a son already old enough to appear in the world; this burdened his house with many expenses and visits of strangers, in which he took little pleasure, not only because

Of the Affection of Fathers

of his desire to save, but even more because, by reason of his age, he had adopted a manner of life very far removed from ours. I said to him one day, somewhat boldly as is my wont,[27] that it would better become him to give place to us and to let his son have his principal house (for there was no other well situated and furnished), and himself retire to a near-by estate of his where no one would disturb his repose, since he could not otherwise avoid our troublesomeness, considering the honour of his children. He followed my advice later and found himself well off.

This does not mean that we thus give them a bond which we can never revoke: I would give them—I, who am in a position to play that part—the enjoyment of my house and of my property, but with liberty to think better of it, if they should give me occasion. I would give them the use thereof because it was no longer needful for me; and I would reserve to myself as much authority in affairs generally as I pleased, having always considered that it must be a great satisfaction to an aged father himself to put his children in the way of managing his affairs; and to be able during his life to overlook their management, supplying them with information and counsel in accordance with his experience of these matters; and himself to entrust the ancient honour and customs of his family to the hands of his successors; and thus to make himself responsible for the hopes that he may form of their future conduct. And to this end I should not wish to shun their society, I should wish to observe them closely, and to enjoy, according to the humour of my years, their merriment and their feasts. If I did not live among them (as I might not be able to do without annoying their gatherings by the gloom of my

Of the Affection of Fathers

age and the thraldom[28] of my ailments, and without also straining and doing violence to the rules and manner of living which I might then be following), I should wish at least to live near them, in a part of my house, not the finest in appearance,[29] but the most convenient. Not as I saw some years ago a Dean of Saint-Hilaire,[30] at Poitiers, given up to such solitude by the discomfort of his melancholy[31] that, when I entered his chamber, it was twenty-two years that he had not stepped outside the door; and yet his faculties were all unimpaired, save for a rheum that had attacked his stomach. Scarcely once a week would he allow any one to come in to see him; he remained always shut up inside his chamber, alone, save that a servant brought him food once a day, who only went in and came out. His occupation was walking about and reading some book—for he had a certain knowledge of letters; he was persistent in remaining in that course till he died,[32] which he did very soon after.

I would try, by pleasant converse, to keep alive in my children a warm affection and unfeigned good-will toward me, which one easily obtains in a well-dowered nature; for if they are wild beasts, of which our time brings forth a harvest, we must detest and shun them as such. I dislike the custom of forbidding children to employ the paternal appellation and enjoining upon them the use of an unfamiliar title,[33] as being more respectful, Nature not having sufficiently provided for our authority. We call God Almighty Father, and disdain to have our children call us so. I have reformed this fault in my family.[34] It is also injustice and folly to deprive children who are grown up of the familiarity of their fathers, and to choose to maintain toward them a harsh and contemptuous austerity, hoping thereby

Of the Affection of Fathers

to keep them in fear and obedience. For it is a most futile pretence which makes fathers wearisome to their children, and—what is worse—ridiculous. They possess youth and strength, and consequently gain the fair wind and favour of the world; and they greet with derision these haughty and imperious airs of a man who no longer has any blood in his heart or his veins—just a scarecrow for birds.[35] Even if I could make myself feared, I should still prefer to make myself loved.

There are so many shortcomings in old age; so much helplessness; it is so open to contempt, that the best acquisition it can make is the love and affection of kindred; authority and fear are no longer its weapons. I have known a man who in his youth was most imperious. Now that he has come to man's estate, although he lives as judiciously as is possible for him, he strikes, he scolds, he swears, the most wrangling master in France; he wears himself out with caretaking and vigilance. All this is only an unreal farce,[36] toward which his very family conspires; of the corn-loft, the wine-cellar, aye, and his purse, others have the greater part of the use, while he has the keys in his wallet, dearer to him than his eyes. While he pleases himself with the frugality and niggardliness of his table, all is prodigality in divers corners of his house, merrymaking and extravagance and talk about the tales of his idle wrath and foresight. Every one is like a sentinel in regard to him. If perchance some menial servant attends carefully on him, he is immediately made to his master an object of suspicion; a sentiment which old age so readily conceives of itself. How many times he has boasted to me of the control he had over his household, and of the entire obedience and respect he received from the members of it; how clear-sighted he **was** about his affairs!

He alone is in complete ignorance.[37]

I know no man who could show more qualities, both natural and acquired, fitted to maintain authority, than he does; and none the less he has lost it like a child. Therefore I have chosen him among many similar cases that I know as the best example. It would be a fit subject for scholastic discussion whether he is better off so, or otherwise. In his presence all things give way to him; this idle effect is permitted to his authority, that they never resist it: they believe him, they fear him, they respect him to his fill. If he dismisses a servant, the man packs his box and is gone — but only out of his sight. The steps of old age are so slow, the senses so dulled, that he will live on and do his work in the same house for a year without being perceived. And when the right time has arrived, letters are made to come from a distance, piteous, imploring, full of promises to do better, by means of which he is restored to favour. Does Monsieur make some bargain or prepare some dispatch which is disapproved? It is suppressed, and later, sufficient reasons are invoked to excuse the lack of performance or of a reply. No letters from outside being brought to him first, he sees only those which seem adapted to his knowledge. If by any chance he gets them into his hands, he is accustomed to rely upon a certain person to read them to him, and the reader instantly finds therein whatever he chooses, and constantly arranges that a person asks his pardon who in the letter insults him. In short, he sees matters only by an image of them planned and arranged, and adapted as much as possible not to arouse his displeasure and his wrath. I have seen, under different forms, many instances of long-continued stable domestic management of exactly similar effect.

Women are ever prone to disagree with their husbands. They grasp with both hands all pretexts for contending with them; the first excuse serves them for plenary justification. I have known one of them who stole largely from her husband, in order, she told her confessor, to make her alms greater. Let who will believe in that pious arrangement. No managing of affairs seems to them to have enough dignity if it comes from their husbands' concession. They must needs usurp it, either slyly or haughtily, and always offensively, to give it charm and authority. When, as in the case I have spoken of, it is in opposition to a poor old man, and for children, then they seize upon this claim and triumphantly use it for their purpose; and, as in a state of common slavery, they easily raise conspiracies against his rule and control. If there are male children, grown up and prosperous, they quickly suborn, either by force or favour, both the steward and the keeper of accounts and all the rest. Those who have neither wife nor sons fall into this unfortunate condition less easily, but even more cruelly and undeservingly. The elder Cato said in his day, as many servants, so many enemies.[38] Consider, regarding the distance of the innocence of his age from ours, if he did not desire to warn us that wife, son, and servant were so many enemies for us. It well belongs to old age to furnish us with the sweet benefit of unperceptiveness and of ignorance and facility in allowing ourselves to be deceived. If we should show anger, how would it be with us, especially in these days, when the judges who have to decide our controversies

Of the Affection of Fathers

are commonly partisans of the young and have a personal interest? In the event that this trickery should escape my notice, at least it would not escape my notice that I am very easily tricked. And can one ever say enough of the value of a friend, in comparison with these civil social connections? Even the image of friendship that I see in the beasts, so undefiled, with what reverence I regard it! If others trick me, at least I do not trick myself into thinking myself capable of guarding against it, or fret my brain to pay it back. I escape from such trickery in my own circle, not by a restless and rash investigation, but rather by turning aside and by consideration. When I hear talk of the condition of some one, I do not think about him; I turn my eyes directly upon myself, to see how it is with me. Whatever comes near him concerns me. What befalls him gives me counsel and opens my eyes in that direction. Every day and every hour we say of another what we should more fittingly say of ourselves if we could as well turn our reflection within as extend it without. And many authors impair in this way the defense of their cause, going forth rashly to meet that which they attack, and casting at their enemies shafts fit to be cast back at themselves more advantageously.

The late maréchal de Monluc, having lost his son, who died in the island of Madeira,—a gallant gentleman, in truth, and of great hope,—made very evident to me, among his other regrets, the trouble and anguish he felt for having never opened his heart to him; and from this humour of paternal gravity and crabbedness, having lost the advantage of insight into his son and of knowing him well, and also of showing him the very great affection that he bore him and the true opinion he had of his virtue. "And that poor boy,"

Of the Affection of Fathers

he said, "never saw aught of me save a stern and disdainful expression, and carried away with him the belief that I could neither love him nor esteem him according to his deserts. For whom did I reserve the knowledge of the peculiar affection which I bore him in my soul? Was it not he who should have had all the pleasure of it and all the obligation? I constrained and stiffened myself to maintain that idle mask; and thereby I lost the pleasure of intercourse with him and at the same time his affection,[39] which can not have been other than very cold toward me as he had never received from me anything but roughness, or known any other than an authoritative deportment." I think that this lamentation was well founded and reasonable; for, as I know by a too positive experience, there is in the loss of our friends no consolation so sweet as that which is afforded us by the knowledge of having forgotten nothing to say to them, and of having had a perfect and complete communion with them. I open my mind to my friends so far as I can; and signify to them very freely the state of my feeling[40] and my judgement concerning them, as concerning every one. I hasten to set myself forth and shew myself;[41] for I would not that any one mistake about me in any respect whatsoever.

Among other customs peculiar to our ancient Gauls was this, as Cæsar tells us: that the [male] children did not appear before their fathers, or venture to be in their company in public, until they began to bear arms, as if it was meant that then was also the time for their fathers to admit them to their familiarity and companionship.[42]

I have observed another sort of bad judgement in some fathers of my day, who are not content with having deprived their children during their long lives of the share that

Of the Affection of Fathers

they ought naturally to have of their fortunes, but still leave after them to their wives the same control over all their property, and permission to dispose of it at their pleasure. And I knew a certain nobleman, one of the chief officers of our crown, who had in prospect by right of succession more than fifty thousand crowns a year, who died in want and overwhelmed with debts at past fifty years, his mother in her extreme old age still enjoying all his property by the disposition of the father, who for his part had lived near eighty years. This seems to me in no wise reasonable. Therefore I think it of small advantage to a man whose affairs are in good order to seek a wife who burdens him with an ample dowry; there is no outside debt which brings more disaster to families; my predecessors have commonly avoided that course very fitly, and I also. But they who advise us against rich wives, for fear lest they may be less tractable and grateful, mistake in losing a real benefit for so worthless an assumption. It costs an unreasonable woman no more to pass over one consideration than another; they have the best conceit of themselves when they are most in the wrong; injustice allures them, as good women are allured by the honour of their virtuous actions; and they are the more affable,[43] the richer they are; as more willingly and vaingloriously chaste because they are beautiful.

It is reasonable to leave the administration of affairs to mothers while the children are not of the legal age to carry the burden; but the father has brought them up very ill if he can not hope that at that age they will have more wisdom and ability than his wife, considering the usual weakness of the sex. Yet it would be, in truth, more contrary to nature to make mothers dependent upon the judgement of their

527

children. We should give them amply the wherewithal to maintain their position according to the state of their family and of their years, because necessity and indigence are much more unsuitable and harder to endure for them than for men. The children should rather be burdened therewith than the mother. Generally speaking, the most sensible distribution of our riches at death is, it seems to me, to let them be distributed according to the custom of the country. The laws have given better thought to it than we; and it is better to let them mistake in their choice than rashly to run the risk of mistaking in ours. Our wealth does not properly belong to us, since, by civil decree and independently of us,[44] it is ordained to certain successors. And, although we have some outside liberty, I hold that it needs a great and very manifest cause to make us take from any one what fortune bestowed upon him, what common justice summoned him to receive; and that it is an unreasonable abuse of this liberty to make it serve our frivolous private desires.

My fate has favoured me in not offering me occasions which could tempt me and divert my affection from the common and lawful ordering of things. I know persons with whom it is time lost to spend long pains in good offices; a word taken amiss effaces the merit of ten years. Fortunate is he who finds himself able to smooth the way for their will at this last passing![45] The latest action carries the day; not the greatest and most frequent services, but the most recent and immediate, do the work. There are people who amuse themselves with their testaments as with apples or rods, to reward or punish every act of those who claim an interest therein. It is a matter of too far-reaching consequence and of too much importance to be thus shifted about every moment, and one in which wise men establish their position once for all, having regard to reason and public custom. We have a little too much at heart these masculine substitutions. And we purpose a ridiculous eternity to our names. We give too much weight also to the idle conjectures about the future that are suggested to us by youthful minds. It would have been an injustice, perhaps, to displace me from my rank because I was more heavy and dull, more slow and uninterested in my lesson, not only than all my brothers, but than all the children of my province, whether the lesson were of mental or of bodily exercise. It is foolish to make special selections on the faith of these presages by which we are so often deceived. If we can set aside the usual prescription, and correct the destinies in the choice that they have made of our heirs, we can do it with more show of justice in consideration of some marked and excessive bodily deformity, which is a persistent, incurable blemish, and to us, great esteemers of beauty,[46] an important misfortune.

The animated dialogue between Plato's legislator and his fellow citizens will shed lustre on[47] this passage. "What, then," said they, feeling their end draw near, "shall we not dispose of what is ours to whomsoever we please? Ye Gods, how cruel, that according as our friends have been of use to us in our sicknesses, in our old age, in our business, we are not at liberty to give them more or less, according to our desire!" To which the legislator replies in this wise: "My friends, who must doubtless die very soon, it is difficult for you both to know yourselves and to know what belongs to you according to the Delphic inscription. I, who make the laws, hold that neither do you belong to yourselves, nor

Of the Affection of Fathers

does that which you enjoy belong to you. Both your possessions and you belong to your family, past as well as future. But even more do both your family and your possessions belong to the public. Wherefore, lest some flatterer, in your old age or in your sickness, or some inclination unsuitably urges you to make an unjust testament, I will save you from doing so. But, having regard both to the interest of the city and to that of your family, I will establish laws and will make it obvious, as being reasonable, that the individual advantage must give way to the general advantage. Depart with gentle and kindly feelings, where human necessity calls you. It is for me, who do not regard one thing more than another, who, in so far as I can, provide for the general interest, to take care of what you leave."[48]

Returning to my subject, it seems to me, I know not why, that in every form predominance over men, save when maternal and natural, is in no wise the due of women, unless it be for the punishment of those who, from some unsoundness of judgement, have voluntarily submitted to them; but this does not at all concern the old women of whom we are now speaking. It is the apparent truth of this consideration that caused us to invent, and so readily give footing to, this law, which no man ever saw, which deprives females of the succession to our crown;[49] and there is hardly any lordship where it is not alleged, as here, by an air of reasonableness which justifies it; but fortune has given it more credit in certain places than in others. It is dangerous to leave to their judgement the disposing of our succession according to the choice they may make among their children, which is often partial and capricious. For the disordered appetite and morbid taste that they have during their pregnancies they have

Of the Affection of Fathers

in their hearts at all times. Usually we see them dote upon the weakest and most miserable, or upon those, if they have them, who are still hanging round their neck. For, not having sufficient strength of judgement to select and embrace that which so deserves, they more easily let themselves go where the impulses of nature are more single, like the animals, which have knowledge of their young only while they are at the breast. Moreover, it is easy to see by experience that this natural affection, to which we give so much authority, has very weak roots. For a very moderate gain, we daily tear their own children from the arms of mothers and make them take ours into their care; we make them abandon their own to some needy nurse, to whom we would not entrust ours, or to a she-goat; forbidding the mothers, not only to nurse them, whatever danger the little ones may incur thereby, but even to have any thing to do with them, that they may devote themselves wholly to the service of our children. And we see in most of them that there is very soon born, through familiarity, a bastard affection more earnest than the natural kind, and greater solicitude for the welfare of children not their own than of their own. And I have spoken about she-goats because it is a common thing in my neighbourhood to see the village women, when they can not nurse children at the breast, call she-goats to their assistance; and I have at this moment two lackeys who were suckled on woman's milk but eight days. These goats are quickly trained to go to these little children, to give them suck; they recognise their voices when they cry, and run to them; if you bring to them another than their nurseling, they reject it; and the child does the same with a strange goat. I saw a child the other day whose goat had just been

Of the Affection of Fathers

taken from him because his father had only borrowed her from a neighbour; he would never suck another one that they brought to him, and he died, doubtless of hunger. Beasts change and corrupt natural affection as easily as we do.

I believe that in what Herodotus narrates of a certain region of Libya there are often mistakes: he says that the men cohabit with women indiscriminately, but that the child, when he is able to walk, finds his father in him to whom, amid the throng, natural instinct guides his first steps.[50]

Now, if we consider this simple reason for loving our children, that we have engendered them, wherefore we call them our other selves,[51] it seems that we bring forth another product which may not be of less value; for what we engender with the mind, the progeny of our intellect, of our disposition and knowledge,[52] are products of a more noble part than the corporeal and are more our own; we are both father and mother in this generation. They cost us much dearer and bring us greater honour, if they have any goodness in them; for the worthiness of our other children is much more theirs than ours; the share that we have in it is very slight; but of these all the beauty, all the charm and value are ours. Thus they resemble us and represent us much more vividly than do the others. Plato adds that these are immortal children who immortalise their fathers, aye, and deify them, like Lycurgus, Solon, Minos.[53] Now, histories being full of examples of the common regard of fathers for their children, it has seemed to me not amiss for me to cull also an example of this other sort of regard. Heliodorus, that good Bishop of Tricea,[54] preferred to relinquish the dignity, the

532

Of the Affection of Fathers

profit, the reverence of so honourable a prelateship, rather than give up his daughter[55]—a daughter who still is very charming, but perchance a little too carefully and wantonly trimmed up[56] for an ecclesiastic and sacerdotal daughter, and of too amorous a nature. There was one Labienus at Rome, a personage of great worth and authority, and, among other qualities, excellent in every sort of literature, who was, so I believe, son to that great Labienus, the foremost of the captains who served under Cæsar in the Gallic War, and who afterward, having gone over to the party of Pompey the Great, carried himself so valiantly until Cæsar defeated him in Spain. This Labienus of whom I am speaking had several enviers of his virtue, and, as is natural, the courtiers and favourites of the emperors of his day were foes of his outspokenness and of the inherited sentiments[57] that he yet retained against tyranny, with which it may be believed he coloured his writings and his books. His adversaries prosecuted him before the magistrate at Rome, and succeeded in having several works of his, which he had given to the world, condemned to be burned. It was with him that this new sort of penalty began, that was afterward repeated at Rome with regard to many others, to punish even writings and studies with death. There would not be enough occasion and material for cruelty, did we not intermingle things which nature has made immune from all feeling and all suffering, like renown and the conceptions of our minds; and did we not bestow material injuries on the teachings and monuments of the Muses. Now Labienus could not bear this loss, nor to survive his so beloved progeny; he had himself taken to, and shut up alive in, the tomb of his ancestors, where he arranged for killing and burying himself

533

at one stroke. It would be difficult to show a more vehement
paternal affection that that. Cassius Severus, a most eloquent man and his familiar friend, seeing his books burn,
cried out that by the same sentence he too should have been
condemned to be burned alive at the same time; for he
cherished and preserved in his memory what they contained.[58] A similar catastrophe befell Greuntius Cordus,
accused of having praised in his books Brutus and Cassius.
That despicable, servile, and corrupt Senate, which deserved
a worse master than Tiberius, condemned his writings to
the flames; he was pleased to bear them company in their
death, and killed himself by abstaining from food.[59] The
good Lucan, being sentenced to death by that wretch Nero,
in the last moment of his life, when more than half his blood
had already flowed out from the veins of his arms, which he
had made his doctor open that he might die; and when
coldness had seized his extremities and had begun to reach
the vital organs, the last thing that he had in his memory
was some of the lines of his book on the Pharsalian war,
which he recited; and he died, having those words last on
his lips.[60] What was this but a loving and fatherly farewell
which he was taking of his children, resembling the adieux
and close embraces that we give to our own when dying,
and a result of that natural disposition which brings to our
remembrance at that supreme moment the things that we
have held dearest during our lives?

Can we believe that Epicurus, who, when dying in torment, as he says, from the extreme pain of the stone, found
his only solace in the beauty of the doctrine that he left to
the world, would have derived as much satisfaction from a
number of well-born and well-bred children, if he had had

Of the Affection of Fathers

them, as he did from the production of his valuable writings? and that, if it had been in his choice to leave behind him a misshapen and ill-born child or a foolish and useless book, he would not have chosen—and not he alone, but every man of like intelligence—to incur the first misfortune rather than the other?[61] It would, be peradventure, impiety in St. Augustine, for example, if it were proposed to him, on the one hand, to bury his writings, from which our religion receives such great benefit, or to bury his children, in case he had any, if he did not prefer to bury his children. And I know not if I should not much prefer to have produced a child perfectly well made, by commerce with the Muses, rather than by commerce with my wife.

To this book such as it is, what I give, I give absolutely and irrevocably, as we give to children of the body; the little service that I have done it is no longer at my disposal; it may know many things that I no longer know, and may hold through me what I have not retained and what it would be necessary that, like any stranger, I should borrow from it if I were in need. If I am wiser than it, it is richer than I. There are few men, lovers of poetry, who would not be more gratified by being fathers of the *Æneid* than of the finest boy in Rome,[62] and who would not more easily endure the one loss than the other. For, according to Aristotle, of all workmen, the poet especially is the most in love with his work.[63] It is not easy to believe that Epaminondas, who boasted of leaving no other posterity than daughters who would one day do honour to their father (they were the two noble victories[64] that he had won over the Lacedæmonians), would willingly have consented to exchange these for the most magnificent maidens in all Greece;[65] or that

535

Of the Affection of Fathers

Alexander and Cæsar would ever have desired to be deprived of the grandeur of their glorious deeds of war for the pleasure of having children and heirs, however perfect and complete they might have been. Indeed, I much doubt whether Phidias, or any other excellent sculptor, would care as much for the preservation and length of days of his natural children as he would for an excellent statue, which, by dint of long toil and study, he had perfected according to art. And as for those vicious and frenzied passions which have sometimes inflamed fathers with love of their daughters, and mothers of their sons, the like is found in this other sort of parenthood: witness what is related of Pygmalion, who, having carved the statue of a woman of singular beauty, became so desperately possessed by frantic passion for this work of his, that it must needs be that the gods, indulgent to his madness, should give it life for him.

> The ivory softens at his touch, and loses its hardness, and yields to his fingers.[66]

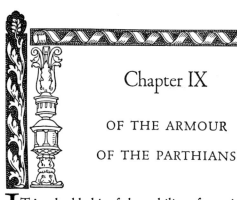

Chapter IX

OF THE ARMOUR

OF THE PARTHIANS

I T is a bad habit of the nobility of our time, and very un-
manly, to put on their armour only at the instant of extreme need, and to lay it off again as soon as there is the
slightest indication that the danger has disappeared.
Whence ensue many disorders. For, with every one shouting and rushing to his arms at the moment of the charge,
some are still lacing their cuirasses when their comrades are
already routed. Our fathers gave their helmets, their lances,
their gauntlets to be carried, and did not put off the rest
of their equipment so long as the business was unfinished.
Our troops are nowadays greatly perplexed and disordered
by the confusion of the baggage and the camp-servants, who
can not leave their masters because of their arms.[1] Livy,
speaking of our people says: *Most intolerant of fatigue,
their bodies could hardly carry their arms upon their
shoulders.*[2] Many nations still go, and used to go in ancient
times, to war without protection for their body, or they protected themselves with useless safeguards,

The covering of their heads being bark torn from
the cork tree.[3]

537

Of the Armour of the Parthians

Alexander, the most venturesome captain who ever lived, very rarely wore armour.[4] And those among us who despise it do not, for that, have much the worse bargain. If we see some men killed for lack of harness, there is a hardly smaller number to whom the embarrassment of their armour has been fatal, they being imprisoned by its weight, or bruised and broken, either by an untimely stroke or otherwise. For, in truth, it seems, considering the heaviness of our armour and its thickness, that we seek only to defend ourselves, and are more burdened than protected. We have enough to do to sustain the load of it, being fettered and constrained, as if we were to fight only with the shock of our armour, and as if we were not as much obliged to protect it as it is to protect us. Tacitus depicts amusingly the warriors of our Gallic ancestors, so armed as only to support themselves, having no way of wounding or being wounded, or of rising when overthrown.[5] Lucullus, seeing that certain Median men-at-arms, who formed the front rank of the army of Tigranes, were heavily and awkwardly armed, as in an iron prison, thence judged that he could easily defeat them, and with them began his attack and his victory.[6] And now that our musketeers are in good repute, I think that we shall invent some means of immuring ourselves to protect ourselves from them, and be carried to war shut up in fortresses like those that the ancients had drawn by their elephants.

This humour is far removed from that of the younger Scipio, who sharply reproved his soldiers because they had scattered caltrops under the water in that part of the moat by which the defenders of the city he was besieging might make sorties against him; saying that assailants should

Of the Armour of the Parthians

think of attacking, not of dreading danger; and he feared, with good reason, that this expedient might lull to sleep their vigilance in keeping guard.[7] He said also to a young man who displayed to him his fine buckler: "It is fine indeed, my son; but a Roman soldier should have more trust in his right hand than in his left."[8]

Now it is only unaccustomedness which makes the burden of our arms intolerable to us.

> Two of these warriors of whom I sing had their corselet on the back and their helmet on the head; neither by night nor day had they laid them aside since they entered their abode; for it was as easy to them to wear these as their garments, such constant use they had of them.[9]

The Emperor Caracalla marched every where completely armed, on foot, leading his army.[10] The Roman infantry bore not only the morion, the sword, and the shield (for as to armour, says Cicero, they were so accustomed to have it on their backs, that it impeded them no more than did their limbs; *for arms, they say, are a soldier's limbs*[11]); but also, at the same time, the provisions that they needed for fifteen days, and a certain number of stakes for making their ramparts, up to sixty pounds weight. And the soldiers of Marius, thus laden, were trained to do five leagues in five hours, and six, if there were haste. Their military discipline was much more rigorous than ours; likewise, it produced very different results. This jest is admirable in this connection: that a Lacedæmonian soldier was blamed because, being on an expedition of war, he had been seen under the shelter of a house. They were so hardened by toil that it was a disgrace to be seen under any other roof than the sky, whatever might be the weather. The younger Scipio, when re-forming his army in Spain, ordered his soldiers always to eat standing, and to eat nothing that was cooked.[12] We should not carry our people far at that price.

For the rest, Marcellinus, a man brought up in the Roman wars, carefully observes the manner the Parthians had of arming themselves, and observes it as being very different from the Roman.[13] They had, he said, armour woven in the fashion of little feathers, which did not prevent the movement of their bodies; and yet it was so strong, that our darts rebounded when they struck it (these are the scales[14] which our ancestors were much accustomed to employ). And, in another place, he says that their horses were strong and able[15] and covered with thick leather; and they themselves were armed from head to foot with great plates of iron, arranged so skilfully that at the joints of the limbs they lent themselves to the motion. You would have said they were men of iron; for they wore head-coverings so exactly fitted, and so closely imitating the shape and features of the face, that there was no way to wound them save through the little round hole which corresponded with the eyes, giving them a little light, or through the slits at the place of the nostrils, through which they breathed with difficulty.[16]

There is a description which much resembles the equipment of a French man-at-arms, with all his bards. Plutarch says that Demetrius had had made for himself and for Alcinus, the chief warrior near him, a complete harness weighing a hundred and twenty pounds, whereas the ordinary ones weighed but sixty.[17]

Chapter X

OF BOOKS

I HAVE no doubt that it often happens that I speak of matters which are elsewhere better treated of by the masters of the art, and more correctly. Here is simply the testing[1] of my natural faculties and in no wise of acquired ones; and he who shall detect me in ignorance will accomplish nothing against me, for I shall hardly answer to another for my opinions[2]—I who never answer for them to myself, nor am ever satisfied with them. He who may seek knowledge from them, let him fish for it where it abides; there is nothing of which I make less profession. These are my imaginings, whereby I do not attempt to make known things, but myself; they will perchance be known to me one day, or have been so at other times, according as chance has carried me to places where they have been made manifest. But I remember them no longer. And if I am a man of some reading, I am a man of no retention. And so I can promise nothing with certainty, save to make known[3] to what point the knowledge that I have of them reaches at this moment. Let not attention be paid to the subject, but to the shape I give to it. Let it be observed whether in what I borrow[4] I have been able to select what will heighten or fitly strengthen the conception, which is always my own. For I make others say, not before me but after me,[5] what I can not say so well myself, from the weakness of my language or from the weakness of my thought.[6] I do not count my borrowings, I weigh them; and if I had desired to give value to them by number, I should have loaded myself with twice as many. They are all, or very nearly all, from names so famous and so ancient, that they seem to me to name themselves sufficiently without me. As for opinions, comparisons, arguments, if I transplant some of those into my fields and mingle them with my own, I have purposely concealed the author, thereby to hold in check the temerity of those hasty judgements which fall upon every sort of writing, especially the recent writings of men still living and in the vulgar tongue,[7] which permits all the world to talk of them and seems to prove the conception and the design to be vulgar, also. I would have them give Plutarch a fillip on my nose, and excite themselves to insult Seneca in me. It is needful to hide my weakness under these great reputations. I shall love any one who is able to unplume me, I mean by clarity of judgement and solely by discrimination of the strength and beauty of the thought. For I who, through lack of memory, often fail to pick them out with recognition of their origin, can yet very well know, by measuring my own capacity, that my soil is in no wise capable of producing any of the more precious flowers I find sown there, and that all the fruits of my own growing would not be worth them. If I encumber myself; if there be emptiness and imperfection in my discourse, which I do not at all perceive, or which I may not be capable of perceiving when put before me, for this I am responsible. For mistakes often escape our eyes, but infirmity of judgement consists in not being able to discern them when another points them out to us. Learning and truth may have their abode in us without good judgement, and so may good judgement be there without them; indeed, the recognition of ignorance is one of the best and surest proofs of good judgement that I know. I have no other drill-master[8] than chance, to arrange my writings.[9] As my thoughts present themselves to my mind, I bring them together; sometimes they come in a crowd, sometimes they drag along in single file. I desire my natural and usual pace to be seen, irregular as it is. I let myself wander wherever I find myself; besides, these are in no wise matters which it is not permissible to be ignorant of, and to speak of casually and at random. I should much like to have more perfect apprehension of things, but I do not choose to pay so high a price as it costs. My purpose is to pass quietly and not laboriously what remains to me of life. There is nothing I care to weary my brains about, not even learning, however great its value. In books I seek only to give myself pleasure by worthy entertainment; or, if I study, I then seek only the learning which treats of the knowledge of myself and which instructs me how to die well and to live well.

This is the goal toward which my horse should strain.[10]

If I meet with any difficulties, I do not bite my nails over them; I give them up, after attacking them once or twice. If I sat down to them, I should waste myself and my time; for I have a nimble[11] wit. What I do not see at the first attack I see even less by persisting about it. I do nothing without animation; and continuation and too earnest effort con-

fuse my judgement, dispirit and weary it. My sight is thereby blurred and bewildered. I must needs withdraw it and
then again suddenly look;[12] just as, to judge of the brilliancy
of scarlet, we are told to pass the eye over it, glancing at it
from several points of view changed rapidly and repeatedly.
If this book wearies me, I take up another; and I give myself to it only at times when the irksomeness of doing nothing begins to lay hold upon me. I care little for new books
because the old ones seem to me fuller and stronger; nor for
those in Greek, because my judgement can not do its work
with imperfect and unskilled comprehension.[13]

Among books merely agreeable, I find, of modern ones,
Boccaccio's *Decameron,* Rabelais, and the *Basia* of Johan-
nes Secundus (if we may place this last in that category[14]),
worth reading for entertainment. As for *Amadis,* and other
works of the like kind, they were not able to interest even
my childhood. I will say this further, if audaciously and in-
discreetly, that this old dull mind can no longer be pleased
either by Ariosto or even by good Ovid; his facility and his
imagination, which enchanted me formerly, scarcely retain
my attention to-day. I utter freely my opinion about all
things, yea, and about those which, perchance, exceed my
capacity, and which I in no wise hold to be within my jurisdiction. And by what I opine about them, I make evident the
measure of my vision, not the measure of the things.[15] If I
find myself without any relish for Plato's *Axiochus,*[16] as a
work lacking in strength, my judgement does not trust itself
about this in regard to such an author; it is not so arrogant as
to oppose itself to the authority of so many other famous ancient judgements, which it regards as its teachers and masters, and with which it is content rather to mistake.[17] It

Of Books

blames itself and condemns itself, either as stopping at the surface, being unable to penetrate to the bottom, or as looking at the thing in some false light. It is content with simply securing itself from confusion and disorder; as for its weakness, it readily recognises and avows that. It studies to give a true interpretation to the perceptions that its apprehension presents to it; but they are feeble and imperfect. The greater number of Æsop's fables have several meanings and significations. Those who expound their symbolism[18] select some aspect which squares with the fables; but, for the most part, it is only the first and superficial aspect; there are others more full of life, more essential and inherent, to which they have not been able to penetrate; behold, it is so with me.

But, to pursue my path, it has always seemed to me that in poetry, Virgil, Lucretius, Catullus, and Horace hold by very far the first rank; and, markedly, Virgil in his *Georgics,* which I esteem the most finished work of all poetry; in comparison with which we can easily see that there are passages of the *Æneid* which the author would have more carefully smoothed,[19] had he had leisure to do so. And the fifth book of the *Æneid* seems to me the most perfect. I like Lucan, too, and willingly frequent him; not so much for his style, as for his proper worth and the truth of his opinions and judgements. As for good Terence, [who embodies] the delicacy and the graces of the Latin tongue, I find him admirable in representing to the life the motions of the soul and the state of our morals and manners; every hour our actions send me back to him. I can not read him so often that I do not find in him some new beauty and charm.[20] They who lived a little later than Virgil objected because some compared Lucretius to him. I am of opinion that it is,

in truth, an unfair comparison; but I have much ado in con-
firming myself in this belief when I find myself occupied by
one of the fine passages in Lucretius. If they were nettled
by this comparison, what would they have said of the ignorant folly[21] and stupidity of those who nowadays compare
Ariosto to him? And what would Ariosto himself say of it?

O senseless and ignorant age![22]

I think that the ancients have even more reason to blame
those who compared Plautus with Terence—the latter is
much more the gentleman—than [the comparison of]
Lucretius with Virgil. It counts much in the estimation and
preference of Terence that the father of Roman eloquence[23]
has him alone of his rank so often on his lips, and the sentence which the foremost judge among Roman poets passes
on his comrade.[24] It has often been in my thoughts, how, in
our times, they who take it upon them to write plays (like
the Italians, who are very successful in that) employ three or
four plots of Terence or Plautus, to make from them one of
their own. They crowd into a single play five or six of Boccaccio's tales. What makes them thus overburden themselves
with matter is the doubt they have of being able to sustain
themselves by their own graces; they must needs find a body
on which to lean; and not having enough of their own wit
with which to interest us, they want the plot to entertain us.
It is quite otherwise with my author: the perfections and
beauties of his manner of expression make us lose the longing
for his subject; his gracefulness and delicacy detain us everywhere; he is everywhere so delightful,—

flowing, and like a pure stream,[25]—

546

Of Books

and so fills our minds with his charms that we forget those
of his fable. This same consideration carries me further: I
see that the good ancient poets avoided the affectation and
the questing, not only of the fantastic flights of the Spaniards and the Petrarchians, but even of the gentler and more
restrained touches[26] which are the ornament of all the poetic
works of succeeding ages. Yet is there no good judge who
finds them lacking in these ancients, and who does not admire incomparably more the smooth polish and the never-
failing sweetness and blooming beauty of Catullus's epi-
grams than all the stings with which Martial sharpens the
tails of his. It is for that same reason that I gave but now, as
Martial says of himself: *he little needed to work his wits;
the subject took the place of them.*[27] Those earlier writers,
without exciting and spurring themselves on, are effective
enough: they find matter for laughter everywhere; they
need not tickle themselves. The later ones require alien aid;
in proportion as they have less spirit, they need more body.
They ride on horseback because they are not strong on
their legs. Just as, at our balls, those men of low degree who
teach dancing seek to gain praise by turning somersaults
and other odd and tumbler-like antics because they can not
imitate the bearing and demeanour of our nobility. And
ladies gain less by their carriage in dances where there are
various irregularities and movements of the body, than in
certain other ceremonious dances, where they have only
to walk at their natural gait and display a simple manner
and their wonted grace. And while I have seen accomplished
clowns, dressed in their everyday clothes and with their
usual bearing, give us all the pleasure that can be derived
from their art, beginners who are not so highly trained need

547

to beflour their faces, disguise themselves, and counterfeit wild gestures and grimaces, to induce us to laugh. This conception of mine is more demonstrable than anywhere else in the comparison between the *Æneid* and the *Furioso:* the one we see on swift wing flying high and strong and always following its course; the other fluttering and hopping from tale to tale as from twig to twig, trusting to its wings only for a very short flight, and constantly alighting, for fear lest breath and strength fail;

He attempts only short flights.[28]

These then are the authors who, as regards subjects of this kind, delight me most. As for my other reading, which mingles a little more profit with pleasure, from which I learn to order my humours and my moods, the books that serve me therein are Plutarch, since he has been French,[29] and Seneca. They have both this marked suitableness for my humour, that the knowledge which I seek in them is treated in disconnected works, which do not require the bondage of long-continued attention, of which I am incapable: such are the minor works of Plutarch, and the letters of Seneca, which are the best part of their writings and the most profitable. It is no great adventure to take them in hand; and I leave them when I please. For they have no connection and dependence one with another. These authors agree together in the greater number of useful and true opinions; as also their fortunes caused them to be born at about the same period, both of them to be tutors to Roman emperors,[30] both to come from foreign lands, both to be rich and powerful. Their teaching is the cream of philosophy, and is presented[31] in a simple and pertinent fashion. Plutarch is more uniform

Of Books

and steady; Seneca more wavering and variable.[32] He takes
great pains, and bends and strains himself to arm virtue
against weakness, fear, and evil appetites; the other seems
not to rate their power so high, and to disdain to quicken
his pace and put himself on guard. Plutarch's opinions are
platonic, mild, and adaptable to civil society; those of the
other are stoical and epicurean, further removed from common usage, but in my judgement more useful for the individual and more solid. It is visible that Seneca leans a little
toward the tyranny of the emperors of his time; for I hold
it certain that it is against his own judgement that he condemns the cause of the noble-hearted murderers of Cæsar.[33]
Plutarch is everywhere unconstrained. Seneca is full of wit
and sallies; Plutarch of substance. The former excites you
more and moves you; the latter satisfies you more and pays
you better. He guides us, the other pushes us on.

As for Cicero, the works of his which best serve my turn
are those which treat of philosophy, and especially of moral
philosophy. But to confess the truth boldly (for when one
has leaped the barriers of audacity, there is no longer any
curb), his manner of writing, and every other like manner,
seems to me irksome. For his preambles, definitions, divisions, and etymologies use up the greater part of his work;
what there is in it of pith and marrow is smothered by these
long-drawn-out preliminaries. If I spend an hour in reading
him, which is a long time for me, and think over what I
have extracted from him of sap and substance, I find oftenest only wind; for he has not yet reached the arguments that
serve his purpose, or the reasons that fitly touch the point I
seek. To me, who ask only to become wiser, not more
learned or eloquent, these logical and Aristotelian arrange-

ments of the matter are not adapted; I would have the last point come first; I understand well enough what death and pleasure are—time need not be spent in analysing them; I seek at the outset good and strong reasons, which will teach me how to withstand their power. Neither grammatical subtleties nor the skilful contexture of words and of arguments are of use here; I would have discourses that give the first charge at the strongest point of the question. His beat about the bush; they are good for the school, for the bar, and for the sermon, where it is permissible to doze, and a quarter of an hour later we are still in time to find the thread. There is need to speak thus to the judges who are to be won over, wrong or right, to children, and to the common people, to whom every thing must be said, to see what will take effect. I do not want time used to make me attentive and to cry out to me fifty times: *Or oyez*, as our heralds do. The Romans said in their worship, *Hoc age,* as we say in ours, *Sursum corda*; for me these are so many words wasted. I come to it[34] quite prepared from my abiding-place; I need no enticement and no sauce; I like meat quite uncooked; and, instead of sharpening my appetite by these preparations and preludes, they dull it, and weaken it.

Will the license of the time absolve me for the sacrilegious audacity of thinking also that even the dialogisms of Plato drag, and too much smother his subject; and of deploring the time that a man who had so many better things to say gave to those long, futile, preparatory interlocutions? My ignorance will excuse me the more since I have no insight into the beauty of his language. In general, I seek books that make use of learning, not those that build it up. The first two,[35] and Pliny and their like, have no *Hoc age*;

550

Of Books

they prefer to have to do with people who have forewarned themselves; or, if they have a *Hoc age*, it is a substantial one, which has its own separate body. I read also with pleasure the *Epistles ad Atticum*, not only because they contain very full instruction about the history and affairs of his time, but much more, to discover therein his personal humour. For I have a singular curiosity, as I have said elsewhere,[36] to know the soul and native judgements of my authors. We must judge their ability, but not their conduct or themselves, by the exhibition of their writings which they display on the stage of the world. I have regretted a thousand times that we have lost the book that Brutus wrote on virtue; for it is well to learn the theory from those who are familiar with the practice. But inasmuch as the exhortation is something different from the exhorter, I like as well to see Brutus in Plutarch as in himself. I should prefer to know truly the talk he had in his tent with some one of his intimate friends, on the eve of a battle, rather than his harangue the next day to his army; and what he did in his study and his chamber, rather than what he did in the public square and in the Senate.

As for Cicero, I am of the common opinion, that, outside his learning, there was no great excellence in his soul; he was a good citizen, of an easy-going nature, as are usually burly men, fond of pleasantry,[37] as he was; but, to tell the truth, of weakness and ambitious vanity he had much. And, indeed, I know not how to excuse him for having deemed his poetry worthy of being brought to light; it is no great imperfection to make bad verses, but it shows imperfection not to have perceived how unworthy they were of the glory of his name. As for his eloquence, it is entirely beyond comparison; I believe that no man will ever equal it.[38] When the younger Cicero, who resembled his father only in name, had command of the troops in Asia, there chanced to be at his table one day several strangers, among others Cæstius, seated at the lower end, where intruders often placed themselves.[39] Cicero enquired who he was, and was told his name. But, like one thinking of other things, he forgot the answer and asked again two or three times over. The servant, to avoid the trouble of repeating the same thing so often, and to make him recognise him by some particularity, said: "It is that Cæstius of whom you were told that he does not think highly of your father's eloquence in comparison with his own." At which Cicero, being suddenly angered, ordered the unhappy Cæstius to be seized, and had him well whipped in his presence.[40] What a discourteous host! Even among those who have judged that eloquence of his, all things considered, to be incomparable, there are some who have not failed to observe faults in it: as the great Brutus, his friend, who said that it was a broken and nerveless eloquence—*fractam et elumbem*.[41] The orators of about his time criticised also in him the careful study of a certain long cadence at the end of his sentences, and noted these words: *it seems to be*,[42] which he used so often. I myself prefer a shorter cadence, cut into iambics. Also he sometimes confuses his measures very roughly, but not often. My ear has been struck by this passage: *I should rather be old less long than old before being so.*[43]

Historians are my right ball;[44] for they are entertaining and easy, and at the same time, man as a whole, knowledge of whom I seek, appears in their work more vividly and more completely than in any other place; the variety and reality of his inner conditions, in general and in detail, the diversity of the methods of his combination, and of the chances that threaten him.[45] Because those of them who write of special lives busy themselves more with counsels than with events, more with what comes forth from within than with what arrives from without, they are fittest for me. That is why, in every way, Plutarch is my man. I am very sorry that we have not a dozen Laertiuses, and also that he was not more expansive or more thoroughly informed.[46] For I am equally eager to know the fortunes and lives of these great teachers of the world and the diversity of their dogmas and ideas. In this study of history, we must turn the leaves of all sorts of authors without distinction, both old and new, those in strange languages and in French, to learn the matters of which they diversely treat. But Cæsar alone seems to me to deserve to be studied, not only for knowledge of history, but for himself, such perfection and excellence has he above all the others, even if Sallust be included. Certainly I read this author with a little more reverence and respect than that with which one reads human works, sometimes considering the man himself in his action and the miracle of his greatness, sometimes the purity and inimitable polish of his language, which surpasses not only all historians, as Cicero says,[47] but, perchance, Cicero himself. With such sincerity in his judgements, even when speaking of his enemies, that, save for the false colours with which he would cover over his bad cause and the ordure of his pestilent ambition, I think that only in this other respect can one find any ground for fault-finding—that he was too chary about speaking of himself. For so many great things can not have been accomplished by him, unless he had had

Of Books

much more hand in the doing of them than he sets down.[48]

I like historians to be either very simple or excelling in worth. The simple ones, who have not the wherewithal to add any thing of their own, and who bring only care and diligence in collecting all that comes to their notice, and in registering every thing honestly, without selecting and without sifting, leave our judgement unimpaired for discernment of the truth. Such is among others, for example, the good Froissart, who proceeds in his undertakings with such frank simplicity that, having made a mistake, he in no wise fears to acknowledge it and correct it at the point where he became aware of it; and who represents to us the very diversity of the rumours that were current and the different reports that were made to him. It is the substance of history, bare and shapeless; every one can profit by it according to his understanding. The historians who excel in worth have the ability to select what deserves to be known; can choose of two reports that which is most probable; from the condition of princes and their humours they deduce their counsels and attribute to them fitting words. They have the right to assume authority to regulate our belief by their own; but certainly that belongs to very few.

Those between the two (which is the most common kind), they mar every thing: they choose to prepare it all for us;[49] they permit themselves to judge and, consequently, to bend history as they please; for when the judgement leans toward one side, it is not possible to keep from turning and twisting the narrative in that direction. They undertake to select the things worthy to be known, and often conceal from us some word, some private action, which would better inform us; they omit, as things not to be believed, those

Of Books

which they do not understand, and sometimes, perhaps, a thing because they do not know how to express it in good Latin or French. Let them boldly display their eloquence and their ideas; let them judge as they will; but let them also leave us the wherewithal to judge after them, and let them neither alter nor omit, by their abridgements and their selections, any part of the substance of their subject, but let them pass it on to us unchanged and complete in its every dimension.[50] Most frequently there are selected for this office, and especially in these days, persons belonging to the common people, for the sole reason that they can express themselves well; as if we there sought instruction in grammar. And they are in the right (having been hired only for this) to concern themselves chiefly with that alone. Thus with fine words they compose a fine mixture of the rumours they pick up in the public squares of cities.

The only good histories are those which have been written by the very men who were at the head of affairs, or who were participants in conducting them, or, at least, who had had the fortune to conduct others of the same sort. Such are almost all Greek and Roman historians. For, several eye-witnesses having written of the same subject (as it happened in those days that eminence and knowledge were commonly combined), if there is a mistake, it must be a wonderfully trivial one and concerning a very doubtful incident. What can we expect of a physician speaking of war or of a scholar treating of the purposes of princes? If we would note the scrupulousness of the Romans in this respect, only this example is needed: Asinius Pollio found even in Cæsar's histories some mistake into which he had fallen because he could not have cast his eye upon every part

of his army, and gave credit to individuals, who often reported to him matters not sufficiently verified; or else because he had not been kept informed carefully enough by
his lieutenants of things they had managed in his absence.[51]
It can be seen by this how delicate a matter is the search
for the truth; and that concerning a battle we can not trust
to the knowledge of him who commanded in it or to the
soldiers, for what happened near them, unless, after the
manner of a judicial enquiry, we confront the witnesses and
hear the objections before admitting as proved the least details of each incident. In truth, the knowledge that we have
of our affairs is far more uncertain. But this has been sufficiently treated of by Bodin,[52] in accordance with my ideas.

A little to aid me in the treacherousness of my memory
and its failure, which is so extreme that it has happened to
me more than once to take in hand, as new and unknown to
me, books which I had read carefully several years before
and scrawled over with my notes, I have for some time
adopted the habit of adding at the end of each book (I mean
of those which I care to use but once) the date at which I
finished reading it and the opinion which I have formed of
it as a whole; so that this may at least show me the character and the general idea that I conceived of the author
while reading it. I will here transcribe some of these anno-
tations. This is what I wrote about ten years ago in my
Guicciardin[53] (for whatever tongue my books speak, I
speak to them in my own): "He is a careful historiographer,
and in my opinion one can learn from him as accurately as
from any other the truth concerning the affairs of his time;
and in the greater part of them he was himself an actor and
of honourable place. There is no indication that from hatred,

Of Books

favour, or vanity, he has disguised any matter; this is confirmed by the frank judgements that he expresses of great men, and notably of those by whom he had been promoted and employed in public offices, as Pope Clement the Seventh. As to the part of his work to which he seems to wish to give the most weight,—I mean his digressions and discourses,—there are some that are good and enriched with fine expressions; but he took too much pleasure in them; for from his desire to omit nothing, having a subject so full and abundant, and almost infinite, he becomes weak and smacks a little of pedantic garrulity.[54] I have also remarked this, that of the many minds and deeds he judges, of the many activities and counsels, he never connects one of them with virtue, piety, or conscience, as if those motives were wholly extinct on earth; and of all the actions, however apparently noble they may be in themselves, he ascribes the cause to some sinful opportunity, or to some profit. It is impossible to believe that, among that infinite number of actions on which he passes judgement, there may not have been one inspired by the process of reason. No corruption can have infected men so universally that some one did not escape the contagion. This makes me fear that a little vice may have been to his taste; that this[55] may have come about because he judged others by himself."

In my Philippe de Commines there is this: "You will find the language smooth and agreeable, of a native simplicity; the narrative unadorned, and in it the author's honesty shines clearly forth, free from vanity when speaking of himself and from partiality and malice when speaking of others; his discourses and exhortations accompanied rather by honest zeal and by truth than by any remarkable ability; and

557

everywhere an authority and seriousness bespeaking a man of good family brought up to great affairs."

In the Memoirs of Monsieur du Bellay: "It is always pleasant to see matters written of by those who have essayed how they should be managed; but it can not be denied that there is clearly to be perceived in these two noblemen[56] a great falling off from the frankness and freedom in writing which shines forth in the earlier writers of their sort; as in the sieur de Joinville, the household friend of St. Louis, Eginhard, Chancellor to Charlemagne, and, of later date, in Philippe de Commines. Here it is rather a plea for King Francis against the Emperor Charles the Fifth, than a history. I do not choose to believe that they have transformed any thing as to general conditions; but they do their best to wrest the judgement of events, often contrary to reason, to our advantage, and to omit all that is questionable in the life of their master: witness the disgrace of Messieurs de Montmorency and de Brion, which are forgotten; and even the very name of Madame d'Estampes[57] is not found here. Secret acts may be covered up; but to keep silent about what all the world knows, and matters which have led to public results, and of such consequence, is an inexcusable offence. Let him who would acquire complete knowledge of King Francis and of the things that occurred in his time look elsewhere, if I may be believed; the profit to be derived from this book is in the detailed narrations of the battles and the exploits of war in which these gentlemen took part; in certain private words and acts of some princes of their time, and in the dealings and negotiations conducted by the Seigneur de Langey, in which there is an abundance of things worthy to be known and of reflections out of the common."[58]

Chapter XI

OF

CRUELTY

IT seems to me that virtue is a different and a nobler thing than those inclinations toward goodness which are born in us. Souls under their own control and of a naturally good disposition[1] follow the same course, and display in their actions the same appearance as the virtuous. But virtue imports a something, I know not what, greater and more active than merely allowing oneself to be led by a happy nature gently and peacefully in the train of reason. He who, from natural gentleness and good-nature, should despise the affronts he received, would do a very fine thing and worthy of praise; but he who, stung and pierced to the quick by an affront, should arm himself with the weapons of reason against his fierce eagerness for revenge, and, after a hard fight, should at last make himself master of it, would doubtless do a much greater thing. The first would do well, the latter virtuously; the one action might be called goodness, the other, virtue; for the name of virtue presupposes difficulty and contention, and that it can not be practised without an adversary. Perchance this is why we call God good, and mighty, and gracious, and just; but we do not call him virtuous; his deeds are all natural and without effort.

Of Cruelty

Of the philosophers, not only the Stoics, but the Epicureans also (and this emphasis I borrow from the common opinion, which is false; whatever was implied in the witty answer that Arcesilaus made to him who taunted him because many persons went from his school to the Epicurean, and never in the opposite direction: "That may well be; capons are made of cocks, but never cocks of capons.")[2]

For, in truth, in firmness, strictness of opinions and precepts the Epicurean sect is in no wise below the Stoic; and a Stoic—showing more honesty than those disputants who, to combat Epicurus and to give themselves the advantage, make him say what he never thought, distorting his words,[3] deriving by the laws of grammar a different meaning from his mode of expression, and a different belief from that which they know him to have had in his soul and in his life[4]—says that he abandoned the Epicurean sect for this reason among others: that he found their path too high and inaccessible; *and they who are called devotees of pleasure are devotees of beauty and of justice, and cultivate and practise all the virtues);*[5] among the Stoic and Epicurean philosophers, I say, there are many who thought that it was not enough to have the soul in a good frame, well controlled and well disposed to virtue; that it was not enough to have our resolutions and our reasonings superior to all the force of fortune; but that, besides, opportunities must be sought for putting them to the proof. These would go in quest of pain, of want, and of contempt, to combat them and to keep their minds vigorous; *virtue is much strengthened by being assailed.*[6] That is one of the reasons why Epaminondas, who was of a third sect,[7] refuses the riches

Of Cruelty

which fortune, by very lawful means, puts in his hand, that he may, as he says, be forced to fight against poverty, in which extremity he always remains.[8] Socrates tested himself, it seems to me, even more severely, making use, for his practice, of the malignity of his wife, which was a test in good earnest.[9] Metellus, alone among all the Roman senators, having undertaken by the power of his virtue to withstand the violence of Saturninus, tribune of the people at Rome, who desired to secure by main force the passage of an unjust law in favour of the common people; and having incurred thereby the heavy penalties which Saturninus had assigned for the recusants, discoursed thus to those who in that extremity surrounded him in the public place: "That to do ill was too easy and too base a thing; and that to do well where there was no danger was an ordinary thing; but to do well where there was danger was the peculiar duty of a virtuous man."[10] These words of Metellus put before us very clearly what I wished to prove: that virtue refuses facility for a companion; and that the easy, gently sloping path by which the even steps of a good natural disposition are guided is not that of true virtue. She requires a rough and thorny road;[11] she desires to have either outside difficulties to contend with, like that of Metellus, by means of which it pleases fortune to interrupt the steadiness of her career; or internal difficulties, which the disordered appetites and imperfections of our nature bring upon her.

I have come thus far at my ease. But at the end of this dissertation it occurs to me that the soul of Socrates, which is the most perfect that has come to my knowledge, would be, by my reckoning, a soul with little to commend it; for I can not conceive in that personage any force of vicious desires. I can not imagine his virtue to have been accompanied by any difficulty or any constraint; I know his reason to have been so powerful and so sovereign in him that it would never have permitted even the birth of a vicious appetite. I can place nothing in advance of a virtue of such high rank as his.[12] I seem to see her marching along with a victorious and triumphant step, in state and at her ease, without hindrance or obstacle. If virtue can be brilliant only through the conflict of opposing appetites, shall we then say that it can not dispense with the assistance of vice, and that it owes to vice the being held in credit and honour? What would betide, also, that noble and generous Epicurean pleasure,[13] which is wont to nurture virtue gently in its lap and to make her frolic there, giving her, for her playthings, shame, sickness, poverty, death, and tortures?

If I assume that perfect virtue is recognised by combatting pain and enduring it patiently, by supporting the assaults of gout without being shaken from her seat; if I give her, as in necessary relation with her,[14] unpleasantness and difficulty, what will betide the virtue which shall have risen to such a point as not simply to scorn pain, but to rejoice in it, and to be pleased by the prick of a sharp colic, like that virtue which the Epicureans instituted, and of which many of them have left by their actions indisputable proofs? As have many others, likewise, whom I find to have, in very fact, gone beyond even the rules of their doctrine. Witness the younger Cato. When I see him dying and tearing out his entrails, I can not content myself with believing simply that his soul was then totally exempt from trouble and terror; I can not believe that he simply maintained himself in that attitude which the rules of the Stoic sect prescribed,

Of Cruelty

tranquil, without emotion, and impassible; there was, it seems to me, in that man's virtue too much lustiness and vigour[15] to stop at that. I believe without question that he felt some pleasure and sensuous delight in so noble an act, and that it was more acceptable to him than any other he ever performed. *So he departed from life, rejoicing that a reason for dying had arisen.*[16] I believe this so completely, that I am in doubt whether he would have wished that the occasion for so fine an achievement had been denied him. And, if the uprightness which made him embrace the public interest rather than his own did not keep me in check, I should readily hold the opinion that he was grateful to fortune for having put his virtue to so glorious a test, and for having assisted that brigand[17] to trample under foot the ancient liberty of his country. It seems to me that I read in his deed I know not what rejoicing of his soul and an emotion of extraordinary pleasure and manly zest,[18] when it considered the nobility and loftiness of his venture.

The more courageous when determined on death,[19]

not spurred on by any hope of glory, as the vulgar and weak judgements of some men have thought;[20] for that consideration is too base to influence a heart so noble, so proud, and so determined; but for the inherent beauty of the thing itself, which he saw much more clearly and in its perfection —he who touched its springs—than we can do. Philosophy has given me pleasure in judging that so noble an act would have been unfitly placed in any other life than in that of Cato, and that for his alone was it meet so to end. Therefore he with reason bade his son, and the senators who attended him, to provide otherwise for their death. *Cato, whom*

Of Cruelty

Nature had endowed with incredible force of soul, which he had strengthened by constant firmness, always had the fixed opinion that death was preferable to looking upon the countenance of a tyrant.[21]

Every death should be like its life. We do not become other by dying. I always interpret the death by the life.[22] And if some one describes to me a death sturdy in appearance, joined to a feeble life, I maintain that it is produced by a feeble cause and conformable to the life. The ease, therefore, of this death, and the facility he had acquired by the strength of his soul—shall we say that it should somewhat detract from the splendour of his virtue? And who, among those whose brains are ever so little imbued with true philosophy, can content himself with imagining that Socrates was simply free from fear and suffering in the mischance of his imprisonment, his fetters, and his condemnation? And who does not recognise in him, not only firmness and constancy (which was his usual condition), but also in his last words and actions I know not what of new-born satisfaction and a playful joyousness? In that thrill from the pleasure that he feels in scratching his leg after the fetters were removed,[23] is there not evidenced a like relief and joy in his soul in being freed from past unpleasantnesses[24] and being about to enter into knowledge of future things? Cato will forgive me, if he so please; his death is more tragic and more intense, but this one is, I know not how, still more beautiful.[25] Aristippus said to those who were bewailing it: "May the Gods send me one like it!"[26]

We see in the souls of these two men and their imitators (for I have great doubt if there ever were any like them) such a perfect habit of virtue, that it had become their na-

Of Cruelty

ture. It is no longer a laborious virtue, or due to the behests of reason, to carry which into effect, the soul needed to brace itself; it is the very essence of the soul; it is its natural and ordinary course. They made it so by long practice of the precepts of philosophy in contact with a noble and rich nature. The vicious passions, which are born in us, find no means of entrance into them; the strength and firmness of their souls stifle and extinguish concupiscences as soon as they begin to bestir themselves.

Now, I think that there is no question that it is a finer thing to prevent, by a high and divine resolution, the birth of temptation, and to have trained oneself to virtue in such wise that the very seeds of vice are uprooted, than to prevent their growth by main force, and, having allowed oneself to be surprised by the first motions of the passions, to arm and brace oneself to stay their progress and conquer them; and that this second state is, again, finer than simply to be endowed with a facile and easy-going nature, of itself disgusted by debauchery and vice. For this third and last sort seems indeed to make a man innocent, but not virtuous; exempt from doing evil, but no sufficiently apt to do well. Moreover, this last condition is so near to imperfection and weakness that I know not well how to discover their confines and distinguish them. The very words Goodness and Innocence are, for this reason, in some sort words of contempt. I see that many virtues, as chastity, sobriety, and temperance, may come to us through bodily failings. Steadiness in danger (if it must be called steadiness), contempt of death, patience in misfortune may come, and are often found in men through failure to judge rightly of such circumstances, and to conceive them such as they are. Lack of apprehension and stupidity thus sometimes counterfeit virtuous conditions; as I have often seen it happen that men have been praised for something for which they deserved blame.

An Italian gentleman once said, in my presence, to the discredit of his nation, that the acuteness of the Italians and the vividness of their conceptions were so great that they foresaw from such a distance the dangers and mishaps that might befall them, that it must not be found strange if they were often seen in war to provide for their safety even before they had perceived the peril; that we and the Spaniards, not being so wary, went on further, and that we needed actually to see and feel the danger before taking alarm at it; and that then, consequently, we had nothing to rely upon; but that the Germans and the Swiss, being more heavy-witted[27] and more dull, had not the sense to bethink themselves, even when they were borne down with blows. This was only a jest, perhaps. Yet it is very true that, in the action of war, the untrained often rush into risks with more recklessness than they do after they have sustained injury;

> not ignorant what the power is of new glory won
> by arms, and of the sweetness of a first victory.[28]

It is for this reason that, when we judge a special act, many circumstances must be considered, and in his entirety the man who performed it, before giving it a name.

To say a word of myself,—I have sometimes heard my friends call prudence in me what was luck; and suppose to be due to courage and patience what was due to judgement and reasoning; and attribute to me one quality for another, sometimes to my gain and sometimes to my loss. Mean-

Of Cruelty

while, I am so far from having attained that highest and most perfect degree of excellence, wherein virtue becomes a habit, that even of the second degree I have hardly given proof. I have not put forth great strength to curb the desires by which I found myself beset. My virtue is a virtue—or innocence, to speak more accurately—casual and fortuitous. Had I been born with a more unruly temperament, I fear that it would have gone miserably enough with me. For I have felt in my soul scarcely the firmness to resist passions if they had been never so little violent. I know not how to breed quarrels and debates in my own breast.[29] Thus I can give myself no great thanks because I find myself exempt from many vices;

> if my nature, otherwise good, is marred by slight faults, but few, as you may find to condemn some spots scattered over a fair body.[30]

I owe it more to my fortune than to my sense. My fortune caused me to be born of a family famous for integrity[31] and of a most excellent father. I know not if some of his dispositions have passed into me, or if the domestic examples and good education of my childhood have insensibly aided therein, or if I was otherwise born so,—

> Whether Libra, or dread Scorpio, the most powerful planet over the natal hour, controls me, or Capricorn, the lord of the western wave;[32]—

but so it is that by nature I hold most vices in abhorrence. The reply of Antisthenes to one who inquired of him what instruction was the best, "to unlearn evil,"[33] seems to be based on this conception.[34] I hold them in abhorrence, I say, with a conviction so inborn and so personal that I have retained the same instinct and impression about them that I brought from infancy; and nothing has ever caused me to change it, no, not even my own reasonings, which, because they have in some matters forsaken the common path, would easily permit me to do things which this natural inclination makes me detest. I will confess something extraordinary; but I will confess it none the less: I find, in many things, more fixedness and regularity in my morals than in my opinions, and my desires less astray than my reason.[35]

Aristippus put forward such audacious opinions in favour of pleasures and riches that he stirred up all philosophy to oppose him. But with respect to his morals, Dionysius the tyrant having offered him three beautiful wenches, that he might choose among them, he replied that he chose all three, and that it had gone ill with Paris for preferring one to her companions; but having taken them to his house, he sent them away without touching them.[36] His servant finding himself overburdened with the money that he was carrying after him on the road, he bade him empty out and throw away so much of it as incommoded him.[37] And Epicurus, whose tenets are irreligious and effeminate, bore himself in his life most scrupulously and laboriously. He wrote to a friend of his that he lived only on coarse bread and water, and asked him to send him a little cheese against the time when he might wish to have a sumptuous repast.[38] Can it be true that, to be really good, we must needs be so by an occult, natural, and universal disposition, without law, without reason, without example?

The excesses in which I have found myself engaged are not, thank God, of the worst sort. I have condemned them

Of Cruelty

in myself, according as they deserve it; for my judgement has not been corrupted by them; on the contrary, it blames them more sternly in me than in another. But that is all, for meanwhile I oppose too little resistance to them, and allow myself too easily to weigh down the other side of the balance, only keeping them in order and preventing the mingling of other vices, which for the most part cling and twine together in him who is not on his guard. Mine I have curtailed and constrained to be as single and simple as possible;

> nor further do I favour error.[39]

For, as to the opinion of the Stoics, who say that the wise man acts, when he acts, by means of all the virtues together,[40] although there may be one or more in evidence according to the nature of the action (and herein the similitude of the human body might somewhat serve them, for the action of anger can not take place unless the whole nature[41] assist, although anger predominates), if from that they wish to draw a like consequence, that, when the sinner sins, he sins by means of all the vices together, I do not so unhesitatingly believe them, or I do not understand them; for I am personally sensible of the contrary. These are ingenious, unsubstantial subtleties, which philosophy sometimes pauses over. I follow after some vices, but I fly from others as much as a saint could do. The Peripatetics likewise do not acknowledge this indissoluble connection and union, and Aristotle holds that a prudent and reasonable man may be both intemperate and incontinent.[42]

Socrates acknowledged to those who perceived in his physiognomy some tendency to vice, that such was in truth his natural propensity, but that he had corrected it by dis-

cipline.[43] And the intimates of the philosopher Stilpo said
that, having been born a slave to wine and women, he made
himself, through reflection, very abstinent in regard to
both.[44]

What there is in me of good I owe, on the contrary, to
the chance of my birth. I derive it neither from law, nor
from precept, nor from any other teaching. The innocence
that is in me is a witless innocence; little strength and no
art. I do hate cruelly, among other vices, cruelty, both by
nature and by judgement, as the worst of all the vices; but
to such a degree of weakness that I can not see a chicken's
throat cut without discomfort, and I can not endure hearing
the cry of a hare in the teeth of my dog, although hunting
is an impetuous pleasure.

Those who have to combat pleasure[45] make use freely of
this argument to show that it is wholly vicious and unreasonable; that, when it is in fullest strength, it so masters us
that the reason can not gain access to it; and they allege the
experience that we have of this in commerce with women,—

When now the body presages sweet joy,
And Venus is about to sow the fields of woman;[46]

in which they think that the pleasure carries us so far beyond
ourselves that our reason cannot then perform its office,
being crippled by the ecstasy of pleasure.

I know that it may be otherwise, and that we may sometimes, by force of will, succeed in that same instant to bring
back our mind to other thoughts. But it needs to be deliberately strained and stiffened. I know that it is possible to
master the violence of that pleasure, and I know it from
personal experience. For I have not found Venus so imperi-

Of Cruelty

ous a goddess, as many men, and those more chaste than I, testify to her being. I do not regard it as a miracle, as does the Queen of Navarre in one of the tales of her *Heptameron* (which is a pretty book for its matter), nor as a thing of extreme difficulty, to pass whole nights, with every opportunity and in all freedom, with a long-desired mistress, keeping the word one has pledged her to be satisfied with kisses and simple contact. I conceive that the example of the pleasure of hunting would be more fitting (while there is less pleasure in it, there is more ravishment and surprise, whereby our reason, startled, has not time to prepare itself for the encounter)[47] when after a long quest the beast suddenly appears in a place where, perhaps, we least hoped for it. This shock and the eagerness of these shouts so affect us that it would be difficult for those who love this sort of hunting to turn their thoughts elsewhere at that moment. And the poets make Diana victorious over the torch and the arrows of Cupid:

Who does not forget, amid these delights, the bitter anxieties that love excites?[48]

[49] To return to my subject—I very tenderly compassionate the afflictions of another, and could easily weep for company if, for any cause whatever, I were able to weep. There is nothing that draws forth my tears, save tears, and not true ones only, but of whatever sort, either feigned or pictured.[50] The dead I scarcely grieve for, and could rather envy them; but I greatly grieve for the dying. Savages do not so much displease me by roasting and eating the bodies of the departed as do those who torture and persecute them when alive.[51] Even the execution of the law, however just it

Of Cruelty

may be, I can not view with steadiness. Some one having to testify to the clemency of Julius Cæsar, "he was," he said, "mild in his vengeance; having forced the pirates to surrender to him, whom they had formerly taken prisoner and held for ransom forasmuch as he had threatened to have them crucified, he sentenced them to that punishment, but it was to be after they had been strangled." Philemon his secretary, who had tried to poison him, he punished no more severely than by mere death.[52] Without naming the Latin author who dares to allege, as evidence of clemency, the simple putting to death of those by whom one has been wronged, it is easy to divine that he was affected by the vile and horrible examples of cruelty put into practice by the Roman tyrants. For my part, even in matters of justice, any thing that is beyond mere death seems to me pure cruelty, and especially in us, who ought to have regard to send men's souls hence in good condition; which can not be when they have been agitated and thrown into despair by intolerable tortures.

Not long ago, a captive soldier, having perceived from the tower where he was that carpenters were beginning to erect scaffoldings in the public square and the populace to assemble there, thought that it was for him; and falling into despair, having nothing else with which to kill himself, he seized upon an old rusty cart-nail which fortune offered him, and gave himself two great cuts in the throat; and seeing that he had not thereby been able to destroy his life, he very soon dealt himself another wound in the belly, after which he fell in a swoon; and in this condition he was found by the first of his guards who came to see him. They brought him to, and to make use of the time before life failed, they read

572

Of Cruelty

him at once his sentence, which was to have his head cut off; by which he was infinitely rejoiced, and consented to take wine, which he had refused; and thanking the judges for the unhoped-for mildness of their judgement, said that the determination to kill himself had come from the dread of some more cruel punishment, the fear of which had been increased by the preparations that he had seen making on the square; and that he seemed to be delivered from death by the form having been changed.

I should advise that this sort of severity, by means of which it is desired to hold the people to their duty, be practised upon the bodies of criminals; for to see them deprived of burial, to see them boiled and quartered, would touch the common people almost as much as the punishments which the living are made to suffer, since, in fact, that[53] amounts to little or nothing; as God says, [*Be not afraid of them*] *that kill the body and after that have no more that they can do.*[54] And the poets emphasise particularly the horribleness of this sight, and more than death.

> Alas! that half-burned remains of a king, the bones laid bare, covered with foul dirt, should be dragged on the ground.[55]

I happened to be in Rome at the time when they dispatched Catena, a famous robber. They strangled him, without any excitement among the spectators; but when they came to quartering him, the executioner gave no stroke that the people did not follow with a doleful moan and cry, as if every one had lent his own feeling to that carcass.[56]

We should practise these inhuman barbarities on what is insensible,[57] not on the living flesh. Thus Artaxerxes, in a

Of Cruelty

somewhat similar case, softened the old laws of Persia, ordaining that the nobles who had done amiss in their office, instead of being whipped as was the custom, should be stripped, and their clothes whipped in their stead; and instead of having their hair torn out, as was the custom, they should only have their high hats taken from them.[58] The so devout Egyptians thought that they satisfied divine justice by sacrificing figures and representations of pigs;[59] a rash conception, to seek to pay God, that so essential substance, with pictures and imitations.[60]

I live in an epoch in which we abound in incredible examples of this vice, from the license of our civil wars; and we find nothing in the ancient histories more excessive than what we experience every day. But this [familiarity] has in no wise accustomed me to it. I could hardly persuade myself, before I had seen it, that there are souls so savage that for the mere pleasure of murder they will commit it, will hew and chop off the limbs of others, will sharpen their wits in inventing unwonted tortures and new kinds of death, without enmity, without profit, and for the sole end of enjoying the pleasing spectacle of the pitiful gestures and motions, the groans and lamentable outcries of a man dying in agony. For that is the extreme limit that cruelty can attain. *That a man should kill a man, not in anger or in fear, solely as a spectacle!*[61] For my part, I have never been able to see without discomfort even the pursuit and killing of an innocent beast, who is without defence and from whom we receive no offence. And as it commonly happens that the stag, finding himself breathless and strengthless, having no other resource, turns back and surrenders to us who are pursuing him, asking mercy from us by his tears,—

covered with blood, and lamenting, and like one imploring,[62]—

this has always seemed to me a very grievous spectacle. I take alive scarcely any beast to whom I do not restore its liberty. Pythagoras used to buy them from fishermen and from bird-catchers, to do the same.[63]

And it was first, I think, by the slaughter of wild beasts that weapons were stained with blood.[64]

Those who are naturally sanguinary with regard to animals give evidence of a natural inclination to cruelty. After they were accustomed, at Rome, to the spectacles of the murder of animals, there came those of men and of gladiators. Nature, so I fear, has herself implanted in man some instinct of inhumanity. No one finds pleasure in seeing beasts play together and caress one another, and no one fails to find it in seeing them destroy and rend one another. And I may not be laughed at for this sympathy that I have for them, since theology herself ordains kindness toward them; and, considering that one and the same master has placed us in this palace for his service, and that they, like us, are of his family, she is justified in enjoining us to have some consideration and some affection for them.

Pythagoras borrowed the doctrine of metempsychosis from the Egyptians; but since then, it has been accepted by many nations, and notably by our Druids:—

Our souls are exempt from death; and always, after leaving their primal seat, they live in new homes, and there dwell, returned to life.[65]

Of Cruelty

The religion of our ancient Gauls held that men's souls, being eternal, never ceased to move and change place from one body to another; with that conception it mingled, too, a certain consideration of divine justice; for, according to the conduct of the soul while it was in Alexander, they said that God ordained for it another body to dwell in, more disagreeable or less so, and suitable for its condition.[66]

> He forces them dumbly to suffer imprisonment in wild beasts; he puts the cruel in bears, robbers in wolves, and hides deceivers in foxes. And after many years, having passed through a thousand forms, by the river of Lethe he at last calls them back to their primordial human forms.[67]

If it had been courageous, it was supposed to be placed in the body of a lion; if licentious, in that of a hog; if cowardly, in that of a stag or a hare; if cunning, in that of a fox; and so with the rest, until, purified by this chastisement, it again took the body of another man.

> In fact, I myself remember that, at the time of the Trojan war, I was Euphorbus, son of Panthous.[68]

As for this cousinship between ourselves and beasts, I make no great account of it; nor of the fact that many nations, and notably some of the most ancient and most noble, have not only admitted beasts to their society and companionship, but have accorded them a rank very far above themselves, sometimes regarding them as familiars and favourites of the gods and having for them respect and veneration as more than human; and other nations acknowledging no other god or other divinity than them;[69] *the beasts, be-*

Of Cruelty

cause of benefits received from them, were deified by the
barbarians.[70]

> In one land they adore the crocodile, in another
> they tremble before an ibis fed on serpents; here
> gleams the sacred image of a golden, long-tailed ape;
> ... here a river fish, there a dog, is venerated by whole
> cities.[71]

And even the interpretation that Plutarch gives of this
error, which is very well conceived, is still to their honour.
For he says that it was not the cat or ox, for example, that
the Egyptians worshipped, but that in those beasts they
worshipped some image of divine attributes: in the latter,
patience and usefulness, and in the other, activity;[72] or,
resembling our neighbors the Burgundians and all Germany, impatience at being confined; and thus they pictured the liberty which they loved and adored above every
other divine attribute; and so with the rest. But when I
meet, among the more moderate views, arguments whose
purpose is to prove the close resemblance between ourselves
and animals, and how largely they share in our greatest advantages, and with how much likelihood they are compared
to us, I certainly then abate much of our presumption, and
readily resign that imaginary sovereignty over other creatures which is attributed to us.

Even if all this were lacking, yet is there a certain consideration and a certain duty of humanity that binds us, not
only to beasts that have life and feeling, but even to trees
and plants. We owe justice to men, and kindness and benignity to other creatures which may be susceptible to it.
There is some intercourse between them and ourselves, and

some mutual obligation. I am not afraid to declare that my feelings are so easily touched, like those of a child, that I can not well refuse my dog the playmating that he offers me unseasonably, or that he begs me for. The Turks have charities and hospitals for beasts. The Romans took public care of the nurture of geese, by whose vigilance their capital had been saved;[73] the Athenians decreed that the mules and asses[74] that had served in the building of the temple called Hecatompedon should be set free and that they should be let graze everywhere without hindrance.[75] The Agrigentines had as a common custom the careful burying of the beasts that they had held dear, such as horses of rare excellence, dogs, and useful birds, or even those that had served as pastime for their children. And the magnificence which was usual with them in all other matters appeared also markedly in the sumptuousness and number of the monuments erected to that end, which remained in their pride for many ages after.[76] The Egyptians buried wolves, bears, crocodiles, dogs, and cats in sacred places, embalmed their bodies, and wore mourning at their death.[77] Cymon gave honourable sepulture to the mares with which he had thrice gained the prize for racing in the Olympic games.[78] Xantippus of old had his dog buried on a headland of that sea-coast which has ever since been named therefor.[79] And with Plutarch it was a matter of conscience, he says, not to sell and send to the shambles, for a small profit, an ox which had long been useful to him.[80]

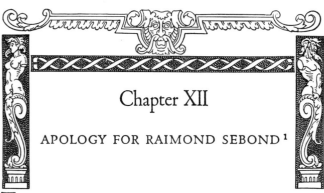

Chapter XII

APOLOGY FOR RAIMOND SEBOND [1]

I N truth, learning is a very useful and powerful ally; they who scorn it prove thereby their stupidity; yet I do not estimate its value as of such extreme importance as is attributed to it by some, like Herillus the philosopher, who placed therein the sovereign good, and maintained that it was in its power to make us wise and happy.[2] This I do not believe, nor what others have said, that learning is the mother of all virtue and that vice is engendered by ignorance. If this be true, it is in need of a long interpretation.

My house has long been open to learned men and is very well known to them; for my father, who ruled it fifty years and more, inflamed by that new ardour with which King Francis the First embraced letters and brought them into esteem, sought with great zeal and expense the acquaintance of learned men, receiving them beneath his roof as sanctified persons who had some peculiar inspiration of divine wisdom, gathering their remarks and discourses as oracles, and with so much the more reverence and devout regard as he had less capacity to judge them; for he had no knowledge of letters, any more than his predecessors. For my part, I care much for them, but I do not adore them.

579

Apology for Raimond Sebond

Among others, Pierre Bunel,[3] a man of great reputation for learning in his time, having stayed some days, with other men of his sort, at Montaigne with my father, presented him, when going away, with a book entitled: "Theologia naturalis sive liber creaturarum magistri Raymondi de Sabonde." And because my father was familiar with the Italian and Spanish languages, and because this book is composed in a sort of Latinised Spanish, he hoped that, with very little assistance, he[4] could turn it to his advantage, and commended it to him as a very useful book, and well suited to the times in which he gave it to him; it was when the new doctrine of Luther was beginning to gain credit, and in many places to stagger our ancient faith. Wherein he was very well advised, foreseeing, by discourse of reason, that this beginning of disease would easily decline to an execrable atheism; for the vulgar[5] not having the ability to judge things in themselves, and being carried on by chance and by appearances, after the courage has come to them to despise and criticise the opinions which they had formerly held in extreme reverence, as those which have to do with their salvation; and when some articles of their religion have come to be questioned and weighed, they at once lightly cast into like uncertainty all the other parts of their belief, which had no more authority or foundation in their minds than those which had been shaken; and they throw off, as a tyrannical yoke, all the impressions which they had received from the authority of the laws or respect for ancient usage,—

For that is eagerly trampled on which before was too much dreaded;[6]

580

Apology for Raimond Sebond

resolving thenceforth to accept nothing to which they have not given their sanction[7] and yielded special consent.

Now, a few days[8] before his death, my father, having by chance found this book under a pile of other neglected papers, bade me put it into French for him. It is easy to translate authors like this one, in whom there is little save the matter to set forth; but those who have much ministered to grace of style and elegance of language are dangerous to undertake; especially to render in a weaker idiom. It was a very strange and novel occupation for me; but being, by chance, at leisure at the time, and being unable to refuse any thing to the bidding of the best father that ever was, I accomplished it as I could; in which he took a peculiar pleasure and ordered that it should be printed; this was done after his death.[9]

I found this author's ideas excellent, the structure of the work well carried out, and his plan full of piety. Forasmuch as many persons take pleasure in reading it, and especially ladies, to whom we owe the most service, I have often found myself able to assist them by exonerating the book from two main objections that are made to it. Its purpose is bold and courageous, for it undertakes, by human and natural arguments, to establish and verify against atheists all the articles of the Christian religion; wherein, truly, I find it so solid and so successful that I do not think it possible to do better in that argument, and I believe that no one has equalled him. As this work seems to me too full of matter and too fine for an author whose name is so little known, and of whom all we know is that he was a Spaniard teaching medicine at Toulouse about two hundred years since,[10] I enquired in other days of Adrian Turnebus, who knew every thing, what might be the nature of this book. He replied that he believed its essential part to be derived from Saint Thomas Aquinas; for in truth that mind, full of infinite erudition, and of a marvellous subtlety, was alone capable of such ideas. However that may be, and whoever is their author and inventor (and there is no justice in depriving Sebond of that title without some greater occasion), it was a very able man, possessing many noble qualities.

The first censure that is made regarding his work is that Christians wrong themselves in desiring to support their belief by human reasons, since it is conceived only by faith and by a special inspiration of divine favour. In this objection it seems that there may be some pious zeal, and therefore we must try with all the more gentleness and respect to satisfy those who put it forward. This would better be the office of a man versed in theology than for me, who therein know nothing. However, I thus conceive, that in a matter so divine and so lofty and so far surpassing human intelligence as is this truth with which it has pleased the goodness of God to enlighten us, there is great need that he still lend us his aid with extraordinary and peculiar favour, to enable us to conceive it and implant it in ourselves. And I do not believe that purely human agencies are in any wise capable thereof; for if they were, so many rare and superior souls in ancient times, so abundantly supplied with natural powers, would not have failed, by their reasoning, to attain this knowledge. It is faith alone which grasps vividly and certainly the high mysteries of our religion. But this is not to say that it is not a very fine and very praiseworthy undertaking to adapt also to the service of our faith the natural and human instruments which God has given us. It must not be doubted that

Apology for Raimond Sebond

it is the most honourable use to which we could apply them, and that there is no occupation and no purpose more worthy a Christian man than to aim by all his studies and reflections to embellish, to extend, and to amplify the truth of his faith. We do not content ourselves by serving God in mind and soul: we owe him also, and render to him, a corporeal homage; we dispose even our limbs and our motions and external things to do him honour. We must needs do the like here and accompany our faith with all the reasoning power that is in us; but always with this understanding, that we do not think it is on us that it depends, or that our efforts and arguments can attain a knowledge so supernatural and divine. If it does not enter into us by an infusion of peculiar nature; if it enters, not only by way of the reason, but also by human influences, we have it not in its dignity or in its splendour.

And truly I fear, howsoever, that we possess it in that way only. If we held fast to God through the mediation of a lively faith; if we held fast to God through himself, not through ourselves; if we had a divine base and foundation, human chances would not have the power to stagger us as they do; our fortress would not then surrender to so feeble an assault; the love of novelty, the compulsion of princes, the good fortune of a faction, the reckless and haphazard changing of our opinions[11] would not have the power to disturb and alter our belief; we should not let it be troubled at the will and pleasure of a new argument and by persuasion —no, not by that of all the rhetoric that ever was; we should sustain these surges with immovable firmness,—

> As a huge rock drives back the broken billows, and by its mass dissipates the roaring waves around it.[12]

If this ray from the divine being touched us at all, it would appear in us everywhere; not our words alone, but our deeds as well, would have the glow and lustre of it. Whatever proceeded from us would be seen to be illuminated by this noble light.

We ought to take shame to ourselves that in human sects there was never a partisan, whatever difficulty and unfamiliarity his doctrine might maintain, who did not in some sort conform his behaviour and his life to it; and so divine and celestial an institution[13] sets a mark upon Christians only in their speech.

Would you see this? Compare our character with that of a Mohammedan or a pagan: you will always find it beneath his; whereas, having regard to the superiority of our religion, we ought to shine with an extreme and incomparable difference of excelling worth; and men should say: "Are they so just, so charitable, so good? Then they are Christians." All other signs are common to all religions: hope, confidence, important occurrences,[14] ceremonies, penitence, martyrs. The peculiar mark of our truth[15] should be our virtue, since it is, moreover, the most heavenly and most difficult mark, and since it is the most worthy product of the truth. Therefore our good St. Louis was well advised, when that King of the Tartars, who had become a Christian, proposed to go to Lyons to kiss the feet of the Pope, and to observe there the sanctity that he hoped to find in our manners and morals, to dissuade him urgently from so doing, for fear lest our reckless manner of living should, on the contrary, make distasteful to him so holy a belief.[16] Yet afterwards it fell out quite otherwise in the case of that other, who, having gone to Rome for the same end, when he

584

Apology for Raimond Sebond

observed there the dissoluteness of the prelates and people of that time, was all the more firmly established in our religion, from considering what great strength and divineness of character it must have, to maintain its dignity and splendour when surrounded by so much corruption and in such sinful hands.[17]

Had we but a single grain of faith, we should move mountains from their foundations, says the Holy Word; [18] our actions, which would be guided and accompanied by the divine being, would not be merely human: they would have in them something miraculous, like our belief. *The formation of an honourable and happy life is soon done by one who believes.*[19] Some men persuade the world that they believe what they do not believe. Others, in greater numbers, persuade themselves of this, not being able to search out what it is to believe. And it seems to us strange if, in the wars which now lie heavy on our state, we see success waver and change in a common and ordinary way. It is because we bring to them only ourselves. Justice, which is with one of the parties, is there only as an ornament and a shield; it is alleged to be there, indeed, but it is neither received there, nor given a place, nor espoused; it is there as in the mouth of a lawyer, not as in the heart and affection of the party. God promises[20] his peculiar aid to faith and religion,[21] not to our passions. Men are herein[22] directors and herein make use of religion.[23] It should be just the opposite. Observe if it be not guided by our hands, to create, as if it were of wax, countless diverse shapes from an ordinance so unswerving and so firm. When was this seen more clearly than in France in our day? Those who have regarded it from one point of view, those who have regarded it from another, those who say it is black, those who say it is white, all employ it in such similar fashion in their violent and ambitious enterprises, and therein conduct themselves in a course so similar in dissoluteness and injustice, that they render doubtful and hard to credit the diversity that they assert of their opinions about matters upon which depend the guidance and regulation of our lives. Can there be seen to issue from one and the same school and teaching, ways of thinking more akin, more identical?

Observe the horrible impudence with which we toss to and fro[24] the divine justifications, and how irreligiously we have cast them aside and taken them up again according as chance has changed our position in these public storms. The so momentous question, whether it be lawful for a subject to rebel and take arms against his prince in defence of religion—remember in what mouths this last year the affirmative was the buttress of one party, and of what other party the negative was the buttress; and listen now from what quarter comes the cry and the teaching of the one and the other; and whether arms clash less loudly for this cause than for that.[25] And we burn those who say that we must needs make the truth submit to the yoke of our need; and how much worse does France do than say it!

Let us confess the truth: he who should cull from the army, even on the legitimate side,[26] those who march therein solely from the zeal of religious emotion, together with those who consider only protecting the laws of their country or the service of their chief, would not be able to form with them a full company of men-at-arms. Whence comes it that there are to be found so few men who have throughout maintained the same mind and the same activity[27] in our

Apology for Raimond Sebond

public commotions, and that we see them sometimes going but at a foot-pace, sometimes galloping at full speed? and, likewise, men sometimes ruining our affairs by their violence and vehemence, sometimes by their coldness, slackness, and heaviness, unless it be that they are impelled by private and casual considerations, according to whose diversity they are actuated? I see this clearly, that we give nothing readily to religion save the services that flatter our feelings. There is no hostility that surpasses that of a Christian.[28] Our zeal does marvels when it seconds our inclination to hatred, cruelty, ambition, avarice, slander, rebellion. Quite oppositely, toward kindness, benignity, temperance,—unless as by miracle some rare disposition direct,—it moves neither hand nor foot.[29] Our religion is formed to extirpate vices; it shelters them, fosters them, encourages them.

We must not *faire barbe de foarre à*[30] God, as they say. If we believed in him, I do not say with faith, but with simple belief, indeed (and I say this to our great confounding), if we believed in him as in other history, as in one of our comrades, we should love him above all other things for the infinite goodness and beauty which shines forth in him; at least, he would stand in the same rank in our affections with riches, pleasure, glory, and our friends. The best of us does not shrink from wronging him as he shrinks from wronging his neighbour, his kinsman, his master. Is there any intelligence so shallow that, having on one side the object of one of our vicious pleasures, and on the other, in equal knowledge and inducement, the prospect of immortal glory, would think of bartering the one for the other? And yet we often renounce this[31] from pure contempt; for what desire attacks us to blasphemy unless, perchance, the desire

of the offence itself? When the philosopher Antisthenes
was being initiated in the mysteries of Orpheus, the priest
saying to him that those who devoted themselves to religion
would receive, after their death, eternal and perfect bliss,
"Why, then, do you not die yourself?" he asked.[32] Diogenes, more roughly, after his fashion,—and outside of our
subject,—answered the priest who exhorted him, in like
manner, to join his order to attain the bliss of the other
world: "You would not have me believe that Agesilaus and
Epaminondas, such great men, will be miserable, and that
you, ass that you are, will be perfectly happy because you
are a priest?"[33]

These great promises of eternal beatitude—if we received
them as of like authority with a philosophical argument,
we should not hold death in such horror as we do.

> Then the dying man would no longer lament his
> dissolution; but rather he would rejoice to go hence, to
> leave his mortal remains as the serpent changes his
> skin, and as the stag, grown old, sheds his too long
> horns.[34]

I would be dissolved, we should say, and be with Jesus
Christ.[35] The force of Plato's discourse on the immortality
of the soul[36] urged some of his disciples to their deaths, the
sooner to enjoy the hope that he gave them.

All this is a very manifest indication that we receive our
religion only in our own fashion and by our own hands, and
not otherwise than as other religions are received. We chance
to be dwellers in the country where it is practised; where we
are influenced by its antiquity or by the authority of the
men who have upheld it; where we fear the menaces that it

addresses to unbelievers, or are allured by its promises. Such considerations as these must be made use of in our belief, but as subsidiary: they are human connections.[37] Another country, other testimony, similar promises and menaces might, by the same means, impress on us a very different belief. We are Christians by the same title that we are Perigordins or Germans.

And as to what Plato says, that there are few men so confirmed in atheism that an imminent danger does not bring them to the recognition of the divine power, that category does not include a true Christian. It is for mortal and human religion to be received through human guidance. What sort of faith must that be which cowardice and faintheartedness implant and establish in us! A droll faith, which believes what it believes only from lack of courage to disbelieve it. An unsound perturbation, like mutability and mental agitation—can this create in our soul any well-ordered production? They established, he says, by the reasoning of their judgement, that what is said of the lower regions and of future punishment is deceitful. But the occasion for testing this presenting itself when age or sicknesses bring them near their death, terror of that fills them with a new belief, from their alarm about their future condition.[38] And because such impressions make men's hearts fearful, he forbids in his laws all teaching of such menaces and inducing them to believe[39] that there can come to man any evil from the gods, except for his greater good, when occasion arises, and with a curative purpose.[40] It is narrated of Bion that, being infected with the atheistical ideas of Theodorus, he had long been in the habit of scoffing at devout men; but that, death taking him by surprise, he gave himself up to the most extreme superstitions, as if the Gods withdrew and reappeared according as it concerned Bion.[41]

Plato and these examples would lead us to the conclusion that we are brought to belief in God either by reason or by force. Atheism being a proposition of an unnatural and unfamiliar kind, and a hard matter also and not easy to establish in the human mind, however insolent and unruly that may be, there are not lacking those who, from vanity and from being proud of holding views that are unusual and reformatory of the world, affect to profess them for appearance's sake,[42] who, if they are foolish enough, are not strong enough to have routed them inwardly.[43] Consequently, they do not fail to lift their hands to heaven if you give them an honest sword-thrust in the breast. And when fear or illness shall have abated and dulled this unbridled fervour of flighty humour, they will not fail to retrace their steps and allow themselves very discreetly to take hold of common beliefs and examples. A seriously considered opinion is one thing; a different thing are these superficial impressions which, being born of the wandering of a disordered mind, swim recklessly and uncertainly in the fancy. Wretched men, indeed, and senseless, who try to be worse than they can be!

The false beliefs[44] of paganism, and ignorance of our sacred truth, allowed that great soul of Plato—but great with human greatness alone—to fall also into this other kindred fallacy, that children and old people are more capable of religion; as if it were born and won belief from our weakness. The bond which should link together our judgement and our will, which should hold fast[45] our soul and join it to our Creator, should be a bond receiving its strands

and its strength, not from our afflictions, from our reasoning and emotions, but from a divine and supernatural compulsion,[46] having but one form, one aspect, and one splendour, which is the authority and the grace of God. Now,
our heart and our soul being ruled and commanded by faith,
it is reasonable that faith should draw into the service of her
scheme all our other faculties according to their capacity.
Also, it is not to be believed that this whole machine[47] has
not some marks stamped by the hand of its great architect,
and that there is not, in the things of this world, some
image resembling, after a sort, the workman who built and
shaped them. He has left on these high works the impress
of his divinity, and it is due solely to our weakness that we
can not discover it. This is what he himself says to us, that
he manifests to us his invisible operations by visible ones.
Sebond laboured at this admirable study, and shows us that
there is no member of the world which belies its maker. It
would wrong the divine goodness if the universe did not accord with our belief. Heaven, earth, the elements, our body
and our soul, all things conspire in this; there needs only to
find the way to make use of them. They instruct us, if we
are capable of understanding. For this world is a very sacred
temple, into which man is introduced to contemplate
images, not the work of mortal hand, but such as the divine mind has made objects of sense,—the sun, the stars,
the waters, and the land,—thereby to represent to us those
things that are objects of the intelligence.[48] The invisible
things of God, says St. Paul, are manifest from the creation
of the world; his wisdom and his divinity from his work.[49]

And, in truth, God himself does not refuse to the

earth the face of the heavens; in its continual revolution he reveals his countenance and form; and he penetrates us with himself and shews himself to us, so that he may be well known, and that, learning by sight what he is, we may consequently learn to observe his laws.[50]

[51]Now, our human reasonings and arguments are as lumpish and sterile matter; the grace of God is their fashioning; it is that which gives them shape and value. In like manner, the virtuous actions of Socrates and Cato remain vain and profitless from not having had for their end, and not having regarded, love and obedience to the true Creator of all things, and from not having known God; so it is with our thoughts and our arguments: they have some body, but it is a formless mass, without shape and without light, if faith in God and his grace be not added to it. Faith, tingeing and illuminating the arguments of Sebond, makes them firm and solid; they are capable of serving to point out the way, and of being the first guide to a learner, to put him in the path of this knowledge; they in some sort fashion him and make him capable of the grace of God, by means whereof our belief is afterwards completed and perfected. I know a man of authority, bred up in letters, who confessed to me that he was led back from the errors of misbelief by means of Sebond's arguments. And if we strip them of this adornment,[52] and of the assistance and approbation of faith, and, accepting them as purely human thoughts, use them to contend with those who have fallen headlong into the dreadful and horrible darkness of irreligion, they will then still be found as solid and as firm as any others of the same nature

that can be brought against them; so that we shall be in a position to say to our opponents,—

If you have any thing better, produce it; if not, submit.[53]

let them submit to the strength of our proofs, or let them shew us elsewhere, and on another subject, any that are more closely interwoven and more full.

I have, unawares, already half entered into the second objection to which I proposed to make answer on behalf of Sebond. Some say that his arguments are weak, and unsuited to establish what he would; and they undertake to overthrow them easily. We must handle these adversaries a little more roughly, for they are more dangerous and more mischievous than the first. We readily arrange the writings of others[54] in favour of the opinions which we have ourselves adopted; an atheist flatters himself upon leading all authors toward atheism; he infects harmless matters with his own venom. These have some preoccupation of judgement that dulls their taste for Sebond's arguments. Besides, it seems to them that they are given a fine chance to be at liberty to combat our religion with purely human weapons, whereas they would not dare to attack it in its full majesty, authority, and command. The means that I take to diminish this lunacy, and that seems to me the most fitting, is to crush and trample under foot pride and human arrogance; to make them feel the inanity, the vanity, and worthlessness of man; to tear from their hands the paltry weapons of their reason; to make them bow their heads and bite the dust under the authority and reverence of the divine majesty. To that power alone do knowledge and wis-

dom pertain; that alone can in itself judge of any thing; and
from it we take what account we make of ourselves and
what value we put upon ourselves. *For God allows no one
but himself to have high thoughts.*[55]

Let us cast down this presumption, the chief foundation of the tyranny of the malign spirit:[56] *God resisteth the
proud, and giveth grace to the humble.*[57] Intelligence exists
in all the gods, says Plato, and in very few men. [58]

Now there is, indeed, much consolation for the Christian man in seeing our mortal and feeble instruments so
fitly suited to our sacred and holy faith, that we employ
them in matters of a mortal and feeble nature; they are not
more accordantly or more forcibly appropriate to them.
Let us see, then, if man has at his command other reasons
stronger than those of Sebond, and if it is in him to arrive at
any certainty by argument and by reasoning. For St. Augustine, contending against people of this sort, has occasion
to upbraid them with inconsistency in that they hold those
parts of our belief to be false which our reason fails to establish; and, to show that there may be, and have been, many
things of which our reason is unable to assign the nature
and the causes, he puts before them certain well-known and
indubitable facts,[59] as to which man confesses that he has
no insight; and this he does, as every thing else, with careful
and keen research.[60] More must be done, and they must be
taught that, to make evident the weakness of their reason,
there is no need of selecting rare instances, and that it is so
defective and so blind that there is no facility[61] so clear that
it is clear enough for it; that ease and difficulty are as one to
it; that all subjects equally, and nature in general, disallow
its jurisdiction and intervention.

Apology for Raimond Sebond

What does the truth enjoin on us, when she enjoins us to fly from worldly philosophy?[62] When she so often inculcates in us that our wisdom is but folly before God;[63] that of all vanities the most vain is man; that a man who presumes on his knowledge knows not yet what it is to know;[64] and that a man who is nothing, if he believes himself to be something, deludes and deceives himself?[65] These sayings of the Holy Spirit express so clearly and so vividly what I desire to maintain, that I should need no other confirmation for those persons who would yield with all submission and obedience to its authority. But these others[66] choose to be scourged to their own cost, and will not suffer their reason to be opposed except by reason itself.

Let us, then, consider now man by himself, without external aid, armed only with his own weapons, and deprived of divine favour and recognition, in which consists all his honour, his strength, and the foundation of his existence. Let us see how much support he has in that fine equipment. Let him make me understand by the force of his reasoning upon what foundations he has set up the great advantages that he believes himself to have over other people. What has made him believe that the wonderful motions of the celestial vault, the eternal light of those luminaries revolving so proudly above his head, and the terrifying motions of the infinite sea were established and continued for many ages for his pleasure and for his service? Is it possible to imagine any thing so ridiculous as this wretched, paltry creature, who, being not even his own master, exposed to the offences of all things, declares himself master and ruler of the universe[67] of which it is not in his power to understand the smallest fragment, far less to govern it? And this prerogative that he attributes to himself, of being the only creature in this great structure who has the ability to recognise its beauty and its parts, the only one who can render thanks to the architect, and keep account of the income and outlay of the world—who has set the seal of this prerogative upon him? Let him show us the letters patent of this noble and great dignity. Were they granted only in favour of the wise? Few people are touched by them. Are fools and wicked men deserving of such extraordinary favour, and, being the worst part of the world, to be preferred before all the rest?[68] shall we believe him who says: *For whose sake, then, shall we say that the world was created? Surely for living beings, who have use of reason. These are gods and men, to whom assuredly nothing is superior.*[69] We can never sufficiently chastise the impudence of this coupling.

But, poor wretch, what has he in himself worthy of such a privilege? When we consider the incorruptible life of the heavenly bodies, their beauty, their grandeur, their continual motion by so exact a rule;

> when we contemplate the celestial vault of the boundless universe over our heads, and the brilliant stars clustered there, and when we meditate upon the revolutions of the moon and the sun;[70]

when we consider the domination and power that those bodies have, not only over our lives and the conditions of our fortunes,—

> For the actions and the lives of men depend on the stars.[71]

but even over our inclinations, our judgements, our wills,

which they govern, impel, and stir, at the mercy of their influences, as our reason teaches us and discovers,—

> and perceives that the stars, beheld from afar, govern us by their silent commanding laws, and the whole universe to be moved by changing relations, and successive destinies run through fixed signs;[72]

when we see that not only a man, not only a king, but monarchies, empires, and all this lower world move with the changes[73] of the slightest celestial motion;

> And what great changes are made by small movements . . . so great is this power that rules even kings.[74]

that our virtue, our vices, our ability and learning, and this very conception that we form of the power of the stars, and this comparison between them and ourselves—that all this comes through their means and their favour:—

> this one is mad with love and can swim across a sea and overthrow Troy; the fate of another is to make laws; see sons assassinate their fathers and fathers their sons, and armed brothers attack with mutual blows. Not due to us is this strife; such commotions and bloody chastisements, with lacerated limbs, are compelled by fate. This too is decreed, thus to weigh fate;[75]

if we hold from the disposition of heaven[76] such share of reason as we have, how can reason make us equal to that? how make subject to our knowledge its essence and its nature? All that we see in those bodies astounds us. *What appara-*

597

Apology for Raimond Sebond

tus, what instruments, what levers, what machines, what labourers achieved so great a work?[77] Why do we deprive them of soul and of life and of reason? Have we perceived in them some settled and senseless stupidity, we who have no commerce with them except that of obedience? Shall we say that we have found in no other creature than man the use of a reasoning mind? What of that? Have we seen any thing resembling the sun? Is it not existent because we have seen nothing resembling it? and are its movements non-existent because there is nothing like them? If what we have seen does not exist, our knowledge is wonderfully curtailed. *How limited are our minds!*[78] Are not these fancies of human vanity, to make of the moon a celestial earth,[79] to dream, like Anaxagoras, of mountains and valleys there?[80] to place human abodes and habitations there, and to plant colonies there for our convenience, as Plato does, and Plutarch? and to make of the earth a light-giving, luminous star? *Among other mortal infirmities is this: a blindness of the mind; and there is in us not merely a necessity of error, but a love of error.*[81] *The corruptible body presseth down the soul, and the earthly tabernacle weigheth down the mind that museth upon many things.*[82]

Presumption is our natural and original malady. The most unfortunate and frail of all creatures is man, and at the same time the most vain-glorious.[83] This creature feels and sees that it is lodged here amid the mire and filth of the world, fast bound and riveted to the worst, the most lifeless and debased part of the universe, on the lowest story of the lodging and the farthest removed from the celestial vault, with these other living beings of the worst condition of the three;[84] and it establishes itself in imagination above the circle of the moon, and brings heaven under its feet. It is through the vanity of this same imagination that he equals himself to God, that he attributes to himself divine conditions, that he selects and separates himself from the crowd of other creatures, shapes the shares of the animals, his fellow members and companions, and distributes among them such portion of faculties and force as seems good to him. How does he know, by the strength of his understanding, the internal and secret stirrings of the animals? By what comparison between them and ourselves does he determine the dulness which he attributes to them? When I play with my cat, who can say that it is not she amusing herself with me more than I with her?[85] Plato, in his picture of the golden age under Saturn, counts among the chief advantages of that time the communication that he[86] held with the beasts, from whom enquiring and receiving instruction, he learned the true qualities of each and the differences between them, whereby he gained a most perfect intelligence and wariness, and by means of this conducted his life far more fortunately than we could do.[87] Do we need any better proof to judge of human impudence with respect to the beasts? This great author was of opinion that, as regards the greater part of the bodily form which Nature has given them, she considered only the custom of such prognostications as in his day were drawn from them.[88]

This deficiency that prevents communication between them and us, why is it not in us as much as in them? It is a matter of conjecture whose fault it is that we do not understand one another; for we do not understand them any more than they us. By this same reasoning they may think us dullards as we think them. It is no great wonder if we do not understand them; neither do we understand the Basques and the Troglodytes. Nevertheless, some men have boasted of understanding them,[89] as Apollonius Thyaneus, Melampus, Tiresias, Thales, and others.[90] And since it is the fact, as the cosmographers say, that there are nations which accept a dog for their king, it must be that they give a definite interpretation to his voice and his motions.[91] We must take note of the parity that there is between us. We have some half understanding of their meaning; so have the beasts of ours, about to the same degree. They caress us, threaten us, and entreat us; and we them.

Touching another point, we very plainly perceive that there is full and complete communication between them, and that they understand one another—not only those of the same species, but also those of different species.

> And the dumb domestic animals, and the species
> of wild beasts are wont to utter distinct and varied cries,
> according as they feel fear or pain, or when joy arises.[92]

By a certain barking of the dog, the horse knows that he is angry; by a certain other tone of his, he is not startled. Even with the beasts that have no voices, from the interchange of services that we observe among them we readily infer some other means of communication; their motions converse and consult.

> For no very different reason, the inability to speak
> is seen to drive children to gesture.[93]

Why not, even as our mutes, dispute and argue and tell stories by signs? I have seen some of them so agile and so well fashioned for this, that in truth they fell in no wise

Apology for Raimond Sebond

short of perfection in ability to make themselves understood;
lovers show anger, are reconciled, entreat, give thanks, make
appointments, and, in short, say every thing with their eyes;

Even silence is wont to have prayers and words.[94]

What with the hands? We request, we promise, summon,
dismiss, threaten, beg, entreat, deny, refuse, question,
wonder, count, confess; we show repentance, fear, shame,
doubt; we inform, demand, incite, encourage, swear, testify,
accuse, condemn, absolve, insult, contemn, defy, affront,
flatter, applaud, bless, humiliate, deride, conciliate, commend, extol, congratulate, rejoice, complain; we express
sadness, discouragement, despair, astonishment; we explain,
keep silent—and what not?—with a variety and multiplicity
that rivals the tongue. With the head: we invite, send away,
avow, disavow, contradict, welcome, honour, venerate, disdain, question, reject, make merry, lament, caress, taunt,
submit, brag, exhort, threaten, affirm, enquire. What with
the eyebrows? What with the shoulders? There is no motion that does not speak, and in a language that is intelligible
without instruction, and in one that is common to all;
whence it follows that, seeing the variety and distinctive use
of other languages, this one should rather be judged the one
best adapted to the nature of man.[95] I pass over what special
necessity teaches, in the way of language, on the instant, to
those who have need of it; and the alphabets of the fingers,
and the grammars expressed by gestures, and the matters
of learning which are practised and expressed only by them;
and the nations which Pliny says have no other language.[96]

An ambassador from the city of Abdera, after having
addressed at great length King Agis of Sparta, said to him:

Apology for Raimond Sebond

"And now, Sire, what reply do you wish me to take back to our citizens?" "That I let you say whatever you chose and as much as you chose without ever saying a word."[97] Is not that a speaking silence, and very intelligible?

As for other matters, what sort of ability of our own do we not recognise in the operations[98] of animals? Is there a government managed with more order, with a greater diversity of labours and functions, and more persistently maintained, than that of the honey-bees? This arrangement of actions and occupations—can we imagine it to be carried on without reasoning and without foresight?

These acts and indications being observed, some declare that bees share divine intelligence and supernal emanations.[99]

The swallows, that we see, at the return of spring, prying into all the corners of our houses—do they search without judgement, and could they choose, without discretion, from a thousand places the one which is most convenient for their abode? And can the birds, in the beautiful and wonderful construction of their buildings, make use of a round shape rather than a square one,[100] of an obtuse angle rather than a right angle, without being aware of the condition and the consequences? Do they use, now water, now clay, without considering that the hardness[101] is softened by moistening it? Do they floor their palaces with moss or with down, without foreseeing that the tender members of their little ones will thus lie more softly and more at ease? Do they shelter themselves from the rain-bringing wind and set their abode toward the east, without knowing the different qualities of the wind and deeming that one is more salutary for them

Apology for Raimond Sebond

than another? Why does the spider make her web thicker in
one place and looser in another? why does she use now this
kind of knot, now that, if she can not deliberate and reflect
and decide?[102] We recognise clearly enough, in most of their
works, how far the animals excel us and how feebly our art
imitates them. We are conscious at the same time, in our
own clumsier works, of the faculties that we employ in
them, and that our minds make use in them of all their
powers; why do we not think that they[103] do as much? Why
do we attribute to I know not what innate and mechanical[104]
inclination the works which surpass all that we can produce by nature and by art? Wherein we unthinkingly give
them a very great advantage over us, in believing that Nature, from maternal kindness, accompanies them and guides
them, as by the hand, in all the actions and utilities of their
life; and that she abandons us to hazard and to fortune and
to seeking, by skill, the things necessary for our preservation, and therewith denies us the power to attain by any
education and effort of the mind the natural ability of the
beasts; so that their brutish stupidity surpasses, in respect
to all utilities, the utmost that our divine intelligence can
effect.

Truly, by this reckoning, we should be quite right in calling her a very unjust step-mother. But it is nothing of the
sort; our government,[105] is not so misshapen and irregular.
Nature has embraced universally all her creatures, and there
is not one that she has not very fully supplied with all the
means necessary for the preservation of his being;[106] for
those foolish complaints that I have heard men make[107]
(as the freedom of their opinions sometimes lifts them above
the clouds, then casts them down to the antipodes), that we

603

are the only animal left naked on the naked earth, bound, fettered, having only the spoil of others with which to arm and clothe itself, whereas nature has covered all other created things with shells, with husks, with bark, with hair, with wool, with quills, with leather, with down, with feathers, with scales, with fleeces, and with silk, according to the needs of their existence; has armed them with claws, with teeth, with horns, for attack and defence; and has herself even taught them what is proper to them—to swim, to run, to fly, to sting; whereas man knows neither how to walk, nor speak, nor eat, nor do any thing but weep, without instruction;

> Then the babe, like a sailor hurled out of the cruel billows, lies naked on the ground, speechless, lacking every further need of life, as soon as nature has brought him forth, by birth-throes, from his mother's womb into the region of light; and he fills the place with lugubrious wails; as well he may, since he must traverse in life so many sufferings of different kinds. But the flocks and the herds and the wild beasts grow up, nor need rattles, or the caressing and soothing accents of the fostering nurse; nor do they seek different garments according to the season; they need not arms or high walls to guard their belongings; for the earth itself and nature give forth abundantly all things for all;[108]

these complaints are unfounded; there is in the administration of the world a greater equality and a more uniform condition.[109] Our skin is provided as sufficiently as theirs with toughness to resist the attacks of weather; witness so

604

Apology for Raimond Sebond

many nations that have never yet known the use of clothes. Our ancient Gauls were scarcely clothed; nor are our neighbours, the Irish, beneath so cold a sky. But we can better judge of this by ourselves; for all those parts of the person which it pleases us to expose to the wind and weather[110] are found able to endure it: the face, the feet, the hands, the legs, the shoulders, the head, according as custom invites us. For if there were any feeble organ in us and one which, it seems, would be likely to dread coldness, it should be the stomach, where digestion takes place; our fathers went with it uncovered; and our ladies, tender and delicate as they are, have it sometimes half bare to the navel. The bands and swaddling-clothes of children are not necessary, either; and the Lacedæmonian mothers brought up their children with entire freedom of movement of their limbs, without binding or swathing them.[111] Our weeping is common to most of the other animals; and there are scarcely any of them which are not known to whine and moan a long time after their birth, inasmuch as it is a behaviour well suited to the weakness that they feel. As for the usage of eating, in us as in them it is natural and untaught;

> For every one feels how far he can make use of his
> peculiar powers.[112]

Who questions that a child, when he has attained the power of feeding himself, knows how to seek food? And the earth produces it without any husbandry and skill, and offers him enough for his necessities; and if not at all seasons, neither does she to the beasts: witness the provision that we see made by the ant and others for the sterile time of the year. Those nations that we recently discovered so abundantly provided, without labour, with natural food and drink, not needing to be prepared,[113] have taught us that bread is not our only sustenance, and that our mother Nature formerly supplied us plenteously with all that we needed, without tilling the ground; nay, as is probable, more amply and more richly than she does now, since we have blended therein our skill;—

> And the earth itself at first produced for mortals luxuriant crops and fruitful vineyards; of itself gave forth sweet fruits and fertile pastures; which things now increase with difficulty, fostered by our toil; and we exhaust our oxen and the strength of our husband-men,[114]—

the excess and unruliness of our appetite always outstripping all the devices that we seek for, to satisfy it.

As for arms, we have more natural ones than most other animals and more various motions of the limbs, and we have more service from them, by nature, and without teaching. Those men who are trained to fight naked—we see them rush into dangers similar to those that we encounter. If some beasts excel us in this respect, we excel many others. And skill in fortifying and protecting the body by borrowed means we have by a natural instinct and admonition. As proving that this is so,[115] the elephant sharpens and whets the tusks of which he avails himself in war (for he has some special ones for that purpose, which he spares and does not use at all for other services). When bulls begin to fight, they raise and scatter dust about them; the boars grind their tusks, and the ichneumon, when he is to come to grips with the crocodile, strengthens his body, besmears it, and encrusts it all over with mud very compactly pressed and well kneaded, as with a cuirass.[116] Why shall we not say that it is also natural for us to arm ourselves with wood and iron?

As for speech, it is certain that, if it be not natural, it is not necessary. Therefore, I believe that a child who had been brought up in absolute solitude, apart from all intercourse (which would be an experiment difficult to make), would have some kind of speech to express his thoughts; and it is not to be believed that Nature has denied us this gift which she has bestowed on many other animals; for what else than speech is the faculty which we see in them of complaining, of rejoicing, of calling upon one another for help, of inviting one another to love, as they do by the use of their voices? How can they not speak among themselves? They truly speak to us, and we to them. In how many ways do we speak to our dogs? And they answer us. We talk with them with other language, with other modes of calling, than with birds, with hogs, with oxen, with horses, and we change our form of speech according to the kind.[117]

So in their brown troop, one ant touches muzzle with another, perchance to spy out their way and their fortune.[118]

It seems to me that Lactantius attributes to beasts, not speech alone, but laughter as well.[119] And the difference in language which is seen amongst us, according to the difference in country, is found also with animals of the same species. Aristotle cites in this connection the different songs of partridge, according to the situation of their dwelling-place.[120]

Apology for Raimond Sebond

> Divers birds utter at different times noises widely different; and some of them change their hoarse songs with the seasons.[121]

But it is still to be known what language that child would speak; and what is said of it by conjecture has not much probability. If it is urged against this opinion,[122] that those who are born deaf do not speak, I answer that it is not solely because they are unable to receive instruction in speech through the ear, but rather because the sense of hearing, of which they are deprived, is related to that of speech, and they are connected by a natural union; in such a way that, whatever we may utter, we must needs utter it first to ourselves, and make it heard within, to our own ears, before sending it forth to the ears of others.

I have said all this to establish the resemblance that there is in human things, and to bring us back and add us to the general crowd. We are neither above nor below the others; all that is beneath the sky, says the wise man, incurs a like law and fortune:[123]

> All are hampered by their fatal shackles.[124]

There is some difference. There are ranks and degrees; but it is within the form of one same nature:

> every thing proceeds by its own law, and all preserve their distinctive differences by a fixed pact of nature.[125]

Man must be restrained and marshalled within the barriers of this control. Wretched being, he has indeed no power to overleap them; he is shackled and held fast; he is

Apology for Raimond Sebond

subject to the same obligations as the other creatures of his class, and in a very mediocre position, without any prerogative, any real and essential preëxcellence. That which he attributes to himself in thought and by fancy has neither body nor perceptibleness;[126] and if it be true that he alone of all animals has this freedom of imagination and this license of thought, representing to him what is, what is not, what he desires, the false and the true, it is a privilege which he buys dear, and upon which he has little reason to pride himself; for thence springs the chief source of the evils which crowd upon him: sin, disease, irresolution, disquiet, despair.

I say then, to return to my subject, that there is no ground for thinking that the beasts do by innate and enforced inclination the same things that we do by our choice and skill. We ought to conclude from like manifestations like faculties, and consequently to confess that the same reasoning, the same way that we follow in working, is also that of animals. Why, when we are not conscious of any such condition, do we imagine in them this natural constraint? Add to which that it is more honourable to be put in the way, and compelled, to act in orderly fashion, by natural and inevitable impulse, and more nearly approaching divinity, than to act rightly from hasty and fortuitous liberty; and safer to leave to Nature than to ourselves the reins of our guidance. The vanity of our presumption causes us to like better to owe our capacity to our powers rather than to her liberality; and we enrich the other animals with natural possessions, and give those over to them, that we may honour and ennoble ourselves with acquired possessions— very foolishly, it seems to me, for I should prize quite as highly favours wholly mine and inborn, as those which I had begged and sought from education.

It is not in our power to acquire a more noble advantage[127] than to be favoured by God and by nature. Consequently, the fox, of whom the people of Thrace make use when they desire to undertake to cross on the ice a frozen river, and send him before them to that end—if we should see him, on the brink of the stream, put his ear very close to the ice, to perceive whether he hears at a long or a short distance the rustle of the water flowing beneath, draw back, or go forward, according as he thus learns the greater or less thickness of the ice, should we not be justified in thinking that there passes through his head the same reasoning that there would be in ours, and that it is a ratiocination and conclusion derived from natural sense: that which makes a noise is moving; that which moves is not frozen; that which is not frozen is liquid; and that which is liquid yields under a weight?[128] For to attribute this simply to a keenness of the sense of hearing, without reasoning and without consequence, is a wild fancy and can not enter our minds. In like manner should be judged the many sorts of wiles and devices with which the beasts protect themselves from our attacks upon them. And if we are inclined to make some advantage of the fact that it is in our power to capture them, to employ them for our service and use them at our pleasure, this is only the same advantage that we have over one another. We have our slaves in this state. And the Climacides—were they not women in Syria who, stooping on all fours, served as foot-stools and ladders for the ladies to mount into their coaches?[129] And the greater number of free persons surrender their life and their existence, for

Apology for Raimond Sebond

very slight benefits, to the power of others. The wives and concubines of the Thracians contend as to which shall be chosen to be killed on the tomb of her husband.[130] Have tyrants ever failed to find enough men sworn to their service, some of them in addition enforcing the obligation to accompany them to death as in life? Whole armies have thus been bound to their leaders.[131] The form of the oath in the untrained company of fighters to extremity[132] contained these promises: "We swear to allow ourselves to be fettered, burned, beaten, and killed with the sword, and to suffer all that regular gladiators suffer from their master, pledging most religiously both body and soul to his service":[133]—

> Burn my head with flame, if you will, and wound my body with a sword, and scourge my back with a rope.[134]

This was a pledge, indeed; and yet, in a certain year there were ten thousand men who entered into it and lost their lives in such wise. When the Scythians buried their king, they strangled upon his body his favourite concubine, his cup-bearer, his equerry, his chamberlain, his usher, and his cook. And on his anniversary they killed fifty horses and mounted on them fifty pages whom they had impaled along the spine to the neck, and left them, thus set in order, around the tomb.[135]

The men who serve us do it more cheaply and for less careful and less kind treatment than that which we give to birds and horses and dogs. What trouble do we not put ourselves to, for their benefit? It does not seem to me that the meanest servants readily do for their masters what princes think it an honour to do for these beasts. Diogenes seeing his kinsmen endeavouring to redeem him from servitude, "They are fools," he said; "he who looks after me and feeds me is my servant";[136] and they who maintain beasts ought rather to be said to serve them than to be served by them.

And also the beasts have this nobler quality, that no lion ever subjected himself to another lion, nor a horse to another horse, from lack of spirit.[137] As we hunt beasts, so do lions and tigers hunt men; and they have a similar mode of action against one another: dogs against hares, pike against tench, swallows against locusts, sparrow-hawks against blackbirds and larks.

> The stork feeds her young on serpents and on lizards found in the open fields . . . but the birds of the noble household of Jupiter hunt hares or wild goats in the glade.[138]

We share the fruit of our hunting with our dogs and birds, as we do the labour and the skill; and near Amphipolis in Thrace, the hunters and wild falcons share their booty in equal halves;[139] likewise, by the Palus Mæotides,[140] if the fisherman does not leave for the wolves, honestly, half of his catch, they immediately tear his nets.[141] And as we have a sort of hunt which is conducted more by cunning than by strength, like that with snares,[142] and fish-hooks, so may be seen similar methods amongst the beasts. Aristotle says that the cuttle-fish ejects from her throat a gut as long as a line,[143] which she casts afar on loosing it, and draws back into herself when she chooses; when she sees some little fish drawing near, she lets him bite the end of this gut, she lying hidden in the sand or the mud, and draws it in bit by bit until the little fish is so near her that with a leap she can catch it.[144]

In the matter of strength, there is no animal in the world exposed to so many injuries as man: there is no need of a whale, an elephant, a crocodile, or any other such animal of which a single one is capable of destroying a great number of men: lice were enough to make vacant the dictatorship of Sylla;[145] the heart and the life of a great and triumphant emperor is the breakfast of a little worm. Why do we say that in man it is learning and knowledge, built up by study and reasoning, that discriminates things useful for his being and for the cure of his maladies from those that are not so; that knows the virtues of rhubarb and polypody? And when we see the goats of Candia, if they have been wounded by an arrow, select, from amongst a million herbs, dittany to cure them;[146] and the tortoise, when she has eaten a snake, instantly seek wild marjoram to purge herself; the dragon rub and brighten his eyes with fennel; storks give themselves clysters of sea-water; elephants pull out, not only from their own bodies and those of their companions, but from the bodies of their masters also (witness the elephant of King Porus, whom Alexander defeated[147]), the javelins and darts which have been cast at them in the fight, and pull them out so dexterously that we could not do it with as little pain[148]—why should we not say that this is learning and skill? For to allege for their disparagement that it is solely through the teaching and guidance of nature that they know these things is not to take them from their title to learning and skill; it is to attribute it to them with more reason than to ourselves, from the honour of so infallible a school-mistress.

Apology for Raimond Sebond

Chrysippus,[149] although in every thing else as scornful a judge of the condition of animals as any other philosopher whatever, considering the movements of the dog who, finding himself at the junction of three roads, being in quest of his master whom he has lost, or in pursuit of some prey that is flying from him, tries one road after another, and after having assured himself about two, and found in them no trace of what he seeks, darts into the third without hesitation—he is forced to confess that in that dog some such reasoning as this takes place: "I have followed my master's trail to these crossroads; he must necessarily have gone on by one of these three roads; he did not go by this one or by that one, therefore he must infallibly have gone by this other"; and that, being assured by this conclusion and reasoning, he no longer uses his scent on the third road, nor searches it, but lets himself be carried on by the force of reason.[150] This purely logical course and this employment of propositions divided and joined and of the just enumeration of parts[151]—is it not as well that the dog should know it of himself as learn it from Trapezuntius?[152]

Yet the beasts are not incapable of being instructed in our way. We teach blackbirds, crows, magpies, parrots, to talk; and the facilities that we recognise in ourselves, with which we make their voice and breath so flexible and manageable as to shape it and confine it to a certain number of letters and syllables, prove that they have a reasoning faculty within, which makes them thus teachable and willing to learn. I think that every one has seen often enough the many kinds of tricks that those who carry dancing dogs about teach them: the dances, in which they do not miss a single cadence of the tone they hear; many different movements and leaps which they are made to perform at the word of command; but I observe with greater wonder the mental action, which is, however, common enough, of the dogs that blind men make use of in the country and in the towns; I have noticed how they stop at certain doors where they are accustomed to receive alms; how they avoid the encounter of coaches and carts, even when, so far as concerns themselves, they have room enough to pass. I have seen one, going along a town-trench, leave a plain smooth path and take a worse one, to lead his master away from the trench. How had that dog been made to understand that it was his office to regard solely the safety of his master, and to neglect his own ease to serve him? And how did he know that a certain path, quite wide enough for him, would not be so for a blind man? Would all this be possible without ratiocination?

We should not forget what Plutarch says that he saw a dog do at the theatre of Marcellus, in the presence of the Emperor Vespasian the father. This dog was in the service of an exhibiter of dogs, who gave a play of several scenes and several characters, and the dog had his part in it. Amongst other things, he had to pretend for a time to be dead from having swallowed a certain drug; after having eaten the bread which passed for the drug, he began soon to tremble and stagger as if he were giddy; finally, stretching himself out and stiffening himself, as if dead, he let himself be pulled and dragged from one place to another, as the plot of the play required; and then, when he knew that it was time, he began first to move, little by little, as if he were coming out of a profound sleep, and, raising his head, gazed here and there in a way that amazed all the spectators.[153]

Apology for Raimond Sebond

The oxen that were employed in the royal gardens of Susa to water them and to turn certain great wheels for drawing water, to which buckets were attached (as is often seen in Languedoc), were ordered to make a hundred turns a day; they were so accustomed to that number that it was impossible, by any compulsion, to make them draw one turn more; and, having completed their task, they stopped short. We are at the age of adolescence before we can count up to a hundred, and we have just discovered nations which have no knowledge of numbers.

There is even more reasoning employed in teaching others than in being taught. Now, leaving aside what Democritus thought and proved,—that we have learned from the beasts most of the arts: as from the spider to spin and sew, from the swallow to build, music from the swan and the nightingale, and from many animals, by imitating them, to practise medicine,—Aristotle holds that nightingales teach their young to sing, and spend time and pains about it; whence it happens that those we bring up in cages, which have not been able to go to school to their parents, lose much of the charm of their song. We can judge by this that it is improved by teaching and study. And even among those that are free, it is not one and the same; each one has acquired it according to his capacity; and in the eagerness of their learning, they strive with such gallant rivalry to excel each other, that sometimes the one vanquished falls dead, his breath failing him rather than his voice. The younger ones thoughtfully ponder and try to imitate certain broken notes. The pupil listens to the instruction of his tutor and very carefully takes account of it; they fall silent, now one, now the other; we hear mistakes corrected and perceive some reproof from the tutor.[154] I once saw (says Arrius) an elephant who had a cymbal hung on each leg and another fastened to his trunk, at the sound of which all the others danced in a circle, rising and stooping at certain cadences, as the instrument guided them; and he had pleasure in listening to that music.[155] In the public shows in Rome there were frequently seen elephants trained to move and to dance at the sound of the voice, in dances with many complications and breaks and varying cadences very difficult to learn. Some have been seen, when alone, to rehearse their lesson and practise carefully and studiously, in order not to be scolded and beaten afterwards by their masters.[156]

But the story of the magpie, whereof we have even Plutarch for authority, is strange. She was in the shop of a barber in Rome, and did wonders in the way of imitating with her voice whatever she heard. It happened one day that some trumpeters stopped in front of the shop and blew there a long time. Afterward, and all the next day, behold this magpie thoughtful, silent, and melancholy, at which everybody marvelled; and they thought that the noise of the trumpets had thus deafened and benumbed her, and that, at the same time with her hearing, her voice was lost. But at last they found that it was profound study and a withdrawal into herself, her thought exercising itself and preparing her voice to reproduce the notes of those trumpets; so that the first sound she uttered was to express perfectly their beginnings, their pauses, and their shifting scales; having, from this new lesson, quitted and disdained all that she could accomplish before.[157] I must not fail to adduce also this other example, of a dog which this same Plutarch says that he saw when he was on shipboard (for, as to order, I am well aware that I confuse it; but I am no more heedful of that, in arranging these examples, than in the rest of all my doings); this dog, being desirous to get the oil that was at the bottom of a jug, where he could not reach it with his tongue because of the narrow mouth of the vessel, sought for some stones, and put them in this jug until he had made the oil rise near to the edge, where he could get at it.[158] What was this, if not the act of a very wily intelligence? They say that the ravens of Barbary do the same thing, when the water they wish to drink is too low.

This action is somewhat akin to what a king of their nation,[159] Juba, told about elephants: that when, by the craft of those who hunt them, one of them finds himself trapped in certain deep pits prepared for them, which are covered with slender branches to deceive them, his fellows, with all diligence, bring many stones and pieces of wood to help him to climb out.[160] But this animal in so many other ways approaches human intelligence that, if I chose to follow out in detail what experience has taught of him, I should easily gain belief for what I am wont to maintain,[161] that more difference may be found between one man and another than between such an animal and such a man. The keeper of an elephant in a private house in Syria robbed him at every meal of half the ration which had been ordered for him. One day the master chose to feed him himself, and poured into his manger the full measure of barley which he had prescribed for his sustenance. The elephant, regarding his keeper with an angry eye, separated with his trunk and put aside the half, thus indicating the wrong that had been done him.[162] And another, having a keeper who mixed stones

Apology for Raimond Sebond

with his food, to increase the measure of it, went to the kettle in which the meat for his[163] dinner was boiling and filled it with ashes. These are individual instances; but every one has seen, and every one knows, that in all the armies which were maintained in Oriental countries, one of the greatest sources of strength consisted of elephants, from whom results were obtained incomparably greater than we now obtain with our artillery, which very nearly takes their place in a ranged battle (this is readily discerned by those who are familiar with ancient histories):—

> their ancestors were trained to serve Tyrian Hannibal and our own generals and the Molossian king, and to carry cohorts on their backs, a part of the armament, and towers that entered into the fight.[164]

They must needs be quite assured of the confidence that those animals deserve and of their intelligence, since they give over to them the vanguard of an army, where the slightest check they might cause, by the great size and weight of their bodies, the slightest fright that might have made them turn round upon their own people, would have been enough to ruin every thing; and fewer instances are known when this has happened, that they fell back upon their troops, than of those when we fall back upon one another and put ourselves to rout. They were entrusted, not with one simple evolution, but with different parts of the battle. As the Spaniards, in the recent conquest of the Indies, did with their dogs, whom they paid and to whom they gave a share in the booty; and those animals displayed as much of skill and judgement in pursuing and checking their victory, in charging or falling back according to the circumstances, in distinguishing friends from enemies, as they did of ardour and fierceness.[165]

We wonder more at unfamiliar things than at common ones, and give more weight to them; and but for that, I should not have spent my time on this long record; for, in my opinion, he who shall observe closely what we commonly see in the animals that live among us may find in them manifestations as wonderful as those which we gather from other countries and ages.[166] It is one and the same nature pursuing its course. He who should intelligently apprehend its present condition could safely deduce therefrom both the whole future and the whole past. I have seen amongst us, in past days, men who have come from distant countries, and, because we did not at all understand their language, and because, moreover, their mode of life and behaviour and clothing were entirely different from ours, who of us did not regard them as savages and brutes? Who did not attribute to stupidity and dulness that they were speechless, without knowledge of the French language, without knowledge of our hand-kissings and our sinuous bowings,[167] our carriage and our demeanour, from which, without fail, human nature should take pattern? Whatever seems strange to us we condemn, and what we do not understand; as happens with the judgement that we form of the beasts. They have many qualities which resemble ours; of these, by comparison, we can form some conjecture; but as to those that are peculiar to them, how do we know what they are? Horses, dogs, oxen, sheep, birds, and most of the animals that live with us, recognise our voice, and let themselves be guided by it; so, too, did Crassus's lamprey, and came to him when he called him; and so also do the eels that

620

Apology for Raimond Sebond

are in the fountain of Arethusa.[168] And I have seen many fishponds where the fishes come in shoals, to eat, at a certain call from those who feed them.

> They have names, and each one comes to his master when summoned by his voice.[169]

We can judge by that. We may say also that elephants have some participation in religion, because, after their ablutions and cleansings, we see them lifting their trunks like arms, and, keeping their eyes fixed on the rising sun, stand a long time in meditation and contemplation at certain hours of the day, from their own inclination, without instruction and without precept.[170] But because we see no such manifestation in other animals, we can not therefore assert that they are without religion, and we can form no opinion about what is hidden from us. As we perceive to some extent in that action which, because it resembles our own, Cleanthes commented on: he says that he saw some ants go from their hill, bearing the body of a dead ant, toward another hill from which several ants came out to meet them, as if to parley with them; and after they had been together some time, the latter went back to consult, you may suppose, with their fellow citizens, and in like manner they made two or three trips because of the difficulty of the capitulation; finally, the last-comers brought to the others a worm from their burrow, as if for the ransom of the dead, which worm the first-comers took upon their backs and carried it home with them, leaving the body of the dead ant with the others.[171] This is the interpretation that Cleanthes gave of this scene, deposing thereby that creatures that have no voice do not fail to have mutual intercourse and communication, in which it is our misfortune that we do not participate; and for that reason, it is foolish for us to express an opinion about it.

Now they achieve still other effects, which greatly surpass our ability, which we are so far from being able to reach by imitation, that even in thought we can not conceive them. Many[172] maintain that in that great and last naval battle which Antonius lost to Augustus, his admiral galley[173] was stopped in mid-course by the little fish which the Latins call *remora*, because of this property it has of arresting every sort of vessel to which it attaches itself. And the Emperor Caligula sailing with a great fleet along the coast of Roumania, his galley alone was stopped short by this same fish, which he caused to be removed from the keel of his vessel, to which it was attached, very much vexed that so small an animal could be stronger than the sea and the winds and the compulsion of all his oars, simply by clinging with its beak to the galley (for it is a shell-fish); and he was also amazed, not without good reason, that, when it was brought aboard the vessel, it had no longer the strength that it had outside.[174] A citizen of Cyzicum formerly gained the reputation of being an excellent mathematician[175] from having learned about the property of the hedge-hog, that he has openings in his burrow in diverse places and toward diverse winds, and foreseeing from what quarter the wind will next come, he closes the hole on that side; observing which, the citizen brought to his city infallible predictions of the wind which would blow next.[176] The chameleon takes the colour of the place where he lies; but the polypus gives himself what colour he pleases, according to circumstances, to conceal himself from what he fears and to deceive what he seeks; in the chameleon it is a passive change, in the polypus an active one.[177] We experience some changes of colour from fear, anger, shame, and other passions, which alter the hue of our faces, but it is involuntarily,[178] as in the chameleon; it is in the power of the yellows[179] to make us yellow, but it is not in that of our will. Now, these qualities which we detect in other animals, greater than our own, bear witness to some superior faculty in them, which is hidden from us; as, it is probable, are many others of their properties and powers of which no appearances reach us.

Of all the predictions of past time the oldest and surest were those which were derived from the flight of birds. We have nothing like it, or so wonderful. That regularity and order in the movement of the wings, from which the consequences of future things were derived, must surely have been guided by some superior influence to so noble an operation; for it is wresting the fact[180] to attribute this great result to some natural command, without there being intelligence, accord, and reasoning in that which produces it; and it is an opinion manifestly false. To prove that it is so: the torpedo-fish has the property, not only of benumbing the limbs that touch her, but through nets and seine[181] she transmits a benumbed stiffness to the hands of those who poke and stir her. Truly, they say, furthermore, that, if you pour water upon her, you feel this sensation rising up against the stream, even to the hand, and deadening the touch through the water. This power is wonderful, but it is not useless to the torpedo; she is conscious of it and uses it, since, to capture the prey that she seeks, we see her hide herself under the mud in such wise that the other fish swimming above, stricken and paralyzed by her coldness, fall into her power. The cranes, the swallows, and other birds of passage, changing their abode according to the seasons of the year, show plainly the knowledge they have of their faculty of divination, and put it to use. Hunters assure us that, to select from a number of pups the one that should be kept as being the best, we need only put the mother in a position herself to select it; for, if they are taken out of the kennel, the first one that she brings back there will always be the best; or, if we pretend to surround the kennel with fire on all sides, it will be that one of the pups to whose aid she runs first. Whence it appears that they have a power of prognostication which we have not, or they have some faculty of judging of their offspring, keener than we have.[182]

The condition of beasts in birth, in begetting, feeding, acting, moving, living, and dying being so similar to our own, all diminishment that we make of their inciting agents,[183] all that we add to our condition to make it appear superior to theirs, can in no wise come from the reasoning of our intelligence. As regards the proper ordering of our health, physicians put before us the example of the beasts' manner of living; and this saying has always been in the mouths of the people:—

> Keep warm the head and the feet;
> In every way live like the beasts.

Generation is the chiefest of natural actions. We have a certain disposition of members which is more suitable for our purpose; yet they recommend us to fall in line with the brutes and adopt their posture and method, as being more effectual:

> For commonly 'tis thought that wives conceive

Apology for Raimond Sebond

More readily in manner of four-footed beast,
Because with breasts beneath and buttocks up,
The seeds can take their proper places.[184]

And they condemn as harmful those indelicate and insolent
motions which the women have introduced into it of their
own invention; referring them to the more modest and
sedate example and usage of the animals of their sex:

For the woman hinders and resists conception
If too joyously she treats the Venus of the man,
With haunches heaving and all her bosom yielding
From plowshare's even course she throws the furrow,
And from its proper place deflects the seed.[185]

If it be justice to render to every one what is his due, the
beasts, who serve, love, and defend their benefactors, and
who pursue and handle roughly strangers and those who
offend them, represent in so doing some imitations of our
justice, as they likewise do in observing a very equitable im-
partiality in distributing whatever they may have among
their little ones. As for friendship, it is with them beyond
comparison more lively and more faithful than with men.
Hircanus, the dog of King Lysimathus, when his master
died, remained obstinately on his bed, refusing to drink or
eat; and the day that they burned the body, he suddenly
ran and jumped into the flames, in which he was burned.[186]
As did also the dog of one Pyrrhus, for he did not budge
from lying on his master's bed after he had died; and when
they took him[187] away, he let himself be carried along with
him, and finally rushed into the fire in which they were

burning his master's body. There are certain affectionate tendencies that are sometimes born in us without the counsel of reason, which are due to a haphazard temerity that others call sympathy; beasts, like us, are capable of them; we see horses form a sort of friendship with one another, to the point of putting us to trouble in making them live or travel apart; we see them fasten their affections upon a particular colour among their companions, as upon a particular face, and when they fall in with it, immediately approach it with flattering demeanour and demonstrations of good-will; and toward some other aspect, show loathing and hatred. Animals, like ourselves, have some choice in their loves and make selection among their females. They are not exempt from our jealousies, or from our extreme and irreconcilable desires.

Carnal longings are either natural and necessary, like drinking and eating; or natural and not necessary, like commerce with females; or they are neither natural nor necessary; of the last sort are nearly all those of mankind—they are all superfluous or artificial.[188] For it is wonderful how little Nature needs to satisfy her, how little she leaves for us to desire. The cooking in our kitchen is not of her appointment.[189] The Stoics say that a man could subsist on one olive a day. Our delicacy of taste about wines is not of her teaching, nor the surcharge that we add to our amorous appetites,—

> she (Nature) never demands a woman descended from a great consul.[190]

These unnatural longings which ignorance of good and a false opinion have instilled into us are so very numerous that they expel almost all the natural ones; neither more nor less than if, in a large city, there were so great a number of strangers that they forced out all the native-born inhabitants, or suppressed their ancient authority and power, usurping it completely and taking possession of it. The animals are much more controlled than we are, and restrain themselves with more moderation within the limits that Nature has prescribed for us; but not so strictly that they have not some consonance with our dissoluteness. And just as we have heard of men being impelled by furious lusts to animal loves, these have sometimes been known to be enamoured of human beings, and to indulge their abnormal affections for others of a different species. Witness the elephant which was a rival with Aristophanes the grammarian in the affection of a young flower-girl in the city of Alexandria, and in no wise yielded to him in the attentions of a very passionate suit; for, going through the market-place where they sold fruits, this beast would seize some of them with his trunk and offer them to her. He would not lose sight of her more than he possibly could, and would occasionally thrust his trunk into her bosom under her cape to feel her breasts. They tell also of a dragon in love with a maid, of a goose enamoured of a boy in the town of Asopus, and of a ram that danced attendance on Glaucia the fluteplayer. Barbary apes are constantly known to be madly enamoured of women.

Among certain animals the males are known to be addicted to loving those of their own sex. Oppianus and others cite examples to show how animals in their marriages, respect the laws of kinship; but experience very often shows us the contrary:

Apology for Raimond Sebond

The heifer thinks no shame her sire to bear
On willing back; the horse his filly leaps;
The goat will pair with them he has begot;
Birds breed by them by whom themselves are bred.[191]

Of malicious cunning was there ever a more manifest example than that of a mule of the philosopher Thales, who, with a load of salt, having followed a river and by chance stumbled in it, so that the bags he bore were all wet, having perceived that the salt, being wetted by this, made his burden lighter, never failed, as soon as he came to any stream, to plunge in with his load; until his master, detecting his mischievousness, ordered that he should be laden with wool; whereupon, finding himself out in his reckoning, he ceased to make use of that trick?[192] There are many animals which naturally present the aspect of our avarice; for we observe in them an extreme eagerness to pounce upon all that they can and to conceal it carefully, although they make no use of it.

As for good husbandry, they not only surpass us in the foresight of storing up and saving for the future, but they have, moreover, many parts of the knowledge which is necessary thereto. The ants spread their grain and seed outside, on a smooth place, to air, and freshen and dry them when they see them beginning to get mildewed and to smell musty. But the caution and foresight they use in gnawing the grain of wheat surpasses all thought of human prudence. Because the wheat does not keep always dry and sound, but softens, moistens, and dissolves as if in milk, proceeding toward germination and reproduction; for fear lest it become seed, and lose its nature and property as a

628

storehouse for their subsistence, they bite off the end at which it is wont to sprout.[193]

As for war, which is the mightiest and most magnificent of human actions, I should like to know if we choose to make use of it as an argument in favour of any prerogative, or, on the contrary, as testifying to our weakness and imperfection; for, truly, in the ability to overcome and kill one another, to despoil and injure our own species, there is not much to make it desired by those beasts who have it not.

> When did a stronger lion ever deprive a lion of life? In what forest did a boar ever expire under the teeth of a stronger boar?[194]

But they are not, however, universally exempt from it; witness the furious encounters of honey-bees, and the enterprises of the chiefs of the two opposing armies:—

> often between two kings great strife begins to be moved, and there can immediately be discerned from afar the anger of the common people, their hearts eager for the fight.[195]

I never read this divine description that it does not seem to me that I there read a portrayal of human folly and futility. For those upheavals of war which astound us with their dreadfulness; that storm of sound and outcries,—

> Then the glitter rises to the sky, and the whole earth around gleams with brass, and a noise is raised by the mighty trampling of men, and the mountains, struck by the shouting, reverberate the sound to the stars of heaven;[196]—

629

that terrifying array of so many thousands of armed men; all
that fury and ardour and courage—one could laugh in noting by what futile causes it is set in motion, and by what
trivial causes suppressed;

It is narrated that Greece was hurled into a long
war against a barbarian country for the love of Paris;[197]

all Asia was ruined and destroyed by the wars arising from
the lust of Paris. The craving of one single man, anger,
sensuality, personal jealousy,—causes which ought not to
excite two fish-wives to blows,[198]—are the soul and the motive of all this vast disturbance. Shall we believe the very
men who are the chief authors and movers? Let us listen to
the greatest, the most victorious Emperor, and the most
powerful, that ever lived, making merry, and turning into a
jest, very amusingly and wittily, many battles hazarded
both by sea and land, the blood and lives of five hundred
thousand men who followed his fortunes, and the strength
and riches of two parts of the world, all exhausted in the
service of his undertakings:—

> Quod futuit Glaphyran Antonius, hanc mihi pœnam
>   Fulvia constituit se quoque uti futuam.
> Fulviam ego ut futuam? Quid, si me Manius oret
>   Pædicem, faciam? Non puto, si sapiam.
> Aut futue, aut pugnemus, ait. Quid, si mihi vita
>   Charior est ipsa mentula? Signa canant.[199]

(I make use of my Latin with a free mind, from the permission you[200] have given me about this.) Now this great body,
with so many aspects and motions, which seems to menace
heaven and earth,—

Apology for Raimond Sebond

As numerous as the waves that roll in the Marmorean sea of Libya, when fell Orion is hidden by the storms of winter, or as the numberless ears of corn that are parched by the young sun in the plains of the Hermus, or in the yellow fields of Lycia, the shields resound, and the earth trembles, agitated by the tread of feet,[201]—

this furious monster with so many arms and so many heads is still man, feeble, unfortunate, and miserable. It is but an ant-hill stirred up and excited;[202]

The black troop goes over the fields.[203]

A gust of adverse wind, the croaking of a flight of ravens, the stumble of a horse, the chance passage of an eagle, a dream, a word, a sign, a morning mist, suffice to overthrow and prostrate it. Let but a ray of sunlight strike its face: lo! it melts away and vanishes; let a little dust be blown in its eyes, as with the bees of our poet: lo! all the standards, the legions, and the great Pompey himself at their head, are broken and shattered; for it was he, if I remember right, whom Sertorius defeated in Spain with that fine weapon,[204] the like of which has served others also, as, for instance, Eumenes against Antigonus,[205] and Surena against Crassus.[206]

This stir of passion and these fierce fights are quieted if a little dust be thrown on them.[207]

Let us but loose some of our flies upon it:[208] they will have both the strength and the courage to scatter it. Within recent memory, the Portuguese besieging the city of Tamly in the province of Xiatime, its inhabitants carried to the walls a great quality of hives, in which they are rich, and with fire drove the bees so vigorously upon the enemy that, unable to sustain their assaults and stings, they were put to rout. Thus victory and the freedom of the city were attained by this novel succour, with such fortune that, on returning from the fight, they found there was not a single one[209] missing.

The souls of emperors and cobblers are cast in the same mould. Considering the importance of the acts of princes and their weight, we are persuaded that they are induced by causes as weighty and important. We are deceived: they are pushed forward and drawn back[210] in their movements by the same springs that move us. The same reason that makes us wrangle with a neighbour brings on a war between princes; the same reason that makes us whip a lackey, acting upon a king, makes him ruin a province. Their will moves as quickly as ours, but they have more power.[211] Similar desires stir in a worm and in an elephant.[212]

As for fidelity, there is no animal in the world so treacherous as man. Our histories narrate the earnestness with which certain dogs have followed up the death of their masters. King Pyrrhus, having observed a dog that was watching a dead man, and having learned that for three days he had been performing that office, ordered the body to be buried and took the dog with him. One day, when he was present at the general muster of his army, this dog, having espied his master's murderers, rushed upon them with great barking and fierceness of anger, and by this first indication led the way to vengeance for that murder, which very soon after was done by course of justice.[213] Not less did the dog of Hesiod the sage, who convicted the children of Ganystor of Naupactus of the murder committed on the body of his master. Another dog, set to guard a temple at Athens, having espied a sacrilegious thief who was carrying away the finest jewels, began to bark at him as loud as he could; but, the guardians not being awakened by that, he undertook to follow him, and when daylight came, he kept a little farther away from him without losing sight of him. If the man offered him food, he would have none of it; and on the other travellers that he met on the road he fawned and wagged his tail,[214] and took from their hands what they gave him to eat. If his thief stopped to sleep, he stopped, too, at the same place. The story of this dog having reached the ears of the church-guardians, they followed on his track, asking news of a dog of that breed;[215] and at last they found him in the city of Cromyon, and the thief also, whom they took back to the city of Athens, where he was punished. And the judges, in recognition of that useful service, ordered from the public store a certain measure of wheat for the dog's sustenance, and bade the priests take charge of him. Plutarch witnesses to this story as well authenticated, and as having happened in his time.

As for gratitude (for it seems to me that we need to bring this word into favour), this one example will suffice here, which Apion[216] narrates as having been himself a witness of it. One day, he says, when the populace were given the pleasure of combats between several unfamiliar beasts, and chiefly lions of unusual size, there was one of these who, by his fierce bearing, by the strength and size of his limbs, and by his superb and terrifying roaring, attracted the eyes of all present. Among the other slaves who were exhibited to the people in this combat of beasts was one Androdus[217] of

633

Apology for Raimond Sebond

Dacia, who belonged to a Roman noble of consular rank. This lion, having spied him from afar, first stopped short, as if struck with wonder, then quietly approached him, in a gentle and peaceable way, as if beginning to recognise him. This done, and having assured himself of what he sought, he began to wag his tail after the fashion of dogs fawning on their masters, and to kiss and lick the hands and thighs of that poor wretch, who was half dead and beside himself with fright. Androdus having recovered his wits by reason of the lion's benignity, and having observed him fixedly and recognised him,[218] it was a singular pleasure to see the caresses and rejoicings that they interchanged with each other. At which the populace having shouted with joy, the Emperor sent for this slave, to hear from him the cause of so strange an occurrence. He told him a novel and wonderful tale.

"My master," he said, "being proconsul in Africa, I was compelled, by the cruelty and severity with which he treated me, causing me to be beaten every day, to escape from him and run away. And to conceal myself securely from a personage whose authority in the province was so great, I thought it best to get to the solitary places and the sandy and uninhabitable regions of that country, resolved, if the means of sustaining life should fail me, to find some way of killing myself. The sun being excessively hot at noon, and the heat insupportable, having come upon a hidden and inaccessible cavern, I entered it. Very soon after, this lion came into it, with a wounded and bleeding paw, moaning and groaning from the pain he was suffering. I was greatly frightened by his arrival; but he, seeing me cowering in a corner of his den, approached me very gently, holding out

634

his injured paw and shewing it to me, as if to ask aid. I thereupon took out a large splinter that was in it, and becoming a little familiar with him, I pressed the wound and squeezed out the matter that had collected in it, wiped it, and cleaned it as well as I could. He, finding himself rid of his trouble and relieved from his pain, betook himself to rest and to sleep, still leaving his paw in my hand. Thenceforward he and I lived together in that cavern three whole years, on the same food; for he brought me the best bits of the beasts that he killed in his hunting, and I cooked them in the sun for lack of fire, and lived upon them. At length, having grown weary of that brutish and savage life, this lion having gone forth one day on his wonted quest, I departed thence; and on my third day's journey I was captured by the soldiers who brought me from Africa to this city, to my master, who speedily condemned me to death and to be given to the beasts. Now, by what I see, this lion was also taken very soon after, who would to-day recompense me for the benefit and cure which he received from me."

This was the tale that Androdus told the Emperor, which he also caused to pass from one to another amongst the people. Whereupon, at the request of all, he was set free and absolved from that sentence, and by popular decree he was made a present of a lion. We saw afterwards, Apion says, Androdus leading the lion by a light leash, going about amongst the taverns of Rome, receive the money that was given him, the lion letting himself be covered with the flowers that were thrown to him; and every one said on meeting them: "There is the lion who was the man's host; there is the man who was the lion's doctor."

Apology for Raimond Sebond

We often weep for the loss of the beasts we love; so also do they, for our loss:—

> Behind comes the battle-horse, Æthon, deprived of trappings, weeping, and his face wet with great tears.[219]

While some of our nations have wives in common, some have each man his own. Is not the same thing true also among beasts? and marriages better kept than ours? As for the association and confederation which they form among themselves, to league themselves together and assist one another, we see in the case of oxen, hogs, and other animals, that, at the outcry of one that you harm, the whole troop runs to its assistance and joins for its defence. When the scarus has followed the fisher's bait, his like gather in a crowd about him and gnaw the line; and if by chance one has been taken in a hoop-net, the others turn toward him, their tails outside, and he seizes hold with his teeth as tight as he can; they pull him out thus, and draw him away. The mullets, when one of their like is caught, put the line across their backs, erecting a saw-toothed spine that they have, with which they saw and sever it.[220]

As for the special offices which we receive from one another for assistance in life,[221] many similar examples may be observed among them. It is believed that the whale in swimming is always preceded by a small fish resembling the sea-gudgeon, which is consequently called the guide; the whale follows him, letting himself be led and turned as easily as the helm makes the ship turn; and, whereas every thing else, whether beast or boat, that enters the horrible chaos of that monster's mouth is instantly lost and swal-

636

lowed up, this little fish, by way of recompense, enters into
it with perfect security and sleeps there; and during his
sleep the whale does not budge; but, as soon as he goes forth,
she follows him again without pause; and if by chance she
is parted from him, she wanders to and fro, often brushing
against the cliffs, like a ship without a rudder; which Plutarch witnesses to have seen in the island of Anticyra.[222]
There is a similar association between the little bird called
the wren and the crocodile: the wren acts as sentinel for
that great creature; and if the ichneumon, his enemy, comes
near, to fight him, this little bird, for fear lest he be surprised in his sleep, awakes him by singing, and by pecking
warns him of his danger. He lives on the leavings of the
monster, who admits him freely into his mouth, and allows
him to peck in his jaws and between his teeth, and take
from them the bits of flesh that have remained there; and
if he wishes to shut his mouth, he first warns him to go
forth, closing it little by little, without squeezing or hurting
him.[223]

The shell-fish that is called the *nacre* lives in the same
way with the shrimp, which is a small creature of the
crab species, acting as her usher and porter, seated at the
entrance of the shell which he keeps always gaping and
open, until he sees some small fish enter in, suitable for their
capture; then he goes into the nacre and pinches her to the
quick, and forces her to shut her shell; then the two together
devour the prey imprisoned in their fortress.[224]

In the mode of life of the tunny-fish there may be observed a strange acquaintance with the three branches of
mathematics. As for astrology,[225] they teach it to man; for
they remain in the place where the winter solstice surprises

637

them, and do not budge until the ensuing equinox; because of this, even Aristotle freely concedes this art to them. As for geometry and arithmetic, they always form their schools in the figure of a cube, every way square, and fashion of it a solid battalion, close and bounded on all sides[226] by six perfectly equal faces; then they swim in this square order, as broad behind as before, so that he who sees and counts one row can easily number the whole troop, since the number of the depth is equal to the width and the width to the length.[227] As for magnanimity, it is hard to give a more visible manifestation of it than in the action of the great dog that was sent from the Indies to King Alexander. They brought before him, first, a stag, to fight with him, and then a boar, and then a bear; he paid no heed to them, and did not deign to stir from his place; but when he saw a lion, he sprang instantly to his feet, showing plainly that he declared that alone worthy to do battle with him.[228]

Touching repentance and acknowledgement of misdeeds, there is a tale of an elephant who, having killed his keeper in an outburst of anger, was seized with grief so extreme that he would never eat again, and let himself die.[229] As for clemency, they tell of a tiger, the most inhuman of all beasts, that, having been given a kid, he endured hunger for two days before being willing to harm it; and the third day he broke the cage in which he was confined, to go in search of other food, being unwilling to attack the kid, his companion and guest.[230] And as for the rights of intimacy and concord which intercourse creates, we frequently bring up cats and dogs and hares together. But that which is known to those who travel by sea, and notably in the sea about Sicily, concerning the condition of the halcyons sur-

Apology for Raimond Sebond

passes all human thought. Of what species of creature has ever Nature so honoured the child-bed, the birth, the travail? For the poets declare that the one island of Delos, being formerly a floating island, was made stationary for the service of the travail of Latona; but God has chosen that the whole ocean shall be stayed, made stationary and smooth, without waves, without wind, and without rain, while the halcyon brings forth her young, which is just about the time of the solstice, the shortest day of the year; and by virtue of her privilege, we have seven days and nights in the very heart of winter when we can sail the seas without danger. The females know no other male than their own, and accompany him all their lives without ever leaving him; if he becomes weak and old, they take him on their shoulders, carry him everywhere, and serve him until death. But no intelligence has yet succeeded in arriving at an understanding of that marvellous substance with which the halcyon builds the nest for her young, or to divine its composition. Plutarch, who saw and handled several of them, thought that it was the bones of some fish, which she joins and binds together, interlacing them, some lengthwise, others across, and adding ribs and roundings, so that at last she shapes a round vessel, prepared for launching; then, when she has completely finished constructing it, she takes it where the waves beat, where the sea, beating softly against it, teaches her to repair what is not well joined and better to strengthen the places where she sees that its structure is disturbed and loosened by the blows of the sea; and, on the other hand, where it is well joined, the beating of the sea presses it together and tightens it,[231] so that it can be neither broken nor crumbled, nor injured by blows of stones or of

Apology for Raimond Sebond

iron, except with the utmost difficulty. And that which is most to be wondered at is the proportion and shape of the concavity within; for it is framed and proportioned in such wise that it can neither hold nor admit any thing but the bird that has built it; for to every thing else it is impenetrable, shut, and secured, so that nothing can enter, not even the sea-water.[232] This is a very clear description of this structure, and borrowed from a good source; but it seems to me that it still does not sufficiently explain to us the complexity of this architecture. Now, from what vanity in us can it proceed that we place below ourselves and interpret disdainfully actions which we can neither imitate nor understand.[233]

To follow out a little further this equality and resemblance between us and the beasts, the privilege our soul glorifies herself on, of reducing to her own condition whatever she conceives, of divesting of mortal and corporeal qualities whatever comes to her, of marshalling the things that she deems worthy of her commerce, so as to remove and divest them of their corruptible conditions, and make them lay aside, as superfluous and mean garments, thickness, length, depth, weight, colour, odour, roughness, smoothness, hardness, softness, and all perceptible accidents, in order to adapt them to her immortal and spiritual nature; so Rome and Paris, which I have in my thoughts—the Paris which I conceive, I conceive and apprehend without dimension and without place, without stone, without plaster, and without wood—this same privilege, I say, seems very evidently to belong to beasts: for a horse accustomed to the sound of trumpets, of musketry, and of battle, whom we see quivering and trembling in his sleep, stretched on his litter as if he were in the fight—it is certain that he conceives in

his thought the beat of the drum without noise, an army
without arms and without body.

> You will see powerful horses, though they lie
> stretched out in sleep, yet often sweat and pant, and
> exert all their strength, as if striving for the prize.[234]

The hare that a greyhound conceives in his dream, in pursuit of which we see him, while he sleeps, panting, stiffening
his tail, moving his legs convulsively, and imitating perfectly the motions of running—it is a hare without flesh and
without bone.

> The dogs of hunters in soft slumber yet often sud-
> denly move their legs, and bark, and repeatedly sniff
> the air with their nostrils, as if they had found and
> were on the track of wild beasts; and when they awake,
> they often chase imaginary stags, as if they saw them
> in flight, until their mistake is dissipated and they
> come to themselves.[235]

The watch-dogs whom we often hear to growl while dreaming, then bark and wake with a start, as if they perceived
some stranger coming—this stranger whom their mind sees
is a ghostly[236] and imperceptible man, without dimension,
without colour, and without existence:—

> and the fawning brood of dogs brought up in the
> house awake from light and fleeting slumber, and leap
> from the ground as if they beheld unknown faces and
> features.[237]

As for bodily beauty, before going further I must needs
know whether we are in agreement as to its description. It

641

is probable that we scarcely know what natural and general beauty is, since we give so many different forms to our own beauty, for which, if there were any natural law, we should all alike recognise it, as we do the heat of fire. We create its forms in imagination, according to our liking.

> The complexion of a Belgian ill becomes a Roman face.[238]

The Indians depict it as dark and tawny, with large and thick lips and a flat, broad nose. And they weight with large gold rings the cartilage between the nostrils, to make it hang down to the mouth; as also the lower lip, with large hoops enriched with precious stones, so that it falls on the chin; and it is with them a seemliness to show their teeth, even below the roots.[239] In Peru the largest ears are the most beautiful, and they stretch them as much as they can by artificial means;[240] and a man of our day says that, in an Eastern nation, he found this sedulousness in enlarging them, as in weighting them with heavy jewels, in such favour, that often he passed his sleeved arm through the hole in the ear.[241] There are nations, too, who blacken their teeth with great care and look with scorn on white ones; elsewhere, they stain them red.[242] Not only in Basque do the women think themselves more beautiful with their heads shaved, but in many other places; and, what is more, in certain very cold countries, so Pliny says.[243] The Mexican women count as a beauty smallness of the forehead; and, although they shave the hair on all the rest of the body, they cultivate it and increase it on the forehead by art; and they hold in such high esteem the largeness of the breast that they try to be able to suckle their children over their shoul-

Apology for Raimond Sebond

der. [244] We should thus depict ugliness.[245] The Italians figure beauty as full and massive; the Spaniards as thin and slender; and amongst us one makes it white, another brown; one, soft and delicate, another, strong and vigorous; this one demands kindness and sweetness,[246] that one, pride and dignity. In like manner, the greater beauty which Plato ascribes to the spherical shape,[247] the Epicureans give rather to the pyramidal, or square, and can not swallow a god shaped like a ball.[248]

But however it may be, Nature has not more privileged us in this matter[249] than elsewise regarding her universal laws. And if we consider ourselves carefully, we shall find that, if there are some animals less favoured in this respect than we are, there are others, and in great numbers, who are more so; *we are surpassed in beauty by many animals*,[250] yes, even terrestrial ones, our compatriots; for, as for those of the sea (setting aside the shape, which can not enter into the comparison,[251] so different is it), in colouring, cleanliness, smoothness, nimbleness, we are much inferior to them; and not less in all qualities to those of the air. And the prerogative, which poets rate high, of our erect posture, looking toward heaven, to which it is akin,[252]—

> And while the other animals, stooping, look down on the ground, he has given men a lofty stature, and has commanded them to regard the sky, and, standing erect, to lift their gaze to the stars,[253]—

is really poetic; for there are several little beasts that have their sight turned wholly toward heaven; and the setting of the head of camels and ostriches I find to be more raised and upright than ours. What animals have not the face high up and have it not in front, and looking straight forward, like ourselves, and do not, in their natural posture, discover as much of the sky and earth as man? And what qualities of our bodily constitution, in Plato and in Cicero, do not bestead a thousand sorts of beast?[254] Those which most resemble us are the ugliest and most despicable of the whole troop; for, as to the outward aspect and form of the visage, they are the apes:—

How like us is the ape, the most ignoble of animals![255]

as to the interior and vital part, it is the hog. Certainly, when I think of man quite naked (yes, and that sex which seems to have the greater share of beauty), his blemishes, his natural tendency to deformities, and his imperfections, I find that we have had more reason than any other animal to cover ourselves. We have been excusable in borrowing from those whom Nature in that respect had favoured more than us, in order to adorn ourselves with their beauty and hide ourselves under what we pillage from them—wool, feathers, skins, silk.

Furthermore, let us observe that we are the only animals whose defects offend our own fellows, and the only ones who have to withdraw from our kind in our natural acts. Truly, it is a fact worthy of consideration that the masters of the profession prescribe as a remedy for amorous passion the complete and unhampered sight of the body that is sought; and that, to cool affection, we need only to see freely the person we love:—

Oft he who viewed the secret parts

Apology for Raimond Sebond

Felt passion cool in full career.[256]

And although this description may perchance proceed from a somewhat fastidious and cold humour, still is it a wondrous token of our weakness that habit and knowledge disgust us with one another. It is not so much pudicity as guile and prudence that renders our ladies so circumspect in denying us admission to their chambers before they are painted and adorned for public exhibition;

> Nor is this unknown to our Venuses; wherefore all the more they themselves hide with the utmost pains all that goes on behind the scenes of life from those whom they wish to retain in the charms of love;[257]

whereas, in many animals, there is no part of them that we do not like and that does not please our senses, so that from their very excrement and from their evacuations we derive not only dainties for eating, but our richest ornaments and perfume. These remarks touch only our common sort of women, and are not so sacrilegious as to intend to include those divine, supernatural, and extraordinary beauties that we see sometimes shining amongst us like stars beneath a corporeal and terrestrial veil.

As to the rest, even the share of the favour of Nature that we, by our own confession, allow to animals, is very much to their advantage. We attribute to ourselves imaginary and fanciful goods, future and absent goods, for which the human understanding can not of itself even be answerable; or goods which we attribute to ourselves falsely, by the license of our judgement, like reason, knowledge, and honour; and

645

we abandon to them,[258] for their share, the essential, easily obtainable, palpable goods: peace, repose, security, innocence, and health; health, I say—the fairest and richest gift that Nature can bestow upon us. So that Philosophy, even the Stoic, actually ventures to say that Heraclitus and Pherecides, if they could have exchanged their reason for health and have freed themselves by that bargain, the one from dropsy, the other from the pest of lice that tormented him, would have done well. Whereby they give even greater value to wisdom, comparing it and balancing it with health, than they give to that other quality which also is theirs. They say that, if Circe had offered Ulysses two kinds of drink, one to change a fool to a wise man, the other, a wise man to a fool, Ulysses should rather have accepted the one causing folly, than consent that Circe should change the human form to that of a beast; and they say that wisdom herself would have spoken to him thus: "Forsake me, depart from me, rather than lodge me under the likeness and body of an ass."[259] What? This noble and divine wisdom—do the philosophers then forsake it for this corporeal and terrestrial veil?[260] It is, then, no longer by reason, by thought, and by the soul, that we surpass the beasts: it is by our beauty, our beautiful colouring and the beautiful arrangement of our limbs, for which we must set at naught our intelligence, our knowledge, and all the rest.

Now, I accept this ingenuous and frank confession. Surely they knew that these qualities, which we extol so highly, are but vain imaginings. If, then, beasts possessed all the Stoic virtues, learning, wisdom, and competence, they would still be beasts; nor would they be comparable to a wretched, wicked, and senseless man. For, in short, whatever is not like us is not to be esteemed.[261] And God himself, to make himself esteemed, must resemble us, as we shall soon see. Whence it appears that it is not from true reasoning, but from a foolish and obstinate pride, that we prefer ourselves to other animals, and sequester ourselves from their estate and companionship.

But, to return to my subject: we have for our share inconstancy, irresolution, uncertainty, sorrow, superstition, solicitude about things to come even after our life, ambition, covetousness, jealousy, envy, unbridled appetites, furious and untameable, war, falsehood, disloyalty, detraction, and curiosity. Surely we have strangely paid too much for this fine reasoning power on which we pride ourselves, and this faculty of judging and knowing, if we have bought them at the price of the endless number of afflictions to which we are incessantly subject. Unless we are inclined to pride ourselves, as Socrates does indeed, on that remarkable prerogative over the other animals, that, whereas Nature has prescribed to them certain seasons and limits for the delights of Venus, she has given us the reins at all hours and on all occasions. *Because wine, while sometimes beneficial, is most often harmful to a sick man, it is best not to offer it to him at all rather than, in hope of a doubtful cure, incur an evident danger. Similarly, I do not know whether it might not have been better had there not been given to mankind at all the quickness of thought, penetration, sagacity, which we call reason,—which are pernicious to many and salutary to few,—rather than to have bestowed them so munificently and widely.*[262]

Of what value can we consider the understanding of so many things to have been to Varo and Aristotle? Did it exempt them from human ills? Were they freed from the misfortunes that lie heavy on a porter? Did they derive from logic any consolation for the gout? From knowing that this humour is lodged in the joints, did they feel it the less? Were they ready to accept death,[263] from knowing that some nations rejoice at it? and cuckoldry, from knowing that women are enjoyed in common in some parts of the world?[264] On the contrary, the one having held the first place in learning amongst the Romans, the other amongst the Greeks, and in the period when learning was most flourishing, we are not told that there was any peculiar excellence in their lives; indeed, the Greek has enough to do to clear himself from some notable blemishes in his.[265] Has it been found that pleasure and health have a greater relish for him who understands astrology and grammar?

Are the muscles of the unlettered less vigorous?[266]

and that shame and poverty are less troublesome?

Doubtless you will henceforth be without sickness or weakness, and escape grief and anxiety, and longer life and happier fortunes will be given you.[267]

I have seen in my day a hundred artisans, a hundred labourers, wiser and happier than University vice-chancellors, and whom I should like better to resemble. Scholarship,[268] in my opinion, holds a place among things of value in life like a great name,[269] nobility of rank, dignity of position, or, at best, like beauty, wealth, and other such qualities, which are indeed of service to life, but remotely, and more through imagination than by nature.

We scarcely need more functions, rules, and laws of

living in our community than the cranes and ants find necessary in theirs. With the few they have,[270] we see that they
conduct themselves in a very orderly fashion without erudition. If man were wise, he would apprehend the real value
of every thing according as it was the most useful and most
suitable for his life. Whoever shall reckon us by our acts and
proceedings will find a greater number of excellent men
among the ignorant than among the learned—I mean, in
every sort of virtue. The old Rome seems to me to have
brought forth men of greater worth, both for peace and for
war, than that learned Rome which was ruined by herself.
Even though the rest should be altogether similar, at least
honesty and innocence would still be found on the side of
the ancient city, for they consort singularly well with simplicity.

But I will leave this train of thought,[271] which would
lead me further than I should care to follow. I will say only
this in addition, that humility and submission alone can
create a man to be respected.[272] The knowledge of his duty
must not be left to each man's judgement: it must be prescribed for him; he must not be allowed to choose it at his
will;[273] otherwise, in accordance with the foolishness and
infinite variety of our reasons and opinions, we should end
by devising for ourselves duties which would bring us to
eating one another, as Epicurus says.[274] The first law that
God ever gave man was a law of pure obedience; it was a
bare and simple commandment, wherein there was nothing
for man to examine and seek the reason for,[275] inasmuch as
to obey is the peculiar duty of a reasonable mind, recognising
a heavenly superior and benefactor. From obedience and

submission every other virtue is born, as every sin from pride. And, on the contrary, the first temptation that came to human nature on the part of the devil, his first poison, insinuated itself into us by the promises he made us of learning and knowledge: *Ye shall be as gods, knowing good and evil.*[276] And the Sirens, in Homer, to beguile Ulysses and to lure him into their dangerous and destructive snares, offer him knowledge as a gift.[277] The deadly disease of man is the belief that he knows. That is why ignorance is so recommended to us by our religion, as a quality belonging to belief and to obedience. *Take heed that no man deceive you by philosophy and vain deceit, according to the elements of the world.*[278]

About this there is a general agreement among all philosophers of all schools, that the sovereign good consists in tranquillity of the soul and of the body. But where do we find it?

> To conclude, the wise man is inferior to Jupiter; rich, free, honoured, well-favoured, in fine, the king of kings; above all, healthy, unless he is tormented by pituita.[279]

It seems, in truth, that nature, by way of consolation for our miserable and beggarly condition, has given us for our portion only presumption. It is what Epictetus says: that man has nothing properly his own save the fashion[280] of his opinions.[281] We have only wind and smoke for our portion. The gods have health in their being, philosophy declares, and disease in their apprehension; man, on the contrary, possesses his goods in his imagination, his ills in his being.[282]

Apology for Raimond Sebond

We have done well to make the most of the forces of our imagination; for all our blessings are only dream-like. Listen to this poor and unfortunate creature bluster. There is nothing, says Cicero, so delightful as the occupation with letters, with those letters, I mean, by which, even in this world, the infinitude of things, the immense grandeur of nature, the heavens and the dry lands and the seas are revealed to us;[283] it is they which have taught us religion, moderation, high-mindedness, and which have snatched our soul out of darkness to show her all things high, low, first, last, and between; it is they which supply us with the wherewithal to live rightly and happily, and guide us to pass our life without doing or suffering harm.[284] Does not this man seem to speak of the estate of God, ever-living and all-powerful? And in reality a thousand simple women in villages have lived more equable, gentler, and more constant lives than was his.

> A god he was, a god, most noble Memmius, who
> first discovered that plan of life which is now called
> wisdom, and who, by trained skill, rescued life from
> such great billows and such thick darkness, and placed
> it in such a calm and bright light.[285]

Here are most stately and glorious words; but a very slight accident put the intelligence of this man[286] in a worse condition than that of the humblest shepherd, notwithstanding this instructing god[287] and this divine wisdom. Of equal effrontery is that promise of the book of Democritus: "I am about to speak of all things";[288] and that absurd title that Aristotle bestows upon us, of mortal gods;[289] and that judgement of Chrysippus, that Dion was as virtuous as God.[290]

651

And my Seneca recognises, he says, that God gave him life, but that he has from himself the living rightly;[291] agreeing with this other: *We justly take pride in our virtue, which we should abstain from if it were a gift from God, not from ourselves.*[292] This again is from Seneca: that the wise man is as free from fear as God, but with human weakness; whereby he surpasses him.[293] There is nothing so common as to find instances of such audacity. There is not one of us who is as much displeased to see himself compared with God as he is to see himself brought down to the level of the other animals; so much more jealous are we of our own interests than of that of our creator.

But we must tread under foot this foolish vanity, and vigorously and boldly shatter the ridiculous foundations on which these false beliefs are built. So long as he thinks that he has any means and any strength in himself, man will never recognise what he owes to his master; he will always make chickens of his eggs, as they say; he must be stripped to his shirt. Let us observe some notable example of the effect of his philosophy. Possidonius, suffering from a malady so painful that it made him wring his hands and grind his teeth, thought to spite the pain[294] by crying out to it: "Do what thou wilt, yet I will not admit that thou art evil." He feels the same tortures as my lackey, but he prides himself upon keeping his tongue at least under the laws of his sect.[295] *After boastful words it was unfitting to succumb to the fact.*[296] When Arcesilaus was ill of the gout, Carneades, who came to visit him, went away greatly concerned; he called him back and, pointing to his feet and his breast, "Nothing has come hither thence," he said.[297] This man takes it with a little better grace, for he feels that he has pain and would like to be rid of it; but nevertheless, his heart is not cast down and enfeebled by that pain. The firmness that the other maintains is, I fear, more verbal than essential. And Dionysius Heracleotes, afflicted with a sharp smarting in his eyes, was fain to forsake these Stoic resolutions.[298]

But even if learning does in fact do what they claim, —somewhat dull and diminish the sharpness of the misfortunes that follow after us,—what does it do that ignorance does not do much more simply and more manifestly? The philosopher Pyrrho, incurring at sea the perils of a great storm, suggested to those who were with him merely to imitate the fearlessness of a pig, which was on the vessel with them and which regarded the tempest without terror.[299] Philosophy, at the end of her precepts, sends us to the examples of an athlete and a muleteer, in whom we commonly observe much less concern about death, pain, and other disagreeable things, and more firmness than learning ever gives to any one not born and prepared for them in himself by a natural habit of mind. How is it that we lance and slash the tender limbs of a child more easily than our own, if it be not ignorance? And those of a horse? How many people has the power of the imagination alone made sick? We often see them having themselves bled, purged, and dosed, to cure ills which they feel only in their fancy. When real ills fail us, then learning lends us hers. That colour and that complexion presage for you some rheumatic inflammation; this hot season threatens you with a feverish attack; this break in the line of life in your left hand warns you of some serious indisposition near at hand. And at last she[300] flatly addresses herself to health itself. This youthful animation and vigour can not remain as it is; we must take from it life and strength, for fear that it do you harm. Compare the life of a man subjected to such fancies with that of a labourer who lets himself go according to his natural liking, measuring things only by his immediate sensations, without learning and without prognostication; who has pain only when he has it; whereas the other often has the stone in his soul before he has it in his bladder; as if it were not time enough to suffer pain when it is there, he forestalls it in imagination, and runs to meet it.

What I say of medicine may be applied generally by way of example to all learning. Thence arose that ancient opinion of the philosophers, who placed sovereign good in the recognition of the feebleness of our judgement. My ignorance gives me as much ground for hope as for fear, and having no other rule for my health than that drawn from the example of others and from happenings that I see elsewhere in like cases, I find them of all sorts, and rest on the comparisons that are most favourable to me. I welcome health with open arms, free, full, and complete, and sharpen my appetite to enjoy it, so much the more because it is now[301] less usual with me and more rare: so far am I from disturbing its peace and pleasantness by a novel and restricted mode of life. The beasts show us plainly enough how the agitation of our minds brings sickness upon us.

That which we are told of the people of Brazil, that they died of nothing but old age, is attributed to the serenity and tranquillity of their climate; I attribute it, rather, to the tranquillity and serenity of their souls, freed from all perturbation and care and laborious or unpleasant occupation, like people who passed their lives in admirable simplicity and ignorance, without letters, without law, without king, without any kind of religion. And whence comes this, which we know by experience, that the grossest and most doltish are the most vigorous and desirable in amorous performances; and that the love of a muleteer often makes itself more acceptable than that of a gentleman, if it be not that in the latter the soul's agitation distracts the bodily vigour, arrests and wearies it, as it also usually distracts and wearies itself? What agitates it,[302] what drives it into madness, more commonly than its quickness, its keenness, its agility—in a word, its own strength? Of what is the most subtle folly made but of the most subtle wisdom? As from great friendships are born great enmities, and from vigorous health, mortal maladies, so from the precious and vivid workings of our minds come the most extreme and most out-of-the-way delusions; it needs but the slightest change to pass from one to the other.

By the actions of insane men we see how easily folly connects itself with the most vigorous operations of our minds. Who does not know how imperceptible is the boundary line between madness and the gallant flights of a free spirit and the condition of a supreme and extraordinary virtue? Plato says that the melancholy-minded are the most teachable and excellent; also, there are none who have so great a proneness to insanity. Numberless minds are ruined by their own strength and pliability. What a fall has just been sustained, due to native emotion and excitability, by a poet more judicious, brilliant, and better formed in the atmosphere of old, pure poesy than any other Italian poet has been for a long time![303] Has he not reason to be grateful to that murderous activity of his mind? to that brilliancy which

blinded him? to that exact and wide[304] apprehension of reason which deprived him of reason? to the over-diligent and
toilsome quest for knowledge which led him to stupidity?
to that rare aptitude for exercises of the mind which has left
him without exercise and without mind? I felt even more
exasperation than compassion, seeing him at Ferrara in such
a piteous state, surviving himself, neglectful both of himself
and of his works, which, without his knowledge and yet in
his sight, have been sent abroad into the world[305] un-
amended and unshaped. Would you have a man sound,
would you have him self-controlled and of a firm and secure
attitude? enwrap him in obscurity, indolence, and dulness.
We must be stultified to become wise, and blinded, to be
led. And if I am told that the advantage of having our sensibility to pains and ills cold and dull brings with it the disadvantage of making us consequently less keen also, and
delicate in our enjoyment of goods and pleasures, that is
true; but the wretchedness of our state is such, that we have
not so much to enjoy as to avoid;[306] and that extreme pleasure does not affect us so much as a slight pain. *Men feel less
keenly what is good than what is ill.*[307] We do not feel perfect health so much as the least sickness.

> The body feels keenly what scarcely harms the
> surface of the skin, while health is not at all perceived
> by it. A man rejoices that neither his side nor his foot
> hurts him; but otherwise he knows hardly at all
> whether or not he is in good health and vigour.[308]

Our well-being is only the absence of ill-being. This is why
the school of philosophy that set the highest value on pleasure, yet placed it as merely freedom from pain.[309] To have

656

Apology for Raimond Sebond

no ill is the greatest good that man can hope for; as Ennius
said:—

A man is too fortunate who has no ill fortune.[310]

For the same delightful excitement and exhilaration[311] that
we feel in certain pleasures, and that seems to lift us above
simple health and freedom from pain; this active, stirring
—and, I know not how, stinging and biting—pleasure; even
this aims only at freedom from pain as its mark. The appetite that drives us to commerce with women seeks only to
banish the distress caused by ardent and fierce desire, and
asks only to satisfy itself and to settle down in repose and in
freedom from that fever. And so with the others.

I say, therefore, that, if ignorance puts us in the way of
having no ills, it puts us in the way of a very fortunate state,
considering our circumstances. But we must not imagine
it so complete as to be altogether without feeling. For Cran-
tor was well advised to combat the freedom from pain of
Epicurus, if its foundations went so deep that even the approach and birth of evils were lacking to it. I do not praise
such freedom from pain, which is neither possible nor to be
desired. I am glad not to be sick; but if I am so, I desire to
know that I am; and if I am cauterised or bled, I desire to
feel it. In truth, he who would destroy consciousness of pain
would at the same time extirpate consciousness of pleasure,
and, in short, would reduce man to nothingness: [312] *This
insensibility to pain is bought at the great cost of inhumanity in the soul and torpor in the body.*[313] Evil is well for man
in its turn. Pain is not always to be shunned, nor pleasure
always to be pursued.

It is a very great gain for the honour of ignorance, that

knowledge herself casts us into its arms when she finds herself unable to strengthen us against the burden of our ills; she is obliged to come to this accord, to loosen the reins, and give us leave to take refuge in the lap of ignorance and to shelter ourselves, under this protection, from the blows and affronts of fortune. For what else does she mean when she enjoins upon us to withdraw our thought from the ills that hold us in thrall and divert it with foregone pleasures; and to make use, as consolation for our present ills, of the remembrance of past goods, and to call to our aid a vanished satisfaction, to oppose it to what presses upon us,[314] *he places the lessening of anxieties in turning away from troubling thoughts and recalling pleasant ones to the mind*,[315] if it be not that, when her strength fails, she is ready to employ craft, and to resort to an agile twist of the leg when strength in the body and the arms has deserted her? For, not to a philosopher only, but to a merely soberminded man, when he is actually suffering the thirst of a burning fever, what coin to pay him is the remembrance of the sweetness of Greek wine? It would rather make his fortune worse;[316]

The remembrance of happiness doubles the grief.[317]

Of the same sort is this other counsel that philosophy offers: to retain in the memory only past happiness, and to expel from it the troubles from which we have suffered;[318] as if we had in our power the art of forgetfulness. And it counsels again what is of still less value:

Sweet is the memory of past labours.[319]

How is it that philosophy, which should put arms in my

hand to contend with fortune, which should strengthen my courage to trample under foot all human adversities, can have the weakness to make me sneak away by these cowardly and ridiculous by-ways? For the memory presents to us not what we choose, but what pleases it. Indeed, there is nothing that impresses a thing so vividly in our recollection as the desire to forget it; it is a good way of giving a thing in charge to our soul and imprinting it there, to solicit her to lose it. And that saying is false: *It is in our power to bury adversities in almost perpetual oblivion, and to remember prosperities joyfully and sweetly.*[320] And this is true: *I remember even what I would not; I can not forget at will.*[321] And from whom comes this advice? From him *who alone dared to declare himself a wise man,*[322]—

Who in intellect surpassed the human race, and quenched all men as the ethereal sun quenches the stars.[323]

To empty and unfurnish the memory—is not this the true and straight road to ignorance? *Ignorance is but a weak remedy for ills.*[324] There are many similar precepts, which permit us to borrow from the common people trivial-seeming truths,[325] when keen and powerful reasoning can not avail, provided they afford us satisfaction and consolation. When they can not heal the wound, they are content to benumb it and cloak it. I think this will not be denied: that if to a condition of life which possesses enjoyment and tranquillity could be added continuance and stability through some weakness and malady of the judgement, this would be accepted:—

Apology for Raimond Sebond

I will begin to drink and scatter flowers, and I will
be content to pass for a very fool.[326]

Many philosophers would be of Lycas's opinion: he, otherwise of well-ordered character, living pleasantly and peace-
ably with his family, failing in no function of his duty toward his dependants and strangers, guarding himself well
from hurtful things, had a strange fancy impressed on his
brain by some failure of reason: he thought that he was per-
petually in the theatre, seeing pastimes, spectacles, and the
best plays in the world. Being cured by the doctors of this
disturbing disorder[327] he almost went to law with them to
reinstate him in the enjoyment of those fancies.[328]

> "By Pollux, my friends, you have killed me, not
> saved me," he said, "from whom pleasure has been
> thus snatched, and a delightful delusion forcibly de-
> stroyed."[329]

A delusion similar to that of Thrasilaus, son of Pythodorus,
who came to believe that all the ships that went out from
and came into the port of Piræus were employed in his service alone; congratulating himself on the good fortune of
their voyages, and joyfully welcoming them. His brother
Crito having caused him to be restored to his better understanding, he regretted that state of being in which he had
lived joyously and free from all trouble.[330] It is as this old
Greek line says, there is much advantage in not being very
wise:—

> The sweetest life consists in taking heed of naught.[331]

And Ecclesiastes: "In much wisdom, much trouble; and he

660

who increases knowledge, to him is increased travail and torment."[332]

Even that to which, in general, philosophy agrees, the last remedy that she ordains for all manner of necessities, which is to put an end to the life that we can no longer endure: *Does it please you? accept it. Does it not please you? depart from it as you will.*[333] *Suffering stings you? or even tortures you? If you are unarmed, present your throat; but if you are protected by the arms of Vulcan, that is, by courage, stand firm;*[334] and that saying at the Greek banquets, which they there followed: *Let him drink, or let him go away*[335] (which sounds more fittingly in the tongue of a Gascon, who freely changes the *b* to *v*, than in that of Cicero),—

> If you know not how to live rightly, give place to those who do. You have played enough and eaten and drunk enough; it is time for you to depart, lest young men, in whom gaiety is more becoming, laugh at you when you have drunk too much, and drive you away,[336]—

what else is it but a confession of her[337] powerlessness and a dismissal, not only to ignorance, there to be under cover, but to very senselessness, non-feeling and non-being?

> When Democritus was warned by his ripe old age that the memory-bringing motions of his mind were languishing, he spontaneously offered his head to death.[338]

This falls in with what Antisthenes said, that provision should be made, either of sense to understand, or of a halter to hang oneself; and what Chrysippus brought forward on this subject from the poet Tyrtæus: To draw nigh virtue or death.[339] And Crates said that love was cured by hunger, if not by time; and, for him whom these two means did not please, by a rope.[340] That Sextius of whom Seneca and Plutarch speak with such commendation,[341] having flung himself into the study of philosophy, all other things laid aside, decided to cast himself into the sea, finding the progress of his studies too slow and too protracted. He sought death in default of knowledge. Here are the words of the law on this subject: If perchance some great misfortune occurs, which can not be remedied, the harbour is near; and safety can be had by swimming out of the body as out of a leaky skiff; for it is the fear of death, not the desire of life, that makes the fool cling to the body.

As life is made more agreeable by simplicity, it is also by it made more innocent and better, as I a while ago began to say. The simple, says St. Paul, and the ignorant rise from the earth and possess themselves of heaven; and we, with all our learning, plunge into the bottomless pits of hell.[342] I care nothing, either for Valentian,[343] the declared enemy of learning and letters, or for Licinius,—Roman emperors both,—who called them the poison and pest of every political state; or for Mahomet, who, as I have heard, forbade learning to his followers; but the example of the great Lycurgus and his authority should certainly have great weight; and veneration for that divine Lacedæmonian government, so great, so admirable, and flourishing for so long a time virtuous and fortunate, without any teaching or practice of letters. They who return from that new world which was discovered by the Spaniards in the time of our fathers can testify to us in how much more strict and more regular a way those nations live, without government and without laws, than our nations do, where there are more officials and more laws than there are other men and lawsuits.

> Their hands and their laps are full of writs and libels and documents and procurations, and great heaps of glosses, consultations, and lectures; thanks to them, the poor people in the cities are never safe; they have before and behind them and on either side notaries, attorneys, and advocates.[344]

It is, as was said by a Roman senator in the later period, that the breath of their predecessors stank of garlic, and their breasts were sweetened by a good conscience;[345] and that, on the contrary, those of his time smelt outwardly only of perfume, stinking within from all sorts of vices; which means, I think, that they had much learning and ability and a great lack of high character.[346] Rusticity, ignorance, simplicity, roughness, are willing companions of innocence; curiosity, cunning, learning, bring evil-mindedness in their train; humility, fear, obedience, kindliness (which are the chief instruments for the preservation of human society) demand a soul untroubled, docile, and thinking little of itself.

Christians have a peculiar knowledge to what extent curiosity is an evil innate and original in man. The desire to increase in wisdom and in knowledge was the first ruin of the human race; it was the way by which it cast itself into eternal damnation. Pride is its destruction and its corruption; it is pride that turns man aside from the common roads, that leads him to embrace novelties and to prefer to be the head of a band wandering and astray in the path of perdition, to prefer to be a master[347] and teacher of error and falsehood, rather than to be a disciple in the school of truth, allowing himself to be led and guided by another's hand into the beaten and straight road. This is, perhaps, what the ancient Greek sentence means, that superstition follows pride and obeys it as if it were its father: *superstition obeys conceit as its father.*[348]

O presumption! how thou dost hinder us! When Socrates was informed that the God of Wisdom had attributed to him the title of Sage, he was astonished at this; and searching and examining himself throughout, he found nowhere any ground for this divine judgement. He knew men as just, temperate, brave, and learned as himself, and more eloquent and more handsome and more useful to the country. At last he determined that he was distinguished from others, and was wise, only because he did not so consider himself; and that his God considered as peculiar stupidity in man his belief in his own learning and wisdom; and that his best learning was the knowledge of his ignorance, and simple-mindedness his best wisdom.[349] Holy writ declares those of us who think highly of themselves to be poor creatures: "Dust and ashes," it says to them, "what hast thou to pride thyself upon?"[350] And again: "God made man like a shadow, of which who shall judge when, by the departure of the light, it shall have vanished?"[351] It is naught but ourselves.[352] Our powers are so far from conceiving the divine height that, of the works of our creator, those best bear his stamp, and are most his, which we understand least. For Christians, to encounter an incredible thing is an opportunity to believe. The thing is so much the more according to reason as it is opposed to human reason. If it were according to reason, it would no longer be miraculous; and if it were in accordance with some precedent, it would no longer be a singular thing. *God is best known by being unknown,*[353] says St. Augustine; and Tacitus: *There is more sanctity and reverence in believing the deeds of the gods than in knowing them.*[354] And Plato thinks that there is some sin of impiety in enquiring too closely both about God and about the world, and about the first causes of things.[355] *But it is, in truth, a difficult thing to discover the creator of this universe; and when discovered, it is sacrilege to proclaim him to the common people,*[356] says Cicero.

We speak of power, virtue, justice; these are words that betoken some great thing; but that thing we in no wise see, nor do we conceive it. We say that God fears, that God is wroth, that God loves,—

Expressing immortal things in mortal speech;[357]

these are all passions and emotions which can not dwell in God in the same form as in us; nor can we imagine the form in him. It is for God alone to know himself and to interpret his works. And he does so in our language unfittingly, in order to lower himself[358] and descend to us, who are prostrate on the ground. How can discretion, which is the choice between good and evil, belong to him, since no evil touches him? How, likewise, reasoning and intelligence, which we employ to arrive, by way of things hard to understand, at what appears as truth,[359] since there is nothing hard for God to understand? Justice, which allots to each one what belongs to him, being created for the fellowship and community of men—how can it exist in God? And how temperance, which is the restraining of bodily pleasures that have no place in divinity? Fortitude in bearing pain, labour, dangers, pertains as little to him; these three things have no access to him.[360] Wherefore, Aristotle holds him to be equally exempt from virtue and from vice.[361] *He is subject neither to love nor to hate, for these are the traits of weak beings.*[362]

The participation that we have in knowledge of the truth, such as it is, it is not by our own powers that we have acquired it. God has taught us that plainly enough by the simple and ignorant witnesses he has chosen from the common people, who instruct us concerning his wonderful secrets; our faith is not our own acquisition; it is a pure gift from the liberality of another. It is not from reasoning or from our intelligence that we have received our religion, but from authority and external command. The weakness of our judgement aids us in it more than the strength, and our blindness more than our clear-sightedness. It is by means of our ignorance more than of our knowledge that we are learned in divine learning. It is no wonder if our natural and earthly powers can not conceive this supernatural and heavenly knowledge; we bring to it naught of our own save obedience and submission; for, as it is written, "I will destroy the wisdom of the wise and will cast down the learning of the learned. Where is the wise man? Where is the teacher?[363] Where is the reasoner according to the time? Has not God rendered foolish the wisdom of this world? For since the world has not by wisdom known God, it has pleased him, by unreasonable prediction,[364] to save believers."

I must also inquire at last whether it is in the power of

666

man to find what he seeks, and whether the quest that he has been engaged in for so many ages has enriched him with some new power and some solid truth. I believe that he will confess, if he speaks honestly, that all the acquisition he has obtained from so long a search is the having learned to recognise his weakness. The ignorance that was in us by nature we have, by long study, avouched and averred. The same thing happens with men really learned that is seen in ears of corn: they grow higher and higher, with heads proudly erect, so long as they are empty; but when they are full and big with grain in their maturity, they begin to humble themselves and to lower their crest.[365] These men who have tested and sounded every thing, having found in that mass of knowledge, and accumulation of so many different things, nothing solid and stable, have renounced their presumption and recognised their natural condition.

It is this with which Velleius twists Cotta and Cicero, that they learned from Philo that they had learned nothing.[366] Pherecides, one of the seven sages, writing to Thales on his death-bed, "I have," he said, "ordered my friends, when they have buried me, to carry my writings to you; if they please you and the other sages, publish them; if not, suppress them; they contain no certain knowledge which satisfies me. And I do not profess to know the truth or to attain to it. I uncover things more than I discover them."[367] The wisest man that ever lived,[368] when he was asked what he knew, replied that he knew this thing, that he knew nothing. He verified what is said, that the greatest part of the things we know is the smallest part of those of which we are ignorant; which is to say, that the very thing that we think we know is a piece, and a very small piece, of our ignorance.[369] We know things as in a dream. Plato says, and in truth are ignorant of them.[370] *Almost all the ancients said that there is nothing to be learned, nothing to be comprehended, nothing to be known; limited are the senses, weak is the mind, short is the course of life.*[371] Cicero himself, who owed to learning all he was worth, Valerius says, as he grew old, began to neglect letters.[372] And, while he had made use of them, it was without being bound to any party, following what seemed to him probable, sometimes in one school, sometimes in another; remaining always within the uncertainty of the Academy. *I speak, but without affirming any thing; I shall be in doubt about many things, and I shall distrust even myself.*[373]

I should have too easy a task if I chose to consider man in his ordinary guise and in gross; and yet I might do so by his own rule, which judges the truth, not by the weight of the voices, but by their number. Let us set aside the common people,—

Who snore, though awake . . . for whom, living and seeing, life is almost death.[374]

who are not conscious of themselves, who do not judge themselves, who let most of their natural faculties lie idle. I would take man in his highest state. Let us consider him in that small number of superior and chosen men who, being endowed with an excellent and exceptional native force, have still strengthened and sharpened human nature by diligence, by study, and by art, and have raised it to the highest point of wisdom that it can attain. They have moulded their minds in every way and on all sides, have supported and propped them with all fitting external aid,

668

and have enriched and adorned them with all that could be borrowed for their benefit, within and without the world; it is in these men that is found the supreme height of human nature. They have ruled the world through governments and laws; they have instructed it by arts and sciences, and still instruct it by the example of their admirable characters.[375] I will take into account only these men, their testimony and their experience. Let us see how far they have gone, and to what they have held fast.[376] The maladies and defects that we find in that company[377] the world may boldly acknowledge to be its own. Whoever is in search of a thing comes to this point, when he says, either that he has found it, or that it can not be found, or that he is still in quest of it. All philosophy is divided into these three kinds. Its purpose is to seek truth, knowledge, and certainty. The Peripatetics, Epicureans, Stoics, and others thought that they had found them. These philosophers set forth the branches of knowledge that we have and discussed them as things certainly known. Clitomachus, Carneades, and the Academics despaired in their search, and concluded that truth could not be apprehended by our faculties. They arrived at weakness[378] and human ignorance. This sect has had the greatest following and the most eminent disciples.[379] Pyrrho and other Sceptics, or Epichists,—whose tenets, many of the ancients thought, were derived from Homer, from the seven sages, from Archilochus, and from Euripides, and connect therewith Zeno, Democritus, and Xenophanes,—say that they are still in quest of truth.[380] These last consider that those who think that they have found it infinitely deceive themselves, and that there is also too bold a vanity in that second kind, which asserts that human faculties are not capable of attaining it. For to do this, to fix the limit of an ability to know and to estimate the perplexity of things, is a great and extreme knowledge, of which they doubt that man is capable.

If any man thinks that nothing is known, he knows not whether even this can be known, that he knows nothing.[381]

The ignorance that knows itself, that judges itself and condemns itself, is not a complete ignorance; to be that, it must needs be ignorant of itself. So thinking, the doctrine of the Pyrrhonians is to waver, to doubt, and to enquire, to be assured of nothing, to answer for nothing. Of the three functions of the mind, the imaginative, the appetitive, and the acceptant,[382] they admit the first two; the last they declare and maintain to be ambiguous, without inclination toward, or approval of, one side or the other, however slight.

Zeno represented by gesture his idea of this division of the faculties of the mind: the hand spread out and open meant what is seen;[383] the hand half closed and the fingers slightly bent, assent; the fist clenched, comprehension; when, with the left hand he closed the first tighter, knowledge.[384] Now this attitude of their judgement, constant[385] and inflexible, accepting all objects without inclination and consent, leads them to their Ataraxy,[386] which is a placid, settled condition of life, exempt from the emotions that we experience by the impress of the idea and knowledge of things that we think we possess. Whence are born fear, avarice, envy, immoderate desires, ambition, pride, superstition, love of novelty, rebellion, disobedience, obstinacy, and the greater number of bodily ills. They are even ex-

Apology for Raimond Sebond

empted thereby from zeal about their doctrine. For they contend in a very mild fashion. They do not fear opposition[387] in their discussions. When they say that what is heavy goes downward, they would be very sorry to be believed about this, but seek to be contradicted, in order to give rise to doubt and suspense of judgement,which is their end. They put forward their propositions only to combat those that they think we believe in. If you adopt theirs, they will as readily adopt the opposite to uphold: it is all one to them; they have no choice about it. If you prove that snow is black, they argue, on the contrary, that it is white.[388] If you say that it is neither one nor the other, they are bound to maintain that it is both. If, as a certainty,[389] you declare that you know nothing about it, they will maintain that you do know. Yes, and if, by an affirmative axiom, you assert that you doubt about it, they will contend with you that you do not doubt about it, or that you can not judge and make sure that you doubt. And by this extreme degree of doubt, which undermines itself, they are separated and divided from many doctrines, even from those which have maintained, in many forms, doubt and ignorance. Why, they say, should they not be allowed to doubt, as among the Dogmatists one is allowed to say green, another yellow? Is there any thing that can be put before you to admit or deny, which it is not lawful to regard as ambiguous? And while others are carried away, as by a great wind, either by the custom of their country, or by the teaching of their parents, or by chance, without reflection and without choice, oftenest indeed before the age of discretion, to this or that doctrine, to the Stoic or Epicurean sect, to which they find themselves pledged, enslaved, and fast joined as something seized upon which they can not let go their hold of,—*whatever philosophical system they are thrown on, as by a storm, they cling to as a rock*,[390] why should it not be likewise granted to these to maintain their liberty, and to consider matters without being bound and subjected? *all the more free and independent because they have complete liberty of judgement.*[391]

Is there not some advantage in being disengaged from the necessity which bridles others? Is it not better to remain in suspense than to be entangled in the many errors that the human imagination has engendered? Is it not better to suspend our conviction than to be mixed up with these seditious and quarrelsome factions? What shall I choose? Whatever you please, so long as you do choose.[392] What a foolish reply, to which it seems, however, comes at last all dogmatism which does not permit us to be ignorant of that of which we are ignorant. Join the party of highest repute: it will never be so secure that, to defend it, you will not need to attack and combat hundreds and hundreds of opposing parties. Is it not better to hold aloof from such a mêlée? You are permitted to embrace, as it were, your honour and your life, Aristotle's belief concerning the eternity of the soul, and to contradict Plato and give him the lie thereupon; and to themselves shall it be forbidden to doubt about it? If it be permissible for Panætius to uphold his private judgement concerning haruspices, dreams, oracles, vaticinations, about which things the Stoics have no doubt,[393] why shall not a wise man dare in all things what this man dares in those things which he has been taught by his masters, and which are confirmed by the common consent of the school of which he is a disciple and teacher? If it be a child who judges, he understands not what it is; if it be a scholar, he is prepossessed. They have kept for themselves a wonderful advantage in the combat, being disburdened of all care of self-defence.[394] It matters not to them that they are struck, so long as they strike; and they make their profit of every thing. If they win, your proposition is lame; if you win, theirs is. If they fail, they verify ignorance; if you fail, you verify it. If they prove that nothing is known, that is well; if they can not prove it, it is well all the same. *And when on the same subject arguments of equal weight are found on opposing sides, it is more easy to suspend judgement on either side.*[395] And they profess to see much more easily that a thing is false, than that it is true;[396] and that which is not, than that which is; and that which they do not believe, than that which they do believe.

They thus express themselves: "I assert nothing; it is no more thus than thus, or than neither the one nor the other; I do not understand it; the probabilities are equal throughout.[397] It is equally permissible to speak for and against.[398] Nothing seems true which may not seem false." Their symbolic word is ἐπέχω[399]—that is to say, I hold on, I do not budge. Such expressions constantly recur with them,[400] and others of like substance. Their result is a pure, complete, and very perfect delay and suspension of judgement. They employ their reason to question and discuss, not to decide and choose. Whoever can imagine a perpetual confession of ignorance, a judgement without tendency or inclination on any occasion whatever, he will have an idea of Pyrrhonism. I describe this humour as fully as I can, because many find it difficult to conceive; and its very authors present it somewhat obscurely and diversely.

673

Concerning the actions of life, they are therein of the common fashion. They yield and adapt themselves to natural inclinations, to the impulsion and restraint of passions, to the decrees of laws and customs, and to the teaching of the arts.[401] *For God chooses that we should not know these things, but merely make use of them.*[402] They allow their ordinary actions to be guided by these things, without any use of opinion or judgement. Which makes me unable to harmonise easily this conception with what is said of Pyrrho.[403] They depict him as dull and emotionless, choosing an untamed and unsociable course of life, standing in the way of being hit by carts, venturing near precipices, refusing to comply with the laws. This is going beyond his teaching. He did not desire to be a stone or a stump; he desired to be a living, investigating, and reasoning man, enjoying all natural pleasures and advantages, employing and making use of all his bodily and mental faculties in regular and right fashion. The fantastic, imaginary, and false privileges which man has usurped, to rule, to regulate, to establish the truth, he in good faith renounced and forsook.

[404]But there is no sect which is not constrained to permit a wise man belonging to it to follow many things neither understood, nor recognised, nor agreed to, if he would live. And when he goes on shipboard, he follows his purpose, not knowing if it will be profitable to him, and trusts[405] that the vessel is sound, the pilot experienced, the weather suitable —conditions that are probable only; in accordance with which he is bound to let himself be moved by outward appearances, provided that they are not of a manifestly thwarting character.[406] He has a body, he has a soul; his senses impel him, his mind stirs him. Although he does not

find in himself the special and peculiar indication for judgement, and although he may discern that he should not pledge his assent, since there may be something false resembling what is true, he does not fail to perform the functions of his life completely and fitly. How many arts are there which avowedly have their being in conjecture rather than in knowledge; which do not decide as to the true and the false, and follow solely after what seems? There is, they say, both what is true and what is false; and there is in us the ability to seek them, but not the ability to determine them by a touchstone. We do much better to let ourselves be guided by the fashion of the world, without inquisition. A soul warranted against prepossession has made marvellous progress toward tranquillity. People who judge their judges and spy faults in them never duly submit to them. How much more docile and easily led, in respect both to the laws of religion and to the laws of civil government, simple and incurious minds are found to be, than the vigilant and pedagogic minds, regarding divine and human causes.

There is nothing of human surmise in which there is so much verisimilitude and utility. This[407] offers man to view, naked and empty, acknowledging his inborn feebleness, fit to receive from on high some degree of foreign force, unfurnished with human knowledge, and so much the better adapted to receive within himself divine knowledge, nullifying his judgement to make more room for faith, neither an unbeliever, nor asserting any dogma contrary to the common observances, humble, obedient, teachable, studious, a sworn foe of heresy, and consequently exempting himself from the idle and irreligious opinions introduced by false sects. He is a blank page, prepared to take from God's hand such manifestations[408] as it shall please him to write upon it. The more we remand ourselves to God and entrust ourselves to him, and renounce ourselves, the better it is for us. Accept things, says Ecclesiastes, in good part, with the aspect and the nature with which they appear to thee from day to day; the rest is beyond your knowledge.[409] *The Lord knoweth the thoughts of man, that they are vanity.*[410]

Here we behold how, of the three general schools of Philosophy, two make express profession of doubt and ignorance; and in that of the Dogmatists, which is the third, it is easy to discern that the greater number assume the semblance of assurance only to make a better appearance. They thought not so much of establishing some certainty for us as of showing us how far they had gone in this hunting for truth: *which the learned imagine, rather than know.*[411]

Timæus, having to inform Socrates of what he knows of the gods, of the world, and of men, proposes to speak of them as man to man, and [says] that it suffices if his reasonings are as probable as the reasonings of another; for not in his hand nor in any mortal hand are accurate reasonings.[412] Which one of his followers has imitated thus: *I will explain these things as I can; not, however, will my words be certain and immutable, like those of Pythian Apollo, but those of a weak man, probabilities following conjectures;*[413] and this on the topic of contempt for death, a simple and everyday topic.[414] Elsewhere he has translated the same thought from Plato: *If, perchance, in discussing the nature of the gods and the origin of the universe, I fall short of the end I have in mind, it will not be surprising; for it must be remembered that both I who discourse and you who judge are men; so that, if I set forth what is probable, nothing more should be required.*[415]

Aristotle ordinarily heaps up before us a great number of other opinions and other beliefs, to compare them with his own, and makes us see how much further he has gone, and how much nearer he approaches probability; for the truth is not determined by authority and by the testimony of others. And therefore Epicurus scrupulously avoided alleging his opinion of other men in his writings. He[416] is the prince of Dogmatists; and yet we learn from him that the much knowing gives cause for the more doubting.[417] We frequently see him of set purpose[418] shroud himself in obscurity so dense and impenetrable that one can detect therein nothing of his opinion. It is in fact a form of Pyrrhonism under a form of decision.[419] Listen to the declaration of Cicero, who explains to us by his own conception that of others: *Those who seek to know what I think about each subject are more inquisitive than is worth while. This dialetic method in philosophy of dissertation about all things, pronouncing clearly on nothing, that was originated by Socrates, renewed by Arcesilaus, strengthened by Carneades, flourishes to our day. . . . I am of those who declare that joined with all truth there is some falseness so much resembling it, that there is no certain quality for assent or dissent.*[420]

Why is it that not Aristotle alone, but most philosophers sought incomprehensibility,[421] unless it were to profit by the emptiness of the subject, and to employ the curiosity of our minds, giving it something to feed upon—that hollow and fleshless bone to gnaw? Clitomachus declared that he had never been able to understand from the writings of Carneades what his opinions were.[422] Wherefore Epicurus avoided clearness for his disciples,[423] and Heraclitus was for this called obscure.[424] Lack of clearness is a coin which learned men use, like jugglers, in order not to lay open the emptiness of their art, and which human stupidity readily accepts.

> Celebrated chiefly among the frivolous for the obscurity of his language; for fools the more admire and like all things which they perceive to be concealed under involved language.[425]

Cicero reprehends some of his friends for being wont to spend more time on astrology, law, dialectics, and geometry than those sciences deserve; and says that this diverted them from more useful and worthy duties of life.[426] The Cyrenaic philosophers equally despised physics and dialectics.[427] Zeno, at the very beginning of his work on the Republic, declared all liberal branches of learning useless.[428] Chrysippus said that what Plato and Aristotle had written concerning Logic, they wrote by way of pastime and for practice, and could not believe that they would have spoken seriously of so unimportant a subject.[429] Plutarch said the same of metaphysics.[430] Epicurus had said this also of rhetoric and grammar, poetry, mathematics, and all the other sciences, except natural philosophy. And Socrates of all save only that which treats of morals and of life.[431] On whatsoever subject he was questioned, he always, first of all, induced the questioner to give an account of the conditions of his life, present and past, which he examined and judged, deeming all other instruction dependent on that, and supererogatory.[432]

Apology for Raimond Sebond

Those studies please me little that have not served to make virtuous those who teach them.[433] Most of the arts have been thus despised by learning itself. But they[434] did not think it inopportune to exercise and recreate their wits, even in matters in which there was no profitable solidity. For the rest, some have thought Plato a Dogmatist, others a doubter, others, on certain subjects the former, and on certain subjects the latter.[435] The leader of his dialogues, Socrates, is always demanding and stirring up discussion, never stopping it, never giving satisfaction, and says that he has no other knowledge than knowing how to take the opposite side. Homer, their fountain-head,[436] has fixed on equal foundations all the schools of philosophy, in order to show how little it matters which way we go.[437] In Plato, ten different sects had their origin, it is said.[438] And in my opinion never was instruction wavering and unasseverating, if his be not so. Socrates said that midwives,[439] by taking up the business of helping others to bring forth, forsook the business of themselves bringing forth; that he, by the title of wise man,[440] which the gods had conferred upon him, had, in like manner, in his manly devotion, wholly of the mind,[441] rid himself of the power of begetting, contenting himself with aiding and befriending with his assistance those who brought forth, opening their organs of generation, oiling their conduits, facilitating the issue of their infant, passing judgement upon it, baptizing it, feeding it, strengthening it, swaddling it, and ordering its movements; employing and using his understanding about the perils and fortunes of others.[442]

It is thus for the most part with the authors of this third category,[443] as the ancients have observed of the writings of

679

Apology for Raimond Sebond

Anaxagoras, Democritus, Parmenides, Zenophanes, and others.[444] They have a manner of writing which is uncertain both in substance and in purpose, rather enquiring[445] than instructing, although they intersperse in their style dogmatic phrases. Is not this also seen in Seneca and in Plutarch? How often is it evident, to those who scrutinise them closely, that they speak now of one aspect, now of another! And those who would bring jurists into agreement should first of all bring each one into agreement with himself.

Plato seems to me to have liked the method of philosophising by dialogues, because of placing more fitly in divers mouths the diversity and variations of his own ideas. To treat matters diversely is as well as to treat them in the same fashion, and better: that is to say, more copiously and usefully. Let us take example from ourselves. Judicial decrees are the highest point of dogmatic and decisive speech; yet those which our parliaments offer to the people, the most exemplary, suited to nourish in them the reverence they owe to that dignity, chiefly from the ability of the persons who exercise it, derive their excellence, not so much from the concluding words, which are usual with them and which are the same with every judge, as from the discussion of the various and contrary ratiocinations which the legal case permits. And the widest field for the mutual recriminations of the philosophers is derived from the contradictions and divergent views with which each one of them is encumbered, either purposely, to show the vacillation of the human mind about every subject, or compelled ignorantly by the volubility and incomprehensibility of every subject.

680

Apology for Raimond Sebond

What means this recurrent thought: "In a slippery and unstable place let us suspend our belief"? For, as Euripides says, —

The works of God in various ways perplex us,—

like that thought which Empedocles strewed freely through his writings, as if moved by a divine frenzy and compelled by truth:[446] "No, no, we feel nothing, we see nothing; all things are hid from us; there is not one, of which we can prove what it is";[447] in agreement with this divine saying: *For the thoughts of mortals are timid, and their devices and counsels are uncertain.*[448] It is not to be thought strange if men, despairing of capturing, have not ceased to take pleasure in the chasing; study being in itself an agreeable occupation—so agreeable that, among other pleasures, the Stoics forbid that which comes from exercising the mind, curb it, and find immoderation in too much knowledge.[449]

Democritus, having eaten at his table figs that tasted of honey, began at once to consider whence came this unusual sweetness in them; and, to enlighten himself concerning it, he was about to leave the table to see the situation of the place where these figs had been picked. His maidservant, having learned the cause of this movement, laughing, told him that he need think no more about that, for it was because she had put them in a dish in which there had been honey. He was annoyed that she had deprived him of the occasion for this investigation, and had robbed his curiosity of an object. "Look you," he said to her, "you have done me an ill turn. I shall not for that stop searching out the cause of this, as if it were a natural one."[450] And he would not have failed to find easily some true reason for a false and suppositious effect. This anecdote of a great and famous philosopher puts before us very plainly that passion for study which keeps us engaged in the pursuit of things of whose acquisition we despair. Plutarch narrates a similar instance of some one who did not wish to be enlightened concerning that of which he was in doubt, in order not to lose the pleasure of seeking it; like that other who did not wish his physician to relieve him of feverish thirst, in order not to lose the pleasure of assuaging it by drinking. *It is better to learn useless things than nothing.*[451] Just as, when we eat,[452] it is oftentimes only for pleasure, and not all that we take that gives us pleasure is nutritious or healthful; in like manner, what our mind derives from learning does not fail to be pleasurable, even if it be neither nourishing nor salutary. This is what they say: Observation of nature is a food adapted to our minds; it elevates and enlarges us, makes us disdain low and earthly things, by comparing them with high and celestial ones;[453] the mere search for things occult and great is very pleasant, especially for him who thereby acquires reverence and awe in judging of them. These are phrases of their doctrine. The empty image of this distempered curiosity is seen still more distinctly in this other instance which they, honouring it, have so often in their mouths. Eudoxus wished and prayed to God that he might once see the sun near-by, to comprehend its shape, greatness, and beauty, on pain of being instantly burned up by it.[454] He desires, at the cost of his life, to acquire a knowledge, the use and possession of which would be at the same moment taken from him; and for the sake of that sudden and fleeing knowledge, to lose all other knowledge that he has and that he might hereafter acquire.

Apology for Raimond Sebond

I can not readily persuade myself that Epicurus, Plato, and Pythagoras gave us for current coin their Atoms, their Ideas, and their Numbers. They were too wise to establish their articles of faith upon matter so uncertain and so debatable. But in the darkness and ignorance of the world, each of those great personages laboured to contribute some sort of luminous conception, and bestirred his mind to invent ideas which should have, at least, a pleasing and ingenious aspect; provided that, false as they are, they could maintain themselves against opposing arguments: *And [inventions] are formed by the mind of each man, not by force of knowledge.*[455] One of the ancients, when he was reproved for making profession of philosophy, of which, however, in his heart he made no great account, replied that that was truly to philosophise. They wished to take every thing into consideration, to weigh every thing, and found that occupation suited to our natural curiosity. Some things they wrote for public utility, for instance, their religions;[456] and it was reasonable, with that end in view, that they did not choose to examine closely[457] common beliefs, purposing not to engender hindrance to obedience to the laws and customs of their country. Plato treats this secret point in a very open manner. For where he writes according to his own thought, he prescribes nothing with certainty.[458] When he acts the lawmaker, he borrows a magisterial and assertive style, and boldly intermingles in it the most fanciful of his conceptions, no less useful for convincing the multitude than ridiculous for convincing himself—knowing how well we are adapted to receive all impressions and especially the most wild and extravagant. And therefore, in his Laws, he takes great care that in public there shall be sung only

683

poems whose fabulous stories tend to some useful end; it being so easy to impress all sorts of false imaginations on the human mind, that it is unfair not to feed it on profitable untruths rather than on untruths that are profitless or harmful.[459]

He says very openly, in his *Republic*, that, to profit men, it is often necessary to deceive them.[460] It is easy to perceive that some schools have more followed truth, others utility, whereby the latter have gained credit. It is the pitiableness of our condition, that often what appears to our imagination as the most true does not appear to us to be the most useful in our life. The boldest schools—the Epicurean, the Pyrrhonian, the New Academic—are still, at the end of the reckoning, compelled to submit to the civil law.

There are other subjects that they have closely examined, this man on one side, that on the other, each one labouring to give some semblance to them, wrong or right. For, having found nothing so hidden that they did not desire to speak of it, they were often compelled to forge feeble and foolish conjectures—not that they themselves took them as a foundation, or to establish any truth, but as a matter of study. *They did not so much believe in the truth of what they said as they desired, it would seem, to exercise their minds on the difficulty of the subject.*[461] And, if we did not take it thus, how should we palliate such great inconstancy, variety, and vanity of opinion, as we see to have been produced by those superior and admirable minds? For, as an example, what is more idle than to seek to conceive God by our analogies and conjectures, and to adjust him and the world in accordance with our capacity and our law, and to employ, to the detriment of the divinity, that small portion of ability which it has pleased him to impart to our natural condition; and because we can not extend our sight so far as to his glorious throne, to bring him down here, to our corruption and our wretchedness?

Of all human and long-existent beliefs concerning religion, that one seems to me to be most probable and most justifiable which recognises God as a power incomprehensible, source and preserver of all things; all goodness, all perfection, receiving and accepting in good part the honour and reverence which human beings render him under whatever form, under whatever name, and in whatever manner it may be.[462]

> Almighty Jupiter, father and mother of all things,
> of kings and of gods.[463]

Such adoration has in all time been regarded graciously by Heaven. All governments have reaped fruit from their godliness. Impious men, impious acts have had always fitting fortunes. Pagan histories recognise authority, method, justice, and miracles and oracles employed for their benefit and instruction in their fabulous religions; God, in his mercy, deigning to foster irregularly[464] by these temporal favours the tender beginnings of a sort of shapeless knowledge of him, which natural reason gave us through the false images of our imaginings. Not false only, but impious also, and harmful, are those that man has fashioned by his own hands. And of all the forms of worship that Paul found in favour at Athens, that which they had dedicated to a hidden and unknown Divinity seemed to him the most justifiable.[465]

Apology for Raimond Sebond

Pythagoras represented the truth as nearly as possible, judging that knowledge of this first cause and being of beings must be indefinite, without limitation, without elucidation;[466] that it was nothing else than the supreme striving of our imagination toward perfection, each one enlarging his conception of it according to his capacity. But if Numa attempted to make the devotion of his people conform to that model, to connect it with a purely intellectual religion without assigned object and without material admixture, he attempted something fruitless: the human mind, wandering among that multitude of formless ideas, could not keep itself in vigour; it must needs bring them together in a special image, fashioned after its will. The divine majesty has thus allowed itself to be circumscribed in some sort for us by corporeal limits; the supernatural and celestial sacraments bear tokens of our terrestrial condition; our worship is expressed by visible rites and audible words; for it is man who believes and who prays. I put aside the other arguments that may be employed about this subject. But it would be difficult to make me believe that the sight of our crucifixes and the depiction of that pitiable martyrdom, that the adornment and ceremonials[467] of our churches, that the voices attuned to the devoutness of our thought, and that the excitement of our senses do not warm people's souls with a religious enthusiasm of very profitable action.[468]

Among those religions to which was given a body as necessity required, amid that universal blindness, I should, it seems to me, have most readily joined with them who adore the sun:

The common light that shines indifferently

686

Apology for Raimond Sebond

On all alike, the world's enlightening eyes;
And, if the almighty ruler of the skies
Has eyes, the sun-beams are his radiant eyes,
That life to all impart, maintain, and guard,
And all men's actions upon earth regard.
This great, this beautiful and glorious sun,
That seasons gives by revolution;
That with his influence fills the universe,
And with one glance doth sullen clouds disperse;
Life, soul of the world, that, flaming in his sphere,
Surrounds the heavens in one day's career;
Immensely great, moving, yet firm and round,
Who the whole world below has fixed his bound,
At rest without rest, idle without stay;
Nature's first son, and father of the day.[469]

Because, in addition to its grandeur and beauty, it is the most distant piece of this machine that we perceive, and, consequently, so little known, that they were pardonable for entering into wonder and reverence toward it.

Thales, who first inquired into such matters, believed God to be a spirit who made all things of water;[470] Anaximander, that the gods were dying and being born at different times, and that they were worlds infinite in number; Anaximenes, that the air was God, that it was engendered and immense, ever in motion. Anaxagoras first maintained that the order and limit of all things is guided by the power and reason of an infinite intelligence; Alcmæon ascribed divinity to the sun, the moon, the stars, and the soul. Pythagoras conceived God as a spirit diffused through the nature of all things, from which our souls are detached; Par-

687

menides, as a circle encompassing the sky, and supporting
the world by the intensity of its light. Empedocles said that
the four elements[471] of which all things are made were gods;
Protagoras, that he had not to say whether they exist or not,
or what they are; Democritus, sometimes that the images[472]
and their circular movements are gods, sometimes the Nature which sends forth those images; and, again, our knowledge and intelligence. Plato disperses his belief in various
aspects; in the *Timœus* he says that the father of the world
can not be given a name; in the Laws, that we must not
enquire about his existence; and elsewhere in these same
books[473] he makes the world, the heavens, the stars, the
earth, and our souls gods, and accepts, moreover, those
which had been accepted by ancient doctrine in every commonwealth. Xenophon reports a like confusion in the teachings of Socrates: sometimes that we must not enquire about
the form of God; and, again, he makes him maintain that
the sun is God, and the soul God; first, that there is but
one, and then, that there are many. Speusippus, nephew of
Plato, makes God a certain force governing all things, and
represents it as animal; Aristotle, at one moment that it is
spirit, at another moment, the world; now he gives another
master to this world, and now calls the ardour of the
heavens[474] God. Zenocrates says there are eight gods: five
nominated from the planets; the sixth composed of all the
fixed stars as his members; the seventh and eighth are the
sun and moon. Heraclides Ponticus does nothing but
wander about among his opinions, and finally deprives God
of sensation, and represents him as changing from one form
to another, and then says that he is the heaven and the earth.
Theophrastus, with like uncertainty, strays about among all

688

his imaginations, ascribing the governance of the world
sometimes to an intelligence, sometimes to the heavens,
sometimes to the stars. Strato thinks that it is Nature,
having power to engender, to augment, to diminish, without form and feeling. Zeno, that it is the law of Nature,
commanding good and prohibiting evil, which law has
life[475] (and he omits the usual gods—Jupiter, Juno, Ves-
ta); Diogenes Apolloniates, that it is the air.[476] Xenophanes makes God round, with sight and hearing, not
breathing, having nothing in common with human nature.[477] Aristo considers the form of God incomprehensible,
deprives him of feeling, and does not know whether he is
a living thing or something else; Cleanthes, sometimes
that he is the reason, sometimes the world, sometimes the
soul of Nature, sometimes the vital heat[478] surrounding and
enveloping all things. Perseus, a disciple of Zeno, held that
the title of God had been given to those who had brought
some noteworthy benefit into human life, and to the beneficial things themselves. Chrysippus made a confused collection of all the preceding opinions, and reckoned, among
a thousand types of gods that he noted,[479] men also who
have been deified. Diagoras and Theodorus denied flatly
that there were any gods.[480] Epicurus makes the gods
radiant, transparent, and unsubstantial,[481] sojourning, as
between two forts, between two worlds, in complete
security, vested with a human form and with limbs like
ours, which limbs are of no use to them.[482]

> I have always said, and shall say, that there are
> heavenly gods; but I am of opinion that they do not
> govern in the doings of the human race.[483]

Apology for Raimond Sebond

Can you trust in your philosophy; can you boast of having found the bean in the cake, when you hear the noisy wrangling of so many philosophic brains? The unsettledness of non-ecclesiastical ways of thinking[484] has gained this for me, that characters and ideas unlike my own[485] do not displease me so much as they instruct me; do not cause me pride in comparing them so much as they humiliate me; and all other liberty of choice than that which comes from the immediate hand of God seems to me a liberty of small advantage. I set apart monstrous and unnatural courses of life.[486] The civil governments of the world are, on this subject, no less various in opinion than are the schools; from which we may learn that fortune itself is not more diverse and variable than our reason, nor more blind and thoughtless.

The things about which we are most ignorant are the most suitable to be deified; therefore, to make gods of ourselves as the ancients did goes beyond extreme weakness of judgement.[487] I should, indeed, have followed rather those who adored the serpent, the dog, and the ox,[488] because their natures and their being are less known to us; and we are more at liberty to imagine what we please about those beasts and to attribute to them extraordinary powers. But to have made gods possessing our own properties, the imperfection of which we know well; to have attributed to them desire, anger, vengeances, marriages, begettings, and relationships, love and jealousy, our limbs and our bones, our fevers and our pleasures, our deaths and burials—all this must have arisen from a marvellous intoxication of the human understanding.

These things are far from possessing divinity, and

are unworthy of being reckoned in the number of the gods.[489]

Their forms, their ages, their garb, their adornments are known; their genealogies, their marriages, their relation-ships, all are brought into the likeness of human weaknesses; for they are represented as disturbed in mind; we accept even the idea of the lusts, the griefs, the angers of the gods.[490] Even as to have attributed divinity, not only to faith, to virtue, to honour, concord, liberty, victory, piety,[491] but also to lust, fraud, death, hatred, old age, ad-versity, to fear, to fever, and to ill-fortune and other mis-haps of our frail and feeble life.

Why introduce morals into our temples? O minds bent to earth, and void of what pertains to heaven![492]

The Egyptians, with an audacious wisdom, forbade, under pain of death,[493] that any one should say that Serapis and Isis, their gods, had formerly been men; yet no one was ignorant that they had been such. And their effigies, representing a finger on the lip, indicated, Varro says, this mysterious command to their priests, to keep silent con-cerning their mortal origin, as by necessary consequence it would annul all veneration for them.[494]

Since man was so desirous to match himself with God, he would have done better, Cicero says, to have given to himself the divine properties and to have drawn them down here below, than to send there on high his corruption and his wretchedness;[495] but, truly apprehended, he has in dif-ferent ways done both the one and the other with equal pride of opinion. When the philosophers scrutinise the

691

hierarchy of their gods and appear eager to point out their alliances, their functions, and their power, I can not believe that they are speaking in earnest. When Plato expounds to us the verger of Pluto[496] and the corporeal pleasures or pains that await us after the destruction and annihilation of our bodies, and makes them agree with the sensibility that we have in this life, —

> From those concealed in solitary paths and hidden
> in a myrtle grove, even in death anxieties do not de-
> part;[497]

when Mahomet promises his followers a paradise hung with tapestry, decorated with gold and precious stones, peopled by maids of surpassing beauty, with exquisite wines and viands, I see clearly that they speak mockingly and adapt themselves to our dulness, to allure and entice us by these beliefs and hopes, suited to our mortal appetites. Yet some in our own day have fallen into like error, promising themselves, after the resurrection, an earthly and finite life, accompanied by all sorts of this world's pleasures and advantages. Do we believe that Plato, he who had such celestial conceptions and such great commerce with what is divine, that the appellation[498] has remained with him, thought that man, that poor creature, had aught in him relating to that incomprehensible power? and that he believed our languid faculties to have the capacity, that our strength of apprehension was forcible enough, to participate in everlasting beatitude or punishment? He should be told by human reason: "If the joys that you promise us in the other life are like those which I have known here below, they have nothing in common with infinity. If all my five natural

Apology for Raimond Sebond

senses should be overflowing with gladness, and this soul possessed of all the satisfaction that it can desire and hope for,—we know her powers,—that would still be nothing. If it be at all human,[499] there is nothing divine. If it is other than what appertains to our present condition, it can not be computed." All satisfaction of mortals is mortal. If the recognition of our parents, of our children, and of our friends in the other world can touch and delight us, if we are still open to such enjoyment, we are in terrestrial and finite conditions.[500] We can not rightly conceive the grandeur of these lofty and divine promises if we can at all conceive them; rightly to imagine them, they must be imagined as unimaginable, unspeakable, and incomprehensible, and perfectly other than things of our miserable experience. Eye has not seen, says St. Paul, nor can enter into the heart of man the fortune that God prepares for his own.[501] And if, to make us capable of it, our being is reshaped and altered (as thou, Plato, sayest by thy purifications[502]), it must be with so extreme and universal a change that according to natural philosophy it will no longer be we.

> It was Hector who fought in battle; but that which was dragged by the horses of the Thessalian [Achilles] was not Hector.[503]

It will be something else that will receive these rewards,—

> What is changed is dissolved; it therefore perishes; for the parts are transposed and quit their order.[504]

For, in the Metempsychosis of Pythagoras, and the change of habitation which he imagined for our souls do we conceive that to the lion in which is the soul of Cæsar are united the dispositions which belonged to Cæsar, or that this animal is Cæsar?[505] If it were he, those would be in the right, who, contesting this belief, in opposition to Plato, cast it in his teeth that the son might be found riding his mother invested with a mule's body, and similar absurdities.[506] And do we think that in the mutations which are made of the bodies of animals to others of the same species, the newcomers are not different from their predecessors? From the ashes of a phœnix is engendered, it is said, a worm, and then another phœnix;[507] this second phœnix—who can imagine that it is not different from the first one? The worms that make our silk—we see them, as it were, die and dry up, and from that same body a moth is produced, and from that another worm, which it would be absurd to regard as being still the first one. That which has once ceased to be is no more, —

> Nor, if time should gather up our material after our death and put it anew in the position in which it now is, this action would not at all concern us, when once our consciousness is interrupted.[508]

And when, Plato, thou sayest elsewhere that it will be the spiritual part of man to which it will belong to enjoy the reward of the other life,[509] thou sayest a thing of as little significance,—

> As the eye torn from its socket can see of itself nothing apart from the rest of the body.[510]

For in this case it will not be man, nor consequently we, to whom that enjoyment will belong; for we are composed of two principal essential parts, the separation of which is the death and destruction of our existence;

Apology for Raimond Sebond

A break in our existence has been interposed, and
motions strayed from the sensations they produced.[511]

We do not say that man suffers when worms devour his
limbs, with which he lived, and that the earth consumes
them,—

And this is nothing to us, who, by the union and
marriage of body and soul, are made all one.[512]

Moreover, upon what basis of their justice can the gods
recognise and reward man after his death for his good and
virtuous acts, since it was they themselves who set in motion
and created them in him? And why should they be displeased and avenge upon him his vicious acts, since they
themselves have created him in this imperfect condition,
and by the slightest action[513] of their will they can prevent
him from doing amiss? Might not Epicurus object this to
Plato, with much show of human reason, if he did not often
take shelter behind the saying that it is impossible to establish by mortal nature any thing certain concerning immortal nature? She[514] but mistakes the road everywhere,
but especially when she intermeddles with divine matters.
Who perceives this more manifestly than we? For although
we have given her definite and infallible principles, even
though we should illumine the steps by the sacred lamp of
the truth, which it has pleased God to communicate to us,
we nevertheless daily see that, however little she may di-
gress from the common path, and turn aside or stray from
the way marked out and trodden by the Church, she immediately loses herself, is entangled and impeded, whirling
about and floating in that vast, disturbed, and fluctuating

695

sea of human opinions, without restraint and without aim. As soon as she loses that broad and beaten road, she wanders about, divided and dispersed, in a thousand different directions.

Man can be only what he is, and can conceive only in accordance with his capacity. It is greater presumption, says Plutarch, for those who are but men to undertake to speak and reason concerning gods and demigods, than it is for a man ignorant of music to attempt to judge those who sing, or for a man who was never in the field to attempt to discuss arms and warfare, presuming to understand by some slight impression the fact of an art which is beyond his knowledge.[515]

Antiquity thought, so I believe, that it was conferring a boon upon the divine mightiness by putting it on a par with man, investing it with his faculties, and endowing it with his fine humours and most shameful necessities, offering our viands to eat, and our dances, our mummeries, and play-acting to amuse it, our garments to clothe it, and our houses to dwell in; charming it with the odour of incense and the sounds of music, with wreaths and nosegays; and, to bring it into agreement with our vicious passions, attributing to its justice a[516] more than human vengeance, delighting it by the ruin and dispersal of things by it created and preserved (like Tiberius Sempronius, who caused to be burned, as a sacrifice to Vulcan, the rich booty and weapons that he had taken from his enemies in Sardinia;[517] and Paulus Æmilius, those from Macedonia, as a sacrifice to Mars and Minerva;[518] and Alexander, when he reached the Indian Ocean, cast into the sea in honour of Thetis many great vessels of gold[519]); heaping up its altars, too, by the slaugh-

ter, not only of harmless beasts, but of men likewise, as
many nations, and among others our own, had in common
custom. And I think that there is no nation exempt from
having made trial of this.

> Then he seized four young men, sons of Sulmo, and
> as many who had been brought up by the Ufens, to
> sacrifice them, living, to the manes [of Pallas].[520]

The Getæ deem themselves immortal and their death to
be simply the beginning of a journey toward their god,
Zamolxis. Every five years they send to him some one from
among them, to ask from him necessary things. This deputy
is chosen by lot. And the manner of despatching him is
that, after they have informed him by word of mouth of his
commission, of those who are with him, three hold erect
as many javelins, upon which the others hurl him with all
their strength. If he is pierced in a mortal part, and dies
quickly, that is to them a sure evidence of divine favour;
if he escapes, they regard him as wicked and execrable, and
depute another of them in like manner.[521] Amestris, the
mother of Xerxes, when an old woman, once caused fourteen youths of the best families of Persia to be buried alive,
to propitiate, in accordance with the religion of the country,
some god of the under-world.[522] Even to-day the idols of
Themistitan are strengthened with the blood of little children; and they care for no sacrifice other than of those pure
infantine souls: justice athirst for the blood of innocence,—

> So greatly can religion counsel ill deeds![523]

The Carthaginians immolated their own children to Saturn; and he who had none bought them, the father and

mother, however, being required to be present at that ceremony, with joyous and satisfied bearing.[524] It was a strange
conception, to seek to pay for the divine kindness with our
affliction; like the Lacedæmonians, who showed tender regard for their Diana[525] by cruel torture of young boys, whom
they caused to be whipped, often to death, in her honour.[526]
It was an extraordinary humour, to seek to gratify the architect by the overthrow of his structure, and to seek to cancel
the penalty due to the guilty by the punishment of the not
guilty; and that poor Iphigenia, in the port of Aulis, by her
death and by her immolation, should absolve before God the
Greek army from the offences that it had committed:—

> And the stainless victim grievously fell, stained
> with blood, in the very season of marriage, offered to
> the gods by a father;[527]

and that those two beauteous and noble souls of the Decii,
father and son, to propitiate the favour of the gods for the
affairs of Rome, should throw themselves headlong into the
thickest press of the enemy.[528] *Was the indignation of the
gods so great that they could not be well disposed to the
Roman people unless such men died?*[529] To which may be
added that it is not for the criminal to have himself whipped
by his own rule and at his own time: it is for the judge, who
considers as chastisement only the penalty he orders, and can
not regard as punishment that which is to the liking of him
who suffers it. Divine vengeance presupposes our entire
repugnance to its decree and to our penalty. And the humour of Polycrates, Tyrant of Samos, was absurd, who, to
interrupt the course of his constant good fortune and to
balance it, threw into the sea the most dear and precious

jewel he possessed, deeming that, by this intended mishap, he should satisfy the revolution and vicissitude of fortune; and she, to deride his folly, caused that same jewel, found in the belly of a fish, to return into his hands.[530] And again, of what use are the rendings and dismemberings of the Corybantes, the Mœnads, and, in our time, of the Mohammedans, who slash the face, the stomach, the limbs, to please their prophet, whilst the crime rests in the will, not in the breast, the eyes, the genitories, the paunch, the shoulders, and the throat. *Greatly is the mind deranged and mastered by madness that thinks to please the gods by exercising cruelties in truth beyond those of men.*[531]

This natural contexture[532] concerns in its use not ourselves alone, but also the service of God and of our fellow men; it is a wrong to others to injure the body knowingly, as it is to kill ourselves on any pretext whatsoever. It seems like great cowardice and treachery to maltreat the body and mar its functions, stupid and servile as they are, in order to spare the soul the perplexity of guiding them according to reason. *Where do those fear the anger of the gods, who think in this way to gain their favour? Some have been castrated for the pleasure of licentious kings; but no one, with his own hand, at the command of a master, has made himself not a man.*[533] Thus they overloaded their religion with many evil details;

> Religion gave birth more often formerly to sinful and unholy deeds.[534]

Now nothing of ours can be compared or likened in any way whatsoever to the divine nature, which does not stain it and mark it with just so much imperfection. That infinite beauty, power, and goodness, how can it admit of any correspondence and similitude with a thing so abject as man, without extreme loss and deterioration of its divine grandeur? *The weakness of God is stronger than men; and the foolishness of God is wiser than men.*[535] Stilpo, the philosopher, being asked whether the gods rejoiced in the honours and sacrifices we pay them, "You are indiscreet," he replied; "let us draw aside if you wish to talk of that."[536] Yet we prescribe for him[537] limits, we hold his power besieged by our reasonings (I call our vain fancies and our dreams reasoning, with the permission of philosophy, which says that even the fool and the sinner are mad by reasoning, but that it is a reasoning of a special kind); we would subject him to the idle and feeble conceptions of our minds—him who created both ourselves and our intelligence.

Because nothing is made of nothing, God can not have been able to make the world without matter. What! has God given us knowledge of the keys and the uttermost extent of his power? has he bound himself not to go beyond the limits of our understanding? Assume, O man, that thou hast been able to observe here some traces of his manifestations: dost thou think that he has here employed all that he is capable of, and that he has made use of all his thoughts[538] and all his ideas in this work? Thou seest only the ordering and the government of this little cave, wherein thou art placed, if, indeed, thou dost see it at all; his divinity has jurisdiction infinitely wider; this part is nothing compared with the whole,—

All things together with heaven and earth and sea are nothing to the whole sum of the universal sums,[539]—

it is a municipal law that thou dost allege; thou knowest not what is the universal law. Fasten thyself to that to which thou art subject, but fasten not him; he is not thine associate or fellow citizen or comrade; if he has in any way imparted himself to thee, it is not by stooping to thy littleness or by giving thee full knowledge[540] of his power. The human body can not fly to the clouds, that is thy concern;[541] the sun runs without resting his regular course; the bounds of the seas and the earth can not be confounded; water is unstable and without firmness; a wall without a breach is impenetrable by a solid body; a man can not preserve his life in flames; he can not be bodily both in heaven and on earth and in a thousand places at once. It is for thee that God has made these rules; it is thou whom they bind. He has testified to Christians that he has done away with them all, when it has so pleased him. Why, in truth, all-powerful as he is, should he have restrained his forces to a certain degree? In whose favour would he have foregone his prerogative? Thy reasoning has in no other matter more truth and foundation than in persuading thee of the plurality of worlds,—

Earth and sun, moon, sea, and all things else that are not single in their kind, but in number past numbering.[542]

The most famous minds of past time believed it, and some of those of our own day, compelled by the evidence of human reason. Forasmuch as in this structure that we behold there is nothing single and one,—

In the sum of all there is no one thing that is begotten single of its kind and grows up single of its kind, and sole,[543]—

701

and all species are multiplied by some number; therefore it seems to be not probable that God has created this sole work without anything resembling it,[544] and that all matter of this kind was used up in this single object;

> Wherefore I say again and again, you must admit
> that there are elsewhere other considerations of matter like this which ether holds in its greedy grasp;[545]

especially if it be a living thing,[546] as its motions make so credible that Plato asserts it,[547] and many in our day either allow it or dare not disallow it;[548] any more than the ancient belief that the sky, the stars, and other parts of the world are creatures composed of body and spirit, mortal by virtue of their composition, but immortal by the decree of the creator.

Now, if there are many worlds, as was believed by Democritus,[549] Epicurus, and almost all philosophy, how do we know whether the origins and regulations of this one are of like kind with the other? They have, perchance, another aspect and another form of government. Epicurus conceives them as in some cases similar and in some cases dissimilar.[550] We see in this world an infinite difference and variety, simply from the distance between places. Neither corn nor wine nor any of our animals is found in that new corner of the world which our fathers have discovered: all there is different. And in times past, consider in how many parts of the world there was no knowledge, either of Bacchus or of Ceres.

For whoever chooses to believe Pliny and Herodotus, there are kinds of men in certain regions who bear very little resemblance to us.[551] And there are mongrel and indefinite forms between human nature and brutish nature. There are countries where men are born without heads, having their eyes and mouth in the breast; where they are all hermaphrodites; where they walk on four feet; where they have but one eye in the forehead, and a head more like that of a dog than like ours; where they are half fish in the lower parts, and live in the water; where the women bear children at five years of age and live only eight years; where their heads and the skin of their foreheads are so hard that a weapon can not cut into them, but is blunted by them; where the men are beardless; nations without use and knowledge of fire; others whose sperm is of a dark colour. What of those who by nature change to wolves, to mares, and then again to men? And if it be true, as Plutarch says,[552] that in some regions of the Indies there are men without mouths who are nourished by the smell of certain odours, how many of our descriptions are false! He[553] is no longer risible,[554] nor, perchance, capable of reason or of society. The arrangement and the cause of our internal structure would be, for the most part, purposeless.

Furthermore, how many things are known to us, which conflict with the fine rules that we have cut out and prescribed for nature? And we would undertake to bind to them God himself! How many things do we call miraculous and contrary to nature! That is done by every man and every nation in proportion to their ignorance. How many hidden properties and quintessences do we find! For to live according to nature[555] is, for us, to live according to our intelligence so far as that can go, and so far as we can see by its means; that which is beyond is outside of nature and irregular.[556] Now, by this reckoning, to the most well-informed and ablest men every thing would be outside of nature; for human reason has persuaded them that it has neither foothold nor any basis whatsoever, not enough even to make it certain that snow is white (and Anaxagoras said that it is black[557]); whether any thing has existence, or nothing has existence; whether there be knowledge or ignorance—which Metrodorus Chius denied that man could say[558]; or whether we be alive; Euripides being in doubt whether the life we are living is life, or whether it is what we call death that may be life:—

Τὶς δ' οἶδεν εἰ ζῆν τουθ ὁ κέκληται θανεῖν,
Τό ζῆν δὲ θνέσκειν ἔστι.[559]

And not without probability; for why do we take our title to existence from that instant which is but a lightning-flash in the infinite course of an eternal night, and so brief an interruption of our perpetual and natural condition, death occupying all before and all after that moment, and even a goodly part of that moment? Others swear that there is no movement, that nothing stirs; as the followers of Melissus (for, if there is but one, spherical movement can not be used by it nor movement from place to place, as Plato proves);[560] that there is neither generation nor distraction in nature.[561]

Protagoras says that there is nothing in nature save doubt; that all things can be disputed for and against this very fact, whether all things can be disputed for and against; Nausiphanes, that, of things which seem to be, nothing is more existent than non-existent; that there is nothing certain save uncertainty; Parmenides, that of that which seems to be, there is no generality, that there is but one;[562] Zeno, that there is not even one, and that there is nothing. If there were one, it would be either in another or in itself; if it is in another, there are two; if it is in itself, there are again two, that which contains and that which is contained.[563] According to these dogmas, the nature of things is but a shadow, either false or nothingness.[564]

It has always seemed to me that, for a Christian man, this sort of language is full of rashness and irreverence: God can not die, God can not contradict himself, God can not do this or that. I do not find it well thus to confine the divine power within the determinations of our phrase-making.[565] And what is understood by these propositions we should express more reverently and devoutly. Our language has its weaknesses and its defects, like all things else. The greater number of the causes of the confusions of the world are grammatical.[566] Our lawsuits arise solely from discussion about the interpretation of the laws; and the greater number of wars, from failure to express clearly the conventions and treaties of amity between rulers. How many quarrels, and what momentous ones, have been caused in the world by the uncertainty as to the meaning of the syllable *Hoc!*[567] Let us take the forms of phrase which logic itself will give us as clearest. If you say, "It is fine weather," and if you speak the truth, it is then fine weather. Have we not here an accurate mode of speech? Yet it will mislead us. That this is so, let us follow up the example. If you say, "I lie," and you speak the truth, then you lie.[568] The skill, the reasoning, the force of this conclusion are the same as in the other; none the less, we are stuck fast in the mud. I observe the Pyrrhonian philosophers, that they are not able to express their general conception by any manner of speech, for they have need of a new language. Ours is entirely composed of affirmative propositions, which are wholly hostile to them; in so much that, when they say, "I doubt," they are immediately at our mercy and forced to acknowledge that, at least, they assert and know this, that they doubt. Thus they have been compelled to take refuge in this medical comparison, without which their humour would be inexplicable: they say that, when they declare, "I do not know," or "I doubt," this proposition carries itself away and, at the same time, the remainder, neither more nor less than rhubarb, which expels the peccant humours, and at the same time carries itself off.[569] This idea is more clearly conceived by a question, "What do I know?" which I employ, with the device of a pair of scales.

See what use is made of this manner of speaking, full of irreverence. In the disputes now going on about our religion, if you press your opponents too far, they will tell you confidently that it is not in the power of God to make his body be in paradise and on the earth and in several places at once. And that ancient scoffer[570]—how he turns it to account! "At all events," he says, "it is no slight consolation to man that he sees that God can not do all things; for he can not kill himself when he would, which is the greatest privilege that we have in our state; he can not make mortals immortal; nor bring back to life those who have gone; nor make it so that he who has lived has not lived, that he who has received honours has not had them; having no other power over the past than oblivion. And—that with this connection between man and God may be associated also amusing instances—he can not make twice ten not be twenty." That is what he[571] says, and what a Christian

Apology for Raimond Sebond

should not let pass his lips. Whereas, on the contrary, it seems that men seek this foolish arrogance of language to reduce God to their measure:—

Let the Father to-morrow cover the heavens with a dark cloud or with pure sunshine; he can not render vain the past, or destroy what the fleeting hour has borne away.[572]

When we say that the infinity of the ages, past as well as future, is to God but an instant; that his kindness, wisdom, power are identical with his essence, our speech so says, but our intelligence does not comprehend it. And always our presumption would make the Divinity pass through our sieve. And hence are engendered all the idle fancies and errors with which the world abounds, reducing and weighing in its balance a thing so beyond its standard of weight.[573] *It is astonishing how far the audacity of the human creature will go, if encouraged by any trifling success.*[574] How insolently the Stoics take Epicurus to task because he maintains that to be truly good and happy belongs to God alone, and that the wise man has only a shadow and similitude thereof.[575] How rashly they linked God with destiny (which, with my consent, none who bears the name of Christian shall ever do again); and Thales, Plato, and Pythagoras enslaved him to necessity. This arrogance of seeking to discover God with our eyes has caused one of our writers of great note[576] to give to the divinity a corporeal form. And this is the reason that it happens every day that we ascribe to God events of importance with a special attribution. Because they are important to us, it seems as if they were important to him also, and that he re-

gards them more fully and more carefully than events which
are slight in our eyes, or of usual occurrence. *The gods concern themselves about great things; little things they heed
not.*[577] Listen to this writer's example; it will throw light on
his thought: *Nor in truth are kings attentive to all the details in their kingdoms.*[578] As if it were more or less to him
to shake an empire or the leaf of a tree; and as if his providence were differently exerted in guiding the result of a
battle and the skip of a flea. The hand of his governance has
a like hold upon all things, with the same force and the
same method; our concern in them adds nothing thereto;
our processes and our proportions do not affect it.[579] *God, so
great an artificer in great things, is not less great in small
things.*[580]

Our arrogance is always putting before us this blasphe-
mous similarity. Because our occupations embarrass us,
Strato endowed the gods with complete immunity from
duties, as are their priests. He makes all things to be produced and nourished by Nature, and constructs parts of the
world with her weights and processes,[581] relieving human
nature from the fear of divine judgements.[582] *A blest and
eternal being is not troubled with affairs, nor deputes them
to others.*[583] Nature wills that like things shall have a like
relation. Therefore the infinite number of mortals deter-
mines an equal number of immortals. The innumerable
things that kill and injure presuppose as many that preserve and benefit.[584] As the souls of the gods, without
speech, without eyes, without ears, perceive among themselves, each what another feels, and judge our thoughts, so
the souls of men, when they are free and loosed from the
body by sleep or by some transport, divine, prophesy, and

see things which they could not see when connected with the body.[585]

Men, says St. Paul, have become fools thinking themselves to be wise, and have changed the incorruptible God into a likeness of corruptible man.[586] Consider a little the trickeries of the ancient deifications. After the grand and stately pomp of the obsequies,[587] when the fire was reaching the top of the funeral pile and caught the place where the dead body lay, at that moment they set free an eagle, which, flying aloft, was a sign that the soul was going to paradise. We have a thousand medals,—and especially of that virtuous woman, Faustina,—in which the eagle is represented as bearing these deified souls up to heaven on its shoulders, like a dead kid.[588] It is a pity that we deceive ourselves with our own pretendings and devices,—

What they themselves create, they are afraid of,[589]

like children who are frightened by their playfellow's face when they themselves have begrimed and blackened it. *What is more unfortunate than man, who is ruled by the phantoms of his own imagination!*[590] It is very far from doing honour to him who made us, to do honour to him whom we have made.[591] Augustus had more temples than Jupiter, served with as much devotion and belief in miracles. The Thasians, by way of recompense for the benefactions they had received from Agesilaus, came to tell him that they had canonised him. "Has your nation," he said to them, "this power of making gods of whom it pleases? Do so to some one of yourselves, that I may see, and then, when I shall have seen how he likes it, I will give you many thanks for your offer."[592]

Apology for Raimond Sebond

Man is indeed mad. He could not fashion a worm, and he fashions gods by the dozen. Hear Trismegistus praising our ability: "Of all admirable things, this is beyond admiration, that man has been able to discover the divine nature and to make it."[593] Look at these arguments of the school of philosophy itself,

> To whom alone it is given to know the gods and the heavenly powers, or to know that they can not be known.[594]

"If God exists, he is animal; if he is animal, he has sensation; if he has sensation, he is subject to corruption. If he is without body, he is without soul, and consequently without action; and if he has body, he is perishable."[595]—There's a trump card![596] "We are incapable of having made the world; so there is some superior nature which has set its hand to it. It would be absurd arrogance to estimate ourselves as the most perfect thing in this universe; so there is something better—that something is God. When you see a rich and stately dwelling, although you may not know who is the master of it, yet you do not say that it was built for rats. And this divine structure that we see of the heavenly palace, is it not to be believed that it is the abode of some master greater than we are? Is not the highest always the noblest? And we are placed at the bottom. Nothing without soul and without reason can bring forth a living being capable of reason; the world brings us forth, so it has soul and reason. Each part of us is less than ourselves; we are a part of the world; so the world is endued with wisdom and reason, and more abundantly than we are. It is a fine thing to have a great government; so the government of the world belongs to some fortunate nature. The stars do us no harm, so they are full of kindliness.[597] We have need of sustenance; so also have the gods, and are nourished by the vapours from here below.[598] Earthly advantages are not advantages for gods; so they are not advantages for us. To offend and to be offended are equally evidences of weakness; so it is folly to fear God. God is good by nature, man by his endeavour, which is more. There is no distinction between divine wisdom and human wisdom other than that the former is eternal; now, duration adds nothing to wisdom; wherefore behold us equals.[599] We have life, reason, and liberty; we value goodness, charity, and justice; so these qualities are in him. In short, the building up and the upbuilding, the conditions of divinity, are arranged by man according to the relation to himself. "What a pattern! Let us stretch and enlarge human qualities as much as we please; puff thyself up, poor man, and again, and again:—

"Not if you burst," he said.[660]

Assuredly, in their thoughts they do not, for they can not, conceive of God; they regard themselves, not him; they compare him, not with himself, but with themselves.[601]

In the things of nature, results but half represent their causes: how about this one?[602] It is above the order of nature; its position is too lofty, too distant, and too commanding, to suffer our judgement to bind and pinion it. It is not through ourselves that we reach it; that is too low a course. We are no nearer heaven on Mont Cenis than at the bottom of the sea, as your astrolabe will show you.[603] They debase God even to the carnal knowledge of women: how many times, how many engenderings! Paulina, wife of Satur-

ninus, a matron of high repute in Rome, thinking to lie
with the god Serapis, finds herself in the arms of a lover of
hers, by the connivance of the priests of that temple.[604]
Varro, the most subtle and most learned Latin author, in his
books on Theology, writes that the sacristan of the temple
of Hercules, throwing dice with one hand for himself and
with the other for Hercules, staked against him a supper
and a wench: if he won, it was at the cost of the offerings; if
he lost, at his own expense. Losing, he paid for the supper
and the wench. Her name was Laurentina, who saw this god
in her arms at night, telling her, besides, that the first man
whom she met the next day would pay her her wage in
divine fashion. This was Taruntius, a rich young man, who
took her home to his house and in time made her his heir-
ess. She, in her turn, hoping to do a thing agreeable to that
god, made the Roman people her heir; consequently divine
honours were given to her.[605] As if it were not sufficient
that Plato was originally descended in a double line from
the gods and had Neptune for the common progenitor of
his race, it was held for certain at Athens that Aristo, having desired to enjoy the fair Periction, was unable to do so,
and was warned in a dream by the god Apollo to leave her
undefiled and untouched until she had been brought to
bed; these were the father and mother of Plato.[606] How
many instances are there in history of such cuckoldries practised by the gods upon poor mortals, and of husbands con-
tumeliously discredited in favour of the children! The
followers of Mahomet believe that[607] there are numerous
Merlins, that is to say, fatherless children, born of the spirit,
divinely conceived in the wombs of virgins; and they bear
a name which in their tongue signifies this.[608]

Apology for Raimond Sebond

It is to be observed that nothing is more cherished and more highly prized by every creature than its own being (the lion, the eagle, the dolphin account nothing more highly than their kind[609]); and that each one compares the qualities of all other things with its own qualities, which we can indeed conceive to be expanded and contracted, but that is all; for beyond this comparison and this faculty[610] our imagination can not go, nor can it divine any thing different; and it is impossible for the mind to go outside of this and to pass beyond it. Thence were derived these ancient conclusions: Of all forms, the most beautiful is that of man; consequently God is of that form. No one can be happy without virtue, nor can virtue exist without reason, or reason dwell elsewhere than in the human shape; consequently God is invested with the human shape.[611] *Our minds are so made and prepossessed that when a man thinks of God, the human form presents itself to him.*[612] Because of this, Xenophanes said, jestingly, that if animals fashion gods for themselves, as it is probable that they do, they certainly fashion them like themselves, and magnify themselves, as we do.[613] For why should not a gosling say this: "All the parts of the universe concern me; the earth serves me to walk upon, the sun to give me light, the stars to breathe into me their influences; I have a certain benefit from the winds, another from the waters; there is nothing that the vault of heaven regards with such favour as it does me; I am the darling of nature; is it not man who maintains me, who houses me, who waits upon me? it is for me that he sows and grinds; if he eats me, so does he his fellow man, and so do I the worms that kill him and eat him"? As much might a crane say, and even more proudly, for the freedom

713

of his flight and the possession of that fair and lofty region; *so flattering a go-between is Nature herself, and, as it were, a procuress to her children!*[614]

So now, in this same way, for us are the fates, for us the world; the light and the thunder are for us; both the creator and the created, all is for us. This is the goal and the mark at which the universality of things aims. Look at the record of celestial affairs that philosophy has kept for two thousand years and more: the gods have acted, have spoken only for man; it attributes to them no other subject of consultation, no other vocation.

Here they are against us in war,—

> The earth-born youths subdued by the hand of Hercules, they from whom the resplendent mansion of old Saturn dreaded danger;[615]

here they are partakers of our troubles, to pay us in kind because we have so many times been partakers of theirs.

> Neptune with his powerful trident shakes the walls and the foundations, and overturns the whole city from its seat; yonder, Juno, most terrible, is the first to hold the Scæan gate.[616]

The Caunians, from zeal for the supremacy of their own gods, arm themselves on their day of worship and go over their whole domain, striking the air here and there with their swords, thus hotly pursuing and expelling foreign gods from their territory.[617] The powers of the gods are limited according to our need: this one cures horses, that one, men; one the plague, one the scurvy, another the cough; one, one sort of itch, one a different sort *(so does su-*

perstition connect the gods with the most trifling things[618]);
this one causes grapes to grow, that one, garlic; one has
lechery in charge, one merchandise (for each class of artisans, a god); one has his province and his renown in the
east, another in the west:

> There were her arms, there her chariot.[619]

*O divine Apollo, who certainly dost govern the navel of
the earth [Delphi].*[620]

> The Cecropides [Athenians] worship Pallas; Crete,
> of Minos, Diana; the dwellers in the land where Hyp-
> sipyle reigned [Lemnos], Vulcan; Sparta and My-
> cenæ, home of the descendants of Pelops, Juno; the
> heights of Mænalis, Faunus [Pan], with his pine-
> crowned head; Mars was adored in Latium.[621]

This one has but one town, or one family, as his possession; that one lives alone, another in company, either voluntarily or of necessity.

> And the temples of the grandson are joined to that
> of his mighty ancestor.[622]

There are some so poor and powerless[623] (for the number
of them reaches to thirty-six thousand) that it needs five
or six combined to produce a blade of wheat, and they derive from it their various names:[624] there are three for one
door—he of the boards, he of the hinges, he of the threshold;[625] four for one child—guardians of his swaddling-
clothes, of his drinking, of his eating, of his nursing;[626]
some about whom there is no question,[627] some uncertain
and doubtful; some who do not yet enter paradise,—

Apology for Raimond Sebond

Whom, since we do not judge them yet worthy of heavenly honours, we at least permit to inhabit the countries that we have given them.[628]

There are among them physicians, poets, statesmen;[629] some of them are midway between divine and human nature, intercessors, intermediaries between ourselves and God; adored with a sort of secondary and diminished order of adoration; there are infinite titles and offices; some good, some evil. Some of them are old and worn out,[630] and some of them are mortal; for Chrysippus believed that, in the final conflagration of the world, all the gods would perish save Jupiter.[631] Man fabricates a thousand agreeable associations between God and himself. Is he not his compatriot?

Crete, the cradle of Jove.[632]

This is the excuse that Scævola, a great pontiff, and Varro, a great theologian, gave us in their day, when considering this subject: that it is needful that the people be ignorant of many true things and believe many false things;[633] *since he seeks the truth in order that he may be free, it is thought expedient for him to be in error.*[634] Human eyes can not perceive things save by the forms with which they are acquainted. And we do not remember the downfall of the unhappy Phaëton for having attempted to manage the reins of his father's horses with a mortal hand. Our mind drops down to as great a depth, and is shattered and crushed in like manner through its temerity. If you ask philosophy of what substance consist the sky and the sun, what will it answer, if not of iron, or, with Anaxagoras, of stone,[635] or some such matter that we use? Does some one enquire of

716

Apology for Raimond Sebond

Zeno what nature is? A fire, he says, artificial, apt to engender, proceeding according to rule.[636] Archimedes, the master of that science which claims for itself preëminence over others in truth and certainty, says: The sun is a god of red-hot iron. Is not this a fine conception, resulting from the beauty and necessary employment[637] of geometrical demonstration! Not, however, so necessary and useful that Socrates did not consider that it was sufficient to know enough of it to be able to measure the ground that one gave and received,[638] and that Poliænus, who had been a famous and illustrious teacher of it, did not, after he had tasted the sweet fruit of the lazy gardens of Epicurus, hold them in contempt as being full of falsity and manifest emptiness.[639]

Socrates, who was esteemed in ancient days to be wise above all other men in matters celestial and divine, says in Xenophon, touching this proposition of Anaxagoras, that he had disturbed his brain, like all men who delve immoderately into branches of knowledge which do not appertain to them. As to his representing the sun as a red-hot stone, he did not reflect that a stone does not glow in fire, and, what is worse, that it is consumed by it; as to his representing the sun and fire as the same, that fire does not turn black those whom it shines upon; that we can look unblinking at fire; that fire kills plants and grasses.[640] In the opinion of Socrates, and in mine also, the wisest way to judge of things above is not to judge of them at all. Plato having in the *Timæus* to speak of divinities, "This is an undertaking," he says, "which goes beyond our scope; those men of old times are to be believed, who said that they were begotten by them; it is contrary to reason to refuse faith to the children of the gods, although what they say be not confirmed

by unquestionable or probable proofs, since they assure us
that they speak of personal and well-known matters."[641]

Let us see if we have a little more clearness in our knowledge of human and natural things. Is it not an absurd undertaking, for those things to which, by our own admission,
our learning can not attain, to devise for them another body,
and ascribe to them a false form of our invention; as is seen
regarding the movements of the planets, to which, inasmuch as our mind can not reach them or conceive their
natural guidance, we ascribe material, clumsy, corporeal
impulsions like ours?

> The pole of gold, the rims of the wheels of gold,
> and the spokes of silver.[642]

You would say there had been chariot-drivers, carpenters,
and painters, who had gone up on high to fashion machines
of various movements and to arrange the wheels and invo-
lutions of the heavenly bodies in diversified colours around
the spindle of necessity, according to Plato.[643]

> The universe is the immense abode of all things,
> which five thundering zones encircle, through which
> a belt adorned with twice six glittering starry signs,
> aloft in the sloping skies, receives the two-horsed car
> of the moon.[644]

These are all dreams and fantastic absurdities. Would
that Nature might be pleased, some day, to lay open her
bosom to us and make us see, as they are, the modes and
guidance of her movements, and there to prepare our eyes!
O God! what deceptions, what errors, we should find in
our paltry learning! I am mistaken if it apprehends a single

thing rightly; and I shall depart hence more ignorant of every thing else than of my ignorance.

Have I not seen in Plato this divine saying, that Nature is naught but enigmatical poetry?[645] as, perhaps, one might say, a veiled and shadowed painting, gleaming with an infinite variety of false lights to employ our conjectures. *All these things are hidden and surrounded by thick shadows, so that no human mind is keen enough to penetrate the sky or the interior of the earth.*[646] And certainly philosophy is naught but adulterated poetry. Whence do those authors derive all their authority save from the poets? And the earliest ones were poets themselves and treated of it[647] in their art. Plato was simply an irregular poet.[648] Timon called him, by way of insult, a great fabricator of miracles.[649]

Just as women make use of ivory teeth when their natural ones fail them, and in place of their true complexion create one of some foreign substance; as they make hips[650] of cloth and felt, and busts[651] of cotton, and in the sight and knowledge of every one embellish themselves with a false and borrowed beauty; so does learning (and even our law, they say, has legal fictions upon which it bases the truth of its justice): it gives us as satisfaction and presupposition the things which, as itself teaches us, have been invented; for these eccentric and concentric epicycles, with which Astrology aids herself in disposing the revolutions of the stars, it[652] gives us as the best that it has been able to devise on that subject; as also, for that matter, philosophy offers us, not what is or what she believes, but what she fabricates that has the most probability and attractiveness. Plato says, in his discourse on the nature of the human body and that of beasts: That what we have said is true, we should be assured if we had thereon the confirmation of a divine voice; we are only sure that it is the likeliest that we can say.[653]

It is not to the skies alone that she[654] sends her ropes, her machines, and her wheels. Consider a little what she says of ourselves and our frame-work. There is not more retrogradation, trepidation, accession, recession, readjustment,[655] in the stars and heavenly bodies than they[656] have fashioned for this poor little human body. Truly they have thence had reason to call this the Little World,[657] so many fragments and forms have they employed to lay its walls and build it.[658] In order to arrange the movements they see in man, the diverse functions and faculties that we feel in ourselves, into how many parts have they divided our souls; lodged it in how many places; in how many ranks and degrees have they disposed this poor man in addition to natural and visible ones; and assigned him how many offices and vocations! They make of him an imaginary republic. It is a subject that they hold to and work over; they are given full power to pull him to pieces, arrange, reconstruct, and fill him out, each one according to his fancy; and still they do not possess him. Not only in reality, but even in imagination, they can not so order it that there is not some cadence or some note that eludes their architecture, quite abnormal as it is, and pieced out with a thousand false and fantastic bits. And it is not reasonable to excuse them. For we pardon painters, when they paint the sky, the earth, seas, mountains, scattered islands, for putting before us only some slight indication thereof, and are content with a sort of shadow and suggestion, as of things not known; but when they draw for us from life any subject which is familiar to us and well known, we require of them a perfect and exact reproduction of lineaments and colours, and despise them if they fail in this.[659]

I am much pleased with the Milesian maid who, seeing the philosopher Thales continually occupied in contemplation of the celestial vault, and [seeing] that his eyes were ever raised upward, placed in his path something to make him stumble, to warn him that it would be time to occupy his thoughts with things that were in the clouds when he had taken heed to those that were at his feet.[660] She surely gave him good counsel—to look at himself rather than at the heavens. For, as Democritus says through the mouth of Cicero,—

No one contemplates what is at his feet; they explore the expanse of the sky.[661]

But it is inherent in our condition that knowledge of what we have in our hands is as far removed from us and as embosomed in clouds, as is that of the stars. As Socrates says in Plato, he who takes part in philosophy can be reproached as that woman reproached Thales, for that he sees nothing of what is before him. For every philosopher is ignorant of what his neighbour is doing, aye, and of what he himself is doing, and knows not what they both are, whether beasts or men.[662]

Those persons who find Sebond's arguments too weak, who are ignorant of nothing, who oversee the world, who know every thing,—

What causes control the sea; what regulates the course of the year; whether the stars move and wander at their own will or by command; what hides the dark-

ened orb of the moon, and what makes it reappear;
what is the meaning and what the power of the discordant harmony of nature,[663]—

did they not sometimes, amidst their books, feel the difficulties that present themselves in understanding their own
being? We see well that the finger is moved and that the
foot is moved; that some parts stir of themselves without our
leave, and that other parts we excite by our direction; that a
certain sort of apprehension causes flushing, a certain other
sort, pallor; one imagination works upon the spleen only,
another on the brain; one causes laughter, another weeping;
a different one appals and benumbs all our faculties and
arrests the movement of our limbs. By one object the stomach is disturbed, by another an organ lower down. But how
a mental impression can so deeply pierce into a compact
and solid subject, and the nature of the connection and
meeting of these admirable springs of action, no man has
ever known, as Solomon says. [664] *All these things are inscrutable to human reason,*[665] says Pliny; and St. Augustine: *The manner in which spirit and body adhere to each
other is altogether wonderful and can not be understood by
man; and this union constitutes man himself.*[666] And yet
no one questions it; for the opinions of men are received in
continuance of ancient beliefs, by authority and on credit,
as if it were a matter of religion and law. We receive as incomprehensible[667] what is commonly held about this matter; we accept this truth, with all its structure and belong-
ings of arguments and proofs, as a firm and solid body,
which is no more to be shaken, which is no more to be
judged. On the contrary, every one, as best he can, plasters

up and strengthens this received belief with all that can be done by the reason, which is a flexible, easily directed tool and adaptable to every form. Thus is the world filled with vapidity and steeped in falsehood. That which causes few things to be questioned is that mere impressions are never tested by us; we never dig to the root, where the mistake and the weakness lie: we argue only about the branches; we do not ask if such a thing is true, but whether it has been thus, or so, understood. We do not ask whether Galen said any thing worth while, but whether he said this, or something else.

Truly it was within reason that this curbing and restraint of the freedom of our judgement, and this tyranny of our beliefs, should be extended even to the schools and the arts. The god of scholastic learning is Aristotle: it is a matter of religion to discuss his decrees, as it was those of Lycurgus at Sparta. His teaching, which is perchance as false as another, is taken by us as supreme law. I know not why I should not accept as readily either the ideas of Plato, or the atoms of Epicurus, or the fulness and emptiness of Leucippus and Democritus, or the water of Thales, or the infinitude of nature of Anaximander, or the air of Diogenes,[668] or the numbers and symmetry of Pythagoras, or the infinite of Parmenides, or the unity of Musæus, or the water and fire of Apollodorus, or the resembling parts of Anaxagoras, or the discord and concord of Empedocles, or the fire of Heraclitus, or any other opinion in that endless confusion of judgements and sayings which this fine human reason brings forth by its certainty and clearness of sight about every thing into which it enters, as I should the opinion of Aristotle on this subject of the ultimate bases of natural things; which bases he built up from three points—matter, form, and privation. For what can be more idle than to make vacuity itself the cause of the production of things? Privation is something negative; by what kind of thought[669] can he have made it the cause and origin of things that exist? Yet this no one would venture to question, except as an exercise in logic. It is in no wise discussed to cast doubt upon it, but to defend the founder of the school from foreign criticisms; his authority is the boundary outside which it is not permitted to investigate.

It is very easy to build upon admitted postulates what one will; for, according to the law and ordering of this beginning, the other parts of the building are easily carried on in harmony. In this way we find our reasoning well grounded, and we discourse on a safe footing; for our masters pre-occupy and gain beforehand in our belief all the room they need to reach the conclusion they desire; in the manner of the geometricians, with their granted demands; the assent and approval that we lend them giving them the means to lead us hither and yon and to whirl us about at their pleasure. Whosoever is believed in his presuppositions, he is our master and our God; he will lay the plan of his foundations so full and so easy to follow that through them he will be able to raise us, if he will, to the clouds.

In this dealing and traffic in learning, we have taken for current coin the saying of Pythagoras, that every skilful man ought to be believed about his art.[670] The dialectician applies to the grammarian for the meaning of words; the rhetorician borrows from the dialectician the arrangement of arguments; the poet, his measures from the musician; the geometrician, his proportions from the arithmetician; the metaphysicians take for their foundation the conjectures of physics. For every science has its admitted principles, by which human judgement is held in check on all sides. If you run up against this barrier, wherein the main error[671] lies, they have at once this saying in their mouths, that there is no arguing with those who deny the first principles.[672] Now, there can be no knowledge of the origin of men[673] if the Divinity has not revealed it to them; of all the rest, both the beginning and the middle and the end, there is naught but visions and smoke. For those who contend by presuppositions, it is necessary to presuppose, on the other side, the very axiom under discussion. Because every human presupposition and every proposition has as much authority as every other,[674] unless reasoning shows the distinction. So we must put them all in the scales; and in the first place, the general ones, and those that domineer over us. The impression of certainty is a certain proof of unwisdom and extreme uncertainty; and there are no more unwise or less philosophical persons than Plato's philodoxes.[675] We must learn if fire be hot, if snow be white, if there be any thing hard or soft within our cognisance. And as for those answers about which old tales were made, as to him who questioned the existence of heat, who was told that he should throw himself into the fire; to him who denied the coldness of ice, that he should put some into his bosom—these are wholly unworthy the profession of philosophy. If they had left us in our natural condition, accepting external seemings according as they presented themselves to us through our senses, and had let us go on according to our simple sensations, regulated by the condition of our inheritance, they would be in the right to speak thus; but it is from them that we

have learned to make ourselves judges of the world; it is
from them that we derive this fanciful idea that the human
reason is controller-general of all that is without and within
the vault of heaven; that it embraces every thing; that it
can do every thing; by its means every thing is learned and
known. Such answer would be appropriate among the Cannibals, who enjoy the good fortune of a long, tranquil, and
peaceful life, without the precepts of Aristotle and with no
knowledge of the name of physics. Such an answer would,
perchance, be worth more and would have more force than
all those that they[676] may borrow from their reason and their
imagination. That answer would fit,[677] with ourselves, all
the animals and all things over which the law of nature
still has pure and simple control; but they[678] have abandoned
it. They are forbidden to say to me: "It is true, for you so
see it and feel it"; they are obliged to teach me whether
what I think I feel I do really feel; and if I do feel it, they
must then tell me why I feel it, and how, and what it is;
they must tell me the name, the origin, the metes and
bounds of heat and cold, the quality of that which acts and
which suffers; or else, let them forsake their profession,
which is to admit or believe nothing save by the way of the
reason: that is their touchstone for all sorts of tests; but
certainly it is a touchstone full of falsity, error, weakness,
and defection.

In what day do we think we can best make trial of her?[679]
Will it not be by herself? If we can not trust her when
speaking of herself, she will hardly be fit to judge of external
things; if she is acquainted with any thing, at the least it
will be with her own self and her domicile. She is in the
soul, and is a part or a product thereof; while the true and

essential reason, whose purloined name we use under false colours, dwells in God's bosom; there is her habitation and her refuge; it is thence that she comes when it pleases God to show us some ray from her, as Pallas issued from her father's head to have intercourse with the world.

Now let us see what human reason has taught us of herself and of the soul; not of the universal soul, in which almost all philosophy makes the heavenly bodies and the primal bodies participants; nor of that which Thales attributed even to the things that are regarded as inanimate, induced by consideration of the magnet,[680] but of that which belongs to us, which we ought to know better.

> For they can not tell what is the nature of the soul:
> whether it is born with the body, or, on the contrary,
> finds its way into men at their birth; whether it per-
> ishes together with us, when severed from us by death,
> or goes to the dark and vast pools of Orcus, or, by
> divine decree, enters the body of an animal.[681]

It taught Crates and Dicæarchus that there was no soul at all, but that the body was moved by a natural impulse;[682] Plato, that it was a substance impelled by itself; Thales, an unresting nature; Asclepiades, an exercitation of the senses; Hesiod and Anaximander, a thing composed of earth and water; Parmenides, of earth and fire; Empedocles, of blood,

> He vomits forth his soul of blood;[683]

Possidonius, Cleanthes, and Galen, a certain heat or ardent temperament,—

> They have a fiery strength and a celestial source;[684]

Apology for Raimond Sebond

Hippocrates, a spirit diffused through the body; Varro, an air inhaled through the mouth, warmed by the lungs, tempered in the heart, and diffused through the whole body; Zeno, the quintessence of the four elements; Heraclides Ponticus, the light; Xenocrates and the Egyptians, a varying number; the Chaldæans, a power without definite form;

> a certain vital state of the body, which the Greeks call *harmonia*.[685]

Let us not forget Aristotle's belief, that the soul is that which by its nature causes the body to move, which he calls *entelechy*; as lifeless a conception as any other, for he speaks neither of the essence, nor the origin, nor the nature of the soul, but observes solely its effect. Lactantius, Seneca, and the better part of the dogmatists confessed that it was a thing that they did not understand. And after enumerating all these opinions, *which of all these opinions may be true, some god must decide,*[686] says Cicero. "I know by myself," says St. Bernard, "how incomprehensible God is, since I can not comprehend the parts of my own being."[687] Heraclitus, who held that the universe was full of souls and spirits,[688] maintained that it is not possible to go so far in knowledge of the soul as to reach it, so secret is its essence.[689]

There is no less disagreement and discussion about its location. Hippocrates and Hierophilus place it in the ventricle of the brain; Democritus and Aristotle, everywhere in the body;

> Just as, when good health is said to belong to the body, yet it is no one part of the man in health;[690]

Epicurus, in the stomach;

728

Apology for Raimond Sebond

Here throb fear and terror; these places are soothed
 by joys;[691]

the Stoics, round about and within the heart; Erasistratus,
adjoining the membrane of the epicranium; Empedocles,
in the blood; as does Moses, which was the reason that he
forbade eating the blood of beasts with which their soul is
connected; Galen thought that each part of the body has
its soul; Strato placed it between the eyebrows.[692] *In truth,
what is its appearance, and where it dwells, we can not seek
to know,*[693] says Cicero. I willingly leave to this man his
own words. Should I desire to change the language of eloquence? Moreover, there is little profit in stealing the substance of his ideas: they are both infrequent and not at all
forcible or original.[694] But the reason why Chrysippus, like
others of his school, argues that it is about the heart, should
not be forgotten: "It is," he says, "because when we wish to
assert something, we put our hand on the stomach; and
when we desire to say ἐγω, which means *I*, we drop the
lower jaw toward the stomach."[695] This passage should not
be passed over without noting the inanity of so great a personage. For not only are these considerations in themselves
infinitely trivial, but the last proves only to the Greeks that
they have the soul in that region. There is no human judgement so on the stretch that it does not sometimes slumber.
What do we hesitate to say? Here are the Stoics, fathers of
human wisdom, who find that the soul of a man, buried
under a ruin, writhes and struggles for a long while to come
forth, being unable to rid itself of the burden, like a mouse
caught in a trap.[696] Some hold that the world was made in
order to give bodies, by way of punishment, to spirits who
have fallen, through their fault, from the purity wherein

729

they were created; and, the first creation having been only incorporeal, according as they are more or less completely removed from their immateriality, they are more or less agreeably or burdensomely embodied.[697] From this comes the variety of so much created matter. But the spirit which was, for its punishment, invested with the body of the sun, must have a very rare and special degree of change. The limits of our enquiry all end in obscurity: as Plutarch says of the way in which histories open,[698] that after the fashion of maps the edge of the known region is occupied by swamps, dense forests, deserts, and uninhabitable places.[699] That is why the most clumsy and puerile utterances are oftenest found in those who treat of the highest and most remote things, they being utterly undone by[700] their curiosity and presumption. The end and the beginning of knowledge are equally possessed by ignorance.[701] See how Plato takes flight into his poetic clouds. See how he uses the language of the gods.[702]

But of what was he thinking when he defined man as an animal with two feet, without feathers, affording to those who desired to make sport of him an amusing opportunity; for having plucked a live capon, they styled it, "a man according to Plato."[703]

And how about the Epicureans? With what ignorance did they first imagine that their atoms, which, they said, were bodies having some weight and a natural downward movement, had built the world; until they were shown by their adversaries, that with that description it was not possible that these atoms should join and cling to one another, their fall being thus straight and perpendicular, and producing everywhere parallel lines. Wherefore there was need that they should afterward add to them a haphazard lateral motion, and that they should also supply their atoms with curved and hooked tails, to make them fitted to unite and fasten themselves together.[704] And even then, do not they who follow them[705] up about this other suggestion, give them trouble? If the atoms have by chance formed so many varieties of figure, why has it never happened to them to make a house or a shoe? Why, in the same way, may we not believe that an infinite number of Greek letters, scattered in the market-place, might attain the contexture of the *Iliad*?[706] That which is capable of reason, said Zeno, is better than that which is not capable thereof; there is nothing better than the world; so it is capable of reason.[707] Cotta, by this same line of argument, makes the world mathematical; and he makes it musical and organical by the other line of argument, also from Zeno: "The whole is more than a part; we are capable of wisdom and are parts of the world; therefore it is wise."[708]

In the reproaches which the philosophers address to one another touching the dissensions in their opinions and their sects,[709] there are numberless like examples of arguments, not false only, but inept, not holding together, and convicting their authors not so much of ignorance as of indiscretion. He who should adequately bring together a collection of the stupidities of human sapience would have wonders to tell. I willingly assemble some of them to exhibit, as being, in their way, not less profitable than more tempered teachings. Let us judge by this what should be our estimate of man, his understanding and his reason, since, in those great personages who have carried human ability to so high a point, there are found failings so manifest and so gross. For my part, I prefer to believe that they treated learning casually, like a toy of various forms, and played with reason as with a useless and trifling implement, putting forward all sorts of conceptions and fancies, sometimes more close in texture, sometimes more loose.[710]

This same Plato, who defined man as a hen, says elsewhere, after Socrates, that he does not in truth know what man is, and that he is a piece of the world as difficult as any to understand.[711] By this variety and instability of opinion they lead us tacitly, as if by the hand, to this decision of their indecision.[712] They openly confess that they do not always present their doctrine with an uncovered and visible aspect; they conceal it sometimes in the deceitful shadows of poetry, sometimes behind some other mask; for our imperfection carries this with it, that raw meat is not always suited to our stomach; it must needs be dried, changed, and spiced. They do the same: they sometimes cast a mist over their real opinions and judgements, and falsify them, to adapt them to public use. They do not choose to make express confession of ignorance and of the imbecility of human reasoning, that they may not frighten the children; but they show it to us plainly enough by the aspect of a confused and wavering learning.

When in Italy, I told a person who had difficulty in speaking Italian that, if he sought only to make himself understood, without desiring in any way to excel, he might use only the first words that came to his lips,—Latin, French, Spanish, or Gascon,—and that, by adding the Italian termination, he would never fail to hit upon some idiom of the country, either Tuscan, or Roman, or Venetian, or Piedmontese, or Neapolitan, and to catch hold of some one of so

many forms. I say the same of philosophy: it has so many
aspects and so much variety, and has said so much, that all
our idle dreams and delusions are found in it. Human fantasy can conceive nothing good or bad that is not there.
*Nothing can be said so absurd that it has not been said by
some one of the philosophers.*[713] And I the more freely allow
my freakish thoughts of this kind to go abroad, because,
although born in my own mind and without pattern, I know
that they will find themselves related to some ancient way
of thinking; and there will not lack some one to say: "See
whence he took it." My opinions[714] are innate; I have not,
in framing them, called to my aid any teaching. But, de-
void of force as they are, when the desire has seized upon
me to declare them, and in order to send them abroad in a
little more seemly guise, I have set about helping them with
arguments and examples, it has been marvellous to me to
find them, by mere chance, conformable to so many philosophic examples and arguments. Of what form[715] my life
was, I did not learn until after it was finished and spent. A
new figure: an unpremeditated and accidental philosopher!

To return to our soul[716]—when Plato placed reason in
the brain, anger in the heart, and lust in the liver, it is probable that it was an interpretation of the movements of the
soul that he intended to make, rather than a division and
separation of it, as of a body, into many members.[717] And
the most plausible of their opinions is that it is always a soul
which, by its inherent power, reasons, remembers, understands, judges, desires, and exercises all its other operations
through various bodily instruments, as the seaman controls
his ship according to the knowledge he has of it, now tight-
ening or slackening a rope, now hoisting the yard, or plying

the oar, by one sole power guiding divers acts; and that it
dwells in the brain: which appears from this—that the
wounds and accidents which touch that part immediately
impair the faculties of the soul; from thence it is not strange
that it flows through the rest of the body,—

> Phœbus never leaves his path in the middle of the
> sky; none the less, he enlightens all things with his
> rays,[718]—

as the sun sheds forth from the sky its light and its influences, and fills the world therewith;

> All the rest of the soul, dispersed through the whole
> body, obeys and moves at the will and inclination of
> the mind.[719]

Some have said that there was a general soul, as it were a
great body, from which all the individual souls were drawn
forth, and to which they returned, constantly reblending
themselves with this universal matter,[720]—

> For God pervades all lands and regions of the sea
> and the deep sky; from him flocks and cattle and men
> and all kinds of wild beasts derive the subtle breath of
> life when they are born; and to him it returns in the
> dissolution of their bodies; and there is no room for
> death;[721]

others, that they were only rejoined and refastened to it;
others, that they were brought forth from the divine substance; others, by the angels, from fire and air. Some believed that they were created at the beginning of all
things;[722] some, at the very hour they were needed. Some

think that they descend from the full of the moon,[723] and
return thither; the generality of the ancients, that they are
begotten from father to son, in the same way and process
as all other natural things, deducing this from the resemblance of children to their fathers,—

> Thy father's virtue is instilled in thee;[724]
> Strong men are begotten strong and good,[725]

and that there are seen to pass from fathers to children, not
only the marks of the body, but also a resemblance of humours, of dispositions, and of tendencies of the soul;

> Finally, why does untamed fierceness belong to the
> surly brood of lions? Why is cunning to the fox, and
> proneness to flight to the deer, given from their fathers,
> why engendered by inheritance, if not because a fixed
> power of mind, derived from its proper seed and breed,
> grows up together with the whole body?[726]

that on this basis rests divine justice, punishing in the children the sin of the fathers, forasmuch as the contagion of the
paternal vices is in some degree stamped upon the souls of
the children, and the disorders of their fathers' will affects
them.[727] Moreover, that if souls came otherwise than in a
natural course, and if they had been something else outside
the body, they would have remembrance of their primal
being, considering the native faculties which belong to
them, of examining, reasoning, and remembering;

> If the soul makes its way into the body at the time
> of birth, why are we unable to remember the time al-
> ready gone, and why do we retain no traces of past
> actions?[728]

735

To estimate the condition of our souls from this point of view,[729] we must presuppose them all to have knowledge when they are in their native simplicity and purity. Consequently, they, being exempt from the prison of the body, would have been, before entering it, such as we hope they will be after issuing forth from it. And this knowledge they would necessarily still remember while in the body; as Plato said, that what we learn was but a remembrance of what we had previously known:[730] a thing which every one, by experience, can maintain to be false: in the first place, precisely because we remember[731] only what we are taught; and if the memory performed her due office, at least she would suggest to us something beyond our learning.[732] In the second place, what the soul knew when in her purity was true knowledge, apprehending things as they are by her divine intelligence; whereas here she is obliged to accept falsehood and error[733] if instructed in them. In which matters she can not employ reminiscence, such idea and conception having never had lodgement in her. To say that the prison of the body so suffocates her native faculties that they are all extinguished is entirely opposed to that other belief, which admits her powers to be so great, and those of her workings which men are conscious of in this life to be so admirable, that therefrom has been inferred her divinity and eternity in the past, and immortality to come.

> For, if the power of the mind is so completely changed that it has lost all memory of past things, that, methinks, differs not widely from death.[734]

Furthermore, it is here, with us, and not elsewhere, that the faculties and the acts of the soul must be considered;

Apology for Raimond Sebond

all the rest of her perfections are for her vain and useless;
it is her present condition that all her immortality must register and recognise, and it is man's life only for which she
must account. It would be injustice to have diminished her
resources and her powers, to have disarmed her, and then,
from the time of her captivity and her imprisonment, her
weakness and sickness,—the time when she was under duress
and constraint,—to pass sentence and a condemnation of
infinite and perpetual duration, and to dwell on the consideration of so brief a time, which is perchance only an hour or
two, or, at the most, a century (which, compared with
infinity, is no more than an instant), in order from that
momentary interval to decree and establish definitely her
whole existence. It would be an iniquitous disproportion, to
receive an everlasting recompense as a consequence of so
short a life. Plato, to escape this undesirable result, has future remunerations limited to a hundred years, relatively
to the length of human life,[735] and many of our own writers
have assigned temporal limits to them. Thus they judged
that the generation of the soul followed the common condition of human things; as, also, her life, according to the
opinion of Epicurus and Democritus (which was most received), based upon these plausible signs:[736] that she was
seen to be born when the body was able to contain her;
that her powers were seen to mount like those of the body;
that there was recognised in her the feebleness of her youth
and, with time, her vigour and her maturity; and then her
decline and her old age, and finally at the end her decrepitude:—

> We perceive that the mind is begotten with the
> body, and grows up with it, and becomes old with it.[737]

737

Apology for Raimond Sebond

They[738] perceived her to be capable of various sufferings and agitated by many painful emotions, whence she sank into lassitude and grief; capable of trouble and change, of vivacity, of dulness, and of langour, subject to her special maladies and to injuries, like the stomach or the foot;

> We perceive that the mind is cured, like the sick
> body, and we see that it can be altered by medicine;[739]

blinded and confused by the power of wine; shaken from her position by the vapours of a burning fever; put to sleep by the use of some medicaments and excited by others:

> The nature of the soul must be bodily, since it suf-
> fers from bodily weapons and blows.[740]

It was seen that all her faculties were benumbed and overthrown by the mere bite of a sick dog, and that there was in her no stability of reason so great, no competence, no courage, no philosophic resolution, no putting forth of her strength, that could exempt her from subjection to such mishaps; the slaver of a common cur, dropped on the hand of Socrates, could unsettle all his wisdom and all his great and so-well-ordered conceptions, could annihilate them to such a degree, that there would remain no trace of his former knowledge,—

> The powers of the soul are disordered and forced
> asunder and torn to pieces by that same poison,[741]

and that poison would find no more resistance in his soul than in that of a four-year-old child; it is a poison capable of rendering all philosophy, were she incarnate, insane and witless; for instance, Cato, so stiff-necked about death itself

Apology for Raimond Sebond

and destiny, would have been overwhelmed with terror and affright at the sight of a mirror or of water, if, from contact with a mad dog, he had fallen into the disease that physicians call hydrophobia:

> The violence of the disease, diffused throughout the frame, agitates the soul, as the foaming waves of the salt sea boil with the mastering might of the winds.[742]

Now, as to this particular, philosophy has well armed mankind for the enduring of all other mishaps, either with patience, or, if that is too hard to find, with an infallible evasion, by stealing wholly away from sensation;[743] but these are methods which are at the service of a soul in command of itself and its forces, capable of reasoning and of deliberation; not possible in that misfortune when the soul of a philosopher becomes the soul of a mad man, confused, overthrown, and past hope of recovery, which several causes may bring about: such as a too violent excitement which, by some strong passion, the soul may engender in herself, or a wound in a certain part of the person, or a fume from the stomach producing giddiness and whirling of the brain:

> Often in diseases of the brain the mind wanders and goes astray; for it loses its reason and talks deliriously; and sometimes, in a profound lethargy, it is carried into deep and eternal sleep, and the eyes and the head droop.[744]

The philosophers have, it seems to me, scarcely touched this thing. No more than another, of equal importance. They have always this argument on the tongue, to console our mortal condition: the soul is either mortal or immortal; if mortal, she will be without pain; if immortal, she will be continually better off. They never touch the other branch —what if she is continually worse off? and leave to the poets the threats of future punishments. But thereby they give themselves an advantage.[745] There are two omissions in their reasoning which often present themselves to me.[746] I return to the first.

The soul loses the experience[747] of the supreme Stoic good, so constant and so stable. Our fine wisdom must needs here surrender and lay down its arms. For the rest, they also judged, from the weakness of human reason, that the commingling and association of two things so diverse as are the mortal and the immortal is inconceivable.

> For to link what is mortal with what is eternal, and to suppose that they can harmonise and can be reciprocally acted upon, is sheer folly. For what can be conceived more incongruous, or more diversified and discordant, than what is mortal eternally linked with what is immortal and everlasting, to endure, united, fierce storms?[748]

Moreover, they felt the soul to be bound to death, like the body,—

> It breaks down at the same time, worn out with age,[749]

and this, according to Zeno, the image of sleep shows us clearly; for he thinks that it is a feebleness and succumbing of the soul as well as of the body: *he thinks that the mind contracts, and, as it were, slips and falls.*[750] And what is per-

Apology for Raimond Sebond

ceived in some persons, that her force and her vigour remain
to the end of life, they referred to the differences in diseases;
as we see men, at that extremity, retain, this man one sense,
that man another; this one the sense of hearing, that one of
smell, without impairment; and there is no enfeeblement
so universal that some organs do not remain sound and vigorous,

Just as the foot of a sick man may ache, his head,
meanwhile, feeling no pain.[751]

The vision of our judgement has the same relation to the
truth that the eye of the owl has to the splendour of the
sun, as Aristotle says.[752] How could we better be convinced
of this than by such gross blindness in such manifest light?
For the contrary opinion of the immortality of the soul,
which Cicero says was first introduced, at all events as
testified to in books, by Pherecides Syrus, in the time of
King Tullus[753] (others attribute the conception to Thales,
and others to other sages), is the part of human learning
treated of with the least openness and most uncertainty.
The most positive dogmatists are, at this point most especially, forced to seek the shelter of the shades of the Academy. No one knows what Aristotle has ordained on this
subject;[754] nor all the ancients in general, who handle it
with a wavering belief; *a most acceptable thing, rather
promised than proved.*[755] He hid himself in clouds of words
and difficult and unintelligible meanings, and left it for his
followers to debate as much about his judgement, as about
the matter of it. Two things made that belief[756] plausible to
them: one, that unless the soul is immortal, there would no
longer be aught on which to base the vain hopes of glory,

which is a consideration of marvellous influence in the world; the other, that it is a very useful impression, as Plato says, that the vices, when they escape from the dim and uncertain eyes of human justice, remain always as a butt for divine justice, which will pursue them, yea, after the death of the guilty.[757]

An extreme desire possesses man to prolong his existence; he has provided therefor by every means. For the preservation of the body there are tombs; for the preservation of the name, glory.[758] He has employed all his wit in rebuilding himself, impatient of his fortune and propping himself up by his conceptions. The soul, by reason of her disquiet and her weakness, having no secure footing, goes seeking on all sides consolations, hopes, and supports, in external circumstances, where she may cling and fix herself; and, slight and fantastic as her imagination fashions them, she rests on them more confidently than on herself, and more willingly.

But those who are most obstinate in this so just and manifest conviction of the immortality of our spirits—it is a wonderful thing how incompetent[759] and powerless they have found themselves to assure it by their human powers. *These are dreams, not of one who teaches, but of one who wishes,*[760] said an ancient writer. Man can recognise by this evidence that he owes to fortune and to chance the truth which he discovers unaided, since, even when it has fallen into his hands, he has not the wherewithal to grasp it and maintain it, and his reason has not the power to make use of it. All things arrived at by our own reasoning and ability, true as well as false, are subject to uncertainty and discussion. It was for the chastisement of our pride, and the instruction of our wretchedness and incapacity, that God brought about the perplexity and confusion of the ancient Tower of Babel. Whatever we undertake without his assistance, whatever we behold save by the lamp of his grace, is but vanity and folly; the very essence of truth, which is unchanging and constant when fortune gives us possession of it, we corrupt and adulterate by our weakness. Whatever course man takes from his own impulse, God directs it to arrive always at this same disorder, the image of which he presents to us so vividly by the just chastisement with which he smote the presumption of Nimrod,[761] and brought to naught the vain attempts at the construction of his Pyramid. *I will destroy the wisdom of the wise, and bring to nothing the understanding of the prudent.*[762] The diversity of dialects[763] and of tongues with which he threw that work into confusion—how does it differ from this infinite and perpetual altercation and discordance of opinions and of arguments which accompanies and confounds the vain construction of human knowledge? And confounds it profitably. Who could restrain us if we had one grain of knowledge? This saint[764] has given me great pleasure: *The obscurity in which is hidden the knowledge of things of interest to us is an exercise of humility and a curb to our pride.*[765] To what degree of presumption and insolence do we not carry our blindness and our stupidity!

But, to resume my subject,[766] it was truly most reasonable that we should be indebted to God alone, and to the benefit of his grace, for the truth of so noble a belief, since from his liberality alone we receive the fruit of immortality, which consists in the enjoyment of everlasting beatitude. Let us frankly confess that God alone has told us of it, and

743

faith; for it is no lesson of nature and of our reason. And he who shall repeatedly examine what his existence and his powers, both inward and outward, would be, without this divine grace; [767] he who shall look upon man without flattering him, will see in him neither ability nor faculty that has any touch of aught but death and the earth. The more we give and owe and render to God, the more truly are we Christians. That which this Stoic philosopher says that he accepts because of casual assent of the popular voice, would it not be better that he should accept it from God? *When we discuss the immortality of the soul, of no light moment to us is the conformity of men who either fear or adore the infernal powers. I rest on this general conviction.*[768]

Now the weakness of human conjectures on this subject is singularly manifest by the fabulous circumstances which they have added in the train of this opinion, to find out of what nature is this our immortality. Let us put aside the Stoics,—*they grant our bodies a length of life like that of crows; they say that our souls will live for a long time, but not forever.*[769] The most universal and generally received opinion, and which endures in divers places to our day, is that of which Pythagoras is said to be the author—not that he was the first to conceive it, but because it derived much weight and credit from the authority of his approval: it is that souls, on their departure from us, did but pass from one body to another, from a lion to a horse, from a horse to a king, proceeding thus incessantly from habitation to habitation.[770] And he said that he remembered having been Æthalides, then Euphorbus, still later Hermotimus, and finally from Pyrrhus to have passed into Pythagoras, having memory of himself for two hundred and six years.[771]

744

Some added that these same souls remount sometimes to heaven, and come down again.[772]

> O my father [Æneas is addressing Anchises],
> must we think that some souls rise hence to heaven,
> and return again to their sluggish bodies? What hap-
> less yearning for the light have these poor wretches?[773]

Origen makes them go and come forever between the good and the evil state.[774] Varro sets forth the belief that when four hundred and forty years have revolved, they rejoin their first bodies;[775] Chrysippus, that this must happen after an unknown and not defined period.[776] Plato, who says he derives from Pindar and from ancient poetry this belief in the infinite vicissitudes of mutation for which the soul is made ready, having none but temporal pains or rewards in the other world, even as her life in this world is but temporal, infers in her a singular knowledge of the concerns of heaven, of hell, and of this world, which she has visited and revisited and abided in throughout many peregrinations:[777] matter for reminiscence on her part. He thus continues elsewhere: "He who has lived virtuously rejoins the star to which he is assigned; he who has lived ill becomes a woman, and if even then he does not mend his ways, he is again changed into a beast of a nature suited to his vicious conditions; and he will not see the end of his punishments until he shall have re-verted to his true condition, having by the force of reason got rid of the coarse and stupid and elemental[778] qualities that were in him."[779]

But I desire not to forget the objection that the Epi-cureans make to this transmigration from body to body. It is amusing. They ask what order would be observed if the

745

crowd of the dying should outnumber that of the newly
born; for the souls dislodged from their abodes would press
upon one another to attain a place first in this new envelope.
And they ask also how they would pass their time while
they were waiting for a lodging to be made ready for them.
Or, on the other hand, if more animals were born than died,
they say that the bodies would be in ill case, awaiting the infusion of their souls, and it might consequently happen that
some of them would die before they had been alive.

> To suppose that souls are at hand during the unions
> of Venus and the births of animals is absurd, and that
> immortal spirits in number numberless wait for mor-
> tal limbs, and contend in rivalry which shall first and
> by preference have entrance.[780]

Others have made the soul abide in the body of the dead, to
give life to the snakes, the worms, and other creatures,
which are said to be born of the corruption of our limbs, and
even of our ashes.[781] Others divide her into a mortal part and
another immortal. Others say that she is corporeal and, notwithstanding this, immortal. Some make her immortal,
without learning and without knowledge.[782] There are those
also who have believed that, from the souls of the damned,
devils are made (and some among ourselves have so considered[783]); as Plutarch thinks that gods are made of those
who are saved; for there are few things which that author
asserts in so assured a manner as he does this, maintaining
everywhere else a hesitating and ambiguous style. "It is to
be thought," he says, "and firmly believed, that the souls
of men virtuous according to nature and according to divine law, from men become saints; and from saints, demi-

gods; and from demigods, after they are thoroughly cleansed and purified as by the sacrifices of purgation, being delivered from all passability and all mortality, they become, not by virtue of any special decree,[784] but in truth, and in accordance with manifest reason, complete and perfect gods, receiving thereby a most fortunate and most glorious end."[785] But he who would see him, who is among the most restrained and moderate of the band, bestir himself more boldly, and tell us miraculous tales on this matter, him I refer to his treatise of the moon and his *Dæmon of Socrates*, where, more clearly than anywhere else, it can be verified that the mysteries of philosophy have many strange matters in common with those of poetry; the human intelligence spending itself idly in desiring to search and inspect all things even to the bottom; in the same way that, wearied and worn by the long course of life, we fall back into a childish condition.

We have now seen the excellent and certain teachings that we derive from human learning on the subject of our souls. There is no less temerity in what it teaches us of the corporeal organs. Let us select one or two examples of this; for otherwise we should be lost in this foggy and vast sea of medicinal errors. Let us ascertain if there is agreement, in this point at least, about the matter whereof men are produced, one from another. For, as to their first production, it is no wonder if, about a thing so secret[786] and so ancient, the human understanding is confused and brought to naught. Archelaus, the natural philosopher, of whom, according to Aristoxenus, Socrates was a disciple and favourite, said that both men and beasts are made from a milky slime, expressed by the heat of the earth.[787] Pythagoras

747

says that the semen is the skimming of our best blood; Plato, that it is the distillation of the marrow of the backbone; which he argues from the fact that this part first feels the lassitude of the labour; Alcmaeon, part of the substance of the brain; and that that is so, he says, is shown by the fact that the eyes of those become dimmed who labour too excessively at that exercise; Democritus, a substance extracted from the whole bodily mass; Epicurus, that it is extracted from the soul and the body; Aristotle, an excrement drawn from the aliment of the blood, the last that is diffused through our members; others, blood cooked and digested by the heat of the genitals, which they conclude from the drops of pure blood that are ejected after excessive efforts; wherein there seems to be more likelihood, if we may derive any probability from such endless confusion. Now, in trying to bring this seed to do its work, how greatly they contradict each other! Aristotle and Democritus maintain that women have no sperm, and that it is only a perspiration exuding in the heat of pleasure and movement, which contributes nothing towards the generation. On the other hand, Galen and his followers hold that generation cannot take place without the meeting of the seeds. Here are the physicians, the philosophers, the lawyers, and the theologians, wrestling pell-mell with our wives about the question as to the length of time which women carry their offspring. I myself, by my own example, support those who maintain pregnancy to be of eleven months. The world is based on this experience; there is no simple little woman who can not give her opinion on all these disputes, and yet we should never be in agreement about it.

This is enough to prove that man is no better instructed

Apology for Raimond Sebond

in the knowledge of himself as to the corporeal than as to the spiritual part. We have put him before himself to be examined by himself,[788] his reason by his reason, to see what she would tell us about it. It seems to me that I have clearly shown how little she herself understands herself. And he who does not himself understand himself—what can he understand? *As if he who knows not his own measure could measure any thing.*[789] Truly Protagoras was talking in the air[790] in making man the measure of all things, who never knows even his own measure.[791] If it be not he, his dignity will not permit that any other creature should have this advantage. Now, he being so in opposition to himself, and one opinion constantly subverting another, this flattering proposition was simply a mockery, which led us necessarily to infer the nullity of the measure and the measurer.[792] When Thales judges the knowledge of man to be very difficult for man, knowledge of all things else is seen to be impossible for him.[793]

You, for whom I have taken the pains to write so at length, contrary to my custom, will not eschew upholding your Sebond by the ordinary manner of reasoning in which you are constantly trained, for the last trick of fence used here must be resorted to only as an extreme resource. It is a desperate thrust, in which you must abandon your weapons to make your opponent lose his; and a secret shift, which must be used rarely and cautiously. It is great rashness to be ready to kill yourself in order to kill another. One need not be ready to die, in order to revenge oneself, as Gobrias was; for, being closely engaged with a Persian lord, Darius coming up, sword in hand, but hesitating to attack for fear of hitting Gobrias, he[795] called out to him to strike boldly even though he should pierce through them both.[796] Arms and conditions of combat so desperate as to make it incredible that either adversary could escape, I have known to be disallowed, when proposed. The Portuguese made prisoners in the Indian sea of fourteen Turks, who, impatient of their captivity, resolved upon setting on fire and reduce to ashes themselves and their master and the vessels, by rubbing some ship's nails against each other until a spark fell upon the barrels of gunpowder that were on board; and they succeeded.[797]

We touch here the limits and final boundaries of all learning, of which what is beyond is erroneous, as with virtue.[798] Keep to the travelled road. It is not in the least worth while to be so cunning and so shrewd. Remember what the Tuscan proverb says: *He who seeks his way too carefully loses it.*[799] I counsel you, in your thought and in your conversation, as well as in your behaviour and in every other thing, moderation and temperance, and the avoidance of what is new and what is unusual. All wandering ways are to me displeasing. You who, by the authority which your high rank confers upon you, and even more by the advantages given you by qualities more your own, can with a glance command whom you please—you should have given this office to some one who made profession of letters, who would much more effectively have sustained you and made more valuable these conceptions.[800] However, here is enough for what you have need of.

Epicurus said of the laws that the worst were so necessary to us that, without them, men would eat one another up.[801] And Plato, in like tone,[802] that without laws we should live like brute beasts; and tried to prove it. Our mind is a

Apology for Raimond Sebond

vagrant instrument, dangerous and rash; it is difficult to bring order and moderation into it; and in these days we see that those minds that have some rare superiority to others, and some unusual activity, are, almost without exception, of a disorderly license in opinions and morals. It is a miracle if one is to be found which is sober and companionable. It is wise to keep the human mind within as narrow limits as possible. In study, as in other things, it is needful to count and regulate its steps; the limits of its hunting grounds must be carefully marked.[803] We bridle and bind it with religions, with laws, with customs, with learning, with precepts, with mortal and immortal punishments and rewards; still it is seen, by means of its swift motion and its laxity, to escape from all these bonds. It is an unreal body, which has nothing by which it can be seized and held; an irregular and misshapen body which can neither be tied nor grasped. Certainly there are few souls so disciplined, so strong and well endowed, that they can be trusted with their own guidance, and can, with moderation and without rashness, sail in freedom of judgement beyond commonly received ideas. It is more expedient that they should be under guardianship. The mind is a dangerous weapon, even to its owner, for him who knows not how to use it as it should be used, and with discretion. And there is no beast upon which it is more truly necessary to put a board before its eyes, to keep its sight under control and narrowed to what is before its feet, and to prevent it from straying hither and yon, outside the tracks which custom and the laws mark out for it. Wherefore it will befit you better to confine yourself to the customary path, whatever it be, than to wing your flight toward this ungoverned liberty. But if any one of these new doctors undertakes to show the sharpness of his wit in your presence, at the expense of his salvation and of yours, this preservative will rid you, in extreme need, of this dangerous infliction which spreads daily in your courts, and prevent the contagion of this poison from injuring either you or those about you.

The liberty, then, and rashness of those ancient minds gave rise—in philosophy and human learning—to many schools of varying opinions, each undertaking to judge and choose, in order to belong to a party. But, now that all men go in one direction,—*who are so addicted and pledged to certain beliefs, that even they are compelled to defend what they do not believe,*[804]—and that we accept the arts[805] by civil authority and decree, so that the schools have but one model and similar circumscribed instruction and discipline, we no longer regard what the coins weigh and are worth, but each man in his turn receives them at the value which common consent and credit[806] gives them. We do not argue about the debasement, but for how much they are current;[807] thus every thing is put on a level. Medicine is ranked with geometry; and jugglings, enchantments, liaisons,[808] intercourse with spirits of the departed, prognostications, domifications,[809] and even that absurd search for the philosopher's stone—every thing takes its place without gainsaying. We need but know that the seat of Mars is in the middle of the triangle of the palm, that of Venus in the thumb, and that of Mercury in the little finger; and that when the table-line cuts the base of the forefinger,[810] it is a sign of cruelty; when it stops under the middle finger and the natural median line makes an angle with the line of life at the same place, it is a sign of a miserable death. That, in

Apology for Raimond Sebond

a woman, if the natural median line is open, and does not close the angle with the line of life, it indicates that she will be unchaste. I call you yourself as a witness whether with this much learning a man may not pass with reputation and favour in all companies.

Theophrastus said that human knowledge, being shewn its way by the senses, could judge of the causes of things to a certain extent; but that, having arrived at the final and primal causes, it must needs halt and draw back, either because of its weakness or because of the difficulty of things.[811] It is a reasonable and agreeable idea that our ability can carry us to the knowledge of some things, and that it has a certain amount of power, beyond which it is rash to employ it. This idea is plausible and put forward by persons ready to make concessions;[812] but it is difficult to set limits to our mind; it is inquisitive and eager, and has no more occasion to stay itself at a thousand paces than at fifty. Having found by experience that where one man has failed to attain, another has arrived; and that what was unknown to one age, the following age has made clear; and that the sciences and arts are not cast in moulds, but rather are gradually formed and shaped by being many times handled and polished, as bears slowly fashion their cubs by licking them;[813] what my strength can not discover, I do not cease sounding and testing, and by dint of repeatedly groping for this new matter and turning it over and over, stirring it and warming it, I open to him who comes after me some facility for profiting by it more at his ease; and I deliver it to him more pliable and manageable,—

as the wax of Hymettus is softened by the sun, and

when worked by the hand, takes on many forms, and is made useful by being used.[814]

As much will the next man do with it for the third; which is the reason why difficulty should not make me lose hope, nor my powerlessness as little; for it is only my own. Man is as able to apprehend all things as some;[815] and if he acknowledges, as Theophrastus says, his ignorance of first causes and of origins,[816] then let him honestly renounce all the rest of his learning; if the foundation is lacking, his reason is overthrown. Disputation and inquiry have no other aim and goal than fundamental causes;[817] if his career be not to this end, he is thrown into infinite uncertainty. *One thing can be comprehended neither more nor less than another, since one definition of comprehending includes all things.*[818]

Now it is probable that, if the soul knew any thing, she would know herself first of all; and if she knew any thing outside of herself, it would be her body and her envelope better than every thing else. If we see, even to this day, the gods of medicine disputing about our anatomy,—

Mulciber [Vulcan] fought against Troy, Apollo for Troy,[819]—

when can we expect them to be in accord about it? We are more akin to ourselves[820] than the whiteness of snow or the weight of stone is to us. If man knows not himself, how can he know his functions and his powers? It is not, peradventure, that some true knowledge has not its abode in us, but it comes by chance. And inasmuch as by the same road, the same manner and guidance, errors are received into our soul, she has not the wherewithal to discern them or to distinguish truth from falsehood.

754

Apology for Raimond Sebond

The Academicians admitted some leaning in judgement, and deemed it incompletely thought out[821] to say that it was no more probable that snow was white than black, and that we were no more certain of the motion of a stone cast from our own hand than of that of the eighth sphere. And to avoid this difficulty and unfamiliar conception, which truly can not easily find a place in our thought, although they asserted that we were in no wise capable of learning, and that the truth is engulfed in deep abysses, where human sight can not penetrate,[822] yet they acknowledged that some things were more probable than others, and admitted this faculty of their judgement, that it could lean rather to one likelihood than to another; they allowed it this tendency, forbidding all decision.

The opinion of the Pyrrhonians is bolder and, at the same time, seemingly more true.[823] For this leaning of the Academicians, and this propension to one proposition rather than to another—is it any thing other than the recognition of some more apparent truth in this than in that? If our understanding can contain within it the forms, the features, the bearing, and the aspect of the truth, it would see her completely not less well than partially, in her beginning, and imperfect.[824] This appearance of verisimilitude which causes them to incline rather to the left than to the right—increase it; multiply that ounce of verisimilitude, which turns the balance, to a hundred or a thousand ounces; it will, consequently, finally come to pass that the balance will entirely decide the matter, and will settle upon a choice and a perfect truth. But how do they allow themselves to yield to the semblance of truth, if they know not the truth? How do they know the semblance of that of which they know not the nature? Either we are able to judge absolutely, or we are absolutely unable to judge. If our intellectual and perceptive faculties are without foundation and footing, if they are but driven by the waves and the wind,[825] to no purpose do we allow our judgement to be affected by any part of their operation, whatever likelihood it seems to offer us; and the safest position for our understanding, and the most fortunate, would be that in which it should maintain itself steady, upright, inflexible, without tottering, and without excitement. *Between true and false appearances, nothing influences the assent of our minds.*[826]

We see clearly enough that things do not find place in us in their real form and in their real nature, and do not enter into us of their own force and authority; because, if it were so, all men would receive them alike: wine would be the same in the mouth of the sick man and in the mouth of the healthy man; he whose fingers are chapped or benumbed would find the same roughness in the wood or iron he handles that another finds. Outside objects, then, submit to us at our discretion; they find such place in us as we please. And if on our part we receive any thing unchanged; if the human grasp were sufficiently powerful and firm to seize truth by our own means, these means being common to all men, truth would be passed from hand to hand, from one to another. And at least there would be found one thing in the world, of so many that are there, which would be believed by men with universal consent. But the fact that there is no proposition which is not discussed and controverted among us, or which may not be, shows plainly that our innate judgement does not grasp very clearly what it does grasp; for my judgement can not make itself accepted by the judgement of my companion; which is a sign that I have grasped it by some other means than by an innate power which is in me and in all men.

Let us set aside this infinite confusion of opinions that we find even among philosophers, and this perpetual and universal discussion as to the knowledge of things. For this is very certainly presupposed, that about no one thing are men—I mean the best-endowed, the most able men—in agreement: not that the sky is over our heads, for they who doubt every thing, also doubt that; and they who deny that we can comprehend any thing say that we have not comprehended that the sky is over our heads; and these two opinions are beyond comparison the most numerous. Besides this infinite variety and division, it is easy to see, from the confusion which our judgement causes ourselves, and from the uncertainty that every one feels within himself, that its position is very insecure. How variously do we judge of things! How often do our inclinations change! What I maintain to-day and what I believe, I maintain and believe with all my power of belief. All my tools and all that I have recourse to, lay hold of this opinion and answer to me for it as far as they can. I could not embrace any truth or maintain it more strongly than I do this. I am entirely possessed by it; I am verily set fast therein;[827] but has it not happened to me, not once, but a hundred, but a thousand times, and every day, to have embraced some other thing with these same tools, in this same manner which I have since judged to be false? A man should at least become discreet at his own expense. If I have often found myself deceived by a similar aspect, if my touchstone is usually found to be false and my scales uneven and inaccurate, what assurance can I

757

feel at this time more than at others? Is it not folly to allow myself to be misled so many times by one guide? None the less, but fortune changes our position five hundred times, let her incessantly empty and fill our belief, like a vessel, with other and other opinions, the one in our eyes, the last one, is the one certain and infallible. For this we must abandon riches, honour, life, and salvation, and every thing;

> The latter changes and destroys our feelings toward the former things.[828]

Whatever is preached to us, whatever we learn, we should always remember that it is man who gives and man who receives; it is a mortal hand that offers it to us, it is a mortal hand that accepts it. The things that come to us from heaven have alone the right and authority to persuade; alone, the stamp of truth; also we do not see this truth with our eyes, nor do we receive it by our endeavours:[829] this great and sacred image could not enter into so mean a habitation, if God did not prepare it for such occupancy, if God did not reshape and strengthen it by his special and supernatural grace and favour.

At least, our faulty condition should make us bear ourselves with more moderation and restraint in our changes. We should remember, whatever we receive into the understanding, that we often receive false things, and that we receive them by these same tools, which often contradict and deceive themselves. Now, it is no wonder if they contradict themselves, being so easily bent and whirled about by very slight occurrences. It is certain that our apprehension, our judgement, and the facilities of the soul in general are affected by the motions and changes of the body, which changes are continual. Is not our mind more alert, our memory more prompt, our conversation more lively, in health than in sickness? Do not joy and gaiety make us receive the subjects that present themselves to our soul in a quite other light than disquiet and melancholy? Do you think that the verses of Catullus or of Sappho delight a miserly and sullen old man as they do a lusty and ardent youth? Cleomenes, son of Anaxandridas, being ill, his friends reproached him for having new and unwonted humours and fancies. "I agree," he said, "for I am not the same man that I was when well; being a different man, my opinions and fancies are different also."[830] In the chicanery of our law courts there is often used this phrase, which is said about criminals who find the judges in a gentle and kindly mood: *Gaudeat de bona fortuna* (let him rejoice in good fortune); for it is certain that judges[831] are found to be sometimes more inclined to condemnation, rougher and harsher, and sometimes more gracious, indulgent, and inclined to excuse the offence. He who brings with him from his house the pain of the gout, of jealousy, or of the thievery of his servant, having his soul all tinged and steeped with anger—it is not to be doubted that his judgement about the case in hand may be affected. That venerable senate of the Areopagus heard causes at night, lest the sight of the suitors should corrupt its justice. The very atmosphere and the serenity of the sky cause some mutation in us, as is said in these Greek verses in Cicero:

> Men's moods accord with the varying light that
> Father Jupiter spreads over the earth.[832]

It is not only the fevers, potions, and great events that up-

759

set our judgement: the slightest things in the world twist it about. And it is not to be doubted, although we are not conscious of it, that, if continuous fever can overwhelm our souls, the tertian, in its measure and proportion, brings some change to us. If apoplexy dulls and extinguishes altogether the power of sight of our understanding, it is not to be doubted that a cold beclouds it; and, consequently, there is scarcely a single hour in our life when our judgement may be found in its proper disposition, our body being subject to so many continual mutations and filled with so many kinds of springs[833] (I believe the physicians about this), that it is almost impossible that there shall not always be some one of them that goes wrong. Moreover, this infirmity does not clearly show itself if it be not quite extreme and irremediable, inasmuch as the reason still works, distorted and limping and disjointed, and works with falsehood as with truth. Consequently, it is not easy to perceive its mistakenness and irregularity. I always mean by "reason" that form of reflection[834] which every one fashions in himself: this reason, of whose nature there may be a hundred different kinds employed about one and the same subject, is an instrument of lead and wax, stretchable, pliable, and adaptable to all curves[835] and all measures; there is needed only the ability to know how to turn it. Whatever good purpose a judge may have, if he does not give careful attention to himself, which few people think of, the leaning due to friendship, to kinship, to beauty, and to revenge, and not only such weighty matters, but that fortuitous instinct which makes us favour one thing more than another, and which, without the permission of reason, gives us a choice between two similar subjects, or some shadow of equality without solidity, may imperceptibly insinuate into his judgement the recommendation or disfavour of a cause, and turn the scale.

I, who watch myself more closely, who have my eyes incessantly fixed upon myself, as one who has not much to do elsewhere, —

> supremely careless as to what king is feared in the cold regions under the Bear, or what causes fear to Tiridates,[836]—

I should hardly dare to say what emptiness and weakness I find in myself. My footing is so unstable and so ill assured, I find it so naturally and so often quaking and tottering under me,[837] and my sight is so disordered that, fasting, I feel myself to be another man than after eating; if my health and the brightness of a fine day smile upon me, you will find me all I should be;[838] if a corn hurts my toe, you will find me frowning, rude, and inaccessible. The same pace of a horse seems to me at one time hard, at one time easy, and the same road now shorter, again longer, and one and the same fashion[839] sometimes more, sometimes less pleasing. One hour I am for doing any thing, another for doing nothing; that which is a pleasure to me at this moment will later be a trouble. There are a thousand ill-advised and casual agitations within me. It may be either a melancholy mood that possesses me, or a choleric one; and at one moment vexation predominates in me by its private authority, at another moment, gladness. When I occupy myself with books, I may perceive in a certain passage excellent graces which touch my soul; let me return to it another day—to no purpose do I turn it this way and that, to no purpose do I twist and manipulate it—it is an obscure and shapeless lump to me.

In my own writings, even, I do not always regain the thought of my first conception: I know not what I meant to say, and often fret myself in correction and giving a new meaning, from having lost the first, which was worth more. I do nothing but go and come; my judgement does not always move forward: it floats, it flits about,

> like a small bark caught on the high seas when the wind is raging.[840]

Many a time, having undertaken, as I am apt to do for practice and for pastime, to uphold an opinion contrary to my own, my mind, applying itself and turning that way, so fixes me there that I no longer find the reason of my first belief, and I abandon it. I lead myself, as it were, in the direction toward which I lean, whatever that may be, and am borne on by my weight. Almost every one would say as much of himself, if he considered himself as I do. Preachers know that the emotion that comes to them when speaking gives life to their belief, and that in anger we devote ourselves more to the defence of our proposition, impress it upon ourselves, and embrace it with more vehemence and approbation, than we do when we are cool and in our sober senses. You tell your case simply to the advocate; he answers you about it hesitatingly and doubtfully; you feel that it is indifferent to him whether he undertakes to defend one side or the other. Have you paid him well to set his teeth in it and to take up your quarrel? does he begin to be interested about it? has he warmed up his will? his reasoning power and his learning become warm at the same time;

Apology for Raimond Sebond

behold a manifest and indubitable truth which presents itself to his understanding; he discovers therein a wholly new
light, and honestly believes it, and so persuades himself.
Truly, I know not whether the ardour born of anger and
obstinacy in the encounter with the weight and violence of
the magistrate and with the danger, or the care of his reputation, has not often induced a man to maintain, even to the
stake, an opinion for which, among his friends and at liberty, he would not have been ready to burn the end of his
finger.

The shocks and stirrings which our soul receives through
perturbations of the body can do much in her; but her own
even more, which have so strong a hold upon her, that it
can perhaps be maintained that she has no other action or
motion than from the breath of her winds, and that, without their agitation, she would remain inactive, like a ship
in the open sea, deprived of the succour of the winds.[841] And
he who should maintain this, following the sect of the Peripatetics, would do us no great wrong, since it is recognised
that the greater number of the finest actions of the soul proceed from, and have need of, this impulsion of the passions.
Valour, they say, can not be perfected without the help of
anger.

> Ajax was always brave, but bravest in his mad-
> ness.[842]

Nor do we assail evil-doers and enemies vigorously enough
if we are not indignant; and it is thought that the advocate
must inspire the judges with indignation, in order to obtain
justice from them. Immoderate desires stirred Themistocles and Demosthenes, and have impelled philosophers

763

to labours, vigils, and peregrinations; they lead us to honour, to learning, to health—profitable ends. And this faintheartedness of soul in enduring trouble and vexation serves to nourish penitence and repentance in the conscience, and to make us feel the scourges of God in our chastisement and the scourges of public correction. Compassion acts as a spur to clemency, and prudence in protecting and restraining ourselves is awakened by our fear; and how many fine actions by ambition? how many by presumption? No eminent and gallant virtue, in short, exists without some lawless excitement. May not this have been one of the reasons that moved the Epicureans to discharge God from all care and solicitude about our affairs, inasmuch as the very works of his kindness could not be executed for us without disturbing his repose by means of passions that are like prickings and solicitations that direct the soul to virtuous actions.[843] Or, indeed, did they think otherwise, and regard them as storms which ignominiously turn aside the soul from its tranquillity? *As the tranquillity of the sea is perceived when no wind, not even the slightest breeze, ruffles the waves, so the calm and quiet of the soul is seen when there is no perturbation by which it can be moved.*[844]

What differences of meaning and of reasonableness, what contrariety of ideas, the diversity of our passions presents to us! What assurance, then, can we have in a thing[845] so unstable and so shifting, subject by its nature to the sway of confusion, never moving save at a forced and acquired pace? If our judgement is at the mercy of sickness and of perturbation; if it is from want of wit and from foolhardiness that it is bound to receive its impression of things, what certainty can we expect from it?

Apology for Raimond Sebond

Is it not bold of philosophy to think that men produce their greatest effects, and those most nearly approaching divinity, when they are beside themselves, and mad, and insensate?[846] We are bettered by privation of our reason and by its torpor. The two natural ways to enter the cabinet of the gods, and there foresee the course of destiny, are madness and sleep. This is amusing to think upon; by the disorder which the passions bring into our reason, we become virtuous; by its extirpation, which madness or the image of death brings, we become prophets and seers. Never could I readily believe this. It is a simple extravagance, which sacred truth instilled into the philosophic mind, extorting from it, contrary to its own assertion, that the tranquil state of our soul, the state of composure, the most helpful state that it can acquire from philosophy, is not its best state. Our waking is more sleepy than sleep, our wisdom more foolish than folly. Our dreams are worth more than our meditations. The worst abode that we can choose is in ourselves.

But does not philosophy think that we have the wit to observe that the word which represents the spirit, when it is loosed from man, as so clear-sighted, so great, and so perfect, and, while it is still in man, as so earthly, ignorant, and tenebrious, is a word uttered by the spirit which is in earthly, ignorant, and tenebrious man, and consequently an untrustworthy and unbelievable word?

I, being of an easy and heavy temperament, have no great experience of these violent agitations, of which the greater number take the soul by surprise, without giving it time to recognise itself. But the passion which is said to be born of idleness in the hearts of young men, although its progress is leisurely and with measured steps, manifests very clearly, to those who have tried to oppose its strength, the force of the conversion and change that our judgement suffers. I have in times past attempted to stiffen myself to resist and repel it (for I am so far from being of those who invite vices that I do not even follow them, if they do not carry me away); I perceived it come to life, increase, and enlarge, in spite of my resistance, and at last lay hold of me and possess me, with my eyes open and all alive, to such a degree that, as in drunkenness, the aspect of things began to seem to me other than as usual: I saw clearly the advantages of the things I was desiring becoming bigger and increase, augmented and puffed up by the breath of my imagination, the difficulties of my enterprise become easy and smooth, my reason and my conscience fall back; but, that fire having vanished, all in an instant, like the brightness of a flash of lightning, [I saw] my soul recover another sort of vision, another condition, and another judgement; the difficulties of withdrawal appeared to me great and insurmountable, and the things themselves of a far other nature and aspect than as the heat of desire had presented them to me. Which was most like the truth, Pyrrho knows not. We are never without sickness. Fevers have their hot and their cold turns; from the conditions of a burning attack we pass into the conditions of a shivering attack. As far as I had been thrown forward, so far am I cast back;

> As when the sea, rushing with ebb and flow, now throws itself foaming on the land, and tosses its waves over the rocks, and waters with its curving flood the whole shore; now, rapidly retreating, engulfing again

Apology for Raimond Sebond

in its whirling depths the stones it brought, and leaves
the beach bare.[847]

Now, from the knowledge of this instability of mine,
I have, by fortune, engendered in myself some steadiness of
opinions, and have scarcely changed my earliest and inborn
ones. For, whatever there may be in the new thing, I do not
easily change, for fear of losing by the change. And since
I am not capable of choosing, I take the choice of others and
keep in the condition in which God has put me. Otherwise
I should not know how to save myself from ceaseless shifting. Thus I have, by the favour of God, without agitation
and trouble of conscience, remained wholly true to the ancient beliefs of our faith, through all the sects and schisms
that our time has produced. The writings of the ancients—
I mean the excellent writings, full and solid—persuade me,
and carry me almost where they wish; he to whom I am
listening seems always to me the most stable;[848] I find them
all to be right, each in his turn, although they contradict one
another. The facility of able minds to make whatever they
please seem probable, and to find nothing so strange that
they do not undertake to give it enough colour to deceive
such unskilfulness as mine, shows plainly the weakness of
their proof. The heavens and the stars were in motion for
three thousand years; every one so believed until Cleanthes the Samian,[849] or, according to Theophrastus, Nicetas
the Syracusan,[850] took upon himself to maintain that it
was the earth that was moved through the oblique circle
of the Zodiac, revolving about its axis; and, in our day,
Copernicus has so well established this doctrine that it is in
common use, with all its astronomical consequences. What

shall we conclude from this, except that it does not matter
to us which of them may be true? And who can say that, a
thousand years hence, a third theory will not overturn the
two earlier ones?

Thus time in its revolution changes the season of
things; what is prized falls wholly out of favour, and
another thing takes its place and emerges from contempt; this is daily more coveted, and, when discovered, thrives in the praises and honour of men.[851]

Thus, when some new doctrine presents itself to us, we have
great reason to distrust it, and to reflect that, before it was
put forth, its opposite held sway; and, as that has been overthrown by this, it may happen hereafter that a third idea
will be born, which will in like manner give battle to the
second. Before the principles introduced by Aristotle[852] obtained credit, other principles satisfied human reason, as
his satisfy us at this moment. What letters patent have these,
what special privilege, that the progress of our invention
should stop with them, and that to them, for all time to
come, should belong the control of our belief? They are no
more exempt from being pushed out of place[853] than their
predecessors were. When a new argument is urged on me,
I may consider that what I can not give a satisfactory answer to, another will answer satisfactorily; for to believe all
the appearances that we can not explain away is great
simplicity. It would come about, in that case, that with all
the common people and the generality of men, their beliefs
would be as variable as a weathercock; for their souls, being
soft and unresisting, would be forced constantly to receive
this and the other impression, the last always effacing the

traces of the preceding one. He who finds himself at a loss
should reply, following the legal style, that he will speak to
his adviser about it, or apply to the wisest men from whom
he received his instruction.

How long has the knowledge of the human body been in
existence?[854] They say that a newcomer, one Paracelsus, is
changing and overturning the whole system of the ancient
rules, and declares that to this hour it has served only to
make men die. I believe that he will easily verify this; but
I consider that it would be no great wisdom to put my life
to the proof of his newly acquired knowledge. We must not
believe every one, says the precept, because by every one
every thing can be said.

A man who openly confesses belief in these new ideas and
in correction of physical conceptions[855] said to me, not long
ago, that all the ancients had evidently been mistaken about
the nature and movement of the winds; and this he would
make me clearly perceive if I would hearken to him. After
I had had a little patience in listening to his arguments,
which were full of plausibility, "How then," I asked, "those
who sailed by the rules of Theophrastus—did they go to
the west when they set sail to the east? Did they go sidewise, or backward?"—"It was a matter of luck," he replied; "all the same, they were mistaken." I told him then
that I liked better to follow facts than reasoning. Now,
these are things which often conflict with one another; and
I have been told that, in geometry, which thinks it has attained the highest point of certainty among the sciences,
there are inevitable demonstrations subverting the truth of
experience; as Jacques Peletier, when visiting me, told me
that he had found two lines wending toward each other as if

to join, which nevertheless, he averred, could never, even
to infinity, come to touch one another. And the Pyrrhonians employ their arguments and their reasoning only to
destroy the verity of experience; and it is marvellous how
far the suppleness of our reason has waited on them in this
design of resisting the evidence of facts; for they affirm that
we do not move, that we do not speak, that nothing has
weight or heat, with a force of argumentation equal to that
with which we affirm the most probable-seeming things.

Ptolomeus, who was a great personage, established the
boundaries of our world; all the ancient philosophers had
thought that they had it measured, save some scattered
islands which might have escaped their knowledge. It would
have been Pyrrhonising, a thousand years ago, to cast a
doubt upon the science of cosmography and the beliefs
which were accepted by every one; it was heresy to avouch
the Antipodes; behold in our time there has been discovered
an infinite extent of terra firma—not an island or a single
country, but a piece almost equal in size to that which we
were acquainted with. The geographers of this age do not
fail to assert that now all has been found and all is visible;

For what we have at the moment is pleasing and
seems to be the best.[856]

It remains to be seen whether, if Ptolemy was mistaken in
other days as to the foundation of his reasoning, it would
not be foolish for me to rely now upon what these say
about it;[857] and whether it is not most probable that this
great body that we call the world is a very different thing
from what we judge it to be. Plato holds that it changes
its aspect in all ways: that the heavens, the stars, and the

sun sometimes reverse the motion that we see in them, changing the east to the west.[858] The Egyptian priests told Herodotus that, since the time of the first king, which was eleven thousand and more years before (and of all their kings they showed him the effigies in statues done from life), the sun had changed his course four times; that the sea and the land change into each other alternately; that the beginning of the world is undetermined.[859] Aristotle, Cicero say the same; and some one of our writers[860] says that the world has been, from all eternity, dying and being reborn, with many vicissitudes; and he calls as witnesses Solomon and Isaiah, to evade these gainsayings—that God was at one time a creator with nothing created;[861] that he was unoccupied; that he betook himself to occupations[862] in putting his hand to this work, and that, consequently, he is subject to change. In the most famous of the Greek schools,[863] the world is held to be a god made by another greater god, and is composed of a body, and of a soul which dwells in its centre, expanding by musical numbers to its circumference, divine, most blessed, most great, most wise, eternal. In it are other gods,—the earth, the sea, the stars, — which linked together in an harmonious and never-ceasing movement and divine dance, sometimes meeting, sometimes drawing apart, concealing and revealing themselves, changing their position, now in front and now behind. Heraclitus affirmed that the world was composed of fire and, by the decree of fate, must some day blaze up and be resolved into fire, and some day be again reborn.[864] And Apuleius says of mankind: *As individuals, they are mortal; as a whole, they are eternal.*[865]

Alexander wrote to his mother the tale told by an Egyptian priest, derived from their records,[866] witnessing to the antiquity of that immemorial race and comprising the veritable birth and progress of the other countries. Cicero and Diodorus said in their day that the Chaldæans had registers of more than four hundred thousand years; Aristotle, Pliny, and others, that Zoroaster lived six thousand years before the age of Plato. Plato says that the people of the city of Sais have written chronicles for eight thousand years, and that the city of Athens was built a thousand years before the said city of Sais;[867] Epicurus, that, at the same time that things here are as we see them, they are wholly similar and of the same fashioning in many other worlds; which he would have said more confidently if he had seen the similitudes and correspondences of this new world of the West Indies with ours, present and past, in such strange instances.

In truth, considering what we have learned of the manner of this terrestrial government, I have often marvelled to see the coincidence, at a very great distance of place and of time, of a vast number of unnatural popular opinions and of uncultivated customs and beliefs, which in no way seem to belong to our natural ideas.[868] Human wit is a great worker of miracles; but this relation has I know not what that is even more unlooked for; it is found also in names, in events, and in a thousand other things. For we find nations that have never, so far as we know, heard of us, where circumcision was held in repute; where high functions and great governments were carried on by women without men;[869] where our fasts and Lent were reproduced, adding thereto abstinence from women; where our crosses, in divers shapes, were held in repute: here, they honoured with them their sepultures; there, they employed them—and notably

772

the cross of St. Andrew—to guard themselves from nocturnal visions, and to place on the cradles of infants against enchantments: elsewhere they[870] found one made of wood, of great height, and adored as the god of rain, and this very far on the mainland. They found there a marked similitude to our confessors;[871] the use of mitres, the celibacy of priests, the art of prophesying by the entrails of sacrificed animals; abstinence in their diet from every kind of flesh and fish;[872] the custom among the priests, when officiating, of using a special tongue and not the vulgar one; and this conception, that the first god was expelled by a second, his younger brother; that they were created with all benefits, whereof, for their sins, they have since been deprived, their territory changed, and their natural condition impaired; that they were of old submerged by the inundation of waters from heaven; that only a few families were then saved, who took refuge in the high caves of the mountains, which caves they closed, so that the water did not there enter, having imprisoned therein many kinds of animals; that, when they perceived that the rain had ceased, they sent out dogs, which having returned clean and wet, they judged that the water was not yet much lower; later, having sent out others and seeing them return muddy, they issued forth to repeople the world, which they found replenished only with serpents. In a certain place, they lighted upon the belief in a day of judgement, which caused them[873] to be highly angered with the Spaniards, who cast abroad the bones of the dead when searching for treasure in the burial-places, the people saying that those scattered bones could not easily be reunited. Traffic by barter, and not otherwise, and fairs and markets for that purpose; dwarfs and deformed persons, for adorn-

773

ment of the tables of princes; the practice of falconry according to the nature of their birds; tyrannical demands for assistance;[874] refinements of gardening; dances; jugglers' antics; instrumental music; coats-of-arms; tennis-courts; games of dice and of chance, at which they often became so heated as to stake themselves and their freedom; no other medicine than charms; the way of writing by figures;[875] belief in a sole first man, the father of all nations; adoration of a god who formerly lived as a man, in perfect chastity, fasting, and penance, preaching the law of nature and the ceremonies of religion, and who vanished from the world without a natural death; belief in giants; the habit of intoxicating themselves with their beverages and drinking as much as they could carry; religious ornaments, with delineations of skeletons and skulls; surplices, holy water, sprinklings; wives and servitors, who present themselves with emulation to be burned and buried with the departed husband or master; the law that the eldest son should succeed to all the property, and no portion be reserved for the younger but obedience; a custom that, on promotion to a certain office of great authority, he who is promoted takes a new name and quits his own; to cast lime on the knee of the new-born child, saying to him: "From dust thou camest and to dust thou shalt return"; the art of augurs.

Those idle shadows of our religion which are seen in some instances bear witness to its dignity and divinity. Not only has it, in some sort, made its way into all the infidel nations on this side of the world by some kind of imitation, but among those barbarians also, by a general and supernatural inspiration. For there was found there, also, the belief in purgatory, but in a new form: what we ascribed to fire they

ascribe to cold, and imagine souls to be purged and punished by the severity of an extreme coldness. And this example reminds me of another odd difference: for, as there
were some nations who found a satisfaction in unsheathing
the end of their member, removing the skin after the manner of the Mahommedans and Jews, there were others who
made so great a scruple about laying it bare, that, very carefully stretching the skin, they brought it up and fastened
it with little cords, for fear lest the end might see the air.
And likewise of this difference, that, whereas we honour
kings and festivals by arraying ourselves in the best clothes
we have, in some countries, to mark complete disparity and
submission to their king, his subjects present themselves
before him in their shabbiest garments, and, on entering the
palace, throw some old torn cloak above their good apparel,
so that all the splendour and adornment may be the master's.

But to proceed. If Nature confines within the limits of
her regular progress, like all other things, also the beliefs,
the judgements and opinions of men; if they have their
cycles,[876] their times, their birth, their death, like cabbages; if Heaven moves them and turns them at its will;
what dominant and permanent authority shall we attribute
to them? If by experience we clearly perceive[877] that the
character of our existence depends on the atmosphere, the
climate, and the soil where we were born, not only our complexion, stature, disposition, and demeanour, but also the
faculties of the soul, *and the region of the air not only
contributes to strength of body, but to that of mind,*[878] says
Vegetius; and that the goddess who founded the city of
Athens chose for its location a climate which made men

775

discreet, as the priests of Egypt informed Solon: *The air of Athens is subtle; and it is for this reason, some think, that the Athenians are sharp-witted; so the air of Thebes is thick, and the Thebans are dull and sturdy;*[879] in like manner, as fruits and animals are born differing, so men are born more or less warlike, just, temperate, and docile; here addicted to wine, elsewhere to theft or to lechery; here inclined to superstition, elsewhere to unbelief; here to liberty, there to servitude; with capacity for one kind of learning, or one art; dull witted or intelligent, obedient or rebellious, good or bad, according to the influence of the place where they dwell; and take on a new nature if we change their location, like trees. This was the reason that Cyrus did not choose to allow the Persians to abandon their rugged and uneven country and betake themselves to another more gentle and more smooth, saying that rich, soft soils produce soft men, and fertile soils unfertile minds.[880] If we see that, by virtue of some celestial influence, sometimes one art, one opinion flourishes, sometimes another; that a certain age produces certain natures and inclines the human race to this or that bent; that the minds of men are, like our fields, sometimes flourishing, sometimes barren, what becomes of all those fine prerogatives that we flatter ourselves about? Since a wise man may be mistaken, and a hundred men and many nations,—and, verily, human nature, in our opinion, has been mistaken for many ages about this or about that,—what assurance have we that sometimes it is not mistaken, and that in this age it may not be mistaken?

It seems to me that, among other evidences of our inability, this deserves not to be forgotten: that man can not, even in desire, find what is needful for him; not in possession, but by imagination and by wish, we could not be in agreement as to what we have need of, to satisfy us. Let our thought fashion[881] at its pleasure, it will not be able even to desire what is meet for this—to give satisfaction;

> With what reason do we fear or desire? What is so fortunately conceived that you do not repent the effort, or even the accomplished desire?[882]

This is why Socrates asked the gods for nothing except to give him what they knew to be salutary for him.[883] And the prayer of the Lacedæmonians, public and private, was simply that good and fair things might be granted them, leaving the selection and choice of these to the divine judgement:[884]—

> We pray for a spouse, and that the wife may have children; but only the gods know what the children and what the future wife will be.[885]

And the Christian prays to God that his will be done, to avoid falling into the dilemma which the poets narrate of King Midas. He besought the gods that every thing he touched might be changed into gold. His prayer was granted: his wine was gold, his bread gold, and the feathers of his bed, and golden his shirt and garments; so that he found himself crushed by the fruition of his desire, and endowed with an intolerable benefaction. He had need to unpray his prayers:—

> Astonished at the strangeness of the evil, at once rich and poor, he would fain flee wealth, and detest that for which he but lately prayed.[886]

Apology for Raimond Sebond

A word of myself. I besought of Fortune, above all things in my youth, the order of Saint Michel; for it was then the highest mark of honour for the French nobility, and very rare. She accorded it to me in a droll fashion. Instead of raising and exalting me in my station to attain it, she treated me much more graciously: she debased it and brought it down to my shoulders, and lower.[887] Cleobis and Bito, Trophonius and Agamedes, having besought, those of their goddess, these of their god, a guerdon worthy of their piety, received the gift of death, so different from our own are celestial ideas regarding our needs.[888] God could confer upon us riches, honours, even life and health, sometimes to our hurt; for all that is agreeable to us is not always salutary for us. If, instead of recovery, he sends us death or aggravation of our ills,—*thy rod and thy staff, they comfort me,*[889] —he does it by the judgement of his providence, which discerns what is fit for us much more unerringly than we can do; and we should take it in good part as from a very wise and very friendly hand;

> if you wish my counsel, let the gods consider what is meet for us and what things are profitable for us; man is more dear to them than to himself.[890]

For, to beseech honours and offices from them[891] is to beseech them to cast you into a battle, or into a game of dice, or some other thing of which the issue is unknown to you and the fruit doubtful.[892]

There is no conflict so violent among philosophers, and so bitter, as that which arises over the question of the supreme good of man, from which, according to Varro's reckoning, two hundred and eighty-eight sects came into

778

being.[893] *Now he who dissents with regard to the highest good raises an argument about the whole subject of philosophy.*[894]

They seem to me, as it were, like three youths at table, who ask for very different dishes according to their different tastes. What shall I offer? what shall I not offer? You decline what another demands; and what you ask for is entirely distasteful and disagreeable to the other two.[895]

So Nature should reply to their contestation and disputes.
Some say that our well-being has its seat in virtue, others in pleasure, others again in submission to nature; this one, in learning; that one, in having no suffering; this other, in not allowing oneself to be led away by appearances (and to this idea, that other of ancient Pythagoras[896] seems very much akin:

To be perturbed by nothing is almost the sole means, O Numacius, that can make and maintain happiness,[897]—

which is the goal of the Pyrrhonian school). Aristotle attributes to magnanimity the being surprised at nothing.[898] And Arcesilaus said that resistance[899] and an upright and inflexible state of the judgement are goods, but yieldings and compliances[900] are vices and evils. It is true that in asserting this as axiomatic he departed from Pyrrhonism. The Pyrrhonians, when they say that the supreme good is ataraxy, which is immobility of the judgement, do not mean it affirmatively; but the same impulse[901] which makes them shrink from precipices, and shelter themselves from the

779

evening air, itself suggests this idea to them and makes them reject any other conception of it.

How much I wish that while I live, either some other, or Justus Lipsius, the most learned man who is left to us, of a most fine and judicious mind, truly akin to my Turnebus,[902] might have the desire and the health and enough leisure to make a compilation of the opinions of the ancient philosophers according to their divisions and their classes, as honestly and carefully as we can distinguish them, on the subject of our being and of our morals; their controversies, the influence and the successions of the different sides, the relations of the lives of the authors and sectators to their precepts, in memorable and typical circumstances.

For the rest, if it is from ourselves that we derive the ordering of our morals, into what confusion do we thrust ourselves! For that which our reason counsels us as having most appearance of truth is, in general, for every one to obey the laws of his country, which is the advice of Socrates, inspired, he says, by divine counsel.[903] And what does our reason mean by that, if not that our duty has only a casual prescription? Truth ought to have a similar aspect everywhere. If man knew any uprightness and justice which had body and a true being, he would not connect it with the condition of the customs of this or that country; it would not be from the opinions held in Persia or in India that virtue would take shape. Nothing is subject to more constant agitation than the laws. Since I was born I have seen those of the English, our neighbours, altered three or four times, not only in state matters, where one is willing to dispense with stability, but in the most important of all matters, namely, religion.[904] By which I am mortified and

Apology for Raimond Sebond

vexed, the more because it is a nation with which those of my province have had in former days so intimate a connection,[905] that there still remain in my family[906] some traces of our old kinship. And here in France I have seen a certain thing, which was formerly a capital offence, become lawful;[907] and those of us who are dependent upon others are in danger, from the uncertainty of the fortunes of war, of being guilty some day of high treason, human and divine, our justice falling into the power of injustice, and after being in possession for a few years, becoming essentially different.

How could that ancient god[908] more clearly indicate in human knowledge ignorance of the divine being, and teach men that religion was merely a thing of their imagining, adapted to bind their society together, than by declaring, as he did, to those who sought, about this, the instruction of his tripod, that the true worship for each man was that which he found to be observed by the custom of the place where he was? O God, what obligation are we not under to the benignity of our sovereign Creator for having shown our faith the folly of[909] these wanderings and uncertain ceremonies, and for having placed it upon the everlasting foundation of his holy word!

What, then, will philosophy say to us in this emergency? That we should follow the laws of our country? That is to say, that fluctuating sea of the opinions of a people or of a prince, which will depict justice to me in as many colours and reshape it in as many forms as there may be in themselves changes of passion? I can not have so flexible a judgement. What goodness is that which I saw yesterday in repute, and to-morrow to be no longer so; and which the crossing of a river makes criminal?[910] What

Apology for Raimond Sebond

truth is that which those mountains bound, which is false-hood to the world beyond them?

But they are amusing when, to give some distinctness to the laws, they say that there are some that are fixed, perpetual, and unchangeable, which they call natural laws, which are imprinted in the human race by the nature of their proper essence. And of these, some make the number to be three, some four; some more, some less: a sign that this badge is as doubtful as the rest. Now they are so unfortunate (for how can I call it other than unfortunate that, of so infinite a number of laws, there is not at least one to be found that fortune and the hazard of fate have permitted to be universally accepted by the agreement of all nations?), they are, I say, so ill off that of these three or four selected laws there is not one single one that is not opposed and disavowed, not by one nation, but by many. Now the only likely sign whereby they could demonstrate some laws to be natural would be the universality of their confirmation. For what nature had veritably ordained for us, that we should doubtless follow by common agreement. And not only every nation, but every private man, would feel the force and violence which would be put upon him by any one who desired to impel him in opposition to that law. Let them bring before my eyes one of this sort. Protagoras and Aristo found no other essential qualities in the justice of laws than the authority and judgement of the legislature; and maintained that, apart from this, the good and the fitting lost their nature, and became but empty names of unimportant things. Thrasimachus in Plato considers that there is no other right than what is well for one's superiors.[911] In nothing else is the world so diverse as in customs and

782

laws. One thing is abominable here which elsewhere brings praise, as in Lacedæmon cunning in thievery. Marriages between those of the same family are forbidden here as a capital crime; elsewhere they are held in honour:

> there are said to be peoples among whom mother and son, and father and daughter, are wedded, and natural affection is increased by the double bond.[912]

The murder of children, the murder of fathers, community of wives, commerce in robbery, license in all sorts of sensualities—there is nothing, in short, so extreme that it is not found to be allowed by the customs of some nation. It may be believed that there are natural laws, such as may be seen in the other creatures; but in us they are lost, since this fine human reason everywhere intrudes, to master and command, confusing and confounding the aspect of things in accordance with its frivolousness and mutability. *And so, nothing is any longer ours; what I call ours is a matter of convention.*[913]

Subjects have divers appearances, divers points to be considered; from this principally is engendered the diversity of opinions. One nation regards a subject by one aspect and stops at that; another by another. There is nothing so horrible to imagine as eating one's father. The nations which, in ancient times, had this custom always held it to be a testimonial of filial piety and true affection; seeking thereby to give to their progenitors the most worthy and honourable sepulture, taking into themselves and, as it were, into their marrow, the bodies and remains of their fathers, vivifying them in some sort, and regenerating them by the transmutation into their own living flesh by means of digestion and nourishment. It is easy to judge what cruelty and abomination it would have seemed, to men permeated and imbued with that superstition, to cast the remains of their fathers to the corruption of the earth and to the nourishment of animals and worms.[914] Lycurgus considered, in theft, the alertness, discretion, boldness, and skill there is in purloining from one's neighbour at unawares, and the utility that redounds to the public in each man's consequently looking more carefully to the safe keeping of what belongs to him; and he considers that, from this double education, in attack and in defence, would ensue profit for military discipline (which was the principal science and virtue in which he desired to train that nation) of greater importance than the irregularity and injustice of acquiring the goods of another.[915]

Dionysius the tyrant offered Plato a robe of the Persian fashion, long, figured,[916] and perfumed; Plato declined it, saying that, being a man, he would not willingly clothe himself in a woman's robe; but Aristippus accepted it with the rejoinder that no apparel could infect an unsullied mind.[917] His friends taunted him with his unmanliness in taking it so little to heart that Dionysius had spat in his face. "Fishermen," he said, "put up with being bathed by the waves from head to foot, to catch a gudgeon."[918] Diogenes was washing his cabbages, and seeing him pass, cried, "If you knew how to live on cabbages, you would not pay court to a tyrant." To which Aristippus retorted: "If you knew how to live among men, you would not wash cabbages."[919] Thus reason justifies differing manifestations.[920] It is a jar with two handles and can be grasped by either one.

O Land that dost receive us, thou hast the air of

Apology for Raimond Sebond

war. This troop of horses armed for war portends war. But yet these same beasts are wont sometimes to come under the yoke and bear the harness of a car; there is hope of peace.[921]

Solon, being exhorted not to shed vain and bootless tears for the death of his son, said: "But it is because they are vain and bootless that I rightfully shed them."[922] Socrates' wife exasperated her lamentation by this consideration: "Oh, how unjustly do those wicked judges put him to death!" "Would you, then, prefer that it should be justly?" he answered her.[923]

We have our ears bored; the Greeks considered that a badge of servitude.[924] We conceal ourselves to enjoy our wives; the Indians do it in public. The Scythians sacrificed strangers in their temples; elsewhere temples are places of refuge.[925]

Hence the madness of the common people, each locality hating the gods of his neighbours, and believing that the only true gods are those which are there worshipped.[926]

I have heard of a judge who, when he met with a sharp conflict of opinion between Bartolus and Baldus,[927] and some subject confused by many disagreements, wrote in the margin of his book: "Question for the friend"; that is to say, that the truth was so entangled and so contested, that in such a cause he could favour whichever one of the parties it might seem well to him to favour. It was only from lack of wit and perception that he could not write everywhere: "Question for the friend." The lawyers and judges of our

Apology for Raimond Sebond

day find in all causes bias sufficient to adjust them as seems well to them. In a science so infinite, depending on the authority of so many opinions, and of a nature so open to caprice,[928] it can not be that there does not arise an extreme confusion of judgements. Thus there is hardly any suit so clear that there are not found differing opinions regarding it. As to that about which one body of men has given a decree, another body of men gives a contrary decree; and itself, at another time, still a contrary one. Of which we see frequent examples in the license (which egregiously mars the solemn authority and lustre of our justice) not to abide by the sentence, but to run from judge to judge to decide the same cause.

As for the freedom of philosophic opinions touching vice and virtue, that is a thing which need not be enlarged upon, and about which there are many opinions that are better unspoken than published to weak minds. Arcesilaus said that in lechery it mattered little on which side or where it was committed.[929] *And Epicurus holds that, if nature demands indulgence in the pleasures of love, they should be guided, not in respect to birth or rank or condition, but in respect to personal qualities, age and appearance.*[930]*—Nor, in truth, that pure loves are to be judged unsuitable for the sage.*[931]*—Let us consider to what age the young should be loved.*[932] These last two Stoic passages, and the upbraiding by Dicearchus of Plato himself about this matter,[933] show to what degree the soundest philosophy permits licenses alien to common usage and excessive.

The laws derive their authority from possession and custom; it is dangerous to trace them back to their origin; they increase in breadth and dignity as they flow on, like our rivers: follow them up-stream to their source—it is only a little spring, hardly recognisable, which becomes thus much prouder and stronger by age. Look at the considerations that, in old time, first set in motion this mighty torrent, fraught with authority, inspiring dread and veneration: you will find them so slight and so weak that it is no wonder if the judgments of those people who weigh every thing and trace it back to reason, and who accept nothing on authority and trust, are often far removed from popular judgements. It is no wonder if people who take for their pattern the primal image of nature, in most of their opinions diverge from the common path. As for example: few of them[934] would have approved the restricted conditions of our marriages; and most of them wished wives to be in common and without ties. They rejected our customary observances.[935] Chrysippus said that a philosopher will make a dozen somersaults in public, yes, and without breeches, for a dozen olives.[936] He would hardly have advised Clisthenes to refuse the fair Agariste, his daughter, to Hippoclides, because he had seen him stand on his head on a table.[937]

Metrocles somewhat carelessly broke wind when arguing in the presence of his scholars, and kept himself hid in his house, for shame, until Crates visited him, and, adding to his consolations and reasonings the example of his own liberty, undertaking to break wind in rivalry with him, he removed his scruples, and furthermore led him to his own more free Stoic sect, away from the more mannerly Peripatetic sect which he had hitherto followed.[938]

What we call decency—the not venturing to do openly what it is decent for us to do in secret—they called foolishness; and to be so delicate as to disown and be silent about acts which nature, custom, and our appetites publish and proclaim, they considered vice. And they held that it was profaning the mysteries of Venus to remove them from the secluded sanctuary of her temple, and expose them to the people's gaze; and that to draw her sports from behind the curtain was to cheapen them. (Shame is a weighty coin. Concealment, reservation, limitation, have their share in its estimation.) They held that voluptuousness very ingeniously protested, under the mask of virtue, against being prostituted in the middle of the highways, trodden under the feet and eyes of the crowd, prizing rather the dignity and convenience of its wonted cabinets. Hence some say that to do away with the public brothels is not only to spread abroad the lechery that was allotted to that place, but by difficulty to spur men on to that vice.

You who were Aufidia's husband, Corvinus, are now her lover; he who was your rival is her husband. Why is it that she pleases you now that she belongs to another, who did not please you as your wife?[939]

This experience is diversified in countless examples.

There was no one in the whole city who would touch your wife, Cæcilianus, when it was easy; but now, being guarded, there is a great crowd of gallants. You are a clever man.[940]

A philosopher who was surprised in the act, and was asked what he was doing, replied, "I am planting a man;" no more blushing at being so caught than if he had been found planting garlic. Solon was, they say, the first who, by his laws, made it lawful for women to make public traffic of their bodies.[941]

I think it was out of over tenderness and respect that a great writer and monk maintained that this action was so necessarily bound up with concealment and modesty, that he could not be persuaded that those shameless embraces of the Cynics were effectual; but that they stopped short at imitating lascivious motions, in order to keep up the reputation for shamelessness which their school of philosophy professed; and that it was still necessary for them to seek the shade to eject what shame had withheld.

He had not seen far enough into their debauchery. For Diogenes, behaving indecently in public, expressed a wish, in presence of the bystanders "that he could as easily satisfy his hunger by rubbing his belly." To those who asked him why he did not seek a more convenient place for eating than the open street, he answered, "Because I am hungry in the open street."

The women philosophers who mixed with their sect also mixed with their persons in all places and without discrimination; and Hipparchia was received into the society of Crates only on condition of following in all things the uses and customs of his order. These philosophers set the highest value upon virtue, and rejected all other rules than those of morality; wherefore in all actions they attributed supreme authority, above the laws, to the judgement[942] of their sage: and set no other restraint upon the pleasures of the senses than moderation and protection of the liberty of others.

Heraclitus and Protagoras, because wine seems bitter to the sick and pleasant to the well, because the oar is

Apology for Raimond Sebond

crooked in the water and straight to those who see it only out of the water, and from similar opposed effects in things, reasoned that all things had in them the causes of these effects, and that there was in wine some bitterness which was related to the sick man's taste; that the oar had a certain curve related to him who saw it in the water.[943] And so with all the rest. Which is equivalent to saying that all is in every thing, and consequently no special quality in any one; for there is no special quality where there is every thing.[944] This theory brought to my mind the experience which we have that there is no meaning or aspect, either straight or bitter or sweet or curved, which the human mind does not find in the writings that it undertakes to search in. From the most clear, pure, and perfect utterance that can be imagined, how much falsity and untruth has been derived? what heresy has not found therein sufficient grounds and testimonies to begin its course and to maintain itself? It is for this reason that the authors of such errors are never willing to depart from the proof afforded by the testimony of the interpretation of words. A person of high position, wishing to confirm to me by authority the quest of the philosopher's stone, into which he had entered deeply, lately alleged to me five or six passages of the Bible upon which he said that he had primarily founded himself for the easing of his conscience (for he is of the ecclesiastical profession); and in truth the idea was not only amusing, but also very fittingly made use of for the defence of that fine science. In this way is acquired the repute of the fables of divination. There is no prognosticator, if he has sufficient weight for it to be thought worth while to turn his leaves, and to seek carefully all the twists and aspects of his words, whom we

790

Apology for Raimond Sebond

can not make say whatever we please, as with the Sibyls. For there are so many methods of interpretation that it is hard for an ingenious wit not to come across, in every subject, either obliquely or directly, some manner of expression that will serve his argument.

Therefore is it that the cloudy and vague style is found in such frequent and ancient use. Let the author be able to succeed in attracting posterity and occupying it with himself (which not merely ability, but, as much or more, the fortuitous interest of the subject may achieve); as to the rest, if he exposes himself, from stupidity or from subtlety, somewhat obscurely and in diverse ways, that matters not at all. A number of minds, sifting and shaking his work, will strain from it a quantity of conceptions, some in accordance with his, some on one side of his, some opposed to his, which will all do him honour. He will find himself enriched by means of his disciples, like the university regents at the Landit.[945]

It is this which has given value to many worthless things; which has brought into credit many writings and laden them with every sort of wished-for matter; one and the same thing receiving thousands and thousands, as many as we please, of diverse forms and considerations. Is it possible that Homer intended to say all that he has been made to say; and that he was embodied in so many and such diverse figures, that the theologians, legislators, soldiers, philosophers, people of every kind who treat of matters of learning, however diversely and contradictorily they treat them, lean upon him, referring to him about these matters: master general of all functions, works, and workers; adviser general in all undertakings? Whoever has had need of oracles and predictions has found them there at his service. A learned personage, and a friend of mine—it is wonderful how many and what admirable sayings he produces therefrom in favour of our religion; and he can not easily relinquish the opinion that such was Homer's design (yet that author is as familiar to him as to any man of our day). And what he finds in support of our religion, many in ancient times found in support of theirs.

See how Plato is handled and moved about. Every one, doing honour to himself by adapting him to his own views, places him on whichever side he desires to have him. They keep him in action and bring him into all the new beliefs that the world receives; and make him differ from himself according to the different course of things. They interpret him as rejecting customs lawful in his day, because they are unlawful in ours. All this eagerly and powerfully, in the measure that the interpreter's mind is powerful and eager.

From the same basis that Heraclitus had, and uttered that saying of his that all things had in them the aspects that were found in them, Democritus derived an entirely contrary conclusion; that things had in them nothing at all of what we found in them; and because honey was sweet to one and bitter to another, he argued that it was neither sweet nor bitter. The Pyrrhonians said that they did not know whether it was sweet or bitter, or neither one nor the other, or both; for they always attain to the highest point of uncertainty. The Cyrenaics held that nothing was perceptible externally, and that that only was perceptible which touched us inwardly, as dolour and pleasure; recognising neither sound nor colour, but certain impressions only which come to us from them; and that man's judgement had no other ground. Protagoras deemed that to be true for each man which seems to each man. The Epicureans place all power of judgement in the senses and in knowledge of things and in pleasure. Plato would have all judgement of truth, and truth itself, taken away from common beliefs and physical perceptions, to appertain to the mind and to cogitation.[946]

This train of thought has led me to the consideration of the senses, wherein lie the greatest source and proof of our ignorance. Every thing that is known is unquestionably known by the ability of the knower; for, since the judgement is derived from the mental activity of him who judges, it is right that he should perfect that activity by his resources and will, not by outside constraint, as would be the case if we knew things by the force, and from the law, of their essential being. Now, all knowledge makes its way in us through the senses: they are our masters,—

The path by which belief finds its nearest way into the human heart and into the regions of the mind.[947]

Learning begins with them and is determined by them. In fact, we should know no more than a stone if we did not know that there is sound, odour, light, savour, measure, weight, softness, hardness, sharpness, colour, smoothness, breadth, depth. Here are the frame and the origins of the whole structure of our learning. And, according to some, learning is nothing else than perception. Whoever can force me to contradict the senses, he has me by the throat, he could not make me fall back further. The senses are the beginning and the end of human knowledge.

You will find that the knowledge of the true is

derived first from the senses, and the senses can not be refuted. In what should we have greater confidence than in them?[948]

Let as little as possible be attributed to them—it will always be necessary to allow them this; that by their means and agency all our instruction makes its way. Cicero says that Chrysippus, having attempted to depreciate the power of the senses and their value, put before himself opposing arguments and objections, so forcible that he could not answer them. Whereupon Carneades, who maintained the opposite side, boasted of making use of the very weapons and words of Chrysippus to combat him; and because of this, cried out to him: "O unfortunate man, your strength has defeated you." There is no greater absurdity, to our thinking, than to maintain that fire does not warm, that light does not illuminate, that there is no weight or solidity in iron, which are pieces of knowledge that the senses bring us; there is in man no belief or learning that can be compared to this knowledge in certainty.

My first consideration on the subject of the senses is that I question whether man is supplied with all natural senses.[949] I see many animals who live a complete and perfect life, some without sight, others without hearing; who knows whether for us also there be not lacking one, two, three, or many other senses? For, if some one of them is lacking, our judgement can not discover the default. It is the privilege of the senses to be the extreme limit of our perception. There is nothing beyond them that can assist us in discerning them; nor, indeed, can one sense discern another.

Can the ears correct the eyes, or the touch the ears?

794

Apology for Raimond Sebond

Can the taste call in question the touch, or can the
scent refute, or the eyes controvert it?[950]

They all together form the outermost line of our ability;

To each is assigned its separate power, to each its
own strength.[951]

It is impossible to make a man who was born blind conceive
that he does not see; impossible to make him desire sight
and regret his lack of it. Wherefore we should derive no assurance from the fact that our soul is content and satisfied
with those senses that we have, considering that she has not
the means of feeling her infirmity and imperfection in this
respect, since it is a part of her. It is impossible to say aught
to this blind man, of reasoning, argument, or similitude,
which can possess his imagination with any apprehension
of light, of colour, and of vision. There is nothing in the
background which can testify to that sense. Those of the
blind from birth whom we find wishing to see—it is not from
understanding what it is they ask for: they have learned
from us that they lack something, that they have something
to wish for which we have, which they name rightly, and
its effects and consequences; but, nevertheless, they do not
know what it is, nor at all apprehend it.

I have known a gentleman of good family, blind from
birth, or, at least, blind from such an age that he knows not
what sight is: he so little understands what he lacks that,
like us, he uses and employs words belonging to sight, and
applies them in a special way that is all his own. They
brought to him a child whose godfather he was; having
taken him in his arms, "Good God!" he cried; "what a fine

795

child! What a pleasure to see him! What a bright face he
has!" He will say, like any one of us: "This room has a fine
view; it is fair weather; the sun shines bright." Yet more:
because hunting, tennis, and shooting at a mark are our
sports, and he has so heard, he likes them and occupies himself with them, and thinks that he plays the same part in
them that we do; he is vexed by them and pleased by them,
and yet knows them only through the ear. Some one calls
out to him, when they are on some level ground where he
can spur his horse, that there is a hare in sight; and again,
they tell him that the hare is caught; and behold, he is as
proud of his capture as he hears others say that they are. He
takes a tennis-ball in his left hand and strikes it with his
racket; he fires a harquebus at random, and is content with
what his people tell him, that his aim was high or wide.

How do we know that the human race does not commit
a like absurdity for lack of a sense; and that, by this default,
the greater part of the visage of things is concealed from us?
How do we know whether the difficulties that we find in
many works of nature are not due to that? and whether
many acts of animals, which are beyond our capacity, are
not the result of the power of some sense that we lack? and
whether some among them have not, in this way, a fuller
and more complete life than ours? We apprehend the apple
by almost all our senses: we find in it redness, smoothness,
odour, and sweetness; beyond these, it may have other
qualities, as drying or astringent, as to which we have no
related sense. The properties in many things that we call
occult,—as that in the magnet of attracting iron,—is it not
probable that there are in nature sentient faculties fit to discern and note these, and that the default of such faculties

causes our ignorance of the true essence of such things? It is perhaps some special sense which manifests to cocks the hour of dawn and midnight, and moves them to crow; which teaches hens, before any acquaintance and experience, to fear a sparrow-hawk, and not a goose or a peacock, which are larger creatures; which warns chickens of the instinct of hostility to them that exists in the cat, and bids them not to distrust the dog: to be on their guard against the miauling of the one,—a rather soothing sort of sound, —and not against the bark of the other, a harsh and quarrelsome sound; which teaches wasps and ants and rats to choose always the best cheese and the best pear before tasting them; and which leads the stag, the elephant, and the snake to the knowledge of a certain herb likely to cure them. There is no sense that may not have a wide sway, and that does not afford us by its means knowledge of an infinite number of things. If we were deficient in the apprehension of sounds, of harmony, and of the voice, that would cause unimaginable confusion in all the rest of our learning. For beyond what is attached to the special knowledge of each sense, how many proofs, consequences, and conclusions do we derive about other matters by comparing one sense with another! Let a man of understanding imagine the human race originally created without sight, and let him judge how much ignorance and confusion such a lack would bring upon it—what great darkness and blindness in our soul! It will be seen by this, of what importance to us in knowledge of the truth is the privation of another such sense, or of two, or of three, if such privation exists in us. We have pictured a truth by consultation with, and the concurrence of, our five senses; but perhaps the agreement and the contribution of eight or of ten senses was needed, to discern it with certainty and in its essence.

The sects [952] that combat man's learning combat it chiefly by the uncertainty and weakness of our senses; for, since all knowledge enters into us by their agency and means, if they err in the report they make to us; if they vitiate or change whatever they bring to us from without; if the light which, through them, flows into our soul is dim in the passage, we no longer have anything to cling to. From this extreme difficulty spring all these visionary ideas: that each thing has in itself all we find there; again, that it has naught of what we think that we find there; and the opinion of the Epicureans, that the sun is no larger than our vision judges it to be,—

> Whatever it is, the form it bears is not at all larger than, as our eyes discern it, it seems to us to be,[953]—

that the manifestations which make a body appear large to him who is near it, and smaller to him who is at a distance from it, are both true,—

> Yet in all this we do not admit that the eyes are at all deceived. . . . Do not attribute to the eyes this error of the mind;[954]

and, determinedly, that there is no deception in the senses; that we must lie at their mercy, and seek elsewhere reasons to explain the difference and contradiction that we find in them; indeed, that a wholly different falsity and vain fancy must be devised (they go as far as that), rather than accuse the senses.

Timagoras swore that, by pressing or turning his eye,

Apology for Raimond Sebond

he had never perceived the flame of the candle to become double, and that this seeming was due to the trickery of the imagination, not of the organ. Of all absurdities, the most absurd to the Epicureans is to deny the power and effect of the senses.

Therefore, whatever is perceived by them at any time is true. And if the senses can not explain why objects, which near at hand seem square, appear at a distance round, it is better in this case to give a false reason for such appearance, than to let escape from your grasp manifest things, and to ruin the elements of belief, and to destroy all the foundations on which life and safety depend. For not only would reason altogether crumble: life itself would at once be overthrown, unless you choose to trust the senses, and to shun precipices and other things of this sort that are to be avoided.[955]

This desperate and so unphilosophical advice means nothing else than that human learning can maintain itself only by unreasonable, foolish, and insane reasoning; but that still it is better that man, to make himself of worth, should avail himself of it and of every other assistance, however fantastic, than avow his inevitable ignorance—so disadvantageous a truth! He can not avoid the senses being the sovereign masters of his knowledge; but they are uncertain and liable to deception on all occasions. It is there that we must needs fight to the uttermost, and, if the lawful powers fail us, as they do, we must resort to obstinacy, rashness, effrontery.

In the event that what the Epicureans say is true, namely,

799

that we can learn nothing if what appears to the senses is false; and if what the Stoics say is also true, that what appears to the senses is so false that they can teach us nothing, we shall reach the conclusion, at the expense of those two great dogmatical sects, that we can learn nothing. As for the error and uncertainty in the operation of the senses, every one can furnish himself with as many examples as he may please, so common are the failures and deceptions which they put upon us. In the echo of a valley, the sound of a trumpet, which seems to come from in front of us, comes really from a mile or two behind us:—

> Mountains that rise from the sea seem to us but a single mass, although really far distant from each other. . . . And hills and fields by which we sail seem to move swiftly past the stern. . . . When a stubborn horse stops with us in the middle of a river, his transversely placed body [when we look down into the water] seems to us to be swiftly carried by some force against the current.[956]

When holding a musket-ball under the second finger, with the middle finger lapped over the other, it is extremely difficult to admit that there is only one ball, the sense of touch gives such evidence of two. For, that the senses are many a time masters of the reason, and compel it to receive impressions which it knows and judges to be false, we see at every turn. I set apart the sense of touch, whose functions are more intimate, more vivid and material, which so often, by the effect of the pain that it brings to the body, subverts all those fine Stoical resolutions, and forces to cry out with the belly-ache the man who has established in his mind, with

Apology for Raimond Sebond

the utmost resolution, this dogma, that the colic, like every other disease and pain, is a thing of no consequence, not having the power to abate any thing of the sovereign good hap and felicity wherein the wise man is housed by his virtue. There is no heart so effeminate that the sound of our drums and trumpets does not make it beat the faster; nor so insensible, that the sweetness of music does not excite and gladden it; and no soul so churlish that does not feel some touch of veneration when beholding the sombre vastness of our churches, the diversity of the decorations and order of our ceremonials, and when listening to the devotional strains of our organs, and the harmony, so solemn and devout, of our voices. Even those who enter them disdainfully feel a certain thrill at the heart, and a certain awe, which makes them distrustful of their state of mind.

As for myself, I do not deem myself strong enough to hear, with senses undisturbed, verses of Horace and Catullus sung in a melodious voice by beautiful and youthful lips. And Zeno was right in saying that the voice is the flower of beauty. Some one tried to make me believe that a man whom all we Frenchmen know had deceived me in reciting to me verses that he had composed; that they were not the same on paper as in the air; and that my eyes would judge of them otherwise than my ears, so much power has utterance to give value and shape to works which lie at its mercy. Wherefore Philoxenus was not blameworthy when, hearing a man give a bad accent to some composition of his, he trampled upon and broke some bricks belonging to him, saying: "I break what is yours, because you spoil what is mine."

For what reason did even the men who procured their

801

Apology for Raimond Sebond

own death, with a fixed determination turn away their faces,
in order not to see the stroke that they caused to be dealt
them? And they who, for their health, desire and order that
they be cut and cauterised, why can not they endure the
sight of the preparations, instruments, and work of the
surgeon, since the sight can have no participation in the
pain? Are not these fitting examples to prove the authority
that the senses have over the reason? We are well aware that
those tresses are borrowed from a page or a footman; that
that rosy tint came from Spain, and that whiteness and
smoothness from the ocean; still sight must needs compel
us to think the person more lovable and more charming
against all reason. For in this there is nothing that is real.[958]

> We are misled by ornament; defects are hidden by
> gems and gold; the girl is of herself the least part.
> Often you must needs seek where, amid all these
> things, is the beloved; with this covering wealthy love
> deceives our eyes.[959]

How much do the poets ascribe to the power of the senses,
who make Narcissus desperately in love with his shadow?

> All is admired by him which in himself is admir-
> able; ignorantly, he desires himself; and what he feels,
> he feels for himself; and according as he seeks, he is
> sought; and equally he himself burns and kindles
> flame;[960]

and Pygmalion's understanding, so perturbed by the impression of the sight of his ivory statue, that he loves it and
adores it as if it had life!

> He gives kisses and thinks them returned; he pur-

802

Apology for Raimond Sebond

sues her and clasps her, and imagines that her limbs
yield to the pressure of his fingers; and he fears that
his embrace may bruise her.[961]

Place a philosopher in a cage of small, far-apart iron
wires, and suspend it at the top of the towers of Notre
Dame de Paris—he will see, by manifest reason, that it is
impossible for him to fall out of it, yet he will be unable (if
he be not used to the tiler's trade) to prevent the sight of
that vast height from terrifying and paralysing him. For it
is difficult enough for us to feel safe in the galleries that are
in our bell-towers if they are open, even though they be
of stone. There are those who can not even support the
thought of them. Let a beam be placed between those two
towers, of such width as we need in order to walk upon it—
there is no philosophic wisdom so firm of will that it can
give us courage to tread it as we should do if it were on the
ground. I have often experienced this in our mountains
hereabout (and yet I am one of those who are very little
dismayed by such things), that I could not bear the sight
of that bottomless depth without dread and a trembling in
my hams and thighs, although I was not near the edge by
quite my own length, and could not fall over if I did not
knowingly place myself in danger. I have there noticed also
that, whatever the height may be, provided in the slope
there appears a tree or a jutting rock to catch the sight a
little, and break it, it relieves us and gives us confidence, as
if it were a thing from which we might receive help in the
fall; but that we can not even look without dizziness upon
the abrupt, smooth precipices,—*so that one can not look
down them without a dizziness both of the eyes and of the*

803

mind,[962]—which is a manifest imposture of the sight. That fine philosopher put out his eyes in order to free his soul from the misleading which it received from sight; and to be able to philosophise more at liberty. But by that reckoning he should also have stopped up his ears, which Theophrastus says are the most dangerous organs that we have, as receiving violent impressions to disturb us and change us; and should have deprived himself, in fact, of all his other senses, that is to say, of his existence and his life. For they all have this power of controlling our reason and our soul. *It often happens that our minds are very deeply impressed by some loud sound, or by song; and often also by anxiety and by fear.*[963] Physicians hold that there are certain temperaments which are excited even to frenzy by some sounds and instruments. I have seen some who could not hear a bone gnawed under their table without losing patience; and there is scarcely any man who is not disturbed by that shrill, piercing noise that files make in rasping iron; just as, upon hearing chewing close by, or hearing some one talk who has an obstruction in the throat or the nose, many persons are moved to anger and hatred. That piping prompter of Gracchus, who softened, steadied, and modulated his master's voice when he harangued at Rome—what purpose did he serve, if the infection and quality of tone had not power to stimulate and change the judgement of his hearers? Truly, there is much cause to brag of the firmness of this fine faculty, which lets itself be managed and swayed by the uncertain motion and chances of so slight a wind! This same cheating that the senses impose upon our understanding they receive in their turn. Our soul sometimes revenges itself in like manner: they lie and are deceived in mutual emulation. What we see and hear when moved by anger, we do not hear as it is;

> And two suns and two Thebes are seen.[964]

The object that we love seems to us more beautiful than it really is,—

> So we often see women who are in many respects deformed and ugly warmly loved and held in the highest honour,[965]

and uglier, that which we detest. To a disquieted and afflicted man the light of day seems overcast and darksome. Our senses are not only changed, but often utterly stupefied, by the passions of the soul. How many things do we see that we do not perceive if our mind be otherwise occupied!

> You must know that even things that are exposed to view, if the mind is not turned to them, are just as if they had always been far removed from you.[966]

It seems that the soul withdraws into itself and arrests the powers of the senses. Thus, both inwardly and outwardly, man is full of weakness and falsehood.

They who have likened our life to a dream were perchance more nearly right than they thought. When we dream, our soul lives, acts, exercises all its faculties neither more nor less than when it is awake; but yet more inertly and vaguely, not by so much certainly that the difference is as that between night and sunlight—rather between night and twilight; in the one condition the soul sleeps, in the other, it dozes. There are always obscurities, aye, Cimmerian obscurities. We sleep when awake, and are awake when asleep.

Apology for Raimond Sebond

I do not see so clearly in sleep; but, as for my waking state, I never find it sufficiently perfect and unclouded. Also sleep, when profound, sometimes quiets dreams. But our waking is never so complete that it wholly casts out and scatters the musings which are the dreams of those who wake, and worse than dreams. Since our soul's reason accepts the imaginations and conceptions which are born in it while sleeping, and authorises the actions of our dreams with the same approval as those of the daytime, why do we not question whether our thinking, our acting, be not another form of dreaming, and our awaking some sort of sleeping? If the senses be our chief judges, it is not ours alone that we must call into council; for in this faculty the animals have as much right as we, or more. It is certain that in some of them hearing is more acute than in man, in others the sight, in others the smell, in others the touch or taste. Democritus said that in the gods and the beasts the faculties of sensation were much more perfect than in man. Now between the action of their natures and ours the difference is extreme. Our saliva cleanses and dries our wounds; it kills the serpent;

> Such is the diversity that exists between things, that what is food to some is deadly poison to others. In fact, often a serpent, if touched by the spittle of a man, wastes away, and gnaws itself to death.[967]

What quality shall we ascribe to the saliva—that which affects us or that which affects the serpent? By which of the two natures shall we prove its true essential quality that we seek? Pliny says that in the East Indies there are fish of a certain kind,[968] which are poisonous to us and we to them, so that by our touch alone we kill them; which is really poisonous, the man or the fish? What shall we believe about it—that man is poisonous to the fish, or the fish to man? Some quality of the air affects man injuriously, which does not harm the ox; some other the ox, which does not harm man: which of the two qualities is, in reality and in nature, a pestilential one? They who have the jaundice see all things yellower and paler than we:[969]

Whatever the jaundiced look at appears yellow.[970]

They who have the disease that the physicians call hyposphagma, which is a suffusion of blood under the skin, see all things red and blood-colour. These humours, which thus change the action of our sight, how do we know whether or not they predominate in the beasts and are usual with them? For we see some of them whose eyes are yellow like our sufferers from jaundice, others whose eyes are red as blood; it is probable that to these the colour of objects appears other than to us. Which of the two judgements is true? For it is not said that the essential character of things has relation to man alone. Hardness, whiteness, depth, and sharpness are of concern in the service and information of the animals as well as in ours; nature has given the use thereof to them as to us. When we partly close the eye, the body that we look at appears longer and more extended; many animals have the eye thus partly closed; this greater length is then, perchance, the true shape of that object, not that which our eyes give it in their usual condition. If we press upon the lower part of the eye, things appear double to us;

Lamps have a double light, blazing with flames, and men's faces and bodies are double.[971]

If our ears are in any way clogged, or the ear-passage narrowed, we receive sounds otherwise than we commonly do; those animals which have hairy ears, or which have only a very small hole in place of the ear, consequently do not hear what we hear, and receive a different sound. At festivals and in theatres we see that, when a glass stained with some colour is placed in front of the glare of the torches, every thing in the place appears to us either green, yellow, or violet;

> And this is the effect that is commonly produced
> by the yellow and red and brown awnings stretched
> over great theatres, and hanging and waving from
> pillars with beams. For they colour all the assembly
> below, and the whole spectacle, the stage, the sena-
> tors and the matrons, and the statues of the gods dye
> them with their changing hues;[972]

it is probable that the eyes of the animals, which we see to be of divers colours, create for them the appearance of objects of the same colour as their eyes.

To judge of the actions of the senses, it would be necessary, therefore, that we should, in the first place, be in agreement with the beasts; secondly, among ourselves; which we are not, in any wise; and whenever one man hears, sees, or tastes something different from another man, we enter into disputes; and we dispute principally about the diversity of the impressions which the senses make on us. By the ordinary law of nature a child hears and sees otherwise and tastes otherwise than a man of thirty years, and the latter otherwise than a sexagenarian. In some persons the senses are more dim and more obscure, and in others more open and more acute. Sick people attribute bitterness to sweet things; from which it is evident to us that we do not receive things as they are but[973] in one way and another, according as we are, and according to our perception. Now, our perception being so uncertain and controverted, it is no longer to be wondered at if we are told that we can declare that the snow appears to us white; but to assert that, essentially and in truth, it is so, this we could not warrant to ourselves; and this commencement being shaken, all the learning in the world necessarily goes down the stream. How if our senses themselves interfere with one another? A picture seems to the sight to be raised; to the touch it seems flat; shall we say that musk is or is not agreeable, which pleases our sense of smell and offends our sense of taste? There are herbs and unguents suited to one part of the body which injure another part; honey is pleasant to the taste, unpleasant to the sight. Those rings which are cut in the shape of feathers, and which in heraldry are called *feathers without end*—there is no eye that can detect their breadth or that can escape the deception that there is an increase of width on one side and a pointedness and diminishing on the other, even when one turns them round the finger; whereas, when handled, they seem to you of even width, and everywhere alike. When those persons who, in ancient times, enhanced their pleasure by using mirrors that enlarged and magnified the objects reflected in them, in order that the members they were about to busy might please the more by the ocular increase, which of the two senses carried the day, the sight which represented those members as big and long as they could wish, or the touch which made them appear small and contemptible?

Is it our senses which impart to the subject these varying

conditions, and has it really but one? As we see with the bread that we eat: it is mere bread, but our using it makes of it bones, blood, flesh, hair, and nails;

> Just as food that has entered our bodies and limbs is destroyed and furnishes out of itself a different substance.[974]

The moisture which the root of a tree sucks up becomes trunk, leaves, and fruit; and the air, although it be but itself, becomes, by being blown through a trumpet, diversified in a thousand sorts of sounds—our senses, let me ask, do they create in the same way diverse qualities in these things, or do the things have such in themselves? And, with this doubt, what can we decide as to their true essential character? Moreover, since the conditions of sickness, of waking dreams, or of sleep, make things appear to us other than they appear to the healthy, the wise, and the waking, is it not probable that our best state and our natural moods have also wherewith to give a being to things related to our condition, and to adjust them to itself, as our disordered moods do? And that our health is as capable as our sickness of imparting a certain aspect to them? Why has not the temperate man some appearance of things peculiar to himself, as the intemperate man has? and will he not equally impress his character upon them? The satiated man attributes to the wine its insipidity; the well-governed man, its flavour; the thirsty man, its refreshingness.

Now, since our condition arranges all things for itself and transforms them according to itself, we no longer know what any thing is in reality; for nothing comes to us other than falsified and changed by our senses. When the compass, the square, and the rule are untrue, all the proportions which are derived from them, all the buildings which are erected according to their measure, are also necessarily defective and lacking. The uncertainty of our senses renders uncertain all that they give birth to.

> As in a building, if from the first the plan is false, and if the square is not true, and the levels are in any part uneven, the whole building is of necessity askew and awry, crooked, bowed, leaning forward, leaning backward, with an ill-fitted roof, and every part seems ready to collapse, and the whole building, betrayed by fallacious decisions, does collapse, so, likewise, your reasoning about things is of necessity defective and false, since it is based on the false evidence of the senses.[975]

For the rest, who can be competent to pass judgement upon these differences? As we say in religious discussions that we must have a judge who is not connected with either one or the other party, who is exempt from preference or partiality, which is impossible among Christians, the same is the case here: for, if he be old, he can not judge of the feelings of old age, being himself a party in that discussion; if he is young, the same; healthy, the same; the same sick, sleeping, and waking. We should need some one exempt from all these qualities, in order that, without preoccupation of judgement, he might judge these propositions as if they were indifferent to him; by that reckoning we should need a judge such as never was. To judge of the manifestations that we receive from things, we should need a judicatory organ; to confirm that organ we must have demonstra-

Apology for Raimond Sebond

tion; to confirm the demonstration an organ; thus we are turning in a circle. Since the senses can not put an end to our dispute, being themselves full of uncertainty, it must be reasoning that does so; no reasoning can be established except by other reasoning; thus we are endlessly driven back and back. Our mental conception is not directly connected with outside things, for it is conceived through the medium of the senses, and the senses do not grasp the outside thing,[976] but only their own impressions; and thus the mental conception is not of the thing itself, but only of the impression on the senses, which impression is some thing other than the thing; wherefore, he who judges by what is manifest to the senses judges by some thing other than the thing itself. And as for saying that the impressions on the senses represent to the soul the nature of outside things by resemblance, how can the understanding be assured of that resemblance, having of itself no commerce with outside things? Just as one who does not know Socrates, seeing his portrait, can not say that it resembles him. Now he who should attempt, none the less, to judge by what is manifest to the senses, if by all such manifestations it is impossible, for they interfere with one another by their extreme differences and discrepancies, as we see by experience,—shall some selected manifestations govern the rest? It will be necessary to confirm the one selected by another selected one, confirm the second by a third, and hence it will all never be done.[977]

Finally, there is no constant existence, either of our own being, or of that of what we observe. Both we and our judgement and all mortal things are incessantly flowing and rolling on. Thus nothing certain can be decided of one or the other, both what is judging and what is judged being in a state of continual change and movement.[978]

We have no intercourse with being, because all human nature is always half-way between birth and death, giving of itself only an obscure manifestation and shadow, and an uncertain and feeble surmise. And if, peradventure, you fix your mind on seeking to seize its being, it will be neither more nor less than one attempting to grasp water; for the more he shall squeeze and compress that which naturally flows in all directions, so much the more he will lose what he tries to grasp and hold. And so, all things being subject to pass from one change to another, the reason, seeking in them a real subsistence, finds itself disappointed, being unable to lay hold of any thing subsistent and permanent, because every thing is coming into being and does not as yet wholly exist, or is beginning to die before it is born. Plato said that bodies never had existence, but, indeed, birth; believing that Homer made Oceanus the father of the gods and Thetis their mother, to show us that all things are in a state of perpetual flux, change, and variation; an opinion common, as he says, to all philosophers before his time, save only Parmenides, who denied that things have motion, the power of which he considers to be of great importance; Pythagoras, that all matter is fluid and unstable;[979] the Stoics, that there is no present time, and that what we call the present is only the junction and blending of the future and the past;[980] Heraclitus, that no man ever entered twice into the same stream; Epicharmus, that he who in times past borrowed money does not owe it now, and that he who was invited last night to come this morning to dine comes to-day uninvited, because they[981] are no longer themselves; they

813

have become others;[982] and that it would be impossible to
find a mortal substance twice in the same state; for through
suddenness and facility of change, sometimes it scatters,
sometimes it reassembles; it comes, and then it goes. So that
which begins to be born never attains a perfect existence,
because this being born never ends and never stops, as being
finished, but from the seed is forever changing and shifting
from one state to another. As from the human seed is formed
first in the mother's womb a formless fruit, then a formed
child, then, having come forth from the womb, a child at
the breast; later, it becomes a boy; then, in due course, a
stripling; afterwards, an adult man; then a middle-aged
man; and, finally, a decrepit old man. So that the following
age constantly destroys and ruins the preceding one.

> Time, in fact, changes the nature of the whole
> world, and in every thing one condition is followed by
> another. Nothing remains the same; all things move,
> and are transformed by the power of nature.[983]

And yet we foolishly dread one kind of death, when we
have already passed, and are passing through so many
others. For not only, as Heraclitus said, is the death of fire
the generation of air, and the death of air the generation of
water, but even more manifestly can we see it in ourselves.
The flower of middle age dies and passes when old age arrives, and youth ends in the flower of an adult man, childhood in youth, and the first existence in infancy; and yesterday dies in to-day, and to-day will die in to-morrow; and
there is nothing which endures and which is always the
same. For, if it were not so, if we remain always one and the
same, how is it that we take pleasure now in one thing and

now in another? How is it that we love things that are contrary to one another, or hate them; that we praise them or blame them? How do we have different emotions, not retaining the same feeling about the same thought? For it is not probable that, without change, we should take other impressions; and that which suffers change does not remain one same thing; and if it be not one same thing, then also it is non-existent. Rather, when one thing thus simply changes its being, it also always becomes different from itself. And consequently the natural senses are deceived and deluded, taking that which is manifest to be that which exists, for lack of well knowing what is that which exists.

But what is, then, that which really exists? That which is eternal, that is to say, which has never had a beginning and will never have an end; to which time brings no change. For time is a thing in motion, which manifests itself obscurely, of a nature always flowing and fluctuating, never remaining stable or permanent; to which these words pertain: "before and after," and "has been," or "will be," which at first sight clearly show that it is not a thing which has existence; for it would be great folly and very manifest error to say that that exists which is not yet in existence, or which has already ceased to exist. And as for these words, "present," "instant," "now," by which it seems that we principally maintain and establish our understanding of time, the reason, laying bare their significance, destroys it instantly; for it[984] forthwith splits time asunder and divides it into future and past, as choosing to see it cut by necessity into two parts. The same thing happens to nature, which is measured by time, as to time, which measures it. For, likewise, there is not in nature any thing which endures, any thing which is subsistent; but all things are either born, or being born, or dying. Wherefore, it would be sinful to say of God, who alone exists, that he has been, or that he will be. For those terms denote deteriorations, phases, or vicissitudes of some thing which can neither last nor remain in existence. From this it must be concluded that God alone exists, not according to any measure of time, but according to an unchangeable and immovable eternity, not measured by time or subject to any deterioration; before which existence nothing was, nor will any thing be afterward, either more precedent or more recent, but an existence actually existing, who with a single now fills the forever; and there is nothing that really exists save him alone; nor can it be said, "He has been," or "He will be"; without beginning and without end.

To this so religious conclusion of a pagan, I desire to add only this saying of a witness of the same condition, as the close of this long and wearisome discussion, which would furnish me with endless matter. "Oh, what a despicable and abject thing is man," he says, "if he does not lift himself above human nature!" This is a wise saying and a profitable desire, but none the less absurd. For to make a handful bigger than the hand, an armful bigger than the arm, and to hope to take a stride longer than the stretch of our legs, this is impossible and unnatural. Neither can man raise himself above himself and human nature; for he can see only with his eyes, and grasp only with his hands. He will be lifted up if God by special favour lends him his hand; he will be lifted up, when abandoning and renouncing his own means and letting himself be uplifted and upheld by purely heavenly means. It is for our Christian faith, not for the Stoic virtue, to aspire to that divine and miraculous metamorphosis.